FOREWORD

This volume is one of a series of handbooks prepared by Foreign Area Studies (FAS) of The American University, designed to be useful to military and other personnel who need a convenient compilation of basic facts about the social, economic, political, and military institutions and practices of various countries. The emphasis is on objective description of the nation's present society and the kinds of possible or probable changes that might be expected in the future. The handbook seeks to present as full and as balanced an integrated exposition as limitations on space and research time permit. It was compiled from information available in openly published material. An extensive bibliography is provided to permit recourse to other published sources for more detailed information. There has been no attempt to express any specific point of view or to make policy recommendations. The contents of the handbook represent the work of the authors and FAS and do not represent the official view of the United States government.

An effort has been made to make the handbook as comprehensive as possible. It can be expected, however, that the material, interpretations, and conclusions are subject to modification in the light of new information and developments. Such corrections, additions, and suggestions for factual, interpretive, or other change as readers may have will be welcomed for use in future revisions. Comments may be addressed to:

The Director
Foreign Area Studies
The American University
5010 Wisconsin Avenue, N.W.
Washington, D.C. 20016

PREFACE

Significant developments occurring since its publication in August 1970 underline the desirability of revising the *Area Handbook for Mexico*. Issues affecting United States-Mexican relations in 1974 included the problem of migrant workers, illicit drug trade, discovery of resources that might make Mexico an oil-exporting nation, the effect of rising Mexican wages on border assembly industries used by United States manufacturers, and Mexican relations with Cuba and other Latin American nations.

This book supersedes the *Area Handbook for Mexico* researched and written by Johnson Research Associates. It represents an effort to provide a compact and objective exposition and analysis of the dominant social, political, and economic characteristics of Mexican society. Consultants with firsthand knowledge of the country have provided data not available in printed sources. The authors alone are responsible for the final draft.

Spanish words and phrases, used only when adequate English equivalents are lacking, are defined at first appearance. If employed frequently, they are listed in the Glossary. Spanish is based on *Appleton's New Cuyas Dictionary* (fifth edition). The spellings of place names are those established by the United States Board on Geographic Names. Unless otherwise stated, tons used in production and commodity figures are metric tons.

COUNTRY SUMMARY

1. COUNTRY: Mexico. Estados Unidos Mexicanos (United Mexican States). Gained independence from Spain in 1821.

2. SIZE, TOPOGRAPHY, AND CLIMATE: Area of 760,000 square miles; third largest country in Latin America. Landmass narrows progressively as it extends southeastward from United States border; narrow Baja California Peninsula points southward from northwest corner, and the blunt Yucatán Peninsula points northward from southeast corner. Northern half dominated by Sierra Madre Oriental and Sierra Madre Occidental mountain ranges and barren intervening Northern Plateau. Central Mexico is volcanic highland region of high peaks and basins. Southern Mexico, where most of major river systems are located, dominated by complex mountain systems. Principal lowlands are narrow Pacific coastal plain, broader coastal plain bordering Gulf of Mexico and Yucatán Peninsula. Subtropical to temperate climate and generally scanty rainful in half of the country lying north of Tropic of Cancer. Wide range of climatic conditions in southern half of country; tropical climate at sea level and temperate conditions in central highland area, where nearly half of population resides. Rainfall from light to heavy. During summer and autumn, both coasts subject to hurricanes.

3. POPULATION: Estimated at 56 million in 1973. Population growth rate of 3.5 percent annually was among world's highest. In mid-1970s government actively engaged in a recently introduced family planning program. Growth rate modified by heavy emigration to United States, most of it illegal. Several million Mexican migrants were believed to be residing illegally in United States.

4. ETHNIC GROUPS AND LANGUAGES: Mestizos (persons of mixed Indian-Spanish descent) are the dominant ethnic group and Spanish the dominant and official language. Monolingual Indians constitute about 7 to 10 percent of the population and speak one of several dozen languages. Largest of these Indian groups are the Maya and Nahuatl speakers. Indians retain largely aboriginal material culture, religion, medical practices, and social structure, whereas mestizo culture favors a modified Hispanic tradition.

5. RELIGION: Roman Catholics constitute over 90 percent of the population, and Protestants about 2 to 3 percent. There is official separation of church and state. Catholicism in Mexico varies from formal Roman Catholicism to folk Catholicism, the latter a blend of indigenous and Roman Catholic beliefs and practices. Mexican church has in past been at odds with the government and anticlerical forces since before inde-

pendence, even to the point of bringing on two civil wars, but in 1974 maintained cordial relations with the government. The church was experiencing reforms from within, and liberal clergy were pushing for greater social justice throughout the society.

6. EDUCATION: During early 1970s over 11 million students enrolled in public and private schools. Primary enrollment had more than doubled since 1960, and enrollments at higher levels had increased still more rapidly. More than 80 percent of total were in six-year primary school program. Most students at all levels were in schools in urban localities; illiteracy remained a serious problem in more remote parts of countryside.

7. HEALTH: Average diet meets minimum nutrition standards, but large proportion of low-income families suffers from malnutrition. Many authorities regard malnutrition and infant mortality as country's most serious health problems. Considerable success in campaigns combating endemic diseases and improvement in medical personnel and facilities reflected in dramatic decline in general mortality rate. Most of personnel and facilities concentrated in major urban centers; plan announced in 1974 for establishment of public health units in farm villages, where traditional medical practices survive.

8. GOVERNMENT: The Constitution of 1917 has been continuously in force since its adoption, although it has been amended more than 100 times. It provides for a federal republic with a strong executive, a bicameral congress, and a judiciary. The powers of the executive far exceed those of the other branches, and the federal government assumes extensive rights to intervene in the affairs of state governments. Political affairs have been dominated by a single official party since 1929.

9. INTERNATIONAL MEMBERSHIPS: Mexico is a member of the United Nations and many of its specialized agencies. It is a member of the International Bank for Reconstruction and Development (IBRD, commonly known as the World Bank), the International Monetary Fund, the Inter-American Development Bank, the Organization of American States, and the Latin American Free Trade Association. It is a party to the Inter-American Treaty of Reciprocal Assistance and to the Treaty of Tlatelolco, providing for a nuclear free zone in Latin America.

10. CURRENCY: Unit of currency is the peso, divided into 100 centavos. Symbol is $, and official rate of exchange in late 1974 was 12.5 pesos equal US$1; this rate had been in effect since 1954.

11. AGRICULTURE AND INDUSTRY: Agriculture employs the largest number of persons but contributes less than industry to the gross domestic product (GDP). Country is nearly self-sufficient in all crops; main crops are corn, rice, beans, sugar, cotton, coffee, fruits, and vegetables. Livestock industry is very large. Industry makes most consumer goods and many intermediate and capital goods.

12. LABOR: Census of 1970 showed 13 million workers in labor force, or less than 27 percent of population. Proportion employed in agriculture

declined sharply; proportion in industry gained moderately; proportion in services gained substantially. Rate of gain in manufacturing was insufficient to absorb influx of majority of job applicants from countryside, who could find work only in marginal service occupations. Moderate unemployment but severe underemployment problem. In particular, as many as half of all agricultural workers were landless farmers and operators of submarginal farm plots who worked so irregularly as to be considered underemployed. Similarly, underemployment high among marginal urban service workers.

13. TRANSPORTATION: Road system is one of most advanced in Latin America. Main roads run north-south between United States border and Mexico City; and all state capitals are connected by road. Government operates most of the railroad system, which connects main population areas with seacoasts and borders. Domestic aviation is well developed, and international service connects Mexico with most world capitals.

14. COMMUNICATIONS: Telephone and telegraph systems are government operated and cover most of country. Satellite communications with rest of world as well as land lines to United States and Canada.

15. IMPORTS AND EXPORTS: Main exports are agricultural products, minerals, shrimp, and manufactured items. No single commodity predominates among exports. Imports are mainly intermediate and capital goods. Few consumer goods imported.

16. ECONOMIC AGREEMENTS AND AID: Mexico is recipient of numerous loans from international organizations, foreign governments, and foreign banks. No grants received since World War II. Mexico has high international credit rating and can obtain adequate capital funds.

17. ARMED FORCES: In mid-1970s all-volunteer armed forces numbered 70,000 to 80,000 officers and men. Army made up about three-fourths of total; small air force and navy played secondary role supporting that of army. Overall size of armed forces was less than it had been immediately after Revolution of 1910 and had increased only slightly since 1960. One year of limited training required of all males reaching age of eighteen years; in addition, a paramilitary force of communal landholders maintained in countryside. Armed forces conditions of service generally excellent, and level of morale high. Principal military roles were maintenance of public order and civic action assignments, such as roadbuilding and disaster relief.

MEXICO

TABLE OF CONTENTS

Chris

Communication—Activities of Foreign Governments

LIST OF ILLUSTRATIONS

LIST OF TABLES

SECTION I. SOCIAL

CHAPTER 1

GENERAL CHARACTER OF THE SOCIETY

The people of Mexico live in a land of striking contrasts—topographic and climatic. Natural features range from coastal lowland jungles to high plateaus and craggy mountains. Access to many areas is so difficult that the inhabitants have remained isolated both culturally and economically.

Most of the rural people live in farm villages or hamlets, clustered in much the same manner as their pre-Columbian ancestors, and the influence of the Aztec civilization, which flourished when the Spaniards arrived in Mexico in the early sixteenth century, is still apparent. More and more rural dwellers, however, have migrated to cities to seek employment and to improve their children's educational opportunities. In 1974 Mexico City, the capital, and a number of other large cities were so crowded that the government was taking steps to relocate industries in order to achieve a more balanced distribution of the people.

Most Mexicans are mestizos—descendants of Spaniards and Indians— and their language and culture contain both Hispanic and Indian elements. After some three centuries of Spanish rule, and almost a century of rule by Mexican dictators, mestizos began to exert their power in the Revolution of 1910. In 1974 mestizos, generally speaking, controlled the government and the economy. The great majority were professed Roman Catholics; and Spanish, spoken by most of the population, was the official language. The social system was one in which values and institutions generated by social change and economic development existed alongside traditional ones.

In 1974 an unprecedented number of people—young and old—were attending schools or institutions of higher education. A low literacy level still constituted a serious problem in more isolated areas, but an extensive adult education program offered a variety of courses. The rapid increase in enrollment in institutions of higher education has resulted in overcrowding of facilities and straining of government education budgets.

Government leaders regard public education as the major instrument for achieving the goals of the Revolution of 1910, particularly the integration of indigenous people—previously neglected by the government —into the national life and development of new programs in urban centers designed to meet the needs of the rapidly expanding urban economy.

1

The revolutionary concept of patriotism and national identity has been incorporated into school curricula and fostered as an incentive to academic achievement.

Patriotism and pride in the country's history are evident in the work of Mexican writers, musicians, sculptors, architects, and painters. Revolutionary heroes, folk arts, traditional dances, and pre-Columbian beliefs provide the inspiration for much Mexican artistic expression. At the same time Mexican artists and intellectuals have been receptive to European and North American influences.

Intellectual expression in Mexico in the twentieth century has dealt extensively with social problems, such as the Indian's place in Mexican society, a major issue in the Revolution of 1910. Likewise painters and sculptors reflect in their work the people's sense of nationalism and a close identification with the country's past. The people hold artists and intellectuals in high esteem; the government has contributed to the support of architects, painters, actors, and dramatists, as well as ballet groups. Intellectuals play a significant role in government—a role more important than that of intellectuals in many nations. They frequently serve as cabinet members and as envoys to other countries.

In 1974 the growing middle class in urban areas and better paid skilled laborers enjoyed a relatively high standard of living, but most of the rural population and poorer urban dwellers lived close to the subsistence level. Among the lower income groups malnutrition was an important factor in the high rate of mortality among children. A problem faced by urban and rural dwellers alike was a severe housing shortage, felt most acutely by lower income urban families living on the fringes of cities in improvised shacks. Most city dwellers could obtain the benefits of public health and welfare services, but in rural areas the availability of such services was limited. Nevertheless, at most levels in Mexican society the family unit provided much of its own welfare protection, medical care, and opportunities for recreation. At all levels of society traditional dances and folk songs were popular and innumerable fiestas were held throughout the country.

One of the most durable elements of Mexican society is the nuclear family, living in a household that may also include aunts, uncles, grandparents, and other relatives. The family may be further extended through patterns of ritual kinship. The importance of the family as an institution is reflected in all classes. Many businesses are run by corporate family structures; and lower class families, when necessary, assume responsibility for individual members in need of assistance.

In remote areas religion plays a major role in the lives of the residents, whose religious practices and beliefs are usually a blend of Roman Catholicism and pre-Columbian beliefs and practices. In urban areas religion plays a less pervasive role in the daily life of the individual. The Roman Catholic Church in Mexico has for centuries stood for traditional thought and ideas, but in the early 1970s liberal elements in the church were advocating social reform to improve the lot of the underprivileged.

A large proportion of the Mexican labor force is employed in agricultural production. Output increased notably after World War II but has barely kept pace with the needs of the growing population. To meet this challenge the government has invested heavily in opening new areas for cultivation and in building flood control and irrigation projects. Over a period of more than fifty years the government has carried out programs of agrarian reform, but in 1974 the vast majority of farms were either in the subsistence category or simply supplied neighboring markets. All of Mexico's agricultural exports are produced by about 1 percent of the farms, and most of the food supplied to urban areas is raised by approximately 15 percent of the country's farms.

In the manufacturing sector domestic production is great enough to meet almost all consumer needs and varied enough to provide intermediate and capital goods. The process of extensive industrialization accelerated during World War II when a scarcity of imports stimulated increased production by existing plants and the building of new plants. The growth of industry has also contributed to the growth of the middle class.

Mexico is one of the world's major trading nations, and the United States has in the past been its dominant trading partner. Although Mexico's imports—principally raw materials, intermediate, and capital industrial goods—have created an annual negative trade balance, earnings of the tourist industry have offset these negative balances. In the early 1970s Mexico was increasing trade with other Latin American countries and Japan and Europe in order to reduce dependence on trade with the United States. In domestic trade, business methods and values are similar to those typical of most industrialized countries. Business dealings are characterized by the sort of courtesy that prevails in social relationships.

Although Mexico had enjoyed significant economic growth during the preceding twenty-five years, in 1974 the country faced serious problems. The government was engaged in efforts to solve an old problem, poverty, and to cope with a new problem, inflation. Although the economy was dominated by a strong private sector, the government operated state corporations, regulated credit, set minimum wages, and carried out other regulatory functions that directly affected operations in which foreign investment has been extensive.

Government regulation of the economy and provision for the basic welfare of the people were themes of the Constitution of 1917, a document that reflected the influence of the Mexican experience of authoritarian rule and social revolution as well as principles of the Constitution of the United States. Although the Constitution of 1917 provided for a division of power among executive, legislative, and judicial branches in a federal system, the powers of the legislative and judicial branches are greatly exceeded by those of the executive; the central government assumes broad powers enabling it to intervene in the states.

The basis for relative stability and continuity that has evolved since the revolution involves a number of apparent contradictions. Among these are an extremely strong president who is barred from reelection; a relatively weak National Congress in which the opposition is guaranteed token representation; general control of political activities by a single party, but by a party with a significantly broad base; and universal suffrage, but with narrow choices for the electorate.

The government party, the Institutional Revolutionary Party (Partido Revolucionario Institucional—PRI), has been undefeated at the polls since its establishment in 1929. The party has usually been able to manipulate the amount of opposition in elections that it is willing to accept. PRI candidates for the presidency are usually picked by the outgoing president in consultation with other party leaders, key businessmen, and heads of labor and peasant unions. Although loyalty to the party is a prerequisite for obtaining a government position, advancement in the party structure may result from achievement in the bureaucracy.

Rivalry for power occurs both within the party and between party leaders and leaders of other interest groups, including labor, the peasantry, the civilian bureaucracy, the military, and small businessmen. Minor parties have proved useful to the party as escape valves for politicians frustrated by the party's official policies. The inner circle of decisionmakers is usually led by the president, and former presidents may be included in the group.

The people's awareness of the political system seems to have increased vastly since the Revolution of 1910. It has been estimated that before the revolution some 90 percent of the people were generally oblivious to the national system, whereas that portion had been reduced to about 25 percent by 1960. President Luís Echeverría, in the early 1970s, was moving discreetly in the direction of increasing participation not only within the official party but among parties in formal legislative bodies.

In the early 1970s the people were served by one of the most advanced mass communication systems in Latin America. Newspapers, radio, television, magazines, and books helped maintain political consciousness, and the government made significant use of radio and television to promote national unity and literacy. Government influence on the media was exercised through a number of channels, including a government newsprint monopoly, purchase of advertising space in the print media, encouragement of the use of official news releases, and pressuring of individual journalists for favorable treatment in their output.

Radio broadcasts reached the great bulk of the population as a result of widespread use of transistor receivers. The greatest concentration of media, however, was found in and around Mexico City, the home of the dominant national television networks and of the magazine, film, and book industries.

Although most Mexicans tend to believe in law and order and to respect the authority of a father or a father figure such as the president, some, particularly older citizens, were concerned that there might be a resurgence of the sort of violence that followed the Revolution of 1910, when private armies fought for control of the country. In the late 1960s and early 1970s threats to internal security arose mainly from massive student demonstrations against the government and from terrorist and guerrilla activities conducted by both leftist and rightist groups dissatisfied with government policies. In 1974 these units were being successfully hunted down by police and the armed forces.

Primary functions of the armed forces, along with maintaining internal order, were civic action projects such as preventive medicine campaigns and road building. The danger of armed foreign invasion was minimal, but the army's civic action programs, carried out in cooperation with the PRI, seemed to make the army an essential factor in preserving the stability of the government. Furthermore, most of the people seemed to regard the military as an institution devoted to the ideals and goals of the Revolution of 1910 that had been effectively pursued by the PRI.

One of the goals of the Revolution of 1910 was establishment of a foreign policy that featured national independence and prerogatives. Conscious of a history of invasions and interventions by foreign troops, Mexicans regard the outside world with caution. One of the factors that triggered the revolution was opposition to the privileged position of United States interests, an attitude that led to the nationalization of United States-owned oil fields in 1938. Discovery of new oil reserves in the early 1970s made it seem likely that Mexico would join the ranks of oil-exporting countries.

Mexican efforts to avoid foreign influence are reflected in the government's rejection of the United States offer of assistance under the Mutual Security Act after World War II. The government has demonstrated its independence by opposing United States efforts to organize the Organization of American States (OAS) as an anticommunist alliance. Likewise it has refused a seat on the United Nations Security Council because of its opposition to intervention by anyone, including the United Nations, in the affairs of sovereign states.

When President Gerald Ford and President Echeverría met along the United States-Mexican border in October 1974, they discussed a variety of economic and political issues. Among these were the problem of illegal immigration of Mexican laborers into the United States, illicit drug traffic across the border, and the discovery of new oil reserves in Mexico.

CHAPTER 2

GEOGRAPHY AND POPULATION

With an expanse of more than 760,000 square miles and a population of well over 50 million, Mexico is third in size and second in population among the countries of Latin America. Most of its mountain ranges, plateaus, and lowlands are continuations of landforms of the southwestern United States. Its demographic characteristics and patterns of settlement, however, are those of Middle America.

Hernán Cortés, the Spanish conqueror, is reputed to have described the topography of the country by crumpling a piece of paper, throwing it down, and saying, "This is the map of Mexico." The same anecdote has been attributed to Christopher Columbus when he was asked for a description of the island of Hispaniola, but the illustration is a valid one. Two-thirds of the country is mountainous, and Mexicans tend to think of directions as up and down rather than in terms of the four quarters of the compass. The mountains have tended to perpetuate regionalism, and access to many areas is so difficult that they have remained economically undeveloped and culturally isolated.

Extending southeastward from its border with the United States, Mexico forms a generally narrowing cone, broken in the northwest by the long, narrow peninsula of Baja California and in the extreme southeast by the blunt peninsula of Yucatán (see fig. 1). A fairly broad coastal plain borders the Gulf of Mexico, and a narrower and broken strip of lowland borders the Pacific Ocean. Great mountain ranges extend roughly parallel to the two coastal lowlands, and between them lies a great interior plateau region. The plateau narrows to the south and terminates in a transverse mountain range consisting of a series of volcanic cones, some of them still active. This zone of volcanoes is a part of the Circum-Pacific Volcanic Ring that circles the Pacific Ocean in a great arc from Japan to the Andes.

This highland region of volcanoes is the heartland of Mexico. Most of the large cities and the densest rural population are located in its basins and valleys. Southward, the range of volcanoes drops away to the basin of the Balsas River flowing into the Pacific. The south, however, is mountainous except in a few river valleys, along the coasts, on the peninsula of Yucatán, and on the low-lying Isthmus of Tehuantepec. Southern Mexico is a relatively undeveloped tropical region in which a predominantly Indian population lives in mountain pockets and along river valleys.

Climatic conditions of Mexico vary as much with altitude as with degree of latitude and include both tropical and temperate. Over half of the country is arid, and even arable land is subject to irregular rainfall, floods, and droughts. Much of it is cultivated under irrigation. The adverse characteristics of climate and topography, however, are offset by great and varied mineral resources. Many of the cities had their origins as mining camps, and nearly all of the states have important mineral reserves.

According to one estimate of land utilization, 12 percent of the national territory is arable, 40 percent is pastoral, 22 percent is forested, and 26 percent has other forms of utilization or is unusable. The indigenous wildlife, much reduced by human habitation, consists largely of North American species, but species common to Middle America predominate in the tropical lands of the south.

The name Mexico is derived either from the Mexica, one of the Aztec tribes, or from Mexitl, an epithet for the god of war in the Aztec pantheon. It is a country of Indian origins, and in the mid-1970s the influence of the Aztecs and other indigenous peoples remained strong in the countryside. The prevailing pattern of rural settlement was one of the farm village or hamlet, in which people lived clustered much as they had in pre-Columbian times.

The dominant factors in Mexican demography during the years since World War II have been rapid population growth and urbanization. With a high birthrate and with a progressively increasing longevity resulting from improved living conditions, each decade of the twentieth century has seen a rise in the population growth rate; in the late 1960s and early 1970s it was among the highest in the world.

This rate of growth has placed increasing pressure on the limited amount of arable land. At the same time, an expanding education system, improved communications, and the growth of industry have tended to draw young people away from the farms and into the cities and towns. In the mid-1970s Mexico City and several other major urban centers had become so crowded that the government was engaged in an effort to decentralize industry in order to lessen urban crowding and to achieve a more balanced distribution of the population.

In 1970 agriculture employed more workers than any other sector of the economy, but this proportion had declined sharply since 1960. Industry registered a substantial gain, but it was in the services sector that the largest gain was recorded as migrants from the countryside took marginal jobs in small shops, as street venders, or as domestic servants.

The capital of the country is known internationally as Mexico City. In the Spanish language, however, it appears simply as México, or as México, Distrito Federal. In addition, México is the name of the state that surrounds the Federal District (Distrito Federal). Moreover, a person identifying himself as a native of Mexico is probably referring to the city rather than to the country.

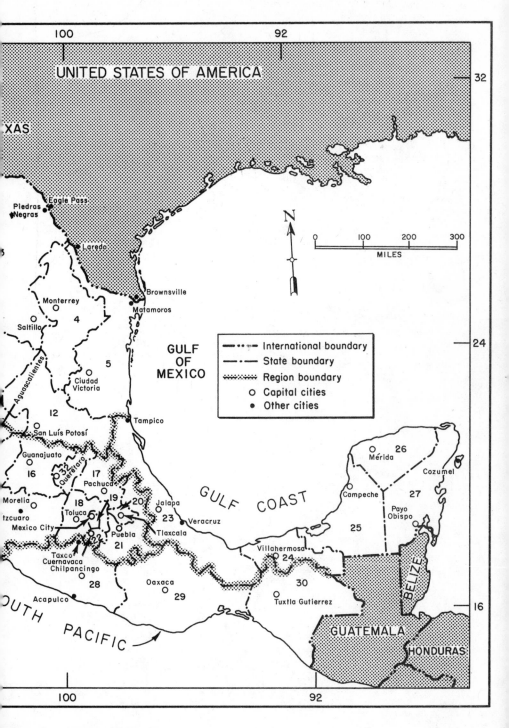

Map labels:

100 92
UNITED STATES OF AMERICA — 32

XAS

Piedras Negras •Eagle Pass
•Laredo

Monterrey O Brownsville
Saltillo O Matamoros 4

GULF
OF
MEXICO

Aguascalientes
5
Ciudad
Victoria

12
San Luís Potosí O Tampico

Guanajuato O
16 32 Querétaro 17
Pachuca•
Morelia O 18 19
tzcuaro • Toluca O 20 Jalapa O
Mexico City 6 23 Veracruz•
Puebla O Tlaxcala
Taxco• 22 21
Cuernavaca
Chilpancingo
28 Oaxaca O 29

Acapulco•

OUTH
PACIFIC

Mérida O 26
Cozumel
Campeche O 27
Payo
Obispo
25

Villahermosa O 24
30
Tuxtla Gutierrez O — 16

GUATEMALA

BELIZE

HONDURAS

GULF COAST

N 0 100 200 300
MILES

	International boundary
	State boundary
	Region boundary
O	Capital cities
•	Other cities

100 92

BOUNDARIES AND POLITICAL SUBDIVISIONS

Mexico's 2,300 miles of border have been fully demarcated. The 1,600-mile boundary with the United States follows the course of the Rio Grande from the Gulf of Mexico to El Paso, Texas. It then follows straight surveyed lines to the Pacific, except for a short distance along the Colorado River. In the south the 160-mile border with Belize (formerly British Honduras) is marked by watercourses and a straight line extending north to south. The 600-mile Guatemalan frontier is marked by straight lines, the deepest channel of the Usumacinta River, and the courses of several other streams.

There are no present border problem areas, although Mexico retains a latent claim to Belize north of 17° north latitude, according to a treaty with Guatemala signed in 1882. The former El Chamizal district of El Paso, Texas, which had been made physically a part of that city by a change in the course of the Rio Grande, was returned to Mexico in 1967, and minor disputes that related to shifts in the Rio Grande and Colorado rivers were settled in 1971.

The border between the United States and Mexico passes through desolate countryside that is a natural barrier more than an area of contact, but this line is probably the most frequently crossed anywhere in the world. In 1972 some 24.5 million authorized crossings into Mexico were recorded at San Ysidro (the California town opposite Tijuana) alone.

In 1951 the United States and Mexico entered an agreement authorizing and controlling the seasonal migration of *braceros* (field-workers). The agreement expired in 1964, however, and since that time an unknown but extremely large and probably increasing number of Mexican workers have entered the United States illegally each year (see Labor Force, this ch.). In 1972 about 500,000 illegal migrants were turned back, but others made the crossing successfully. The United States Immigration Service authorities estimated that 1.3 million Mexicans were living in the United States illegally, and other estimates ran as high as 4 million.

These migrants, known as wetbacks because many enter by swimming across the Rio Grande, are in many instances recruited and brought into the United States by contractors operating along the border who are known as chicken herders. In the early 1970s wetbacks were estimated by César Chavez of the United Farm Workers Union to hold 20 percent of all farm labor jobs in California. They are said to make up almost all of the potato harvest working corps in Idaho and to hold 100,000 urban jobs in Los Angeles.

The wetback problem has been the subject of a great deal of diplomatic discussion between representatives of the two countries. Mexican and United States border authorities, however, have worked in general harmony in attempting to control the traffic (see ch. 12). The length of the border and the wide stretches of unoccupied territory impose a heavy burden on the world's busiest customs and immigration posts on both sides of the border, however, and an illicit trade in narcotics and other contraband goods is also heavy. In early 1973 United States and Mexican agents participated in a five-week drug enforcement operation code named "Operation Cactus," which resulted in the arrest of 100 persons and the seizure of twenty-four tons of marijuana and 9.3 pounds of uncut heroin.

Little control is possible over movement across the jungle frontiers with Belize and Guatemala. No specific data regarding crossings are available, but in 1973 the governor of Chiapas was reported as estimating the number of illegal migrants from Guatemala at 20,000 annually. In particular, English-speaking migrants who have crossed from Belize later attempt to cross into the United States. The migrants from Guatemala are believed to include a considerable number from other Central American countries who, as citizens of Central American Common Market states, can move freely into Guatemala.

Mexico claims jurisdiction over territorial waters to a limit of twelve miles and over the Gulf of California as an inland sea north of Tiburón Island. At the 1972 meeting of the fourteen-member Caribbean Nations Conference on the Law of the Sea, however, the country outlined its future position as one involving "patrimonial" rights to offshore waters to a distance of 200 miles. Fishing and seabed rights would be reserved to the patrimonial state, but innocent passage of vessels between the twelve-mile limit and the 200-mile limit would not be affected. Mexico was joined by Venezuela and Colombia in sponsoring this patrimonial concept, as opposed to the more generally supported territorial 200-mile principle, at the third United Nations Law of the Sea Conference that met at Caracas in July 1974. The conference ended inconclusively, and the parties resolved to meet again in Geneva in 1975.

Mexico is compartmentalized internally into thirty-one states and the Federal District—an enclave in the state of México. The newest of the states, the former territories of Baja California and Quintana Roo, achieved statehood in October 1974. The big states of the North and the North Pacific and the political subdivisions of the Yucatán Peninsula are divided by straight surveyed lines. Elsewhere, internal borders sometimes follow such natural features as watercourses or highland ridges, but colonial property lines are also used. Only to a limited extent do political subdivisions reflect natural features or facilitate national integration.

The rugged character of the country has given rise to an extreme degree of regionalism and a tendency toward anarchy that, in turn, has made the establishment of a strong centralized government necessary. Mexicans have developed a strong sense of nationalism. They feel allegiance not only to the *patria* (nation) but also to the *patria chica* (little nation). The latter is less likely to be the artificially bounded state than the particular community or subregion, such as a basin or valley, where

12

the ethnic pattern of the rural population can be identified by accent, food preferences, and dress.

NATURAL FEATURES

Highlands and Lowlands

The predominant structural features of Mexico are the southward continuations of the more northern parts of the North American continent. On the east, the Sierra Madre Oriental range is an extension of the Rocky Mountain range and, on the west, the Sierra Madre Occidental range is an extension of the Sierra Nevada range of the United States. Between the two Sierra Madres the lofty Northern Plateau, made up of highlands and intermontane basins, extends northward from near Mexico City to become the western tablelands of the United States. Eastward from the Sierra Madre Oriental, the coastal lowlands of the Gulf of Mexico are a continuation of the coastal plain of Texas, and the structure of the Yucatán Peninsula resembles that of Florida. The depression known as the Salton Trench in the United States continues into Mexico and becomes the body of water known internationally as the Gulf of California and by Mexicans as the Mar de Cortés. On the western coast of the mainland the outliers of the massive Sierra Madre Occidental—the country's most extensive mountain system—descend almost directly to tidewater, leaving only a narrow and discontinuous coastal plain and a few river deltas. West of the Gulf of California the barren peninsula of Baja California is a continuation of the Coast Ranges of the United States.

Between the parallels of 18° and 20° north latitude lie a series of volcanic peaks that terminate the southward extension of North American physiographic features (see fig. 2). Some geographers regard this volcanic fracture zone, a region of frequent and sometimes serious earthquakes, as the termination of the North American continent. The loftiest peaks lie on the southern flank of this zone and form a kind of mountain range that extends laterally from the Pacific almost to the Gulf of Mexico. It is known variously as the Cordillera Neovolcanica, the Sierra Volcanica Transversal, and the Cordillera de Anahuác.

The range is anchored on the east, not far from the Gulf of Mexico, by the perfect volcanic cone of Orizaba. With an elevation of nearly 19,000 feet, it is the country's highest mountain. The second and third in height, Ixtacihuatl and Popocatapetl, respectively, are visible from Mexico City. Most of the country's highest peaks are in this chain. Nearly all of the volcanoes of the fracture zone are extinct, but some volcanism continues. Ixtacihuatl last erupted in the eighteenth century, but its crest is still sometimes topped by a plume of smoke. The new volcano of Paracutín first erupted in 1943 in a cornfield 250 miles southwest of Mexico City. Before ceasing activity in the early 1950s, it had reached an elevation of 1,700 feet.

South of the fracture zone, the land descends to a broad depression formed by the Balsas River and its tributaries, and between this depression and the Pacific coast lies the Sierra Madre del Sur range with altitudes of up to 10,000 feet. This range is not related to the mountain systems of northern Mexico but resembles the submerged chain of mountains whose peaks appear as the islands of the Greater Antilles. East of the Balsas River depression, the interior is occupied by a complex system of ranges known as the Oaxaca Highlands; on the Gulf of Mexico the coastal lowlands are broken by an isolated upland called the Tuxtlas mountains, the highest Atlantic coastal elevations south of Labrador.

At about 95° east longitude, Mexico narrows to form the lowlands of the Isthmus of Tehuantepec in which altitudes do not exceed 500 feet. Beyond this isthmus, the Sierra Madre de Chiapas extends to the Guatemalan border, separated from the Pacific by a fairly broad coastal plain. The remaining major mountain system, the Chiapas Highlands, occupies most of the interior east of the Isthmus of Tehuantepec and south of the peninsula of Yucatán. Along the northern flank of both the Chiapas and Oaxaca highlands lies a narrow band of folded ranges that resembles the Sierra Madre Oriental and may thus be considered a far southern extremity of the Rocky Mountains.

Geographic Regions

Geographers see Mexico as divided in different ways into geographical regions. For some statistical and administrative purposes, however, the Mexican government has devised a system of five regions consisting of the North Pacific, the North, Central Mexico, the Gulf Coast, and the South Pacific (see fig. 1).

The arrangement is imperfect in the sense that the regions bear only a limited relationship to natural features, and the small South Pacific state of Colima is left as a coastal enclave flanked by two states of Central Mexico. Climate, land utilization, and population distribution patterns do generally conform to the arrangement, however, and it is adaptable for use in the preparation of statistical tables.

The North Pacific

Second largest but least populated of the regions, the North Pacific, is made up of the three coastal states lying west of the Sierra Madre Occidental plus the peninsula of Baja California. It is located principally between the parallels of 20°N and 30°N and, like all west coast regions in this latitudinal range in both northern and southern hemispheres, it consists largely of desert.

Nearly half of the region is occupied by the large state of Sonora. Most of it is the Sonoran Desert, which continues southward into Sinaloa. Desert conditions terminate in Sinaloa with an increase in rainfall, but the physiography of the desert zone is repeated in southern Sinaloa and in Nayarit. It consists of ancient foothills of the Sierra Madre Occidental

14

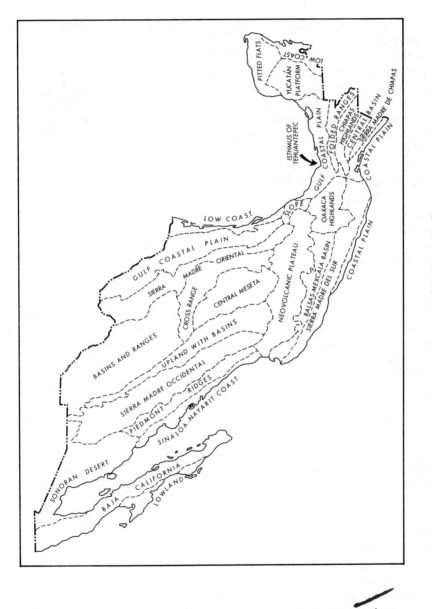

Figure 2. Mexico, Physiographic Zones

that have been buried by waste washed down from that range. A narrow coastal plain extends inland for a distance of only ten to fifteen miles. This plain, however, is one of the country's most productive commercial farming areas, particularly on the alluvial fans created by the Sonora, Yaqui, Fuerte, Sinaloa, and Culiacán rivers and several other rivers and streams.

The Morelos Dam on the Colorado River at the head of the Gulf of California has converted the desert land of the Mexicali Valley into an important agricultural area devoted primarily to cotton farming. In the far west the narrow finger of the Baja California Peninsula is a desert on which block mountains with elevations of up to 9,000 feet drop abruptly into the Gulf of California and descend to a narrow plain only on the southern part of the Pacific coast. The upper half of the peninsula is the state of Baja California, and the lower half is the state of Baja California Sur.

The North

Extending eastward from the crests of the Sierra Madre Occidental to the Gulf of Mexico, the North has more than 40 percent of the country's territory but less than 19 percent of its population. The Sierra Madre Oriental lies almost entirely within the region. The coastal state of Tamaulipas is situated to the east of this range and is physically similar to the states that make up the Gulf Coast region. Its general aridity, however, is unlike that of the Gulf Coast but similar to the other states of the North.

The other six states of the region comprise the great Northern Plateau of Mexico. The terrain includes extensive flat areas, but it is broken by numerous hill ranges, most of them longitudinal. It narrows somewhat from north to south, and elevations increase as the plateau of Central Mexico is neared. At approximately its midpoint, the plateau is interrupted by a series of cross ranges between the two Sierra Madre systems.

South of these ranges, in an area occupied principally by the states of Zacatecas and San Luís Potosí, the land is more arid than that of Central Mexico, and the population is less dense. The pattern of settlement, however, is similar to it in the sense that it is made up of population clusters in intermontane basins. This portion of the Northern Plateau as a whole is sometimes referred to as the Central Meseta, or central tableland.

To the north of the cross ranges, the land becomes progressively more arid and the population scantier. The states of Chihuahua and Coahuila are at once the country's largest and least densely populated. It is a dry pastoral countryside of great desert basins known as bolsons. These depressions drain internally to salty lakes or salt flats bordered by gradually sloping shallow alluvial fans and rimmed by steeply sloped hill ranges. The largest of these, the Mayarán Bolson, has an elevation of about 3,600 feet; a chain of interconnected basins known collectively as

16

the Mapimí Bolson straddles the borders of the states of Durango, Coahuila, and Chihuahua at elevations of a little more than 3,000 feet.

The poor quality of the soils, resulting in particular from the absence of humus, and the scanty rainfall limit farming to a few oases. The area does, however, produce herbaceous and xerophyte vegetation that permits extensive animal husbandry. Much of the land reclamation through irrigation projects has taken place in the North, particularly in areas sufficiently close to the United States border to use the waters of the Rio Grande. One of the largest irrigation projects fans out from Matamoros in Tamaulipas State and is located near the mouth of the river. Close to the city of Torreón the Coahuila Bolson includes an old lakebed that has become the extensive La Laguna irrigation district. It is the North's principal irrigation area away from the Rio Grande, but the irrigation complex was not carefully planned and neither its extent nor its productivity has met expectations.

Central Mexico

Third in size among the regions, Central Mexico contains almost half of the country's population. It is physiographically the southern end of the Northern Plateau and consists mainly of a volcanic zone that is sometimes called the Neovolcanic Plateau.

Central Mexico is the heartland of the country and borders on all other regions. Its southern perimeter is fairly well defined by the decline from the plateau to the Balsas River depression, but its other flanks merge imperceptibly into other regions. On the west, the coastal areas of the states of Jalisco and Michoacán are physiographically part of the South Pacific region and, on the east, the plateau slopes almost to the Gulf of Mexico in the Gulf Coast region. Northward, the plateau merges into the North region without perceptible change other than the gradual disappearance of the old volcanoes and the increasing aridity in the area.

Central Mexico was an ancient center of civilization and is one of world's loftiest areas of concentrated population after those of Tibet and the Andean countries. The terrain consists principally of rolling hills and the dissected cones of thousands of old volcanoes interspersed by broad basins and valleys with floors at elevations of 5,000 to 8,000 feet. The seven largest and most important of these basins and valleys extend westward in a transverse chain from the Basin of Puebla on the east through the Valley of México; the basins of Toluca, Guanajuato, and Jalisco; and the valleys of Morelos and Aguascalientes. The distinction between the terms *basin* and *valley* is one based on common usage rather than on distinctive difference in configuration of the areas.

The Valley of México is drained internally, and the Basin of Puebla drains to the Pacific Ocean through streams of the Balsas River system. The remaining five valleys are drained to the Pacific through the Lerma River system. The basins west of Toluca are interconnecting and form a subregion that terminates in mountains west of the city of Guadalajara. This area of relatively level land is known as the Bajío and consists of rich volcanic ash and the lacustrine soils of old lakebeds. These soils and a relatively long growing season make the Bajío the most productive agricultural zone of Central Mexico.

There are many other smaller basins and valleys and pockets of arable land at higher elevations. Among the largest is the high and rather arid basin of Tlaxcala that lies directly to the east of Mexico City. The small but famous basin in which the picturesque tourist town of Taxco is situated lies between mountains not far from Mexico City in the South Pacific state of Guerrero.

The Lerma River rises in highlands northwest of Mexico City and flows westward to Lake Chapala on the outskirts of Guadalajara. It is the country's largest lake and a popular vacation and retirement center. Lake Chapala empties into the Santiago River, which flows northwestward to the Pacific. Although the Lerma-Santiago river system is only seventh in the country in terms of runoff, it is of particular importance because of its location in the country's heartland.

The Gulf Coast

The Gulf Coast is made up of the states of Veracruz and Tabasco plus the political subdivisions of the Yucatán Peninsula, which is sometimes considered a separate region. The interior of Veracruz extends to the watershed of the Sierra Madre Oriental, and its coastal slopes are patterned by a string of plantations and commercial farms. The fairly broad Veracruz coastal plain is interrupted by outliers of the range that extend almost to tidewater a little north of the city of Veracruz. These lowlands are fertile but hot and marshy and once so insect-infested that Veracruz was known as the "City of Death." Drainage of swamps and other health and sanitation programs, however, have made the coastal plain of both Veracruz and Tabasco an area of rapid population growth. Tabasco is for the most part a lowland state in which the countless streams that form the delta of the Grijalva and Usumacinta rivers have created Mexico's most extensive coastal swamplands.

The Yucatán Peninsula is a low platform of barren limestone soils on which elevations seldom exceed 500 feet of undulating lowland. Physiographically it is similar to Florida and unlike anything else in Mexico. The northeastern tip is a desert, but rainfall increases to the south, and a dense tropical rain forest covers Quintana Roo Territory and the base of the peninsula.

There is virtually no surface drainage, but the northern part of the peninsula is pitted by countless small depressions called cenotes formed by the collapse of the ceilings of the enormous subterranean limestone reservoirs. Water is drawn to the surface by windmills. The cenotes become fewer to the south, and the population obtains water from rainwater ponds and numerous small lakes. Beyond a wave-built barrier reef off the northern and western coasts, the bank of Campeche is the most extensive part of the Mexican continental shelf.

The South Pacific region is made up of the states of Guerrero, Oaxaca, and Chiapas plus the state of Colima, which is situated as a coastal enclave in the region of Central Mexico. It is the most rural and slowest growing of the regions and the one in which Indian life most nearly continues unaffected by the twentieth century. Cut off from the rest of the country by the plateau of Central Mexico, its natural features resemble those of Central America.

The South Pacific region is extremely mountainous; but the Grijalva and Usumacinta rivers that rise in Guatemala and flow across the region to the Gulf of Mexico, the Balsas river that crosses its northern flank, and many other rivers and streams give it a greater flow of water than the other regions of Mexico. The basin of the Papaloapán River in the state of Oaxaca is the site of the large Miguel Alemán Reservoir and an extensive farm colonization area.

Climate

The country is bisected laterally by the Tropic of Cancer and at sea level is half inside and half outside the tropics. Well over half of the territory is located in uplands, however, and the climate is sometimes described as vertical rather than longitudinal. Prevailing winds—primarily tradewinds—blow out of the northeast across the Gulf of Mexico and influence most of the landmass. Extratropical cyclones crossing the Rocky Mountains cause occasional rain in the northern deserts. On the Pacific coast, light land and sea breezes as a rule occur during the winter and early spring, and short gales and squalls are common during the remainder of the year.

During summer and autumn both coasts are subject to hurricanes. The most common hurricane pattern is one that curves clockwise across the Caribbean Sea to batter the Mexican Gulf Coast and go on with diminished fury to the cities of the Texas coast. In 1959, however, a Pacific hurricane caused 1,500 deaths in the coastal portions of Jalisco and Colima.

Degree of longitude, elevation, and prevailing winds are modified extensively as climate conditioners by local physiography. Cool water currents tend to make the Pacific coastline cooler and drier than the Atlantic. The sharp escarpments of the Sierra Madre Oriental form a vast rain shadow that contributes to the aridity of the northern plateau. In Central Mexico the relatively adequate moisture in the Valley of México contrasts with the aridity of the adjacent basins of Tlaxcala and Toluca as a consequence of local configurations of terrain. In a single intermontane basin or valley in any part of the country, climatic conditions may vary sharply from one mountain slope to another.

The importance of elevation as a conditioning factor in climate is underlined by the fact that since pre-Columbian times the population of tropical Mexico has been concentrated at elevations above 3,000 feet in what is known in tropical countries of Latin America as the *tierra templada* (temperate land). The earlier population centers were in the volcanic plateau of Central Mexico, on the eastern slopes of the Sierra Madre Oriental, and in the valleys and basins of the southern highlands.

Temperate-land climate is at its most pleasant in Central Mexico. In Mexico City the year-round average temperature is about 60°F, and there is light but adequate rainfall. A considerable diurnal temperature range results in cool evenings and nights, but the small ten-degree range between the coldest and the warmest month contrasts with the more than thirty-six-degree range registered at El Paso, Texas, which lies at about the same elevation.

Rainfall ranges from extremely scanty in the deserts of the North Pacific and the North regions to extremely heavy in the tropical, wet climates of the southeastern slopes of the Sierra Madre del Sur and portions of the Gulf Coast. Mexico is a generally dry country, however, and according to one classification, less than 10 percent of the country has adequate rainfall throughout the year. More than 50 percent suffers from a deficiency throughout the year, and in nearly all of the remaining 40 percent the winter rains are inadequate. In most of the country the rainy season extends from late May to October or November, and its onset is so sudden that May rather than one of the summer months is the hottest of the year. It also falls with so great an irregularity that a Mexican agricultural official has called it the country's most serious agricultural problem, particularly in the temperate areas where as much as 90 percent of the cultivable land requires irrigation for fully efficient utilization.

Mineral Resources

Mineral resources are abundant and varied in nearly all parts of the country; only the Yucatán Peninsula is generally lacking in known reserves. Precious metals were mined by pre-Columbian Indians, and there were reports of gold that first led Spanish expeditions to the Mexican mainland. Silver production soon replaced gold in importance, but the value of precious metals production was replaced by that of other minerals only well after the start of the twentieth century; and in the mid-1970s substantial reserves of both still awaited exploitation.

Gold is found principally in veins in the Sierra Madre Occidental, but some placer deposits are worked. Mexico is one of the world's leading producers of silver, which is often found in conjunction with other ores. There are deposits in a large majority of the states. The most extensive occurrences are in the states of Chihuahua, Hidalgo, Zacatecas, and Durango, but a single nugget found in Sonora weighed more than 1 ton. A mine in Guanajuato, developed in the early 1970s, was the first new silver property opened in more than fifty years.

Some 1.5 billion tons of primarily low-grade copper reserves are widely distributed, but many are so located that exploitation is difficult. Half or

20

more of the production comes from deposits in Sonora, but there are important reserves in the states of Baja California, Zacatecas, Guanajuato, Jalisco, and Michoacán. The mineral also exists in Guerrero, Oaxaca, and Chiapas.

The country is among the world's leaders in lead and zinc production. Lead exists in at least twenty-three states, but most of the output and known reserves are in Chihuahua. Zinc, frequently produced in conjunction with lead or as a by-product of silver ores, is found principally in Chihuahua, Coahuila, Durango, Guanajuato, Guerrero, and Zacatecas.

Although Mexican iron ore production is not sufficient to meet the demands of its growing steel industry, there are more than 100 deposits with proven ore reserves totaling more than 250 million tons. Estimates of total reserves run as high as 700 or 800 million tons, but only about 20 percent of the known deposits have proven reserves in excess of 1 million tons. Most of the production comes from Durango and Coahuila.

Manganese is produced in limited quantities in both of the northern Sierra Madre ranges and in the state of Baja California Sur. Some tungsten and molybdenum are mined in Sonora; there are deposits of mercury in the Sierra Madre del Sur; and tin, cadmium, and bismuth are found in widely scattered deposits.

In the early 1970s the extent of Mexico's uranium resources remained in question. Deposits were reported in Durango, Sonora, Nuevo León, and other northern states, and total ore reserves were estimated on the basis of current information at 4.6 million tons. The National Nuclear Energy Institute, however, announced in 1974 that, although there was reason to believe that large reserves existed, several years of intensive exploration had failed to produce any major discoveries.

Mexico is the world's second largest producer of sulfur, the country's most important nonmetallic mineral. It occurs in at least eighteen states, but the largest deposits are in the saline domes of the Isthmus of Tehuantepec. Exploration carried out in a single five-year period during the late 1960s and early 1970s resulted in a tripling of the known reserve in this area. There are major fluorspar deposits in San Luís Potosí and Coahuila; and barite, dolomite, clays, and construction materials are widely distributed. Salt is produced by solar evaporation in the state of Baja California Sur, and the salt pans of Oaxaca are used by the chemical and pharmaceutical industries. In addition, there are salt domes along the coast of the Gulf of Mexico.

Opals are found in Querétaro and on the Pacific coast; amethysts come from Guerrero, turquoise from Zacatecas, agates from around the United States border, and onyx from the Baja California Peninsula and Puebla. A pearling industry in the state of Baja California Sur was being revived in the mid-1970s, and volcanic glass and quartz crystal are used in fashioning handicrafts. The Aztecs used large quantities of jade in fabricating jewelry and artifacts, but one of Mexico's mysteries is the fact that no jade deposits have been discovered since the conquest.

The largest of the known coalfields and nearly all of the bituminous coal production are concentrated in the Sabinas Coal Basin in Coahuila and in smaller adjacent fields. There are also some bituminous reserves in Chihuahua, Chiapas, Jalisco, and Veracruz, and small quantities of anthracite coal are found in Durango, Michoacán, Puebla, Sonora, and Tamaulipas.

Known and possible petroleum reserves occur in a series of sedimentary basins that extend from near the United States border in Nuevo León and Tamaulipas in an almost unbroken chain across those states, Veracruz, and Tabasco and into Campeche. There are numerous producing fields including the important Reynosa natural gasfield in the north.

Farther to the west, a zone of possible petroleum resources flanks these sedimentary basins in a wide strip that extends from near El Paso, Texas, across the Sierra Madre Oriental and southeastward to Campeche. The remaining parts of Coahuila, northern Chihuahua, the remainder of the Yucatán Peninsula, the west coast of Baja California Peninsula, and the interior of Chiapas are also considered possible petroleum zones. In early 1974 the new Reforma field in Chiapas had twenty-three producing wells, and other adjacent fields were reportedly being developed.

After a period of stagnation, the Mexican petroleum industry in the early 1970s was in another growth stage. During the 1960s Tabasco had become a major producing state with four fields, and the submarine extension of the Gulf Coast fields off the mouths of the Pánuco and Tuxpan rivers near Tampico were under exploration. In 1973 it was speculated that as little as 10 percent of the zones likely to produce petroleum had been fully prospected, and exploration was reported in progress in twenty-three states as well as in the continental shelf off the peninsula of Baja California. In 1974 important new strikes were reported in the southern state of Chiapas.

Vegetation

The indigenous population had a high regard for its forests, and a striking number of Indian-language place-names include the word *tree*. Excessive cutting for charcoal and slash-and-burn agriculture practiced over millennia have seriously depleted the woodlands, however, and it has been made a misdemeanor to cut a tree without a license. Conifer, cedar, and oak predominate in the northern mountains, especially in Durango where the largest pine-forest reserves are located. At lower levels, grass-covered savannas are dotted with palm and palmetto, and poplar and willow grow along river banks. Mahogany, cedar, rosewood, ebony, and logwood are found in the tropical rain forest that borders the Gulf of Mexico in a broad band that extends southward from Tampico across the base of the Yucatán Peninsula and the northern part of Oaxaca. Seasonal tropic forest and dry scrub prevail elsewhere in the

22

Gulf Coast and in the lowlands of the Pacific Coast. A small town in Oaxaca has grown up around a famous single *ahuehuetl*, or giant, cypress tree that has a bole more than 160 feet in circumference and is believed to be the oldest living thing in the Americas.

Dry scrub and grassland are characteristic of most of the flatter lands of the North, the North Pacific, portions of Central Mexico, and the Isthmus of Tehuantepec. The most conspicuous of the vegetation species are the cacti. A cactus appears on the Mexican coat-of-arms, and various kinds of cacti are characteristic features of the Mexican landscape. The saguaro is a giant arboreal growth that reaches fifty feet or more in height, and columns of the cereus cactus stand like fences with heights of twenty to twenty-five feet. The nopal, or prickly pear, familiar to the southwestern United States, produces a fruit that is eaten raw or used in making candies. The pulpy-leafed maguey cactus is a kind of agave cultivated on plantations in Jalisco for use in the preparation of the alcoholic beverages pulque and tequila; and henequen—another agave— is cultivated on the Yucatán Peninsula for the production of fiber.

Some temperate grassland occurs in the northern part of the North Pacific, on the coastline of Tamaulipas, and in Central Mexico. Savannas made up of subtropical and tropical grasslands and scattered trees are found along the coastlines of Central Mexico and the South Pacific, and mangrove thickets line the Bay of Campeche.

Flowers grow everywhere and are an important part of Mexican life. The floating gardens of Xochomilco Park in Mexico City are among the world's most famous floral displays, and the management of a hotel in the Veracruz mountain town of Fortín de las Flores (Little Fort of the Flowers) scatters thousands of fresh gardenias in its swimming pool each morning. There were two important flower gods in the Aztec pantheon, and frangipani and magnolia were reserved for the Aztec nobility. Throughout the country the blue blossoms of jacaranda trees and purple and red bougainvillea line the streets and adorn the walls of cities and towns. Most of the cacti produce vivid flowers, and wildflowers carpet the northern deserts after the occasional rains. An early United States ambassador introduced the Mexican Christmas flower—the poinsettia— to North America; and cosmos, snapdragons, marigolds, dahlias and myriads of orchids are indigenous. More than 800 species of orchid, most of them found in the jungles of Chiapas, have been classified.

Mexico's tropical forests gave the world chocolate (from the cacao trees of Chiapas) and vanilla. The word *chocolate* is derived from the Aztec word *chocolotl* and the word *vanilla* comes from Mexico through the Spanish word *vaina* (pod). The chicle used in preparation of chewing gum comes from the latex of the sapodilla tree, and wild rubber and sarsaparilla are gathered in the forests. Among the herbs that were known to the pre-Columbian Indians are the foxglove plant used in making digitalis, barks used in the preparation of purges and disinfectants, and a multitude of plants that are part of the standard pharmacopoeia. A plant that grows only in Mexico, the Discorea composita, is gathered in Veracruz, Oaxaca, Tabasco, and Chiapas for preparation of a vegetable hormone that is the essential ingredient of the contraceptive pill.

Wildlife

The Isthmus of Tehuantepec serves as a kind of wildlife dividing line separating the Middle American mammalian species to its south from the Northern American species. Indigenous mammals of the northern part of the country are almost identical to those of the southwestern United States. There are several varieties of deer, bobcat, puma, lynx, marten, gray fox, bear, mule sheep, coyote, porcupine, peccary, skunk, badger, rabbit, and squirrel. The predominantly tropical species of the south include ocelot, jaguar, tapir, howler and spider monkeys, opossum, large and small anteaters, paca, agouti, armadillo, and kinkajou.

The Tehuantepec line separating the northern and southern species is not a distinct one. Most southern species are found throughout the tropical lowlands and some, such as the opossum and the armadillo, are seen as far north as the southwestern United States. Similarly, northern mammals sometimes penetrate the higher elevations of the southern mountain systems.

Marine turtles were once plentiful off both the eastern and western coastlines. They are still found off the shores of the peninsula of Baja California, but a sharp increase in their catch during the 1960s because of demand for their skins and shells indicated endangerment of the species. In general, Baja California is one of the world's most important sanctuaries of marine mammalian wildlife. Guadalupe Island is the only known home of elephant seals, and the only known mating and nursery grounds of gray whales is in Magdalena Bay. Dolphins are also common off the coasts of Baja California.

The small Mexican eagle is the country's national symbol, and the sacred bird of the Mayas, the quetzal, can still be occasionally found on the Yucatán Peninsula. The most familiar large bird of Mexico, however, is the *zopilote*, a turkey buzzard that is a useful scavenger. The doves of Mexico are famous, and there are many quail and pheasants. During the colder months North American bird species migrate to Mexico, and parrots, parakeets, and macaws are plentiful in the southern tropical lowlands.

Several kinds of rattlesnake are common in the deserts of northern Mexico, and in tropical latitudes a common snake is the *palanca*, related to the fer-de-lance. Alligators are sometimes found in the southern rivers and streams. Lizards range from the five-foot tropical iguanas that are prized as food both for their chicken-like flesh and for their eggs to the tiny nocturnal lizards of the Gulf Coast. Among the amphibians are salamanders, frogs that include a tree-climbing variety in the southern jungles, and a marine toad that measures up to eight inches in length.

Among the insect pests, the most pernicious are the mosquitoes that once spread malaria and yellow fever on the Gulf Coast and have not entirely been exterminated. Crop-destroying pests are only gradually being controlled by sprays and other means; in 1960 it was calculated that almost 700,000 acres of agricultural production were lost because of pests. Army ants, common in Central Mexico, have a direct bearing on the agricultural cycle. Agronomists have found that the reluctance of peasants to plant corn during a certain phase of the moon is not superstition; it is during this phase that army ants are on the march. The *garrapata* is a particularly tenacious tick of the northern deserts, and the stings of the many scorpions are always painful and sometimes fatal. Scorpions are traditionally most lethal in Durango where craftsmen demonstrate a perverse pride by imbedding these creatures in glass and selling the products as jewelry and ashtrays. An ant common to Tlaxcala produces an egg much prized as a kind of caviar. The appreciable number of workers in this generally impoverished state who earn a marginal living gathering ant eggs during one season of the year subsists during another season gathering the equally edible and prized maggots that inhabit the maguey cactus.

A lack of fondness for fish—a prejudice shared by most Latin Americans—is a cause of concern for Mexican nutritionists (see ch. 7). A great number of many varieties of fish are found off both coasts and in the inland lakes and streams. Among the freshwater species, rainbow and brook trout, silversides, and catfish are familiar; and the European carp has been introduced. The most highly regarded, however, is a particularly delicate kind of whitefish found in Lake Chapala and Lake Pátzcuaro, where the picturesque butterfly-shaped nets of the fishermen are favorite subjects of photographers.

Marine fishing grounds on the Pacific coast are at their best off the coast of the Baja California Peninsula, where warm southern waters merge with subarctic currents from the north. The resulting diversity of marine flora and fauna and water temperature combine with depth of ocean beds and coastal irregularities to produce one of the world's finest fishing grounds. On the Gulf of Mexico almost correspondingly fine fishing is found in the waters of the Campeche bank.

Mexican waters as a whole contain more than 100 important marine species, including those common to tropical and temperate climates and to coastal and deep waters. The species also include the surface and ground feeders and the sedentary and migratory.

Among the more important of the Gulf and Caribbean species are shrimp, oysters, jewfish, croaker, swordfish, snapper, pompano, king mackerel, snook, mullet, sea bass, and haddock. In the Pacific waters the most important are shrimp, crayfish, spiny lobster, sardine, croaker, tuna, skipjack, sea bass, hake, and anchovy. In terms of the volume of catch in marine waters, shrimp, sardines, and oysters make up over half of the total. In addition, some of the world's best deep-sea sport fishing is found on the coast off the North Pacific region and off the Caribbean coast of the Yucatán Peninsula.

SETTLEMENT PATTERNS

Central Mexico comprises only 14 percent of the national territory, but in 1970 nearly 50 percent of the population resided there. The North, with more than 40 percent of the territory, had less than 19 percent of the population; and the 8 percent that lived in the North Pacific occupied 21 percent of the territory. Only in the small Gulf Coast and South Pacific regions did population density approximate the national average. In both population and territorial extent, each made up about 12 percent of the national total (see table 1).

Since pre-Columbian times, this irregularly patterned settlement has been concentrated in the *tierra templada* intermontane valleys and basins where the amount of arable land, availability of water, and climatic conditions have encouraged habitation. In the oases of the great northern basins, in the smaller basins of the central part of the country, and in the intensively farmed intermontane pockets of southern Mexico the steepest mountain slopes as well as bottomlands have been occupied since antiquity. The coastal lowlands contain the country's richest soils, but until after World War II they remained sparsely populated. Improved health and sanitation in the once pestilential coastlands of the Gulf of Mexico and the building of roads and the development of irrigation on the alluvial deltas of the Pacific coast, however, have resulted in a relative increase in the rural populations of these coastal areas. Between 1960 and 1970 the rural populations of all Gulf Coast states other than Yucatán increased at rates greater than the national average.

A simplified land-utilization map shows a concentration of plantation agriculture in the Mexicali Valley near the mouth of the Colorado River, in the drainage basin of the lower Rio Grande, along the northern Pacific coastline, along the full length of the Gulf of Mexico, and in the central lowlands of Chiapas. Subsistence agriculture predominates in the volcanic plateau and in most of the remainder of the country lying to the south. Pastoralism occupies the Northern Plateau and the remainder of the north; portions of the Sierra Madre Occidental are little developed. Although pasturelands make up more than two-fifths of the national territory, little more than one-third of this proportion consists of low hills and plains well adapted to stockraising; the remainder is made up of steeply sloped highland terrain.

Population is scantiest in the pastoral areas and heaviest in areas where subsistence agriculture prevails, although much of the commercial produce comes from very small farms. Except in the sparsely populated pastoral areas, the prevailing pattern of settlement is that of the nuclear farm village; except for some parts of northern Mexico, almost no one lives on isolated farms.

Table 1. Mexico, Geographic Regions by Territorial Extent and Populations for
1960 and 1970
(distribution in percent)

Regions and Political Subdivisions	Territory	Population 1960	Population 1970	Increase 1960-70
Central Mexico:				
Federal District.........................	0.1	13.9	14.2	41.1
Aguascalientes	0.3	0.7	0.7	39.0
Guanajuato	1.6	5.0	4.7	30.8
Hidalgo	1.1	2.8	2.5	20.0
Jalisco	4.0	7.0	6.7	34.9
México................................	1.1	5.4	7.9	102.0
Michoacán.............................	3.0	5.3	4.8	25.3
Morelos	0.3	1.1	1.3	59.5
Puebla	1.7	5.7	5.2	27.1
Querétaro	0.6	1.0	1.0	36.8
Tlaxcala..............................	0.2	1.0	0.9	21.3
Subtotal............................	14.0	48.9	49.9	41.9
Chihuahua............................	12.5	3.6	3.3	31.4
Coahuila	7.7	2.6	2.3	22.8
Durango	6.1	2.2	1.9	23.4
Nuevo León	3.3	3.1	3.5	57.1
San Luís Potosí	3.2	3.0	2.7	22.3
Tamaulipas	4.1	2.9	3.0	42.3
Zacatecas	3.8	2.3	2.0	16.3
Subtotal............................	40.7	19.7	18.7	33.6
North Pacific:				
Baja California........................	3.6	1.5	1.8	48.5
Baja California Sur.....................	3.6	0.2	0.3	75.8
Nayarit	1.4	1.1	1.1	39.5
Sinaloa...............................	3.0	2.4	2.6	51.1
Sonora...............................	9.4	2.2	2.3	40.3
Subtotal............................	21.0	7.8	8.1	49.5
Gulf Coast:				
Campeche	2.9	0.5	0.5	49.5
Quintana Roo	2.1	0.1	0.2	75.7
Tabasco	1.3	1.4	1.6	54.8
Veracruz	3.7	7.8	7.9	39.9
Yucatán..............................	2.2	1.8	1.6	23.5
Subtotal............................	12.2	11.6	11.8	47.7
South Pacific:				
Chiapas	3.8	3.5	3.2	29.6
Colima	0.3	0.5	0.5	46.6
Guerrero	3.2	3.5	3.3	34.6
Oaxaca...............................	4.8	4.9	4.5	16.7
Subtotal............................	12.1	12.4	11.5	26.4
Total	100.0	100.0	100.0	38.5

Source: Adapted from Organización de los Estados Americanos, Instituto Interameri-
cano de Estadística, *América en Cifras 1972, Situación Física: Territorio y Clima*,
Washington, 1972, pp. 18–19; and Kenneth Ruddle and Donald Odermann (eds.),
Statistical Abstract of Latin America, 1971, Los Angeles, 1972, Table 8.

The farm-village pattern predates the Spanish conquest, and the villages, most of them with populations of less than 300, have similar appearances. There is a central plaza, a town hall, a parish church, a store or two, a bandstand, and a village well. Some of the larger villages have grown into towns, but they retain their distinctively rural characteristics.

The basic pattern of village land tenure is that of the *ejido* (see Glossary), an institution established in the Constitution of 1917 for distribution of the lands of the confiscated haciendas. In a few localities the *ejidos* are organized as collectives, but in a large majority the *ejido* unit is a quasi-private farm that is worked individually and can be inherited; it cannot, however, ordinarily be subdivided or sold. If a farmer moves away, his land remains with the communal governing body. In 1970 nearly 820,000 farm operators and almost half of the employers and self-employed workers who engaged in agriculture were *ejidatarios*. There were *ejidatarios* in every state and territory of the country and in the Federal District, but the largest numbers were in Veracruz, Chiapas, Yucatán, México, Michoacán, Guanajuato, and San Luís Potosí. The *ejido* plots vary in acreage with the productivity of the property, but most are small or submarginal in size.

Another form of rural land tenure was added in 1947 with the passage of legislation permitting establishment of small private farms in farm colonies on expropriated rangeland or on land brought into production through reclamation or irrigation. The private farm properties are also usually small but, in these as well as in *ejido* units, relatives often are proprietors of adjacent plots and operate the several properties as units, and entire communities may agree to grow the same crop. Thus, a large proportion of the commercial crops continue to be grown on *ejidos*, and the pattern of settlement continues to be dictated by the kind of land utilization. In rangeland, for example, the ownership of enough land to support 500 head of cattle is permitted, an amount sufficient for members of a family or a group of ranchers to maintain a ranch on the barren Northern Plateau covering an enormous area (see ch. 13).

Since World War II all regions of the country have been experiencing a relative decline in rural population, as country people have flocked to the cities and towns. In 1950 more than 57 percent of the population was rural. Rural and urban sectors were virtually equal in population in 1960, and in 1970 some 57.7 percent of the people lived in urban localities. Between 1960 and 1970 the urban and rural sectors gained in population by 52.5 percent and 15.3 percent, respectively. Although birthrates were probably higher in the countryside, the rural rate of population was less than half the national average rate of demographic growth.

Mexican statisticians define an urban locality as one with 2,500 or more inhabitants, a considerably greater number than that used by most countries. Moreover, there are increasing numbers of small industrial centers with populations of less than this number that are unrealistically classified as rural. Conversely, however, a very large number of farm villages have grown to more than 2,500 in population without losing their rural characteristics, and on the fringes of the largest cities an uncounted but large number of urban farmers continue to live under rural conditions. In the early 1970s some authorities argued that far less than half of the Mexican population could realistically be considered urbanized.

The degree and dynamics of urbanization vary by region and by state and do not necessarily correspond to the overall density of the population in the state or in the region. For example, Chihuahua in 1970 had a population density that was only about one-fourth of the national average, but almost two-thirds of that population was urban. Between 1960 and 1970 its urban population had grown by 67 percent while the rural population had remained almost unchanged. It was in the North as a whole that the country's heaviest rural out-migration occurred between 1960 and 1970. The rate of rural out-migration was somewhat lower in the South Pacific, but there were no large cities in that region to attract migrants and, as a consequence, its rate of population growth as a whole was the lowest of the five regions.

Despite the fact that the states of Central Mexico are the most densely populated in the country, much of their population is made up of subsistence farm families crowded on small plots. The small state of Hidalgo, for example, had a 1970 population density more than twice the national average, but little more than one-fifth of its population was urban, and it was one of the few states of the country in which the rate of rural population growth exceeded that of the urban sector between 1960 and 1970. In general, the relative decline in the rural population of Central Mexico was due less to out-migration than to the rapid growth of its cities as a consequence of migration from other regions.

Urbanization in the North Pacific and the Gulf Coast, the two fastest growing regions, was strikingly different in character and degree. In 1970 all political subdivisions of the North Pacific were predominantly urban, and all those of the Gulf Coast were predominantly rural with the exception of Campeche. Both had rural population growth increases relatively higher than the national average, but the urban increase in the North Pacific was the higher of the two. The large cities of Tijuana and Mexicali grew faster than the Gulf Coast cities of Veracruz and Mérida and, more importantly, the growth of smaller urban localities along the Pacific coast was faster than in any other part of the country (see Cities of Mexico, this ch.).

In 1970 there were fifteen cities with populations in excess of 200,000 (see table 2). Including their metropolitan areas, they had a total population of 15 million, well over half of the entire urban population. The true big city total was probably greater than 15 million; data on metropolitan populations outside the city proper are not always available, and in many instances the physical location of Mexican cities is such as to place limits on the extent to which the city itself can grow.

When the more desirable available land in a small pocket or basin has been occupied, population tends to spill over surrounding ridges to adjacent areas. In addition, fast growth may cause new cities to appear in one metropolitan area. The new city of Netzahualcóyotl in the state of México is a case in point. A fast growing working-class municipality, it is part of the Mexico City urban complex.

An exact count of the true size of all of the large urban conglomerates is not possible, but they represent a large and growing majority of the urban population. The migrants from the countryside who continue to swell the populations may previously have migrated to smaller centers, close to their rural place or origin. Unable to find work in these smaller centers, they move on to larger centers and, ultimately, to one of the major cities, most frequently to Mexico City, where in 1970 about half the population had been born elsewhere.

Among the individuals who engage in this urban migration, women appear to outnumber men by a very small margin. No statistical count of migrants by sex is available, but since the number of males and females in the country in 1970 was virtually equal, the fact that 51.7 percent of the population of Mexico City was female was almost certainly the result of urban migration. In thirty-seven major urban centers, women were in a majority in all but three but in no instance was the majority significant. The extent to which women migrants outnumber men is moderate for Latin America where, as a general rule, there is little rural employment opportunity for females, and girls and young women in large numbers come to the cities in search of employment. For example, in 1970 nearly 54 percent of the population in Buenos Aires was female.

The migrants are young. A 1971 survey of selected migrants to Mexico City at various levels of income found the average age at the time of migration to have been about twenty-one. Those who had come from other urban localities had an average of one year's education more than the average of natives of the city. The proportion occupying white-collar or higher positions far exceeded that of the city born, and the upward social mobility of the children of interurban migrants exceeded that of the children of natives. Migrants who had come directly from the countryside had better educations than the rural average, and many had acquired skills and found stable employment.

During the years since World War II the Mexican government has become increasingly concerned over the rate of urban growth. It has placed heavy burdens on public services and schools, given rise to severe housing shortages, and caused a variety of social problems.

In an effort to slow the exodus from the countryside, between 1965 and 1970 alone, the government created additional *ejidos* in order to provide land for 375,000 landless farm workers. It has also opened up additional agricultural land through extensive irrigation and land reclamation projects. Between 1930 and 1960 the acreage of *ejido* and other farm properties was increased by nearly 17 percent. One of the

Table 2. Mexico, Population of Principal Cities in 1970 and Percent of
Increase Since 1960[1]

City	State	Population	Percent Growth
Mexico City	Federal District	6,874,165 (8,587,630)[3]	29.1[2]
Guadalajara	Jalisco	1,193,601 (1,455,824)[3]	62.0
Monterrey	Nuevo León	858,107 (1,213,479)[3]	16.4
Netzahualcóyotl	México	580,436	....[4]
Ciudad Juárez	Chihuahua	407,370	55.3
Puebla	Puebla	401,603	39.1
León	Guanajuato	364,990	73.8
Tijuana	Baja California	277,306 (327,400)[3]	82.2
Mexicali	Baja California	263,498	50.3
Chihuahua	Chihuahua	257,027	71.3
San Luís Potosí	San Luís Potosí	230,039	43.7
Torreón	Coahuila	223,104 (322,557)[3]	23.9
Veracruz	Veracruz	214,072	47.8
Mérida	Yucatán	212,097	24.0
Tampico	Tamaulipas	179,584 (270,414)[3]	46.3

[1] The following 18 cities had 1970 populations between 100,000 and 200,000: Acapulco, Aguascalientes, Ciudad Obregón, Colónia Agrícola, Culiacán, Cuernavaca, Durango, Hermosillo, Irapuato, Jalapa, Matamoros, Mazatlán, Morelia, Nuevo Laredo, Poza Rica, Querétaro, Reynosa, Saltillo, Toluca.

[2] Growth of Federal District.

[3] Figures in parentheses include population of metropolitan area; only growth of city proper included in percentile growth 1960-70.

[4] Not incorporated as a city in 1960.

Source: Adapted from *Demographic Yearbook, 1972*, New York, 1973, Table 7; and Unión Panamericana, Instituto Interamericano de Estadística, *América en Cifras 1967, Situación Demográfica: Estado y Movimiento de la Población*, Washington, 1968, Table 201-07.

earliest and best known of these undertakings developed in the valley of the Papaloapán River in the interior of Veracruz and was modeled on the Tennessee Valley Authority project in the United States. During the early 1970s the thrust of rural resettlement activity of this nature was directed toward the interior of the South Pacific region.

In addition to attempting to relieve urban crowding by dissuading country people from coming to the cities, the government has tried to slow the rate of growth of the largest cities by a decentralization of industry. In 1970 about 60 percent of production was concentrated in Mexico City, Guadalajara, and Monterrey. The petroleum and petrochemical industries were centered in Tampico and cities of the Gulf Coast, and there was considerable industrial development in the cities along the United States border in connection with the so-called border-industries program (see ch. 13). In general, however, the spread of industries was limited.

Some decentralization had occurred as early as the 1950s when a few industrial enterprises based on the utilization of local raw materials were established in heavily populated rural areas and drew on the surrounding farm villages for their unskilled labor. The decentralization program in its current form, however, dates from a 1971 law that established a schedule of tax reductions, depletion allowances, and other incentives encouraging regional industrial development. A July 1972 decree issued pursuant to this legislation divided the country into three zones. Mexico City, Guadalajara, and Monterrey, and surrounding areas were ineligible for program benefits. Certain other areas, all located in Central Mexico, were to receive limited benefits, and the remainder of the country was to benefit fully from the program. In addition, a 1971 decree provided for subsidies to small and medium-sized industries established along the country's northern border.

By the end of 1972 numerous new industrial centers planned under the decentralization program were on the drawing boards or under construction. They were to be located not in remote rural areas but in the vicinity of the large cities where they could draw on existing transport and other facilities, but at sufficient distance for them to exist as separate entities and to draw surplus labor away from the parent city. One of the most important, named Cuautitlán Izcalli, was under construction in what had been corn and alfalfa fields about twelve miles north of the limits of the Federal District on an express highway connecting Mexico City and Querétaro. The new city was to reach a projected population of 1.6 million in the early 1980s.

CITIES OF MEXICO

Mexico City is one of the great urban centers of the world and ranks with Buenos Aires, Argentina, and São Paulo, Brazil, as the largest in Latin America. The 1970 census listed the population of the city proper at 2.9 million, but a 1972 decree had the effect of incorporating other districts *(delegaciones)* of the Federal District in it, and at least five contiguous municipalities of the state of México are part of its metropolitan area. This entire urban complex is usually considered part of Mexico City, which President Luís Echeverría in 1972 estimated to have more than 10 million inhabitants.

Founded in the early thirteenth century on the several islands of Lake Texcoco in the Valley of México, Mexico City was the capital of the Aztecs and is believed to be the oldest continuously inhabited urban locality in the Americas. There are evidences of human habitation beneath the Pedregal, a lava flow on the southern perimeter of the city, and stone weapon heads have been found near the city in proximity to the bones of prehistoric animals.

Mexico City is located at an elevation of more than 7,000 feet and is surrounded by some of the country's highest peaks. Several are located within the confines of the Federal District, where densely urbanized districts are mixed with a small amount of remaining farmland. In 1970 about 4 percent of the Federal District was classified as rural.

After the Spanish conquest, the canals of the Venice-like island capital of the Aztecs were gradually filled, and in the seventeenth century Lake Texcoco was partially drained by construction of a ditch and tunnel across a low divide to the waters of the Pánuco River system. The continuing process of land reclamation and the gradual elimination of the lake have given the city a highly unstable foundation that has been worsened since World War II by a lowering of the water table as a result of increasing requirements for water for industrial and domestic use. Many of the colonial buildings have become badly tilted and sunken, and the newer high-rise architecture has been constructed on piles and literally floated on great subterranean caissons. The technique, which appears to have been fully successful in accomplishing stability, has also made the buildings highly resistant to the frequent and severe earthquakes to which the city is vulnerable. In general, however, the threat of earthquakes has limited the heights of buildings to five or fewer stories.

Among the numerous plazas of Mexico City, the centrally located square named the Zócalo can be considered the center of the country as well as of the city in the sense that in many if not most of Mexico's cities and towns, the central plaza has been given the same name. In the immediate vicinity of the Zócalo much colonial architecture remains. Elsewhere in the inner city old mansions have been replaced by modern architecture, and old residential areas have become part of the downtown business district. Within the Federal District, the numerous clusters of working-class and middle and upper class residential neighborhoods are in some cases separated by stretches of open land. Some of the finest of the newer residences are scattered around the Pedregal lava bed, built of the same lava rock on which their foundations are laid. There are also enough factories both inside and outside the Federal District, and a sufficiently heavy flow of automotive traffic, to give Mexico City a serious smog problem that is aggravated by its bowl-shaped site.

In the contiguous metropolitan municipalities of the state of México, the same mixed pattern of settlement is continued. The ancient town of San Angel has cobblestone streets and colonial Spanish houses but is entirely surrounded by factories, shantytowns, and areas of low-cost housing. There are some fine residential neighborhoods in the outer suburbs, but the most conspicuous features of the area are the serried blocks of low-cost dwellings. The government has located many of its housing projects in this outer suburban area, which in the early 1970s was the fastest growing part of Mexico City and probably of Mexico.

Guadalajara is the country's second city in size and one of its fastest growing. It has a well balanced economy based on the processing of local agricultural production, manufacturing of goods for an extensive hinterland, production of handicraft, and service as a transport and communications center. It has an attractive setting and climate, is a cultural and educational center, and is the place of origin of the famed mariachi street musicians. Many old buildings survive, but industrial development and demographic growth since World War II have been accompanied by much widening of streets and construction of new business and residential buildings.

Also located in Central Mexico and the country's sixth city in size, Puebla (its seldom-used full name is Puebla de Zaragoza) is the country's most Spanish city and perhaps its most traditional. The national women's costume, the *china poblana* (literally, Chinese girl of Puebla), originated there (see ch. 7). Its industrial growth since World War II, however, has been greater than that of any city other than Mexico City, Guadalajara, or Monterrey. As a consequence, there has been much modernization and damage to the colonial atmosphere.

The other large cities of Central Mexico, León and Querétaro, are both located in the Bajío. León lies in a fertile agricultural district and derives much of its importance from its status as a market center. It is also a shoe manufacturing center and is noted for its fine leather handicraft. Querétaro was an important pre-Columbian settlement and is a picturesque city of old buildings and winding streets. It has little manufacturing but serves an important agricultural hinterland; it is a railway and highway center and is famous for its silver.

The third urban center of the country in size and the largest city of the North is Monterrey, a name familiar to millions of North Americans because of the perennially popular romantic song "It Happened in Monterrey." But Monterrey is a city of hard work rather than romance. Most of Mexico's great cities had their beginnings either as market towns or as mining camps. Monterrey, however, was colonized in the seventeenth century without the advantage either of agricultural hinterland or mineral wealth with the deliberate intent of establishing a settlement in the bleak and empty countryside of the Sierra Madre Oriental on the rim of the Northern Plateau.

Monterrey is an industrial city of breweries, textile mills, and glass and paper factories. It is a place of conservative values, and there are good-natured jokes about the thriftiness of its generally well-educated and skilled inhabitants. It is located in a small mountainside pocket in which the smog accumulation rivals that of Mexico City. The architecture of the city proper tends to be drab, but attractive suburbs have pushed their way up the surrounding mountain slopes, and in 1970 nearly one-third of the metropolitan population lived in three urban municipalities located outside the city.

Smaller but faster growing than Monterrey, the city of Chihuahua also lies on the Northern Plateau and has similar disadvantages of natural setting and climate. It is a ranching and mining center, however, and irrigation has made its hinterland an important producer of wheat and cotton. Located little more than 100 miles southwest of the United States border, it is an important railroad and highway junction and has an atmosphere in many ways similar to that of North American cities.

Two other large cities of the Northern Plateau are San Luís Potosí and Torreón. The former originated as a mining camp. It remains an important mining center and has an extensive agricultural hinterland. The latter is located in the great Mayarán Bolson and is the principal city of the La Laguna irrigated wheat and cotton district. The La Laguna irrigation project has failed to meet expections, however. The area is one of rural out-migration, and the city's growth has been relatively slow.

The large cities along the United States border are distinctively different from all other Mexican cities. Tijuana and Mexicali are located in the North Pacific, and Ciudad Juárez and the smaller cities of Matamoros, Reynosa, and Nuevo Laredo are located in the North. They resemble one another and owe much of their identity to their location on the border.

The border cities exist largely as centers for Mexican-American trade and as attractions for one-day tourists; as a consequence they are commercial cities with a great many shops, restaurants, and bars of varying degrees of excellence. During the 1960s and early 1970s, however, they were also becoming industrialized. Mexicali and Matamoros, in particular, had become centers for prosperous irrigated agricultural hinterlands.

Tijuana, the fastest growing large urban center in the country, has traditionally been a city of tawdry shops and bars, sleazy motels, and activities of dubious morality. During the 1960s and early 1970s its character changed substantially, and the change was accelerated in 1972 by completion of the dorsal highway linking the city with Cape San Lucas on the southern tip of the Baja California Peninsula. In the mid-1970s it remained essentially a tourist city, but the quality and nature of the tourist attractions had substantially improved.

All of the coastal cities with populations in excess of 200,000 in 1970 were located on the Gulf of Mexico. Veracruz, the largest, is the only major port in a country where most of the international movement of goods is overland to the United States. Veracruz is a mixture of the old and new, in which varicolored old stucco and wood buildings with overhanging balconies are mixed with a few factories and modern shops and houses along the winding streets. Tampico is located on the coast at the border between the North and Gulf Coast regions at a point where two major rivers flow into the Gulf of Mexico. It is the country's principal oil refining and shipping center and is an exportation point for tropical fruits and products. Mérida, the only urban center of importance on the Yucatán Peninsula, is located a few miles inland from the small port city of Progreso. It is the center of the henequen industry. A modern and conspicuously clean city, Mérida is visually peculiar because of the enormous number of rooftop windmills (reputedly, some 15,000) that draw water from the cenotes that are characteristic of that part of Yucatán.

There are no large cities on or near the Pacific coast other than those located on the United States border. Smaller coastal cities and towns, however, experienced a remarkable growth during the 1960s and early 1970s as tourist centers. The entire Pacific coastline from Acapulco northward was becoming known as the Mexican Riviera.

Acapulco is the prototype and largest of these new urban resorts. Isolated from the rest of Mexico by the Sierra Madre del Sur mountains, it was the departure point for the Manila convoy during the colonial era but remained little more than a village until after World War II. By 1970, however, its population had reached 174,000. The countless hotels catered to persons of modest as well as lavish income, and it was the first choice of middle-class Mexican vacationers as well as many world travelers.

Some 500 miles to the northwest of Acapulco, Puerto Vallarta was a smaller but even faster growing tourist center. It was the natural vacation spot for residents of Guadalajara, where newspapers regularly carried advertisements concerning Puerto Vallarta hotels and real estate. Farther north still, the small cities of Mazatlán and Guaymas were growing rapidly in response to the increasing tourist trade, and in various coastal localities entire new tourist centers were planned or under construction. On the Baja California Peninsula alone, in 1974 the Mexican government had plans for the dredging of five deepwater ports, the installation of seventeen desalinization plants, and the paving of airport runways to accommodate visitors to twenty-six new tourist centers.

POPULATION STRUCTURE AND DYNAMICS

The 1970 census showed that Mexico had a population of more than 48 million, and an unofficial correction for underenumeration brought the total to more than 50 million. Earlier census figures show the rate of growth to have risen from about 1 percent annually at the time of the 1910 Revolution to 1.7 percent during the 1930s and to 3.4 percent during the 1960–70 intercensal period.

The scattered information available in 1974 indicated that the rate of population growth was still advancing and that the number of people in the country was, if anything, more than the census and its adjusted estimates had indicated. There were several 1973 population estimates of 56 million people, and 1973 annual growth was estimated at 3.5 percent or higher. During the early 1970s Latin America as a whole had a growth rate of slightly under 3 percent (see Population Problems, this ch.).

Vital statistics are frequently registered after a year or more of delay, and the proportion registered varies substantially by region. Under-registration of infant mortality in 1970 was estimated to have varied from nil in the Federal District to more than 50 percent in the state of Oaxaca. The best data available, therefore, are approximations that are valuable principally as indicators of trends.

The number of births per 1,000 inhabitants declined from 48.1 in 1940 to 43.4 in 1972. The overall death rate, however, dropped far more sharply, from 17.8 per 1,000 inhabitants in the 1945–49 period to 8.9 from 1965 to 1970, and in 1972 it was reported at 8.2. Life expectancy at birth increased sharply from a 41.5-year average for both sexes in 1940 to an anticipated 64.6 years for the 1970–75 period. During the years 1965 to 1970 it was calculated at 61.0 years for males and 63.7 years for females.

Between 1960 and 1970 the proportion of the Mexican population under the age of twenty increased from 54.3 to 56.7 percent of the total (see table 3). The country shared with Colombia, Ecuador, and the Dominican Republic the distinction of having the youngest population in the Americas. The proportion in the wage-earning age span of between fifteen and sixty-five years declined from more than 56 percent in 1930 to almost 50 percent in 1970. The increasing youthfulness of the population has placed an increasing burden on wage earners. In the early 1970s it also became a factor of increased political significance when the voting age was reduced from twenty-one to eighteen years.

The two sexes are about equal in number, and the proportions showed no change during the 1960–70 intercensal period. Males were in a majority in both census years through the age of fourteen but females outnumbered males in all subsequent age groups. Overall, the male and female sectors of the population were nearly equal in number in both 1960 and 1970.

Immigration, which formerly played an important part in determining the composition of the population, was of progressively decreasing

Table 3. Mexico, Population by Age-Group and Sex, 1960 and 1970
(in percent)

Age Group	1960			1970		
	Male	Female	Total	Male	Female	Total
0 to 4	8.4	8.1	16.5	8.6	8.3	16.9
5 to 9	7.7	7.5	15.2	8.2	7.8	16.0
10 to 14	6.4	6.1	12.5	6.8	6.5	13.3
15 to 19	5.0	5.1	10.1	5.2	5.3	10.5
20 to 39	13.0	14.0	27.0	12.6	13.2	25.8
40 to 64	7.4	7.5	13.9	6.8	7.1	13.9
65 and over...........	1.9	1.9	3.8	1.7	1.9	3.6
TOTAL*	100.0	100.0	100.0	100.0	100.0	100.0

*Figures may not total because of rounding.

Source: Adapted from Estados Unidos Mexicanos, Dirección General de Estadística, *Anuario Estadístico de los Estados Unidos Mexicanos, 1968–1969*, Mexico City, 1971, pp. 33-34.

significance after World War II. In 1970 only about 0.4 percent of the resident population was foreign born.

During the 1960s and early 1970s the number of people entering the country with immigrant visa documentation remained stable at a little more than 2,000, but this number did not represent the total addition of foreigners to the population. An unreported additional number entered with temporary documentation and later applied for resident status.

Retired United States citizens, estimated at 40,000 in the late 1960s, make up the largest resident alien group. Most of them live in and around Guadalajara, but there are also sizable colonies in Mexico City, Cuernavaca, Taxco, and several other localities. In the fast-growing Pacific tourist resort of Puerto Vallarta one neighborhood is referred to popularly as "gringo gulch."

Immigration law is restrictive as applied to those seeking to earn a livelihood unless they are members of diplomatic and consular missions or representatives of foreign companies. In any business organization, 90 percent of the personnel must be Mexican. Retired persons retain the legal status of immigrant *(inmigrante)* for five years but, after that time, they become permanent residents *(inmigrados)* who may seek employment.

During the 1960s and early 1970s the small inflow of immigrants was far outmatched by emigration, most of it to the United States. In 1972 about 64,000 emigrants departed for legal admission to the United States, but a far larger number probably crossed the border illegally in search of jobs that might pay seven times as much as they could hope for at home (see Boundaries and Political Subdivisions; Labor Force, this ch.).

POPULATION PROBLEMS

In the mid-1970s excessive urbanization, the uneven geographical distribution of the population, and a continuing sharp decline in the size of the labor force in relation to the size of the population as a whole were population problems of major concern to the Mexican government (see Settlement Patterns; Labor Force, this ch.). These considerations, however, were largely outgrowths of the basic problem of runaway population growth. Mexico ranked only ninth among the twenty-two Latin American and Caribbean countries in population density, but its growth rate was one of the highest in the world. Surveys in the late 1960s and early 1970s indicated that Mexican women regarded four children as about the ideal family size.

Historically, public policy and individual inclination have been *poblacionista* (favoring population growth), and the General Law of Population had provided specifically that "measures shall be taken . . . to increase the birth rate." In 1965, however, the private Foundation for Population Studies was founded as an affiliate of the London-based Planned Parenthood Federation. During the late 1960s it operated some forty family planning clinics and conducted training courses in conjunction with several university medical schools. In addition, the private Association for Maternal Health furnished planning services, and some assistance was furnished by the Rockefeller Foundation, the Church World Service, and Oxfam of Canada. The Mexican government permitted the Foundation for Population Studies to use some public health facilities in connection with its program. There was also a limited distribution of contraceptives, but the government avoided involvement in family planning, and the pertinent legislation in force remained favorable to large families.

President Echeverría, himself the father of eight children, entered office in 1970 after having taken the position that population growth was needed for economic development. Perhaps influenced by the findings of the 1970 census, he announced in 1972 that steps to encourage lower fertility would be initiated, and in January 1973 Mexico launched the program Integrated Family Planning (Planificación Familiar Integral). At that time it was calculated that 80 percent of the country's families did not have access to family planning services.

The government emphasized the voluntary nature of the new program. Such terms as *birth control* and *population control* were avoided, and no change was made in a highly restrictive abortion law. The National Union of Heads of Families, a Roman Catholic lay organization with a claimed membership of 500,000 people, reacted negatively to the new official attitude, but unexpected support may have been received from the Mexican Council of Bishops. In late 1972 that organization issued a widely publicized statement interpreted differently by various reporters. The consensus, however, indicated at least that the council recognized the existence of a problem and left to individual families the determination of their positions regarding family planning. Traditional objections to family planning continued during the early 1970s. More frequently heard, however, were criticisms directed specifically at what was said to be mass distribution of contraceptive devices to peasant women who had not been given adequate prior education in responsible parenthood.

At the beginning of 1973 the Directorate General of Maternal-Infant Medical Care was charged with general coordination of the new program. Participants included the social security agencies and all official and semiofficial organizations providing medical services, as well as the university medical schools and the two private planning entities that were already in existence. Early in 1974 a new General Law of Population was enacted and a National Population Council was created to prepare and implement projects relating to the planning of population growth.

In his 1973 annual message to the legislature, President Echeverría drew attention to the gravity of the population problem. In its 1973 congress the National Academy of Medicine had stressed the importance of family planning, and a former Mexican minister of foreign relations was named secretary general of the World Population Conference of the United Nations that met in Bucharest in August 1974. A mass circulation (270,000 copies) comic book called *Los Supermachos* (The Supermales) underlined the extent to which the man in the street had at least become aware of the existence of a population problem by devoting an issue to the somewhat scatological treatment of the family planning program.

LABOR FORCE

Structure

The 1970 census showed the labor force to have consisted of slightly over 13 million workers. Some 39.2 percent were engaged in primary or agricultural and related activities; 22.9 percent in secondary or industrial (mining, manufacturing, construction and public utilities) activities; 31.7 percent in tertiary or services activities, such as commercial, transport, and personal; and 6.2 percent in poorly identified activities or in personnel seeking work for the first time. Comparison with figures from the 1960 census showed a sharp decline in agricultural employment and substantial gains in both the industrial and the services sectors. Because the proportion engaged in poorly identified activities was much higher in 1970 than in 1960, however, the data from the two census years are not fully comparable (see table 4).

The labor force as a proportion of the total population fell sharply from 32.4 percent in 1960 to 26.9 percent in 1970, continuing a decline that had commenced during the 1950s. During the earlier decades of the twentieth century, the size of the labor force had grown at about the same rate as that of the population as a whole.

The downward trend, which appeared to have been arrested during the early 1970s, resulted in part from the increasing youthfulness of the population as a whole and from a larger proportion of school-age children remaining in school. Some authorities, however, had expected the labor force in 1970 to be made up of as many as 3 million more workers than were counted in the 1970 census. The participation rate was much lower than that in other Latin American countries with fast population growth and expanding school systems. It appears possible, however, that a large number of Mexicans did not join, or dropped out of, the labor force during the 1960s because of the inability to find jobs.

Agricultural workers in 1970 made up half of the country's employers and self-employed persons, nearly one-third of the wage and salary earners, and a large majority of the unpaid family workers. The distinction between the self-employed workers and the wage earner is not a clear one, however, since a large proportion of the agricultural labor force is made up of small farmers who work seasonally for hire in their own village or elsewhere in the country. Others leave the agricultural sector altogether on a part-time basis to engage in handicraft production or work in factories or construction projects.

The distinction between members of the agricultural labor force and economically inactive persons is also unclear. The 1970 census showed that about 1 million fewer workers were engaged in farming and related activities than in 1960. Several million country people had migrated to urban localities during the period, but the rural population had registered an increase sufficiently large to make an actual decline of 1 million in rural employment improbable. It appears likely that a more restrictive definition of labor force membership was employed in 1970 than in 1960. A large proportion of the farm population is made up of landless farm workers and of operators of submarginal farm plots who must work for hire during part of the year. According to a 1972 estimate, half of the 8 million people engaged in agriculture were in these two categories. These peasants, who worked an average of 100 or fewer days in the year, were estimated to constitute 65 percent or more of the agricultural labor force in the states of Baja California, Sonora, Tamaulipas, Guanajuato, Jalisco, and Michoacán.

In the mid-1970s manufacturing concerns ranged in size from Mexican Petroleum (Petróleos Mexicanos—PEMEX), the government petroleum company with 78,000 workers, to a great many one-man or one-family shops. In 1970 a government banking agency estimated that between 1.5 million and 2 million families worked in rural areas and small towns in the production of arts and crafts that ranged from objects of daily use to creations of high artistic merit.

Since World War II industry has had a healthy record of growth, but the increasing use of capital-intensive machinery has limited its ability to absorb additional industrial manpower. During the late 1960s and early 1970s the most encouraging new source of manufacturing employment was located in the cities of the northern border where, under a 1965 arrangement, United States companies were establishing assembly plants. For the most part, they were twin installations paired with manufacturing plants on the other side of the border. In 1972 most of the approximately 100,000 employed in these plants were women. United States labor unions voiced some complaint over the border-industries program, but the number of installations increased from 179 in 1970 to more than 400 in 1974.

Although handicraft employment is on the decline in other Latin American countries, it has been growing in Mexico in response to increasing tourist demand for products. It is a skilled and specialized vocation, particularly in the states of Central Mexico, in Yucatán, and in Chiapas. No accurate count of the number of craftsmen is possible because many are also farmers or engage in other occupations, and others work too infrequently to be considered regular members of the labor force.

In the tertiary or services sector, employment in commerce experienced a slight relative decline between 1960 and 1970, but employment in personal and other services registered so sharp a gain that in Mexico in the early 1970s it was common practice to refer to the *tercerización* of the labor force. In Mexico City, in particular, the availability of cheap labor was such that even families of moderate income had at least one domestic servant.

The poorly differentiated composition of the Mexican labor force is demonstrated again in the tertiary employment sector where most of the marginal jobs are found. Industry has not developed to a degree sufficient to absorb its proportion of the urban migrant job seekers, and make-do employment has developed in which people divide their time between such personal services jobs as shoe shining and small commercial enterprises. There are many petty merchants, some in tiny shops or market stalls and some ambulatory. Every plaza and zócalo in Mexico has one or

Table 4. *Mexico, Structure of the Labor Force, 1970*

Branch of Economic Activity	Males	Females	Total
Employers and Workers on Own Account:			
Agriculture, forestry, hunting, and fishing..	1,981,587	94,285	2,075,872
Mining and quarrying	12,526	1,515	14,041
Manufacturing	319,510	111,640	431,150
Construction...........................	102,582	2,684	105,266
Electricity, gas, water, and sanitary services	5,462	556	6,018
Commerce..............................	404,012	129,209	533,221
Transport, storage, and communication....	97,140	3,155	100,295
Services...............................	326,774	222,544	549,318
Activities not adequately described	157,969	80,918	238,887
Total employers and workers on own account	3,407,562	646,506	4,054,068
Salaried Employees and Wage Earners:			
Agriculture, forestry, hunting, and fishing .	2,382,125	117,329	2,499,454
Mining and quarrying	151,665	11,560	163,225
Manufacturing	1,355,801	310,964	1,666,765
Construction...........................	440,349	14,103	454,452
Electricity, gas, water, and sanitary services	42,574	4,065	46,639
Commerce..............................	400,452	167,527	567,979
Transport, storage, and communication....	245,418	13,363	258,781
Services...............................	1,077,809	864,151	1,941,960
Activities not adequately described	315,134	140,433	455,567
Total salaried employees and wage earners	6,411,327	1,643,495	8,054,822
Family Workers:			
Agriculture, forestry, hunting, and fishing..	473,153	55,040	528,193
Mining and quarrying	2,444	465	2,909
Manufacturing	46,237	24,922	71,159
Construction...........................	10,298	990	11,288
Electricity, gas, water, and sanitary services	539	89	628
Commerce..............................	58,473	37,205	95,678
Transport, storage, and communication....	8,866	871	9,737
Services...............................	33,596	39,908	73,504
Activities not adequately described	36,305	16,766	53,071
Total family workers	669,911	176,256	846,167

Branch of Economic Activity	Total Labor Force[1]				
	Males	Females	Total	Percent 1960	1970
Agriculture, forestry, hunting, and fishing	4,836,865	266,654	5,103,519	54.2	39.2
Mining and quarrying	166,635	13,540	180,175	1.2	1.4
Manufacturing	1,721,548	447,526	2,169,074	13.7	16.7
Construction.................	553,229	17,777	571,006	3.6	4.4
Electricity, gas, water, and sanitary services	48,575	4,710	53,285	0.4	0.4
Commerce...................	862,937	333,941	1,196,878	9.5	9.2
Transport, storage, and communication	351,424	17,389	368,813	3.2	2.8
Services....................	1,438,179	1,126,603	2,564,782	13.5	19.7
Activities not adequately described..................	509,408	238,117	747,525	0.7	5.7
Persons seeking work for the first time	22,655	36,704	59,359	....[2]	0.5
Total labor force	10,511,455	2,502,961	13,014,416	100.0	100.0

[1] Includes 59,359 workers (22,655 male and 36,704 female) classified as "others and status unknown."
[2] Not listed.

Source: Adapted from *Year Book of Labour Statistics, 1970*, Geneva, 1970, pp. 88-89; and *Year Book of Labour Statistics, 1973*, Geneva, 1973, pp. 74-75.

more boys or old men selling Chiclets. This North American chewing gum is manufactured in Mexico and packaged in small lots in deference to the limited capital of the vendors and the limited purchasing power of their buyers.

During the 1960s and early 1970s the fastest growing and most encouraging area of employment in the services sector was provided by the tourist industry where the building of new hotels also accounted for much of the substantial growth in construction employment. It was calculated that a single hotel with 777 rooms completed in Acapulco in 1973 would result directly in 1,600 new jobs and would contribute indirectly to many other new positions. In mid-1974 tourist authorities estimated that it would be necessary to train a minimum of 70,000 additional personnel concerned directly with tourism in the next five years (see Cities of Mexico, this ch.).

In 1970 about 407,000 individuals, or a little more than 3 percent of the labor force, were government workers. Data by category of public employment are unavailable or unreliable, but a very large proportion of the country's civil servants hold relatively highly paid positions usually identified by labor writers as those involving trust and confidence. In government offices in Mexico City the trust and confidence personnel in many instances far outnumber the base-level manual workers. At lower levels the acceptance of *mordidas* (bribes) for public services performed has not entirely been eliminated; but professionalism in the civil service dates generally from the regime of President Miguel Alemán, and in the mid-1970s the corps was generally recognized as a highly skilled and dedicated one.

Age and Sex Distribution of Labor Force

In 1970 almost one-half of the labor force was under the age of thirty. Some 3.4 percent were between the ages of twelve and fourteen, about 14.6 percent, were between fifteen and nineteen, and 15.8 percent were between twenty and twenty-four, the age bracket in which the largest number of workers was concentrated. The proportion decreased progressively in each older five-year bracket to 4.8 percent for those between the ages of fifty and fifty-five. The 12.6 percent aged fifty-five and over were listed in a single age grouping.

The participation rates for males and females were 43.8 and 10.5 percent, respectively, in 1970 as compared with 53.4 percent and 11.6 percent in 1960. The moderate decline in female participation in the labor force as compared with the very sharp decline in male participation probably is a reflection of urban migration and the greater availability of jobs for women in urban localities than in the countryside. In addition, however, it suggests that the more restrictive definition of an economically active person used in the 1970 census eliminated a primarily or exclusively male group, probably seasonal agricultural workers.

By age group, male participation reached a maximum of 93 percent of the male population between the ages of thirty and fifty. The 83 percent of the population active over the age of fifty was only slightly lower than the 84.5 percent active between the ages of twenty and twenty-nine.

The rate for women was 14.3 percent between the ages of twelve and nineteen and 21 percent between twenty and twenty-nine. It then declined irregularly to less than 14 percent among those fifty years of age and over. The pattern is unusual for Latin America in that it does not show the sharp decline in participation by women in their middle twenties, usually as a consequence of marriage and family responsibilities. The participation rate for Mexican women in general is rather low, but a high proportion of those who enter the labor force remain in it.

The census data include only employment of workers aged twelve or over. According to an authority at the National Autonomous University of Mexico, however, in 1973 there were 105,000 working children between the ages of eight and eleven; and 372,000 children of the approximately 450,000 between the ages of twelve and fourteen were employed in violation of the constitutional limitation on employment in this age group. The source concluded that nearly 2 million children under the age of sixteen were employed illegally or under conditions below the standards prescribed by the law. It was noted, however, that strict enforcement of the law would deprive the children involved of their means of eating regularly and suggested that, if stricter enforcement were undertaken, it should take the form of heavy fines to be applied to provision of support for indigent children.

Skills and Productivity

The Mexican worker learns quickly and has an intuitive skill in mechanical tasks. He is, for example, extremely adept at repairing old automobiles. His inherited Spanish sense of individuality, however, limits his ability to work cooperatively in a group. He stresses technical efficiency and prefers challenging tasks that provide outlets for his Indian artistic sense. A dislike for repetitiveness and drudgery is reflected in a resistance to mass-producing handicraft items.

The level of skills is lowest in agriculture. Per capita productivity is much lower than in other economic sectors and has registered a progressive decline in relation to those sectors. During the 1960s it was lowest in Central Mexico and the South Pacific because of the proliferation of very small subsistence farms in those regions. A gain in productivity in the North Pacific was the result of irrigation rather than of an increase in skills.

Poor soils, limited amounts of land available, lack of capital, oversupply of labor, and lack of education all militate against the acquisition of rural skills. In addition, the relatively well educated and more ambitious young people who are best equipped to acquire rural skills are also those most likely to leave the countryside altogether and to migrate to cities and towns where they first are employed in domestic service, in custodial assignments, in small shops, or as street vendors. These people constitute an industrial reserve, however, and those who eventually find jobs in factories respond to the opportunity offered. Absenteeism and turnover in Mexican border-industry plants in the early 1970s, for example, were lower than in corresponding plants in the United States, and per capita production was said to be higher.

Skills are acquired on the job rather than in the classroom, but Mexicans more than most Latin Americans view a lack of education as a serious deterrent to job advancement. Moreover, surveys covering a period from 1940 to the mid-1960s showed the quality of labor performed to have been improved with progressing rapidity. They also showed that higher rates of improvement have been progressively registered by those with better educations.

Before 1950 the greatest advances were registered in jobs requiring two or three years of schooling, sufficient to attain literacy. After 1950, however, the greatest advances were among those who had completed primary school and those who had some secondary schooling. Workers who had completed secondary school and those who had some university-level education also showed progressive improvement, but the greatest demand continued to be for enough education to provide a background for skilled workers, foremen, and middle-level technicians. The industrial sector had yet to develop to a point where it could absorb more than a small fraction of the best educated; it was estimated in the early 1970s that 80 percent of all the graduates of universities and higher technical schools were employed in the services sector, many in jobs that bore little relevance to their professional educations.

Unemployment

During the week preceding the 1970 census about 415,000 people, or 3.2 percent of the labor force, were reported unemployed. The figure was higher than the 1.5 percent reported in the 1950 census but well below the level of most countries of the world. The 1970 census figure, however, may have been conservative to an extreme; in 1973 a major North American journal fixed the total at 2.2 million, about 16 percent of the working population. Unemployment was principally an urban phenomenon and was probably heaviest in the border cities; some 15 percent of the labor force in Juarez and half of the total in Nogales had been reported out of work in 1968. Unemployment was heaviest along the border because of the large number of migrants entering the area during the late 1960s and early 1970s in hopes of finding jobs in the new border factories.

Only 2 percent of the unemployed in 1970 reported themselves as having been out of work for more than one year, and a substantial majority had been seeking work for less than four weeks. It appears, therefore, that the large number of seasonal farm laborers who must have been out of work on the day of the census were not considered unemployed. The reported rate was actually lower among workers over the age of forty than among those between the ages of twenty and twenty-nine. Older workers have difficulty finding work in most countries of the world, however, and Mexico has an active National Association of 40 Plus Executives (Asociación Nacional de Ejecutivos Plus 40), a self-help employment group similar to the "40 Plus" clubs of the United States.

Underemployment is far higher than unemployment, and has been widely recognized as a serious problem. In the early 1970s it was the consensus that 3 million or more workers were underemployed. It is a rare phenomenon in sparsely settled rural areas, such as Quintana Roo and Baja California, but underemployment is characteristic of most or all of the landless farm workers and the operators of submarginal *ejido* farm plots, amounting to perhaps half of the agricultural labor force. Urban migration has also made underemployment increasingly heavy in urban centers where new arrivals can find work only in the most marginal occupations. For example, thousands of families earn a precarious living, particularly in the cities along the United States border, scavenging trash heaps for such discarded articles as tire casings and tin cans. Known as *pepenadores*, they have even organized a labor union.

Underemployment serves as an alternative to a much higher rate of open unemployment. The government often requires or encourages the overstaffing of offices and investment in less productive undertakings because of the relative ability of these operations to absorb workers. In the city this may take the form of investment in a relatively uneconomic

46

labor-intensive factory. In the countryside, it may take the form of growing labor-intensive crops on land that might more productively be used for cattle raising.

Labor unions argue that both unemployment and underemployment would be reduced by a reduction of the forty-eight-hour working week to forty hours. Employers contend, however, that this would only accelerate the already existing trend toward mechanization that has been in progress since the end of World War II and point out that the inauguration of a forty-hour week in banking and certain other fields has not brought about employment gains.

The core of the employment problem is industry's inability to create a sufficient number of new jobs. This cannot be accomplished while half of the population remains outside the market economy, and the problems of unemployment and underemployment that already exist would be far greater were it not for the massive escape valve provided by the illegal movement of wetbacks into the United States (see Boundaries and Political Subdivisions, this ch.).

CHAPTER 3

HISTORICAL SETTING

The impact of history on modern Mexican society is apparent in the makeup of the population, in the people's language, and in their religion, their art, and their government. When Hernán Cortés conquered Mexico during the years 1519 to 1521 he encountered an advanced Indian civilization. In their zeal to introduce Roman Catholicism the Spaniards destroyed many of the symbols of the Indian civilization—notably magnificent temples and well-planned cities. Today, nevertheless, Mexicans, most of whom are of mixed Indian and Spanish descent, take pride in the remaining monuments of their Indian forebears; many Mexicans practice folk Catholicism, a combination of ancient Indian religion and Roman Catholicism.

The effect of the Spanish conquest is clearly evident in varying degrees in all sectors of modern Mexican society. Spanish, the official language, is spoken by the majority of the people. Most Mexicans are professed Roman Catholics. The Hispanic tradition is widely reflected in social customs and thought, and in literary, artistic, and architectural styles.

The democratic form of government in modern Mexico reflects the aspirations of leaders who, after nearly 300 years of Spanish rule, established the republic in 1822. For practical purposes, democratic procedures were not brought into being until the Revolution of 1910. Between 1822 and 1910 the people were ruled by authoritarian leaders, among whom were General Antonio López de Santa Anna, who controlled Mexican politics between 1833 and 1855; Benito Juárez (1858–71); and Porfirio Díaz (1876–1911).

During the nineteenth century the mestizos (of Indian-European descent) changed the racial composition of Mexico and grew in numbers and power. They became the backbone of indigenous liberal movements and advocated the elimination of race and inherited social position as bases for status.

The Revolution of 1910 was generated by economic and social problems that had existed since colonial times. Among the leaders of armed uprisings were Francisco I. Madero and Venustiano Carranza—both landowners—Pancho Villa, a mestizo peon, and Emiliano Zapata, an Indian tenant farmer.

The Constitution of February 5, 1917, promulgated during the "continuing revolution," remained in force in the early 1970s. It provided for separation of powers into independent executive, legislative, and judicial branches of government. And the Revolutionary Party, eventually known as the Institutional Revolutionary Party (Partido Revolucionario Institucional—PRI), in the early 1970s continued as the most powerful political force in the country.

Mexico's continuing economic growth has reflected emergence from a primary production economy based on agriculture and mining to the economic structure of a substantially industrialized nation. Nevertheless, the government's most acute problem in the early 1970s was deeply rooted in the past—the problem of raising the living standards of the people.

NATIVE ROOTS OF MEXICAN CULTURE

Before the Spaniards arrived, much of what is present-day southern Mexico as well as parts of contemporary Honduras and Guatemala and all of Belize were occupied by Maya peoples, whose highly developed civilization had its beginnings centuries before the Christian Era and had reached its greatest heights between the fourth and tenth centuries A.D.

During about six centuries (A.D. 325 to 925) known as the Classic Period, the Maya civilization probably surpassed all other pre-Columbian civilizations of the Americas in the development of hieroglyphic writing, in architectural sculpture, in painting, and in astronomy, chronology, and mathematics. They established city-states ruled by nobles and priests. The cities competed in trade, but there is little evidence that their rivalry led to wars.

The principal food of the people was corn, and the surplus raised by the planters was collected and sold in the cities, where the proceeds supported the priest-scientists and made possible the construction of great religious and civic centers. Maya civilization in the Classic Period was centered on a belt that reached from Copán in present-day Honduras through the Petén jungle in Guatemala and extended to the north into Belize and Mexican states of Campeche and Quintana Roo.

When the Spaniards arrived in the region where Maya civilization had flourished, they found only the ruins of cities; and it appeared that the natives lacked any knowledge of their ancestors. The mystery of the dissolution of Mayan civilization has yet to be solved. Speculation among scholars raises questions as to whether it was famine, civil war, invasion by foreign enemies, or pestilence; or whether peasants, tired of forced labor in the fields and on the construction of palaces and temples, rose up against their rulers and, after killing them or driving them away, failed to govern successfully.

About the sixth century A.D. a group of Indians known as the Toltecs, who may have been related to the Maya, entered the Valley of México. The Toltecs may have been the vanguard of the Nahuas, hunters and warriors, who had lived on the Pacific coast, thousands of miles to the north.

In the tenth or eleventh century the Toltecs in the Valley of México were conquered by the Chichimec peoples, who appear to have adopted the Toltec civilization. Then, probably in the twelfth century, the Aztecs, a group of Nahuatl-speaking nomads, moving in from the north, conquered the Valley of México and started to extend their power to other parts of Mexico. They formed a great confederation ruled by an emperor. From 1440 until the arrival of the Spaniards the Aztecs and the city government of Tenochtitlán, present-day Mexico City, exercised hegemony over the confederation.

The Aztecs practiced human sacrifice in the temples on the tops of their pyramids, and they worshiped many gods. Crafting gold and silver objects and weaving were developed to a high degree, and mining and agriculture were important sectors of the economy. Trade was carried on throughout the confederation. The Aztecs employed a remarkably accurate calendar, recorded their ideas in picture writing, engaged in a variety of athletic activities, and enjoyed the dance and dramatic productions (see ch. 4).

In 1502 there ascended to the throne of this strong but still diffuse hegemony Montezuma II, a complex and meditative ruler, not the single-minded militarist and powerful organizer typical of the previous Aztec kings. His beliefs were increasingly pervaded, as was the Aztec religion, with an obsession with death and tragedy and an inherent sense of pessimism and doom. He was under the influence of astrologers, who saw grave portents in the stars and natural phenomena. When word was received of the landing on the coast of mysterious strangers with horses and fire-belching weapons, the warnings of the astrologers were confirmed. An empire with tens of thousands of warriors under arms was about to be conquered by invaders whose original strength was about 600 soldiers.

THE COLONIAL PERIOD

The Conquest

In April 1519 Hernán Cortés landed at a spot on the Gulf Coast of Mexico that he named Veracruz (True Cross) for the holy day (Good Friday) of the Spanish arrival. He had been chosen by the Cuban governor, Diego Velásquez, to lead an expedition to Mexico. Velásquez, however, once having selected Cortés, became suspicious of him. Aware of the governor's desire to replace him, Cortés stole away from Santiago, the capital of Cuba, and completed preparations in Havana. The expedition set out with 508 swordsmen, 100 sailors, thirty-two crossbowmen, thirteen musketeers, fourteen cannons, and sixteen horses. After the initial landing at Veracruz, Cortés cut off communications with Velásquez, had himself chosen captain general of the new town, sent one ship directly to Spain to secure royal ratification, and burned the remaining ten ships.

Montezuma, receiving word of the newcomers, soon realized that they were human but feared that they were the symbols of otherworldly forces. Religious factors aside, the inherent weakness in Aztec governance through a tributary confederation undermined any serious long-range defensive posture. The pueblos, or city-states, between the Valley of México and the coast were independent, if tributary, communities. Thus, as the Spanish conquistadores marched inland, they were able to exploit not only spiritual but also political weaknesses in the Indian realm. Many tributary tribes welcomed the advent of the conquistadores as an opportunity for revolt. The independent Tlaxcalans, on the other hand, tested them twice in battle, lost, and became the most important and loyal of Cortés' Indian supporters. At Cholula, a religious center connected with Tenochtitlán, the Spaniards were met as friends; but in a political maneuver, perhaps instigated by Montezuma, the Cholulans secretly plotted the destruction of Cortés' forces. Suspecting this, the conquistadores counterattacked in a well-planned massacre. This massacre in Cholula is frequently mentioned when Mexicans speak of Cortés. They admire his leadership and military abilities, but they feel that such massacres destroyed the possibility for a quiet and peaceful blend of the two cultures.

Cortés arrived at Tenochtitlán on November 8, 1519. Both practical and psychological considerations induced Montezuma to allow the conquistadores to enter the capital in peace, but Cortés seized Montezuma, hoping to control the Aztecs through the king. This triggered a mass resentment against the Spaniards. Just at this juncture Cortés was forced to leave for the coast to counter the arrival of a force under Panfilo Narváez sent by Velásquez to relieve Cortés. The trouble brewing in Tenochtitlán broke during his absence. Perhaps in the mistaken belief that a gathering of the Aztecs for a celebration of the feast of Huitzilopochtli was a prelude to an attack on the Spaniards and their Tlaxcalan allies, Pedro de Alvarado, left in command, massacred the celebrants. The city rose up and drove the Spanish forces to cover. Having routed Narváez, Cortés returned with an enlarged force to find the garrison besieged. Because the ceremonial character of Aztec warfare did not envisage the splitting and separate destruction of an adversary's army, Cortés and his reinforcements were allowed to rejoin the beleaguered Alvarado.

Unable to break from the surrounded refuge, Cortés attempted to have Montezuma pacify the people, but they bitterly turned on their king, stoning him fatally. The Aztec nobles then elected Montezuma's brother as king, and the Aztec will to fight was revived. On the night of June 30, 1520, the Spanish and Tlaxcalans attempted to steal out of Tenochtitlán. Discovered, the allies were set upon by the whole male population of the capital, and within a few days three-quarters of the Spanish army was lost. The Aztecs failed to follow their advantage and destroy the remnants of the conquistadores; instead, they spent time plundering the dead and recovering stolen Aztec treasures.

The exhausted Spaniards, many of them wounded, fled, only to be intercepted and set upon at Otumba by the Texcocans. Because the Indians would not break their ceremonial battle formation, they could not overcome the mobility and tactical superiority of the Spaniards, who routed them after a desperate fight. Reaching Tlaxcala, Cortés rested his army and then set about consolidating his position by launching two new campaigns, one eastward toward the sea and the other southward and westward into present-day Morelos.

In his subsequently renewed offensive against the Aztecs, Cortés, through luck and the defection of the Texcocans to the Spanish side, was virtually assured of victory. The defection gave the conquistadores a base on Lake Texcoco. From there they launched an attack on Tenochtitlán by a fleet of small galleys that had been constructed in Tlaxcala, armed with cannon, and brought overland to be assembled on the lake. The naval attack was launched on May 26, 1521, in concert with land attacks along the three causeways into the capital. Tenochtitlán was slowly starved out. Its people retreated into the center of the city, which allowed the Spanish to raze building after building and then fill the canals with the debris, thus providing themselves with maneuvering room. In their religiously inspired efforts to capture the invaders alive, the Aztecs often gave them a chance to escape, a fact that helped to seal the Aztec defeat. The siege ended on August 13 with Tenochtitlán completely destroyed. The conquest of the Valley of México had now been consummated—some 2½ years after it had started.

The siege of Tenochtitlán produced one of the great national heroes of Mexico—Cuauhtémoc, last king of the Aztecs, elected after the death of Cuitláhuac. Cuauhtémoc is revered as a personification of dignity and valor, Indian heritage, and heroism because of his courageous last stand during the siege of Tenochtitlán, his subsequent stoicism in the face of captivity, and then his bravely faced execution as a conspirator against Cortés. For many Mexicans, Cuauhtémoc is the "young grandfather"—the original patriot.

The Consolidation of the Conquest in the Center and South

Cortés fought, on his own responsibility, against the will of his superior but in the name of and on behalf of the king of Spain. In Cortés' mind and in the minds of his soldiers were the opposing concepts of service to the crown and the Roman Catholic faith, and self-serving gain of glory and personal wealth.

With the fall of Tenochtitlán, Cortés, without royal sanction until 1522, began the rebuilding of his new capital on the ruins of the old city. Cortés' view was feudal; he rewarded his fellow conquistadores for their services through the Spanish baronial land grant system. This creation of individual fiefdoms served to confirm the king's suspicions of Cortés' independent aspirations; Cortés was soon relieved of his leadership and replaced by the first viceroy in Spanish America.

Conquest and colonization radiated outward from central Mexico. Two factors tended to determine the course and direction of the first territorial conquests, generally completed by about 1540: first, the location of concentrations of Indian population, the source of both labor and tribute for the feudal land grant system; second, the major sources of preconquest tributary gold, the southern highlands and the northern Caribbean slopes of Central America. In their search for gold, Spaniards moved into the densely populated, cacao-rich Coatzacoalcos region in the Isthmus of Tehuantepec. The religious orders and lay Spaniards followed the conquistadores into these areas, administering and controlling the Indian population through the founding of towns at strategic points.

Expansion to the North

Movement north beyond the Indian agricultural line and into the Gran Chichimeca, or Tierra de Guerra (Land of War), did not occur until after 1540. Occupation of these lands was a difficult and slow task, taking over 200 years to accomplish. Among the intractible nomadic Chichimecs, neither the land grant system (which was legally but not effectively abolished in 1542) nor tributary subjugation could be carried out. The labor force, therefore, had to be imported from the south, recruited from among the Indians of the central highlands. Settlement was not in towns but in mining camps, later major cities (Zacatecas, Guanajuato, Parral, Chihuahua, and San Luís Potosí). The persistent raids by the desert Indians meant that the Spanish administration of the north was usually in the hands of the military, through a series of forts stretching along the invasion routes. Where minerals were lacking, however, the church, active among the Indians of the north, frequently became the more important force.

Two events opened the way for the first northward conquest and colonization: first, the driving back of the Guachichil nomads north of Guadalajara in the Mexton War of 1541; and second, the discovery in 1546 of silver at Zacatecas. The Zacatecas mines, together with the Guanajuato silver mines opened in 1563, brought in Indian farmers, Spanish missionaries, and ranchers who fostered the establishment of the market centers of Celaya and León. From this base the first important northward path was pushed along the eastern foothills of the Sierra Madre Occidental, through the great silver belt of northern Mexico. Via this route traveled the expedition that settled the upper Rio Grande Valley of New Mexico and established the town of El Paso del Norte, present-day El Paso, Texas.

The second defeat of the Zacateco-Guachichil Indians in 1562 opened up a second major route, which was slowly extended northeastward from Zacatecas through Saltillo (1577), Monclova, Monterrey, Cerralvo, and beyond the Rio Grande to San Antonio (1717). These areas remained sparsely settled and poor, dependent on stock raising, throughout most of the colonial period. Direct contact was not opened with Mexico City until the founding of San Luís Potosí in 1592. Government-sponsored settlement of the northeastern coastal area was not initiated until the mid-eighteenth century, when the French and British had begun to threaten the frontier from the Mississippi Valley.

The third major route was opened by Jesuit missionaries. It proceeded northward up the western slopes of the Sierra Madre Occidental along an ancient Indian trail and through Sonora to the Colorado Plateau. This trail had been used in 1540 by Francisco de Coronado on his expedition seeking the legendary Seven Cities of Cíbola. Baja California was opened through the establishment of missions in the late seventeenth and early eighteenth centuries. The threat of Russian expansion from Alaska caused the Spaniards in 1769 to begin, through the Franciscan friars, the colonization of upper California.

Indians in the Colonial Period

One fundamental concomitant of Spanish colonization was the decimation of the Indian population (see ch. 4). After the first 100 years of Spanish occupation the native population of occupied areas was reduced to a fraction of its preconquest numbers. This incredible mortality was caused by warfare, harsh treatment, dislocation, disruption of normal food production, slavery, and the introduction of Old World diseases.

In the sparsely populated rural north the Jesuit and Franciscan missions came to be the basic instruments of administration. The large Indian nations of the center and south were broken up and reduced to their constituent city-states, now under the administrative leadership of the chief, who had been the native ruler of the village or town during the preconquest period. Thus, in these densely settled high cultures the secular native city-state became the unit into which was introduced the Spanish concept of town government.

Differentiation between the Indians in the administrative centers and those in the outlying communities gradually became less important. The resettlement of scattered Indian communities into more compact towns was in large part the product of gradual appropriation by, and encroachment of Spanish landed interests on to royally decreed "public lands" and "wastelands" created through the great population decline of the sixteenth and seventeenth centuries. While the ultimate effect of Spanish rule was to destroy stratification in Indian society and in its stead to bring all native classes to the level of the former commoner class, distinctions continued to survive in Indian society as some native nobility retained rank and holdings, if not power, until after independence. This was because the Spanish ruled the Indian towns through native leaders and, as a consequence, provided social privileges for the Indian nobility. Although the powers of the local chiefs lasted longer than those of the Spanish colonial leaders, these Spaniards evolved into a property-based class, a transition made by few Indians.

The conversion of the Indian was more extensive in urban areas. There he came into closer contact with both the Spaniard and the Roman Catholic Church. In the more rural areas Roman Catholicism was outwardly accepted, but Indian rites and practices were carried on underground. The Indian has never fully lost his traditional beliefs and has never fully accepted the strongly individualistic attitudes of Western man, a fact that has strongly colored the ongoing revolution (see ch. 5).

The Negro

It is estimated that nearly 250,000 Negroes were brought to New Spain, although in any given year the incoming number seldom exceeded 35,000. They were brought as slaves in response to the labor shortage resulting from the decimation of the Indians.

The monarchy integrated the Negro as it had the Indian into the structure of colonial society. Thus, royal decrees and church proclamations were handed down providing that the slaves be allowed to purchase their freedom, that family solidarity and marital sanctity be guaranteed as a Christian obligation, that the disciplinary authority of the master be restricted, and that the African be hispanicized to bring him into community with his master. Over time the Negro has virtually disappeared as an identifiable element in the population.

The Mestizo

In 1810, despite racial mixing, probably as much as 60 percent of the population of New Spain was still of pure Indian blood. The Indians' rank in the Hispano-Catholic social order was higher than that of the Negroes but lower than that of the mixed-blood peoples, the zambos (Indian-Negro), the mulattoes (Negro-European), and the mestizos (Indian-European). The pure Indian, however, was a ward of the state and the church, a "child," needing protection. The mestizo, on the other hand, usually was left outside both Indian and Spanish communities; because his features were generally distinctive, he had little chance of moving to a higher station in life (see ch. 5). To avoid the degeneration and social deprivation of the urban areas, many mestizos migrated north to Durango, Coahuila, and Nuevo León, becoming cowboys, ranchers, miners, or tenant farmers—the backbone of the northern stock of the contemporary Mexican people.

Spanish Sources of Power

In general, the "subject races" became the laboring base of society, thus reinforcing the Spanish notion that manual work was a symbol of servility, and associating both with race. It was the Spaniards, both Iberian-born and native-born (criollos), who wielded power and controlled the wealth of New Spain. This power, however, was severely circumscribed by the Spanish crown. The structure of colonial jurisdiction was designed to consolidate the absolute power of the monarch, assisted by his Council of the Indies (Consejo de las Indias).

The Bureaucracy

The crown used three institutions to maintain its authoritarian rule, the bureaucracy, the church, and economic monopoly. The royal power in New Spain was ostensibly maintained through an administrative hierarchy headed by the viceroy. The colony was divided into provinces administered by governors (who sometimes also held the title of captain general), and these were subdivided into smaller political and juridical units entrusted to magistrates or mayors. The lowest governing unit was the town or city council, the only institution to possess any measure of self-government. Unlike all other positions, whose offices by law were required to be held by the Iberian born, the city council membership consisted largely of the native born. As a consequence, the councils had little effective authority. The administration of such a complex government, however, meant that certain practical flexibilities began to evolve. First, the slow communication with the mother country meant that edicts promulgated by the crown could easily be evaded or ignored. Often an official would simply either fail to implement directives or postpone their execution until clarification of the local situation was sent to and passed upon by the courts.

The sale of offices in the town councils became common but did not essentially encroach upon royal authority because the powers of the councils were limited. The sale of offices did provide, however, the means whereby the landed oligarchy gained control of the local, minor administrative apparatus—a control that came to burden the common people so heavily that it was to serve as an impetus for the Revolution of 1910. Once an oligarchy became entrenched in public office, it resorted to graft and nepotism and to increasing the number of jobs under its patronage—perhaps the beginning of an inordinate desire to attach oneself to the public payroll, which has persisted in contemporary Mexico.

Spanish colonialism was town centered. Spanish towns in Mexico were created by corporate charter instead of growing up naturally. There was, thus, an artificial character to the Mexican town, a duality underscored by the regulations on municipal configuration contained in every civic charter. The specified urban grid patterns were characterized by a sense of subordination to a central will, symbolized by the plaza, the focus of the town; around it were the symbols of Spanish dominance—the church, the town hall, and the residence of crown officials.

In an attempt to curtail corruption, the Spanish crown made no less than five changes in the administration of New Spain between 1758 and 1804, the most important for municipal government being the system of provinces and provincial administrators adopted in 1786. The purpose was to coordinate colonial administration in Mexico, the provincial administrator in effect assuming the powers of the governor, the magistrate, and the mayor. This official exercised control over the principal governmental functions of the town, especially in the field of municipal finance. Obviously, the town council became dependent on his authority. The general effect of this reform was to weaken the council even further as the empire grew older. Yet, the town council remained the only organ of government open to the native born, and the tradition of the open town council was never forgotten; the institution quickly revived during the independence period and was the avenue through which the men of native birth began to assert their influence.

The Spanish Constitution of 1812 introduced the concept of decentralized administration by regions headed by provincial governors, officials who—in the fashion of bosses—usurped the powers of the town and city councils. Bossism later came to haunt Mexico during the regime of Porfirio Díaz; the provincial boss, in his region, perpetuated electoral fraud, "prepared" the tax lists, and supervised and directed many other jobs as well as the town councils themselves. A principal cause of the Revolution of 1910 was popular dissatisfaction with the bosses; the country has had, however, great difficulty in overcoming this heritage of weak municipal government run by a privileged few.

The Roman Catholic Church

The second major source of royal authority was derived from the king's relation to the church. The church was an integral part of the power of the state in New Spain. It enjoyed special privileges as "a state within a state," which compensated for the spiritual authority the church provided as a buttress to the king. The alliance of church and crown was sanctioned by the institution of royal guardianship for the church, whereby the king received from the papacy the right to make all ecclesiastical appointments and to control ecclesiastical revenues. This interrelationship was underscored by the requirement of reading before the Indians of New Spain a proclamation that demanded absolute allegiance to the church as well as to the crown.

The enormous task of modeling New Spain after the Hispanic pattern devolved largely upon the church, through its monopoly not only of education but also of most social services. The church was also able to enforce intellectual and political orthodoxy through the Office of Holy Inquisition, established in New Spain in 1571. As the colonial period progressed, however, the church tended to become somewhat estranged from the imperial order as it came to participate directly in the economy of New Spain. The church became an avenue to security for many native-born men who could not otherwise find a place within the colonial political or economic order.

Its use of Indian labor, the privileges it received from the crown, and innumerable gifts both from the crown and rich laymen made the church the wealthiest corporation in New Spain. Its enterprises, in particular the extremely successful Jesuit accomplishments in agricultural production and in manufacturing based on Indian crafts, were models of early capitalistic organization. Because of its enormous revenues and its corporate functioning, toward the end of the colonial period the church controlled most of the liquid capital in New Spain; as a result it became the main lending agency in the colony, especially for the large land-owners. Because of foreclosures on unpaid loans, the church held approximately one-half the total real estate of New Spain by the beginning of the nineteenth century.

Thus, despite its initially close relationship with the crown, the growing power of the church in the New World began to pose a threat to the royal authority—one difficult to challenge because of the legal rights enjoyed by the clergy, including the exclusive jurisdiction of the clerical law courts. Unsurprisingly the crown began to move toward anti-clericalism, initially manifested in the royal decree of 1717 directing that no further conventual establishments be created in the Indies. Finally, in 1767 the king ordered the Jesuits expelled from the Indies.

Some of the lower clergy were receptive to liberal ideas, even to the point of becoming influential in the movement toward independence. The leaders of the church, however, continued to use their immense influence to support conservative political principles as well as orthodox religious beliefs. This conservatism eventually led to the prolonged series of conflicts between the church and the secular elements of society after Mexico had achieved independence from Spain.

Mercantilism

The third element upon which Spanish authority depended was a mercantilist conception of economics. The royal power was strengthened directly by a vast increase in the crown's revenues and indirectly through an increase in the capacity of the population to contribute. The New Laws of 1542, abolishing the land grants, were an attempt to eradicate an institution whose feudal autonomy challenged the authority of the central power. The further purpose of the New Laws was to preserve the Indian population as the labor mass upon which the economic foundation of royal power in New Spain could be maintained.

The core of the Spanish mercantilist system was the Spanish monopoly on trade with the colonies established through the House of Trade (Casa de Contratación) situated in Seville, the only port in Spain legally authorized to handle shipping to and from the Indies; annual or twice-yearly fleets in which all goods to and from the Indies had to be carried; and, most importantly, the powerful merchant guilds that monopolized trade with the Indies. The crown, however, did maintain direct monopoly rights over the production and sale of a number of items on which excise taxes provided a valuable source of revenue to the king. Outside the royal monopolies, production and sale of those goods of particular importance in New Spain, livestock and minerals, were assisted by special guilds. The powerful guild of livestock owners was transferred to New Spain, and the special privileges allowed to livestock owners were attractive both economically and in terms of status.

The mining industry was regulated by codes of law, the specificity of which had prevented mining techniques from developing much beyond their original level. By 1760, in spite of new and rich strikes, the decline in production and royal revenues from silver mines had become a serious concern to those in charge of revenues. In 1777 a royally chartered mining guild, dominated by the native born was created in an attempt to revitalize the mining industry and give it a comprehensive structure. The operations of the guild served to establish mineral production as the traditional basis of royal and state income, tending to reinforce the economic concept that silver mining was the real basis of Mexican and royal prosperity—an attitude that blighted the expansion and diversification of the Mexican economy until well into the twentieth century.

The middle groups of colonial society—the mixed-blooded peoples and the native-born, lower status people—were unprotected by the crown, had little access to land, labor, or capital, and were dependent on the wealthier native-born entrepreneurs for their livelihood. The local crafts were governed by a rigid monopolistic guild system, of the classic European pattern, and regulated by a series of anachronistic directives issued by the town councils and sanctioned by the viceroy. If a craftsman was a member of a guild, he had access to the group of masters and employers who controlled the industry; if not, he was barred from the craft. Although the effect of the guilds on local industry was recognized as early as the beginning of the seventeenth century, the system was not abolished until 1861; traces of it remained in the early 1970s, however, in such industries as glassblowing and silverwork.

Directly linked to the mercantilist economic structure and thus beneficiaries of royal privilege were the powerful merchant-consuls, closed groups of the Iberian born that were given a monopoly in import-export operations. Because of their dependence on oceanic trade with Spain, the merchant-consuls were strongly oriented toward royal and Spanish policies. Their purview was the purchase and sale of goods at wholesale, but through close collaboration with the colonial government they came to control the flow of goods; this made them able to increase prices drastically and to generate large profits. The nature of the merchant-consuls, their monopoly of international trade, and their fostering of the rising local prices stood in the way of the growth and development of colonial industry and commerce. They became the favorite target of attacks on Hispanic dependency from both the less privileged native born and the staunchest partisans of resistance to change.

Land and the Failure of Mercantilism

The tradition of the gentleman on horseback made land a prerequisite for social prestige. The taint placed by the Spanish system on manual and commercial activities helped to reinforce this traditional approach to social status. Thus, particularly in the regions distant from the viceregal capital in Mexico City, a Mexican landed elite came to thrive on the basis of municipal land grants, assertions of de facto rights to vacant lands, sequestration of municipal common lands or Indian common holdings, or purchase of lands from the local Indian chiefs. This was to become the basis of the estate system, typical of nineteenth-century Mexico and a primary grievance in the Revolution of 1910. The estate owners found on their remote estates a de facto independence from the centralized state. Yet, they governed their lands with much the same paternalistic attitudes, giving the legally free Indian labor access but no rights to land while holding them in bondage through a system of peonage or quasi-forced labor based on systematic, chronic indebtedness. The estate owners, in their desire for more autonomy, joined forces with others beginning to push for independence from Spain toward the end of the colonial period; from their position evolved both oligarchic and localistic trends that prevailed in Mexico until the Revolution of 1910 and beyond.

The mercantilist system proved to be the weakest link in the structure of royal rule because its success required both naval supremacy and an expanding market in Spain to absorb colonial production; both were in decline in the eighteenth century. Worse, the system of taxes became more onerous, and the venality of high officials and the merchant-consuls increased. The reform of the provincial administrations in the late eighteenth century was meant to forestall collapse, but the new freedoms only helped in the long run to undermine the waning authority of the Spanish crown.

EVOLUTION OF A NATION

Rumblings of Revolt

The wealth and importance of New Spain by the end of the colonial period made it by far the prize possession of the crown, but the more liberal reforms of the monarchy came too late and only reinforced the restive spirit. Democratic ideas were adopted by a Mexican group made up principally of lawyers and the lower clergy, including many members of the Literary and Social Club of Querétaro. Father Miguel Hidalgo y Costilla, José María Morelos, Vicente Guerrero, Ignacio Allende, Andrés Quintana Roo and his wife Leone Vicario, Juan Aldama, and Miguel Dominguez were all destined to play key roles in the independence movement. These were the "reasoning gentlemen" who were influenced by the French rationalists—particularly Baron de Montesquieu, François Marie Arouet Voltaire, Denis Diderot, and Jean Jacques Rousseau—and by Adam Smith's *Wealth of Nations*. Many were anticlerical Free-masons, as were their sympathizers (the lower clergy included). They adopted the ideas of the *Philosophical and Political History of the Indies* of the Abbé Guillaume Raynal, who bitterly attacked Spain's treatment of American Indians. Alarmed by the content of the new writings, the Inquisition in the 1790s attacked both the printing and discussing of these ideas, forcing the liberals underground where they became even more imbued with the ideas of the French Revolution.

The far larger group of Mexicans, however, were anxious to keep the

Indians subjugated and favored independence primarily in the hope of ousting the Spanish and becoming the new ruling class. They resented the fact that the Mexican elite were socially, politically, and economically subordinate to the Spanish. Excluded from the most profitable businesses by the monopolistic merchant-consuls, suffering under the restrictive policies of the crown, and politically unrepresented except in the weak town councils, the Mexicans became estranged from the Spanish colonial system, increasingly assertive of their "rights," and impatient with royal dictation.

In the cities that experienced a subordination both to the Spanish bureaucracy and to the monopolistic merchants, social exclusion and, above all, economic motives came to predominate over political alignments. A particular grievance grew out of an 1805 royal decree, known as the consolidation. This was a move to transfer the wealth of the religious orders to the royal treasury for shipment to Spain. Since the religious orders of New Spain were the owners, lessees, money lenders, and principal mortgagors on landed property, the ensuing recall of all advances made by the church hit its Mexican borrowers hard. On the other hand, the French Revolution had alarmed the Mexican elite who, although wanting independence, mistrusted and feared the eventual stirring of the subject peoples.

The Struggle for Independence

The trigger for revolt was Napoleon's occupation of Spain in 1808 and his attempt to establish his brother Joseph Bonaparte on the throne. The absence of the legitimate monarch justified a reversion of sovereignty to the people. The Spanish, fearing a movement for independence, supported as the legitimate authority the committees that governed the parts of Spain not occupied by the French. The Mexicans, on the other hand, asserted that sovereignty devolved on the people.

The conservative group, seeking moderate reform by existing authority and constituted law, sent delegates chosen by the town councils to Spain to take part in a constitutional convention. The liberal group insisted that natural rights and equality were basic and that the people created sovereignty. The liberal group moved first. On September 16, 1810, Father Hidalgo y Costilla called his followers to rebel against the Spanish. The uprising of Indians against whites which ensued was joined by Querétaro club members Allende, Aldama, and Dominguez; the rebels sacked San Miguel el Grande (now San Miguel de Allende), Celaya, and Guanajuato.

The violence and the rise of the long-feared race war frightened many of the Mexicans away from the Hidalgo movement; the propertied elite, in particular, preferred to cling to the security of Spanish law and order rather than risk their wealth and religious faith under independence. By November of 1810, Hidalgo had 50,000 followers and had marched into the Valley of México. By hesitating to strike into the Spanish-dominated heartland, he destroyed the morale of his movement, which dissolved. The Spanish seized the initiative, gave chase, and crushingly defeated Hidalgo in the battle of Calderón near Guadalajara in January 1811. Hidalgo was tried by the Inquisition and recanted, but he was defrocked and shot as a traitor. His severed head was hung for ten years on a fortress wall in Guanajuato. Not for years could the damage caused by the desertion and destruction of mines and fields be repaired. Likewise, grievances of race against race had long-term effects.

The spirit of rebellion had not died. Father Morelos organized a band of raiders out of the southern highlands, taking Acapulco and "liberating" most of Oaxaca in 1813 and harassing traffic on the Mexico City-Veracruz road. In November 1813 he called a congress at Chilpancingo to declare the independence of his Republic of Anahuac.

The next year, in a congress held in Apatzingan, a constitution rejecting the Spanish Constitution of 1812 was drawn up largely by the veteran revolutionaries Carlos Bustamante and Andres Quintana Roo. The constitution provided for racial equality, the abolition of clerical and military privileges, and the distribution of land from the estates to the peasants. During 1814 and 1815 the fugitive band of revolutionaries went from town to town briefly instituting the new constitutional regime. In November 1815, Morelos was caught by Spanish troops and shot, having faced the Inquisition without recanting. His programs later influenced those of the Revolution of 1910 and the ensuing reforms. The death of Morelos was followed by a rapid disintegration of the liberal wing of the independence movement, although a few revolutionaries, notably Guerrero, continued to lead guerrilla forces in the southwestern highlands of Oaxaca.

The socioeconomic recovery of New Spain was well under way by 1820. Mines were coming back into operation, and Indian laborers were returning. Then came the news of an uprising in Spain, with its call for restoration of the liberal Constitution of 1812, which the Spanish monarch had failed to maintain. This alarmed many of the higher clergy and elite for it evoked memories of Hidalgo's race wars and Morelos' constitutional ideas. Rather than attempt to work out a compromise with the Spanish government, the more conservative Mexicans seized the initiative to head off the development of liberal strength.

The leader was Agustín de Iturbide, a well-to-do Mexican landowner, who had been an officer in the Spanish army. Obtaining troops from the viceroy on the pretext of destroying the remnants of the Morelos forces, Iturbide instead joined up with Guerrero. In February 1821 the two issued the Plan of Iguala, announcing the independence and sovereignty of New Spain, the supremacy of the Roman Catholic Church, the principle of monarchy with a dynasty separate from that of Spain, the equality of rights of Mexican and Spaniard, and the absence of property confiscation. The plan became the rallying point of the nineteenth-century conservatives. The rebel army moved with enthusiastic popular support; the viceroy soon capitulated, and independence was won.

Faced with a movement to select a European prince as sovereign, Iturbide gathered sufficient support to claim for himself the position of emperor of Mexico. In May 1822, he was crowned Agustín I. His "empire" included not only Mexico, but also the modern Central American republics. Although he seized available capital—then in desperation issued worthless paper currency—he still failed in financing his government and was forced to abdicate in March 1823, and the Central American states broke away permanently. Not long afterward a convention proclaimed Mexico to be a federal republic, through the Constitution of 1824, patterned notably after the Constitution of the United States.

Regionalism Versus Centralism

The nineteenth century was characterized by a continuing struggle between the central authority and regional autonomy. The major power struggle was between Guadalajara, the stronghold of regionalist-federalism, and centralist Mexico City. Unlike Puebla and Veracruz, Guadalajara was not strongly dependent on the trade markets of the capital. It commanded the mining wealth and commercial markets as far as Aguascalientes and Bolanos. Its commercial influence determined the fates of the Pacific ports of Mazatlán, San Blas, and Manzanillo. Zacatecas, however, challenged Guadalajara's control over the Bajío, to the north of Zacatecas, which had developed its rich agricultural resources in close interdependence with the mines. This territory north of Zacatecas had long been unfamiliar to the inhabitants of the center and south and, as a consequence, had developed a distinctive mining-ranching complex all its own. Oaxaca and Chiapas also had been remote and removed from the Valley of México long before the conquest, and they continued to remain isolated and independent well into the twentieth century. The Yucatán Peninsula, too, had been far out of the mainstream, and Mérida and Campeche both attempted to establish their rights to the trade along the Gulf Coast historically dominated by the Veracruz-Puebla-Mexico City monopoly. These historic regional influences are still apparent.

Conservatives Versus Liberals

Under the influence of the Constitution of 1824, the two political factions that were to dominate Mexico for the next fifty years began to take shape. The liberals supported a federal system, a strong middle class that developed through agrarian reform and promotion of broad-based industrial growth, separation of church and state, secular education, and abolition of clerical and military privileges. The conservatives advocated centralized and authoritarian government and maintenance of church and aristocratic power.

The political conflict was intensified by the rivalry between the United States minister, Joel Poinsett, and the British chargé d'affaires, Henry

Ward, who personified the desires of their respective governments to achieve a dominant influence in Mexican affairs. Poinsett, who wanted Mexico to emulate the United States, gravitated toward the liberals; Ward tended to favor the conservatives. The battle lines were thus drawn that were to divide the republic within eight years of the signing of the Constitution of 1824.

The first president of the republic was Guadalupe Victoria, a hero of the independence struggles whose chosen pseudonym derived therefrom. With him appeared a new national flag, the red, white, and green tricolor of Iturbide's army with the traditional Aztec eagle-snake-cactus symbol. This is still the Mexican national flag. Victoria presided over a country sinking into anarchy.

A conservative was elected in 1828 and, fearing a challenge, attempted to seize the government. But the liberals incited an uprising of Mexico City Indian beggars and put the aged Guerrero into the presidency. Guerrero was immediately confronted by a Spanish expeditionary force sent by Ferdinand VII to reconquer Mexico. Long aware that the invasion was coming, the Mexican government had offered the Spaniards in the country the choice of leaving or becoming naturalized citizens. Large numbers of them were deported, depriving Mexico of much of its small middle class and of considerable capital, which the Spaniards took with them. The Spaniards' attack at Tampico, when it came, was easily repulsed by General Santa Anna—making the latter a potent national figure. However, Guerrero's ineptitude in handling the crisis undermined his power; he was replaced by his conservative vice president, Anastasio Bustamante, who proved unable to prevent Mexico from slipping deeper into anarchy.

THE ERA OF SANTA ANNA

Between 1832 and 1855 Santa Anna was president of Mexico eleven times. A showman, an opportunist, and an egocentric, he nonetheless had a talent for sensing the mood of soldiers and politicians and gaining their support. He also had the advantage of the proximity of his plantation, Mango de Clava, to Veracruz and thus of being able to seize the city's customhouse, the only source of income for the Mexican government. Santa Anna, with the cooperation of the liberal federalist Valentín Gómez Farías easily unseated Bustamante as his inauguration drew near; however, Santa Anna withdrew to Veracruz, pleading illness, and left Gómez Farías in the presidency to carry out the liberals' program.

Santa Anna allowed Gómez Farías to assume power initially as a test of public sentiment. The Gómez Farías government passed the Reform Laws of 1833, which, consistent with the Constitution of 1824, continued the abolition of the Inquisition while maintaining Roman Catholicism as the only religion of the Mexican nation. The reforms were aimed at decreasing the power of the army; creating a civilian militia; reforming the prisons and courts by striking out at the surviving privileges of the army, church, and landed aristocracy; abolishing tithes; weakening the church and its mission through secularization and retention of the state's privilege of nominating bishops; and establishing a system of lay education. The reforms were not, however, to be carried through. The church proclaimed the cholera epidemic of 1833–34 a sign of divine punishment for a godless administration. With great fanfare, Santa Anna then emerged from Mango de Clava, expelling both Gómez Farías and the Liberal Congress, rescinding the Reform Laws of 1833, and drafting the centralist constitution known as the Seven Laws.

Texan Independence

Toward the end of 1835 the province of Texas, whose population of settlers from the United States then totaled more than 30,000, threatened to secede from Mexico, fearing that a centralist regime would threaten its autonomy. Collecting an army of some 8,000 men from the environs of Mango de Clava, Santa Anna marched north. The Texas declaration of independence on March 2, 1836, precipitated the Mexican attack on the Alamo, in which the fort was overwhelmed and all of its defenders killed. In pursuit of the fugitive Texas government, Santa Anna massacred 500 Mexicans suspected of rebellion. The Texans were in total disarray, and an effective follow-up might have quelled the rebellion. But Santa Anna halted at San Jacinto Creek without elementary perimeter precautions, and the Texans routed the Mexican army. Captured, released, and finally negotiating the independence of Texas (although already unseated as president of Mexico), Santa Anna returned to his estate, defeated and humiliated.

The conservatives maintained control of the formal structure of government with the support of the church and the army, but there was no true national government. Military bosses controlled the states, and the central government functioned only at the will of the army. Tyranny and corruption were universal, and everywhere the socioeconomic system showed signs of retrogression. The enormous debt owed, or allegedly owed, by the Mexican government was staggering. Nonpayment of French loans precipitated the French-Mexican War of 1838 and 1839. Lodged in the San Juan de Ulloa fortress, the French army could not be ousted. Again, Santa Anna appeared from his retreat to "save" the nation. The country continued to sink deeper into chaos, and Santa Anna, after a bloody coup, drew up the new centralist Constitution of the Organic Bases and assumed the presidency again in 1843. A military revolution once more ousted him in 1844; he was deported to Cuba, and a moderate was installed as head of government.

Mexican-American War

The Texas problem had never been settled; Mexico had never recognized Santa Anna's "settlement," and the United States had not incorporated the territory. The election victory of James Polk brought on the annexation of Texas in 1845. War broke out in 1846 as General Zachary Taylor met and defeated a Mexican force situated in the disputed area between the Río Nueces and the Rio Grande. Suddenly Santa Anna reappeared in the country and, at the head of a large army, moved north to confront Taylor in the Saltillo area. In the battle of Buena Vista, after having apparently captured most of Taylor's strong points, Santa Anna inexplicably withdrew, leaving the field to the United States forces. Santa Anna nonetheless returned to the capital as though he had been victorious and ousted the liberals.

Under Winfield Scott, a United States expedition then landed at Veracruz and followed the route of Cortés in a march through Puebla to the capital. Hard-fought battles saved Mexican honor, but Scott was victorious. The United States attack on the military college at Chapultepec Castle gave Mexican children and the Mexican nation a new set of national heroes in the Boy Heroes, the teenage cadets killed in the defense. Santa Anna left the country once more, leaving the problem to a provisional president. Mexico City fell; Taylor swept down through the north and General Stephen Kearny through Texas and New Mexico to California, where General John Frémont had already taken over. The final peace settlement of the Treaty of Guadalupe Hidalgo ceded to the United States all Mexican territory north and west of the Rio Grande in return for US$15 million. Stunned and resentful, their national pride devastated by the loss of nearly half of their territory, Mexicans became more hostile to the United States.

After the war, the ultraconservatives seized power and recalled Santa Anna from exile to provide authoritarian rule in preparation for plans to place a royal prince at the head of the Mexican government. Assuming an almost monarchical role under the title of serene highness, Santa Anna spent lavish sums on trappings and bribery. Lacking ready funds, he finally sold a strip of land along the then ill-defined border to the United States for US$10 million (Gadsen Purchase). The liberals, growing bolder, in early 1854 expressed their renewed hopes in the Plan of Ayutla. The runaway economic, political, and social degeneration of the country finally and irrevocably undermined Santa Anna's power. In August 1855 he fled out of the country.

La Reforma

The Plan of Ayutla, proclaimed by the aging Indian guerrilla Juan Alvarez, was the opening of *la reforma* (the reform) in Mexico, that period of the nineteenth century dominated by liberal thinkers with great faith in the power of words. In November 1855 Alvarez, a liberal constitutionalist, became the provisional president. His Indian minister of justice, Benito Juárez, immediately promulgated a law making civil equality basic to the Mexican system by abolishing special privileges and raising the civil courts above those of the church, the army, and the great landowners. The bitter opposition of the church and the conservatives created such popular uproar that Alvarez retired.

Alvarez was replaced by a lawyer, Ignacio Comonfort, a moderate whose cabinet nonetheless unexpectedly adopted anticlerical laws. Comonfort's minister of finance, Miguel Lerdo de Tejada, in 1856 issued a decree calling for the forced sale of corporate landholdings. Although chiefly aimed at the church, which still controlled one-third of the cultivated land in Mexico, the law's phraseology also permitted the redistribution of the communal holdings of the Indians. The plan was to auction off the properties in anticipation of creating a peasantry of small, free farmers and thus to finance the government by means of a transfer tax in a way no previous Mexican administration had been able to do. It was not the landless who obtained these properties, however, but the speculators, the great landowners, and the local political bosses.

The work of a constituent assembly made up of moderates and liberals culminated in the Constitution of 1857; an affront to the conservatives, it survived in form, if not in practice, until 1917. Aside from incorporating the anticlerical and antiaristocratic ideals of Juárez and Lerdo de Tejada, the chief purpose of the document was to prevent a presidential dictatorship of the sort typical of the Santa Anna period—an objective that was not to be achieved for several decades.

The strong liberal faith in the power of words was reflected in a long list of inalienable rights and in the design of a federal system imbued with more central power—this in a country whose local political bosses increasingly controlled effective political action. The signing of the constitution represented a call to arms for the conservatives. Pope Pius IX issued an extraordinary condemnation of it, and the church hierarchy promised denial of the sacraments to all who upheld the works of *la reforma*. Nearly all important figures in the government were excommunicated. In December 1857 a group of conservatives under General Felix Zuloaga seized both President Comonfort and the new vice president and chief justice, Juárez. Escaping to Querétaro, a group of congressmen and members of the liberal administration set up a rump government.

The tensions exploded in January 1858 into a bloody three-year civil war, the War of the Reform. Juárez, released and at the head of the liberal regime, set up a government of the Republic of Veracruz, which only the United States, among the more influential world powers, recognized. This civil war pitted traditionalists against reformers, Central Mexico against the provinces, and even Europe against the United States. During the height of the battle in July 1859, Juárez issued the Laws of the Reform, which confiscated all church properties except buildings used for worship; suppressed all religious orders; ended tithing; required civil marriages and registration of births and deaths (thus depriving the church of an important source of funds); completely separated church and state; and even restricted any reinstatement of the traditional state Roman Catholicism in favor of the principle of religious equality.

These laws were carried out wherever the liberals occupied territory, and the consequence was persecution and counterpersecution in the name of Roman Catholicism. For nearly three years the conservative forces held the upper hand. But by controlling Veracruz, Mexico's major seaport—to which the United States kept the sea lanes open—the liberals maintained an advantage that was to prove decisive. Juárez entered Mexico City in January 1861.

As president, however, Juárez was faced with innumerable problems. There was neither enough money in circulation to gather taxes nor enough sales of church property to produce a significant amount of hard currencies. The old claims of foreign debt were revived, for the Europeans despised Juárez as an Indian bandit who had robbed and looted Europeans during the civil war. The European demands were intensified by the intrigue of conservative exiles all over Europe; the United States had become preoccupied with its own Civil War. At first, Juárez attempted to scale down the debt demands but, encountering only stubborn protests, he stopped payment completely for two years. The incensed creditors demanded that the governments of Great Britain, France, and Spain take action.

In late 1861 and early 1862 the Spanish, British, and French governments sent expeditionary forces to Veracruz, either to collect the debt through impounding customs receipts or to frighten Juárez into repaying. The British and Spanish, after lengthy negotiations, withdrew in April 1862. But the French had been approached by Mexican royalists; Napoleon II, coveting the wealth of Mexico and aspiring to leadership of the Latin world, decided to establish a puppet monarchy in Mexico.

The French army, moving inland from Veracruz, was badly beaten at Puebla on May 5, 1862 (see ch. 17). Sending a new commander and massive reinforcements, Napoleon redoubled his efforts, finally forcing the Juárez government out of Mexico City in June 1863 and establishing a provisional regime. Napoleon persuaded Archduke Maximilian of Austria, brother of the Hapsburg emperor, Franz Josef, to ascend the Mexican throne by showing him false evidence of overwhelming popular support from a rigged plebiscite. Maximilian arrived at Veracruz in July 1864. Falling in love with the country, Maximilian and his wife adopted Mexican clothes and Mexican customs. Well-meaning Maximilian attempted to make Mexico a showplace of progress and tolerance, but he was overcome by the country's chronic lack of capital, made worse by the French seizure of funds, mines, lands, and business houses in the collection of its claims. Likewise, he enraged the church by refusing to restore the lands and privileges of the clergy and by appointing Mexican moderates and liberals to high office.

At the end of the United States Civil War, Secretary of State William

Seward put heavy diplomatic pressure on Napoleon to withdraw French troops from Mexico, backing his demands by shipping great quantities of surplus war supplies and large numbers of "volunteers" to the Mexican republicans, who were cornered at a spot across from El Paso, Texas, now the site of Ciudad Juárez. Alarmed by the rising power of Prussia, Napoleon withdrew French troops in January 1867. Deserted but refusing to admit defeat, Maximilian was surrounded at Querétaro by Juárez' troops. He was tried and executed—one of perhaps 50,000 deaths attributable to Napoleon's adventure. Maximilian is generally viewed as a well-intentioned but misguided man.

Juárez, having won the battle against the forces that threatened the consolidation of the Mexican nation—the church and the French army— entered Mexico City with his stature immensely enhanced. Having driven out the invaders, he became the personification of Mexican nationhood. Symbolically, for the modern Mexican, the circle of national unity broken by the conquest was finally closed when a full-blooded Zapotec Indian drove out the last of the foreign powers to attempt domination of Mexico. Thus, Juárez has become the most important Mexican national hero (see ch. 17).

Mexico could now get on with the job of nation building. Juárez, reelected in 1867, tried to implement the Constitution of 1857. Retaining the loyalty of key army units through his minister of war, Juárez was able to demobilize two-thirds of the military challenges to his authority. The economy, however, did not easily revive from the ravages of civil war and intervention. Mineral production remained low, and agricultural yields had seriously fallen off after the transfer of church lands into private hands. Education suffered as a result of the drastic depletion of clerical teachers, the disbanding of the ecclesiastical orders, and popular resistance to Protestant missionaries.

Juárez was, however, able to inaugurate the era of railroad building by contracting with British firms for the Veracruz-Mexico City line, to promote a school system, and to give Mexico its first period of truly stable government since viceregal times. Reelected to the presidency in 1871, Juárez served only a few months before his death in July 1872. The short period of stability and growth was soon shattered by political and military struggles.

A revolt broke out in Jalisco directed against Juárez' successor, who was from Veracruz and thus a symbol of the hated Veracruz-Mexico City trade monopoly. It was in part by taking advantage of the uprising that one of the president's generals, Porfirio Díaz, in 1876 overthrew the government. The advent of the Díaz regime marked the end of *la reforma*. Juárez' ideals, though never entirely obscured, were deemphasized during the succeeding decades of the *porfiriato*—the long rule of Porfirio Díaz—only to be resurrected and fulfilled by the Revolution of 1910 and the subsequent evolution of modern Mexico.

THE PORFIRIATO

A mestizo of Spanish and Mixtec blood, Porfirio Díaz came from a Oaxaca family of modest circumstances, was a pupil of Juárez in law school, and was an extremely courageous officer in the ranks of the liberal Mexican army. Díaz had defied the 1854 plebiscite "set up" for Santa Anna and had been a key leader in Mexico City after the withdrawal of the French army in 1867. Díaz' Plan of Tuxtepec, which initiated the final overthrow of *la reforma* in 1876, was ostensibly a model of liberal thought—denouncing the idea of presidential reelection, calling for effective suffrage, and criticizing the extensive presence of foreign capitalists.

Díaz ruled through an informal political apparatus in which the major state and local leaders depended on Díaz not only for their economic well-being but for their freedom. Each district and city was ruled by a local boss, whose accountability to the national leader was even greater than it had been under the colonial system. The national congress and judiciary were staffed with obedient and loyal clients who did their benefactors' bidding. This political apparatus was sustained by spying and spoils and backed by an army that maintained internal order and forced subservience.

Military power was retained not only because of the great respect officers and enlisted men had for Díaz but also because of his appointment of men he could dominate, his largesse for those in his favor, and his frequent shifting of commands. Perhaps as nearly powerful, however, was the highly centralized police force, the mainstay of which was the rural police.

Incorporating bandits into the well-armed mounted rural police, Díaz brought rural crime and banditry under control for the first time, but he also created a tool for terrorizing political enemies and troublesome citizens. The whole system was built around the slogan "Bread or Club" (for those who cooperated, "bread"; for those who rebelled, "club"). This practice was often the product of the escape law, which permitted the shooting on the way to jail of those who "attempted escape." This political apparatus completely controlled the Mexican government from 1876 to 1911. The only ostensible lapse in power was the administration of General Manuel Gonzales Praia (1880–84), which was allowed in order to fulfill Díaz' original commitment to no immediate reelection.

The *porfiriato* was not unpopular—at least until its last years. Even his critics admitted Díaz' skill in assuming, in the popular mind, the mantle of Juárez. Of particular importance in sustaining popular regard was the regime's ability to create and maintain a high level of material and economic growth in Mexico. By 1894 Díaz was able to announce the first balanced budget in the history of the republic. Mexico attracted great sums of foreign money, matched by the growth of governmental concessions to foreign enterprise.

First railroads, then telegraph, and later the telephone brought in large amounts of foreign capital. There followed the reemergence of the mining industry, which in turn stimulated more railroad construction, opening up regions that had become stagnant since independence. The growth in these latter regions spurred the expansion of the livestock and agricultural industries to the north. The growing national wealth created urban demands for streetcars, electrical systems, and massive public utility projects. Finally came the discovery in 1900 of the rich oil pools of the Gulf Coast, stretching from Texas to Veracruz and centering on the port of Tampico. This contributed to the rapid growth of the city of Monterrey, opening up a new and serious regional challenge to the central monopoly of Mexico City and Veracruz (see ch. 2).

The pattern of growth, despite prosperity, tended to nourish an ever-ripening xenophobia. The foreigner was protected from the police and law courts, and government censorship and tax structure worked to his advantage. Between 1902 and 1911, for example, United States holdings in Mexican railroads approximately doubled to almost US$650 million. Total United States investment in Mexico by 1912 was more than US$1 billion, exceeding the total amount of capital invested by the Mexicans themselves.

Labor and even the church shared in a growing displeasure with foreign "colonization." Knowing the Mexicans as a whole were neither anti-Roman Catholic nor anticlerical, Díaz had allowed the Laws of the Reform regarding the church to fall into disuse. As a result, the church began to regain some of its properties and accumulate moderate cash reserves. But even the native clergy had its complaints. Although the number of priests rose from 3,000 to 6,000 during Díaz' period of power, most of this increase was accounted for by a heavy immigration of Spanish, French, and Italian clerics. This growth tended to please the church hierarchy, but it tended to arouse the resentment of the lower ranks of the native-born Mexican clergy.

Díaz had little sympathy for labor; he viewed union organizers as public enemies and treated them severely. As material progress spread, the industrial working class grew; as it expanded, its grievances against government and industry swelled. As early as the 1890s Ricardo Flores Magón, an anarchosyndicalist, began to attack the Díaz regime with demands for economic equality for Mexican workers. In all, some 250 strikes occurred under the Díaz regime, mainly in the textile, railroad, and cigar industries, all largely in the hands of foreign capitalists. The strikes were put down quickly and ruthlessly, which created a strongly anti-Díaz and antiforeign attitude among the Mexican working classes.

Perhaps the greatest indictment leveled against the *porfiriato*, however, was that of the outraged liberals against the regime's flavor of white supremacy. The notion of white racial superiority was an outgrowth of quasi-scientific notions introduced into Mexico at the end of *la reforma*. These ideas, however, were not in the long term a practical position for the controlling groups. During the nineteenth century they had become a progressively smaller proportion of the total population. The mixing of the Mexican population, though gradual, was irreversible.

The nineteenth-century liberal based his formula for rapid agricultural development on small private holdings, not on the corporate holdings of the church or the Indian communal holdings. Díaz continued this policy by applying the anticorporate provisions of *la reforma* laws to the Indian communal holdings. As before, however, the lands did not become small private farms but were quickly bought up by wealthy Mexicans or foreigners. The result was that foreigners were able to gain control of large areas. Thus, although more than two-thirds of the population remained engaged in agriculture, production declined, and increasingly toward the end of the *porfiriato* the country required importation of foodstuffs.

Just as the white-to-nonwhite ratio tended to work against the maintenance of a white supremacist philosophy, so the landholder-to-peasant ratio worked against the economic philosophy of depending upon large agricultural landholdings. In fact, both weaknesses tended to work hand-in-hand to undermine the *porfiriato*. Some 80 percent of the Mexican population in 1910 was rural and dependent upon the land for subsistence. Yet, over 95 percent of this rural population was landless and depended almost entirely on the few thousand large landowners for their livelihood. The peasant had to buy necessities from his estate's store. As a result, virtually all peasants were in perpetual debt, debt peonage that would seemingly never allow them to break free. Should they strike or riot in protest, the army and the rural police were ready to suppress them.

After the beginning of the twentieth century, protest rose sharply, but the end of the regime was triggered by Díaz himself and a United States magazine correspondent. Díaz had turned seventy in 1900 and concern grew about the problem of a successor. In the 1904 election, Díaz installed a vice president as a concession to those who thought he was too old to guide the country. In February 1908, James Creelman, a reporter for *Pearson's Magazine,* implied in an article that in a private interview Díaz had expressed a desire to retire in 1910 at the end of his term and that under no circumstances would he run again for reelection. The reprinting of what has come to be known as the Creelman Report in the Mexico City newspaper *El Imparcial* stirred political activity as opponents and friends alike began to group their forces for the coming election. Díaz some months later informed his cabinet he would indeed seek another term. This interchange, however, caused Francisco I. Madero in 1908 to write *The Presidential Succession in 1910,* a highly popular book that was to prove the undoing of the *porfiriato* and the making of Madero. Encouraged by his own growing popularity and disillusioned by a personal interview with Díaz, Madero declared himself a candidate for the presidency under the slogan "Effective Suffrage—

No Reelection."

Díaz had Madero jailed in San Luís Potosí and then carried the election off on schedule. It was announced that Madero had received 196 votes to Díaz' 1 million votes. Released in October 1910, Madero fled to the United States, where he issued the so-called plan of San Luís Potosí calling for the overthrow of the *porfiriato* and its replacement by a political system providing for land reform, social justice, and no reelection of the president. The plan caused rumblings among the leaders of the Indian and mestizo masses of the north and south. Government reaction was too slow, and the end came within six months in May 1911. Emiliano Zapata, with his army of landless Indian peasants from Morelos and Guerrero, marching under the banner of "Land and Liberty," captured the important railroad center at Cuautla. Pancho Villa and his private army and irregular bandit forces stormed Ciudad Juárez. News of these rebellions brought on army mutinies and riots in Mexico City. Díaz resigned on May 25, 1911, and set sail for Europe.

THE REVOLUTION

Francisco I. Madero, from an aristocratic Coahuila family of wealthy Díaz supporters, entered Mexico City on June 7, 1911. The masses hailed him as a deliverer who would provide them with "Land and Liberty." The popular euphoria was, however, ill founded, for it swirled around a man with little experience in public affairs and none in government. His political plans went little beyond free and open elections and the establishment of a democratic system, but the desire for social change had prompted swelling demands, from all sides, that went far beyond this. Although Madero was elected president on November 6, 1911, and subsequently swept away much of the old Diaz bureaucracy, he also attempted a balancing of all factions and thus moved too slowly for the taste of those who wanted to remake the social order overnight.

Generals, local chiefs, and radicals all over Mexico, freed from restrictive controls, responded to the welling up of popular resentment against the controlling aristocracy, both foreign and domestic. Zapata, a tenant farmer, had been leading his peasant army over the Morelos countryside, killing landowners and dividing up their lands. He feared a reaction might cheat the peons of these properties. In November 1911 he issued his Plan of Ayala, denouncing Madero as having joined forces with the followers of Díaz and thus being unfit to govern. Soon there was a southern Indian revolt against Madero's administration. When Madero continued to take no positive steps toward social reforms, Pascual Orozco, a storekeeper, and his army of the north revolted in March 1912. Although the Orozco revolt was put down by General Victoriano Huerta, the social ferment raging among the lower classes of the north, particularly in the state of Chihuahua, was not effectively countered. It soon became clear that, although Madero put political reform above social and economic reform, the latter held highest priority for the revolutionary elements epitomized by Zapata and Orozco.

Madero could not reestablish order. Three individuals involved in his downfall were Huerta, Madero's commanding general; General Felix Díaz, nephew of the recently deposed autocrat; and Henry Lane Wilson, the United States ambassador to Mexico. Díaz had unsuccessfully attacked the presidential palace. Rebuffed, he joined Huerta, whom Madero had appointed to lead the forces loyal to him. Together, on February 9, 1913, they began a siege of Mexico City that lasted for ten days (the "tragic ten"). Ambassador Wilson stepped in to mediate between Madero and Huerta, hoping to achieve peace, to provide safety for American citizens, and to reestablish the flourishing United States enterprises that had operated during the *porfiriato*. Wilson pressured Madero to resign and encouraged a Huerta coup by informing the general's representatives that the United States would recognize any regime that could restore order to the city and countryside. On February 18 Huerta arrested Madero and proclaimed his own assumption of the presidency until elections could be held.

Despite promises of safe passage out of Mexico, Madero was assassinated on the night of February 22 as he was being removed from the presidential palace. Although no evidence linked Wilson to the plot, to many Mexicans it appeared that he bore responsibility, in that the coup he encouraged led to the murder. This and other grievances induced violent hostility to the United States among the Mexican revolutionaries. Madero's assassination raised the stature of this unsuccessful president to that of a martyred father of the revolution.

Huerta ruled by force, bribery, and a liberal construction of the fugitive law. His claim of a lack of popular demand for new elections in October 1913 caused Zapata to break away and the surviving followers of Díaz to denounce his dictatorship. Having escaped prison to reenter Mexico from the United States, Villa, a revolutionary with a private army constantly eluding the grasp of Huerta's military forces, broadened his power base in Chihuahua. Huerta's most serious problem, however, was the American president, Woodrow Wilson.

By April 1914, Wilson had lifted the United States embargo on arms to Mexico. This aided the rebel armies of Villa and of Alvaro Obregón in Chihuahua and Sonora; they gained control of virtually the entire northern border zone and, with the aid of Zapata, the central states of Morelos, Guerrero, and Michoacán and parts of the regions to the north and east of Mexico City. All of these were under the general leadership of Venustiano Carranza. In the face of this threat, Huerta's strategy was to maintain fortified cities along the rail lines from the United States border to Mexico City. But during late 1913 and early 1914, the *constitucionalistas*, as the forces of Villa, Obregón, and Carranza came to be called, descended from the north following those same rail lines.

The fatal blow to Huerta's cause, however, came from President

Wilson's strong reaction to the arrest of some United States sailors in Tampico; Wilson ordered United States naval forces to seize and hold the customshouse of Veracruz and so bring on the financial collapse of the Huerta government. In an attempt to deprive Huerta of a shipment of arms in Veracruz, a party of United States marines and sailors was landed, only to be forced to withdraw by a group of citizens led by 200 cadets from the Mexican Naval Academy. The next day three United States cruisers bombarded the Veracruz defenses into submission.

These acts generated indignation among some Mexicans, but Huerta was unable to turn the inflamed Mexican nationalism into support. Surrounded and without financial resources he fled to the United States in July 1914. This triggered an interlude of anarchy. As the revolutionary forces approached the capital, a wave of violence broke out. Being wealthy became punishable by death. Estates, factories, villages, and mines were ravaged.

Obregón's army of the northwest reached Mexico City first, followed by Carranza, who had by this time broken with Villa. In an attempt to unify the movement, the leading factions under Villa, Zapata, Obregón, and Carranza met in October 1914 in Aguascalientes to organize a government. General Eulalio Gutiérrez, the presidential choice of Villa and Zapata, was elected, causing Carranza and Obregón to repudiate the proceedings and to withdraw to Veracruz where they set up a regime "in exile" and began building a military force to oust Villa and Zapata.

President Gutíerrez soon gave up his position and went over to the Carranza-Obregón side. Zapata and his followers returned to their southern homeland. In February 1915, joined by a sizable force of radical laborers, Obregón drove Villa from Mexico City and gave chase until a final battle at Celaya in April broke the back of the Villa forces.

In a desperate attempt to wrest control of the revolution from Carranza, Villa attempted to provoke a general United States invasion by a series of border raids. President Wilson sent General John Pershing with a large force of United States regulars and militia into Chihuahua to chase Villa. Although Carranza strongly objected to the United States chase of Villa's "bandits," there was little he could do to control Villa or Pershing.

The withdrawal of United States troops in February 1917 came almost simultaneously with the publication by the British secret service of the so-called Zimmerman note, in which Germany offered Mexico an alliance against the United States (anticipating American entrance into World War I) in return for territory lost by the Mexican Cession of 1848. The offer was not accepted, but the resulting outcry in the United States and the galvanizing of Mexican antipathy to the United States proved an asset to Carranza.

The Carranza government convened a constitutional convention in Querétaro in late November 1916, in an attempt to attract peasant and worker support and to restore legality to political affairs. Within little more than two months Carranza proclaimed the completion and ratification of the Constitution of 1917, the most hallowed document of the Mexican revolution. The provisions of the new constitution incorporated political elements found in most nineteenth-century Western constitutions—effective universal male suffrage, no reelection of the president, division of powers, a bicameral legislature, an independent judiciary, separation of church and state, federalism, and compulsory free education.

On matters of economic and social welfare, however, the revolutionary intellectuals had their way, incorporating the collectivist principle in the constitution to a degree unparalleled before the Russian Revolution. The state was to take precedence over the individual. The precolonial communal farmlands of the central and southern Indian villages were to be restored and enlarged. "Oversized" individual holdings were to be subdivided. The Constitution of 1917 guaranteed the right of agricultural and industrial workers to unionize and strike and proclaimed limits to working hours and bases for minimum wages. Both debt peonage and child labor were abolished. The church was to own no property whatsoever, including houses of worship. Monastic orders were outlawed, and priests were severely restricted. Most of all, the church was to have no influence on public education.

Once in the presidency, Carranza governed under a conservative interpretation of the constitution. Bothered by the persistence of Zapata-led revolts demanding "Land and Liberty," Carranza tried to capture the peasant leader; his subsequent involvement in the assassination of Zapata undermined his popular support, and his attempt in 1920 to dictate to his successor, Obregón, completed public disaffection, even to the extent of causing Obregón to summon the people, through his Plan of Agua Prieta, to resist the imposition of the successor. Carranza attempted to get to Veracruz in a train loaded with national treasure, only to have the train derailed and to be hunted down and murdered. On July 20, 1923, Pancho Villa was ambushed in Parral by a relative of one of the victims of his banditry. By mid-1923 Madero, Zapata, Carranza, and Villa, four of the five noted heroes of the Mexican revolution, were dead. The last, Obregón, would soon follow.

THE RISE OF THE MESTIZO SPIRIT

By 1920 many Mexicans were beginning to feel that once again the continuing revolution was falling back into reaction. It seemed as if the revolutionary promises and ideals were going to be lost in the violence and confusion that prevailed. But Alvaro Obregón assumed the presidency, salvaging the revolution and consolidating its divergent forces. He established the so-called Sonoran dynasty that was to rule Mexico for the next fifteen years.

By manipulating the three new bases of power—the revolutionary generals, the agrarian spokesmen, and the labor leaders—Obregón solidified the program of the revolution. He reduced the size of the armed forces drastically while inducing many generals to accept status as a pensioned class of wealthy individuals. Most of the generals responded by remaining strongly loyal to Obregón and the new system throughout their lifetime.

It was much more difficult to organize and bring under control the agrarian elements. As a northerner, Obregón saw land reform primarily in terms of small private plots, but he allowed an old Zapata follower, Antonio Díaz Soto y Gama, to influence his policies to the extent that some 4 million acres of land were redistributed, mostly in the form of common lands to Indian communities.

It was in labor matters that Obregón was to achieve his greatest national acclaim. He supported Luis Morones in 1918 in his attempts to establish a national trade union confederation, the Regional Confederation of Mexican Workers (Confederación Regional Obrera Mexicana—CROM). Under Obregón, Morones and the CROM had the full and enthusiastic support of the government in forcing hesitant workers into unions and in backing union claims against entrepreneurs.

It was under Obregón that Mexico's vast attempt at mass education of the illiterate really began (see ch. 6). His minister of education, José Vasconcelos, was a writer and philosopher of high repute; his conception of the racial superiority of the Mexican intermixture of Indian, Negro, and white blood was to take on a very special importance in the attempt to create a mestizo society and a sense of national greatness. In this process, the search for national identity emphasized the glorification of the Indian past. This was a period of unprecedented intellectual freedom and artistic flowering that brought forth great muralists, composers, philosophers, and a wealth of poets and novelists—all of whom glorified the Indian past (see ch. 8.)

The principal instrument involved in the creation of a mestizo society was public education. Thousands of new schools were started and staffed with hastily trained primary teachers. Obregón had infused with missionary zeal the attempt to establish a fully literate Mexican society. Vast numbers of itinerant teachers moved out over the countryside; cultural missions brought hygiene to remote villages; and children were taught the folk arts and dances of ancient Mexico (see ch. 6). Moreover, Obregón, in his agricultural program, stimulated the education of farmers in modern methods and techniques.

With the aid of United States arms and permission to pass through Texas in a flanking maneuver, Obregón was able to put down a revolt and to ensure the 1924 presidential installation of his friend and fellow-Sonoran, Plutarco Elías Calles (president, 1924–28). Calles pursued essentially the same policies as did Obregón, but perhaps with even more vigor. Agrarian reform gained greater momentum, as more than 20 million acres of land were redistributed to the Indian communities over the decade in which Calles directly controlled government policy. The school building program moved ahead rapidly. The movement attracted increasing numbers of workers, and Calles continued to support the CROM.

It was with regard to the church, however, that Calles demonstrated what many considered to be true revolutionary virtue. In 1926 he suddenly ordered strict compliance with the various anticlerical clauses of the Constitution of 1917, particularly those requiring the registration of all priests and the closing of seminaries. The government hunted down and registered clandestine communities of friars and nuns and confiscated church property, funds, and art objects.

On July 31, 1926, all church bells were silenced, and for the next three years no church services were held in Mexico, although the church buildings remained open for individual worship. Devout citizens, mainly centered in Jalisco and Guanajuato, rebelled against the "godless republic," assassinating officials and attacking revolutionary leaders. By 1929 the conflict was temporarily halted through the mediation of United States Ambassador Dwight Morrow. The federal government, did not, however, prevent the governors of such states as Sonora, Tabasco, Veracruz, and Yucatán from expelling or deporting most of the priests in their domain.

During the first two or three years of his presidential term, Calles brought the monetary and fiscal system of Mexico directly under the control of the state, establishing the Bank of Mexico in 1925, creating a general controller's office for overseeing national budgetary matters, and levying Mexico's first income tax. For the first time since the Díaz regime, Mexico showed signs of attaining financial and monetary stability (see ch. 13). In 1926 Calles created Mexico's first postrevolutionary development bank. He broadened this agrarian program by establishing the national Irrigation Commission and subjected the electric power industry to strict government regulation. In addition, he attempted to link all parts of the nation through a road network.

In December 1925 Calles ordered all oil companies to exchange their titles of ownership for fifty-year leases. The long and acrimonious controversy that ensued was again settled by Morrow. He was able to achieve an agreement whereby companies that had performed positive acts of exploitation before 1917 should not be disturbed, but the state's ownership of the subsoil was reaffirmed in principle.

In the 1928 presidential elections, Calles tried to return his old partner, Alvaro Obregón, to power, but before his inauguration Obregón was assassinated by a religious fanatic. All the great military heroes of the revolution were now dead; maintenance of revolutionary spirit and direction could no longer depend on personalities but needed the institutionalization of the revolutionary process. Therefore, Calles created the National Revolutionary Party (Partido Revolucionario Nacional—PRN), officially making Mexico a one party state. Calles assumed the role of directing the PRN, initiating the process of direct central control over all levels of government and grouping all political parties and regional political associations into a single national entity. The agrarian forces, still relatively weak politically, were easily brought into the party. The army was a different matter. On the one hand, Calles and his loyal generals took to the battlefield to defeat dissident generals in the last rebellion of regular army elements against the central government. On the other hand, labor, by way of the CROM, was left out, largely because of Calles' feelings about Luis Morones, whom he had come to consider overly ambitious.

The interim presidency of Emilio Portes Gil was followed in 1929 by the election of Pascual Ortiz Rubio to the remainder of the presidential term. Hamstrung by a growing power struggle between his own few supporters and those loyal to Calles and his generals, Ortiz Rubio resigned in 1932 and was replaced through congressional selection by Abelardo Rodríguez, who served until the term ended in 1934.

The pressures of the more liberal elements of the PRN were strong enough to make it necessary for Calles to select as the presidential nominee Lázaro Cárdenas, whom Calles felt he could control. Cárdenas assumed the presidency in late 1934 with a Calles-approved cabinet. But the new president proved to have strong attitudes of his own—closing gambling casinos and brothels, backing labor in a sudden series of strikes, and announcing a series of far-reaching educational and social reforms without the advice or consent of Calles. Viewing these acts as a challenge to his authority, Calles began to hint that Cárdenas might be forced into a resignation. Cárdenas stood his ground, and on June 19, 1935, dissolved the original cabinet and appointed one committed both to him personally and to his program of economic and social reform. On the same day, a government aircraft flew Calles to Mazatlán and retirement. Thus ended the Sonoran dynasty.

The official party brought under its wing the giant national labor organization, the Mexican Workers' Federation (Confederacíon de Trabajadores Mexicanos—CTM), created out of the ruins of the old CROM by the Marxist intellectual, Vicente Lombardo Toledano. Although the CTM has undergone ups and downs in government favor, it has remained the largest labor group in Mexican commerce and industry.

Cárdenas saw land reform in terms of rejuvenating the ancient Indian communal lands and through his vast land-distribution program created more communal-land farmers than there were workers in the entire industrial labor force. From this he created the agrarian pillar of the restructured party, the National Confederation of Campesinos (Confederación Nacional de Campesinos—CNC), membership in which became obligatory for every communal-land farmer in the nation. Finally, Cárdenas created the Government Employees Union (Federación de Sindicatos de Trabajadores al Servicio de Estado—FSTSE), a civil servants and teachers organization, the membership of which was solidly committed to the official party.

Outside the official party, interest groups were created among bank employees, small independent farmers, cooperative labor, and chambers of commerce. These groups, although not part of the official party, were to be consulted frequently by the president on decisions of great national or particular importance. Essentially, the newly reorganized party rested on a functional occupational structure. Overall direction of this party and, therefore, of national affairs was lodged in the hands of the president, advised by a committee made up of the four secretaries heading up the four party sectors. This basic design still characterizes Mexico's "one-party democracy."

Although Cárdenas came to symbolize the implementation of the most revolutionary clauses of the Constitution of 1917, he began, in 1936, to relax the restrictions against the church's participation in education and began a revamping of the Mexican educational system. By 1945 President Manuel Avila Camacho was able to call for and obtain the passage of a constitutional amendment that called for a patriotic education, a greater tolerance of private and parochial schools, and a revision of textbooks.

This relaxing of strong revolutionary anticlerical sentiment was balanced by a strict adherence to revolutionary land-reform objectives. By 1940 Cárdenas had redistributed nearly 45 million acres as communal lands. Although nearly three times as much land remained in private hands, predominantly in large estates or in commercial farms, the area held communally included almost half of the land actually under cultivation. In social terms, the effect of the Cárdenas program was to make the rural peasant, particularly the southern Indian, feel that the federal government had his interests in mind (see ch. 14).

Cárdenas became a living legend among the poor of Mexico and the Left. In 1937 he brought the masses into the political structure by revamping the official party, changing its official designation from PRN to the Mexican Revolutionary Party (Partido Revolunionario Mexicano— PRM). The object was to create a set of interest groups through which the PRM might become more responsive to popular demands—although the final word would continue to be that spoken by the president of the republic. The aim of Cárdenas was to achieve a functional democracy, centered on a single party and giving primary voice to the labor, agrarian, military, and "popular" sectors but also incorporating other broadly based national interest groups.

Cárdenas backed the labor movement strongly. A case in point was the nationalization of the railroad system. He placed management in the hands of the railroad workers' union. Inefficiency, featherbedding, and costs mounted drastically, as did the accident rate. This interlude proved so unworkable that Cárdenas finally brought the railroads under the direct control of an autonomous government agency.

Cárdenas' most famous implementation of his program of national socialism was the strict enforcement of states' constitutionally decreed

81

subsoil rights. A protracted dispute between American and British oil companies and the CTM—whose members in the petroleum industry were striking for higher wages, fringe benefits, and better living and working conditions—brought government pressure on the companies to submit to labor's demands. The companies refused a court settlement and appealed the decision over Cárdenas' head, through full-page advertisements in Mexican newspapers. Cárdenas, using Article 27 of the Constitution of 1917, announced the expropriation of the foreign oil properties in 1938. (Indemnification of US$24 million was eventually agreed to in 1941). The nationalized oil fields and refineries became a government monopoly, Mexican Petroleum (Petróleos Mexicanos—PEMEX). This achievement was to make Cárdenas a symbol of Mexico's break with foreign domination.

The acute shortage of manufactured goods available for import during World War II stimulated sharply the upsurge in domestic manufactures already started under Cárdenas. By the end of the war, as a result of heavy exports of minerals and fibers to the United States, Mexico had a significant positive balance of trade. Building on this backlog and accumulation of domestic capital reserves, the social and political power of Mexico's industrialists grew substantially. Within the PRI structure they were typically centrist. "Their" president was Adolfo Ruiz Cortines who, with his finance minister, Antonio Carrillo Flores, kept the momentum of Mexico's industrial growth going in the 1950s by judicious use of tariffs, quotas, and legal controls on the amount and character of foreign investment. The net effect of all this was a great strengthening of the power of the Center in PRI, with concomitant weakening of both Left and Right.

There was little change in the formal political framework after Cárdenas, with the exception of the enfranchisement of women by President Ruiz Cortines in 1954 and the dropping of the military as such from the party structure in conjunction with the institutionalization of the popular sector by Avila Camacho (see ch. 10). After this latter structural change, the PRM in 1946 had changed its name to its present-day designation, the Institutional Revolutionary Party (Partido Revolucionario Institucional—PRI), a verbalization of the institutionalization of an ongoing peaceful Mexican revolution.

Thus, succeeding governments modified institutions of the revolution solidified by the Cárdenas administration, but the basic system has changed little since. Under the system the president is nominated by the heads of the party and the outgoing president after consultation with sector leaders, strong interests outside the party, and other individuals powerful in their own right. After Cárdenas, five presidents completed their terms—Manuel Avila Camacho (1940–46), Miguel Alemán (1946–52), Adolfo Ruiz Cortines (1952-58), Adolfo López Mateos (1958-64), and Gustavo Díaz Ordaz (1964–70). These men were drawn from all factions of the PRI (see ch. 10; ch. 13).

The pattern that prevailed in 1970, when Luís Echeverría became president, had felt the cumulative effect of forces set in motion by Cárdenas. First, the process of restoring the traditional communal lands had broken the power of the estate owners as a class. The displaced rural elites had moved to the cities where they had become urban real property investors, merchants, or industrialists. This in turn had broken the traditional resistance against economic protectionism and permitted the establishment of tariffs and controls aiding domestic industry. Second, the pensioning of the revolutionary generals and their soldiers, usually with land, had tended both to remove them from the political scene and to give them a stake in the continuance of the PRI system (see ch. 10; ch. 12).

CHAPTER 4

ETHNIC GROUPS AND LANGUAGES

The vast majority of Mexicans are mestizos, a point of national pride since the Revolution of 1910. In language and culture mestizos represent the flowering of the Hispanic heritage. Their values, kinship patterns, class structure, and Roman Catholicism bear close resemblance to mestizo cultures throughout Latin America (see ch. 5). Mexican mestizos control the economy and the government, and society reflects their values. Nevertheless, there are many remnants of Indian culture to be found alongside this Hispanic heritage, and it has been estimated that over 50 percent of the Mexicans are of predominantly Indian extraction. Indian traits survive in the national language, art, handicrafts, folklore, and cuisine, as well as in the indigenist movement, which has spurred more widespread interest in Mexican origins than has any parallel movement in the Western Hemisphere.

Mexico has one of the proportionally smaller indigenous populations in the Western Hemisphere. The Indian minority has decreased drastically since the Spanish conquest and in 1974 constituted no more than 5 or 10 percent of the population. It remains, despite this reduction, regionally and culturally diverse, but the various Indian groups share certain characteristics that distinguish them from the rest of the society: indigenous language, low literacy levels, housing and material culture, relationship to the land, and folk Catholicism—a blend of aboriginal and Roman Catholic beliefs.

Indian groups exist outside the mainstream of Mexican society, living mainly in the more marginal geographic areas in their own settlements. Indian ethnicity cannot be maintained outside the family or village unit and requires a community of interpersonal and organizational relationships. The sociopolitical or civic-religious hierarchy that exists in many Indian villages is a remnant of pre-Columbian times and is structured differently from mestizo organization.

The quality and breadth of studies of the different Indian groups vary, and in some matters there is no scholarly consensus. The basis for classification may be ethnographic, linguistic, historical, or regional, or a combination. Using regional criteria as a starting point, five groups can be identified: those of the Yucatán Peninsula and Chiapas; the Southern Mexican Highlands; the Central Mexican Highlands; Western Mexico; and Northwest Mexico. Similarities and differences among the Indian groups in these regions can be discussed in terms of seven factors:

language, community type, material culture, economic organization, family and kinship, village government, and religion.

Despite the impact of the revolution on the nation, traditional attitudes toward the Indian have persisted on the local level. Therefore, though officially the Indian is the equal of any other citizen—occasionally the government has even made special dispensation for him—in reality, he is unequal to his mestizo neighbors in many respects. The character of interethnic relationships is conditioned by the superior economic position of the mestizos, the differential access to power of mestizos and Indians, the limited socialization of the Indian into the national society, and the perceived inferiority of Indian race and culture. In Oaxaca and a few other areas, Indians enjoy considerable political and economic power. But usually the close relationships between rural mestizos and Indians, for which the latter depend upon mestizos as social, economic, and political brokers or intermediaries, is exploitive.

Mexican ethnic history is a series of attempts to integrate the Indian into the national society, first by religious conversion and political control and later through incorporation of the Indian as a vital part of the cultural heritage. Bringing the Indian into Mexican society has been central to revolutionary philosophy. Efforts toward integration have greatly increased since 1914 and have included programs of land reform, bilingual education, and technical instruction.

Combined pressures and incentives make efforts by individual Indians to merge into mestizo society increasingly common. Indians who wish to acculturate do so by "passing"—that is, adopting certain mestizo characteristics, such as Spanish surname, mode of dress, and values. It is also advantageous to marry a mestizo and imperative to speak Spanish in the process of "passing."

EVOLUTION OF MODERN ETHNIC GROUPS

By 1974 Mexico had evolved into a mestizo nation—ethnically, linguistically, and culturally. Present-day ethnic configuration is a series of overlays and gradations ranging from Indian to European, which blend almost imperceptibly into each other. Elements of both cultures, including language, are found throughout all groups and classes of society and in all areas of the country. For the Indians this evolutionary process began with Indian migrations and tribal wars long before the arrival of Hernán Cortés in 1519 (see ch. 3). Hundreds of groups, speaking a variety of languages, splintered off and migrated to new areas, developing enclaves of noncontiguous language groupings throughout the area. Although the principal language groups placed the Indians in some sort of general category, a strong tradition of local variation fostered by village specialization and climatic differences has complicated the ethnic picture for Mexican historians and anthropologists alike.

The results of the conquest were cataclysmic for the Indian social system. The Indians lost their best lands, water supplies, and a large portion of their population. Their society underwent a tremendous reduction in social complexity during the sixteenth and seventeenth centuries. The massive disappearance of Indian elites created a vacuum in the political, religious, and military organization as well as in the realms of Indian art and architecture. Such vacuums were filled by Spanish overlords. There was only a slight impact of Spanish peasant culture; New Spain became a society of Spanish upper class, including both Iberian-born Spaniards *(gachupines)* and American-born Spaniards (criollos) and Indian lower class. Governmental and religious changes were imposed in a superficial way by the Spanish, but the Indians retreated both geographically and socially and thus remained basically Indian.

The repatterned Indian community emerged as a new entity, a corporate organization composed entirely of local peasants. These communities became bastions of cultural homeostasis and self-sufficiency. All factors served to reinforce the social and cultural homogeneity and to discourage the development of internal class distinctions and heterogeneous behavior and interests. Exploitation by the Spanish further enhanced the solidarity of Indian communities and values. Rules, such as marriage within the community and prohibition of sales of land to outsiders, made it difficult for any outsiders to become members of the village society.

The greatest retention of pre-Hispanic traits is thus found at the family or village level, whereas the formal religious and political organization is largely Spanish. Some of the Indian characteristics to survive with minor alterations have been language, family organization, religion, material culture, private cults and beliefs connected with the life cycle or land, and technology of the family or village production unit. In some areas village hierarchy and patterns for ascending it retain an Indian cast, although the ultimate position may be one created by Spanish influence. In most cases village-level organization has come to act as a liaison between the national society and local interests.

Few, if any, Mexican Indians live as their ancestors did 500 years ago. Present-day Indian culture is a synthesis of colonial and aboriginal cultures all remade and redefined in terms of each other. Nothing is entirely Spanish or entirely Indian. What is implied by the word *traditional,* then, is the evolution and subsequent retention of Spanish colonial and Indian traits. For example, traditional Maya communities continue to practice ritual offerings to the maize (corn) and rain gods, which incorporate the forms of a Roman Catholic communion by filling a calabash with bark beer rather than using a chalice and sacramental wine.

Ethnic evolution in Mexico has probably done more to alter the genetic character of its Spanish descendants than its Indian population. The result of early and extensive miscegenation has been the mestizo. His heritage has been shaped by his early dominance as a racial type, his pride in his Indian heritage, and the Revolution of 1910. There are a few Middle Easterners, Europeans, and Asians in the country, although these are found in isolated enclaves as fairly recent immigrants. Most of the black population has become racially integrated into the larger mixed population, although a few enclaves remain, particularly in Tampico and other Gulf Coast areas.

ETHNIC DIVISIONS

Mestizos

Mestizos, or ladinos as they are called in Chiapas, form the great bulk of the population—an estimated 75 to 90 percent of the total. They are found in all geographic areas, occupations, and social classes and at all levels of economic well-being (see ch. 5). They range from the poor ladino farmers of Chiapas to the urban industrialists of Mexico City. Moreover, mestizos control the reins of government at all levels, from the presidency to officials in mixed Indian-mestizo villages. The vast majority are Roman Catholics, at least nominally, and their value system and personal relationships conform to the general Hispanic legacy found throughout the Southern Hemisphere.

The vast differences between Mexican mestizos are bridged by one important factor: a common pride in the Revolution of 1910 accompanied by a strong awareness of Mexican nationhood. In theory, all Mexicans have equal access to the political system, but only the mestizos have gained an understanding of how that system works. In addition, all mestizos speak Spanish and not infrequently another language, such as English or French. They are constantly in touch with the national political, social, and economic system through a fairly extensive network of communications and transportation. Moreover, they are aware of Mexican nationhood in relationship to other nations, particularly nations of other hemispheres.

Indians

The 1950 census was the last attempt to racially distinguish Indians from the rest of society in the national census. Consequently, estimates of the Indian population in the mid-1970s ranged from 2.5 million to ten times that number. Several indexes tend to make the lower figure more believable. For example, a study of *ejidatarios* (those living on *ejidos*— see Glossary) in 1960 showed that 96.4 percent spoke Spanish, an increase of 2 percent in twenty years. Thus, less than 4 percent were monolingual in Indian languages. A 1967 estimate claimed 10 percent of the population as monolingual Indian, and in 1972 President Luís Echeverría stated that some 4 million, or 7 percent of the population, could be considered as members of Indian communities. These figures are probably more accurate than higher estimates, as there has been a gradual and steady decline of the Indian population over the last 450 years.

Moreover, the Indians remaining are not evenly distributed throughout the country. It has been estimated that 94 percent live in one of three regions: 36 percent on the Central Plateau, mostly in Puebla, Hidalgo, and México; 35 percent in the South Pacific, in Oaxaca, Chiapas, and Guerrero; and 23 percent on the Gulf Coast, mostly in Yucatán and Veracruz.

Part of the confusion over the number of Indians rests in the definition of the term *Indian* and in the distinction between Indian and mestizo characteristics. One of the foremost Mexican sociologists, Antonio Caso, has defined the Indian as "he who feels he belongs to an Indian community" and an Indian community as "that in which exists a predominance of non-European physical elements, where language is preferentially Indian, possessing within its material and spiritual culture a strong portion of Indian elements, and finally, having a social feeling of being an isolated community within surrounding ones, distinguishing it from white and mestizo ones." Thus, the essence of being an Indian lies in the quality of the relationships found in certain kinds of communities, as well as in the self-image of individuals who identify with these communities. Such communities have a corporate nature and consist of people bound by certain duties and rights who have their own systems of social control and particular political and religious hierarchies and beliefs. Finally, such communities are neither totally isolated nor self-sufficient. They interact in varying degrees with the dominant society through mestizos or mestizoized Indians who act as intermediaries.

Indians are distinguished from their mestizo neighbors through social rather than racial differences, although local concepts of race may still influence one's perceptions of another (see Interethnic Relationships, this ch.). Language, literacy, surname, kind of housing and material culture, place of residence, various customs, and differing relationships to the land are commonly mentioned distinctions between the two groups. Speaking an Indian tongue as a first language identifies one as an Indian. The ability to use Spanish as a second language does not alter this identity.

Low levels of Indian literacy reflect in part the fact that few Indians know Spanish. Native languages have been provided with alphabets, but the formal education system makes little use of them. The indigenous surname is a valid criterion of Indian status in many areas, although many rural mestizos—and even upper class urban Mexicans—frequently bear Indian names through custom or choice. The trend, however, is still for mestizos to use Spanish surnames and for mestizoized Indians to adopt them.

The Indian hut *(jacal)* made of vegetal and (or) cheap materials is a common Indian home, whereas mestizos reside in homes of more solid or modern construction. Dress is also a distinction that remains in many areas. Semiofficial pressure and type of occupation may serve to weaken adherence to native costume. In the more isolated areas, traditional dress may change more slowly, where many remain *de huipil* (literally, of *huipil*, a tuniclike garment worn by many Indian women in southern Mexico) and *de caites* (literally, of sandals) as opposed to *de vestido* (literally, of dress, referring to Western dress) with regular shoes instead of rubber tire *caites* (see ch. 7).

Patterns of residence have some diagnostic value; Indians are rural dwellers, and mestizos are semirural or urban dwellers. Many towns are mixed; but even so, each group tends to live in a special section, the mestizos at the center of the village and the Indians on the periphery. Indians are strongly religious and adhere to various forms of folk Catholicism, which are tied to a politicoreligious hierarchy frequently based on pre-Columbian concepts. Moreover, they do not give the appearance of having social classes as does the larger mestizo society (see ch. 5).

Mestizo and Indian relations to the land and the national economy are areas of obvious and often tension-producing difference (see Interethnic Relationships, this ch.). Most relationships emphasize the fact that the Indians are less advanced, both economically and agriculturally. As subsistence farmers, they always secure their maize crop first; they may then cultivate commercial crops, land and time permitting. This traditional procedure has changed little regardless of the economic advantages of doing it in reverse. Moreover, Indians tend to rely on traditional second crops like squash and beans rather than investing the extra time and capital in a cash crop like coffee. Mestizos, however, frequently supplement farming with commerce or other economic specialization and frequently hire Indians to work their land for them.

The basic difference between the Indians and rural mestizos arises from differing attitudes toward land and its use. The Indian belongs to a society that draws its social and religious, as well as economic, life from the land. He ceases to be an Indian psychologically and loses his ethnic identity when separated from it. Indians regard their land as nontransferable property and as a means of production—not as merchandise or liquid capital. An Indian will never break ties with his community of origin if it can be helped.

There is great diversity among the Indians themselves. Much of the visible cultural difference among them is connected to the differences in natural environment. The most important crops—maize (corn), beans, and squash—are widely adaptable and have become nearly universal throughout Mexico. These are supplemented with a variety of other vegetables and domestic animals. Nevertheless, variations in animal husbandry and agriculture, for example, are related to water supply, soil quality, elevation, and climate. Agricultural techniques are also related to surrounding environment and vary from slash-and-burn to relatively sophisticated plow techniques.

Where the land is richer there is greater population density. This results in more intensive marketing efforts and specialization—in short,

90

more development—than in poorer areas. Village specialization is common in many more developed areas and typical of peasant economy, and villages can be classified by crop or craft.

Both similarities and differences among the Indians can be outlined in terms of seven factors: language, community type, village government, material culture, economic organization, family and kinship, and religion. The size of communities varies greatly. Moreover, settlements may be scattered or nucleated, depending upon the prevalent agricultural system. Nevertheless, almost every community includes some sort of civic-religious center housing a statue of the local patron saint. A distinction is frequently made between village or town administrative units and hamlets. The former is an autonomous unit with its own political administration. It consists of a nucleated settlement, the land surrounding it and, not infrequently, dependent hamlets. Such a unit may be a *municipio*, where its autonomy has a strong legal base and local officials are determined in a more traditional manner by more traditional criteria.

The village has historically been the most important political and culture-carrying unit because jurisdiction over land, ceremonial and political organization, and basic integration into the Indian social unit goes on at this level. When village or *municipio* control is in the hands of non-Indians, the Indian's seat of culture is placed in the surrounding subdivision, that is, hamlets or families. Political and ceremonial organization at the hamlet level may also be weakened by the presence of mestizos. From the colonial period to the mid-1970s there has been a tendency to split Indian political units into smaller and smaller subdivisions. This has caused village life to become increasingly diversified among Indian groups, especially in areas of stratification, ceremonial life, and political organization.

The material culture of the modern Mexican Indian clearly reflects the retention of pre-Hispanic technology and corresponding loss of ceremonial upper class elements. Thus, the farming techniques, cooking, housing, dress, and craft production are still largely aboriginal, but the high quality of public art and architecture present at the time of the conquest has disappeared. Important crafts still include weaving, pottery making, and metallurgy. Whereas techniques and styles used in metallurgy have changed, pottery making has remained basically aboriginal. Glazing techniques and the potter's wheel are gaining slow acceptance over traditional methods. Textiles and dress styles were heavily influenced by European methods, although native spindles and primitive looms continue to be used in some areas.

The growth of the non-Indian population, assimilation, and development of new forms of agricultural activity have continuously restricted the Indian population to smaller and even more marginal areas. Moreover, rural underemployment and overcrowding have developed in many high-density areas. Here the restriction to marginal areas does not signify isolation and self-sufficiency but more dependence on and vulnerability to the national economy. In addition, as common lands disappear and other communal traditions break down, such as communal labor for public works, general support for fiestas, and sponsorship of political and ceremonial offices, other aspects of Indian culture will also lose importance, and social identification as an Indian will be lost.

The modern hamlet or village is the primary social division regardless of ethnic or kinship basis. Below this is the household unit, usually consisting of a nuclear family. The Indian family is hierarchical with regard to age, generally with male dominance. Both lines of descent are recognized, but the tendency is patrilineal in transmitting names and property. Marriage tends to be negotiated by elders or a go-between and is characterized by ritualized visits, exchange of presents, and formal speeches. Serial monogamy is not uncommon, that is, until children arrive, and then it is generally stable. *Compadrazgo* (ritual godparent relationship) is an important pattern of social relationships; in fact, the importance of the social and psychological functions of this system helps to explain its universal acceptance and retention for over four centuries (see ch. 5). Access to *compadrazgo* is open to all, both Indians and mestizos, and therefore may serve to formally bind relationships. Moreover, *compadrazgo* provides a model for all interpersonal relationships and an organization to set them in action, as well as giving security and satisfaction to the participants. Finally, where ethnic or status differences are present, it helps to bridge cultural and socioeconomic problems. It may provide a system of mutual help among equals and a system for borrowing or getting ahead for those with wealthy *compadres* (coparents) (see Interethnic Relationships, this ch.).

Despite the lack of systematized social classes, there are considerable differences in prestige owing to wealth, power, and personal achievement. Prestige and the age hierarchy among males are notable and are tied to performance in the civil-religious hierarchy. The personnel of local government—either Indian or mestizo, or a combination—forms a hierarchy of officials, the top members of which are recognized by the government of the national state. The political offices are closely interwoven with a similar religious hierarchy serving the local Roman Catholic church and its ritual activities (see Indian Groups and Languages, this ch.). In both hierarchies there are annual ritual changes of office. One result of ascending the hierarchy may be the depletion of personal wealth and simultaneous surge in personal prestige for the participant. Thus, this situation not only encourages leadership responsibility but also exercises social control by preventing wealthy villagers from getting far ahead of their neighbors in material goods.

The life cycle events of importance are baptism and marriage; there are no puberty rites of consequence remaining. Death is accepted as normal and frequently is followed by a Roman Catholic wake. Conceptions of the causes of disease are unsystematic. They include air and wind invasions of the body and identification of illness with disturbed emotional states and periods of delicacy—such as childhood—when illness frequently strikes. Maintaining a balance between the polarities of heat and cold and strength and weakness is used in diagnosing and curing illness. Curers are specialists who may have the ability to do harm as well as good.

The degree of integration into the national society and the number of Spanish versus Indian traits are particularly apparent with respect to the Indians' religion. The foremost factor in shaping the character of modern Indian religious faith was the forced nature of the conversion by the Spanish. Total conversion was rare, and in fact Spanish conversion practices enhanced pre-Columbian patterns of incorporating new gods and cults within a larger religious context. Indian rituals and beliefs centering on the family level of integration—namely, rites of passage and "curing" practices—have survived largely intact; public performances centering on the Roman Catholic Church and the cult of the saints have been superimposed.

Another important process has been the meshing of indigenous and early Christian concepts. The world view is animistic, peopled with ghosts, spirits, witches, and souls that can affect daily lives. The various supernatural forces that affect decisionmaking include omens, dreams, talismans, and witchcraft. Both Christian and native supernaturals patronized human activities or groups and took an interest in human welfare. Religious buildings and images centered on them. This has evolved into a vague hierarchy of deities, frequently with the Christian God at the apex. Below him are various saints, who possess a synthesis of pagan and Christian attributes and powers, and some pagan forces, who are identified with nature and the elements. A strong saint cult has evolved that is centered in the housing of images on home altars and in temples. In most cases ancient gods have lost connection with anthropomorphic deities of pre-Columbian times and have become nature spirits.

The examples of this syncretism are numerous. Similar characteristics in a pagan spirit and a Christian saint will lead to their being mutually identified. For example, in one village the image of the local fire god blended with that of Saint Joseph or Saint Simon, as all were perceived as old men.

Remnants of indigenous belief and practice have to do mainly with life cycle events, treatment of disease, and technological activities. Related rituals are closely tied to the nature spirits of air, wind, and lightning; shrines are located in natural sites, such as caves and lakes. Some Indian groups have retained more of these traditional beliefs than have others. Among the more traditional groups, for example, are those found on the Central Mexican Highlands, as well as in more conservative villages in Oaxaca and among the Mazatec, Mixe, northern Zapotec, and many Maya speakers.

Groups that have retained fewer indigenous beliefs and practices are found in more populated and accessible areas—in the valleys of México,

Puebla, and Morelos and among more acculturated groups, such as the Tarascans and the valley Zapotec. Private rituals among these groups are relatively fewer and as much Roman Catholic as pagan in character. Surviving indigenous elements are found in the realms of curing and weather lore.

Witchcraft is used for both good and evil purposes and includes both *curanderos* (native healers) and shamans or witches. It is still a serious concern among modern Indians, but its results befall only those who break social rules or who are otherwise outstanding or enviable. Three commandments enforced by the threat of witchcraft are: shun excessive personal wealth, respect the rights and properties of others, and do not alter or deny the Indian heritage by failing to participate in community life. The witch can be a man or woman, depending on local tradition, and can be a relatively harmless thief or a serious spell caster. Powers accorded to the latter are the ability to inflict illness, cast the evil eye, become a vampire, or change into an animal. Zapotecs, for example, believe witches can take the form of vultures, black burros, dogs, or cats. Witches receive their powers from a variety of sources. The Tzotzil, for example, believe they receive it from Pukuj, the Maya god of death. Both Nahuatl-speakers and the Tzotzil identify witches as poor men who lack sufficient lands, animals, and crops for sustenance and, therefore, must prey on the good fortunes of others.

Others

Although the general tendency has been toward absorption of immigrants, various ethnic enclaves are still found throughout rural and urban Mexico. Blacks and mulattoes are found largely on the coasts of Guerrero, Oaxaca, and Veracruz; Chinese descendants are found in the Baja California Peninsula and Sonora, although in smaller concentrations than in the past. The Chinese, many of whom were settled on land owned by a North American railroad company, were physically moved by the Mexican government during the 1920s. They were given land elsewhere and in the 1970s lived in scattered settlements throughout the country.

European enclaves are found along the Gulf Coast and the central regions where there was demand for industrial workers. Most such groups have been assimilated, but some, such as the descendants of Cornish miners who settled in Real del Monte, Hidalgo, in the nineteenth century, were still visible in 1974. Others, such as the descendants of Italian immigrants to Veracruz, retain their proud ethnic heritage even though their surnames have been mexicanized. The thousands of French who remained after the fall of Emperor Maximilian, as well as English and German immigrants, helped to pour capital into a growing Mexico during the nineteenth century. The importance of these Europeans is seen in the number of their descendants who occupied important economic and political positions in the second half of the twentieth century. One group of Europeans, Spaniards from the Second Republic of

Spain, have retained their ethnicity to a surprising degree. Many have not been assimilated but have retained Spanish citizenship and even passed this on to their children, who may obtain passports as exiled citizens of the Spanish Republic. In the late 1960s they numbered about 330,000, and their cohesiveness was underlined through their closely knit social gatherings and Spanish regional clubs.

There is a relatively large enclave of North Americans residing in Mexico, numbering close to 100,000 in the early 1970s. They are found in three predominant categories: retired people and their dependents, those married to Mexicans, and those stationed with North American companies. Another group, those from the southern United States who migrated after the Civil War with their dependents and slaves, have been largely assimilated into Mexican society.

Immigration to Mexico speeded up after the revolution, especially among Jews, who came to view the revolution's experiment in social justice as a favorable sign. The first overture by Mexico to attract displaced European Jews was made in 1922, the only stipulation being that they become Mexican citizens. By 1925 an estimated 10,000 had arrived, most of them settling in Mexico City and forming a cohesive ethnic zone that was viewed with disfavor by the rest of the society. During the years of social reform that followed the 1920s there was some repression of Jewish Mexicans, and at one point there was speculation about a law requiring them to rear "Mexican mestizo families," that is, to marry Indians. After the regime of President Lázaro Cárdenas (1939–40) the situation was less serious, however, and has remained so into the 1970s. Throughout this time Jews have contributed to the rise in the Mexican economy and in 1974 played an important role in many of the country's industries, such as textiles, furniture manufacture, chemicals, and the film industry.

INDIAN GROUPS AND LANGUAGES

The classification of literally hundreds of indigenous ethnic and linguistic groups continues to be a matter of controversy, and authorities have not agreed as to boundaries and groupings. This is because of the overlapping and noncontiguous nature of many of these communities and their lack of conformity with geographic boundaries. One of the leading authoritative works on the subject, the *Handbook of Middle American Indians*, has established five major Indian groupings based on a compilation of all data relevant to linguistic and cultural kinships. These regions include: the Mayance (Maya-speaking) peoples of Chiapas and Yucatán; the Southern Mexican Highlands of Oaxaca, Guerrero, and parts of Puebla, Veracruz, and adjoining coastal regions; the Central Mexican Highlands, which include the southeastern part of the Central Meseta and its eastern slopes and coastal plain; Western Mexico, which contains the Tarascan Indians of Michoacán; and Northwest Mexico, including Baja California.

Maya-Speaking Indians

With the exception of the outlying Huastec who live in northern Veracruz, the descendants of the people who developed the great Maya culture still reside in relatively contiguous sections in Guatemala, the Yucatán Peninsula, and the Mexican states of Chiapas and Tabasco. The gaps in distribution, especially in lowland regions and highland basins, are now inhabited by ladinos. Compared to the other four regions, the Mayance area still contains large numbers of Indian communities. In fact, in the size of their population—estimated at 2 million—and in the solidarity of their distribution, they rank next to the Quechua speakers of Bolivia, Peru, and Ecuador in being the most impressive surviving native culture in the Western Hemisphere. Logically, it would seem that Maya would be the most widely spoken Indian language in Mexico but, because of the numerous mutually unintelligible dialects in the Maya language, this distinction belongs to the Nahuatl speakers farther north.

Mayan origins are traced to northwestern Guatemala and the year 2600 B.C. A dozen migrations over the next 3,600 years from the central core gave rise to the numerous dialectic differences found in 1974. Throughout this time the Mayans have remained a physically homogeneous group. They are short, averaging five feet four inches for men and less for women, slender of build, but muscular. Such slenderness, along with small hands and feet, is deceptive, because Maya physical strength lies in the legs, neck, and back.

For all their reputed passivity, the Mayans were one of the most intransigent groups encountered by the Spanish conquerors. Major upheavals against the white man occurred as late as 1847. Other persecuted groups retreated to isolated areas in an attempt to preserve their culture. Consequently, the remaining Mayance vary greatly in degrees of acculturation. The main distinction occurs between highland and lowland groups. The highland area includes Chiapas and contains the Tzotzil, Tzeltal, and Tojolabal, the three largest Mayance groups remaining in central Chiapas. The lowland area includes the Yucatec Maya of Yucatán, Campeche, and Quintana Roo and the Lacandon Maya of eastern Chiapas, as well as the Chontol, Chol, and Kekchi. The Huastec inhabit a separate lowland area and are sometimes considered a separate group even though they are culturally and linguistically Maya.

The general settlement pattern is one in which the ladinos occupy the major towns and the Indians the outlying rural *municipios*. Each *municipio* has distinctive dress styles, local dialects, and a patron saint. The smallest social unit is the domestic group, which among the much studied Zinacantecos (Tzotzil Indians) is a nuclear or extended family sharing a single cross. This cross is a three-foot-high wooden structure that is decorated with pine boughs and flowers for family rituals and major fiestas. The next larger unit is one consisting of two or more related domestic groups; somewhat larger is the waterhole group, those sharing a single source of water. The most important deities for the

Zinacantecos are the ancestral gods of the living, who provide examples of good lives; the Earth Owner, a nature deity portrayed as a large, fat ladino; and the Roman Catholic saints.

The Yucatec Maya have undergone varying degrees of acculturation, and groups among them range from the modern to the primitive. The latter is located in the forests of Quintana Roo, the only place on the peninsula where independent tribal government still exists. Another primitive group is the Lacandon Maya, who have lost all knowledge of the Western calendar and follow only the seasons. By watching the stars and observing changes in plants and animals, they determine when to plant their corn. Because of their historic isolation, they have been little affected by Christianity; they have various gods and venerate the site of a sacred stone. This primitive group had only begun to wear Western dress in the 1960s; before that, both men and women wore long, white hand-woven tunics.

The final group of Maya is the Huastec. This group, which extended the Maya culture to its northernmost limit, experienced a drastic reduction in the twentieth century. In 1950 there were only five towns in Veracruz and an equal number in San Luís Potosí that could claim a population of 18 percent or more Huastec inhabitants, and no town had over 72 percent Huastec residents. Their rapid dissolution can be measured in terms of the decrease in monolingual Huastec speakers and changing customs. Hunting, once important, is now a minor occupation. The white muslin shirts and pants once favored by the men are being replaced by factory-made clothes on the younger generation. Even up to the late 1800s each village considered itself a republic, but the widespread attendance of Huastec children in the rural schools has encouraged the Huastec to become integrated into the national scene.

Southern Mexican Highlands

The second major ethnic region, the Southern Mexican Highlands and adjacent coastal areas, contains Indian cultures with more linguistic and cultural diversity than any other area. Within the region Indian cultures may be grouped together by language similarities, indicating historical ties and common origin. The modern period since 1920 and the government's efforts on the Indian's behalf have greatly affected this region, the recovery of land bringing economic stability and the growth of the rural school system bringing change. Nevertheless, the majority of Indian communities still retain much of their closed corporate status. Although mestizo shopkeepers are penetrating traditional Indian markets and the involvement in improving transportation and communication systems is breaking down isolation, Indian cultures are proving quite resilient. Outside pressures to abolish ritual labor and religious systems have been fairly unsuccessful.

The remaining native population is much larger in the state of Oaxaca than in other parts of the country. In 1960 Indians constituted a population of approximately 684,000 out of a total population of 1,727,000. Estimates differ, however, as do definitions, and one anthropologist claimed that 75 percent of the population of Oaxaca lived in a so-called Indian-colonial style. In any event, the Indian heritage in Oaxaca is prevalent and proud, as evidenced by the number of people who speak Zapotec as a second language and by the pride in former President Benito Juárez, a full-blooded Zapotec Indian and native of Oaxaca.

The two largest linguistic groups in this region are the Macro-Mixtecan, including Zapotec, Mixtec, Popolocan, and others, and the Macro-Mayance, including members of Zoquean-speaking groups and the Mixe. Other groups in the Southern Mexican Highlands are the Chontol of Oaxaca, Tlapanec, Cuitlatec, and Nahua, close relatives of the Nahuatl speakers farther north.

The largest modern group in the area, and one of the more frequently studied, is the Zapotec, numbering 250,000 in 1950. They are found throughout the eastern and southern part of Oaxaca, interspersed with small enclaves of Huave and Chontol Indians, as well as Spanish speakers. Various Zapotec-related language groups exist in the area, some of which are not even mutually intelligible, reinforcing the cultural and linguistic diversity that has characterized them for centuries. Marketing is vitally important—as it is elsewhere in Oaxaca—and the Zapotecs are famous throughout Mexico for their shrewd business sense. Zapotec women frequently do the buying, selling, fishing, and even the governing.

Based on economic criteria, three types of Zapotec communities may be distinguished. One type of community produces cash crops for national and international markets. Another type is the town, in which economic activity centers in the marketplace. Both of these categories have more contact with the outside world than the third, which is a village community that produces for its own consumption using slash-and-burn or other techniques. Only small, local markets exist in this setting.

Whatever their structure, communities are usually corporate and closed and have a distinctive value system. Three major qualities—humility, trust, and respect—organize this system of mores and beliefs along the lines of good and evil. These values are inculcated in the young to preserve the tightly knit community where concepts of unity and equality of the group are favored over personal ambition.

Humility among the Zapotecs is defined as a pervasive sense of egalitarianism and an absence of selfishness. It is a recognition that all are equal and equally poor. Trust involves a person's character, which is ideally straightforward and unchanging. The highest insult one Zapotec can offer another is to imply that he is untrustworthy. Respect is shown when the prevalent social hierarchy is manipulated to show a person deference, regardless of his relative social position. The definition of a good man is one willing to do another a favor. Envy is the opposite of these characteristics; it is the dark side of village life that fosters witch-

98

craft and fear. Deviance within this system is, therefore, the inability to be a good neighbor or kinsman, and it is handled through both Mexican law and village pressures, as well as through magic.

Second in size to the Zapotec are the Mixtec, who are found mainly in western Oaxaca and nearby Guerrero. Both groups were extensive contributors to the pre-Columbian culture. Despite their broad similarities of life-style and organization, many shades of difference exist in ritual, belief, personality, and organizational structure. The markets that are so important to the Zapotec also characterize the Mixtec, and village specialization is also characteristic of both. The trading network is extensive, reaching well beyond linguistic boundaries. The market at Oaxaca probably integrates the largest number of different groups of any place in the region.

The Popolocan consist of several subgroups including the Mazatec. They are similar in life-style to the Zapotec and Mixtec. Although they are reputed to have fewer Spanish speakers than Zapotec or Mixtec groups, many of the Mazatec men speak up to three other Indian languages.

The Macro-Mayance group is considerably smaller and less complex. It contains several members of the Zoquean family, the largest subgroup of which is the Mixe. Again, these are peasant farmers with a culture similar to their Zapotec neighbors. Another subgroup, the Popoluca of southern Veracruz, is considered a linguistic unit in spite of the fact that they are divided into four mutually unintelligible language groups—three of which are within a five-mile radius and the fourth only an hour's distance away.

Central Mexican Highlands

The Central Mexican Highlands is the seat of the ancient Aztec Empire, as well as the core of urbanized modern Mexico. The Indians here have been more influenced by the non-Indian population and by the economic and cultural transformations of the colonial and republican periods than any other region in Mexico. This area has always been at the apex of both population density and economic development—starting with the flowering of Indian civilizations and continuing with the establishment of Spanish cities, such as Mexico City and Puebla, mining centers, sheep ranches, haciendas and, later, vast industrial complexes. From the nineteenth century on, the Indians of this area became increasingly integrated into the Mexican mestizo society. Ethnic consciousness and solidarity as well as the indigenous languages have been on a rapid decline, and in 1974 the Indians of this region existed only as marginal and scattered groups, both geographically and socially.

Three remaining linguistic families are Uto-Aztecan, Otomian, and Totonacan. Nahuatl—the language of the Aztecs—is the only surviving Uto-Aztecan language in the area, although a relatively large population over a considerable geographic area still speaks it. Otomian includes two major subgroups, Otomi and Mazahua. Other groups have only limited distributions in the states of México and Guanajuato. Otomi is spoken mainly in the western part of the state of México and the Mezquital Valley of Hidalgo, although there are small concentrations elsewhere. Mazahua is spoken only in the western part of the state of México and in a few adjacent villages in Michoacán. The Totonacan group is smaller and includes Totonac, a language spoken by some people in Puebla and Veracruz, and Tepehua, spoken by a very few in Hidalgo.

This once solidly indigenous ethnic region had only five areas of concentration in the early 1970s. The largest includes the most conservative groups (Nahuatl, Totonac, Tepehua, and Otomi) and is found on the eastern slopes of the Central Plateau. The Otomi speakers in the Valley of Mezquital are another dense concentration. A third is the western part of the state of México, containing Otomi, Mazahua, and Nahuatl. Nahuatl speakers also reside on the slopes of Popocatapetl and Malinche in the regions of Tlaxcala and Puebla. A final concentration of Nahuatl speakers is found on the southeastern edge of Puebla.

The Nahuatl speakers, estimated at over 1 million in the 1960s, follow the Mayance speakers as the most impressive surviving aboriginal group. In fact, Nahuatl is said to be the most widely spoken language in Mexico after Spanish. The largest monolingual group is found in Puebla, the heart of the ancient Aztec empire, and the Valley of México contains the most bilinguals.

Modern spoken Nahuatl contains a large number of Spanish loan words, particularly if the speaker is bilingual. Bilinguals prefer the convenience of using Spanish terminology for new things rather than exercising the power of spontaneous coinage. Spanish words are commonly borrowed for agricultural tools, garments, money, measures, ritual kinship, disease concepts, remedies, political offices, and administrative divisions. Mexican Spanish has adopted many Nahuatl words as well. This is probably because in early colonial days Nahuatl, as the Aztec language, was common to many diverse tribes in the area and as such was used as an early lingua franca.

Nahua Indians—those who speak Nahuatl—carry on many preconquest customs although their life-style has been significantly remodeled by their nearness to the Spanish and, later, mestizo, population. Their religion, for example, is a syncretism of Aztec and Christian beliefs symbolized by the miraculous appearance of the dark-skinned Virgin of Guadalupe—who spoke Nahuatl and was also called Tonantzin, the name of the Aztec earth goddess. Saints are the most important supernatural beings in the lives of individuals, and the village patron saint occupies the supreme position in the religious hierarchy. Every village member is expected to contribute time, money, and devotion to fiestas honoring this saint.

Religion plays such an important part in the life of the Nahua that the characteristic feature of their settlement pattern is the location of the church in the center of town with streets leading out to surrounding homes in four directions in the shape of a cross. Each of the four quarters bears a Nahuatl name and takes the responsibility of supplying compulsory collective labor on the village land dedicated to the support of the church.

Nearly every village has specialists in curing, midwifery, and witchcraft. Craft specialization is also present. Weaving is the outstanding craft of the Nahuatl peoples, and some of the finest serapes in Mexico are handwoven in their villages. The weavers are usually men who devote full time to their craft, which is performed on an antiquated Spanish upright loom.

Western Mexico

Because of the pressures of acculturation, there is only one major group remaining in the Western Mexican ethnic region, the Tarascans of Michoacán. They occupy the west central section of that state, and their numbers are small. As a group they are more integrated into the national society than many other indigenous peoples because they occupy territory on an important transportation route between Mexico City and Guadalajara. The completion of this highway in the 1930s and 1940s exposed the Tarascans to new influences, and urban visits became commonplace. Moreover, governmental efforts directed at their integration and change have proved quite effective. Such programs have included elementary instruction in the Tarascan language, improvement of water supplies, and health and agricultural reforms.

The mestizoization of Tarascan towns and the concomitant decline in the number of Tarascan speakers is one result of the push for integration. Bilinguals far outnumber monolinguals, who number less than one-third of the Tarascan speakers and occupy isolated areas of the sierra. Other customs, especially those pertaining to the material culture, are also changing rapidly toward mestizo standards. Despite acceptance of some technological changes and some increase in the value of education, the main core of Tarascan culture has suffered little change and remains relatively uncorrupted. In the areas of folklore, belief, patterns of living, crafts, music, and dance, the Tarascans have retained particular solidarity. They are noted for their extensive craft specialization—wood products, weaving, and pottery. They have been noted for woodworking since preconquest times. Another area of specialization is lacquer-work pottery, and some potters are so devoutly traditional that they will only ply their trade on special feast days.

Agriculture and livestock raising supply most of the food plus a surplus. These activities are supplemented by fishing, forest exploitation, handicrafts, wage labor, and trading. In the past fishing was of major economic importance to the Tarascans. In fact, the Nahuatl word for the area, *mechuacan*, meant "land of the fishers." Because of drainage and desiccation of the lakes, however, fishing has declined, and fish now constitute a major import into the region.

Tarascan religion is folk Catholicism with no identifiable remnants of pre-Columbian belief. This is in contrast to most other Indian religions throughout Mexico. Moreover, the religious fiestas are more orthodox, and the roles of religious leaders stand apart from the civil-religious hierarchy found in most communities. In the 1970s the ceremonial organization followed a functional classification of rituals and fiestas: church, community, occupational, and private with little or no overlapping. At one time they probably possessed the combined political-ceremonial organization found in other communities, but in the present day they are purely ceremonial. The major power roles in a Tarascan village are frequently filled by mestizos, that is, outsiders. These include the priest, mayor, school director, social worker, and owners of artisan industries. People occupying these roles act as mediators for the community and nation and in a sense help to preserve the cohesiveness of Tarascan culture.

The cohesive nature of these communities is further enhanced by their world view and values. Most sanctions are concerned with transgressions against authority. People exhibit a sense of fatalism—the conviction that a person's efforts count for little in the final outcome. Emphasis is placed on reciprocal obligation, such as that found in *compadrazgo*, and security is found in the acceptance of the status quo.

Northwest Mexico

The ethnolinguistic data for this sparsely populated but ethnically complicated area are less complete than for the other regions. Further, Northwest Mexico was never a geographic or cultural unit. Two unrelated groups were present at the time of the conquest: the Uto-Aztecan speakers, who had long dominated both the mountains and the desert from Nayarit to Arizona in the United States; and the relatively few Hokan speakers of the western regions. With the exception of the occupants of Baja California and the Sonora coast, most of the Indians spoke a Uto-Aztecan language when Cortés arrived. Population shifts and declines have changed this original picture, and the wide differences between figures of decline and increase emphasize the wide variety of contact conditions. Native populations in the states of Baja California, Sinaloa, and Nayarit, for example, have declined rapidly, whereas in Sonora the decline is less marked, and in Chihuahua indications show the population has actually increased.

Hokan groups persist in hunting and gathering, and Uto-Aztecan groups engage in agriculture. The major effect of the Spanish conquest on this ideal grazing area was the introduction of cattle and horses. This allowed the Indians to be less reliant on wild food and more sedentary, diversifying farming with livestock. The Jesuits had a profound effect on the Indians of this area, helping to settle them in ranches and missions. Those who escaped these influences continued to roam the area, living a marginal existence for the next 400 years. They adopted the Western clothing and occasionally certain implements and fishing equipment but continued to live into the mid-twentieth century with only minor alterations of their social and religious life.

There are still three language families extant of Uto-Aztecan stock in the area—the Taracahitan, the Piman, and the Aztecoidan. From these there have developed numerous subgroups. The Taracahitan is the largest family in Northwest Mexico, and Cahitan is its largest subfamily. Modern Cahitan has in turn diverged into two important languages—Yaqui and Mayo. Another subfamily of Taracahitan is Tarahumara, which has less differentiation than Cahitan and is spoken in southwestern Chihuahua. A third subfamily, Opatan, is found in north, central, and eastern Sonora.

The second group or family is Piman, which is divided directly into the Piman and Tepehuan languages. At one time this group extended from Jalisco to the Gila River with little differentiation. The Tepehuan speakers are farmers or herders living in the state of Durango; they have little urban specialization or acculturation. Their religious figures include the Dios Padre (God the Father), identified with the sun; Jesús Nazareno (Jesus the Nazarene), identified with the moon; and Madre María (Mother Mary), whose various helpers include the Virgin of Guadalupe. The final family, Aztecoidan, is divided into the subfamilies of Cora and Huichol. These Indians reside in the states of Jalisco and Nayarit. They have been more resistant to acculturative pressures than other groups, and their religion remains basically indigenous with a Roman Catholic overlay of rituals and beliefs in baptism, saints, and the ritual calendar.

INTERETHNIC RELATIONSHIPS

Before 1910 interethnic relations were characterized by a caste system in which Indians and mestizos coexisted in apparent equilibrium. Premises of biological origin maintained the positions of the castes and conditioned future interaction. This stable situation was eroded through constructive interest in the Indian plus the social and scientific speculations on the national level that ran counter to prevalent opinions regarding him. Although the change affected governmental attitudes tremendously, it has taken over half a century to filter down to interpersonal relationships between members of different ethnic groups. Officially, the Indian is regarded as any other citizen, but remnants of traditional thought and behavior persist, effectively maintaining functional inequality between Indian and mestizo (see ch. 5). This situation persists despite social legislation and the disapproval of most educated and upper class and middle-class Mexicans.

These inequities are a result of the superior economic position of the mestizos; the cultural duality that overvalues the mestizo language and culture and undervalues that of the Indian; the perceived racial duality, which values "white" blood and deprecates Indian ancestry; and the differential access to power, which effectively keeps Indians on the periphery of political interaction.

Perceived racial difference is the oldest and most tenacious element affecting interethnic relationships. In some ways it is also the most pervasive. Rural ladinos and mestizos distinguish themselves from their Indian neighbors through ascribed superiority of race, blood, and genealogy. They attribute certain superior cultural qualities to their white race and blood, and they undervalue the Indian's dark skin and alleged mixture of races. Mestizos perceive cultural differences as a consequence of natural inferiority on the part of the Indian, and from the Indian point of view they represent distinctions that are natural and indelible, based on biological heredity. Frequently, biological mixture is considered by mestizos as undesirable "contamination," but some hold that such mixture actually improves the Indian race.

Mestizos also tend to undervalue Indians as a group, despite the fact that they have little intimate knowledge of Indian customs. They regard Indian beliefs and customs as backward and crude. The degree of contempt varies inversely with the degree of Indian acculturation. The greatest contempt is found among the Indian's closest mestizo neighbors. Middle-class and upper class urban mestizos—especially the young— usually have positive feelings, if any, toward the Indian. They carry this view because it was inculcated with the Revolution of 1910, however, not because of personal contact with Indians. Their knowledge of aboriginal Mexicans is probably even less than that of rural mestizos.

Indians generally accept their ascribed inferiority and view the differences as normal. It is considered both possible and desirable to change, however, and given sufficient outside pressure, Indians may move to acculturate. Cultural change is invariably from Indian to mestizo; it is never the reverse.

Inequality of status between the two groups is seen in ethnic terminology and in social expressions and rules of conduct by which the mestizo receives deference from the Indian but does not return it. The word *indio* (Indian) is universally recognized as a term implying inferiority, whereas names given mestizos, such as *gente de razón* (people of reason), connote superiority. Moreover, mestizo paternalistic attitudes are manifest in diminutive nouns of address or in usage of the familiar *tú* instead of the polite *usted*. With possible exceptions in Oaxaca and Yucatán, a mestizo will never refer to a high status Indian as "sir," although formal and polite usage is always expected from the Indian in return.

Despite the fact that the indigenous economy is often self-sufficient, patterns of joint participation weld Indian and mestizos together in all economic activities. Most frequently this is an exploitive relationship on the part of the mestizos. The limited number of modern skills among Indians keeps the division of labor complementary rather than competitive. Coupled with the Indians' low standard of living and particular

104

customs, it also limits the number of jobs for which mestizos will hire them. Consequently, the mestizo is the agricultural landlord or foreman, and the Indian is the laborer. Exceptions occur in such states as Oaxaca, where it is common for Indian artisans to be assisted by mestizos, or where acculturated Indians may employ mestizos.

Labor legislation, although designed for both groups, has been applied unequally and does not really protect the Indians. Moreover, the quality of service received by the Indian is often poorer because of his ignorance, status, or the amount paid. One anthropologist insisted that, among the differing kinds of relationships, commercial ones were the most important since the mestizo was invariably able to act as the middleman. The Indian, who participates as producer and consumer, cannot protect himself against the mestizo as trader, middleman, and creditor. The mestizo position is reinforced by his own sense of cultural superiority, his knowledge of price mechanisms, laws of the country, and the Spanish language.

Mestizo merchants tend to exploit their Indian customers who have no choice but to buy from them. The more isolated the community, the more likely mestizos are to retain their status because there will be less opportunity for Indians to become aware and to circumvent this commercial disadvantage. Finally, this situation perpetuates the Indian's reliance on his own closed system and his lack of interest in dealing with outsiders. Although the success of rural mestizos as a group can be attributed to their exploitation of differences between the peasant and national economies, the local success of town mestizos is due to their ability to combine commerce with landownership. Multifaceted mestizo enterprises include sharecropping, selling timber, raising livestock, making rum, and market gardening. These additional activities, for which Indians are employed as laborers, make the difference between merely meeting costs and turning over a profit.

In places like Oaxaca, where Indians possess greater commercial astuteness and where sociocultural differences between the two groups are less, exploitation is neither as severe nor as one-sided. Both Indians and ladinos take advantage of the consumer's ignorance, regardless of ethnicity.

Differences in tradition, interests, social position, and religion set off the two groups in social situations. Certain activities—for example, street congregations, recreation, school and public parties, social visits, wakes, weddings, baptisms, and religious observances—are activities where each group may participate in a segregated fashion, or where both groups participate but the Indians remain on the periphery. Indian religiosity and the nature of their folk Catholicism cause them to be regarded by mestizos as superstitious and ignorant. The priest, a mestizo by definition, plays a limited role among Indians themselves but a key role in the personal relationships between the two groups.

Compadrazgo crosses ethnic boundaries and, despite the reciprocity of the relationship, tends to reinforce inequality. The Indian gets favors and protection in return for expanded services and heightened deference. The Indian, as such, and as a beneficiary of the ritual service is doubly indebted and must be even more respectful to the mestizo who, in turn, may be even more condescending. Aside from *compadrazgo* and casual sex relationships, personal relationships are more limited than impersonal ones because of obvious factors related to language, customs, and differing status.

In general, interethnic relationships run the gamut from peaceful and friendly to permanently conflictual, accompanied by fear, threats, hostility, and even open violence. In the more peaceful communities, breaking with tradition is a cause for conflict. In hostile communities, conflict results from land problems, economic and cultural competition, or political dominance of one group over another. Life in towns is especially hazardous during religious festivals, when Indians or mestizos become drunk and threaten to attack each other. Indian carnivals occasionally give rise to rumors of imminent rebellion, frightening mestizos who fear retaliation.

ACCULTURATION AND INTEGRATION

It has been suggested that two main elements have guided ethnic relationships—exploitation and acculturation. Mestizo efforts to transform the Indian have been from the angles of religious conversion and political control and, since the revolution, from the point of integration. As societal attitudes toward the Indian have changed, so have the demands upon him. He is no longer required as a conscripted labor force in non-Indian enterprises or as an important source of tribute. In fact, his participation as a producer and consumer is small, and his numbers are growing steadily smaller. In 1810, 60 percent of the population was still pure Indian. A century later this had been reduced to 13 percent, and it has continued to decline. The current situation is one in which Indian communities are faced with adapting to the industrial and urban culture of modern Mexico. They are largely affected by the technological changes around them: sewing machines, corn mills, radios, automotive transportation, and factory-made clothing.

The struggle that began with the agrarian revolution catapulted Mexican Indians into a new phase of acculturation and integration. Accompanying the merging of criollo and mestizo elite was the acceptance of the Indian heritage and its utilization as part of new nationalistic ideologies. For one thing, this movement led to extensive support for archaeology and applied anthropology. Indianist action increasingly stressed integration, that is, full economic, social, and political participation in addition to the traditional goal of acculturation. Indianists further stressed that the cultural heritage of the Indian must not be lost, and consequently they stress the Indian over the Spanish legacy. In practice, however, greater emphasis has been placed on the merging of the Indian into the mainstream of Mexican life than on the preservation of his culture.

There have been two general forces encouraging the Indian to acculturate, the favored position of mestizo culture as opposed to the disadvantaged one of the Indian and the incentives offered by the national government. This carrot-and-stick situation has brought increasing numbers of Indians into the national society. Movement is accompanied by "passing" or acquiring some prestigious cultural traits and by separating oneself from close ties with the Indian group. "Passing" is easier for the wealthier Indian with extensive mestizo contacts already established. He may change to a Spanish surname, adopt Western dress, and marry a mestizo woman. In all cases, "passing" requires speaking Spanish and adopting a mestizo outlook. Even so, the man himself may not be fully accepted as mestizo, although his children most likely will be.

Government incentives have generally dealt with distributing land—the *ejido* program—or improving educational opportunities and have also done something to increase political participation. In 1936, under President Lázaro Cárdenas, the Autonomous Department of Indian Affairs was established, followed the next year by the Department of Indian Education. Despite opposition, the former group was able to redistribute an additional 45 million acres to the Indians by 1940. To help Indians make full use of their land, the government in 1942 established Indian brigades to instruct communities in modern agricultural methods. The brigades offered instruction in crop diversification, animal husbandry, pest and disease control, and the use of modern agricultural machinery. They helped organize producer and consumer cooperatives, repair old roads and build new ones, and install better telecommunications networks.

In 1947 the previous Indian agencies were brought under the Ministry of Public Education, and the following year the National Indian Institute (Instituto Nacional Indigenista—INI) was created. The central purpose of the INI was to nationalize the Indian; it was considered essential that the Indians become aware of belonging to the Mexican state. This has continued to be the most important source of directed social change, concentrating on the improvement of realistic educational facilities, health programs, agriculture, and communications, while making no direct effort to manipulate the symbolic and belief structure or social system of the Indians. The INI has frequently been aided by the United Nations Educational, Scientific and Cultural Organization and the Organization of American States through pilot or training projects.

Formal education is officially recognized as an important means to integration (see ch. 6). It signifies, to a great extent, the transmission and adoption of mestizo culture and values. Indian attitudes toward schools and teachers vary from the extremely negative viewpoint held in some isolated areas to unconditional acceptance by those who see education as a means for change. Teachers are usually mestizos, occasionally mestizoized Indians, and only rarely Indians. The latter two groups may have trouble gaining acceptance, since communities feel they may be poorly trained.

Integration of Indian ethnic groups into the national culture is thus progressing fairly rapidly. The ability of local groups to set their own patterns of village organization is breaking down. There are increased limitations of the authority of the local village headmen in favor of centralized national authority, in an effort to make the community responsive to national rather than local needs. Mestizo acquisition of large landholdings in Indian core areas has resulted in a reorganization of agricultural production that is incompatible with the older village organization. Racial and ethnic groups are becoming increasingly intermingled, especially at the village level.

The attractions of the cities, combined with population pressures on the land, have drawn large groups away from their ancestral homes. In some cases, entire groups move into urban areas at one time and live in one neighborhood. Under the pressure of adjustment to urban life and economic diversification, Indian ethnicity breaks down.

CHAPTER 5

SOCIAL SYSTEM

In the mid 1970s the Mexican social system was one in which traditional values, institutions, and patterns coexisted with those arising from economic development and social change. The role of the Revolution of 1910 as a catalyst in the process of expansion cannot be underestimated. Not only did the revolution erode the Hispanic elitist element in the system, but it set about arranging new goals that would provide for an equal, democratic, and integrated society. Mexicans have been only partially successful in attaining these goals, although the revolution was instrumental in opening a relatively closed society and cementing the separatist character of church-state relations.

The traditional elite has been destroyed and replaced by mestizos, the middle class has grown, and the size of the lower class has been reduced. This shift has been accompanied by substantial population growth, general movement of the population from country to city, and expansion of the occupational structure—that is, an increase in both the number and the kinds of jobs available. Mexican scholars distinguish between so-called participants in economic development—those who have profited from it—and the so-called marginals, who have not. The former are the people who have really reaped the benefits of the revolution; they have gained political clout within the one-party system, they can understand and to varying degrees manipulate the economic system, and they enjoy certain distinguishing educational and cultural advantages.

The marginals, by contrast, reap few benefits, whether materially or otherwise, from the industrial process, which excludes them. Members of the marginal group are typically lower class and rural. The center of the group are the Indians, whose aboriginal life-style and language are obstacles to communication with other Mexicans. A few marginal people are recent migrants or poor urban dwellers living in tenement slums or squatter settlements. There marginals have a better chance to move into participant society than do their rural counterparts.

Three social classes may be distinguished. The upper class, though relatively landless compared to its counterparts elsewhere in Latin America, owns much of the means of production and holds the highest political positions in the country. The middle class is small, emergent, and heterogeneous and occupies mid-level professional and bureaucratic positions. Commercial expansion and a growing public bureaucracy have both become strongholds of the middle class. The upper and middle classes are both essentially urban. There is more economic and cultural variation in the lower class, the largest, than in the other classes. Members range from isolated and primitive Indians to blue-collar workers in Mexico City. One-third of the class may be considered in transition from marginal to participant status.

The society is relatively fluid; individual status can and does change in a single lifetime. Some members of the upper class were born into the middle class, and some people of middle-class status have risen from the working class. Various opportunities for rising in the social scale exist, and the conviction that upward mobility can occur encourages the ambitious to take advantage of such means.

The family remains one of the strongest and most adaptable institutions in Mexico and seems to show less disintegration than other family structures in Latin America. The core unit is the nuclear family of parents and unmarried children, but the household may include aunts, uncles, grandparents, or related children. The *compadrinazgo* (ritual kinship) system extends the family even further and may formalize special relationships within the family or with friends. Moreover, it is common practice in Mexican society for close friends to refer to each other as *compadre* (coparent), a term usually reserved for ritual kin. Parents' friends may also be elevated by the child to the status of aunt or uncle.

Family relationships are equally strong at all levels of society and remain so even when individual life-styles change. A large number of Mexican businesses are run by closed, corporate family structures. Lower class families are also tied by economic bonds but of a different sort. For example, family ties assume a special importance for the rural migrant newly arrived in the city, as he may be totally dependent upon relatives for economic and psychological support as well as for socialization into the new environment.

In most sections of Mexico Roman Catholicism, the predominant faith, is somewhat mixed with preconquest indigenous beliefs and practices. This fusion manifests itself in beliefs and practices that are often far removed from Roman Catholic dogma. Religion in remote areas tends to pervade all aspects of life, while in urban areas the tendency to compartmentalize religion is often evident.

Contemporary Roman Catholicism in Mexico must contend with a myriad of problems including interecclesiastic disagreements and a lack of priests. There is also the task of trying to keep church traditions, beliefs, and values intact yet relevant and viable in a society of rapidly rising population, changing social structures, and increasing secularization. Despite and partially because of the problems and handicaps faced by the church, its activities have greatly increased since the 1940s, and in 1974 Roman Catholicism was in many respects more robust in Mexico than in any other Latin American country. Construction of new churches, numerous religious processions and pilgrimages, flourishing religious orders, and seminaries and church schools attest to the vitality of the church.

Although for centuries the church represented conservative ideas and thought, in 1974 it was being brushed by the winds of change. Liberal clerics were denouncing the status quo orientation of the past in favor of radical social change and elimination of social injustice. They were countered by conservative elements who wanted the church to remain traditional. Although relations between church and state remained very cordial, it was not known how the state would react to increasing church pressure for social reform.

SOCIAL STRATIFICATION

The Revolution of 1910 did more to alter the stratification system and relax class lines than any single event in Mexican history. It broke with the past—when 1 percent of the population owned 97 percent of the land and 96 percent of the population owned 1 percent—and projected Mexico onto a path of economic development and social change. The revolution destroyed land tenure patterns, stripping elite *hacendados* (land-owners) of ancestral holdings, and broke from Mexico's Hispanic heritage in favor of its Indian past. The revolution eased social mobility, built a new sense of Mexican nationhood, and prepared the society for stepped-up economic developments. The erosion of the political, social, and economic power of the traditional elite created a vacuum in which new criteria for class membership, particularly middle-class and upper-class membership, were emphasized. The social consequences of the revolutionary changes included the movement of increasing numbers of people from stagnant, usually rural, to dynamic, usually urban, regions of the country. The patterns of internal migration to more developed areas reflected the prevalent opinion that upward social mobility occurred only in the city.

Although the revolution destroyed much of the old structure of society, it did not create an entirely new one but left vestiges of prerevolutionary and even colonial society. This has led some scholars to call it the "incomplete revolution" and others, the "bourgeois revolution." Moreover, although the political revolution took place in 1910, the effects of social change were delayed nearly three decades while the mechanisms of agrarian, educational, and occupational reform were set in motion. The greatest development has occurred within the urbanized middle and upper classes, which have been in the best position to take advantage of technological expansion.

In the postrevolutionary era, different variables have come to be emphasized in determining social rank. Whereas before 1910 ethnicity and family background were of overriding importance, education, occupation, and income have since become the prime criteria, and value orientation and life-style have retained some significance.

Mexican society, however, is not stratified in a simple way. The system has been a dynamic and developing one in which concepts of marginality and participation, rural and urban inequalities, and regional differences have all played a part. Many Mexican scholars have been particularly concerned with the issue of participation, since the integration of marginal people—the Indians in particular—was one of the most important goals of the revolution. Marginal groups, made up predominently of rural inhabitants who have not benefited from industrial growth, characteristically lack the capacity for organized action and are thus unable to redress the socioeconomic imbalance affecting them.

The Mexican census provides a statistical framework for distinguishing marginal peoples from the rest of the population as well as for measuring the relative decrease over time of certain aspects of marginality. A high incidence of illiteracy, a lack of shoes, low school attendance rates, and the absence of milk, meat, and fish in the diet are correlates of marginality. The core group among the marginals is still the Indians, who constituted about 7 to 10 percent of the population in the 1970s (see ch. 4). Not only do they exhibit the usual correlates of marginality, but they also retain aboriginal cultures and languages that place them outside the dominant mestizo culture.

In 1910 the marginal group encompassed 90 percent of the population. Since then marginals have increased in absolute numbers, but they constitute a decreasing proportion of the total population and are gradually being absorbed into the participant sector. Moreover, some aspects of marginality such as illiteracy have shown considerable decline.

Census figures tend to corroborate the evidence of continuing inequalities between rural and urban areas. They show the phenomenal growth of industrialized centers, the higher growth rate of industry and commerce compared to agriculture, and the population shifts from poorer to more developed areas. For example, regional breakdowns in the 1960s showed that standards of living in the Federal District and in some northern districts were far higher than in the South Pacific region and certain Central Mexico states surrounding the Federal District. This correlated with another study of poverty that indicated that 80 percent of the families in the Central Mexico and South Pacific regions would be considered "needy"; 60 percent, in the Gulf Coast and North regions; and 33 percent, in the Federal District and the North Pacific region.

The criteria for ranking people include education, occupation, and wealth, as well as their value orientation and their life-style. Membership in a traditional social elite that emphasizes Hispanic heritage, so important to the value system of other Latin American countries, however, has relatively little importance in postrevolutionary Mexico.

Class breakdown is generally considered in terms of upper, middle, and lower classes, although boundaries and proportions are by no means clear. It is generally conceded that the participant sector encompasses upper class and middle-class elements and the part of the lower class that may be considered urban workers. This last element has been designated "transitional" by some authors, because it constitutes a group whose marginal status is on the wane.

Estimates of the size of the upper class fifty years after the revolution range from 0.5 percent of the population to a generous 6.5 percent, the latter estimate constituting a jump from 1.5 percent at the beginning of the century and the former, a decline of 0.1 percent over the same period. Estimates of the middle class are just as varied—17.1 to 33.5 percent of the population, both from a starting point of about 8 percent. The lower class constitutes from 60 to 82.4 percent of the population, the transitional element being the upper third of this class. These great differences of opinion in estimating class makeup result from differing criteria.

UPPER CLASS

The revolution did more to alter the composition of the upper class than any other group by removing the double-edged power base of the traditional rural elite: land and Spanish heritage. The members of this social elite—who also occupied positions of political and economic power—based their position in a hereditary aristocracy on the purity of their Spanish blood. They were deposed in favor of the mestizo and the building of a sense of "Mexicanness" based on aboriginal culture and values. Many who had formerly displayed their Spanish heritage with pride doffed this hat in the revolutionary winds and replaced it with one emphasizing their indigenous origins—thus deemphasizing their European background. Sixty-four years after the revolution, the upper class was still stressing its native background, although some noticed the beginnings of an open resurgence of pride in the Spanish element as well.

Some of the prerevolutionary elite were able to convert land to cash or another commodity before the revolution, but the majority lost their land without compensation and were forced to rely on other economic sources or on family help. Their recognition that the new order would be dominated by urban political leaders led many more to move to urban areas and cast their lot with the growing entrepreneurial class there. Enterprising Mexicans of mestizo origins who lived through and profited economically by the revolution constituted a nouveau riche element whose children are now full members of the upper class.

Although the ancestral holdings of the upper class were largely expropriated, land remains a commodity valued by the upper class, as it is by all Mexicans. The security of owning land is desired because it is thought to be something that will never decrease in value. Thus, large landholdings—in urban as well as rural areas—are beginning to be built up within governmental limits, and extra income may be used to buy land.

Studies show that there are regional differences between upper class members, just as there are within the society as a whole. The inhabitants of Monterrey, known as *regiomontanos* to the rest of the Mexicans, are stereotyped as industrious and stingy people. Not only do they accept this designation, but they are proud of it and their widespread reputation for being hard workers. This attitude is somewhat of an anomaly in Latin America as a whole, where elite attitudes based on disdain for manual labor and openly remunerative activity have tended to inhibit interest or investment in industry and commerce.

The fact that Monterrey's upper class is dominated by a small number of family capitalists affiliated with business associates and a few professionals has led them to be considered a cohesive industrial bourgeoisie. The top industrial and financial firms are linked by family ties and mutual interest, enabling them to function as a bloc. The ascetic character of the industrial elite is still part of a general mystique surrounding Monterrey's capitalism. Families have retained control in two ways: by refusing to sell out to multinational corporations and by retaining decisionmaking power rather than delegating it to hired managers. Family businesses are prevalent throughout Mexico, and many represent the efforts of penniless Italian or French migrants whose Mexicanized descendants now reside in luxury because of their enterprising ancestors. In many parts of Mexico the business and political elements of the upper class form a cohesive unit with common and sometimes overlapping interests. In Monterrey, however, the two are differentiated, and the local leaders of the Institutional Revolutionary Party (Partido Revolucionario Institucional—PRI) serve as intermediaries between the business elite and the federal government.

MIDDLE CLASS

The middle class is heterogeneous and emergent, and it has flourished in the last generation. Like the upper class, it has changed in composition. As a class it has benefited greatly from the industrial expansion and free public education. Older and more independent groups, such as small entrepreneurs, merchants, traditional professionals, and small landowners, have been joined by new occupational groups that have arisen in response to the increased bureaucracy and mid-level managerial positions. These include technicians and white-collar managers in business, government, and services. Although most members of the middle class are employed in white-collar occupations, some skilled workers may be included.

That obstacles to rising from lower class to middle-class status are not overwhelming is attested to by the heterogeneous nature and social origins of the middle segment. This is especially true of the Gulf Coast and larger industrial cities where the sons of European immigrants and rural mestizos vie for occupational advancement in a fairly fluid society. Moreover, many middle-class people continue to come from working-class origins. It is also true that there are fewer obstacles to rising from middle-class to upper class status in Mexico than in other Latin American countries. This is largely because of the absence—or at least minimized

114

importance—of traditional elite criteria regarding family, ethnic background, and prestige.

In the smaller and less developed towns the small size of the middle class is accounted for by the restricted commercial development and public bureaucracy, which are both middle-class strongholds. A middle class does not even exist in the remote rural areas, except as poor middlemen in relation to their even poorer Indian neighbors.

One study that tried to differentiate the middle class from the working class found that the former had certain core values that indicated a "modern" outlook on the world. They included: activism, a weaker integration with relatives than the working class, a preference for urban life, individualism, a perception of the system as being open rather than tightly stratified, and a high interest in the mass media. Moreover, education is viewed as the prime mover in social status, and most members of the middle class aspire to a college education for their children.

Members of the middle class have a primary education and frequently a secondary or even college education. They live in dwellings of three rooms or more with running water and electricity and have access to a radio or television or both. New appliances and other consumer items are made for the middle class, and they have learned to spend more than they earn through credit. Among the wealthier segments of the middle class, more money is available for travel, entertainment, and education.

The Mexican middle class has not gone far in developing a specific ideology or common goals. They feel a strong, if somewhat ephemeral, sense of nationalism that psychologically aligns them with all other Mexicans. They are proud of the economic progress their country has made and are reaping the benefits of their fathers' struggle. Moreover, they are seemingly content with the one-party system, which represents their economic frame of mind. It is expected that, if their interests were seriously endangered, the middle class would form a more cohesive and forceful unit (see ch. 10).

LOWER CLASS

The lower class is not only the largest group—comprising at least half of the population—but it is also the most complex. Members of this class range from the Indians, whose hard-core marginality is reflected in their cultural differences and lack of national identity, to urban workers, whose transitional status puts them on the edge of the middle class. The Indians are exclusively rural people engaged in subsistence farming, handicraft production, and occasional rural labor projects (see ch. 4). In contrast to the other classes, the greatest concentration of the lower class is found in the country, and a smaller but mushrooming proportion is found in industrial centers.

Agricultural workers, who include small farmers, *ejidatarios* (see Glossary), sharecroppers, tenant farmers, and day laborers, as well as wealthier farmers engaged in commercial crops, still earn far less as a group than the urban working class. For example, the mean annual per capita income in the rural sector in 1960 was one-fourth of that in all parts of the urban sector. Although this gap had decreased by the mid-1970s it still presented a striking contrast of income and life-styles.

The rural mestizos frequently have a local stratification system in which the Indians are on the periphery. Stratification is influenced by such factors as landownership, income, occupation, education, and family background. Although traditional ethnic criteria play a greater part than they seem to in the city, the high value placed on wealth and property by the mestizos permits an Indian who becomes wealthy to be adopted slowly into the mestizo community as a full participant. The condition of the independent farmer is much envied, and in many communities he still represents a kind of local aristocracy associated with good families, higher education, political control, and frequently big business or commerce. These people are only prosperous relative to other rural dwellers, however, and cannot be considered part of the upper class. Their status is nontransferable to urban localities because their wealth and sophistication are relative to their locale. They do, however, join with rural professionals in acting as interpreters and liaisons between the national and local social structures and constitute an upper stratum within the rural lower class. Moreover, this stratum is frequently linked to commercial or even industrial interests of national scale.

The working class is a substratum of the lower class. In Mexico it seems to command more respect than in many other Latin American countries where aristocratic Spanish values predominate. This is particularly true in the industrialized areas, where labor is actually esteemed and many workers earn more than their white-collar counterparts in the middle class. This situation makes for more egalitarian, impersonal class contacts, especially in a situation where mobility between the lower and middle sectors is not unheard of.

Nevertheless, the division of the working class has handicapped the development of a strong class consciousness and prevented workers from becoming unified politically or even socially. Moreover, the political force that works to integrate them into the participating section of the society, the PRI, brings them into basically supportive political roles (see ch. 10). Through unions they are subject to the current PRI president, and strikes are therefore carefully monitored. When the president is prolabor, more strikes are likely to occur because they will carry greater weight, indicating that the workers' movement is closely tied to the chief executive's policy and is protected by his power.

The reformist, conformist, and generally conservative nature of the working class—relying on government policy and suppressing separatist tendencies—has also handicapped the development of class identity with other lower class elements. The integrated and participatory section of the working class may actually, if inadvertently, support the

116

inequalities in labor market participation. Those in secure positions feel threatened by the crush of migrants searching for the privilege, security, and high pay they enjoy so, far from backing migrants' demands for integration, the integrated sector may contribute to the exclusionist policies of unions and employers who would reduce job competition.

The growth of large, mechanized farms that produce such export crops as cotton, sugar, and wheat has allowed the growth of a rural working class. Although smaller than its urban counterpart, this segment is characterized by a similarity of organization and interests. Most members of the rural working class are assured of minimum wages and some benefits concerning hours and vacation time. Some are even provided with hospitals, schools, and housing. The rural labor organizations help to unite interests and articulate grievances and are somewhat effective in integrating rural workers into the participant sector.

There is great heterogeneity among working-class Mexicans, especially with respect to working conditions. In the areas of greater industrial growth, such as Monterrey, the proportion of wage earners to self-employed workers increases. Among the wage earners there is further differentiation of skill and of the kind of enterprise. Workers in large industries—both public and private—are better paid, have more job stability, and get more benefits than workers in smaller, more traditional plants or those in commerce or services. They enjoy a higher standard of living and greater prestige than their counterparts in the more traditional industries. Wages also vary greatly among the different categories of workers. Someone employed in a steel company or nationalized electric plant may earn five times what is paid a construction worker and will receive far better benefits in housing, health care, and education for his children.

One study conducted in the early 1970s among several thousand industrial workers along the northern border indicated that the majority were women, usually unmarried. For these women and their families the job was vitally important, and a daughter might even replace her father as the family's main breadwinner. Conversely, loss of her job could mean economic hardship for her family. Her family's moral support, along with her own sense of responsibility and desire to retain her new life-style, serve to keep her in her job and make her a good company risk. When a woman leaves her traditional post in the home, she finds many expanded opportunities for a freer and more acquisitive life-style. She may obtain a visitor's card to travel to the United States; some factory workers along the Texas border spend up to 70 percent of their incomes in the United States.

These female factory workers may postpone marriage because of several factors: they fear losing their newly gained social independence; they cannot find suitable husbands among the small number of available bachelors; most realize that their husbands would forbid them to work

117

outside the home once they married; and many factory managers dislike employing married women. Many managers hire unmarried women specifically because they consider them better workers than men. They are more easily disciplined and directed. Moreover, they develop a sense of loyalty to the company analogous to that they feel for their family. Despite their growing sense of independence, their loyalty still lies at home, where their behavior is closely supervised outside working hours. Often women are even escorted to and from work by their fathers and brothers, thus prolonging the perception that the single woman invites danger when she is alone.

SOCIAL MOBILITY

The existence of upward mobility and the increasing integration of the marginal population are two related phenomena substantiated by census figures and social science research. That this process is accelerated the higher up the social ladder one goes is also evident. The belief in upward social mobility pervades all levels of society and to varying degrees is accompanied by belief in education and migration as factors influencing mobility.

Vertical movement up the social scale is a pattern obvious to even the most isolated Indian groups in Mexico. The peasants of yesterday are the laborers of today, and their children may enter a profession. The consciousness of all people has been affected in some way by the possibility of individual opportunity through adopting mestizo values or moving from country to city or from underdeveloped to developed region or by the possibility of rising from one class to another through education, work, or luck. The fact that increasing numbers of the lower class are participating in economic progress increases the individual's hope for self-betterment and reinforces the national pattern. It also creates pride in the nation and its development.

Education has accelerated participation by increasing literacy since the revolution, but it has not brought about a revolutionary change in the patterns of mobility. Education tends to reinforce social status and, only if one can break through the various economic barriers to higher education or technical training, can one achieve significant mobility. Determinants of educational achievement are socioeconomic status of the family, father's and mother's level of education, size of community, and age. Thus the wealthier the family, the more urbanized the locale, and the younger the child, the more likely he is to advance through the grades and enter a university.

Education is the most relevant criterion for the first job, especially among migrants, and this in turn affects all subsequent jobs. The age span between fifteen and thirty years is frequently the period of highest mobility, so that the more education attained at an early age the better. One study showed that a man's chances were not affected by his age at marriage or the number of his children; they were affected, however, if he was a member of the lower class, by his wife's education. Getting married to a better educated woman was associated with upward movement in the occupational scale for many migrants as well. The importance of a wife's education diminishes higher up the social ladder.

Although a large percentage of the urban working class may be trapped in marginal positions, few are trapped for life, much less for generations. This is the basic difference between urban marginality, where the relative fluidity and expansion of the economic sector allows for upward mobility, and rural marginality, where advancement is hampered by decreasing availability of land and lagging development. The answer to this problem for millions of rural Mexicans has been migration to urban centers. In a city like Monterrey or in a dynamic region like the northern border, many are able to fulfill their hopes for social mobility.

If migration nearly always lives up to the migrant's hopeful expectations, it is not because he compares himself with other workers in the city but because he compares himself with his relatives back home. Many are able to become factory workers with the help of relatives or friends who have preceded them. Whereas the migrants themselves probably did not get past primary school, sacrifices are made so that their children will attend school—even though the child is old enough to contribute financially to the household. Expectations for children run high. In one study, two-thirds of the migrants interviewed (compared to four-fifths of the natives) expected their sons to hold nonmanual positions.

Many factors ease migration from country to city. Most important is the basic continuity of rural-urban areas, which decreases the fear of making the transition. Although the urbanization process modifies migrants' behavior, there is little evidence of large-scale alienation because of mutually exclusive rural and urban value systems. Moreover, migrants are usually prepared for what they will find in the city either through step migration—moving to increasingly larger urban concentrations—or through trial visits to relatives or friends in the city. Once the move is made, migrants tend to reside in the same *colonia* (residential section) as their former townsfolk and maintain close ties with relatives.

Often the *colonias* are squatter settlements that have mushroomed illegally at the outskirts of the city or near a main highway. Lots are purchased or merely claimed by the squatter, thus making everyone an "owner"—an important criterion for status in these settlements. The houses are built of adobe, brick, or cement and are not usually equipped with water, sewage, or electricity until they are recognized by the municipal government. As many as a dozen people may occupy a one-room dwelling, which usually has a patio for pigs and chickens and occasionally a small contiguous cornfield. As it is for all classes, the ownership of land is a focal value in the lives of the migrants, no matter how small or inconveniently placed the plot is. When the final decision is made to remain in the city, migrants may even sell land back home in order to buy a plot in a squatter *colonia*.

The family is one of the strongest institutions initiating the migrant in the ways of city life. Some scholars say ties are even strengthened owing to the need for friendly connections in the new environment. The family provides economic as well as psychological support and frequently is responsible for getting the migrant his first job. Ritual relationships like *compadrazgo* (ritual godparenthood) flourish in the city as in the country. They take on added importance, as the bonds of *compadrazgo* ensure solidarity and provide security. Most migrants also tend to retain ties with their community of origin and, distance and finances permitting, try to pay a return visit at least once a year—frequently for the town's patron saint day. They not only keep in contact with rural relatives in this manner but also, provided they are successful, provide a positive example to other potential migrants.

Another way in which integration is eased is through the formal and informal organizations open to the migrant. Certain regional organizations, such as the Coalition of the Oaxacan Mixtecans (Coalición de Pueblos Mixtecos Oaxaqueños) of Mexico City, protect the interests of their member communities in both the city and the hinterland. These clubs serve a social function as well and are often headed by the oldest or wealthiest migrants of the area. Military service also tends to integrate rural dwellers and is a key factor in inculcating a sense of Mexican nationality and pride.

FAMILY

Structure and Function

The nuclear family consists of parents and their unmarried children. As each child marries, he leaves the parental household and establishes a new residence. Usually a son will locate his new home in the vicinity of the parental household. Although the great majority of households are based on nuclear family units, members of the extended family or other kin are often included.

Families are strong, cohesive units held together by bonds of loyalty, common economic goals, interdependence, stability of marriage, prospects of inheritance, and the significant absence of other social groups to which the individual can turn in time of need. Family unity and stability are perpetuated by the method of child rearing and the nature of parent-child relations. Disruptive factors in the functioning of the family, such as adultery of one of the spouses, sibling rivalry, of favoritism of the parents toward one of the children, are overshadowed by the positive attributes of the funtioning unit.

There is some disagreement among scholars as to whether the urbanization process has had a disintegrating effect on the Mexican nuclear family. Some say that the higher rate of abandonment by fathers of wives and children and the higher separation rate, as well as the larger percentage of violent crimes, are endemic in the city and that the stresses and strains of lower class existence show basic erosion of the family. Nevertheless, other studies of migrants show that the family is indeed changing but not necessarily suffering a breakdown or decline. The fact that the extended family is still strong is demonstrated by the fact that the family is the key institution socializing migrants in the city.

The stability of the family as an institution under change is impressive, as is the relative uniformity in rural and urban environments and across lines of social strata. The degree of family cohesion, extent of kinship interaction, and fundamental values do not vary widely between urban and rural communities, rich and poor, or older and younger families. Moreover, kinship ties are so strong that movement up or down does not seem to sever relationships. Family ties and obligations continue to be of vital importance. Thus, even though the upwardly mobile are not expected to pull their kin up with them, they may choose to help out financially, even though to do so may deflect from economic goals and constitute an economic drain. Even those who do not choose to help financially are still expected to maintain close social contact.

The family functions as a basic economic unit and is characterized by a sexual division of labor—except in times of intensive labor in the rural areas, when women may work in the fields alongside the men. The traditional activities of the mestizo wife center in the household, where she is in charge of child rearing and other domestic duties, whereas her husband's labor is outside the home—in the rural areas in crafts, agriculture, and commerce and in the urban areas in manufacturing, business, or a profession. In some rural areas such as the state of Oaxaca, men till the fields while women run the marketplace.

The family functions as an autonomous unit in child rearing and socialization. Cultural values and behavior patterns are transmitted from generation to generation within the nuclear family. The father maintains the power to regulate behavior through physical punishment. Respect and authority are emphasized in parent-child relations. Children are reared to respect and obey their parents. Responsibility to the family is important because an individual's status and security originate in the family. Often the success or disgrace of a member of the family reflects on the father's responsibility for the children. Thus, regardless of age or marital state, a son is under the father's authority as long as he remains in the household. Another example of the recognition of hierarchical powers and duties within the family is the dominance of older brothers over younger ones.

Generally, relations of the nuclear family with the immediate relatives of the extended family may be limited, except in the upper classes. Geographical proximity and frequency of contact are the most influential factors in the relations within the extended family. Although relations outside the nuclear family are not elaborated, the family will turn to close relations, *padrinos* (godparents), or *compadres* in time of crises.

Family structure is enlarged with the recognition of ritual kin ties in a system of *padrinos* and *compadres*. *Compadrinazgo* emphasizes the pattern-valued behavior of respect between individuals and represents a model for social interaction at all levels. *Padrinos* and *compadres* perform economic and social functions by assisting in child rearing and providing economic help in emergencies.

Another function of the family is to socialize the children in accepted sexual roles. In the past this has meant a high degree of personal freedom for both sexes up to adolescence and then differential training patterns. Boys were taught to be assertive, brave, honorable, and protective—in short, to manifest all those qualities embodied in machismo. Conversely, women were taught to submit to their fathers and later to their husbands, to be pious, and to base their lives in the domestic sphere. Since the revolution, however, sexual roles have been in flux, especially those of women.

In his 1974 state of the union address, President Luís Echeverría announced sweeping reform legislation to end discrimination against women: "It is necessary to break the barriers that impede women from achieving their total development within the political, economic and social life, and which obstruct the internal advancement in Mexico." This was the first time a Mexican president had given women such importance in a state of the union message and the first important legislation to affect women since they were granted the right to vote in the mid-1950s. In a direct criticism of machismo, President Echeverría further stated that laws alone would not change the system and that mental attitudes would have to change in order to reduce the unjust situation. The forthcoming legislation included a plan to expand job opportunities and equalize pay scales. It accompanied a basic change in attitude among a large segment of the female population. Many upper class and middle-class women pursue careers outside the home as teachers, physicians, lawyers, and dentists.

Marriage

There are three types of marriage in Mexico—civil, religious, and free union—but only the first is recognized by the state. Although the church marriage has the greatest prestige and is thought to be the only form of marriage by the older generation, fewer young people are being married in the church. If a family can afford it, both a civil and a religious ceremony may take place.

When a man and woman cohabit without church or civil sanction, the marriage is termed a free union. Although the free union is not a legal form of marriage, it is not uncommon, especially in second marriages. The informal marriage establishes no contractual bonds. Civil authorities, however, have recognized a partial right of inheritance by the

122

woman if the couple has lived in monogamous union for five years preceding the death of the husband, and if the woman has borne the man's child or children. Although many free unions are later formalized, such marriages are often unstable; desertions and remarriages are frequent in informal unions, and one man may head several households with children in each.

According to civil and church authorities, the children of the illegal free union are illegitimate. Nevertheless, in both urban and rural environments these marriages are socially acceptable, and the children are officially regarded as illegitimate only if they are not recognized or supported by the father. Civil law allows children born to unwed parents legitimate status if the parents are later married. Most children who are illegitimate are born of free unions or religious marriages not accompanied by civil ceremonies; illegitimate children born of casual relationships are not significant in numbers. Children born of free unions usually have *hijo natural* (natural son) put on the birth certificate along with the father's name.

The frequency of free union and illegitimacy is greater in the northern and southern regions of Mexico than in the central region. Free union and illegitimacy are more prevalent among the poor, the rural, and the Indian populations, whose conservative attitudes result in the maintenance of older customs that have been abandoned by the middle and upper classes. With increasing literacy and educational levels, civil marriage is gaining advocates, especially in the urban centers. Other factors, such as the prerequisite of stable families in qualifying for low-cost housing and installment credit, have influenced this trend in the urban context.

In 1972 President Echeverría's wife continued a campaign aimed at legalizing the thousands of free unions and millions of illegitimate children. It was estimated that some 90,000 Mexican couples living out of wedlock would take advantage of the program, called the Mexican Family. The civil registry office waived normal fees for processing marriage papers to encourage couples to join the wedding ceremonies, which would be held en masse on certain days. The civil ceremonies were to take place in municipal offices across Mexico.

Ritual Kinship

In Mexican culture, kinship status is extended to nonkinsmen in the *compadrinazgo* system. This system formalizes all the relationships between *padrinos*, their godchild, and the child's parents. During the celebration of church rituals, such as baptism and confirmation, a kinlike relationship, *padrinazgo*, is established between the child and his *padrinos*. At the same time a relationship, *compadrazgo*, is created that binds the *padrinos* and parents of the child as *compadres*.

The dual relations of *compadrinazgo* are characterized by mutual rights and duties that reflect the concept of respect. Thus, behavior and attitudes that create respect and affection while maintaining distance and avoiding conflict are reinforced. Interaction based on respect emphasizes the ritual nature of *compadrinazgo* and is significant in the social structure.

The *padrinos*, who are chosen by the parents, give the child his first status by introducing him to society at the baptismal celebration. Ideally the duties of the *padrinos* include socialization of the child in the church. Actually they provide a relationship in which the child practices behavior that reflects the fundamental value of respect. The child learns respect for age and for ritual experience and is encouraged to participate in other rituals which in turn reinforce the system.

Like the *padrinazgo*, the *compadrazgo* adds new status and increases the total number of statuses of the individual. Satisfaction for the individual lies in the relationship of *compadres* involving new rights and duties, not in the position as rank. There is a tendency in mestizo communities, however, to use *compadrazgo* to link poor and wealthy families for the material and prestige benefits that may result; in such communities the reciprocity characteristic of the relationship may be destroyed because the *compadres* are no longer on the same social level.

Of the two sets of relationships in the *compadrinazgo*, the *compadrazgo* is the more important, for it continues throughout life. In contrast, the duties of the baptismal *padrino* tend to weaken after the marriage of the child. There is asymmetry in the relations between *compadres*, as more respect is given to the *padrino*. *Compadrinazgo* brings separate, sometimes extended, families together in formal, kinlike relationships. Terminology approximates but does not parallel that of the kinship system, for it ignores generational variations. The *padrinazgo* mirrors the nuclear family in terminology and partially in function. It supports the child with affection through benevolent and unquestioned authority. By exemplifying the desirable, it socializes the child in the behavior patterns of the culture. It also functions to mitigate strains within the family and provides economic help in times of crisis.

RELIGION

Development of Church-State Relations

Serving the spiritual needs of the Spanish conquerors and converting Indians to Christianity were the primary responsibilities of the missionaries who followed the conquistadores to the new world. These spiritual conquerors were usually as intelligent and resourceful as their military counterparts and considerably more compassionate. Beginning their evangelical efforts in 1522, the friars converted thousands of Indians by the end of the century and millions by the end of the colonial period. By that time all but the most inaccessible natives had been at least nominally Christianized, and Roman Catholicism in Mexico was nearly universal.

With notable exceptions, the priests who followed the first wave of friars were not as zealous or eager to Christianize and help the Indians but served the spiritual needs of the rich Spanish landlords who, upon dying, bequeathed the priests property, cattle, and large endowments of gold and silver. The clergy became richer and less conscientious, and the increase in wealth accompanied a decline in morals. By the end of the eighteenth century the church owned almost two-thirds of all money in circulation and more than one-half of Mexico's land.

Much of the accumulating wealth belonged to the secular or higher clergy who handled administrative responsibilities for the proliferating parishes set up by the lower clergy. Each secular priest was the highest civil authority in his village, and *fueros* (immunities) put him beyond the reach of civil courts and invited abuses of power. The higher clergy were Spanish born, loyal to the crown and opposed to the new and heretical ideas of nationalism, liberty, and equality originating in France. The lower clergy were mainly Mexican born, often mestizos, and as impoverished as their parishioners, and they identified with them. To these men the French ideas did not seem beyond reason or unacceptable. It was two of these lower clergymen, Miguel Hidalgo y Costilla and José María Morelos, who helped initiate the struggle that eventually led to Mexico's independence.

Mexico's first independent government acknowledged the state religion to be universally Roman Catholic, and for a time the church was allowed to maintain its powers and privileges. Yet without the backing of the crown its position was in jeopardy. Increased anticlerical feelings caused by intraclergy conflicts, the envy-arousing wealth of the church, the liberal reforms of the American and French revolutions, and a growing belief that the church's affluence and power made it a strong rival political force led government leaders to begin stripping the church of its temporal powers.

In 1833 acting President Valentín Gómez Farías leveled the first attacks on the church. He secularized education and suppressed the university because it was under ecclesiastical control. The small but influential and intense group of liberals were impervious to pious protests against Gómez Farías' statutes, for they were determined to free the nation from centuries of clerical domination. The recently enacted church restrictions were followed by others—measures restricting the jurisdiction of ecclesiastical courts and prohibiting the church from owning real property. This wave of anticlericalism culminated in the 1857 Constitution under the presidency of Benito Juárez. The constitution explicitly reiterated the previously stated restrictions and also declared that members of the clergy were ineligible to run for president or national representatives and that governors were to designate buildings to be used for religious services.

What followed these anticlerical moves was a wave of intrigue and eventually civil war. As the fighting raged among the church-military alliance, an essentially conservative group, and the liberal constitutional-ists, the anticlerical laws were expanded even further. Sacred cere-monies held outside the church were forbidden; monastic orders, religious holidays, and the ringing of church bells were regulated. The laws eventually established complete separation of church and state. Much of this legislation was selectively ignored when Porfirio Díaz came to power in 1876 with clerical support. This tacit consent of revitalized church influence acted as a catalyst to the latent discontent of the liberals, and it was a potent cause of the Revolution of 1910.

The Constitution of 1917 contained stringent restrictions that went far beyond those of its 1857 predecessor. In an attempt to drive the church out of politics, destroy its social influence, and confine it to strictly religious activities, the Constitution gave state legislatures the power to determine the number of clergy needed in each locality. It also excluded foreign priests and placed further limitations on the political and property rights of clergymen. If these and other measures had been strictly enforced, the very existence of the church would have been threatened.

The antichurch clauses, however, were not activated until 1926 under the administration of Plutarco Elías Calles. Beginning that year and extending to 1929 there was a virtual civil war between the administra-tion and the church. Convents were raided, and hundreds of foreign priests were deported. Congress ratified laws that declared that no priests could teach primary school, wear religious garb in public, or speak out against the government or the Constitution. The passing of these new laws and the enforcement of older ones brought a backlash from the pro-Roman Catholic middle class, who formed a guerrilla group called the *cristeros* (defenders of Christ). The *cristeros* attacked army garrisons, burned buildings, and once even dynamited a train, killing 100 passen-gers in the explosion and fire. The *cristero* rebellion was finally put down after a series of conferences between church officials and the Mexican president, the United States ambassador acting as intermediary, brought a gradual conciliation in 1929.

Although disagreements continued throughout the 1930s, by the end of the decade both sides had sufficiently moderated their positions to alleviate most of the tension. Major friction-producing issues, such as clerics in politics, church ownership of private property, the number and nationality of priests, and parochial education, were ameliorated. More-over, as the revolutionary government grew in strength and confidence and as Mexican-born priests rose in the Roman Catholic hierarchy—replacing the deported foreign-born priests—a flicker of empathy began to develop between the two. Although no Roman Catholic political parties as such were permitted in Mexico, various church-oriented political groups were tolerated in the mid-1970s.

The Constitution declares all churches, rectories, and convents government property; gives individual states the power to control the number of clergymen permitted within their boundaries; and prohibits foreign-born priests. The government's permission is required before a new church structure may be built. In most states the clergy have no difficulty in securing building permits, though some states still occasionally deny petitions. Once constructed a church becomes national property. Church officials have said that a constitutional amendment allowing them to own new church buildings used exclusively for worship should be enacted. Clergymen also maintain that allowing states to determine the number of priests contradicts the constitutional guarantee of religious liberty. Without changing the laws the revolutionary government has decreased the tension these issues produce by overlooking some violations of the religion-suppressing statutes. The noticeable number of foreign-born Jesuits active in several parts of the country is an example of the de facto privileges tacitly granted to the church by the government.

Contemporary Religions and Their Organization

Roman Catholicism is the predominant faith in Mexico with 50 million or more followers in the mid-1970s. The proportion of Roman Catholics in the total population had decreased slightly, from 97.8 percent in 1930 to 90 percent in the mid-1970s.

Mexican Roman Catholicism has social and regional variations in ritual and sacramental observances. Upper classes adhere to formal Roman Catholic doctrines and look with disdain on lower class pious practices, which are often a fusion of Christian and other elements, held over tenaciously from preconquest indigenous religions (see ch. 4). Generally, Christian elements prevail in the northern states and in major urban areas while Indian beliefs and practices are prevalent in the Yucatán Peninsula and in peripheral population regions.

It is interesting to note that the strongest Roman Catholic areas in the mid-1970s were generally those where the main thrust of sixteenth-century missionary activity occurred, whereas the weaker Catholic regions correspond to the areas of least intensive missionary work. Many of the anticlerical personnel of the revolution came from the weaker regions. Their opposition, however, came from intensely Roman Catholic areas.

Protestants constituted about 1.9 percent of the population in 1960, though estimates varied from 1.6 to 3.1 percent. Presbyterians, Methodists, Baptists, and Pentecostals are the most active denominations; other groups include Lutherans, Episcopalians, the World Gospel Mission, and Wycliffe Bible translators. Protestant faiths have made their greatest appeal to the lower classes in both rural and urban areas and have had little effect on the upper classes.

Mexico's Jewish population, 90 percent of whom lived in the capital, accounted for about 3 percent of the 1960 population. The Jewish people are mainly middle-class businessmen engaged in trade and commerce.

There are also a number of Jewish Indians who speak Hebrew and attend synagogues. They are dispersed in the lower class throughout the states of Puebla, México, Veracruz, and the Federal District.

Other religious beliefs are held by approximately 0.3 percent of the population, including several thousand Mennonites, who are mainly farmers in north-central Mexico, Mormons, Quakers and others. In 1960 over 192,000 people had no religious affiliation.

In 1969 Mexico had 5,947 inhabitants per priest, about average for Latin America. There were 8,600 priests, of whom about three-fourths were diocesan priests, and the remainder were members of various orders. There were over 3,800 brothers and 23,600 nuns. Rural priests are often village counselors and in isolated areas even provide medical aid for their parishioners. They supervise the various lay functionaries of the church, such as sacristans and cantors. Sacristans act as caretakers of church buildings and as personal aides to the priests. Cantors, or church singers, are in charge of church musical task, which involve singing during masses and leading hymns.

International, national, regional, and local lay Roman Catholic organizations abound in Mexico. Catholic Action movements promote church-oriented social welfare programs. Rural and urban youth groups participate in housing, sanitation, recreation, and community improvement programs. Thousands of lay teachers and missionaries are working to raise literacy figures and standards of living in lower class city slum areas and in isolated rural regions. Private groups of the faithful from trade unions, housing settlements, towns, and villages make regular pilgrimages to the Shrine of the Virgin of Guadalupe in Mexico City. The Christian Family Movement (Movimiento Familiar Cristiano) works to improve family stability and conjugal harmony through spiritual exercises and weekend retreats. Numerous lay associations function on a local level in villages and towns, organizing fiestas and promoting religious activities.

Although the Mexican Roman Catholic Church is regarded as one of the strongest in Latin America, numerous problems hinder its organization and operation. These include insuficient numbers of clergymen, inadequate financial resources, widespread religious indifference, ever-increasing secularization, and clerical conflicts of ideology.

The consequences of these problems are that many isolated villages do not see a priest more than once every five years. In peripheral parishes most Roman Catholics receive baptism, but masses and religious teaching are rare because the priests find it impossible to serve the spiritual needs of all the villages in their territory. In urban areas recent mass migrations to cities have caused considerable overcrowding of parish precincts. Unable to carry out their religious functions effectively in these crowded situations, priests are often discouraged while religious ignorance, indifference, and secularization are encouraged. Mexican church leaders are acutely aware of these problems, but differences in outlook among the hierarchy occasionally precipitate further problems instead of solutions.

The church has been conservative throughout Mexican history. While attempting to conserve and preserve the status quo, the church consistently condemned changes in society because change was thought of as inimical to the existing faith. In contemporary Mexican society, rapid social change became an inexorable and often unsettling fact, and the church was often associated with static backwardness.

The church has slowly been transforming this traditional image of conservatism by identifying itself with more liberal policies. Yet a rift in the hierarchy exists between progressive and conservative elements, priests usually being in the former category and bishops in the latter. In the early 1970s, however, many reform-minded priests were being joined by like-minded bishops.

In many ways the church had come full circle from its conservative stance in earlier days. A report was prepared in 1971 for the World Synod of Catholic Bishops in Rome on the social and economic state of Mexico sixty years after the revolution. The report, entitled "Justice in Mexico," reached the conclusion that there was little social or economic justice in the country and that this condition was partially brought about by the lack of interest in the church. Ironically, whereas clergy had found themselves allied with conservative elements one-half century earlier, this report encouraged the more conservative laity to side against the proposed church reforms. Heading this conservative alliance was the powerful national trade union, the Mexican Workers Federation, which accused the authors of the report of trying to bring about a new church-state conflict.

The theme of social justice continued to be important for all levels of clergy in the mid-1970s, causing further rifts between conservative and liberal elements within both the church and the laity. Liberal priests found support from such powerful men as the bishop of Cuernavaca. Roman Catholicism in Mexico was itself going through a revolution in which it was becoming much more aware of the need for temporal justice. This move in the church, which is frequently expressed in liberal terminology, cannot help but affect Roman Catholic thought and action in Mexico.

In the 1970s the Presbyterians, in addition to carrying out missionary work among the Indians and the poorer rural sector, operated a large publishing house, a scholarship program, and miscellaneous health and educational services. The Baptist, Episcopal, and other denominations supported seminaries, and a large number of Bible schools were supported by Pentecostal groups. One of the most ambitious Protestant projects was the Summer School of Linguistics located at the Wycliffe Bible Translators Institute in Mexico City. A staff of several hundred specialists created and distributed dictionaries, grammars, and Bible translations and promoted the scholarly study of Hispanic cultures.

Problems confronting the Protestant denominations included confusion in the minds of the people caused by the variety of Protestant groups and their differences in Gospel interpretation, vestigial Roman Catholic resistance to their activities, and widespread secularization. A number of interdenominational organizations, such as the Committee on Cooperation in Latin America, espoused coordination among the Protestant bodies and discussed common problems. Nevertheless, Protestantism was prospering in Mexico.

Religious Practices and Beliefs

Generally, religious practices and beliefs are strongly imbued with paganism in the remote Indian villages and in other isolated areas; a fusion of Roman Catholic and pagan elements prevails in most rural mestizo communities and in lower middle-class densely populated areas; and traditional Roman Catholic practices, devoid of indigenous influence, are observed by Mexico's urban upper classes. Certain symbols and observances are meaningful in all three of the environments—isolated, rural, and urban—including the image of the Virgin of Guadalupe, patron saints (santos), fiestas, churches, domestic shrines, and crosses.

The Virgin of Guadalupe is the most widely recognized and universally worshiped of all Mexican saints. During the early days of the conquest she appeared in a vision to a poor Indian named Juan Diego. The dark-skinned virgin asked him to build a church in her honor so that she could be near his (the Indian) people to protect and love them. The apparition appeared directly over a destroyed Indian shrine to Tonantzin, the Aztec earth goddess. The new virgin enabled the Aztecs to indianize the white man's religion and make it their own. This miracle was officially endorsed by the Roman Catholic Church, and the Virgin of Guadalupe became the patron saint of all Mexico. The shrine is the holiest in Mexico, and large crowds congregate daily in the plaza near the basilica. Upon entering they kneel and crawl forward to a spot where they can gaze at the image and pray.

Even more important than Our Lady of Guadalupe to average Catholics are the local patron saints. They are protectors of the villages, and their images are displayed prominently in every church. The villagers look to the patron saint to save crops, stop epidemics, still earthquakes, bring children to barren women, and solve countless problems. They have personal qualities, and their images are worshiped directly as divine beings rather than just symbols of living saints. Some local saints have extraordinary miraculous qualities and gain prominence over a wide region. These regionally important saints become the object of pilgrimages and special veneration. Parishioners show gratitude for their protection and special favors by the saint by holding annual fiestas in homage to them.

Churches are a ubiquitous feature of Mexican cultural landscapes. They usually tower above other village and town structures, and in them are found the highest artistic contributions of the community. Elaborate and sumptuous altar decorations, vivid drawings and carvings, and rich interior colors contribute to the awe-inspiring atmosphere and appeal to the Mexican's aesthetic sensitivity. They are also refuges from the outside world, and upon entering churches the people feel themselves to be in another little universe, free from temporal tribulations and cares.

Domestic shrines are found in many Mexican homes. They usually consist of a picture or small effigy a favorite saint to whom the family turns in time of need or when it is impossible to attend church and pray to the saint there. The small shrines often occupy one corner of a room. Near the image of the saint may be found candles, incense, a vase of flowers, and a cross.

Crosses are among the most widespread of Mexican religious symbols. Besides being conspicuously displayed in churches, domestic shrines, and cemeteries, they are frequently found along crossroads and trails throughout the countryside, so that persons traveling from one town to another may stop to pray. Crosses are generally thought of as powerful protective symbols, though their significance, like that of other sacred symbols and observances, often varies from isolated to rural to urban religious environment.

The Indians make no distinction between religion and culture or between Roman Catholicism and paganism, and they are not aware that such differences exist. Indigenous worship is full of modified Roman Catholic ritual but, although they accepted certain rites, they rejected Christian monotheism because it is too abstract and because it conflicts with their view of afterlife. The Indians view the universe as inhabited by innumerable supernatural beings and many of the features around them, such as the wind, rain, mountains, sun, and moon, as spiritual and personal. When "Christianized," these people have replaced the old gods with the new saints, but their function remains the same.

The Indians deeply venerate the Virgin of Guadalupe and other sacred symbols. They believe that crosses protect the faithful from fright, thieves, and all undesirable phenomena. They communally observe hundreds of holy occasions each year and constantly engage in spiritual activities from baptism to extreme unction. The neglect of ritual obligations subjects the individual or the whole community to punishment in the form of sickness, crop failure, or other misfortune. (see ch. 4).

CHAPTER 6

EDUCATION

During the early 1970s more than 80 percent of the students enrolled in the regular school program were in the primary grades, and primary enrollments had more than doubled since 1960. The rate of growth had been still faster in middle-level schools, however, and the rise of enrollments in institutions of higher education in the late 1960s and early 1970s overcrowded existing facilities and severely strained federal and state education budgets. Outside the regular system, an extensive adult education program provided a wide variety of literacy, basic education, and vocational courses, but illiteracy remained a serious problem in the more remote rural parts of the country.

In both quantity and quality, the schools were unevenly distributed. Above the primary level, nearly all were located in urban centers, and a large proportion of the rural units offered only a few grades of primary school. At all levels the most extensive facilities, the best trained teachers, the highest level of student enrollment, and the best student performance and retention rates were found in the larger urban centers, particularly in the Federal District and the large cities of Central Mexico, the North, and the North Pacific.

A university was established in Mexico not much more than a half century after the discovery of America, but education during the colonial period and the formative years of the republic was available to few children other than those of the elite, and education did not reach into the countryside. The modern educational era began only with the spread of schools and democratization of education that followed the Revolution of 1910.

Schooling was seen as the paramount instrument for achievement of the revolutionary goals, and during subsequent years these goals have remained fundamental in the evolution of educational philosophy and programs. Until about 1940 the emphasis of educational programmers was placed on rural primary schooling and literacy classes directed toward the revolutionary goal of integrating the previously neglected indigenous population into the national life.

Later, the establishment and improvement of rural schools continued at a slower rate as the thrust shifted to the introduction and improvement of new programs in urban localities in response to the needs of the rapidly developing urban economy. Continuously, however, the revolutionary concept of national identity and pride in country has been reflected in school curricula and has been deliberately encouraged in students as an incentive for their achievement of academic excellence.

Although the educational program is generally a centralized one, there has been relatively little overall planning, and an intricate system has developed with overlapping functions and responsibilities and an interweaving of federal, local, and private authority. Above the primary level, a relatively clear dividing line is drawn laterally between academic and technical studies, but the division between middle-level and higher education is blurred.

ADMINISTRATION AND FINANCE

The principal educational authority at the federal level is the Ministry of Public Education (Secretaría de Educación Pública—SEP). Certain specialized schools are administered and funded by the ministries of defense, navy, agriculture, and health. The basic authority resides in the federal government, which enacts legislation assigning degrees of responsibility to local administrations. The educational system has evolved as a generally centralized one, in part because the financial resources of many of the states never permitted them to develop their own programs.

Beneath subsecretariats for general education, technical and higher education, and cultural affairs, the SEP is composed of more than thirty directorates general (including four for primary schools in the Federal District), committees, and councils. Since World War II the senior officials of the ministry have had university or equivalent schooling and for the most part have been drawn from the educational community. They have tended to retain their appointments during the term of office of the incumbent president, and changes at the ministerial level have not substantially altered the pattern of the educational program.

The SEP has original authority for prescribing and coordinating administrative procedures, curriculum contents, requirements for admission, and graduation from schools. State and municipal governments assume day-to-day responsibilities and operate a considerable number of schools, particularly at the middle and higher levels.

Linkage between the individual schools and higher authority is provided by corps of school inspectors staffed by senior teachers who provide both academic and administrative inspection services. Each directorate general with responsibility for a group or category of schools at the primary or secondary level maintains its own inspection corps.

The legal charter of the educational system is set forth in Article 3 of the Constitution of 1917, which has been amended several times. The Organic Law of Public Education implements the constitutional provisions, and some institutions of higher education operate under their own organic laws.

Private education is authorized under the Constitution. Instruction in private schools must be entirely secular, however, and the state retains the authority at any time to withdraw recognition of a private institution. The schools must conform to the established standards of the public system with respect to such matters as objectives, programs of study, and examinations and must reserve 5 percent of their vacancies for scholarships to needy students designated by the government.

In 1972 less than 9 percent of the primary enrollment was in private schools. Current data for enrollments at the middle level were not available, but in 1968 about 26 percent had been in private units. A small number of schools are operated on a mixed or cooperative basis in small localities in which the cost of construction and payments of the staff are contributed to by patronage committees or associations of parents. Attendance may or may not be free, appointments of teachers are controlled by the federal or state government, and the principal must be an SEP appointee.

The largest of the institutions of higher education, the National Autonomous University of Mexico (Universidad Nacional Autónoma de México), is an autonomous institution operating under its own organic legislation. The other public universities are state institutions, although some of these also are autonomous.

A majority of the private universities are under indirect supervision of the public institutions; by virtue of their laws, the National Autonomous University of Mexico and the state universities are entitled to "incorporate" private universities in order that the studies pursued and degrees granted by them be recognized. Private universities may also receive recognition from the SEP or be granted the status of "free universities" by the federal government. Several are incorporated both with the SEP and with a public university. The Autonomous University of Guadalajara, the largest of the private institutions, is a "free university" with federal charter and operates under authority of the General Universities Council.

In Mexico the relationship between the upper middle school and the university is unlike that in other countries. Public universities maintain their own upper middle units, and schools in the private sector must become "incorporated" with universities in order that their credentials be accepted for university matriculation. Both public and private universities maintain this system. Because a similar pattern exists between technical schools at the middle and higher levels, the entire fabric of administrative relationship between middle and higher education in both public and private institutions is closely interwoven.

The National Polytechnic Institute (Instituto Politécnico Nacional) is at once the largest higher technical institution and the focal point of technical education throughout the country with broad responsibility for planning and establishing technical programs, planning curricula, and granting certificates and diplomas at all levels. In addition the National Polytechnic Institute supervises higher level regional technical institutes scattered about the country.

Funds for public education come from federal and state tax revenues and from some gifts and donations. During the late 1960s and early 1970s the federal government bore about 70 percent of all educational costs, and the states bore a little less than 20 percent. The remainder was borne by the private school system. Federal expenditures were relatively heavier in the states with lower tax revenues, and some of the private institutions received public subsidies.

In 1971 some 46 percent of the federal education budget was devoted to preprimary and primary schooling. Middle-level education took 19 percent, and higher and technical education took almost 17 percent. Other kinds of education, library and museum services, and other cultural services took less than 6 percent, and approximately 12 percent was allotted to school construction and maintenance. The proportion for construction and maintenance was significantly higher than the average for the 1960s; the rate of school building had accelerated after about 1970, and in late 1974 it was reported that during the preceding four years the Administrative Committee of the Federal School Construction Program —the public school construction authority—had built 60 percent of all schoolrooms constructed since the institution's establishment in 1968.

Expenditures for education at the national level rose irregularly from 16 percent of the total federal outlay in 1961 to 24 percent in 1966 and to 29 percent in 1970. The 2.5 percent of the gross domestic product (GDP) devoted to education in 1970 was not significantly higher than the average for the 1960s and below the level of earlier predictions. It was also below the then current average for Latin American countries. In 1974, however, the 17.8 billion pesos (12.5 pesos equal US$1) budgeted for public sector expenditure on education and culture was more than twice that budgeted for public health and related programs and almost five times that budgeted for national defense.

EDUCATION IN THE SOCIETY

The limited amount of education available during the colonial period was classical in content, controlled by the Roman Catholic hierarchy, and designed for children of the aristocracy. After the achievement of independence, in 1810, civil authority replaced the ecclesiastic, and there was some expansion and democratization of the small school system. The long regime of President Porfirio Díaz (1876–1911) created the economic base on which a modern educational program was later to develop, but capital formation during that period was matched by social retrogression. At the time of the outbreak of the Revolution of 1910 no more than one-fourth of the primary-age children attended school, and not more than one child in ten attended in rural localities.

The revolution heralded the beginning of the modern era in education, and the famous Article 3 of the Constitution of 1917 was an expression of the new national view of what education should accomplish and be. Education was to be free, mandatory at the primary level, and truly universal. Religious teaching and schools were to be separated, and practical courses of study were to be emphasized. Underlying the constitutional provisions was an almost mystical conception of education as both the symbol of the revolution and the means for achieving its goals through the collective and patriotic participation of all people in the pursuit of national identity.

Until about 1940 the new educational program gave first priority to bringing literacy and primary schooling to the countryside, particularly to the physically isolated Indian villages where Spanish was to many an unfamiliar language. It proved to be a singularly important assignment, for the self-contained traditional communities had their own cultures to which schools were extrinsic and the goals of the revolution were irrelevant. The acceptance of schools by these villages constituted a kind of cultural watershed beyond which the villagers were gradually transformed into patriotic Mexicans with an appreciation of the value of schooling and often unrealistically high educational aspirations for their children. At this stage in cultural orientation, the schoolhouse often replaced the church as the center of village life.

The program for establishment of primary schools in remote rural localities continued with slackened but still considerable intensity during the 1950s and 1960s. In the early 1970s, however, there were still rural communities with no school or in which the school was still an extrinsic element and where the goals of the revolution were still irrelevant.

The cultural watershed that acceptance of education represents is not a sharply defined one, and it is not found only in isolated rural localities. Rural migrants newly arrived in cities and towns tend to bring their cultural values with them, to live first in self-contained neighborhoods, and often only belatedly to be receptive to schooling. For the urban migrant, the watershed is crossed less through familiarization with such urban devices as motion pictures or radios than through interpersonal communication, job experience, and a growing awareness of the higher income and upward social mobility that may result from learning to read and write, and perhaps a little more.

Extension of the primary system in rural areas was at first severely handicapped by a shortage of trained and willing teachers, and the regular staffs were supplemented by a system of cultural missions. These organizations consisted of teams of dedicated specialists who traveled around villages teaching, instructing the poorly trained teachers, and assisting in community activities. After World War II the focus of their activity shifted somewhat toward community development, but in the early 1970s the missions were still active in the countryside. Together with social brigades of university students on vacation performing similar functions, they continued to represent pursuit of the revolutionary goals through popular participation.

During the 1920s there were few complete primary schools in the rural parts of Mexico and virtually no schools above the primary level.

Middle-level schools were being established in the cities and towns, however, and in 1923 the government created a federal agency for the administration of technical schools at this level. This step came in response to demands of the laboring classes, who were not interested in the classical curricula of the existing schools and wanted something more relevant to their own occupations and ambitions.

The technical school system spread rapidly, and by 1930 nearly 70 percent of all middle-level public school students were enrolled in it, one of the highest proportions ever recorded in a Latin American country. Enrollment in schools of this kind experienced a progressive relative decline during subsequent years as academic or general enrollments rose proportionately, but their popularity during the 1920s indicates that Mexicans did not share the prevailing Latin American lack of interest in education in manual skills. Moreover, a subsequent relative decline in technical enrollments can at least in part be attributed to rising educational aspirations; as a rule, the courses did not qualify their graduates for matriculation in institutions of higher education.

The relatively high value placed by Mexicans on practical education is in part based on their ability to take advantage of it; they are receptive to training and readily become expert workmen (see ch. 2). The country's physical closeness to the United States is also probably in part responsible. Mexicans are acutely aware of the high wages commanded by skilled labor in the United States; in addition, their school-nurtured patriotism encourages them to learn skills that will help their country's economy catch up with that of their neighbor. The appreciation of practical education is in evidence at all levels of schooling; in the early 1970s the proportion of university-level students studying practical disciplines was among the highest in Latin America (see The Educational System, this ch.).

The educational program during the 1920s was highly nationalistic in its content and objectives. During the administration of President Lázaro Cárdenas (1934–40)—the "socialist" period in Mexican political history—the program remained essentially unchanged, but it was adapted to socialist objectives. An educational catchword of the time was *igualización*, the equalization of all Mexican people. The concept involved was essentially an adaptation of the revolutionary aim of making all the people of the country Mexican into one of making all Mexicans equal. Behavioristic techniques were employed in the "socialist" schools of the period, and the name of Ivan Pavlov became as well known in Mexico as it was in the Soviet Union.

A new emphasis on athletics and the plastic and performing arts during this period has been cited as illustrative of the force of the Pavlovian influence. The new emphasis survived the short-lived socialist experiment, however, and has served to underline the Mexican school system's ability to adapt itself to different interpretations of the continuing pursuit of the revolutionary goals.

The socialist period ended in 1940, not with a reversal of the political trend but on a stable plateau. Similarly, the educational program retained many of the reforms that had been introduced, and it was not felt necessary to abrogate the several amendments that had been made to Article 3 of the Constitution. The Cárdenas government had adapted rather than changed the preexisting program, and the principal visible change that followed its termination was the gradual abandonment of the socialist catchwords.

During the 1920s and 1930s the principal objective of educational planners had been not the achievement of maximum economic returns to education but the social achievement of education for all. After about 1940, however, there was a change in priorities, and the extension of basic schooling in the countryside surrendered first place to the promotion of urban middle-level and higher education. In a sense, this was a move away from the goals of the revolution, but it could also be defined as no more than a change in the means of seeking these goals. The urban middle class was growing increasingly important, the country itself was changing from a rural to an urban one, and the revolutionary goals were being pursued in the new urban setting.

The political party of President Cárdenas remained in power after the conclusion of his terms of office in 1940, but its name was changed from the Mexican Revolutionary Party to the Institutional Revolutionary Party (Partido Revolucionario Institucional—PRI). It was an apt change in name, for the party was to prove successful in capturing the ideals and symbols of the revolution as its own. It has remained continuously in power and, in so doing, has profoundly affected education's role in the society (see ch. 9).

Public education has remained the principal instrument for establishment of the nationalist ideology. Schools have continued to teach Mexican history, Mexican geography, and the lives of the popular Mexican heroes; schoolhouses have continued to be the scene of patriotic holiday celebrations; and pageants have continued to symbolize unity, participation, and commitment to the continuing revolution. Although still given emphasis, education is no longer the symbol of the revolution, however, and its role as the agent of social change has been correspondingly restricted.

The progress of education under successive PRI administrations has brought about significantly increased rates of social participation and mobilization, but the failure of these to result in an increased demand by educated people for social change has been disappointing to the proponents of change. A mid-1960 survey of carefully selected white-collar workers of various ages and both sexes in Mexico City showed a persistent survival of traditional values. Those with the most education were only slightly more liberal in their orientations than those with less, and attendance at the "socialist" primary schools of the 1930s had produced no discernible effect on subsequent attitudes.

At the university level, students in the 1960s and early 1970s demonstrated an increasing dissatisfaction with the political status quo, but much of their resentment was based on such deficiencies in the educational program as crowded classrooms, poor teaching, and lack of individual attention. A 1960s study of National Autonomous University of Mexico students found that about half belonged to the ideological center and that those to the right outnumbered those to the left by a proportion of two to one.

There were violent politically oriented disturbances in the universities, particularly during 1968, when riots between leftist and pro-government students resulted in considerable bloodshed and some fatalities. Only a minority of the students are politically active, however, and a variety of factors limit both the intensity and the effectiveness of their activism.

Family ties are usually powerful in Mexico, and a large majority of the university students come from well-to-do families. According to a report published in 1971, the families of 66 percent of the National Autonomous University of Mexico enrollment had incomes in the highest 5 percent in the country, and 95 percent had incomes in the highest 15 percent. The income level of families of students in the state universities was somewhat lower; the more affluent parents elsewhere in the country preferred to send their children to the more prestigious institutions of higher education in Mexico City. The political attitudes of students in the state institutions, however, were generally more moderate than those of students in the capital city; and in the generally conservative private universities, the quest for social change was not a significant student concern.

For graduating university students in search of jobs in the early 1970s, an attitude at least of tolerance toward the status quo was a practical necessity. With the continuing rise in university enrollments, the production of new professionals had outstripped industry's practical needs for them, and a large majority found employment in the federal bureaucracy (see ch. 2). Those securing private employment found it in a business community functioning in harmony with, and through, the PRI.

In the early 1970s the government, on occasion, abridged the autonomy of the National Autonomous University of Mexico by sending police onto its campus to quiet disturbances, and in 1974 student activity was restricted. President Luís Echeverría, early in his administration, however, made a point of making himself available to student groups for discussions and has appointed many relatively young university graduates to high government posts.

The students and teachers who make up the educational community, like the business community, have been able to make their influence felt, and their objectives achieved, only through the government. The existence of a single governing party, the ideological weight of the revolution, and the continuing expression of this ideology by the state have combined to limit the independence of their role.

THE EDUCATIONAL SYSTEM

By an official estimate, in 1970 about 72 percent of the country's population between the ages of six and fourteen attended school. Between the ages of fifteen and nineteen the proportion attending school declined sharply to 23 percent of the national total, and between the ages of twenty and twenty-four it declined still further to 4.3 percent.

Three years of kindergarten *(jardín de niños)* are available to children between the ages of four and six, but kindergarten attendance is optional. The standard primary school entrance age is six years, and attendance is mandatory between the ages of six and fourteen or until the primary cycle has been completed.

Beyond the primary level, the ages of students in the several grades of school vary substantially. For example, the three-year basic cycle of middle school is designed for students between the ages of twelve and eighteen, and the two- or three-year upper cycle is designed for those between the ages of fifteen and twenty-one. So many of the university-level students are full-time or part-time workers who can devote only a few hours weekly to their classes that a Mexico City newspaper referred seriously to the students in those institutions as customarily being under the age of thirty-four. Young people in Mexico attend school under circumstances different from those that prevail in the United States, and their ages at all levels of instruction tend to be considerably older.

Dates for the beginning and end of the school year formerly differed in the hot and temperate climatic zones of the country. Since 1970, however, all preprimary, primary, and middle-level school years have commenced in September and terminated in July. Including Christmas and other vacations, the school year consists of about forty-one weeks. Preprimary classes are held during three hours, and primary classes during five hours, of a five-day week. Middle-level schools formerly held six hours of classes daily during a six-day week, but in 1974 they too adopted the five-day schedule. University-level schools have varying schedules for class attendance.

In the lower primary grades girls nearly equal boys in enrollment. In the higher primary grades and in the more advanced levels of schools, they are progressively fewer. At all levels females are somewhat younger than males, and at all levels a large majority of the oldest students are male.

Statistical reporting of school enrollments entails certain special considerations. In technical schools, enrollments are sometimes reported without reference to the scholastic level, and administrative and functional mixing of middle and higher programs of study is such that annual statistical reviews list the two together under the summary heading of postprimary education. As in North America, the school year includes portions of two calendar years, but the school year cited is customarily the year in which classes commence rather than the one in which they conclude.

141

In 1974 official consideration was being given to a proposal that the six grades of primary school and the first three grades of schooling at the middle level be combined in a single nine-year cycle of basic studies during which attendance would be mandatory. The proposal was widely criticized on grounds that the enactment of legislation requiring children to attend school for nine years would be visionary at a time when the constitutional requirement of six years of schooling was still unenforceable because of the lack of a sufficient number of complete primary schools.

The critics missed the point. The change was a logical one in the sense that the curricula of the lower middle cycle were already more closely coordinated with those of primary school than with those of the upper middle cycle, which was seen largely as preparation for matriculation in institutions of higher education. The proposed reform was designed less to compel attendance by legislation than to encourage more students to remain in school for an additional three years.

It would make the progression from the first through the ninth grade a continuous one, uninterrupted by the completion of studies at one level of school and the possibly traumatic transfer to another school in another place. During the late 1960s and early 1970s similar reforms had been introduced for precisely this purpose in the school systems of Argentina, Brazil, Bolivia, and Peru. In supporting the proposal, the minister of public education had acknowledged that its mandatory provisions could not be made effective for some time to come but had urged that Mexico not forever remain a country of *primarios* (persons on a primary school level).

Preprimary and Primary Schools

Three grades of kindergarten constitute an integral but optional part of the Mexican school system. The preprimary program is better attended than in any other Latin American country, and children who have received an introduction to education through it are found to be at a definite advantage among those commencing primary studies. In 1972 some 409,000 children were enrolled in kindergarten as compared with 230,000 in 1960. Girls slightly outnumbered boys, and a large majority of both sexes were either four or five years of age. Nearly all institutions were in large urban centers, and about one-third were concentrated in the Federal District.

Between 1970 and 1972 enrollments in the six-year primary school program increased from 8.8 to 9.5 million students (see table 5). In 1960 less than 5 million had been enrolled. In the early 1970s boys slightly outnumbered girls, nearly all the units were coeducational, and a little less than 1 percent were in night schools.

The comprehensive curriculum stresses "learning by doing" (an educational catchword at the primary level) and aims at total personality development. It includes Spanish language and literature, an introduction to the natural and social sciences, civics, geography, music,

Table 5. Mexico, Primary Education, School Years 1970 and 1972

	1970	1972
School Units:		
Public:		
Urban	8,233	8,964
Rural	31,637	33,303
Subtotal...............................	39,870	42,267
Private:		
Urban	2,569	2,530
Rural	376	367
Subtotal...............................	2,945	2,897
TOTAL	42,815	45,164
Teachers:		
Public:		
Urban	96,557	106,301
Rural	58,472	70,503
Subtotal..............................	155,029	176,804
Private:		
Urban	17,786	18,446
Rural	800	1,146
Subtotal..............................	18,586	19,592
TOTAL	173,615	196,396
Students:		
Public:		
Male.....................................	4,099,146	n.a.
Female	3,710,238	n.a.
Subtotal..............................	7,809,384	n.a.
Private:		
Male.....................................	355,767	n.a.
Female	374,311	n.a.
Subtotal..............................	730,078	n.a.
TOTAL	8,539,462	n.a.
Students:*		
Urban:		
Male.....................................	2,895,259	3,098,112
Female	2,719,542	2,915,766
Subtotal..............................	5,614,801	6,013,878
Rural:		
Male.....................................	1,677,368	1,866,516
Female	1,473,915	1,647,814
Subtotal..............................	3,151,283	3,514,330
TOTAL	8,766,084	9,528,208

n.a.—not available.
*Revised data.
Source: Adapted from Organización de los Estados Americanos, *Boletín estadístico*,
No. 99, Washington, September 1973, Table 5-B; and Organización de los Estados
Americanos, Instituto Interamericano de Estadística, *América en Cifras 1970,
Situación Cultural: Educación y Otros Aspectos Culturales*, Washington, 1973,
Table 501-36.

manual training for boys, and domestic economy for girls.

The government maintains a free textbook program for primary (but not higher) schools. Use is compulsory, and official text and exercise books are in use throughout the country. Between 1965 and 1970 nearly 100 million texts were distributed, and an additional 54 million were issued in 1971 alone. In addition to books devoted to the standard curriculum subjects, guidebooks for teachers and bilingual primers for Indian children unfamiliar with Spanish are provided.

The books encourage devotion to the country and awareness of the national heritage and have for that reason been criticized as somewhat doctrinaire. An adequate supply of free schoolbooks is a relative rarity in Latin America, however, and their availability is an important asset to the national primary program. The aim of primary educational planners is not only to provide most texts and other school material free of charge but to require that children furnish a small proportion of the items in order that they become accustomed to the idea of contributing.

The median age of the primary student in 1972 was between nine and ten years. About 9 percent were under the age of six, however, and nearly 5 percent had passed their fifteenth birthdays. Boys were older than girls in all grades and, among those over the age of fifteen, boys were in a majority by a margin of nearly two to one.

Promotion at the end of the school year is determined not by standardized examinations but by the teacher's evaluation of performance, aptitude, and behavior. Both the proportion of children promoted and the proportion who drop out during the course of the school year appear to be substantially lower than in most other Latin American countries. In 1970 the retention and promotion rates varied widely by region, but the nationwide average for completion of the school year was 93 percent, and the average promotion rate was 84 percent. In 1974 the Mexico City press attributed to the SEP a report that 95 percent of the children completing the year had been promoted and that in the sixth grade the promotion rate had been 96.5 percent.

In 1972 the number of students enrolled in the sixth and final year was less than 37 percent of the number that had commenced the primary cycle five years earlier. This overall retention rate compared favorably with that in other Latin American countries, however, and concealed a wide divergence between urban and rural retentions. The proportion of rural children beginning primary classes was not far below that of urban children, but only a small proportion of the rural schools offered the full six years of primary education.

In 1970 a few urban institutions were still incomplete units, but nearly 90 percent offered the full six years. In the countryside, however, less than 10 percent of the units were complete schools, more than half had three or fewer years, and a scattering had only a single grade. In 1974 the Mexico City press reported that there were still 25,000 rural primary schools in which children could not progress beyond the third grade and estimated the primary school completion rate at 15 percent in rural localities.

Middle Schools

Enrollments at the middle educational level increased from 1.2 million in 1970 to more than 1.4 million in 1972 (see table 6). According to a Mexico City newspaper report, enrollments had quintupled during the preceding fifteen years, and one authority predicted an enrollment of 2.5 million by 1980. In the early 1970s boys outnumbered girls by a ratio of about four to three. Private education was more extensive at this than at any other level. Current enrollment data were not available, but in 1968 about 27 percent of the students had been enrolled in private institutions.

The organizational structure of schools at the middle level is a complicated one in which the nomenclature employed can cause confusion. The schools themselves are referred to here as *middle* rather than the more commonly used *secondary*, because that term has a specific and restrictive meaning. Similarly, the term *vocational* is applied not to schools providing instruction in a particular skill or trade but to upper level middle schools preparing students for university-level matriculation in a technical field.

There is no single term corresponding to *vocational school* as it is applied in the United States, since the closest equivalent—the term *technical school*—can be applied either to an institution offering terminal middle-level training in a practical skill or preparation for further study in a technical school at the higher level. In addition, the term *subprofessional* is applied regularly to terminal technical studies at the basic middle-school level and is also sometimes applied to upper cycle technical studies that may or may not lead to further schooling at the higher level. Unfortunately, available data rarely are segregated to a point where enrollments in each kind of technical and academic institution can be distinguished. Distinction is customarily made only between students preparing for further study at the university level in arts and sciences, students in middle-level normal schools, and students in schools of agriculture, industry, and commerce of all kinds.

Articles in the Mexico City press reported that the proportion of primary school graduates entering middle-level schools edged upward from 77 percent in 1965 to 79 percent in 1972 but that in 1974 the students who completed the first three years—or lower cycle—of middle school represented only 15 percent of the number who had commenced primary school nine years earlier. In middle as well as in primary schools, promotion is based on the teacher's evaluation of class performance rather than on examinations. In 1969 the average rate of grade promotion was 89 percent, and girls achieved somewhat better records than boys.

General Schools

The term *secundario* (secondary) is reserved specifically for students

145

in the three-year basic cycle of general studies leading to further study at the middle level and eventual matriculation in arts and sciences programs in an institution of higher education. The varied curriculum continues most of the primary studies and adds biology, chemistry, and physics as well as a foreign language, usually English or French. English is used extensively in Mexico, is spoken by most university graduates, and is esteemed as an instrument of economic and social advancement even in the most remote communities.

On completing the *secundario* cycle, students receive a certificate of course completion and are eligible for admission to a two-year preparatory cycle in a specialized course of study that will later be continued at the university level. Since the upper cycle school is administered as a part of one of the universities, the passage from the *secundario* to the preparatory cycle is a significant one, which in a sense marks the commencement of the student's university career.

Not usually counted statistically with the *secundario* schools, but comparable to them, are the basic-level schools preparing students for study at institutions of higher education in technical fields. The three-year cycle is in *secundario-técnico* (technical-secondary) units that were known as prevocational schools until 1967. The curriculum is similar to that in the *secundario* but includes a scattering of technical subjects.

The two-year upper cycle that corresponds to the preparatory is called the vocational and leads to matriculation in one of the university-level technological institutes. Students graduating from the preparatory schools receive a *bachillerato* (baccalaureate) certificate while those graduating from the vocational schools receive an equivalent preparatory *(preparatorio)* certificate. Both qualify recipients for admission to institutions of higher education, however, and both kinds of upper level general school are sometimes referred to as *bachilleratos*.

Technical Schools

A majority of the students in these schools are enrolled in terminal programs, usually three years in duration, for which a primary school certificate or evidence of aptitude is required. Courses of study are offered in the agricultural, industrial, and commercial sectors. Commercial schools attract the largest number of students, and private institutions are in a majority. The position of bilingual secretary is a prestigious one in Mexico, and many of the schools offer language instruction to predominantly female students. Statistical series do not ordinarily include separate listings for schools in the other economic sectors, but enrollment in industrial schools appears to be much higher than that in agricultural units. There is also a scattering of lower middle schools in specialized technological fields. In particular, in 1973 there were reported to be about thirty small fisheries schools, some of them with boarding facilities, and the Directorate General of Fishing Education Technology had been established.

In addition, there is a small enrollment in upper level technical schools,

Table 6. Mexico, Middle-Level Education, School Years 1970 and 1972

	1970	1972
School Units:		
Public:		
General	1,442	1,681
Commercial	91	99
Industrial, agricultural, and other	592	612
Normal	136	124
Subtotal	2,261	2,516
Private:		
General	1,329	1,702
Commercial	614	660
Industrial, agricultural, and other	186	197
Normal	99	100
Subtotal	2,228	2,659
TOTAL	4,489	5,175
Teachers:		
Male:		
General	41,402	51,275
Commercial	3,305	3,211
Industrial, agricultural, and other	8,177	9,182
Normal	4,817	3,297
Subtotal	57,701	66,965
Female:		
General	23,974	27,415
Commercial	3,109	3,501
Industrial, agricultural, and other	2,881	3,442
Normal	2,512	2,351
Subtotal	32,476	36,709
TOTAL	90,177	103,674
Students:		
General:		
Male	550,026	681,355
Female	332,487	419,633
Subtotal	882,513	1,100,988
Commercial:		
Male	28,804	30,404
Female	63,611	75,532
Subtotal	92,415	105,936
Industrial, agricultural, and other:		
Male	102,058	97,502
Female	61,222	64,555
Subtotal	163,280	162,057
Normal:		
Male	25,621	26,782
Female	40,091	42,533
Subtotal	65,712	69,315
Total Student Enrollment:		
Male	706,509	836,043
Female	497,411	602,253
GRAND TOTAL	1,203,920	1,438,296

Source: Adapted from Organización de los Estados Americanos, *Boletín estadístico*, No. 99, Washington, September 1973, Table 5-C.

which offer three-year courses to students who have completed *secondario* or technical studies at the basic level. There are also upper level schools of agriculture, nursing, fine arts, and social work. Graduates of the agricultural and nursing schools are eligible for matriculation at institutions of higher education.

Normal Schools

Normal, or teacher training, schools at the middle level provide instruction for teachers in the primary schools. The three-year course of study is open to students who have completed the basic-cycle secondary course, and its graduates are eliglble for admission to institutions of higher education for further teacher training. During the 1960s and early 1970s enrollment fluctuated in a narrow range without showing any pattern of growth. In some years as many as one-third of the students had been unqualified teachers—most of them from rural schools—receiving in-service training at the Federal Institute for Teachers' Qualification, which was established in 1944 for that propose.

Graduates of the regular normal schools qualify as teachers in kindergartens and regular primary courses. Special normal schools train physical education instructors and teachers of handicapped children. Separate urban and rural units provide basically similar training that differs somewhat in course content in order to meet the needs of city and country children. Graduates of urban institutions may teach in primary schools throughout the country, but rural normal school graduates must qualify for urban assignments by completing additional courses of study.

In 1972 about three-fourths of the normal school enrollment was in public institutions. During the 1960s the proportion of female students increased gradually and reached 61 percent of the total in 1972. During the late 1960s students in normal institutions had better retention records than those in any of the other kinds of middle-level school.

Institutions of Higher Education

Between 1959 and 1973 enrollments in courses of study in institutions of higher education leading to undergraduate and graduate degrees increased from about 62,000 to 307,000. An undisclosed additional number of students in nondegree courses of study at the higher level together with students in associated middle-level schools increased in number from about 46,000 in 1959 to 282,000 in 1973 (see table 7).

There is a heavy concentration both of schools and of enrollments in the largest urban centers, particularly in the Federal District, Guadalajara, and Monterrey. In 1960 about 60 percent of the degree students were in the Federal District alone. A decentralizing trend set in at approximately that date, but in 1973 the concentration had been reduced only to 47 percent.

In the mid-1970s the great urban universities had become crowded to a degree that severely limited student-teacher relations, and the quality of instruction was reported to be deteriorating. It was the consensus,

148

Table 7. Mexico, Enrollment in Institutions of Higher Education, Selected Years, 1959, 1966, and 1973

	1959		1966		1973		Growth in Percent	
	Number	Percent	Number	Percent	Number	Percent	1959-66	1966-73
University Level								
Federal District..........	20,084	32.3	53,526	46.9	144,272	47.0	167.0	170.0
Rest of country	42,046	67.7	60,556	53.1	162,816	53.0	44.0	169.0
TOTAL	62,130	100.0	114,082	100.0	307,188	100.0	83.6	169.2
Other*								
Federal District..........	23,821	51.9	59,915	51.4	113,711	40.3	151.5	89.8
Rest of country	22,076	48.1	56,597	48.6	178,263	59.7	156.4	215.0
TOTAL	45,897	100.0	116,512	100.0	291,974	100.0	153.8	142.0

*Nondegree undergraduate courses and associated upper middle schools.

Source: Adapted from Universidad Autónoma de Puebla, "A la Opinión Pública: El Nuevo Rol de la Universidad," *Excélsior* [Mexico City], V, No. 20925, July 1974, p. 13-A.

however, that the best higher education in Mexico was available in these schools to students anxious to work for it. The smaller institutions in the interior could not match their offerings, and parents who could afford to do so continued to send their children to universities in such centers as Mexico City, Guadalajara, and Monterrey.

Mexican universities for the most part recruit their teaching personnel on a part-time basis from the civil service and the business community and, as a consequence, the availability of qualified teachers in Mexico City and a few other urban centers is not equaled elsewhere in the country (see The Teaching Profession, this ch.). Educational authorities who, on the one hand, recognize the need to decentralize higher education in order to give greater opportunity to young people in smaller localities and to avoid overcrowding in the large urban institutions, on the other hand, fear that too much decentralization will reduce the quality of education offered.

By far the largest, most influential, and probably the best of the Mexican universities is the National Autonomous University of Mexico, one of the largest institutions of higher education in the world. Established in 1910 in the Federal District and given autonomy in 1929, it developed from a colonial university founded in 1553. Previously housed in a group of buildings clustered in the center of Mexico City, it was moved in 1955 to a spacious campus on the edge of the city on the Pedregal lava field. The world-famed campus consists of some eighty modern structures including a fifteen-storied administration building and features impressive outdoor murals executed by Diego Rivera, David Alfaro Siqueiros, and Juan O'Gorman. The arts building is more than 400 yards in length, and some of the principal athletic facilities are on a scale measurable by the fact that they were constructed for use in the 1968 Olympic games.

During the school year ending in 1974 the National Autonomous University of Mexico, where President Echeverría was once a law professor, was reported to have 6,000 graduate students in addition to 126,000 undergraduates. Well over 100,000 attended the affiliated middle-level preparatory schools. Since the late 1960s all categories of enrollment had more than doubled.

The university's other credentials were correspondingly impressive. It had more than 18,000 teachers and an administrative staff of more than 14,000. Its libraries included the National Library of Mexico and the Central Library, with combined resources of 1.8 million volumes, plus about forty specialized libraries. The university published more than thirty journals. In addition to ten faculties and schools offering 100 or more courses of study and its system of preparatory schools, it had thirty-four attached research institutes and centers.

The largest of the state universities, the Autonomous University of Guadalajara, had a 1973 enrollment of about 40,000. Also having enrollments in excess of 10,000 were the University of Nuevo León, located in Monterrey, the Veracruzan University, the Autonomous University of Puebla, the University of Coahuila, and the Autonomous University of San Luís Potosí.

The largest of the private institutions is the Autonomous University of Guadalajara. Founded in 1933 by a group of dissident students and teachers from the state-operated University of Guadalajara, it is a conservative institution that had only 2,700 students in 1966. A US$3 million Alliance for Progress loan and assistance from United States foundations made possible expansion of facilities and sharp enrollment increases during the late 1960s and early 1970s, however, and its enrollment in 1974 had reached about 13,000. Other private universities with 5,000 or more students were the Universidad Michoacana de San Nicolás in Morelia and the Iberoamerican University in the Federal District. Unlike the public institutions, many of the private universities maintain dormitories for their students. They more frequently are located on central campuses, and they have a far higher proportion of full-time teaching personnel (see The Teaching Profession, this ch.).

The two large higher technical schools with university status are the National Polytechnical Institute and the Monterrey Institute of Technology and Advanced Studies, a private institution founded in 1943 by a group of Monterrey industrialists and patterned after the Massachusetts Institute of Technology. In 1973 it offered a wide variety of courses of study, in arts and sciences as well as in technical fields, to an enrollment of about 21,000.

The National Polytechnical Institute plays a role in higher technical education comparable to, and perhaps even more extensive than, that of the National Autonomous University of Mexico in higher education in the arts and sciences. Also located in the Federal District, it was founded in 1922 as an adjunct to the practical education program at the middle level, but its status and organization have been revised several times. Its enrollment in 1973 was estimated at about 100,000. The 1969 enrollment in schools offering university-equivalent degrees, however, was less than 30 percent of the total. The remainder were in preparatory and terminal technical courses of study at the middle-school level.

A decentralized part of the National Polytechnical Institute system is a network of small regional technological institutes scattered throughout the country. These schools, the first of which were formed in 1948 but which were greatly expanded in number during the early 1970s, were developed to provide basic technical schooling at the primary and middle levels. The regional institutes, however, have been devoted increasingly to studies on the higher level, particularly in the field of industrial engineering.

The principal higher institution for the study of agronomy and veterinary medicine is the National School of Agriculture, located at Chapingo, near Mexico City. Maintained by the Ministry of Agriculture, it supports a graduate as well as an undergraduate program. A seventy-day strike by its students and teachers ended in August 1974 when the

Mexican government agreed to demands that the institute be given autonomous university status.

The other institutions of higher education are the more advanced teacher training institutes and numerous small schools serving a variety of specialized purposes. They include several independent technological institutes and schools of public health, nutrition, anthropology and history, librarianship and archives, and advanced studies of several kinds. Several engage extensively in advanced research and grant advanced degrees. In general, institutions of higher education other than the universities and the university-equivalent higher technical institutes are referred to as *colegios* (colleges). This term can lead to some confusion, since the term *colegio* in Latin America is customarily a high school, and even in Mexico the term is sometimes used with this meaning.

Located as it is on the southern rim of the North American continent, Mexico probably receives a far larger number of university-level students from the United States and Canada than do all the other countries of Latin America combined. Ordinary tourist documentation is sufficient for students taking short courses of a semester or less in duration, and about a dozen United States universities conduct summer sessions in Mexico. A large number of Mexican institutions offer special study programs—some in the English language—and maintain special relationships with universities and higher educational organizations of the United States. In particular, several Mexican schools are members of the Southern Association of Colleges of the United States.

The National Autonomous University of Mexico operates a school for foreigners on a year-round basis with courses in the Spanish language and literature, history, anthropology, and technology, as well as non-academic courses in crafts, folklore, and music. Among its affiliated research institutions is the Center for Anglo-American Studies. The University of the Americas (its official name is in English) at Cholula in the state of Puebla is virtually a transplanted North American institution. It had its origins in Mexico City as a high school for the children of foreign residents, and in the early 1970s about half of its student body of 1,500 came from the United States.

The Allende Institute at San Miguel de Allende in the state of Guanajuato, formerly devoted to the study of fine arts at the graduate level, in the early 1970s added an undergraduate program designed for children of foreign residents and for Mexican students preparing for further study abroad. A large proportion of its courses are conducted in English, and its study program is approved by the United States Office of Education. The Institute of Iberoamerican Studies at Saltillo in the state of Coahuila offers instruction in English and courses leading to bachelor of arts and master of arts degrees.

The Iberoamerican University conducts summer courses in the English language, and the Anahuac University offers intensive courses leading to entrance to the University of Southern Illinois. Perhaps the most notable as well as the largest program for North American students, however, is conducted by the Autonomous University of Guadalajara, where as many as 3,000 medical students from the United States were expected to enroll for the fall semester in 1974.

In the mid-1970s nearly two-thirds of the applications for admission to United States medical schools were being refused, and schools of medicine in Europe that had formerly maintained a policy of ready acceptance of foreign students were becoming increasingly selective. In 1974 the Autonomous University of Guadalajara had more medical students from the United States than from any other foreign country. It maintained one of the largest United States medical student groups in existence. More than fifty visiting physicians from leading United States universities were to teach short courses in specialized fields, but most of the instruction was in the Spanish language, and the students were required to pay tuition fees that were high even by United States standards. A continued rise in the enrollment of students from the United States during the late 1970s, however, was expected.

The universities are presided over by rectors. In the state universities they are appointed by the governors of the states, but in the National Autonomous University of Mexico and the other autonomous institutions they are elected by the university councils. These councils, the highest internal governing bodies in both autonomous and state schools, are made up of elected representatives of the teaching and administrative staffs and student representatives. The proportion of student representation varies; it amounts to one-third of the voting membership in the National Autonomous University of Mexico but is as high as one-half in the state institutions.

Functionally, the universities are divided into faculties and schools. The faculty is an academic division comparable to the academic department in most North American universities, but it has more internal autonomy, offers students a complete course of study, and in some instances is made up of studies in a large number of related disciplines. The faculties of philosophy and letters, for example, are responsible for a wide range of programs in the humanities.

The school is similar to the faculty in composition; the faculty was originally distinguished from the school by virtue of its authority to grant advanced degrees, but this distinction appears to have become blurred with time. Private universities and the *colegios* tend to have more centralized internal organizations, and in some the administrative patterns resemble those of the academic departments in United States universities.

University courses of study vary from three to six or seven years in duration, but so large a majority are for five years that this number of years is considered standard. Many of the students are employed on a full-time or part-time basis, however, and additional years are often required for completion of the courses of study. Some institutions have academic schedules specifically designed for part-time students, whose days are evenly divided between school and work. The enrollments include many young people taking a single course, or a few courses, who do not plan to qualify for degrees.

Most of the institutions of higher education operate on a semester basis in which the school year commences in September and concludes in June. Some have other opening and closing dates, however, and in the mid-1970s there was talk of lengthening the school year as one means of accommodating the increasing demand for university admission. In 1974 the new Autonomous Metropolitan University opened in the Federal District on a trimester basis that would reduce the regular five-year course of study to four years. In the new university, classes were to be held in a morning *(matutino)* session commencing at 7:00 A.M. and an evening *(vespertino)* session concluding at 10:00 P.M. Because of the large number of part-time professors holding regular jobs in government and industry and the large number of working students, this system of early morning and late evening classes is customary in Mexican institutions of higher education.

During the middle years of the twentieth century, the most popular university studies were medicine, law, and—increasingly—engineering; and there was relatively little interest in the social sciences and the humanities. The trend in orientation, however, was already away from the traditional prestige disciplines and toward those increasingly in demand by the developing economy. Between 1940 and 1962 enrollments in medicine had declined from about 38 percent to 15 percent of the total; law enrollments declined from 20 to 13 percent, and enrollment in faculties of philosophy from 1.6 to 1.1 percent of the total. The proportion of the student body in schools of engineering had risen from 21 to 25 percent, however, and social science enrollments were up from 2 to more than 6 percent. In general these trends continued during the late 1960s, medical and law enrollments gaining at rates much slower than those of universities as a whole.

Enrollments in schools of engineering soared, however, and a still more rapid gain was registered in the social sciences faculties and schools where the principal courses were in economics, accounting, and business administration. In 1970 one-half of all the university and university-equivalent enrollments were in engineering and the social sciences; and these, plus law and medicine, represented nearly 80 percent of the total. Enrollments during the late 1960s and early 1970s, however, were not necessarily reflections of preferences. Medical and technical faculties and schools requiring a substantial outlay per student in laboratories, demonstration fees, and experiment material were finding it necessary to turn away qualified applicants while some of the less sought-after disciplines where the only need per student was a seat in a lecture hall had unfilled vacancies.

The retention rate of students in institutions of higher education is a matter for debate. On the basis of what appear to have been incomplete data, a major Mexico City newspaper reported that university graduates in 1973 represented only 15 percent of the original matriculants. The article led promptly to replies pointing out specific discrepencies in the claim, and a ranking SEP official in 1974 stated that 63 percent of the students in institutions of higher education were completing their courses of study. The figure, however, presumably included courses not leading to an undergraduate or equivalent degree and, perhaps, courses in the associated upper middle schools. In general, the completion rate appears to have been highest in medicine and in such fields as architecture and accounting, which prepare students for specific professions, and lowest in the more theoretical studies such as the humanities.

Teaching systems within the universities and other institutions of higher education vary widely, but a majority of the programs consist largely of lectures and note taking. Tutorial instruction is relatively rare, although it is employed in an increasing number of university seminars. In the late 1960s and early 1970s the system of teaching by lectures was under growing criticism as one in which the lecturer did little more than repeat what the student could find in books and one that minimized the amount of personal student-teacher communication. There seemed, however, to be little immediate prospect of an early reform in teaching methods during a period in which enrollments were increasing so rapidly and in which the bulk of the professorial staffs were professionals who spent only limited periods of time in the classrooms (see The Teaching Profession, this ch.).

LITERACY AND ADULT EDUCATION

The rate of literacy among Mexicans fifteen years of age and older rose from 59.4 percent in 1960 to 74.6 percent in 1970. It was highest among those between the ages of fifteen and nineteen and declined progressively in older age-groups to less than 50 percent among those aged sixty and over. The United Nations and most countries employ fifteen years as the base age in reporting adult literacy. The Mexican census of 1970 reported literacy of the population ten years of age and older, however, and previous censuses reported it on the basis of those six years of age and older. As a consequence, Mexican literacy rates officially reported frequently differ slightly from those just cited.

The degree of literacy varies in direct proportion to the size of the locality; it is highest in the large cities and lowest in the smallest and most remote hamlets. This pattern is modified somewhat, however, by the continuing infusion into the cities and towns of often illiterate migrants from the countryside. Literacy is highest in the Federal District and adjacent parts of the Valley of México. The rate is only moderately high in Central Mexico as a whole, however, because of the large rural population in that region. It is high in the North Pacific and North, particularly in the zones adjacent to the United States border, which are regions of large cities and scanty rural populations. It is generally lower in the Gulf Coast and is lowest in the South Pacific, a region where there are no large cities and the pattern of widely dispersed farm villages predominates.

The 1970 adult literacy rates for men and women were about 78 and 72 percent, respectively. There was no significant difference between the two sexes in the large cities, but male literacy predominated in smaller places and was substantially the higher of the two in the remote villages. A study made in about 1960 of a fairly large but remote and traditional Indian village of the South Pacific found that the enrollment of girls in the local three-grade school almost matched that of boys but that the effective literacy rate of male adults was about three times that of females. Men had tended to find some use for reading and writing in connection with travel to other localities for seasonal employment and through other means, but women had remained at home, and those who had acquired the skills of literacy had tended to lose them.

Although exposure to literacy training and the need for it increase with the size of the locality, the disadvantages of illiteracy in the urban environment are not insurmountable; and techniques developed for accommodating to illiteracy rather than eradicating it have acted to some extent as disincentives to learning to read and write. The increasing exposure to radio, television, and motion pictures has provided recreational outlets for illiterates, and symbols have been devised that are easy for illiterate people to understand. Many manufacturers have designed easily identified trademarks, for example, and laundries and dry cleaning shops have installed systems for marking clothing with colored yarn that make possible the hiring of illiterate workers.

At the time of the 1910 Revolution, the literacy rate probably did not exceed 15 percent. It had reached 37 percent by 1940, principally through the growth of the primary school system, supplemented in the country-side by the dedicated work of the cultural missions. The first countrywide literacy program commenced in 1944, when the government inaugurated a "one teach one" campaign in which each literate Mexican was required to teach one illiterate to read and write, a technique that claimed extension of literacy to 1.3 million people by 1947. Literacy training continued in various forms during succeeding years, and in 1970 about 1 million individuals were enrolled in 27,000 adult education centers.

In 1965 the SEP extended the scope of the program by inaugurating a radio and television training project called "Alfabetización," which by 1970 was broadcast over some 130 radio and television stations. Its basic guide, a free workbook called *I Can Do It*, outlined a series of lessons to be taken over a six-month period by radio classes and a four-month period by television viewers. The courses could be completed at home, but voluntary civic and fraternal organizations soon began to sponsor and organize classes in which they could be studied. By the end of 1968 some 2.5 million copies of the workbook had been distributed, and 60 percent of the students formally enrolled in the course had completed it. Perhaps optimistically, it was claimed that nearly all of these had learned to read and write at least at the third grade level.

The third grade level might not have been enough, although it was the minimum generally recognized by the world's educators as needed to instill permanent and functional literacy, particularly in rural cultural environments where access to and use of written material is limited. In a 1972 address, a ranking SEP officer stated that four years of primary school had been proved to be needed and that 7 million Mexicans who had attended school had not progressed beyond the third grade. In the late 1960s and early 1970s even in the largest urban centers it was still possible to find *evangelistas* (public letter writers) who charged the equivalent of eight cents for setting down a business letter and up to twenty cents for a love note.

Literacy training courses have often been combined with studies in the acquisition of basic education and practical skills by adults as well as by children, particularly in rural localities where the need has been greatest and the facilities the fewest. Rudimentary practical skills were taught in the new primary schools of the 1920s and 1930s, and the cultural missions provided guidance in handicrafts and hygiene as well as in reading and writing to people of all ages.

The opportunities for education of young adults as well as children in the regular school system substantially increased during the 1930s with the establishment of a large number of middle-level night schools limited to employed individuals and those over the age of fifteen. Night school enrollments declined after 1930 but, even at the primary school level, more than 250,000 students in regular schools were fifteen years of age or older in 1972. Age data are not available for enrollments in post-primary schools, but a large proportion of the students are regularly employed individuals in their late teens or older.

Apprenticeship programs have not contributed substantially to adult education. In 1970 it was determined that the existing system for training apprentices did not meet the country's expanding technical education needs, and new legislation was enacted requiring employers or groups of employers to organize training programs for their workers.

In stages during the early 1960s the National Productivity Center was organized as a joint venture between the government and private enterprise. Courses for the agricultural and services sector, as well as for industry, are offered to workers and employees at all levels and to young people not yet employed. Among the several branch operations established by the center, the Monterrey unit is reported to have been the most successful.

In 1968 the government inaugurated middle-school television classes offering a standard school curriculum but not considered part of the regular school program. By 1973, 39,000 students were reported to have completed the course of study, which was transmitted from a station in the Federal District and repeated by stations in seven states. A 1974 announcement that the service would be extended to all forty-three outlets of the national cultural television network, however, was immediately followed by complaints that the poor quality of the instruction offered was seriously weakening the program.

An informal kind of adult schooling was introduced in 1965 in the Chapultepec Park of Mexico City in the form of an open-air program teaching unskilled peasants means of becoming self-supporting. It promptly attracted municipal support, and by 1973 about 7,000 students were enrolled and paying a nominal fee to cover administrative costs. A more ambitious informal program was announced in 1974 by the National Council of Technical Education in a report stating that textbooks were being prepared for courses in middle-level technical education for people of all ages who were unable to attend school. The books were to be distributed at cost and would serve as the basis for study by groups meeting in homes and in improvised schoolrooms or out of doors; persons completing the program would be accepted by institutions of higher education.

A similar kind of program was being developed in 1973 and 1974 by the National Autonomous University of Mexico. Named the Open University and patterned on programs recently introduced in the United States and in Great Britain, it would include both upper middle and university courses of study and would lead to acquisition of an undergraduate or equivalent degree. No class attendance would be required, students would not be required to meet specific time schedules, and promotions would be based on computer-graded examinations. The only classrooms would be bulletin boards on which assignments, grades, and other necessary information would be posted.

THE TEACHING PROFESSION

In 1972 there were 13,000 kindergarten teachers, 196,000 teachers in primary schools, and 104,000 teachers in middle-level establishments. Women constituted 67 percent of the teachers in kindergartens, 61 percent in primary schools, and 35 percent in middle-level units.

The student-teacher ratio in 1972 was about thirty to one in kindergartens, forty-eight to one in primary schools, and fourteen to one at the middle level; since 1960 the ratio has declined in kindergartens and has remained stable in middle schools, where it compared favorably with ratios in other Latin American countries. In primary classes, however, it edged upward and in 1972 was among the highest in Latin America. In a summary report concerning the status of Mexican education prepared by the SEP for a 1971 United Nations Educational, Scientific and Cultural Organization publication, it was stated that there was no lack of teachers in primary schools. This assertion appeared to be at odds with the large number of primary students the average teacher was required to instruct. In 1973, however, the minister of public education reported that some 2,000 qualified teachers were without jobs. The volume and rate of enrollment growth during recent years has been such that neither funds to pay the instructional personnel nor school-rooms to accommodate them could be found. During the first seven months of 1974, however, it was reported that 60,000 new teachers had been appointed, as compared with 37,500 during the preceding period of six years.

Qualified *(titulado)* primary teachers are graduates of the middle-level normal schools or qualify through in-service instruction in a special normal school established for that purpose. In particular, a large number of teachers in rural localities have been unqualified; the proportion declined only from 90 percent in 1932 to 71 percent in 1960, but the rate of in-service training accelerated during the 1960s and, by 1972, 97 percent of all primary teachers were reported to have the requisite qualifications.

Middle-level teaching personnel were trained in the faculties of philosophy and letters at the National Autonomous University of Mexico and several other universities and at the higher teacher training schools in courses four years or more in duration. About 79 percent were qualified in 1965, but rapidly rising enrollments in the middle-level schools made it necessary to employ increasing numbers of unqualified instructors during the late 1960s, and in 1972 only slightly over 50 percent met the required standards.

The staffing of rural schools has presented a particular problem. Teachers have been reluctant to accept assignments in the more remote Indian villages, where the amenities of life have been minimal and where it has frequently been necessary to teach students the Spanish language as well as reading and writing. The teacher has traditionally been a poorly educated schoolmaster whose wife informally assists in the classroom assignments. As the education system has gradually spread in the remote countryside, however, more adequate school facilities have been installed, and a progressively warmer and more cooperative attitude toward the teacher has developed. In the early 1970s a majority of the new primary teachers appointed were assigned to rural units, and in 1973 some 200 new bilingual normal school graduates were added to the staffs of rural boarding schools and technical training centers in areas with predominantly Indian populations. It appeared that in the mid-1970s the average student-teacher ratio in country schools approximately equaled that in urban establishments, a rarity in Latin American educational systems.

The Mexican government stresses the right of the schoolteacher to be considered a professional. Only to a limited extent are primary teachers recognized as having professional status, however, and recognition accorded to some middle-level personnel is based more on their possession of university-level education than on their school assignments. Teaching provides a large number of jobs for women in a labor force that offers relatively few opportunities for female employment, however, and the Mexican educational system provides unusual incentives as well as challenges to dedicated teachers. The relatively generous supply of free textbooks in primary classes, the responsibility given to teachers in making student performance evaluation, and a high degree of latitude permitted in planning the content of course material make it possible for the teacher to play an important and personalized part in the education of his or her students. In rural localities the role of the teacher is a particularly demanding one, but it is also one in which the teacher may achieve a position of great community importance and prestige.

Teachers are appointed by the SEP and, after appointment, can be removed only for insubordination, lack of probity, scandalous behavior, or conviction by a criminal court. Benefits to which they are entitled include medical care, maternity leave, eligibility for retirement at any age after thirty years of service, and life insurance.

A 1971 publication quoted the SEP as listing the beginning monthly salary at 1,150 pesos for qualified and 780 pesos for unqualified primary teachers. Beginning middle-school teachers, many of whom worked on a part-time basis, received from 26 to 30 pesos per hour. In addition to seniority salary increases, personnel at both levels received compensatory allowances amounting to up to 100 percent of their basic salaries for assignment to remote or unhealthy localities or to localities where the cost of living was unusually high. In the early 1970s representatives of teacher unions complained that salaries were so low as to encourage defection to other professions, but in 1973 the minister of public education expressed to a meeting of primary teachers the belief that salaries were at levels sufficiently high to be attractive to entering personnel.

According to a statistical summary prepared by the Organization of American States, nearly 28,000 teachers were employed in institutions of higher education, not including the teaching staffs in attached middle-level schools. More than two-thirds were in degree-granting institutions, and about one-tenth were women.

Although a large proportion of the teachers, particularly in the universities, hold graduate degrees, there is no regular program for their academic preparation, and procedures for their recruitment and appointment vary. In the public institutions, professors are seldom employed on a full-time basis. In the 1974 school year at the National Autonomous University of Mexico, for example, about 1,100 of the teachers were career professors (profesores de carrera), and 17,000 were part-time personnel (profesores de asignatura), a category made up of civil servants, young professionals, and newly graduated individuals. Considerable prestige attaches to possession of a teaching appointment, and a part-time staff can be assembled at relatively little cost.

University teaching is traditionally regarded as a part-time occupation throughout Latin America, but in Mexico some of the private universities have been able to afford the cost of assembling their staffs largely on a full-time basis. In particular, the Monterrey Institute of Technology and Advanced Studies maintains a full-time staff with salaries comparable to those offered in industry and government.

Educators recognize the need for securing a larger number of professors devoting all or a large part of their time to teaching, but an important aspect of the traditional Latin American reliance on the part-time university professor is the high value placed on the contribution to education that only the professor who also practices his profession can give. Among the goals of a reform program initiated by the National Autonomous University of Mexico in 1966 was attainment by 1980 of a regime in which 40 percent of all class hours would be presided over by career professors, a proportion apparently considered optimum.

CHAPTER 7

LIVING CONDITIONS

Mexico during the mid-1970s was moving toward the economic and social goals of the 1910 Revolution, but they had yet to be fully achieved. The growing urban middle class and the families of the better paid skilled workers were able to acquire the necessities and luxuries associated with a relatively high standard of living. Poorer urban families and most of the rural population, however, continued to live close to the subsistence level.

Although the per capita diet was better than adequate, malnutrition was common among lower income groups and was a major contributory cause of the heavy rate of mortality among young children. A serious housing shortage affected town and country dwellers alike, but its greatest impact was felt by the countless lower income urban families who lived in communities of jerry-built shacks on the fringes of the cities. Public health and welfare programs were available to most city dwellers. They were available only to a very limited extent in the countryside, but 1973 legislation had extended broad social security coverage to the rural sector, and an extensive network of rural health units was planned.

A single element common to the living conditions of all Mexicans is the degree to which traditional customs and practices survive. While subsistence farmers and the urban poor live through necessity on a diet consisting largely of the traditional corn and beans, well-to-do families often eat dishes based on corn and beans through preference. The urban well-to-do as well as the rural subsistence farmers continue sometimes to wear traditional costumes and articles of apparel, and the most prosperous urban housewife still visits the herb market to purchase an ancient herbal remedy. As a consequence of the traditional closeness of family ties, the family unit in Mexican society as a whole provides much of its own medical care, welfare protection, and recreation. Folk songs and dances are universally popular, and the countless traditional fiestas celebrated throughout the country are important recreational activities for all Mexicans.

DIET AND NUTRITION

During 1969 the average daily diet included more than 2,600 calories and seventy-two grams of protein, nearly twenty-three of them of animal origin. These averages exceed internationally recognized minimum standards and are considerably higher than the Latin American average.

There had been a substantial improvement in the diet; some thirty years earlier the average consumption of calories had been estimated at no more than 1,700 per day.

The diets of some persons are more ample and nutritious than the average, and the diets of many are deficient. It was estimated by an international agency that during the 1960s half or more of the population suffered from some degree of malnutrition. The condition affected many lower income families in urban localities but was most prevalent in the countryside, where little animal protein was available and half or more of the farms did not produce enough food to satisfy the needs of the farmer and his family. In addition, poor distribution and storage facilities limited the amount of food available. In 1973 the National Council of Science and Technology estimated that 30 percent of the crops and perishables produced were lost in the field.

Corn and beans are Mexico's basic foods and make up most of the diet of the poor; traditional dishes based on them are frequently enjoyed by the well-to-do. Beans, of which there are many varieties, supply carbohydrates and are rich in vegetable protein. They are the principal or only source of protein for the many families unable to afford meat. Corn is all important, and some writers contend that Central Mexico was first settled because corn grew well there. In 1970 corn constituted more than three-fourths of all grain consumed. A moderate wheat and rice consumption is increasing, but half of all Mexican farmland is devoted to corn, and without it half of the country's population would be in danger of starvation.

Mexicans are not heavy meat eaters, and some can afford to eat meat only on rare occasions. According to the 1970 population census, about 20 percent of the population had eaten no meat during the week that preceded the census, and doctors working in the countryside observe that many countryfolk eat meat only on the local saint's day. In the early 1970s it was estimated that one-third of all meat was consumed in the Federal District. Beef is the most popular meat but, except in the modern urban butcher shops, it is freshly killed and is not cut in the prime ribs, porterhouses, and sirloins known in the United States. Other meats include lamb, mutton, surprisingly good goat meat, and venison from the Yucatán Peninsula and some other localities.

During the precensus week in 1970 only 30 percent of the population had eaten fish, and the per capita consumption was less than eight pounds annually. The country's lakes and rivers provide excellent freshwater varieties, and the waters of both coasts abound in many kinds of saltwater fish and crustaceans. Government officials argue that the low fish consumption results from ignorance and poor marketing and distribution systems. In the mid-1970s a concerted public effort to increase the national seafood consumption was in progress.

During the course of the 1970 precensus week 23 percent of the population had not eaten eggs, and 32 percent had not drunk milk. During the early 1970s the per capita egg consumption was a little more than 130 eggs annually, and the per capita milk intake was a little less than half a pint daily. Both rates were fairly high in comparison with Latin American averages and had been on the rise. The increasing milk consumption during the early 1970s caused demand to exceed supply, and it became necessary to import substantial quantities in dry and evaporated form.

Although the Mexican consumption of garden vegetables is light by United States standards, it is relatively high by the standards of Latin America. Most important are vegetables belonging to the squash family. The traditional Indian garden is one that grows corn, beans, and squash. Also of particular importance are tomatoes: the tomato is believed to have originated in Mexico (see ch. 2). In addition, great use is made of onions, garlic, and chili peppers. Green vegetables are primarily used as ingredients in dressings and in soups and stews rather than served separately.

Numerous fruits are consumed in moderate quantity. They include temperate climate products, such as pears and peaches, as well as pineapples, mangoes, and less known items such as *zapotes*, the fruit of the tree that produces chicle for chewing gum.

An annual per capita consumption of nearly eighty pounds of sugar during the early 1970s made Mexico one of Latin America's heavier consumers. It was a relatively inexpensive commodity, and low-income families consumed almost as much sugar as more prosperous ones.

Mexican cookery in general is a blend of the Indian and the Spanish. The most popular food, however, is the tortilla, originated by the pre-Hispanic Indians. It is made of dried corn kernels, slaked in a mild lime solution, ground to a paste, and hand-patted into a thin cake baked on a metal sheet. It can be eaten like bread or used as the basis of an endless variety of dishes. A taco is a tortilla filled with chopped meat or other ingredient, then rolled and fried. A tamale is similarly prepared but placed in corn husks or banana leaves and steamed. The enchilada is a taco covered with chili sauce or other hot condiment and sprinkled with grated cheese. Meat, cheese, tomatoes, chili peppers, onions, and garlic are the most common additions to the dishes based on the tortilla, but sweets are also sometimes used.

Dishes based on beans are as characteristically Mexican as those based on tortillas. They also take many forms, but commonly the beans are reduced to a paste and served with rice.

The Mexican farmer rises before the sun and works in the fields for several hours before breakfast, which consists of a corn and bean dish that is brought to him by his wife or eaten cold. It is accompanied by coffee or a hot cornmeal drink called *atole*. The main meal is eaten in the middle of the day and may include a stew, beans, and tortillas. Supper, eaten in the early evening, is a matter of leftovers and a beverage. Tortillas take the place of bread. During the 1960s and early 1970s bread made of wheat was increasingly favored as a substitute for

165

tortillas. The traditional thin corn pancake remained valuable as a substitute for a spoon, however, it could be folded and used for scooping food from the bowl.

In well-to-do urban homes breakfast is served from 7:00 A.M. to 9:00 A.M. It is a substantial meal that frequently includes eggs, a circumstance unusual in Latin America, where the light continental breakfast of a breadstuff and coffee or tea is customary. The principal meal of the day is served in the early afternoon. In well-to-do homes it consists of three or four courses, including a soup, a starchy dish of rice or pasta, a vegetable, and a light dessert. The heavy midday meal probably results from the fact that the country's civilization evolved in the high elevation of Central Mexico, where food digests slowly. A heavy evening meal at these elevations would be less conducive to a comfortable night's sleep.

Between 5:00 P.M. and 7:00 P.M. the *merienda* (snack), a light meal consisting of a beverage and various sweet rolls of the country, is eaten. Increasingly, however, it is being replaced by a simple cup of coffee or an aperitif. Supper, served between 8:00 P.M. and 10:00 P.M., is a light meal, even in the more prosperous homes.

The traditional Mexican intoxicant is pulque, or cactus beer, made from the juice of the maguey cactus. The juice ferments quickly to form a beverage containing alcohol. It is inexpensive, takes the edge off hunger and misery, and is reputed to contain vitamins that supplement an otherwise inadequate diet. Pulque must be drunk fresh because fermentation continues and the liquid cannot successfully be corked. *Pulquerías* (shops selling pulque) are gradually disappearing from the towns and villages as beer consumption mounts. Mexico produces several excellent varieties of beer, and 1971 beer consumption amounted to about thirty quarts per person. The national distilled liquor, tequila, is also made from the maguey cactus. Once a very strong raw liquor, it is now carefully controlled and has an alcoholic content of 88 or 92 proof. Numerous mixed drinks are concocted from it, but traditionally it is taken straight, followed by a pinch of salt and a taste from a wedge of lime.

CLOTHING

In the large cities the dress of both sexes is conservative and resembles that worn in the cities of Europe and North America. Colors tend to be subdued, and sports clothes and casual wear are reserved for resort areas and weekend outings. Men wear coats, ties, and hats. Women customarily go bareheaded, a custom that dates from the Revolution of 1910, when the wearing of hats by women was considered European and ostentatious.

Younger urban women wear colorful sweaters, suits, and semitailored dresses. Because of the closeness of family ties, older women are frequently seen in the unrelieved black of mourning. Some widows wear black for the remainder of their lives and, because Mexican women tend to marry men considerably their senior, widowhood is often long.

Some traditional garments are still worn. Women of all classes wear the rebozo, a graceful stole or scarf woven of silk or cotton. The well-to-do wear their beautiful silk rebozos as evening shawls; those of moderate income wear them as an alternative to a sweater; and the poor wear them as an overcoat shawl, as a protection for the head against the sun, or as a convenient way of carrying the baby. The colorful serape, the bulkier man's equivalent of the female serape, is also worn in all parts of Mexico but is less frequently seen in urban environments.

National costumes for both sexes continue to be worn on ceremonial and other special occasions and to be a cherished part of the wardrobe of those who can afford them. The *charro*, or gentlemen cowboy, costume is worn by ranchers but also by business and professional men dressing up for an occasion. It consists of a short bolero jacket with decorative buttons, a flowing bow tie, high-waisted and flared trousers, high-heeled boots, and a wide-brimmed sombrero. *Charro* is a somewhat opprobrious word in dictionary Spanish, but it is an elegant one in Mexico, and the *charro* costume is worn at the most elegant and festive of times.

The traditional female costume is the *china poblana*, named for the perhaps mythical Chinese princess said to have been brought in captivity to the city of Puebla and to have captivated the people of that colonial city. It, too, is worn for special occasions. It consists of a green cotton skirt with red yoke, an elaborately embroidered white blouse, and a rebozo of green, red, and white stripes. These are the national colors.

Traditional Indian dress is seen with increasing rarity in urban localities, but it can still often be observed in the more remote countryside, and modified traditional costume is still common among rural visitors to towns and sometimes among urban migrants. Still generally worn is the straw hat that was derived from the low-crowned felt headgear of the Spanish conquerors, but it has acquired distinctively regional characteristics. In Veracruz, for example, its high crown and relatively narrow brim give it the appearance of a homburg; in Michoacán it is low crowned, flaring-brimmed, and decorated with ribbons.

The stereotype of the Mexican countryman is one in which his costume consists of a wide sombrero and white, pajama-like shirt and trousers. It remains a true picture, although blue jeans or chino pants are also often worn and the pajama-like garb has numerous regional variations. One of the most striking of these occurs on the Yucatán Peninsula, where the white shirt is a *guayabera*, a starched and pleated garment worn with a colorful scarf at the neck. Baggy pantaloons complete the costume. The costume of rural Chiapas is made up of short pants, an embroidered shirt, and a short wool jacket fastened at the waist by a leather belt.

A common traditional outergarment worn by countrywomen of southern Mexico is the *huipil*, a kind of tunic that is usually worn long and is often heavily embroidered. Colored and embroidered blouses are also common, and there is always a rebozo. The color of the garments, the amount and kind of embroidery, and the way a woman drapes her rebozo indicate her regional origin.

In the mid-1970s it was still possible to see Indians belonging to half a dozen different tribes visiting the open-air market in towns of Chiapas dressed in as many distinctive traditional costumes. In general, however, the colorful traditional garb tends increasingly to be reserved for fiestas and other special occasions and to be worn more frequently by women than by men. Factory-made clothing or garments made in the home from factory-produced materials are increasingly worn by both sexes, although cotton and wool are still spun and woven by hand in rural areas where Indian culture predominates.

The peasant mestizo woman migrating from country to town may continue for some time to wear her customary rural clothing. For men, the transition in costume is quicker. In order to find work, particularly in an office position, it may be necessary for a male urban migrant to acquire an inexpensive suit with lapels and creased trousers as a replacement for the pajama-like garb of the countryside.

During the years after World War II the factory production of shoes increased at a rate many times greater than that of population growth, and a footwear survey conducted as part of the 1970 population census found that 80 percent of the population wore shoes, 13 percent wore huaraches—the traditional Mexican sandals—and 7 percent went barefoot. It appears likely, however, that the peasant owning a single pair of shoes reserved for special occasions classified himself as a shoe wearer when, in fact, as a matter of convenience and comfort he customarily either wore the traditional huaraches or went barefoot. Huaraches of families of more modest income frequently have soles made of old automobile tires. One observer during the late 1960s speculated that one-half of the nation walked on worn-out car treads.

HOUSING

A total of 8.3 million housing units were counted in the 1970 census, compared with 6.4 million in 1960. The increase of 1.9 million, or about 30 percent of the 1960 total, was less than the rate of population growth during the period. Moreover, much of the new construction appears to have been in the form of flimsy shacks built on the outskirts of the cities by urban migrants.

Most of the housing units counted in 1970 were small. Nearly 40 percent consisted of a single room. Some 29 percent had two rooms: 18 percent had three rooms; and only 14 percent had four rooms or more. These statistics did not include service spaces, such as hallways, porches, bathrooms, and kitchens.

Since more than two-thirds of the population lived in one- or two-room units, the reported average 1970 occupancy rate of 5.8 persons per unit indicated considerable crowding. These crowded conditions were in large measure the consequence of a severe housing shortage, but in part they resulted from social causes. Mexican families are large, and it is common practice for grown and sometimes married children to remain in the parental home. In addition, room is frequently made for uncles, aunts, and other relatives.

The extent of the housing shortage was officially estimated at 4 million units in 1970. Overall, the shortage was about equally severe in urban and in rural localities. In the countryside, however, it was qualitative in the sense that it consisted principally of occupied units that were considered unfit for habitation. In the cities and towns it was principally quantitative; there was a severe absolute shortage in the number of units needed to house the fast-growing population.

In Mexico City, where the shortage was most severe, it was both qualitative and quantitative. An enormous number of new units were needed, and among those in existence it was calculated in 1970 that only 16 percent were fully adequate. An additional 13 percent were adequate in construction, repair, and sanitary facilities; but they were too small to accommodate the number of people living in them. Some 64 percent were considered deficient, and the remainder were considered unfit for human habitation.

About 65 percent of the exterior walls of the housing units in existence in 1970 were constructed of brick or adobe. Wood followed with 16 percent and clay with 5 percent. Stone and other materials made up the balance. Although stone was of limited statistical importance, the lava rock available in Mexico City and some other localities is an excellent building material and is used in many of the finer houses.

More than 34 percent of the roofs were of cement, and 21 percent were of oval tile and similar materials. Over 15 percent were of palm and thatch, and 11 percent were wooden. Various materials made up the remainder. Over 40 percent of the floors were earthen. Specific data were not available on other floor materials used, but many of the more substantial dwellings have stone or tile floors, and cement is replacing earth in the floors of many of the newer working-class residences.

Adobe is the traditional rural building material. It is made simply in the villages by mixing mud with straw and shaping the bricks to wooden molds that are placed in the sun to dry. They are then arranged in truncated pyramids around which branches are stacked and ignited to fire the sun-dried bricks. Adobe walls make dwellings resistant both to summer heat and to winter cold. Some adobe houses more than a century old are still in excellent condition, and an authority at the National Autonomous University of Mexico has urged that the use of an improved adobe brick rather than the other materials currently being used would go far toward alleviating the housing shortage, particularly in rural areas.

According to a paper prepared for a 1973 meeting of Latin American housing authorities, 38.8 percent of the Mexican homes had running water inside the housing unit, 10.6 percent had water outside the home but within the building, and 11.6 percent had easy access to a public tap or well. The remaining 39.0 percent had no specific source of supply. In some urban localities, the easy-access-facility included baths or showers with hot water. Some 32 percent of the units had bathrooms with toilets, and 43 percent had sewage-facility connections.

The 1970 census found that 74 percent of the units had cooking facilities inside the home. Some 44 percent of these used wood or coal, 44 percent used gas or electricity, and 12 percent used oil. Nearly 59 percent of all units had electrical connections. The actual number with electricity was probably somewhat higher, since the shanty dwellers living on the fringes of the cities are adept at tapping electric lines.

The two basic traditional styles of housing in Mexico are Spanish and indigenous in origin, the former predominating in cities and towns and the latter predominating in the countryside. With a few exceptions, both the materials and the construction methods employed have been in use for centuries. Newer houses tend to be in different styles, but many examples of the older architecture remain.

The traditional urban house consists of several rooms opening on a central patio, much used by the family and often containing a flower garden. Each room is designed for a specific use, such as sleeping or the preparation of food. Although the houses built in this traditional Spanish style are often large, they seldom exceed two stories in height. They permit a maximum of sunshine and circulating of air, and their thick walls provide protection against heat and cold.

In the older neighborhoods of Mexico City and the other large centers there are still some Victorian houses with turrets and stained glass windows. Among the modern houses the most popular of the styles is one developed in Mexico but borrowed by California and known internationally as Californian. The houses, varying in size, are set back from the street, have one or two stories, are finished in stucco, and have oval tile roofing.

The massive old urban residences are dwarfed by the increasing number of high-rise structures. Apartment living is increasing, but in Central Mexico it is limited by the vulnerability of that region to serious and frequent earthquakes. In the mid-1970s the likelihood of earth tremors in Mexico City generally limited housing construction to five stories. Architects, however, have apparently solved the capital city's vulnerability to earthquakes by placing the newer high-rise buildings on great subterranean caissons that float the structures in the watery subsoil (see ch. 2).

In Mexico City, in particular, the old mansions in the downtown area have tended to deteriorate into *vecindades*, or tenements. In a 1974 issue, a Mexico City newspaper estimated that 1 million residents of the Federal District lived in these old buildings. Dwellings of ten to fifteen rooms have become occupied by as many families, with communal baths and, sometimes, communal cooking facilities. The inflow of migrants from the countryside has increased the demand for these inner-city slums, and the progress of conversion of old mansions into tenements has been accompanied by a process of tacking on additional rooms to the existing structures. Inner-city tenements are most prevalent in Mexico City, but they exist also in the other major centers. In Guanajuato, for example, a sixteenth-century inn and the old house that was the birthplace of Diego Rivera have become tenements.

The newer and more numerous of the slum or substandard neighborhoods are suburban. In some cases the occupants of the properties are owners or renters, and in others they are squatters. In all cases the housing units are flimsily built of scrap or substandard materials, and public services are deficient or lacking. The communities are referred to by such names as *ciudades perdidas* (lost cities) or *colonias proletarias* (proletarian neighborhoods). Groups of squatters often move into unoccupied areas and erect their shanties almost overnight. As a consequence they are known as *paracaidistas* (parachutists).

There are various estimates of the number of people living in these communities. According to a 1972 estimate there were 657,000 squatters in Mexico City, 86,000 in Monterrey, and an overall squatter population making up 7 percent of the urban total. Newspaper reports in 1974 estimated that 500 *ciudades perdidas* and an uncounted number of *colonias proletarias* occupied 40 percent of the area of metropolitan Mexico City and had a total of 4 million inhabitants. It was also reported that 80 percent of the people of the fast-growing Pacific coast city of Mazatlán lived in improvised homes.

The traditional rural dwelling is an adobe rectangle that may or may not be divided into two or more rooms. It has an earthen floor and a roof of palm thatch or other material readily available locally. Glass is prohibitively expensive for the lower income farm family, and as a consequence windows are usually lacking in places with colder climates. The houses of shopowners and other particularly prosperous village residents have several rooms, including a kitchen, an outhouse, and a simple brick or tile floor. These houses are usually close to the center of the village, and some manufactured materials are used in their construction.

There is little variety in basic construction patterns in a single village or locality, but regional differences are pronounced. The typical adobe walls and flat roofs of villages in the Valley of México are located adjacent to a highland zone in which stone and timber walls and split-log roofs are common. In another adjacent zone the walls are made of logs fitted in log cabin style, and the roofs are of fired tile. In general, tile roofing is possible only where timber for a strong roof support is locally available. In barren portions of the North and North Pacific regions where heavy timber is scarce, a traditional form of architecture involves roofs made of closely laid willow branches over which several inches of earth are packed.

Still other traditional forms of rural housing include an oval wattle and daub dwelling in areas that were occupied by the Mayans, houses in tropical localities with walls of lumber or bamboo separated to permit free passage of air, and the *jacales* of Indians in the South Pacific region that are little more than lean-tos. The simplest of all rural housing units, however, are those of certain Indians in the Sierra Madre Oriental range who live in caves that are sometimes extended by stone verandas.

Although the housing shortage has caused some inconvenience for the well-to-do, it has not constituted a serious problem for them. In 1974 the Mexico City press carried numerous advertisements for the sale of condominium high-rise apartment buildings in the hills surrounding Mexico City and attractive new suburban houses. The principal impact of the shortage was felt by families of limited income, and the traditional attitude of business had been one of approving the concept of low-cost housing but of opposing efforts to force business organizations to finance it.

After World War II the old attitude began to change, and during the 1960s the business community showed an increased willingness to participate financially. Government pressure was increasing, but there was also an increased awareness that good housing would contribute to political stability and good labor relations. Businessmen in Monterrey had begun to build homes for their workmen in cooperation with a government agency, and in the late 1960s the Center for Promotion of Housing was created by the National Chamber of the Construction Industry and supported by business leaders.

This venture proved to be abortive, probably because a new labor law, enacted in 1970, required that employers provide adequate housing for their workers by 1973. The business community protested, and the provision was later rescinded in legislation substituting a 5-percent payroll tax to be paid by employers. The funds generated by this tax were to be used for public housing construction by the Institute for the National Fund for Worker Housing (Instituto del Fondo Nacional de la Vivienda para los Trabajadores—INFONAVIT), which was created by the same legislation. Worker, employer, and government representatives made up the general assembly of INFONAVIT.

In the early 1970s most of the public housing program projects were located on the fringe of the major urban localities, particularly in the vicinity of Mexico City. In 1972 it was reported that over half of the land acquired by a government agency for housing projects was in the Federal District, and most of the remainder was in or close to other large centers.

Public housing programs have been focused primarily on the construction of low-cost housing for families with moderate incomes. The poorest urban families and the bulk of the migrants of the countryside have had so little income that it has been impossible to provide housing for them on anything but a charity basis. Between the mid-1920s and the mid-1960s no more than 150,000 homes for low-income families were constructed, and in 1970 the National Bank of Public Works and Services (Banco Nacional de Obras y Servicios Públicos—BNOSP) reported that 46 percent of the families living in the Federal District had incomes too low to permit them to purchase units in the public housing projects then in progress.

The BNOSP pointed out, however, that it would be psychologically undesirable as well as financially impossible to attempt to place the urban migrants in the closely spaced individual housing units or in apartments. The migrants preferred to remain in the suburban slum communities, where there was some space in which household animals could be kept. Instead, the BNOSP was assisting the inhabitants of the suburban slums to improve their shanties by such measures as offering inexpensive prefabricated bathroom and kitchen units that could be attached to the existing dwellings.

In the mid-1970s the rate of public housing construction appeared to be on the increase, but the bulk of the new building remained in the private sector, where 220,000 houses had been constructed in 1970 alone. INFONAVIT had been launched in 1972 with an ambitious target of 100,000 units a year. Its initial activities had been slowed by bureaucratic delay, however, and despite the accumulation of a fund equivalent to more than US$300 million, in mid-1974 it was reported to have completed only 20,000 units since 1972 and to have an additional 80,000 at some stage of financing or construction. INFONAVIT was the largest of the public housing agencies, but several others were active in the field. Among the others was a program established in the Federal District to provide dwellings for low-income workers who did not qualify for INFONAVIT participation. In general, the increase in the housing shortage seemed to be slowing, but it had not yet been reversed.

HEALTH

Medical Personnel and Facilities

In the early 1970s Mexico's medical personnel were generally well trained, and hospitals and outpatient facilities were generally adequate. The number of both in relation to the number of people in the country, however, no more than approximated the average for the countries of Middle America and was substantially lower than the average for South America.

Personnel and facilities were heavily concentrated in the large urban centers, and in much of the countryside no modern medical care was available. Even in the cities, however, the care available was not always fully utilized. The urban migrant occupying a job covered by a social security medical program might visit a social security hospital only for a required physical examination or in order to establish eligibility for work-accident benefits. At other times he might rely on ministrations within his home or visit a neighborhood pharmacist or a medicinal herb market.

The number of Mexicans with ready access to modern medical care is a matter for debate. In 1974 one Mexico City press article stated that it was available to about 35 million people, a little more than half the population. Another, however, stated that the number of doctors must be doubled and the number of hospital beds quadrupled in order to match the standards of developed countries.

Workers in private industry and their dependents receive care supplied by the Mexican Social Security Institute (Instituto Mexicano de Seguro Social—IMSS), which maintains its own system of personnel and facilities. Government workers are covered by a separate system, and the government-owned Mexican Petroleum and the armed forces provide their own services. Persons not eligible for care under any other government program may receive free attention, where available, from personnel and facilities of the Ministry of Health and Welfare. Some large business enterprises have their own medical programs, however, and some people who can afford to do so rely on private medical personnel and facilities, either directly or through one of several private health insurance programs similar to those in operation in the United States.

Medicine is an ancient profession in Mexico. Sculptured figures that long predate the Spanish conquest show trepanning operations, and there is some evidence that cesarean deliveries were made. Medicine is traditionally one of the most respected professions in Mexico and one of the most sought after courses of study in the universities. The number of doctors in practice increased from 24,000 in 1966 to 29,000 in 1970. About 75 percent were employed in the public sector. Homeopathic medicine is popular throughout Mexico, and there are numerous homeopathic doctors. The National Polytechnical Institute offers a course of study in homeopathic medicine, and there is a homeopathic hospital in Mexico City.

In the early 1970s there were more than 150 public and private maternity and pediatric care facilities in Mexico City alone, and more than 10 percent of all practicing physicians in the country were either obstetricians or pediatricians, more than in any other specialty. The membership in the medical corps included specialists in all major fields, however, and in early 1974 the chief of clinical instruction at a major university expressed concern that a sufficient number of general practitioners were no longer being trained.

During the late 1960s and early 1970s the proportion of university matriculants enrolling in the six-year course in medicine was on the decline. The actual number increased; however, classrooms were crowded, and laboratories and demonstration and experimental equipment were in short supply. About twenty of the universities maintain medical schools, including a school of homeopathic medicine at the

174

National Polytechnical Institute. The largest and most prestigious is in the National Autonomous University of Mexico. The fast-growing medical school is at the Autonomous University of Guadalajara. It attracted particular attention during the mid-1970s because of the large number of students from the United States; as many as 3,000 were expected to enroll for the school year beginning in late 1974 (see ch. 6).

Medical students are required to serve a term of duty in rural medical facilities, and in 1974 the minister of health and welfare announced plans for recruiting 1,000 doctors annually to work in poverty-stricken sections of the countryside. Young doctors, however, are reluctant to take up rural practices. The amenities of life are relatively few, the shortage of modern laboratories and equipment in the few rural facilities limits the extent to which professional competence can be improved, and the extent to which rural people continue to rely on traditional medical practices limits the demand for their services.

Although numerous universities offer five-year courses of study in dentistry, there is little demand for dentists in Mexico, and the ratio of 0.7 dentists per 10,000 of the population in 1968 was considerably below the average for Latin America. A large majority practice in the major cities, and most of their patients are well-to-do. Lower income people visiting a dentist usually require extractions. The limited demand for dental care, however, may in part result from the fact that most Mexicans have good teeth. The calcium contained in the lime solution added to the corn kernels in the grinding of cornmeal may be an explanation for the firm, white teeth that are often cited as a Mexican attribute (see Diet and Nutrition, this ch.).

Nurses are trained in nursing high schools and in university programs. The regular university course of study is three years in duration; a fourth year is required for a licentiate, the equivalent of a bachelor's degree.

There were about 9,000 graduate nurses and 40,000 nursing auxiliaries in practice during 1968. The numbers, as proportions of the total population, would be regarded as seriously inadequate in other North American and European countries, but in almost all of Latin America nursing has yet to be fully recognized as a profession, is poorly paid, and has only limited attraction for young women. There were indications, however, both that this attitude was changing and that the number of nurses was increasing rapidly in Mexico during the early 1970s. The number of schools of nursing in the universities had increased to a point at which it approximately equaled the number of university medical schools. In 1974 it was announced that 1,300 additional midwives had completed training in an intensive program and that the social insurance medical program for government workers had during the past year increased its nursing staff by 67 percent to a total of 5,000.

In 1969 the 4,721 hospital units in the country had a total of 69,494 beds. Many of the units were health centers with a few hospital beds. The number of beds per 1,000 of the population was 6.6 in Mexico City and

1.5 in the remainder of the country. A large majority of the hospitals are in the public sector. The relatively few private hospitals provide service at rates far below those charged in the United States; in the early 1970s the full cost of a private room was comparable to that charged for a room in a good Mexico City hotel.

As part of a ten-year national health plan inaugurated in late 1974, the hospitals and sanatoriums operated by the two social security systems and the facilities of decentralized government agencies such as Mexican Petroleum were integrated in a nationwide system. Activities of private hospitals accepting social security beneficiaries as patients were to be coordinated with it.

The oldest existing hospital in the Americas, the Jesús Nazareno Hospital in Mexico City, was founded by Hernán Cortés and maintained by an endowment in his will. The largest hospital in the country is the great Medical Center of Mexico City maintained by the IMSS. It is a complex consisting of laboratories, research centers, and a chain of eight hospital units. Each is concerned with a particular form of illness, and the units have from 100 to 1,000 beds. The most extensive of the several medical facilities under construction in the mid-1970s was the "city of health" that was to be associated with the Autonomous University of Guadalajara. Scheduled for completion in 1980, it is to include a chain of hospitals, doctors' offices, classroom facilities, and the administrative offices of the university's medical school.

In 1974 the Ministry of Health and Welfare reported that there were 100 urban, 500 suburban, and 1,500 rural health centers, which offered an assortment of outpatient medical services. The available human resources were insufficient to permit construction of health centers in all rural localities, but the current health plan called for construction of a new kind of unit, a *casa de salud* (literally, a house of health), in each of the country's 12,500 rural communities with populations of between 500 and 2,500 people. These units were to furnish limited care including such services as first aid, simple medications, and attention to normal deliveries.

Health Hazards and Preventive Medicine

In 1971 some 37.9 percent of all deaths reported in the country resulted from infections and parasitic and respiratory diseases; 15.3 percent resulted from ailments of the circulatory system and cancer; and 7.6 percent resulted from violence. Of greater significance than statistics concerning specific causes of death, however, are the data concerning the state of mortality among young children.

In the mid-1960s about 45 percent of all reported deaths involved children under the age of five years. The principal causes reported for mortality in infancy and early childhood were gastritis, enteritis, and related diseases; influenza and pneumonia; bronchitis and other infectious and parasitic diseases; and measles. In Monterrey during the

1968–70 period nearly half of all deaths of children under the age of five resulted from diarrhea and other infectious and parasitic ailments.

Malnutrition contributed to many of these early deaths. According to a mid-1970s estimate attributed to the National Academy of Medicine, some 350,000 of the more than 2 million infants born in 1974 were destined to die in infancy or early childhood as a direct or indirect consequence of malnutrition, and many of the survivors would suffer physical or mental retardation. Life expectancy at birth for those with dietary deficiencies was estimated at forty-two years, compared with seventy years for those whose family incomes made adequate nutrition possible.

During the years since World War II the achievements of Mexican medicine in lowering the general death rate and in extending the average life span have been impressive. The sharp rise in the rate of population growth during those years has been a consequence of a progressively lower death rate rather than a rising rate of birth. The reported rate of mortality in Mexico is not higher than the Latin American average, and the rate for children between the ages of one and four years is high but by no means the highest. Mexican medicine, however, has been far less effective in reducing the incidence of deaths among infants and young children than it has in reducing the incidence in older age-groups (see ch. 2).

Statistics assembled by the Pan American Health Organization concerning the incidence of notifiable and communicable diseases show Mexico to have rates generally below the Latin American average. The relatively high incidence of such childhood diseases as whooping cough and measles calls further attention to the seriousness of the health problems of young children. Among the few other diseases with relatively high incidence are typhus and typhoid. Mexico is one of a minority of Latin American countries reporting both endemic and epidemic louse-borne typhus. During the late 1960s and early 1970s the incidence of typhoid was not excessively high, but the mortality rate was the highest in Latin Americas. In 1971 a strain of *Salmonella typhi* that was resistant to antibiotics caused an epidemic that resulted in more than 2,600 deaths.

In much of rural Mexico, diseases with high rates of incidence cannot always be exactly identified. For example, a complaint known as *pulmonía* is the cause of much illness and some infant mortality among the Indians of the Baja California Peninsula. The word means pneumonia, but in Baja California it is an all-inclusive name for any ailment that causes a high fever and affects the chest.

Of the several preventive medicine campaigns in progress during the mid-1970s, the most energetic was directed at the reduction of maternal, infant, and early childhood mortality and the general improvement of maternal and child health. The program had received new impetus through the country's decision in 1972 to establish a family planning program. It was decided to emphasize the positive aspects of family planning by teaching responsible parenthood and the improvement of maternal and child health (see ch. 2).

The preventive medicine departments of the IMSS and the Ministry of Health and Welfare conduct an extensive inoculation program, particularly against communicable childhood diseases. A commission made up of directors of the two agencies prevents duplication of effort. As soon as cases of contagious disease are reported, mobile units are dispersed to track down persons who have been exposed.

The IMSS has permanent health units that follow the brigades of migrant sugar workers, who work under what may be the country's worst sanitary conditions. In addition, its clinics distribute to their patients educational material prepared by the Medical Center of Mexico City concerning malnutrition, venereal diseases, rheumatic fever, diarrhea and dysentery, diabetes, and breast and uterine cancer.

Campaigns against malaria, polio, certain tropical skin ailments, tuberculosis, measles, whooping cough, and diphtheria have been outstandingly successful. Malaria, which was once the country's leading killer, has been eradicated from all but a small portion of the areas in which it was endemic. Polio has almost been eliminated, and Mexico produces enough vaccine to supply all of Latin America. Measles remains a major cause of infant and child mortality, but in 1974 it was officially estimated that in a year's time inoculations had prevented the death of 10,000 children from this disease.

Traditional Medicine

Medicine is practiced at several levels. At the apex is the professional physician, a university graduate. The second level is occupied by the neighborhood or village druggist. Pharmacies are rated as first, second, or third class, and only the first-class units have registered pharmacists qualified to prepare prescriptions. Irrespective of their qualifications, however, druggists are regularly called on to prescribe dosages and treatments. At the third level are the traditional practitioners—the *yerberos* (herb dealers) and the *curanderos* (native healers). At different times a person with a medical complaint may seek aid at all three of these levels.

Well-stocked herb markets are to be found in every city and town, and herb sellers are fixtures in the open-air village markets. One prosperous Mexico City herb merchant in the early 1970s carried an assortment of some 1,800 different medicinal plants in a main store and several branches that had a collective daily turnover amounting to thousands of pesos. The markets have changed little since Aztec times, and their stocks in trade include varieties believed to cure complaints ranging from bed-wetting to cancer. Some have only superstitious value, but the Mexican countryside abounds in plantlife essential to the practice of modern medicine. Among the useful plant remedies known since ancient times are ipecac against amoebas, quinine against malaria, valerian as a tranquilizer, and castor beans for the production of castor oil. In addition to the wide varieties of plantlife of real or presumed value, the herb market stocks include amulets and other curiosities such as dried devil-fish used as lightning rods.

A few *curanderos* continue to practice in the more remote parts of the countryside. They are well versed in herbal cures, but their treatments rely heavily on traditional supernatural beliefs. Many of these involve the concept of balance. Illness is a form of imbalance resulting from improper food or other cause, and good health is restored by a regaining of balance. It is also believed that strength and weakness in the body must be kept in balance and that strong emotions cause disequilibrium.

The traditional concept of balance has survived in the form of a homespun psychotherapy practiced as often by well-to-do as by poor families. A common kind of ailment suffered usually by women is called *bilis*. Literally, this means biliousness, but in fact it is a matter of being out of sorts. It is a real, if emotional, ailment that is cured promptly within the family circle by a great deal of sympathy and comforting.

WELFARE

Mexico's principal social welfare agency, the IMSS, was established in 1943 for the benefit of workers in private industry and their dependents in the Federal District. The program has since been expanded from time to time to include workers in various categories in other parts of the country. The number of direct participants increased from 136,000 in 1944 to 2.9 million in 1969. In 1969 about 9.2 million people were covered by the program. Some 32.0 percent were directly insured workers, 65.4 percent were family members, and 2.6 percent were pensioners. By the end of 1972 some 11.4 million workers and their dependents were covered.

Benefits are available to insured personnel, legal wives, common-law consorts after five years, children under the age of sixteen (twenty-five if full-time students), and dependent parents. The IMSS program is funded by quotas paid by workers and employers plus a federal subsidy. Federal social security costs regularly amount to over half of all social infrastructure costs in the federal budgets.

The quotas paid by employer, worker, and government were originally equal. The proportions have changed over time, however, and employers have paid a progressively larger share. In 1971 the employers' share was almost tripled by expanding the pay on which contributions were based to include a wide variety of fringe benefits. In 1974 the distribution of the contributions on behalf of industrial workers included 62.5 percent from the employer, 25 percent from the worker, and 12.5 percent from the government. Changes in quotas have also involved raising the maximum assessable wage. This technique has been repeatedly employed as a small and not too unpalatable means of narrowing the gap between the incomes of the highest and lowest paid workers.

Benefits are divided into the three major categories of medical, economic, and social. Medical care is provided in cases of occupational illness and work accidents, nonoccupational illness, and maternity. Economic benefits include sick pay, work accident indemnification or pensions, marriage expenses, assistance to nursing mothers, old-age and disability pensions, funeral expenses, and pensions for widows and orphans. Social benefits are provided through centers for social welfare; social, youth, and vocational training centers; vacation centers; and housing programs including housing loans and low-cost houses for workers. Overall, payment in goods and services rendered have far exceeded money payments.

The extension of social security coverage to rural workers has presented particular problems; it has, however, been regarded as of particular importance by successive governments as essential to achievement of the goals of the continuing Revolution of 1910. In 1954, the year in which social welfare was first effectively extended to rural localities, about 2,300 rural workers were enrolled. This coverage increased gradually, but in 1967 the total rural enrollment remained slightly under 300,000. Pressure groups urged that the limited available funds be expended in improving the benefits available to those already nominally covered rather than in enrolling additional groups who in practice could not receive adequate protection. A new social security law in 1973, however, specifically included all organized farmworkers on a mandatory basis. The limitation that farmworkers be organized did not imply that they belong to a labor federation; it required only designation of some local farm cooperative group.

The IMSS serves only workers in private industry. In 1960 the Institute of Social Security and Services for Government Employees (Instituto de Seguridad y Servicios Sociales de los Trabajadores del Estado—ISSSTE) was created to provide federal personnel with social welfare coverage. Later legislation extended this protection to some state government workers, personnel of the federal legislative branch, other public elements, and some workers under government contract. The number of beneficiaries, including dependents and pensioners, increased from about 500,000 in 1960 to about 1.5 million in 1970 and to 2 million in 1973. The ISSSTE program is generally similar to that of the IMSS but offers some additional benefits, such as a variety of loans, low-rental apartments, and life insurance. Like IMSS, it operates its own system of hospitals and outpatient facilities.

Participants in the public social security programs may also benefit from other programs, such as those offered by mutual benefit societies and those granted by the major industrial firms as fringe benefits. A 1974 survey of sixty-two large industrial firms by the American Chamber of Commerce of Mexico City showed these fringe benefits to be important ones. Among the benefits offered by varying numbers of firms were payment of their workers' IMSS quotas, separate pension retirement programs, and medical services in addition to those of the IMSS. Other benefits included loans for car purchases, vacation time in excess of that legally required, supplemental vacation pay bonuses, Christmas bonuses in excess of those legally required, payment of at least 50 percent of the cost of cafeteria meals, discounts of 20 percent or more on company goods, assistance in payment of the cost of education for workers' children, and productivity or sales bonuses.

The civil association *(asociación civil)* is a peculiarly Mexican institution that engages in a variety of charitable and educational undertakings. It is a legally constituted nonprofit organization registered with the municipality of domicile and carrying the letters *A.C.* after its title. The civil associations operate with small staffs and little publicity, customarily represent a particular sector of industry, are associated with the employer associations, and work closely with the government. Civil associations have existed throughout the century but have greatly increased in number during the years since World War II, particularly in the Federal District.

A large number of social and professional organizations of businessmen perform such voluntary functions as disaster relief and contributing to charitable causes. Among these in the early 1970s were nearly 100 junior chambers of commerce, more than 500 Lions clubs, and more than 150 Rotary clubs. The activities of these organizations, as well as the welfare-related fringe benefits conferred on workers in the big industrial enterprises, are sometimes criticized as paternalistic and obstructive to social progress. Patron-client relationships, however, are an enduring part of the national culture. They carry some advantage for all, and the scope of the fringe benefits offered by Mexican industry suggests a conceptual relationship to the extended family (see ch. 5).

The closeness of the ties that bind the Mexican family has considerable welfare significance. Aged parents are cared for unquestioningly, and room can usually be found in the home for an indigent aunt or uncle. The rate of child abandonment in Mexico is far lower than that in most other Latin American countries because the abandonment of a child by both parents is an extreme rarity, and children who have lost their parents or whose parents are destitute are readily given homes, even by distant relatives.

PATTERNS OF LIVING AND LEISURE

Holidays and Business Hours

Sunday is a day of rest. The working week is forty-eight hours in duration, and Saturday is a working day. Banks are closed on Saturdays, however, and in the mid-1970s labor unions were demanding a forty-hour week. There are fifteen days regularly observed as national holidays. These are: January 1, New Year's Day; February 5, Constitution Day;

March 21, Birth of Benito Juárez; Holy Thursday, Good Friday, and Holy Saturday (movable holidays); May 1, Labor Day; May 5, Battle of Puebla; September 15 and 16, Independence Days; October 12, Columbus Day; November 2, All Souls' Day (not an official holiday but generally observed); November 20, Anniversary of Revolution; December 12, Our Lady of Guadalupe (not an official holiday but generally observed); and December 25, Christmas Day. Also, a working day occurring between two holidays may be declared a *puente* (literally, bridge; day of rest). For example, when a national holiday falls on a Tuesday, the preceding Monday may be made a *puente*. In addition, the day of the patron saint of each city, town, and village is the occasion for a fiesta lasting a day or several days during which business comes to a virtual halt.

Shopping hours are customarily from 9:00 A.M. to 6:00 P.M. in Mexico City but are much more flexible elsewhere in the country. Professional people and businessmen may commence work at 8:00 A.M. and work into the early afternoon. The custom of the late luncheon and an afternoon siesta is still frequently observed, and business people may return to their offices in the late afternoon to continue work until 8:00 P.M. or 9:00 P.M.

Banks are open from 9:00 A.M. to 1:00 P.M. Mondays through Fridays, and most government offices work from 8:00 A.M. to early afternoon in a continuous shift. Luncheon is eaten in the early afternoon, and restaurants are open for the midday meal between 1:00 P.M. and 4:00 P.M. They open for dinner at from 8:00 P.M. to 9:00 P.M. and often remain open until after midnight.

Business hours vary between localities. For example, a British travel publication notes approvingly that in the businesslike industrial city of Monterrey the hours of business are roughly the same as those in Great Britain. In general, the flexibility of hours is suggested by the custom of referring to an engagement in which promptness is essential as a *cita inglesa* (English appointment).

Consumption Patterns

A 1973 government publication observed that 50 percent of the country's population had purchasing power; the other 50 percent had none and was thus unable to participate in the developing economy. The statement was a deliberate oversimplification that called attention to the fact that there are two Mexicos. In one, primarily urban and dominated by the rapidly growing middle class, a consumer society is in a fairly advanced state of development. In the other, primarily rural, families exist at or near the subsistence level.

In addition to the urban middle class and the relatively few elite, unionized workers to varying extents can be considered members of the consumer society. Most of the country's skilled workers are union members who by virtue of their skills command fairly high wages, and unions usually obtain for their membership higher wages than those paid

182

to the balance of the labor force. In the early 1970s about 40 percent of the nonagricultural labor force was unionized.

The remainder of the urban population, much of it made up of recent migrants has simple consumption patterns that are dictated by necessity and resemble those of the subsistence farmers and farmworkers who make up most of the rural population. Not all of the rural population, however, lives at the subsistence level. A small but growing middle class is made up of prosperous commercial farmers, farm managers, and successful businessmen in the larger villages. There is also a small rural elite, but its members frequently visit cities and sometimes maintain city residences, and their consumption patterns do not differ significantly from those of the urban well-to-do.

Data from the 1970 census indicate that the per capita income derived from agriculture and related activities was little more than one-fourth of the national average. At this level of income, the farmer necessarily lived largely outside the mainstream of national life and outside the national economy.

The basic expenses of the subsistence farmer are purchases of food not produced at home and clothing. Although money income is low, there is a tendency to spend a considerable portion of it on recreation. In Indian villages where traditional customs prevail, considerable prestige attaches to sponsorship of the fiesta celebrating the local saint's day. This is an expensive matter, and a prosperous farmer may spend a year's income for this purpose. In less remote places, when crops have been marketed and there is a little money on hand, after purchasing the necessary household staples and clothing the farmer is likely to spend any remaining funds on a spree in the nearest city or town.

Such visits cannot be enjoyed by all country people. About 8 million live in so-called desert zones where the land is often too poor to produce crops. These people engage in gathering and handicraft production. Baskets and ropes of maguey fiber, bundles of mesquite for use as firewood, wild herbs, and chunks of limestone are taken to market to be sold or bartered for the corn and beans essential to survival.

In urban localities the growth of the middle class has been accompanied by a corresponding increase in advertising, installment buying, and the use of credit cards. Under the influence of these modern techniques, a large part of middle-class income is spent on such products as television sets, washers, modern kitchen conveniences, and cosmetics. In 1970 about half of all homes in Mexico with electricity had both radio and television sets. Changing patterns are indicated by a large factory in Monterrey where in the late 1960s a bicycle rack was replaced by a parking lot.

Because of the cheapness of unskilled labor, a large proportion of urban families are able to afford domestic servants. Even the moderately well-to-do maintain a retinue, and some families living in slum neighborhoods are able to afford domestics who come by day to clean and do

183

laundry work.

The consumption pattern of the lower income urban family is somewhat more varied than that of the family of the subsistence farmer but is basically similar to it. Food and clothing are the principal expense items, and some money is expended on recreation, such as attending motion pictures or sporting events. City merchants accommodate the limited purchasing power of these families by selling cigarettes by the unit, thread in lengths of a few yards, and spices in packages the size of stamps. Purchasing power, however, has been rising sufficiently to permit a progressively fuller participation in the consumer economy. Between 1954 and 1969 the minimum wage index for workers in the largely unskilled construction industry rose from 100 to 323.1; during the same period the cost-of-living index for working-class families in Mexico City rose only from 100 to 189.9.

The government engages in a variety of operations aimed at protecting and strengthening the limited purchasing power of the lower income families and bringing them more fully into the market economy. In particular, the National Company of Popular Subsistences (Compañia Nacional de Subsistencias Populares—CONASUPO) operates a great many urban and rural outlets selling basic foodstuffs and clothing at moderate prices. In addition, in 1974 a public agency was established to provide working capital to the numerous stores operated by large companies for the benefit of their workers, and plans were announced for the establishment of low-cost retail outlets for the use of government workers (see ch. 15).

During the same year the National Guarantee and Promotion Fund for Workers was established to enable workers with limited incomes to obtain low-interest loans for the purpose of purchasing durable consumer goods. The several programs were opposed by the private food and retail stores but were viewed with cautious approval by the producers of durable goods, who hoped that a new market for their products would be created.

Recreation

All Mexicans love music and find a great recreational outlet in various musical activities. Every town and village has a bandstand, and people of all social levels in all parts of the country find release from everyday cares in playing, listening to, and dancing to music. The love for it traces directly to the Indian heritage, and many of the musical instruments still in use are of indigenous origin (see ch. 8).

There is music for all tastes, and even those who profess to look down on popular music are deeply affected by the authentic folk songs that are still regularly played and sung. Classical music and opera are available in the larger cities, and even the small and relatively isolated Yucatán city of Mérida has its own symphony orchestra. Even the more remote towns sometimes have not one but several municipal bands, and a group of musicians is often a part of the market-day scene in the villages.

Among the several kinds of musical groups, the best known are the strolling mariachi musicians, who originated in Guadalajara but are popular in many parts of the country. Sunday morning masses in Cuernavaca are accompanied by a special mariachi troupe. Also of great popularity are the bands formed around a marimba, a giant xylophone-like instrument that is played by seven men on one side and three on the other.

The store of Mexican romantic and popular songs is enormous. Folk songs are incorporated in the composed music, and many of the popular songs have endured for generations. They are often extremely melodic, and their appeal has reached far beyond the borders of the country. Mexico's Agustín Lara may be the best known popular composer of Latin America.

Music is a basic necessity to Mexicans and, like other basic necessities, was under price control during the inflation-plagued year of 1974. In the Federal District the union of mariachi musicians petitioned local authorities for permission to raise the price of a song from fifteen to twenty pesos.

The love of music is interwoven with a love of dancing. The Ballet Folklórico—the national folklore ballet company—is certainly the best known and probably the best organization of its kind in the world. In addition to performing in Mexico City during the October-to-May season, its three troupes perform in major cities throughout the world.

Everyone dances in Mexico. The dances include the Spanish flamenco, the Afro-Cuban, the North American, the waltz, the polka, and countless traditional native dances. There are large dance halls in Mexico City, and "dime-a-dance" partners are available. Among the traditional dances, the most famous is the *jarabe tapatío* of Jalisco, known internationally as the Mexican hat dance. Others include the deer dance of the North, in which the dancer wears a breechcloth and a stuffed deer head; the *sandunga* of Tehuantepec, a kind of waltz; and the staccato *jarana* of Yucatán.

Each locality has its own traditional dance. With the urbanization of the country and the heavily increasing inflow of tourists, the traditional performances are to an extent becoming commercialized. The dance exists for the pleasure of the performers and their audiences, however, and the fact that a group of village musicians or a dance group receives a few pesos from tourists has not destroyed the recreational value to the whole village.

For Mexicans of modest income, music and dancing are most fully enjoyed at fiestas. Virtually every day there is a fiesta somewhere in Mexico. A majority honor the day of the local patron saint, and every village as well as the barrios (working-class residential neighborhoods) of the cities have patron saints. Fiestas range from those celebrated countrywide on the national holidays to those of the individual village. They may celebrate anything of religious or historical significance, and any recreational gathering of Mexicans for which admission is not charged takes on the aspect of a fiesta.

Festivities last from a day to a week or more. Planning is usually ragged, but the entire community participates, and the fiesta gives country people their best chance to see people from neighboring towns and villages, to sell a few pieces of handicraft or tacos, and otherwise to enliven a monotonous existence. The entertainment involves pilgrimages, special masses, shows of horsemanship, games, bullfights, giant papier-mâché puppets, and fireworks. Although most of the fiestas have a religious origin, in some the original meaning has become blurred by time, and the occasion is simply given over to singing, dancing, feasting, and drinking. In others, much of the original Christian and pagan pageantry has remained.

Supplementing and closely related to the fiesta is the open-air market that is held weekly in villages and towns and daily in cities. Most of the villages with populations in excess of 1,000 have set market days that attract farm families from considerable distances. Their arrival transforms the village into the scene of a pageant in which the buying and selling of the produce are less important to many than the social significance. The event is of particular importance in the central and southern parts of the country. In northern Mexico the institution of the weekly market has been displaced by the local store.

In Mexico, as in most other Latin American countries, soccer is the most popular sport. In 1970 the quadrennial World Cup games were held in Mexico in the 105,000-seat stadium that had been built for the 1968 Olympic games. Baseball follows soccer closely in popularity. It is played professionally by an eight-team league, and the quality of play is suggested by the fact that during the 1972 season there were ten Mexican players on teams of the United States major leagues, half of them regular players. Mexico's Roberto Avila was the first player from a Latin American country to win a major league batting title in the United States.

Mexico is the only Latin American country to play football on a regular basis. The National Autonomous University of Mexico and several other Mexican schools play against one another and United States teams. Basketball is popular, and in 1974 Mexico fielded men's and women's teams in the World Volleyball Championship matches. Among the other sports with considerable followings are gymnastics, swimming, and cross-country running. Especially popular among the imported United States television programs is sports coverage.

Mexican teams participate regularly in Davis Cup tennis competition, and in 1973 Mexico played host to the North American zone finals. Golf has only a limited appeal and there are no public courses, but equestrian sports of all kinds including polo are popular, and horseraces at Mexico City's Hipódromo de las Américas are well attended. The deep-sea sport fishing may be the best in the world, particularly the fishing for sailfish and marlin off the coast of Baja California and tarpon off the coast of Yucatán. The hunting season, where it exists, is longer than in the United States. White-tailed deer are common, and coyote, ocelot, fox, jaguar, and mountain lion can be bagged.

Jai alai, known locally as *juego de pelota* (ball game), is a very popular spectator sport played by professionals in Mexico City. A form of jai alai called *fron-ténis* in which tennis rackets are used rather than the regular *cestas* (baskets) is played by many Mexicans.

Professional boxing matches are held Wednesday and Saturday nights in Mexico City's Arena Coliseo, and cockfights have been popular since colonial times. The premier Mexican sports spectacle, however, is the bullfight. There are two bullrings in Mexico City; one of these, holding 48,000 spectators, is the largest in the world. There are bullrings in Tijuana and several other cities, and improvised bullfights are frequent features of country fiestas. Bullfighting has ceded first place to soccer in popularity, but it continues to attract more interest in Mexico than in any other country in the world except Spain.

The most peculiarly Mexican of all sporting events is the *charreada*, the Mexican version of the rodeo. It is an amateur institution in which the performers are ranchers, businessmen, and professionals who belong to *charro* clubs. In the more elaborate meetings, one *charro* club competes against another, and there are no specialists; everyone competes in everything. The largest and most affluent clubs are in Mexico City, Guadalajara, and Monterrey, but in the early 1960s there were a reported 365 clubs scattered about the country. The *charreadas* take place in open fields or in miniature stadiums, and admission is free or at moderate cost. The atmosphere is informal and festive to an extreme. The traditional *charro* costume is worn, a mariachi band plays, and the events are sometimes interspersed by folk dance exhibitions.

The theater in the city of Puebla, built in 1550, is the oldest in the New World, but the legitimate stage does not offer productions matching those in the musical arts in quality. Mexico City has many small legitimate theaters in which shows change frequently, and the Xola Theater is a center for the classical Spanish drama.

Mexico has more motion picture theaters than any other Latin American country except Brazil, and the average per capita attendance at eight films a year during 1968 was close to the highest, in the Western Hemisphere; it exceeded that in both the United States and Canada. There are theaters in the larger villages as well as in cities and towns, and the government-controlled prices of admission are so low that attendance at an occasional motion picture is within the reach of even the poorest families.

United States films with Spanish subtitles predominate, but Mexico has a substantial motion picture industry of its own. The names of Mexican stars are better know abroad than those of any other Latin American country; and although the industry has suffered from the competition furnished by television and other forms of entertainment, it continues to lead Latin America in the production of motion pictures (see ch. 11).

Mexican family ties are close and warm, and it is often remarked that the favorite Mexican toy is a baby. Leisure activity centers in the family, and it is not easy for a stranger to find his way into a Mexican home. Family events have great recreational value for people of all social classes, and great occasion is made of birthdays, saints' days, first communions, weddings, and funerals. Weddings in particular can be elaborate affairs. A village wedding may involve the groom's mock abduction of the bride and a triumphant return celebrated with a band performance and fireworks. Mariachi bands are said to have originated as performers at wedding feasts, and their name is believed to have come from *mariage*, the French word for marriage.

Courtship also has considerable recreational value. In a weekly event known in most localities as a *serenata*, young men promenade in an outer circle around the local plaza as girls walk in an inner circle in the opposite direction. Eventually, the promenade disintegrates, and the participants stroll about the plaza in pairs. In an ancient variation sometimes encountered in rural Oaxaca, the boy throws a fishnet over the girl. Although the *serenata* is observed with decreasing frequency, it still can be seen in some towns and villages.

The neighborhood city plaza, as well as the central plaza of the town or village, is the focal point of leisure activity to an extent unparalleled elsewhere in Latin America. In addition to serving as the site of the *serenata*, it is the town meetingplace. Music and dancing take place in it, and it is in the plaza that most of the fiesta events take place. In the open-fronted cafés surrounding it people play chess or dominoes or simply observe the passersby. Others gather in the plaza pool hall, which serves as a kind of men's club.

City people take great pleasure in weekend family outings. In Mexico City the favored locations for these strolls and picnics are University City—the campus of the National Autonomous University of Mexico—Chapultepec Park, and the world-famous Floating Gardens of Xochomilco. Chapultepec Park is the parade ground and backyard of the working-class family, and its numerous attractions include the world's highest roller coaster, a breathtaking amusement that requires both a lap bar and a seat belt. The Xochomilco gardens were originally laid out by the Aztecs and are of particular attractiveness to the countless families that visit them because of their magnificient floral display. Flower gardens are common throughout Mexico, and the Mexican love of flowers is such that flower gardening is a significant kind of informal recreation.

Ownership of a vacation retreat at Acapulco or some other vacation resort is possible only for the well-to-do, but the government maintains a network of moderate-cost vacation centers scattered about the country; the largest and best equipped of these—at Oaxtepec, near

Cuernavaca—accommodates more than 1 million visitors annually.

Participation in the national lottery provides excitement for those with a desire to gamble, and the heavily attended drawing at the National Lottery Building in downtown Mexico City has a carnival atmosphere. Drawings are held three nights each week, except during three weeks of the year when a single lottery is held for higher prizes.

CHAPTER 8

ARTISTIC AND INTELLECTUAL EXPRESSION

In Mexico, perhaps more than in any other Latin American country, artistic and intellectual expression has been a reflection of the country's history through the attempt by its artists and intellectuals to establish a national identity, a sense of uniqueness. The pride of Mexicans in their history is evident in all the arts. They sing of revolutionary heroes; they retain traditional dances and folk arts, many of which incorporate their Indian and Spanish heritage. Sculpture, architecture, and contemporary painting emphasize pre-Columbian Indian traditions. Philosophers have sought to reinterpret Indian thought. This pride is not insular, however; Mexican artists and thinkers have been open to European and North American influences and have adopted them to fit Mexican needs.

Because of its strong association with history, artistic and intellectual expression in the twentieth century has tended to focus on social problems rather than universal questions. The dominant theme has been the Revolution of 1910 and its aftermath, for it was with the revolution that a national character emerged. Revolutionary goals and ideals were the principal subjects of writers during the first decades of the century; the betrayal of these goals and ideals occupied them for some time thereafter. Writers were deeply concerned with the Indian's place in Mexican society, first decrying his exploitation before the revolution and later treating problems of incorporating him into modern society. Painters and sculptors also treated social, economic, and political subjects inspired by the revolution, reflecting the society's identification with its past and the people's strong sense of nationalism. Philosophers examined human conduct rather than theories of knowledge, becoming intimately concerned with the revolutionary tradition and the spread of nationalism.

As the national identity became more firmly established, creative expression began to include other subject matter. With increasing modernization in the country, the clash between traditional and modern values started to occupy attention. Intellectual and artistic pursuits have also been modified since the mid-twentieth century by the special interests of the society. The Indianist movement, for example, has promoted interest in and support for archaeological research into pre-Columbian civilizations. The doctrine of the Roman Catholic Church, the church of virtually all Mexicans, has influenced the social and physical sciences, tending to promote interest in philosophical rather than empirical questions.

Artists and intellectuals are highly regarded by the Mexican people. The government has contributed much to their support. Painters and architects are often commissioned by the government; actors and dramatists are supported by a number of national theatrical organizations. The Ballet Folklórico and several other dance groups have received active government encouragement. In 1961 the Center for the Experimental Arts was founded in Mexico City. Schools have been established by the government in various parts of the country for the training of painters and sculptors.

Their influence in government is generally greater than that of their counterparts in many European and Latin American countries. Many intellectuals teach part time at the university level, although the number is decreasing; their occupations outside the university provide them with influential contacts throughout society, and they serve as a bridge between society and the university. Moreover, many intellectuals have been elevated to important posts in the cabinet and in international service; many have even become ambassadors. The influence of such prestigious men and women has often been felt during political crises.

There is a large degree of occupational and professional diversification among artists and intellectuals, although these groups display a high degree of unity and of autonomy in their dealings with the rest of society. Moreover, many artists and intellectuals are in active communication with their counterparts throughout Latin America, Western Europe, and the United States. Many have traveled extensively, which lends to the artistic and intellectual community an air of cosmopolitanism. United States and European universities welcome Mexican artists and scholars as visiting lecturers and professors.

LITERATURE

Mexico's literary tradition begins with the poetry and sacred writings of the Maya and Aztec civilizations. Parts of the Popol Vuh (sacred writings of the Quiché Maya) survive, as do fragments of poetry written by Nezahualcoyotl, the fifteenth-century king of Texcoco. A good deal more literature is believed to have existed; most, however, was destroyed by colonial churchmen on the grounds that it was inspired by paganism and retarded the progress of the Indians toward Christianity.

The most important literary work of the early colonial period was *The Chronicles of Bernal Díaz de Castillo*. A firsthand account of the conquest, it is rich in description and accurate in detail; it remains one of the best and most colorful sources of information on the conquest of Mexico.

Most extraordinary of all literary colonial figures was perhaps Sor Juana Iñez de la Cruz. Born in the late seventeenth century near the capital, she became a nun at eighteen. She wrote verse, secular and religious plays, and essays on the laws of nature and studied astronomy and music. She collected a library of 4,000 volumes, and her convent became

192

a gathering place for the most distinguished and learned people of New Spain.

Colonial literature was in the tradition of Spain almost entirely in both style and subject matter. Toward the end of the colonial period, there was increased stylistic influence introduced from eighteenth-century French literary circles. During the nineteenth century the influence of French romanticism was marked. Romantic novels were extremely popular; historical novels were almost unknown. Poetry was almost entirely dominated by French influence. The output of the large number of Romantic novelists of the nineteenth century was relatively small, it made a considerable impression on the French-dominated literate community of the time.

With the Revolution of 1910 came the beginning of a uniquely Mexican literature. Realistic novels appeared treating themes of social protest, the heroism of revolutionary figures, and the Indian not as local color but as the central character in Mexican development. Poetry, unlike the novel, broke away more slowly from European influence. Although some poems dealt with social disaffection, many still reflected the concerns of French romanticism.

Mariano Azuela (1873–1952) initiated the "novel of the revolution" in 1915 with *Los de Abajo* (The Underdogs), which, by realistically portraying the exploitation of the Indian, made the Indian the prime focus of the revolutionary movement. Martín Luis Guzmán continued the novel of the revolution into the 1920s with *El Águila y la Serpiente* (The Eagle and the Serpent), telling of the adventures of such revolutionary heroes as Pancho Villa.

The revolutionary fervor that produced novels of social protest began to wane in the 1940s. Younger novelists influenced by European and United States stylists began exploring new techniques. José Revueltas (b. 1914) used the stream of consciousness technique in *El Luto Humano* (Human Grief), published in 1943, to tell the story of a group of Mexican peasants trapped by floods. The era of revolution had not been forgotten, however. In *Al Filo del Agua* (The Edge of the Storm), published in 1947, Agustín Yañez conveyed the anguish of a church-dominated Indian town on the eve of the revolution. Since then he has written novels on Mexican society both before and after the revolution.

The influence of the novelists of the revolution, particularly Azuela, Guzmán, and José Rubén Romero, remains evident in the work of contemporary authors in the selection of themes, the creation of backgrounds, and the techniques of characterization. In *Pedro Páramo*, Juan Rulfo (b. 1918) tells of a young man returning to his village in search of his father, Páramo. *Páramo* (wasteland) alludes not only to the barren setting of the novel but perhaps to the sterility of the prerevolutionary period. The father, deposed by the revolution, had been a *cacique*, a man of much influence and power over a large region. Rulfo speaks of man's relationship with his past—the past in this case being the revolution, which to many Mexicans marks the emergence of their national and unique identity.

In the 1950s and 1960s the social protest themes of the early revolutionary period had evolved into criticism of those who would betray revolutionary ideals. One of Mexico's foremost contemporary novelists is Carlos Fuentes (b. 1929). In one of his earlier novels, *Las Buenas Conciencias* (Clear Consciences), published in 1959, Fuentes focuses on this theme through the story of a man who grows to manhood, corrupted during the period just before and during the revolution. *La Muerte de Artemio Cruz* (The Death of Artemio Cruz), published in 1962, chronicles the deathbed thoughts of a fighter in the revolution who has prospered at the expense of his revolutionary ideals by exploiting others. The novel spans a long period of Mexican history, from the age of Antonio López de Santa Anna to the 1960s. None of the several works he has published since that time have been as successful in the creation of an unforgettable character. In his more recent works, such as those published in the late 1960s, he has interwoven two epochs, the present and the Middle Ages.

Other present-day novels attack corruption through the presentation of a gap between generations. The young are often presented as pure and honest, while the older characters are corrupt, dogmatic, or life denying. Many novels treat the dilemma presented by the coexistence of traditional and modern societies; the values of the closed Indian communities inevitably clash with those of the modernized, urban middle class.

The works of Juan José Arreola (b. 1918), a contemporary of Rulfo, are representative of the trend toward universal—as opposed to national—themes. He is best known for his short stories, in which he weaves subtle social satire into fantastic settings. The world he portrays, with ironic and poetic style, is one in which the foolish acts of foolish men set the tone of life. A volume of his works published in 1971 contained short stories, satirical discourses, proverbs, epigrammatic expressions, and phrases that can be read backward as well as forward. It has been well received by critics.

Stylistic experimentation since the mid-1960s has included attempts to draw the reader into vicarious participation in the creative process. For example, Salvador Elizondo's (b. 1932) *El Hipogeo Secreto* (The Secret Hypogeum), published in 1968, is a novel about a novel. As the author writes, the reader is invited to guess what will come next in the novel, and characters, author, and reader become part of the same world.

An even more extreme form of experimentation is found in Carlos Páramo's *Los Huecos* (The Holes), published in 1970. Seeking rhythm and imagery, Páramo discards punctuation and violates the rules of syntax and the structure of words. For most of the younger generation of novelists, however, experimentation has not meant a rupture with national literary traditions. José Agustín, for example, whose rich imagination was first revealed in 1966 with the publication of *De Perfil*

(From the Side), has forcefully acknowledged his debt to Revueltas. In his case, Agustín maintains, the generation gap does not exist.

Mexican poets broke away from French romanticism more slowly than novelists. The first to make the break, and the most widely recognized contemporary poet, is Octavio Paz (b. 1914). He has been deeply influenced by translations of Aztec religious poetry. His early poems consider the nature of creation and the subconscious sources of poetry, which he later identified with pre-Columbian sources. His most famous poem, "Piedra del Sol" (Sun Stone), treats history as a cyclical process; the sun stone on which the Aztec calendar was inscribed is an integral part of the Mexican historical cycle.

Since 1945 Mexican poetry has followed lines developed by Paz but with considerable independence of style and theme as well. Alí Chumacero (b. 1918) treats themes of nihilism and frustration. Jaime Sabines (b. 1925) speaks for the transitional Indian caught in the confusion and mercilessness of city life, yet dominating it through the force of his legends. Rosario Castellanos (1925–74) also speaks from the Indian's point of view. Castellanos, ambassador to Israel at the time of her death, is one of the many examples of literary figures who have been drawn into government service. Antonio Montes de Oca (b. 1932), like Paz, is concerned with the nature and sources of poetry.

Throughout his career Paz has also been noted as a literary critic and essayist. His most famous essay, "El Laberinto de la Soledad" (The Labyrinth of Solitude), presents a scathing analysis of Mexican character and particularly of the obsession with machismo.

Mexican poets and literary critics have given considerable attention to the historical development of the country's poetry and its relationship to the nation's maturity. José Emilio Pacheco's *La Poesía Mexicana del Siglo XIX, Antología* and Carlos Monsiváis' *La Poesía Mexicana del Siglo XX*, both published in 1966, have been acclaimed as the most comprehensive and best presented anthologies of the poetry of any country in Hispanic America.

While Mexican folk drama continues to emphasize traditional Indian themes, the lives of religious saints, and church rituals, much of modern drama shares with postrevolutionary novels and poetry the themes of social protest and the problems of man in the modern world. A search for a national identity of character has been the subject of some playwrights, while others have concerned themselves with the effects on man of modernization and changing values. European and United States influences are to be found, especially in stylistic and production innovations.

The modern theater in Mexico had its inception in 1928, with the foundation of the Teatro Ulises, an experimental group of dramatists. These men, important not only in their own right but also as teachers of the present generation, include Celestino Gorostiza, whose work focuses on an exploration and definition of the Mexican character. Many consider his *Corona de Sombra* (Crown of Shadows) and *El Gesticulador* (The

Face Maker), written in 1945 and 1947, respectively, among the best productions of the contemporary Latin American theater.

Since World War II interest in the theater has increased markedly. The Department of Theater of the National Institute of Fine Arts, the School of Dramatic Arts, and National Theater Festivals have all been founded since that time. Probably the most famous of contemporary dramatists is Emilio Carballido, whose output ranges from *Rosalba y los Llaveros* (Rosalba and the Turnkeys), which in 1950 introduced to Mexican audiences the possibility of treating serious problems in a comic fashion, to *Medusa* (1965), a complex vision of man's spiritual death in the modern world.

Other important members of the current group of dramatists include Luisa Josefina Hernández, Sergio Magaña, Elena Garro, and Carlos Solórzano. Hernández is concerned with provincial life, the role of women in Mexican society and, of late, social criticism. Magaña is noted for unusual experiments in form. Garro is closely related to the theater of the absurd. Solórzano, influenced by French playwrights, has moved toward a concept of total theater, which is the focus for his vision of man's eternal struggle against human and cosmic repression.

A number of women were prominent in the theater in the early 1970s. Maruxa Vilalta, in addition to being a drama critic, was also a director. Among her best known plays were *El Nueve* (Nine), a foreboding of the mechanization of men in the world of the future, and *Esta Noche Juntos Amándonos Tanto* (Together Tonight Loving Each Other So), an unusual approach to the eternal themes of love and loneliness. For the latter play she won the Juan Ruíz de Alarcón Prize in 1970, which she shared with Marcela del Río. Del Río's share of the prize was awarded for her tragedy *El Pulpo* (The Octopus), based on the assassination of John F. Kennedy. She has also written a number of avant-garde plays.

Vigorous and effective efforts were being made in the early 1970s to inspire young dramatists and to expand the social base of both participants and audience for the theater. The theater department of the National Institute of Fine Arts was regularly sponsoring young authors, actors, and directors. The Mexican Social Security Institute was offering free drama courses at each of its family welfare centers, and the most promising participants were given the opportunity to present their plays in the numerous theaters maintained by the institute. The institute, in collaboration with the Federal District, has also been bringing theater to the poorest and most isolated areas of the city. There has also been considerable expansion of theatrical activity by and for children. This popular theater, as it is called, has become just that, and the number of theaters sponsoring live performances is approaching the number of cinema theaters in the Federal District. Prices range, although many are popularly priced (equivalent from US$0.40 to US$0.80), and some are even free.

INTELLECTUAL EXPRESSION

Before the revolution, most Mexican philosophical thought tended to serve the needs of church, state, school, or industry. It is with Antonio Caso and José Vasconcelos that twentieth-century Mexican philosophy, as an independent field of inquiry, began. Both Caso and Vasconcelos were influenced by the French philosophers Blaise Pascal and Henri Bergson. Caso's Christian philosophy of the world attempts to resolve strains in the Bergsonian philosophy.

Vasconcelos rejected the materialism of the positivist thought that had been embraced by the most influential philosophers of the late nineteenth century. He sought instead to articulate a philosophy that, although unusual, would be rooted in Spanish American culture. This aspiration was expressed in his best known work, *La Raza Cósmica: Misión de la Raza Iberoamericana* (The Cosmic Race: Mission of the Iberoamerican Race), published in 1925.

Historically, Mexican philosophy was conditioned by a number of factors different from those that affected most of Western Europe (except Spain) and North American Indian preconceptions retained a considerable hold in Mexico. In addition, the theological doctrines of the Counter-Reformation encountered no philosophical challenges. Enlightenment thought, which spread across Europe in the eighteenth century, did not reach Mexico until the latter part of the nineteenth century; when it did arrive, it was in a form much diluted with romanticism.

Mexican philosophical effort expresses itself in the search for political, social, and artistic goals and ideals. It is not as much concerned with problems of phenomenology, epistemology or methodology as is Western European and United States philosophy. Like most of the philosophical thought in Latin America, Mexican philosophy tends toward a tragic view of life in which the individual is perceived as being in eternal conflict with himself and the world around him. This conflict cannot be resolved, and the individual cannot win. Man must find his place between the conflicting elements of circumstance and the needs of his own personality. Mexican thought is thus dominated by problems of human conduct, not by problems of knowledge.

Caso and Vasconcelos, influenced by French Romantic philosophy, dominated philosophical thought from 1900 to 1925. Since that time the dominating influence has been the Spanish philosopher José Ortega y Gassett, as interpreted by Mexicans Samuel Ramos and José Romero Muñoz. Ortega y Gassett provided the conceptual framework for the attempt by the generation of philosophers coming out of the revolution to develop a uniquely Mexican philosophy of life. Ortega y Gassett's perspectivism argues that each nation must produce a unique philosophical image of its own values and consciousness, its ideals and aspirations, and its system of social and political thought. Mexican philosophers continue to attempt to interpret the tenets of Ortega y Gassett to fit Mexican needs. In his *Hacia un Nuevo Humanismo: Programa de un Antropología Filosófica* (Toward a New Humanism: Program of a Philosophical Anthropology), Ramos admonishes his countrymen to combat the subhumanity engendered by bourgeois capitalism and materialism and signals the need to rally generous, spirited youth behind the values of humanism.

Humanities faculties exist in many of the country's thirty universities. Degrees are granted in music, architecture, art (including painting and sculpture), literature, and history. The humanities continue to operate under scholastic methods of instruction that emphasize memorization; teaching centers on a lecture rather than a tutorial system. A notable exception is the internationally respected work in anthropology and archaeology centered at the National Autonomous University of Mexico and the National Museum of Anthropology in Mexico City. Much empirical research has been carried out in the area of pre-Columbian civilizations. Students from all over the world are attracted to the National Autonomous University of Mexico to take part in this program.

In archaeology, the central Mexican highlands and the Maya area were receiving considerable attention in the early 1970s, and there was a growing interest in iconography, particularly in Olmec art. In ethnology, studies had generated a debate on the ethical questions relating to the cultural integration of the Indian.

The social sciences (with the exception of anthropology) are metaphysical rather than empirical in orientation. Sociology is influenced to a large extent by the metaphysical German school. Among the more highly regarded recent works of applied social research is *Disyuntivas Sociales* (Social Alternatives), edited by Miguel S. Wionczek and published by the Ministry of Public Education in 1971. Political science emphasizes the history of Western political thought. Medieval thought is studied closely, especially that of Saint Augustine and Saint Thomas Aquinas, reflecting the influence of Roman Catholicism in the country.

The field of economics is particularly forward looking; the problems of modernization are studied, and training is given in practical policy decisionmaking, business enterprise, and banking (see ch. 6; ch. 14). Theoretical attention was focused in the early 1970s on agriculture and income redistribution. These two subjects were combined in *Bienestar Campesino y Desarrollo Económico* (Peasant Welfare and Economic Development), a masterful study by Ifigenia M. de Navarrete, published in 1971. Navarrete has also played a part in government and in the 1970s was a senior member of a government ministry.

In the general field of Mexican history, an inordinate proportion of the scholarship of the past fifty years has centered on the revolution. The output of historical literature in the first three decades after the revolution tended to focus on individual caudillos and to glorify the feats of the revolutionaries. In the view of one critic, historians of this period, given the option of being candid or being loved, chose the latter. The output of the post-World War II period, however, has reflected greater attention to methodology and broader frames of reference. The findings of the social sciences, for example, have been integrated into historical works. The historiographical enterprises improved markedly during the decade of the 1960s. A number of perceptive essays, such as Enrique Florescano's "Las Investigaciones Históricas en México" (Historical Research in Mexico), published in 1968, have been helpful to students seeking a conceptualization of Mexican historical literature.

The physical sciences are not as empirically oriented as in Europe or the United States; little original research is done. With increased laboratory space and modern facilities, especially at the university level, it is probable that an empirical approach will begin to develop.

PAINTING, SCULPTURE, AND ARCHITECTURE

Mexican art and architecture have evolved through three distinct periods: the pre-Columbian period, the era of Spanish or European influence—roughly the colonial and early independence period—and the period following the Revolution of 1910. Each of the first two has contributed something of lasting value to the third, which has emerged as a synthesis of Indian, European, and national elements entirely unique to the Mexican character. The cultural legacy of ancient or pre-Columbian Mexico is now recognized as one of the great treasures of mankind and one of the bases of a modern, nationalistic art movement unlike anything else experienced in the Western Hemisphere (see ch. 3).

Archaeological finds throughout the 1960s and 1970s continued to push the beginnings of Mexican art further and further back. In the late 1960s some cave paintings were found in the state of Guerrero that were estimated to be 4,000 years old. Ceramic figures of a similar vintage have also been found to support this date. The figures are of such quality and detail that one archaeologist said, "There is nothing in all of Mesoamerican art which can compare with the intensity of movement and the electric feeling of rapport, of these figures"; and compared to these vivid portraits much of the later work seems stiff and stylized. After the cave paintings and the terra-cotta figurines came pottery, murals, sculpture—mostly bas-relief—and other artistic expressions in a durable medium. As a consequence of the durability of these relics, archaeologists have been able to assemble fairly complete pictures of these ancient cultures.

Architecture was also an extremely important means of artistic expression to the pre-Columbian peoples and was often combined with bas-relief carvings and painted murals. The effect was to achieve a perfect synthesis of architectural function and artistic form. These structures were often pyramid shaped and built to serve a religious or administrative function. Among the most impressive architectural feats are those of the Toltec, Maya, and Aztec cultures.

One of the outstanding examples is the Pyramid of the Sun, found thirty miles northeast of Mexico City in the ancient city of Teotihuacán. It is one of the largest monuments in pre-Columbian America, and it measures 720 by 760 feet at the base, has five terraces, and rises to a height of 216 feet. Originally the entire surface was decorated and painted. The Mayans were also outstanding architects, constructing many of their cities in the dense tropical forest of the Yucatán Peninsula. A characteristic and exclusive feature of Mayan architecture is the corbeled, or false, arch constructed by setting up two parallel piles of stones and gradually bringing them closer together until they meet at the top. Mayan painting also attained a high artistic and technical level, most of it being fresco painting used to decorate temples and palaces. Such frescoes served as an impetus to the young artists in the post-revolutionary period who were looking for a touchstone for a new art movement. The art of the Aztecs, which found no really valid or original expression in pottery or painting, may be summed up as basically a sculptor's art. The Aztecs developed an imposing new style of sculpture that was energetic and often austere and managed to incorporate much of it architecturally. The Aztec genius found a perfect form of expression in the carving of bas-reliefs, in which a feeling for draftsmanship and detail predominates.

The Spanish conquest began another period in Mexican art and architecture, one in which the European—especially the Spanish—influence predominated. The first important buildings were the monasteries of the various Roman Catholic orders, and they were followed by hundreds of churches. The sixteenth century became known architecturally as the century of cathedrals. The need to decorate the growing number of religious buildings made Mexican artists indispensable, as well as those Flemish, Spanish, and Italian artists who came to New Spain. An entire school of religious art with its own techniques and style thus grew up to meet the demands of architecture. This devotion to religious themes and Roman Catholic expression has also been a point of controversy for many of the postrevolutionary artists.

Throughout this second period, which was to span some five hundred years, Romanesque, Gothic, Renaissance, baroque, neoclassic, and Romantic elements became intertwined with Indian and Mudéjar (Islamic) influences. Baroque, in its final and most exuberant phase, was the language of innumerable works of art throughout the country. It combined several contemporary trends, including rococo and Churrigueresque, which was named after the Spanish architect José de Churriguera. The combination of the Spanish-Latin temperament with the native made Mexico the home of baroque at its most expressive, and many churches still bear the soaring towers, imposing facades, and gilded, colorful interiors of this style. The reaction against baroque, which was thought of as a style officially imposed by Spain, led to the neoclassical style, which itself was a reflection of the French Revolution. Toward the end of the nineteenth century, artists were beginning to emerge who would be the forerunners of the independent muralists. José Guadalupe Posada (1852–1913) and Saturnio Herrán (1877–1918) were both predecessors.

The Revolution of 1910 ushered in the modern period in Mexican art and had a greater effect in expanding Mexican self-awareness than any other movement before or since. The revolution strove to bring back and upgrade the Indian culture, and this doctrine was accepted as the cultural program of the revolution and its aftermath. For thirty years the artistic establishment in Mexico was dominated by concepts of nationalism and social realism as portrayed by the muralists, and the revolution itself became as obligatory a theme as Christianity had been earlier. Shortly after the outbreak of the revolution José Vasconcelos, minister of education under President Alvaro Obregón, organized the first official support that made the muralist movement possible. Because of this official support the doctrinaire nationalism of the muralists represented the official view of art in Mexico throughout the first half of the twentieth century. It has also been a difficult current to challenge, as many new and aspiring artists have discovered.

The visible effects of the cultural program were brought out by three muralists who also played a large part in the revolutionary setting: Diego María de la Concepción Juan Nepomuceno Estanislao de la Rivera y Rodriguez, more commonly known as Diego Rivera (1886–1957); José Orozco (1883–1949); and David Alfaro Siqueiros (1896–1974). Lesser known but nonetheless important to the movement was Gerardo Murillo (1877– 1964), who was commonly known as Dr. Atl, after the Aztec word for water. Dr. Atl was the revolutionary artist who set the example of using art as political propaganda. He was also heavily involved as a militant organizer even before the outbreak of the revolution. Under his leadership two important precedents were established while Porfirio Díaz was still in power: the association of artists under militant leadership and the painting of murals in public buildings as a group project under government sponsorship. He also set the example of seeking his techniques abroad and his subjects at home and awakened in students a sense of individual and national identity.

The shift from easel to mural painting, coupled with the subordination of form and color to exciting subject matter, was the decisive turning point in the history of Mexican painting. For Rivera this meant rediscovering the lost art of fresco painting. Rivera traveled to Italy to study fresco paintings of the Italian Renaissance. Upon his return to Mexico he was commissioned with several other muralists, including Siqueiros and Orozco, for a mural at the National Preparatory School in Mexico City. In this first major mural, completed in 1922, there were many individual styles but one common theme—Mexico. Rivera continued to dominate the muralist school, by the sheer volume of his work if nothing else—at the time of his death it was said to cover 4,000 square meters. In subject matter Rivera exalted the revolutionists, the Indian, and the Mexico of the Aztecs; he defamed the representatives of capitalism, the church, and the conquest. His major work was the National Palace in Mexico City (1930–35), the subject of which was the history of Mexico from the pre-Hispanic era to the present.

Orozco was overshadowed by Rivera during his lifetime but is the only one of the muralists whom the newer generations recognize as a seminal force and spiritual ancestor. Moreover, Orozco's work has been posthumously enhanced through the praise of critics. Orozco first dedicated himself to social caricature, and in a 1916 exhibition he portrayed a sick society of dwarfs, cripples, and prostitutes in need of transformation through the work of revolutionary heroes. His later work concentrated on the tragic and cruel aspects of life, often depicting events of desperate energy during the revolution. As a dissenter from the muralist movement, Orozco declared that the emphasis on nonaesthetic content would lead to purely descriptive or anecdotal painting.

Siqueiros was the most politically active of the three. He was a man who associated himself with polemics, manifestos, class struggle, and communism. He took an active part in the revolution and twelve years later organized the Syndicate of Technical Workers, Painters, Sculptors, and Similar Guilds, an organization intended to promote solidarity among artists and the working class. The group issued a manifesto that set forth the ideology of the Mexican revolution: "to liquidate the decadence of modern art, to socialize artistic expression, and to destroy bourgeois individualism." Later he criticized this manifesto and pointed out that none of the artists wanted to give up bourgeois easel painting; they merely changed its name to "movable" painting. Apart from his political leanings, Siqueiros is known as the foremost innovator in contemporary Latin American painting techniques. Among his most notable works are *Retrato de la Burguesía* (Portrait of the Bourgeoisie), located in the Electricians' Union headquarters, and *Por una Seguridad Completa y para Todos los Mexicanos* (In Behalf of Complete Security for all Mexicans), located in the Social Security Hospital in Mexico City.

Murals did not entirely monopolize the world of art. Although their work was degraded as an aristocratic form of art, many artists continued in the field of easel or "movable" painting. They largely reflected the prevailing international currents of the time: surrealism, Dadaism, and neoromanticism. None of these, however, became an important national current or created international interest because of the firm grip the muralists had on the world of Mexican art. In fact, it is significant that the leading exponent of surrealist art in Mexico has been an artist of English origin. Purely abstract art was slow to emerge and has never been a dominant tendency.

What these countercurrents needed and eventually found was an artist of sufficient stature to confront muralist popularity. Two such artists emerged, Carlos Mérida (b. 1891) and Rufino Tamayo (b. 1899). Mérida, a native Guatemalan, was an artistic leader in both Mexico and Guatemala and was referred to as "the poet of the pallet." He discarded the picturesque image of native art in favor of a synthesis of folklore, archaeology, and plastic concepts. In 1919 he went to Mexico, and there he became influential in initiating semiabstract figuration and the inventive use of indigenous motifs. His personal evolution led him to become both abstract and figurative, and he consistently avoided any sort of naturalistic nativism or social realism. Nevertheless, he also did documentary work on Mexican folklore, including two sets of colored lithographs depicting traditional Indian dances and fiestas. As he became increasingly interested in art as an integrated part of architecture he branched into murals, and some critics consider this his best work.

Tamayo was the first Mexican artist of note who was not a muralist. His early works include the whole indigeneous-folkloristic category. As a young man he was appointed head of the Department of Ethnographic Drawing in the National Museum of Anthropology, and this gave him encyclopedic knowledge of the Mexican peoples. Nevertheless, in contrast to other artists, he did not feel that being Mexican and participating in international currents in contemporary art were mutually exclusive. In 1960 Tamayo even criticized the older school by saying, "There is no place for art in political or ideological manifestations." He was himself heavily influenced by Pablo Picasso and Georges Braque and incorporated certain of their stylistic elements, such as Picasso's exaggeration of parts of the body. His work is marked by flexibility, increasing abstraction of the human figure, and subtle colors.

Tamayo's works were the bridge between the older muralists and the newer generation born around 1920. Three of the most important artists in the 1960s and 1970s have been Ricardo Martínez (b. 1918), Juan Soriano (b. 1920), and Pedro Coronel (b. 1923). Martínez is a self-taught painter, whose emphasis on the nude human subject has become his hallmark. His matured style emerged after 1959, the emphasis increasingly being placed on the primordial and timeless aspects of his subjects. Maternity, fecundity, and man's dependence on nature are elemental themes.

Soriano made early and favorable beginnings as a figurative painter—largely landscapes and children's portraits in Mexico City. A trip to Rome turned him toward semiabstraction, which has remained his style. One of the best examples of his style is *The Fish*, now in Mexico City's Museum of Modern Art, which is outstanding in the use of hallucinative and original colors. He has managed to incorporate both figurative and abstract styles into a unique dualism of curvilinear forms.

Pedro Coronel (b. 1923) and Rafael Coronel (b. 1932) are two brothers who have greatly contributed to contemporary Mexican art. Pedro's first one-man show in Mexico won critical acclaim from such eminent intellectuals as Octavio Paz. His paintings depict a metaphysical interpretation of man and his universe in which the sun is a central symbol and cubist treatment is the vehicle. In his work there are references to myths, magic rituals, and the realm of the primitive. His brother Rafael has remained within the figurative mode, making human beings his central subject. Other objects on the canvas are only hinted at. He prefers to paint people of humble origins, dwelling on their humanity and individuality rather than making them representatives of their social class. In one phase of his work he turned to expressionism and distortion. During this time his paintings verged on the macabre, representing fear, confusion, and dissolution.

Several Mexican artists have moved beyond surrealism and into the world of fantasy, among them Alberto Gironella (b. 1929). Gironella, the son of a Mexican mother and a Spanish father, uses the heritage of the Spanish masters as a point of departure for all of his work. He is an extremely versatile artist: oil painting, mixed media, drawing, engraving, sculpture, or three-dimensional objects. He works from specific paintings, taking them through a series of changes and media—a gradual decomposition of the original model that results in its ultimate transformation. The model undergoes all kinds of decomposition and recomposition, such as style, texture, form, color, medium, and even essential being.

José Luis Cuevas (b. 1933) is considered the master of pen and ink drawing in Mexico. His first exhibit was in 1947 in an open-air lot in Mexico City, and his first gallery show was six years later. Since 1960 he has become much in demand, and his illustrated books in limited editions are expensive. Cuevas did not go along with the postrevolutionary nationalism and social realism. Nevertheless, he has been aligned with other Mexican artists because of what one critic called a "passionate, cruel sense of truth." Cuevas himself admitted that the theme of insanity has long been a dominant one in his work.

Since 1960 there has been tremendous growth in the field of sculpture. Variety in style and media also has been impressive. This ranges from the traditional stone sculptures to works using scrap metal, machine parts, and miscellaneous pieces of junk that the artists have salvaged. The work of Helen Escobedo stands out in sculpture—particularly her bronze pieces—and in the creating of environments. One of her critics described her as creating a space that is musical and then filling it with music. One of her most famous pieces is just that—a fish that contains a radio deep inside.

Pedro Coronel and Soriano, already described as artists, have also made important contributions in sculpture, Coronel in stone of monumental proportions and Soriano in ceramics. Coronel has used the figure of a hooded female in two of his more prominent works, omitting detail in favor of hollow spaces delineated only by the curves and folds of the garment. Soriano, in his use of ceramics, has felt a sense of affinity with the primitive cultures of Mexico. Although he does not reproduce Indian themes per se, he does use the spirit and symbols of these ancient peoples.

204

Architecture, like art, was uplifted by the revolution and modernist currents of the twentieth century. After Churrigueresque, the neoclassical movement began to impose formalism on Mexican tastes, and this led to a decline of inventiveness. With the reform and confiscation of church property in the second half of the nineteenth century, many good buildings of colonial style fell into decay while the nouveaux riche built new mansions in the Second Empire style. Of this particular period one critic said, "All that was worst in French municipal taste went in the public buildings during the age of Porfirio Díaz (1876–1910)."

With the revolution, two distinct and sometimes conflicting architectural styles developed, functionalism and nationalism. Functionalists rid themselves of the empire style in favor of clean lines and a plain unadorned style that stressed practicality and comfort. They desired to see modern styling and techniques spread throughout Mexico. The functionalist era was launched in the late 1920s and early 1930s by José Villagrán García (b. 1901) and Juan O'Gorman (b. 1905). Villagrán García started the movement and was appointed director of the newly created National School of Architecture in 1932. O'Gorman was converted to functionalism by Villagrán García and became a militant advocate of utilitarian architecture based on science and technology. In 1929 O'Gorman built a combination house and studio for the muralist Rivera in the style of the French architect Le Corbusier. This became celebrated as being among the first "functional" houses to be built in Mexico. To lighten the austerity of his functionalism, O'Gorman chose bright colors, such as blue, rose, red-brown, and Venetian red, for his exteriors.

Practicality, efficiency, and minimum expenditure dominated this architectural style, which was thus very popular in government-sponsored projects. Many architects devoted themselves to creating large edifices able to withstand earthquake shocks. Others built elementary and technical schools and became interested in low-cost housing for workers. Nevertheless, functionalism was attacked by nationalists who wanted Mexican architecture to reflect nationalist traits in an overt manner and by those who felt functionalism stifled personal creativity. Even O'Gorman eventually repudiated his association with functionalism and became highly decorative and nationalistic in orientation.

Although modern architecture began as functionalism, this did not prove the ultimate solution, as it left unsatisfied an ingrained love of the baroque—a touch of the extravagant and the irrational. Eventually functionalism declined or was absorbed into new expressions less austere in character. Since the early 1950s, especially, architecture in Mexico has flourished and has produced some of the finest buildings in contemporary Latin America. This has been caused by several factors: the establishment of the National School of Architecture as a part of the National Autonomous University of Mexico, supplemental training abroad, an abundance of talent, a balance of individual and group efforts, strong support from both government and private sectors, and a highly ingenious blending of ancient Middle American and modern international trends.

The most celebrated achievement in Mexican architecture is the University City of the National Autonomous University of Mexico, located on the outskirts of the Federal District and covering an area of 1,500 acres. Over 100 architects participated in its construction, which was begun in 1950 under the general direction of Carlos Lazo, Mario Pani, and Enrique de Moral. It stands as one of the major accomplishments in Latin American architecture. The most impressive building in the complex is the Central Library; it is also the most successful example of integration of the arts in the University City. Stone mosaics designed by O'Gorman cover all four sides of the structure. This oblong block rises above a wider and more open structure, which contains a lava-stone wall enclosing a garden courtyard. The materials used in its construction —lava, sandstone, onyx, and the multicolored stones of the mosaics— were gathered from every Mexican state.

The museums of anthropology and modern art also stand as solid achievements in the field of creative architecture. If the University City represents Mexico's confrontation with the modern age, the new National Museum of Anthropology represents its confrontation with the past. In building this museum the principal criterion was to achieve a massive and monumental effect in keeping with the form and character of ancient Middle American architecture and sculpture. The Museum of Modern Art, located in Chapultepec Park (Bosque de Chapultepec) and begun in 1964, includes beautiful gardens as an integral part of the environment. The architectural aim is to induce the visitor to prolong his stay in the galleries by providing a constantly attractive outlook.

Emotional architecture—the antithesis of functionalist puritanism— has in the last two decades found many advocates in Mexico. Among them is O'Gorman, who coined the phrase organic architecture—meaning that which is in harmony between man and nature—and built his own house along these lines. The main portion of the house is built into a natural grotto of lava rock, and the rest of the house is constructed around it. Mathias Goeritz (b. 1915, in Germany) is another architect interested in achieving "a unified totality in art." At various times in his life he has worked as an artist, sculptor, architect, teacher, and writer. When working as an architect, he likes to combine his talents with others, constructing experimental museums on vacant lots and modernistic cathedrals in planned cities. As artistic adviser to the Organizing Committee for the 1968 Olympic Games held in Mexico, Goeritz was able to use his favorite architectural feature, concrete towers. One of the architects who has worked with Goeritz is Luis Barragán (b. 1902) who, despite the lack of a degree in architecture, has become one of the most successful and internationally famous Mexican architects; he specializes in landscape architecture.

Félix Candela (b. 1936, in Spain) has become known as the master of curvilinear forms. He strongly advocates the use of flowing aesthetic lines as opposed to the boxlike rectangular structure favored by current international architects. He began to build concrete shells in 1949 and over the years has developed various uses and ramifications for this versatile form. One of his most outstanding achievements was in the building of the Cosmic Rays Pavilion for the University City in 1951. Structural problems demanded that the crown of the shell have no more mass than eight pounds per square foot. Candela designed and built a saddle-shaped vault, with a span of thirty-three feet and a thickness at the crown of seven-eights of an inch, which has since become known as the "thinnest shell in the world."

FOLK ART

Well-developed folk art is the natural expression of a proud and artistic people. Official recognition of the value and significance of popular arts and crafts came soon after the revolution when in 1921 the first folk art exhibit was organized by Dr. Atl and others. This exhibit began the current of expansion and popularization of all Mexican folk arts into cultural as well as economic realms. It was estimated in 1970 that as many as 2 million families, mainly rural, were dedicated to the production of arts and crafts. An estimate in 1968 placed production at 2.4 billion pesos (12.5 pesos equal US$1), 1.1 billion of which was placed on the internal market and 1.3 of which went to foreigners in Mexico and abroad (see ch. 2).

The fact that much of the artisan work is absorbed at home attests to the utility and quality of the work, as well as the national popularity of folk arts among all classes. It must be emphasized that it is not the revival of dead crafts but the continuation of a living and utilitarian art. In fact, some experts say that the finest examples are still used by the families that made them. Moreover, increasing numbers of middle and upper class Mexicans take pride in displaying national folk art in their homes, where once European art predominated.

Spurred by such achievements as the creation of the Popular Arts and Crafts Board in 1951 and the National Arts and Crafts Council in 1968, folk art production has increased in quality, quantity, and ease of distribution. The board—charged with the conservation, protection, and encouragement of folk arts—has undertaken several ambitious projects. It has established workshop-schools where promising young artisans may perfect their craft in an atmosphere stressing traditional techniques. In order to restore the use of primary materials, the board undertook the cultivation of cochineal and indigo, very important in the dyeing of pre-Columbian cloth. The council arose as a response to the National Arts and Crafts Congress, which was called by the Ministry of Industry, Commerce, and Fisheries to discuss problems concerning folk arts. The council, an organization made up of craftsmen from all over Mexico, undertook such tasks as the creation of regional agencies, the first census of folk art categories and craftsmen, and a program to resolve the most immediate problems—primarily those related to financing.

Production is varied and abundant, and it is estimated that twenty-four different branches of folk art exist. The principal production centers are in the states of Jalisco, Michoacán, México, Puebla, Oaxaca, Chiapas, and Yucatán, as well as in the Federal District. Products include pottery, textiles, metalwork, woodwork, palm fiber products, glassware, toys, and leatherwork. Pottery making occupies the largest number of craftsmen and is of two types, clay pottery fired at low temperatures and ceramics baked in high temperature kilns. For the variety of styles and techniques in pottery, Mexico has few rivals in the world. Clay pottery found in the Valley of Oaxaca, for example, is primitive and shaped by ancient methods. The famed figurines of Teodora Blanco and the large jars and pitchers of other artisans bring many tourists to the area every year. In contrast to the Valley of Oaxaca is the village of Tonalá, located near Guadalajara, which has experienced a revival of the potter's art. Much credit for this revival is given to Jorge Wilmot, who enlivened and expanded traditional designs and introduced high-temperature kilns into the area. Among his trademarks are highly glazed birds and animals painted with free-flowing leaf motifs.

Textile production is classified according to the kind of fiber used in three major groups: cotton, wool, and hard fibers. Cotton garments with embroidery and openwork are popular as ceremonial dress in Indian communities as well as for tourists and urban Mexicans. The making of cotton or wool *rebozos* (shawls) and *sarapes* (blanket-like outer garments) is popular throughout Mexico, the *sarapes* of the Yaqui Indians of north Sonora being of especially fine quality. The Yucatán Peninsula is the major henequen-growing region and, therefore, the producer of the greatest number of colorful baskets, rugs, and accessories.

Mexico possesses a long tradition of gold and silver work dating to pre-Columbian times, when precious metals were used as adornments and religious items. Gold and silver still occupy a large portion of artisan talents. Silver is still worked with the old manual techniques and is used for table services, such as cutlery and other large pieces, and jewelry. The most important production centers are Taxco, the Federal District, and Guadalajara. In the same vein, lapidary work is also practiced, especially in Querétaro and areas where semiprecious stones—opals, amethysts, turquoises, and agates—are mined.

MUSIC AND THE DANCE

Music has long been preeminent in Mexican culture. The Aztecs possessed a variety of instruments. Those that have been discovered recently indicate that the ancient tribes knew of harmony 200 years before it evolved in Europe. Aztec composers and musicians were part of the staff of a palace. When the Spaniards introduced stringed instruments, the Indians showed great eagerness and aptitude in learning to play them.

When President Luís Echeverría made a state visit to Venezuela in July 1974, he carried with him a collection of Mexican instruments to be put on permanent loan to the Interamerican Institute of Ethnomusicology and Folklore in Caracas. The exhibit contained seventy-eight pieces and was divided into three sections: pre-Hispanic, colonial, and contemporary. Some pieces included were mud timbrels 1,100 years old and *jaranas* (small guitars) and harps found in modern Veracruzan bands.

Today, a guitar appears at almost any gathering. Almost no village, however small, is without a band (see ch. 7). Mariachis (wandering musicians) dressed as *charros* (Mexican cowboys) and players of the marimba (a percussion instrument similar to the xylophone) are present at markets, celebrations, and private parties. *Corridos* (ballads) tell of tragic love affairs, catastrophes, or the exploits of revolutionary heroes and bandits—the assassination of Francisco I. Madero, the pursuit of Pancho Villa, or the killing of Emiliano Zapata. History and new events thus are told in music for the illiterate thousands. Radios and jukeboxes are common and transmit not only Mexican music but popular music derived from European and United States sources. Popular composer Agustín Lara and singer Pedro Vargas are internationally known.

The National Symphony orchestra has a repertoire of European classical compositions but specializes in music of contemporary Latin American composers. The most influential contemporary Mexican composer is Carlos Chávez (b. 1899), who has produced nationally inspired music distinct from the European concept of nationalism in music. Chávez' nationalism is of a social character, born of the revolution. He uses revolutionary songs in his scores and attempts to accentuate the Indian contribution to Mexican music. More recent composers, such as Daniel Ayala (b. 1908), Blas Galindo (b. 1910), Miguel Bernal Jiménez (b. 1910), and Pablo Moncayo (b. 1912), have remained attached to the nationalist and revolutionary tradition begun by Chávez.

A new musical trend has appeared, which is a reaction to the traditional nationalism of earlier composers. Leading figures in the new trend are Rafael Elizondo, who applies a clean and formal style to Mexican themes and writes mainly for the ballet; Leonardo Velásquez, who has done musical scores for motion pictures; Manuel Enríquez, a violinist-composer; and Eduardo Mata (b. 1942), who is both a conductor and a composer. This new generation of composers seeks untouched forms of expression, feeling that the themes of nationalism have been overworked.

The dance in Mexico has also been highly nationalistic in character. Many traditional Indian dances survive, such as Los Viejitos (The Little Old Men) and the spectacular Los Voladores (The Flyers). In the latter, five men costumed as hawks leap from a tall pole to which they are tied and, as the ropes unwind, the men appear to be flying to the ground. Other dancers combine elements from the country's history. The feather dancers of Oaxaca dance and act stories of the conquest. Another dance reflecting Spanish influence depicts the struggle between the Moors and the Christians. The Shell Dancers of the Central Plateau dance to honor the four winds and also the *mesa santa* (communion table). The national folk dance, the *jarabe tapatío*, is a heel-and-toe rhythm dance, which ends with the music of the bullfight. The widely acclaimed Ballet Folk-lórico of Mexico City, which has toured internationally, incorporated many of the traditional Indian folk dances into its repertoire.

SECTION II. POLITICAL

CHAPTER 9

GOVERNMENTAL SYSTEM

During its first half century of independence, Mexico experimented with, or was subjected to, at least forty forms of government, including federal and centralized organization, constitutional monarchy, dictatorship, and representative democratic government. Nevertheless, the country has had only three constitutions, those of 1824, 1857, and 1917. The Constitution of 1917 has been continuously in force since its adoption, although it has been amended more than 100 times. It reflects both the influence of the United States Constitution and the Mexican experience of dictatorship and social revolution.

As an expression of the government's intentions to regulate the economy and to provide for the basic needs of its citizens, the 1917 document was by far the most radical of its time in the Western Hemisphere. Such plans for pushing forward toward revolutionary goals called for a strong executive and a strong central government; thus, although the Mexican Constitution sets forth a tripartite division of power—among executive, legislative, and judicial branches—and a federal system, the powers of the executive far exceed those of the other branches, and the federal government assumes extensive rights to intervene in the constituent states. The actual distribution of power in the political system has served to reinforce these structural asymmetries.

The formula for continuity and relative stability in government that has evolved since the revolution is replete with seeming contradictions: a very strong president who is barred from reelection; a weak national congress in which token representation of the opposition is guaranteed; elected state governors with considerable local autonomy but only as long as they remain unquestionably loyal to the president; monopolization of political activities by a single party but one that is broadly based; and universal suffrage but little choice for the voters. With the vast apparatus of the state behind it, the Institutional Revolutionary Party (Partido Revolucionario Institucional—PRI) has been invincible at the polls since its inception in 1929 as the government party. Thus, it has generally been able to determine how much and what kind of opposition it will encourage or tolerate. In fact, its leaders have insisted upon maintaining token opposition. In accordance with a curious electoral law passed in 1964, opposition parties are allocated a minimum number of seats in the Chamber of Deputies irrespective of the vote.

In the matter of presidential succession, the function of the election itself is largely ceremonial. The crucial choice of the PRI candidate is generally made by the outgoing president, who has taken into account the opinions of other party leaders as well as the political climate in the country as a whole as he perceives it. Consultation with ex-presidents, business leaders, and the heads of labor and peasant unions is a well-established part of the process.

As no one is allowed to hold the same elective office for more than six consecutive years, it has been estimated that there is a turnover of approximately 18,000 elective posts during every six-year period. As newly elected officials choose to be assisted by their own loyalists, the turnover of appointive posts is even greater, amounting to about 25,000. The disruptive consequences of such a system are obvious, but there is also a larger sense in which the frequent turnover contributes to stability. Participation is broad, and most activist PRI members can anticipate at some time having their share of the perquisites—if not the power—of public office.

The federal government offers a broad range of welfare, public works, agrarian, and general financial services designed to benefit both urban and rural areas. As a consequence of the proliferation of such services, it appears that the locus of power has gradually been moving away from the extraofficial organs of the PRI and toward the formal machinery of the executive branch of the government, that is, the bureaucracy (see ch. 10). Although being a loyal party member remains a virtual prerequisite for acquiring a position in government, successful performance in the bureaucracy has also become a prime means of getting ahead in the party.

CONSTITUTIONAL DEVELOPMENT

The criollos (Mexican-born Spaniards) who led the movement for independence in 1821 faced several large political issues, including those of liberalism versus conservatism, centralism versus federalism, and the intertwining of church and state versus their separation. The Constitution of 1824 was influenced by the liberal Spanish 1812 Constitution of Cádiz, which had in turn been strongly influenced by the French Revolution. Inspired also by the United States Constitution, it provided for a federal republic, a tripartite division of powers, and a bicameral legislature. Nevertheless, the 1824 document contained a provision whereby in emergencies the chief executive could have overriding authority; this provision was exercised extensively, effectively abolishing federalism and other legal constraints on the power of the chief executive.

A reform movement, which reached its zenith in the 1850s, resulted in the promulgation of a series of laws restricting the privileges of the clergy. These laws were incorporated into the Constitution of 1857, which sought to destroy the church's temporal power base by depriving it of all of its real property except that specifically used for churches and related ecclesiastical institutions. It provided for civil marriage and for civil registries of deaths and births, removed cemeteries from clerical control, and required priests to celebrate the sacraments for people without regard to their ability to pay.

While the liberals were in the ascendancy, federalism was reestablished, together with a bicameral legislature with sufficient power to counter that of the executive. The Constitution of 1857 was similar in form to that of 1824, but it abolished the special ecclesiastical and military courts, called for the direct popular election of the president, and provided many guaranties of personal liberty. Strife between liberals and conservatives continued, however, leading to the War of the Reform, in which liberal leader Benito Juárez and his followers engaged proclerical elements in costly battles. Juárez became president in 1861, but it was a short-lived victory. French intervention, eventuating in the installation of Maximilian as emperor, followed soon after (see ch. 3). Even during the relatively effective constitutional government of Juárez, some of the regional *caciques* (men of much influence and power over large regions) continued to rule arbitrarily.

During the long dictatorship of Porfirio Díaz—which followed the death of Juárez in 1872, the collapse of the reform movement, and the interlude of Maximilian's rule—the Constitution of 1857 gradually ceased to be the functioning organic law of the state, and the constitutional guaranties of personal liberty were effectively abrogated. The clergy and landed gentry once again dominated the state and the government along with Díaz' intellectual advisers *(científicos*—literally, scientists). Thus rule by edict almost entirely supplanted constitutional processes between 1877 and 1911.

The far-reaching goals of the Mexican revolution, which began in 1910 with the attempt to depose Díaz forcibly, were reflected in the Constitution that emerged in 1917. President Venustiano Carranza called a constitutional assembly into being in 1916; the following year it produced a constitution, which is still the organic law of Mexico. Many of the features of the Constitution of 1857 were carried forward to the 1917 document, but features designed to institutionalize revolutionary change were added.

THE CONSTITUTION OF 1917

In the Constitution of 1917 a great many matters of public policy are treated explicitly. The clergy, for example, are prohibited from engaging in political activities, and procedures for the redistribution of land are detailed.

Article 27 ascribes to the nation original ownership of land, waters, seas, natural resources, and sources of power and fuel. Ownership by aliens of land in specific zones and of certain industries is prohibited, and the exploitation of many natural resources is limited to Mexican nationals. Article 123 of the original text contained enlightened provisions on labor and social security, which have been elaborated and further liberalized over the years through amendments. The article sets forth the principle that labor is entitled to a share of profits and that government employees are entitled to the protection of general labor legislation.

Reelection is prohibited for the president, and consecutive terms are disallowed for the National Congress. A very strong executive emerges, and the total pattern is repeated and detailed in the state constitutions so that the strong central executive extends across and into the state and local governments.

Thirty-one states and the Federal District constitute Mexico. The formal federal-state relationship leaves the states with little autonomy. The present federal regime is not the result of a compact between independent states; rather the states have been created by the government of the republic.

The states have legal equality. They do not have a right to secede. They are represented in a two-house national congress. Admission of new states and the conversion of territories into states are under the authority of the National Congress. States may fix their boundaries by mutual agreement and with the consent of congress. Congress may adjust state boundaries except in cases where there is a justiciable controversy, when the decision is left to the Supreme Court of Justice.

In late 1974 the two remaining territories, Baja California Sur and Quintana Roo, became states. A bill to create the two new states passed the Chamber of Deputies in October 1974, and local elections were to be held before the end of the year to select delegates to state constitutional conventions.

The tax structure of the republic is one of the most complicated facets of federalism. Since two or all three of the levels of government perform or participate in financing a number of services, there is no standard way of determining which will do what and by what method of financing. Thus there are many special arrangements among the three levels for certain services in particular states and localities. The striking factor about government spending in Mexico, however, is the preponderance of the federal role at all levels (see ch. 13).

Interpretation of constitutionality is the exclusive province of the federal court system, which includes forty-six district courts, six circuit courts, and the Supreme Court of Justice. The judicial provisions of the states stand on their own as long as they do not violate the Constitution or federal laws. The Federal District has local judicial systems established by federal law (see ch. 16).

The first twenty-nine articles of the Constitution of 1917 contain civil rights guaranties that limit the powers of the states and municipalities as well as of the federal government. The Mexican *amparo* is the legal concept that gives teeth to the bill of rights. Literally, *amparo* signifies protection, assistance, a human refuge. *Amparo* actions in other countries in Latin America tend to be primarily habeas corpus writs. The Mexican version not only champions the right of physical liberty but safeguards personal equities and property rights as well (see ch. 16). These protections, however, have often been denied to persons accused of subversive activities.

The enabling legislation for *amparo* is found in Article 103 and Article 107 of the Constitution and in the subsequent implementations of the law of *amparo*. Its objectives are the settlement of controversies arising from laws or acts of federal or state authorities that allegedly violate guaranties of individual liberty, laws or acts of federal authorities that allegedly injure or restrict the sovereignty of the states of the union, and laws or acts of the states that allegedly violate the federal sovereignty. "Acts" of authorities include denial of justice in civil or criminal suits or in final judgments of the courts and illegal acts or acts beyond the authority of government officials in the discharge of their functions. Most *amparo* actions in the federal courts have been in connection with violations of the constitutional guaranties of individual rights. But in all three categories they are effective only as to individual plaintiffs (natural or corporate) who request the protection of *amparo*. In conflicts between laws of the states and those of the republic, the only question to be solved by the court concerns the injury caused to an individual thereby and not the equity or inequity of the law or act itself (see ch. 16).

THE FEDERAL GOVERNMENT

The Executive Branch

The president must be a native born of Mexican parents and must be at least thirty-five years of age. There is no vice president and, if the president dies, a provisional president is elected by the Senate. Under Article 89 the president has broad appointive powers reaching well into the military establishment and many regional offices. Although he does not appoint state governors, he has an almost unlimited power to remove state and local officials. He has total control of foreign relations. The president orders the introduction of laws in congress and has a total or item veto over all legislation that is passed by congress. The Constitution provides no means for the Mexican congress to override a presidential veto. One of the president's most powerful executive tools is control over the budget, which is usually approved by congress. The president also legislates by executive decree in certain economic and financial fields.

The full extent of decisionmaking power structurally vested in the presidency has led one analyst to refer to the office as a six-year dictatorship. It appears, however, that for the most part this power remains latent. It is conceivable that without violating the Constitution a particularly bold and imaginative president might strike out in radically new policy directions without first generating a consensus among lesser power holders. Some observers have in fact seen the presidency of Lázaro Cárdenas (1934–40) in this light. What appears to be more commonly the case, however, is that the very weight and complexity of the job leaves its occupant little time and energy for creative departures.

The president becomes quite dependent upon the bureaucrats who assemble the data on the basis of which decisions must be made. He has little means of judging on his own, for example, whether the budget requests from the various agencies are reasonable. He is more likely to be engaged in greasing the wheel that happens to be squeaking than in contemplating the problems and needs of the society as a whole. And the constant bombardment of cross-pressures threatens to reduce him to the role of manager or arbiter. Compromise is not always possible, and the need to accommodate groups with greatly varying or conflicting interests often makes it appear that the president is following a zigzag course or that policy statements and governmental action are utterly disassociated.

The cabinet of President Luís Echeverría, who was elected in July 1970 and began serving his term of office in December, consisted of twenty-three ministries *(secretarías)*. The most powerful of these by far was the Ministry of Government (Secretaría de Gobernación), an office roughly equivalent to a combination of the departments of justice and of the interior of the United States, with various additional administrative functions; it has generally been the second most sought after post in the competition for power in the Mexican system. President Gustavo Díaz Ordaz held this post before his selection as the PRI presidential candidate in the 1964 elections, and Echeverría held it in the cabinet of Díaz.

In addition to the ill-defined and politically sensitive role of maintaining social order and internal security, the Ministry of Government carries out many of the functions that in some systems would be assigned to a presidential staff or executive office. Much of the president's information is collected and processed by this ministry. It assembles reports from the other ministries, for example, for the use of the president in his annual message to the opening session of congress, a message in which he presents the general outlines of future policy. It also advises the president on needed legislation, drafts bills to be submitted to the congress, and makes recommendations on bills adopted by congress and awaiting the president's signature.

Other ministries and agencies that have considerable influence or discretionary power include those with responsibility in the fields of finance and commerce. The Ministry of Finance and Public Credit, for example, may approve petitions of individual businessmen for tariff increases, and the Ministry of Industry, Commerce, and Fisheries is charged with import licensing. As a consequence, such entities are always under intense pressure from lobbyists.

Although national debates relating to public administration have tended to focus on those ministries and agencies engaged in making and

216

implementing economic policies, other ministries have from time to time found themselves engulfed in controversy. The Ministry of Public Education, for example, which annually receives about 30 percent of the federal agencies' share of the budget, has often served as a focal point of debate over such broad issues as the goals of the revolution vis-à-vis the Índian and the revolutionary or counterrevolutionary consequences of officially sponsored political indoctrination. The ministry has been torn from its inception in 1921 between the assimilationists who would accelerate the cultural integration of the Indian by teaching only in Spanish and the pluralists who have sought to facilitate the early learning process as well as to preserve indigenous cultures through bilingual education. The assimilationists have predominated historically, but the pluralists appeared to be gaining some ground in the early 1970s.

Political indoctrination carried out through the public education system was seen by the victorious revolutionaries as a means of consolidating their gains at the expense of the defenders of the prerevolutionary status quo. Contemporary critics of the PRI see it as a means of perpetuating the status quo and discouraging original thought. Their protests have been to little avail, however, as the ministry continues to expand its activities into cultural and vocational spheres previously beyond its purview.

Two new ministries were created during the session of the National Congress ending in December 1974. The Department of Tourism was upgraded to become the Ministry of Tourism, and the Department of Agrarian Affairs and Colonization became the Ministry of Agrarian Reform. The latter was expected to merge ultimately with the Ministry of Agriculture.

The extensive involvement of the government in economic development projects and social welfare services has generated a virtually uncontrollable bureaucracy. The numerous decentralized agencies were established largely in order to bypass the red tape of the regular ministries. But such decentralization has also resulted in duplication, nonuniformity in procedure, minor empire building, and sometimes frustration of national policy.

The general policy outlines of presidents intent upon enhancing social welfare services have on occasion been negated by the tendency of credit institutions to follow traditional banking procedures. The National Ejidal Credit Bank (Banco Nacional de Crédito Ejidal), for example, has tended to lend only to the most prosperous *ejidos* (see Glossary) because they would be more likely to repay the loans. One distraught minister said in 1959, "The decentralized agencies are practicing feudalism. Each one manages its own affairs for its own account and risk, only occasionally giving notice of its activities."

An interministerial committee created to facilitate coordination failed to achieve its objectives because its members were subordinates whose decisions had to await ministerial ratification. So many coordination plans had been designed for the decentralized agencies that it was being suggested in the early 1970s that there was a need to coordinate the coordinators.

A law promulgated in December 1970 was designed to increase the control of the federal government over autonomous agencies and state-affiliated enterprises by expanding the powers of the Ministry of National Properties. Nevertheless, the president does not have time to supervise even the work of all the ministries, much less of the decentralized agencies, and therefore many important decisions are left to ministers or administrators and their aides. Recognizing this, lobbyists for most interest groups approach the bureaucracy first and turn to the presidency itself only as a last resort.

The Legislative Branch

The federal legislature is bicameral: the Senate has two members from each state and the Federal District; the Chamber of Deputies had 210 members after the elections of 1970. The minimum membership of the chamber is a function of the population. In general, one deputy represents 200,000 people, although an electoral district may have as few as 100,000. Minority parties, however, are granted special representation in the form of deputies named by the parties. Their numbers vary with the voting percentage achieved in such a way that the Chamber of Deputies can have a maximum of 258 members. Resignations and deaths also contribute to fluctuation in the membership of the Chamber of Deputies.

Each deputy and his alternate are elected by direct popular vote of a congressional district for a period of three years. Consecutive terms are prohibited, but an alternate and a deputy can sometimes switch jobs from term to term. The senators are elected for a six-year term to correspond with that of the president. They, too, are barred from reelection. The congress has a permanent committee of twenty-nine members that attends to the interest of the legislative branch when congress is not in session.

Both the Chamber of Deputies and the Senate have some exclusive prerogatives, but these are relatively inconsequential in view of the strong executive system. The chamber approves the annual budget, discusses taxes, and verifies election returns. It considers accusations made against public officials and can bring impeachment proceedings before the Senate. The latter body has the exclusive power to ratify treaties as well as high presidential appointments. It can also declare that the constitutional powers of a state have "dissolved" or that a "conflict of arms" disturbing to constitutional order has arisen, permitting federal intervention to designate a provisional state administration.

Legislation may be introduced into congress by the president, by senators or deputies, or by an act of a state legislature. A bill so introduced is given a preliminary reading and then referred to an appropriate commission or subcommittee for study and recommendation to the house of congress in which the bill was introduced. Upon being passed by one house, a bill is automatically submitted to the appropriate committee of the second house (without an additional formal reading) for consideration. A procedure similar to that in the United States Congress then ensues in which joint committees of the two houses must work out a compromise version of a bill passed in different versions by both houses. A bill rejected by one house is considered dead until it has been reintroduced. A regular calendar of approved bills (those that have cleared committee) is maintained, but a two-thirds vote of the members of either house is sufficient to amend the order established on a given calendar. Private interests seeking to introduce legislation may present their positions to the presiding officer of either legislative branch and through him have their legislation introduced by a qualified member of that house.

Both houses of congress have been controlled by the PRI without serious challenge since the party's inception. The congress has generally been passive. It has made no effort to assert its prerogatives vis-à-vis the executive branch. The frequent contact, however, between legislators and interest group leaders, as well as officials of the executive branch, suggests that the role of the legislators is somewhat more than that of a legitimizing agent.

The Judiciary

The judicial branch of the government consists of a twenty-one member supreme court and a system of federal and state courts. In addition, there is a system of labor-management, quasi-judicial tribunals known as the arbitration and conciliation courts. With approval of the Senate the president names the judges of the Supreme Court of Justice, who in turn appoint judges for the lower courts. According to the Constitution a federal judge may be removed only by impeachment. In actual practice, however, the political system offers numerous ways of removing justices (see ch. 16).

The supreme court is organized into four general chambers *(salas)*, corresponding to substantive areas: civil, criminal, administrative, and labor. Five justices sit in each of the four chambers. The position of chief justice is rotative; he is elected annually by the membership of the court and may be reelected.

Mexican law depends upon absolute principles that are compiled by legislatures and jurists—in the Roman as contrasted to the English common law tradition. Civil law is a comprehensive system characterized by voluminous codes and strictures.

Because of the superior power of the executive branch, the courts have not generally been major agents for socioeconomic change. They have provided a forum, however, for those who have felt most severely disadvantaged by the redistributive efforts of the executive branch. The

Constitution of 1917 permits the confiscation of private property for payment of delinquent taxes or fines, but it also contains a due process clause, which provides that no one shall be deprived of property except by a judicial proceeding before competent and duly established tribunals. Thus the Federal Fiscal Court (Tribunal Fiscal de la Federacíon) was established in 1936 specifically to deal with controversies arising in fiscal matters between an individual and the government. Within certain limitations, the decisions of this court, composed of fifteen magistrates, have the force of stare decisis; that is, they stand as precedent.

The Civil Service

According to the Federal Labor Law for Public Employees of December 27, 1963, still in force in 1974, all employees of the federal government, including those in decentralized agencies, fall within the purview of the civil service. Since the concept of a civil service was first expressed in legislation in 1934, government employees have been permitted to strike under certain conditions, as interpreted by the Federal Court of Conciliation and Arbitration. Legislation of 1940 drew a distinction between the responsibility of higher officials and that of other public servants and specified seventy-two kinds of misconduct in office, including omissions as well as acts, for which officials may be punished. The measure provides that higher officials are to be tried by congress and lesser officials by a special federal jury.

Mexico has no competitive merit system of examination for civil service appointments in the usual sense. Recruitment and training of personnel occur within a relatively limited circle of PRI members. Whether a person is considered a professional civil servant is largely a function of the amount of time he has been able to spend in the service. Especially for such managerial personnel as bureau executives, rotation in office on the basis of patronage is the rule. It is also the rule for politically sensitive positions, such as military and police personnel. In addition to membership in the PRI, family ties continue to be important in civil service appointments.

As the governmental apparatus becomes more complex, the middle-level *técnicos* (technicians) in the many bureaus and agencies gain increasing leverage. Although they tend to be reluctant to submit proposals that their politically appointed superiors might find objectionable, their control over information and capacity to choose the technical alternatives from which their superiors must select the means of implementing a policy gives them considerable power. This power is furthermore reflected in their prestige within the PRI. The civil service as a whole tends to be relatively highly regarded (see ch. 2).

STATE AND LOCAL GOVERNMENT

Reserved powers are conceded by the Constitution to the states, but the power of the states is curtailed by the concurrent powers that the states share with the national government and by the obligations and prohibitions that the Constitution imposes on the states. The states must have a popular representative government that is republican in form. In local government the basic unit is a free municipality. The states must not, without the consent of congress, levy import or export duties, maintain permanent troops, or make war except in case of invasion or its imminence. Under no circumstances may the states usurp any of those powers exclusively delegated to the National Congress. The states must surrender criminals wanted in other states, publish and enforce federal laws, and grant full faith and credit to the public acts, registries, and judicial proceedings of the other states.

The states are given specific powers to grant professional licenses, to acquire and use real property for public purposes and for taxation, and to expropriate agrarian properties within their areas. With the consent of congress the states may settle their boundary questions and may initiate legislation in the federal congress.

The central government has the constitutional obligation to protect the states against uprising or turmoil. Article 122 provides that, upon the request of the governor of a state, protective intervention from the federal government may be made available. The federal government has in the past intervened in the affairs of a state under Article 76 without any such request and without affording any protection of the state's rights through the federal courts. The effect of Article 76 is to give the Senate powers to decide whether the governor of a state should be replaced and then, by a two-thirds vote, to approve a nominee for the gubernatorial replacement, who is selected by the president.

State governments consist of elected governors and chambers of deputies. Before the revolution and the establishment of the PRI, state governorships tended to fall into the hands of powerful local *caciques* who either ignored or actively intrigued against the federal government. Under the contemporary system, selection of the PRI candidate, which is tantamount to election, follows a pattern of the reconciliation of federal and local interests. The president, or presidential candidate, who has the final word, will want to fill the governorships with persons fully loyal to him, but he must also find a candidate who is acceptable to the local PRI leadership.

Provision of public services to urban areas is largely a function of the state governments, which levy taxes, receive federal subsidies, and in turn make subventions to municipalities. The basic taxes that support state regimes are levies on property, sales and consumers, gasoline, alcohol, interest and inheritance; income tax on salaries; and special assessments for public works.

The municipalities have relatively little power to tax or to mobilize fiscal resources through bonded indebtedness. Sales taxes belong to the state and federal governments, and the property tax is a state prerogative; so the only remaining tax base for the municipality is the issuing of business licenses and various permits for street vendors and miscellaneous small-scale activities.

Several major services are provided on a shared basis between federal, state, and local levels of government. Main highways and state roads are constructed and maintained by the federal highway department, the state governments, and local private initiative, each contributing one-third. Private initiative, in this case, may be a local government or, more usually, a local civic group. A similar arrangement prevails in financing domestic water service, in which the three levels of government assume respective shares of 20, 50, and 30 percent.

THE ELECTORAL SYSTEM

The Ministry of Government sets up a federal election commission that supervises the lesser electoral tribunals in the management of elections. Elections for president and for congress take place on the first Sunday in July every six years. Additional elections are held every three years for the Chamber of Deputies. In addition to the federal offices, state governorships, state and municipal legislative offices, and mayorships are filled through elections.

The Constitution of 1917 abolished literacy requirements for voting, and subsequent amendments have further expanded suffrage. An amendment extending the suffrage to women was approved by a majority of the state legislatures in 1953. It was approved by the National Congress and became law in 1954, and women voted for the first time in the congressional elections of 1955. Another amendment, passed in December of 1969, lowered the age of full citizenship rights, including suffrage, to eighteen. Previously, unmarried citizens had been ineligible until the age of twenty-one.

The president is elected by direct popular vote. Although the victory of the PRI candidate has never been in doubt, candidates campaign vigorously. The campaign serves to expose the candidate to a broad cross section, both social and geographic, of the people and their problems, and to give the president-to-be a chance to explain his program and cultivate a popular image. Under the pressures of the office, personal popularity may prove a most valuable asset. Despite the preordained outcome of the contest, voter turnout in presidential elections has increased steadily over several decades, from 5.3 percent of the population in 1917 to 27.6 percent in 1970.

Although opposition parties have never been represented in the Senate, PRI leaders have generally considered it desirable for opposition parties to have token representation in the federal and state chambers of deputies. The "mixed" system of proportional representation that went into effect at the federal level in 1964 was designed to facilitate the entry of opposition parties into those bodies. In his address to the Mexican Chamber of Deputies in September 1974, President Echeverría expressed satisfaction that this change in the electoral laws had increased popular participation in government, and reported that more than half of the states had begun changing their constitutions in order to establish such a system at the state level. In October he announced that he was sending to congress a bill to provide for similar "institutional representation" of the opposition in the Senate.

The federal law instituting proportional representation applies only to the Chamber of Deputies; senatorial seats, two from each of the states and two from the Federal District, are won by popular plurality vote. A registered party can win seats in the chamber either on the basis of a plurality in an individual electoral district or on the basis of deputies at large, known as *diputados de partido*.

To secure election of deputies at large, a party has to win at least 2.5 percent of the total national vote for deputies. This rule is a means of eliminating parties that contest in only a few states. A party that wins this percentage receives five deputy seats, and one additional seat is awarded for each additional 0.5 percent of the vote up to a limit of twenty seats. In the elections of July 1970 the PRI won all Senate seats and 175 seats in the Chamber of Deputies. Three minority parties won a total of thirty-five at large seats.

CHAPTER 10

POLITICAL DYNAMICS

The Mexican political system since the consolidation of the revolution in the 1920s and 1930s has been considered one of the most unusual in the world. For several decades it was generally viewed as a stable democracy dominated by a single party. By the 1970s, however, in light of the stern repression of student demonstrations in 1968, many observers had concluded that the persistence of the revolutionary ethos has served to camouflage a generally benign, in many respects enlightened, but increasingly "bourgeois" and decidedly authoritarian system. Competition for power and its perquisites occurs on at least two levels, within the party and between the party and other powerful interest groups, but both recruitment to leadership roles and mobilization of mass support for policies are initiated at the top of the power structure.

Since its inception in 1929 the official party—designated the Institutional Revolutionary Party (Partido Revolucionario Institucional—PRI) in 1946—has held the presidency, all state governorships, and all federal senatorial seats and has controlled the federal Chamber of Deputies, all state legislatures, and almost all municipal governments. Within the party structure are the selected or approved representatives of organized labor, headed by the Mexican Workers' Federation (Confederación de Trabajadores Mexicanos—CTM), and of the peasantry, headed by the National Confederation of Campesinos (Confederación Nacional de Campesinos—CNC), as well as an amorphous body known as the popular sector. This sector, embracing the civilian bureaucracy, the military, the liberal professions, small businessmen, and others, is by far the strongest.

Although some elements of the popular sector, such as the military, also articulate their interests through extraparty channels, attempts by labor and peasant groups to assert autonomy or to exert influence through other political parties have been unsuccessful. The carrot-and-stick options at the disposal of the National Executive Committee (Comité Ejecutivo Nacional—CEN) of the PRI have been formidable, and defectors have generally allowed themselves to be co-opted once again into association with the party. Although some urban laborers and peasants have been represented in the bargaining process, others, especially among the still unintegrated Indians, are not represented. The multisectoral nature of the alliance has made it possible for a relatively small number of participants in the development process to control the marginal groups, who in fact constitute a majority of the population.

Minor parties participating at the behest, or at least at the sufferance, of the PRI have served as an escape valve for frustration with official policies. But the PRI controls the electoral machinery, and it is not inclined to let opposition get out of hand.

The National Action Party (Partido de Acción Nacional—PAN) is the preferred opposition; the PRI is more fearful of opposition to its left, which it commonly discourages through refusal of legal registration. Opposition parties tend to weave in and out of the PRI structure much in the manner of ambivalent factions; the fact is that they have nowhere else to go.

The Roman Catholic Church has theoretically been viewed as an enemy of the revolution, but most observers contend that it weighs into the bargaining process at the top. Like most other groups, representatives of big business and big finance have legally prescribed relationships with the government, but they enjoy considerably greater autonomy than labor or middle-class groups. As a result they bargain with, rather than through, the party. This relationship has been somewhat blurred, however, by the proliferation of interlocking directorates among public and private enterprises and party and bureaucratic leaders.

The membership of the decisionmaking inner circle, or what one scholar has designated the "Revolutionary family," is apparently rather fluid as it is more often dependent upon personal relationships or political cliques (camarillas) than on formal party or governmental roles. Its patriarch at a given moment is usually, but not necessarily, the president, and former presidents figure prominently in the group. It has been estimated that beneath the top twenty or so leaders of national or regional political cliques is another layer of about 200 individuals representing a variety of interests, and below them in the structure is the formal apparatus of national and party government.

Revolutionary symbolism appears to have been effective in generating identification with the political system. It has been estimated on the basis of one survey that, whereas before 1910 nine out of ten Mexicans might have been beyond the reach and generally oblivious of the national system, by 1960 that number had been reduced to about 25 percent of the population. Although only about 10 percent were found to consider themselves participants in the system in 1960, about 65 percent considered themselves affected by it.

If the measure of democracy in the Mexican system is indeed as limited as some critics have claimed, the ruling group could ill afford a precipitous expansion of interest in participation. The attempts of Carlos Madrazo, as president of the CEN in the mid-1960s, to introduce primary-level competition in municipal elections proved so successful that he lost his job and was widely criticized by other party leaders. Nevertheless, President Luís Echeverría, who assumed office in 1970, has moved cautiously in the direction of expanding participation, both within the official party and among parties in formal legislative bodies.

THE MYSTIQUE OF THE REVOLUTION

Over the course of more than six decades, the Mexican revolution appeared to be virtually all things to all people. The sector that has profited most from the demise of the feudal structure is the bourgeoisie, but each of the major socioeconomic sectors has been favored by some administration under the revolutionary rubric. Before the social upheaval that began in 1910 most of the arable land was concentrated in large uneconomic units, first under the control of the Roman Catholic Church and later under the landed aristocracy. The economic gains that had taken place under the long rule of Porfirio Díaz had accrued mostly to a small local elite and to foreigners. For this the Díaz regime was widely condemned as the "mother of foreigners, stepmother of Mexicans." The nascent labor movement had been held in check, and the educational system had been foreign oriented and reserved to the well-born (see ch. 3).

The goals of the original instigators of the revolution were primarily political, as exemplified in their slogan "Effective Suffrage, No Re-election," but a subsequent, apparently spontaneous uprising by the peasants of the state of Morelos, led by Emiliano Zapata, adopted the slogan "Liberty and Land." Thus the goals of the revolution were as multifarious as the groups that became involved in its consummation. Although urban labor was free to organize under Francisco Madero and was instrumental in bringing Venustiano Carranza to power and although agrarian reform and labor benefits were incorporated in the Constitution of 1917, it was not until the presidency of Lázaro Cárdenas (1934–40) that urban labor and the peasantry were to reap the benefits of the revolution. The consolidation of the revolution in the 1930s opened up new channels of political expression, making it imperative that previously ignored sectors of the population be taken into account in the formulation of policy.

The agrarian reform probably benefited the incipient national bourgeoisie as much as the peasantry, as it forced the landed aristocracy to seek investment opportunities in new financial and industrial undertakings. It also drew much of the rural population out of its former isolation, changing consumption patterns in such a way as to enlarge the market for commercial products. It also made the peasant class vulnerable to the forces of cultural change, open to the development of new loyalties as well as to cultural fragmentation and alienation.

The PRI, which, with its adherents, has dominant influence on the national communications media, has traditionally presented itself as the embodiment of the symbols of nationalism and group attachment that were generated by the revolution; it represents itself as sole claimant to continuity with revolutionary leadership and ideals and has proved sufficiently flexible to include in its membership a broad spectrum of political beliefs. Since the 1960s a new wave of political forces has to some extent eroded the strength of the PRI but has not threatened its continued dominance.

The PRI has been largely responsible for the socialization process in which Mexicans have learned respect for the symbols of group attachment that unite their nation. Public and private holidays and festivals, official acts, dedications, and sporting events are occasions on which national values are paid homage. Newspapers and magazines regularly devote space to the treatment of historical and patriotic themes. The educational process, especially in the elementary grades, dedicates considerable attention to the patriotic legacies of Benito Juárez, the Revolution of 1910, and many other such themes. All of this is intended to build psychological links between the Mexican citizen and his nation. The socialization process and the control thereof are intimate parts of the competition for popular support within the Mexican political system.

POLITICAL FORCES AND INTEREST GROUPS

Private Enterprise

The groups that have been the most consistent beneficiaries of Mexico's economic growth over the last three decades have no official representation in the PRI. Such organizations as the Confederation of Industrial Chambers (Confederación de Cámaras Industriales— CONCAMIN) and the National Confederation of Chambers of Commerce (Confederación Nacional de Cámaras de Comercio— CONCANACO), nevertheless, enjoy semiofficial status and extensive influence on government. Although the influence of business organizations is certainly felt within the party, it appears that the most prestigious of these organizations negotiate with the party, rather than through it, at the highest levels of government for policies favorable to them.

The first private enterprise group to establish a highly advantageous working relationship with the government was the National Chamber of Manufacturing Industries. It emerged in the 1930s and 1940s when the pace of industrialization was accelerating rapidly and by the 1950s had become an effective advocate of tariff protection, tax incentives, and government subsidies to new industry. In exchange for such favors, it accepted PRI initiatives in land reform and social welfare measures.

By the mid-1960s the older sectors of the business community, represented by CONCAMIN and CONCANACO, had recognized the advantages of continuous and intimate contact with the government. Since the 1940s members of the business community have increasingly accepted appointments to positions in government, especially to positions on regulatory and advisory commissions. The federations and their constituent chambers, either on their own or at the invitation of the government, regularly express their demands in the form of proposals for new legislation or for amendments to pending legislation. Most of the influential members of the business community have consistently supported the PRI rather than the more conservative PAN.

Organized Labor

Organized labor has had an important role in Mexican politics since the revolution. Likewise, the government has had an important role in the affairs of organized labor since the unstable years from 1910 to 1930. In those years labor bosses were able to mobilize the support crucial to the victory of one revolutionary faction over another, and the victorious political faction was in turn in a position to support the organizational activities of one labor group while suppressing the efforts of contending groups.

By the time the forerunner of the PRI was founded, the pattern of collaboration between the government and the favored unions or confederations, as well as of the co-option of labor leadership, had been institutionalized. The administration of Cárdenas swelled the numerical strength of organized labor but also left it more dependent on the government.

The country's largest labor federation, the Mexican Workers' Federation (Confederación de Trabajadores Mexicanos—CTM), claimed a membership of about 2 million in the early 1970s. It had been dominant in the labor movement since it was founded as the Regional Confederation of Mexican Workers (Confederación) Regional Obrera Mexicana—CROM) by Luis Morones in the 1920s. It received international recognition in the late 1930s when its leader, Vicente Lombardo Toledano, founded the Latin American Workers' Confederation (Confederación de Trabajadores de America Latina—CTAL). At odds with the business-oriented governments that followed that of Cárdenas, Lombardo Toledano led a splinter group out of the CTM, and in 1949 CTM leadership passed to the more conservative Fidel Velázquez.

In the 1950s the CTM joined a number of lesser confederations and independent industrial unions to form a front known as the Workers' Unity Bloc (Bloque Unido de Obreros—BUO). In response, rival confederations to the left of the BUO united in opposition as the National Confederation of Workers (Central Nacional de Trabajadores—CNT). In addition to the CTM, one of the most powerful components of the BUO is the 400,000-member Government Employees Union (Federación de Sindicatos de Trabajadores al Servicio de Estado—FSTSE). In terms of salaries, fringe benefits, and patronage positions held, the FSTSE occupies an elite position within the labor movement and bargains through the popular rather than the labor sector of the PRI.

Some individual unions have supported such opposition parties as the Popular Socialist Party (Partido Popular Socialista—PPS), but most

229

adhere to the labor sector of the PRI. Rewards to labor leadership for cooperation with the government are abundant. CTM leaders, for example, have held seats in the National Congress on a regular basis for thirty years.

Peasant Groups

The complex pyramidal organization of the 3-million-member agrarian sector of the PRI is theoretically rooted in free elections within each *ejido* (see Glossary), but the charges of imposition of leadership have been widespread and continuous for forty years. Leadership at the municipal and state levels appears to be dictated by, or at least subject to the veto of, state governors. The national leaders of the National Confederation of Campesinos (Confederación Nacional de Campesinos—CNC), the predominant organization within the agrarian sector, are designated by the president.

The creation of the CNC during the Cárdenas administration made the peasants for the first time a nationwide political force to be dealt with, and the confederation has since served to mobilize rural support for the PRI. It has represented itself as the defender of the interests of the rural poor against the large landholders, and it has been expected to protect its members from fraudulent practices on the part of the National Ejidal Bank and the Department of Agrarian Affairs and Colonization. But the increasing incidence of land seizures and other forms of more or less spontaneous protest in rural areas suggests that its representation has been less than adequate.

Unrest had been greatest among the landless rural labor force, which amounted to over 3 million people by 1960 and was expected to reach 5 million by 1980. The problems of unemployment and underemployment were becoming increasingly grave, and standards of living for the group, already near the subsistence level in the early 1960s, have apparently continued to drop. This situation has been reflected in internal strife within the CNC as well as in the germination of opposition groups.

One such group was the Independent Peasant Confederation (Confederación de Campesinos Independientes—CCI), formed as an offshoot of the CNC in 1963. It was factionalized almost from the beginning, however, over the issue of collaboration with the PRI. One of its leaders who opposed collaboration, Ramón Danzós Palomino, was imprisoned, and its intellectual mentor, Lombardo Toledano, lost much of his following when he allowed himself to be co-opted by the PRI. The incarceration of Danzós Palomino and the deaths of Lombardo Toledano in 1968 and Cárdenas, another titular leader, in 1970 have left the CCI lacking dynamic leadership.

Another opposition group, the General Union of Mexican Workers and Peasants (Unión General de Obreros e Campesinos Mexicanos—UGOCM), which was responsible for the invasion of large landholdings throughout northern Mexico in the 1960s, suffered a similar fate. Its leader, Jacinto López, had been co-opted by the PRI, and the group had fallen into organizational chaos. In December 1974 the CNC, the UGOCM, the CCI, and a fourth peasants' organization, the Mexican Agrarian Council, pledged to unite, thereby bringing the process of co-option a step further, to the absorption of all peasant organizations into a single PRI-controlled central.

The Roman Catholic Church

Throughout much of Mexico's history the struggle between the church and its conservative supporters and the anticlerical liberals has amounted to virtual protracted warfare, grievances feeding upon themselves until both sides were irrational in their assaults. In the years following independence the church, favoring centralism and authoritarianism, met relatively ineffective opposition from the liberals, who favored federalism and representative government. The church's political and economic domination continued to expand until by the mid-nineteenth century it controlled about one-third to one-half of the national wealth, and the state found itself in the position of pleading with the church for loans.

Church privileges were curtailed from time to time when the liberals were in office. Most of the important reform legislation of the 1850s was aimed at breaking the grip of the church on national life, but the effects of such legislation were not always the intended ones. The Lerdo Law of 1856, for example, proclaimed that corporate bodies could not own land or property other than that used in the practice of the cult. The church, however, managed to escape the rigors of the law, and it was the *ejidos* that suffered most, as their land was absorbed by private large landowners.

The polarization that sparked the War of the Reform (1857–60) was such that the church was accused of seeking to impose a medieval theocratic state, while the liberals were accused of seeking the extinction of the church. Liberal victories were short-lived, and the church prospered under the Emperor Maximilian (1864–68) and the long dictatorship of Díaz (1876–1911).

Anticlericalism, then, was one of the cornerstones of the revolution, and the stable state that finally emerged from that upheaval had the power to enforce laws curtailing the role of the church in society. Some administrations, however, have chosen to enforce those laws less strictly than others. The most serious clash between church and state since the revolution was the so-called revolt of the *cristeros* (defenders of Christ) in the late 1920s (see ch. 5).

The power of the church reached a low ebb in the 1930s—when there were only about 500 priests in the entire country. It has grown steadily stronger since that time, and in the early 1970s there were over 8,000 priests. The issue of church versus state had been confused and blunted, however, by polarization within the church itself. Criticism of the government by the church was arising from both the Right and the Left.

Intrachurch controversy was deepened in 1971 when the Episcopal Commission for Social Action published a document castigating the church for its failure to attack social injustice in Mexico. Conservative clergymen, along with some trade union leaders and politicians, accused the reformists of violating the Constitution, which prohibits church involvement in political matters. President Echeverría dampened the controversy in early 1972 by expressing the view that political statements by priests were "within the wide range of liberties in Mexico."

The Military

Military officers continue to be extensively involved in the formal apparatus of the political process but generally as an expression of individual ambition rather than of institutional prerogatives or factional competition. The number of officers holding important policymaking positions has decreased steadily since the consolidation of the revolution (see ch. 17).

When the last of the general-presidents turned over the highest office to a civilian in 1946, the post of chairman of the CEN of the PRI became a military sinecure. But that post, too, has been held by civilians since 1964. Whereas in 1948 fifteen of the twenty-nine state governors were military officers, only two military men were governors in 1969. The chief of police of the Federal District, his assistant, and the head of the Federal Judicial Police, however, were generals.

The military as an institution has had considerably less autonomy in Mexico than in most other Western Hemisphere countries. Nevertheless, its political significance as a protector and defender of the PRI has been great, and the military position on certain issues has been forcefully presented both through the party and directly to the top policymakers. It was generally believed for example, that the military had strongly advocated the harsh measures that were taken to suppress the student movement in 1968.

University Students

Although Mexican students have a long tradition of political activism, their role as advocates of national policy since the 1940s had been muffled; it had consisted largely of the projection of ideas without the organizational muscle to turn those ideas into demands. Militant advocacy had generally been reserved for issues relating directly to university instruction. This was due in part to the seeming invulnerability of the PRI and in part to the atomization of student groups (see ch. 6).

Before 1968 the two main concentrations of students in the capital, the National Autonomous University of Mexico (Universidad Nacional Autónoma de México) with some 80,000 students and the National Polytechnical Institute (Instituto Politécnico Nacional) with about 50,000, had little to do with each other beyond a generalized sense of rivalry. The official student organization of the National Polytechnical Institute, the National Federation of Technical Students, was government financed and generally considered, especially by students of the National Autonomous University of Mexico, to be government controlled. Political activity at the autonomous university centered in the schools of law, economics, social and political sciences, and philosophy, but groups from these schools had little contact with each other and less with students from the traditionally apolitical schools of architecture, business, and engineering.

Virtually every political organization to be found in the larger community has its campus contingent. Communists, anarchists, Christian Socialists, Falangists, and many other such groups were to be found at the university, along with numerous organizations that existed only on campus. The PRI had attempted to extend its control over the university system through its own youth groups as well as through undercover agents. It had been less successful, however, in co-opting the academic community than it had been with other groups that were actual or potential articulators of political demands. The increasing incidence in the 1960s of the use of troops to quell student demonstrations at state universities had generated considerable animosity between students and the government. But student groups remained disunited and generally ineffective until 1968.

The impetus for a massive citywide student movement in the capital in 1968 was apparently a series of clashes of escalating seriousness between students and police. Special riot-trained police (*granaderos*) were sent in to break up a minor scuffle among students in July 1968 and in the process chased students into their school buildings, indiscriminately beating up students, professors, and janitors. This led to student demonstrations against riot police, who once again forcefully dispersed the students.

As student arrests, injuries, and deaths increased, representatives of each of the schools of the polytechnical institute and the university met and organized the National Strike Council (Consejo Nacional de Huelga —CNH). The six basic demands of the CNH remained the same throughout the period of turmoil: repeal of the articles of the penal code that allowed authorities to jail people for their words or beliefs; freedom for all political prisoners; dismissal of the chief and deputy chief of police of the Federal District; establishment of responsibility for the authorization of the use of riot police and the army against students; abolition of the riot police; and compensation for wounded students and for the families of those killed in previous clashes.

Student brigades representing the CNH fanned out to factories and villages and appeared to be gaining considerable public sympathy, and demonstrations drew successively larger crowds. The last one organized by the CNH drew several hundred thousand people in front of the National Palace on August 27, 1968. The government's anxiety regarding

233

the movement was magnified by the fact that in October the eyes of the world were to be focused on Mexico as the host of the Olympic Games.

On September 18, for the first time in forty years, troops occupied the grounds of the autonomous university, and several thousand students and professors were arrested. The climax of this confrontation was the Tlatelolco Massacre of October 2, in which troops fired into a crowd of demonstrators, killing a large number of students and wounding many more. The incident appeared to have broken the back of the student movement. Hundreds of students and professors remained in jail or went into exile. Some went underground and joined guerrilla units. Most returned sullenly to their studies.

THE PARTY SYSTEM

The Institutional Revolutionary Party

The assassination of President Alvaro Obregón in 1928 provided an impetus for Mexico's political leaders to band together into an enduring institutional arrangement whereby the nation could spare itself a repetition of the anarchy and bloodshed that had marked the Revolution of 1910. As a consequence, in 1929 a new party was formed, the National Revolutionary Party (Partido Revolucionario Nacional—PRN).

Under Cárdenas, the party was renamed the Mexican Revolutionary Party (Partido Revolucionario Mexicano—PRM). It was organized into four sectors: agrarian, labor, popular, and military. The agrarian sector contained a number of subsidiary organizations designed to integrate peasants and small landholders into the party. The most prominent of these groups was the CNC. The labor sector was integrated around the CTM under the leadership of the socialist intellectual Lombardo Toledano. The popular sector appealed primarily to urban small business-men, professionals, students, and public employees; the military sector was meant to represent and contain the armed forces.

Under President Manuel Avila Camacho in 1946 the PRM became the Institutional Revolutionary Party (Partido Revolucionario Institucional —PRI). The military sector of the PRI was absorbed by the popular sector in 1940 at the start of Avila Camacho's administration as a gesture of demilitarization in Mexico's growing commitment to a civilian steward-ship of the revolution. The official party, PRI, thus emerged as the all-encompassing structure that it is today.

Because of the intimate relationship between the PRI hierarchy and the Mexican governmental process, the structure of decisionmaking and accountability within the party is most important. Immediately beneath the president of the republic (who is also the titular head of the PRI) is the National Executive Committee (Comité Ejecutivo Nacional— CEN). The president of the CEN is traditionally thought of as the second most powerful man in the PRI. Next there is the Grand Commission, or the National Council, which exercises a watchdog function between meetings of the principal representative body of the PRI, its National Assembly. The National Assembly, through an extensive and complicated subsystem of regional and local units, is intended to be the popular voice of PRI. It convenes once every six years to establish party policy and to ratify the party's nominee for the presidency. The National Assembly may also be called into an emergency session by the CEN, although this has rarely been done.

The CEN has more power within the PRI than either the National Assembly or the National Council. The principal functions of the CEN are convocation of national assemblies and specifying criteria for choosing delegates; convocation of the National Council and establishing criteria for selecting delegates; supervision of party discipline with respect to both groups and individuals; establishment of special investigatory commissions to deal with regional political problems; and control over a broad range of local and regional political organisms including the state and municipal party committees. The CEN conducts programs of public education and citizenship training and is the nucleus of promotional activity on behalf of party unity and recruitment.

The party's presidential candidate polls about 90 percent of the vote. In 1970 PRI candidate Echeverría received 11.9 million votes to 1.9 million for his only opponent. The PRI also won all sixty Senate seats and 175 of the 210 seats in the federal Chamber of Deputies. Of the more than 2,300 mayoralties, only seventeen were held by other parties in 1969, and the PRI controlled all but twenty-three of the 700 municipal councils. Furthermore, between 1952 and 1967 the percentage of the total vote accruing to the PRI increased in all but three of the twenty-nine states, an average increase of 11 percent.

The Opposition

Although the National Action Party (Partido de Acción Nacional—PAN) is considered by most observers to be Mexico's principal opposition party, there are other groups that are registered as legal parties. Among these are the Authentic Party of the Mexican Revolution (Partido Auténtico de la Revolución Mexicana—PARM) and the Popular Socialist Party (Partido Popular Socialista—PPS). The PARM is often viewed as a conservative appendage of the PRI. It usually collaborates with the dominant party and enjoys representation in the Chamber of Deputies. The PPS, founded by labor leader Lombardo Toledano, also enjoys representation in the Chamber of Deputies. The PPS and the PARM entered candidates in a number of federal, state, and local elections in 1970, but the total vote for the PPS was only 123,330 and that for the PARM, 75,921. The PARM appeared on the verge of disbanding in late 1974.

Mexico also has several parties and political groups that cluster about the fringe of the legally recognized system but do not have legal registration permitting them to appear on electoral ballots. Examples of such groups are the National Union of Anti-Anarchists (Unión Nacional Sinarquista—UNS), the National Liberation Movement (Movimiento de Liberación Nacional—MLN), and the Mexican Workers' Party (Partido Mexicano de Trabajadores—PMT). These groups are not recognized as legal political parties by the Mexican government because of their failure to satisfy membership requirements as prescribed by law. Therefore, their function is generally limited to the role of pressure and propaganda activities.

Since 1940 the most significant formal opposition to the PRI has been offered by the PAN, which emerged as part of the conservative reaction to the socialistic reforms of the Cárdenas regime during the 1930s. Principal targets of their attack were the sweeping nationalizations of industry, the stricter enforcement of the anticlerical provisions of the Constitution of 1917, and the hastened distribution of the agricultural lands through the use of *ejidos*. The PAN was formed at a Mexico City convention in 1939. Since its founding the PAN has always offered presidential and congressional candidates, except in 1946 when it chose not to contest the presidency. The PAN expresses support for the Constitution of 1917, except for the anticlerical provisions, and charges that the controlling PRI has violated the Constitution through administrative abuses of liberty.

The members of the PAN include the old families of distinguished ancestry whose wealth and position have been reduced or threatened by the PRI, some of the more recently successful business and professional people, many of the upwardly mobile middle class, and an uncertain base of peasants and artisans that church influence has placed within PAN ranks. The PAN has never been officially credited with more than 12 percent of the vote in a presidential election and has not posed a major threat to the PRI in the past.

A study of recent voting patterns indicated a trend toward decreasing voter turnout and an increase in blank or null ballots. The lowest voter turnout and the highest votes for opposition parties have tended to be in the states experiencing the highest degree of economic development. Some observers have seen this as indicative of an increasing alienation of the middle class from the PRI, of which the PAN has been the major beneficiary.

In addition to the governorship of Sonora, which it claims to have been denied, the PAN in 1967 won the mayoralties of Hermosillo and Mérida, and in 1968 it won those of Tijuana and Mexicali. After a disputed state election in Yucatán in November 1969, the PAN charged the government with fraud and threatened to boycott the presidential election in 1970. It ultimately chose, however, to run a candidate, Efraín Gonzalez Morfin; it was the only opposition party to do so. The party won twenty seats in the federal Chamber of Deputies in the 1970 elections. Both the PAN and the PPS gained at the expense of the PRI in local elections in the state of Puebla in 1974.

236

To the right of the PAN is the UNS, which is largely confined to San Luís Potosí. The term *sinarquista* is a corruption of two words, *sin* and *anarquía*, meaning "without anarchy" or "with order." All Sinarquistas are said to be ardent Roman Catholics. Sinarquistas are disciplined members of a militant theocratic sect and frequently use the word *soldier* in self-description. The ideology *sinarquismo* embraces a strong economic conservatism.

To the left of the PRI is a loose configuration of Marxist-oriented groups whose principal ideological bond is a common dissatisfaction with PRI policies. In August 1961 a convention of prominent leftists, including representatives of the Mexican Communist Party, the PPS, and a number of other splinter groups, was held in Mexico City. Former President Lázaro Cárdenas served as the ideological mentor for this convention. These meetings displayed a broad consensus in favor of nationalization of all natural resources, expulsion of most foreign capital investments, closer ties with Fidel Castro's Cuba, and a broad "go-it-alone" policy. The convention also decided that a new leftist entity was needed to cement and coordinate the efforts of the various groups into a unified front. Thus a new movement, the MLN, was proclaimed.

The MLN called itself a grass-roots organization, but this image was short lived. During the first year of the MLN, Lombardo Toledano took the PPS out of the movement. His action resulted partly from rivalry between himself and Cárdenas. The General Union of Mexican Workers and Peasants (Union General de Obreros e Campesinos Mexicanos— UGOCM), headed by Jacinto López, also pulled out of the MLN under pressure from Lombardo Toledano. MLN adherents countered this blow to their prestige by trying to capitalize on the prestige of Cárdenas; they proclaimed a radical campaign to renew his vigorous agrarian reform measures of the 1930s.

Until the death of Lombardo Toledano in 1968 and Cárdenas in 1970 the Mexican Left was divided principally between supporters of the two men. The PPS has dominated Mexico's Left because of its willingness to come to terms with the PRI on matters of potential ideological cleavage. In the presidential campaign of 1964 the PPS, which had existed since 1948, became an "official" opposition party to the PRI and was inscribed as a legal political party by the government. In return, Lombardo Toledano promised to support the PRI presidential candidacy in exchange for assured seats in congress. This rapprochement further widened the breach between the PPS and the MLN, which formed its own campaign front, the Popular Electoral Front (Frente Electoral del Pueblo—FEP), and ran Danzós Palomino for the presidency. Danzós Palomino, who was also an official of the Mexican Communist Party, was denied inscription as a legal candidate, as was the honored painter David Alfaro Siqueiros, who campaigned for the Senate from his jail cell in Mexico City as a protest gesture. By the early 1970s the MLN was practically defunct.

The followers of Heberto Castillo constituted the PMT in September 1974, but some observers believe the new party will be merely a convenient instrument for the personal ambitions of its leaders. Rather than transgress the PRI's unwritten rules on tolerable opposition activity by taking issue with government goals and policy, the party exhorts the government to go further in the same direction of control of foreign investments, agrarian reform, and "anti-imperialism."

THE ECHEVERRÍA LEADERSHIP

The Echeverría administration has attempted to remain at the center in an increasingly polarized society. Most observers felt that, after the conservative rule of Gustavo Díaz Ordaz, public opinion and the traditional pendulum pattern of the presidency dictated a swing back toward the center. It appears, in fact, that despite his conservative record Echeverría has tried to isolate the alienated fringes of both Right and Left by alternately appealing to the business community, professionals and other elements of the center-Right, and the groups of workers and peasants that make up the center-Left.

In particular, the president has addressed himself to the need to expand agricultural production and raise rural standards of living and to expand educational opportunities and participation in party affairs. He also pledged industrial expansion to create more jobs and an independent foreign policy.

Echeverría promised early in his term to end the tension between the government and the universities but, since he, as minister of government in 1968, was blamed by many of the students for the Tlatelolco Massacre, this has proved no easy matter. He suggested a private dialogue with student leaders, but the students demanded a public one. Sporadic student demonstrations continued in the early 1970s and, although the government's response was less overt and dramatic than in the late 1960s, suppression of student dissent became more systematic.

Furthermore, a right-wing paramilitary gang, known as *los halcones* (the falcons), continued to operate boldly. On one occasion in 1971 the group attacked some 10,000 peaceful protestors with submachine guns, killing thirteen and wounding some 200, while the police watched and refused to intervene. President Echeverría denied that the gang had any connection with his administration and even suggested that they might be backed by right-wing elements attempting to discredit him or force his hand. He also proceeded to release the student leaders who had been imprisoned since 1968 and to remove the chief of police of the Federal District. But the continuing animosity between students and the government was reinforced when police invaded the campus of the National Autonomous University of Mexico in August 1973.

The Echeverría administration has supported various measures to expand participation in the country's political life and has had some success in enhancing the image of the PRI. The congressional elections

238

of 1973 represented a defeat for the old guard of party leaders and an infusion of well-educated middle-class and lower class young men who owed their loyalty to the president.

In 1974 the government was plagued by both a spate of political kidnappings and a sudden upsurge in inflation, unofficially estimated at an annual rate of 40 percent. The latter had frustrated the government's essentially incremental efforts to reverse the trend toward overconcentration of wealth. President Echeverría has alienated much of the business community by imposing price controls and expressing sympathy with labor's demands for wage increases. But labor has been less than content because the wage increases actually negotiated have fallen short of increases in the cost of living.

In his speech to the opening session of the National Congress in September 1974, the president criticized those who had been sending capital out of the country in the hope of causing a devaluation of the peso. He also expressed the suspicion that the extreme Right might be provoking a climate of violence in order to "bring on repressive measures and hold back the advance of our constitution and the exercise of our liberties." And he warned that this climate of violence might reflect an intent to support foreign intervention.

CHAPTER 11

MASS COMMUNICATION

By the mid-1970s Mexico had developed one of the most complex and advanced mass communication systems in Latin America. Word-of-mouth communication was still vitally important in the transmission of ideas and information—especially in the rural areas—but technological advances and the transistor radio had brought mass media channels and messages to all but the most isolated. Newspapers, radio, films, and television had all experienced a surge in growth since World War II. Only film production had seen a relative decline since 1950; the growth of all other media had accelerated at a rapid rate. The press and, to a large extent, the radio and television broadcasting facilities were privately owned.

The government, nevertheless, was able to influence the content of printed media through both subtle and overt controls. For example, it held a monopoly on the distribution of newsprint, allocating it to newspapers and magazines through a quota system based on circulation figures. The government advertised heavily, and it pressed for the use of official news releases. Overt censorship had occurred but less frequently than in other Latin American countries. A more common practice was self-censorship, whereby news managers assumed that certain subjects would be considered sensitive and simply did not print them.

The expansion of the literate population has fostered the growth of the press. All existing newspapers were established after the Revolution of 1910, and most of these since the 1940s. Magazines have also proliferated, especially women's magazines, scholarly journals, and government publications. General-interest magazines, such as the Spanish version of the *Reader's Digest*, and news magazines are also popular.

Radio and television both started slowly, largely because of mountainous terrain and the expense of building transmitters. By the 1960s, however, these media were flourishing, having overcome initial problems and setbacks. Although television remained a means of communication that only the middle or upper classes could afford, it was said to have potential for becoming the most important medium.

The government has viewed radio and television as instrumental in the push for literacy and national unity. It has required broadcasting stations to allot at least thirty minutes per day to government programs although it has seldom supplied enough material to all stations to fulfill this quota. The principal program handling the government material has been "The

National Hour" (La Hora Nacional), which is aired on radio for an hour every Sunday night and consists of news and cultural items. The government also owns one television station, which is run as an educational station. Several programs have been aired on both radio and television that teach literacy and courses at the secondary education level.

Mexico had advanced far enough by 1965 to meet the stringent minimum media standards set by the United Nations Educational, Scientific and Cultural Organization (UNESCO) for developing nations—ten copies of daily newspapers, five radio receivers, and two television receivers per 100 inhabitants—standards that still remained unmet by many other Latin American countries in 1974. In that year both newspapers and television receivers per 100 people exceeded the standards, and the standard for radio had been achieved fifteen years earlier. Despite this growth, there is still great regional imbalance. The largest and most important media are concentrated in the Federal District. It was the seat of the nation's film, magazine, and book industries and also the headquarters of the dominant national television networks.

THE GOVERNMENT AND THE MEDIA

Freedom of the press has been guaranteed in every constitution since independence and is preserved along with other constitutional guarantees in the Constitution of 1917. Articles 6 and 7 proclaim freedom of the press, the former limiting this freedom in cases of moral attack, rights of third parties, and provocations to commit crimes or disturb the public order. Article 7 declares that the right to write and publish on any topic is inviolate and forbids prior censorship. It further states that press freedom has no limitation except for respect for private life, morality, and public peace.

Because of the conditional nature of the basic guarantees of freedom of the press, specific laws can restrict and have restricted this freedom. Although all presidents have acknowledged this freedom, some have been more liberal than others in allowing it to flourish. States of war or political instability, for example, have promoted the imposition of restrictive measures. Penalties have been imposed on those who disturb the public order through the press and the broadcast media.

The government circulates official reports and occasionally engages in prepublication censorship. Sometimes it attempts to suppress a story that appears to be detrimental to the public interest and if unable to do so may confiscate an issue of a publication in which such material appears.

Within the constitutional framework, the government exerts an influence on the press by a number of means including the distribution of advertising revenue, dissemination of its own news releases, and control of newsprint through the government's monopoly, the Producer and Importer of Paper (Productora y Importadora de Papel—PIPSA).

In addition, publishers and journalists generally impose self-censorship, voluntarily excluding material they know would offend authorities. Self-censorship has given way to open criticism principally when a newspaper's economic interests have been threatened by governmental reforms. The mere mention of tax reform, for instance, has invariably produced numerous headlines quoting prominent businessmen claiming that such measures could wreck the country's economic stability.

Self-censorship has been practiced particularly with respect to the chief executive and his activities. To show disrespect for the president has been a serious offense. Moreover, whereas sly references to public figures and humorous epithets have been common, the president has usually been excluded from published caricaturization. This pattern began to change in the late 1960s after a series of student strikes were put down by the executive authority. The repression of these strikes loosed a wave of criticism and made way for a liberalization and an opening of press-state relations in the early 1970s.

Political discussion in general was more open under this regime than its predecessors, and the media benefited greatly. Whereas open discussion of terrorist activity, corruption at the governmental level, or official foibles would have brought threats of seizure in the past, these criticisms were increasingly tolerated. In 1971 President Luís Echeverría ordered the release of several journalists and authors who had been jailed for their writings and expressed the desire for constructive criticism from the media.

The government's desire for feedback and public opinion reflected a broader mood of national self-examination. Not everyone agreed with its decision to solicit public opinion, however, including some members of the business community. When criticism of business became too abrasive, the business community set up an advertising boycott against its main critic, the liberal newspaper *Excélsior*. To compensate the newspaper for financial losses, the government itself advertised more heavily, allowing *Excélsior* to continue its criticisms. Eventually the boycott was abandoned because business was suffering more than the newspaper. In late 1974 there were some indications that this relatively relaxed attitude was hardening.

Much of what is presented as news in the printed media is derived from publicity releases and articles prepared by the government. State and local government offices issue and encourage the use of such material, which includes texts of speeches, official notices, and reports.

Three large government advertisers are Air Mexico (Aeroméxico), the National Lottery (Lotería Nacional), and the National Development Bank (Nacional Financiera), a chief investment development agency of the federal government. The government also lent money to newspapers through the National Development Bank, which in 1970 owned 20 percent of the stock of *El Universal*, a leading Mexico City daily. Favorable publicity to promote the interest of certain individuals within the ranks of the government party or the government is planted in the news media.

PIPSA was established in 1935 and was authorized to purchase newsprint in large quantities to sell to periodicals at wholesale prices, free from import duties. Control of PIPSA is vested in both the government, which holds majority stock, and private interests; publishers of leading journals have served on PIPSA's board of directors. Not only is PIPSA the sole agent authorized to import newsprint, it also grades, stores, and sells it and assures periodicals of adequate supplies during times of political stress. During its forty years of operation PIPSA has become an efficient and effective way of assuring its clients of a steady supply of relatively inexpensive newsprint. In 1974 virtually all Mexican newspapers and magazines were PIPSA clients.

It is possible for an individual firm to bypass PIPSA and buy newsprint directly from another newspaper that has exceeded its newsprint quota or from a foreign supplier, but an import license must be granted by the government, and an 80-percent ad valorem tax would have to be paid by the purchaser. Only a few have attempted this course.

PIPSA supplies newsprint on credit and, at its own discretion, may extend very favorable terms of payment, even to the point of carrying a debtor indefinitely. It may also rescind any such privileges at any time. In 1965, when PIPSA's original thirty-year charter expired, a number of publishers petitioned to have it extended. The cost of privately imported newsprint would have run many publishers out of business, and many owed PIPSA large sums in back payments. PIPSA officials have declared that, as long as newsprint is available, they will sell to any publisher except for those "not in observance of the law" or those not using their newsprint in accordance with original understandings.

PIPSA may grant consumption quotas far in excess of amounts actually needed. This surplus is then sold to other companies unable to obtain a quota assignment from PIPSA. This income garnered from selling newsprint is substantial, frequently amounting to as much as 40 percent of a publication's gross receipts.

The 1940 Law of General Ways of Communications gave the government exclusive regulatory jurisdiction over broadcasts, prohibited foreigners from owning or controlling broadcast stations, forbade the broadcasting of news contrary to the security of the state, the laws of the country, public order, and international harmony, and prohibited attacks on individual honor or the constituted government. Intervenors were provided to monitor content, their job being to examine programs before they were aired and to compare actual broadcasts with approved scripts.

Most of the provisions of the 1940 law were incorporated in the 1960 Federal Law of Radio and Television that superseded it. The 1960 law, however, stated in addition that broadcasting waves are public domain, that they are part of the public interest, and that the state should see that the media perform in the best public interest. In order to perform this function, states should do four things: enhance respect for moral principles, human dignity, and family ties; avoid programming detrimental to children's development; contribute to the cultural level of the people; and contribute to national integration by strengthening democracy.

The 1960 act also specified certain categories of broadcasting stations, such as commercial and cultural—which included governmental, experimental, and radio schools—and gave the Ministry of Communications and Transport the right to assign more categories and determine the characteristics of each. Government licenses to broadcasting stations may run for up to thirty years, but they may be revoked. Freedom from government censorship is assured, but a large number of injunctions establish kinds of broadcasts permitted and priorities regarding government information. For example, government announcements related to security, defense, and public order must be given priority. Certain kinds of programs are designated disruptive and are prohibited. There is a regulation against cheap comedy and offensive sounds. If broadly interpreted, the exercise of the regulatory power in these laws could effectively prevent the transmission of almost any kind of information. Most broadcasters stay well within the limits of what is acceptable, however, and rarely risk action by the intervenors.

As of the late 1960s the regulation of broadcasting was divided among four federal ministries: communications and transport, government, health and welfare, and public education. The Ministry of Communications and Transport was primarily concerned with assigning licenses and broadcast frequencies and ensuring that stations complied with all technical regulations. The Ministry of Government had the responsibility of seeing that broadcasters respected individual rights of privacy and personal and moral dignity and that the broadcasts did not disturb public order and were in the best interests of the federal government. One of its most important functions was administering a provision of the 1960 federal law requiring broadcasting stations to provide at least thirty minutes of free broadcast time daily for educational, cultural, or social purposes. A broadcasting station is so obligated only if the government provides material to fill the air time, as it seldom does.

Subordinate to the Ministry of Government is the National Council of Radio and Television. It is composed of one representative from each of the four ministries involved with the regulation of broadcasting, two owners or managers of broadcasting stations, and two other representatives from the broadcast industry. This council is charged with promoting and organizing broadcasts ordered by the president in addition to serving as a consulting body to him.

The jurisdiction of the Ministry of Health and Welfare extends to the regulation of advertising of potentially harmful products: medicines, therapeutic apparatuses, and insecticides. The Ministry of Public Education has probably been the agency most concerned with the media's social role as educator and agent for integration. Two major programs produced by this agency have been a basic literacy course and a program of secondary-level academic work, both produced under the direction of the General Administration of Audiovisual Education.

The basic literacy course first went on the air in 1965 and used a workbook as its core. The workbook, which was given free to any illiterate person who requested it, enabled the person to follow lessons on radio or television in his own home or in small classes. Some of these classes have been sponsored and financed by public and private organizations, including factories, Lions clubs, and the Junior Chamber of Commerce. The entire course could be completed in four months with a television set and in six months with a radio. It has been carried throughout most of Mexico and apparently throughout parts of the southwestern United States as well, as shown by letters received from students across the border. An analysis of the program in the late 1960s showed that approximately 40 percent of those who began the course did not complete it. Of the 60 percent who did complete it, 97 percent "passed"—that is, learned to read and write.

The more advanced secondary-level program was started in 1968 to educate through television students in rural areas who were unable to afford a secondary school or a teacher. Subjects taught were mathematics, history, Spanish, biology, English, civics, geography, and technology. Students could attend one of several hundred television classrooms or could watch at home. Surprisingly, early studies of the program's effectiveness indicated that its students ranked even higher on achievement tests than students in regular secondary schools.

Another program produced by the federal government has been "The National Hour," a one-hour radio program of music, poetry, and government announcements. The program is on the air every Sunday between 10:00 P.M. and 11:00 P.M., and stations equipped to carry it are required to do so.

NEWSPAPERS

Mexico had the first printing press in the Western Hemisphere, but the growth of journalism has been a slow and sporadic process. There was little or no freedom of the press under three centuries of Spanish rule, and another century of domestic problems further inhibited growth. The Mexican press has developed from a religious and literary one during the colonial era to a political one after independence and an information press after the Revolution of 1910. Few newspapers survived the cataclysmic effects of the 1910 Revolution, and by 1974 none of the prerevolutionary newspapers remained in existence. Of those in existence, a great many had begun publication after World War II, many of them as recently as the 1960s and early 1970s.

Estimates of the number of daily newspapers being published ranged from fewer than 200 to as high as 240. Over half of the total number of daily newspapers were published in Mexico City, Guadalajara, and

Monterrey and, although the large newspapers of the capital city—*Excélsior, Ultimas Noticias, Novedades, La Prensa, El Universal, El Sol,* and *El Heraldo*—circulated in the interior, their provincial circulation averaged one-fourth of the total. Most of these newspapers had circulations of over 130,000.

Excélsior has undergone a remarkable journalistic metamorphosis. Founded in 1917 and organized as a cooperative in 1932, it is generally regarded as Mexico's leading newspaper and the nearest thing to a national newspaper. It was also one of the largest newspapers, with a circulation of over 150,000 in 1973. It has been ranked among the world's top thirty newspapers and is subscribed to by all major libraries, top government officials, and prominent educators in Mexico. Before 1968 *Excélsior* was regarded as conservative, but under new editorial direction its stance has moved toward the center-Left, and some of its writers have directly attacked the government. In turn, *Excélsior* has been attacked by more conservative newspapers and has even been called communistic by the powerful conservative Colonel José García Valseca, owner of a large newspaper chain.

There are three categories of newspaper ownership—independent, cooperative (where ownership is collectively held by key employees), and chain. Several influential owners control a large portion of the media through chains. The greatest chain ownership is found in the areas of greatest population concentration and in the centers of business and wealth. In 1970 about 35 percent of the daily newspapers were chain owned. There were a number of small chains, each having from two to four newspapers; in 1970 eleven small chains controlled 11.4 percent of all dailies.

In 1970 two of the larger chains accounted for a large percentage of ownership: García Valseca Periodicals (Periódicos García Valseca) and the O'Farrill newspaper chain. García Valseca Periodicals is the largest chain in Mexico and in the Spanish-speaking world. It carries the name of García Valseca, who refers to himself as the William Randolph Hearst of Mexican journalism. In 1973 the chain was composed of three dailies in Mexico City and thirty-one dailies and three sports weeklies throughout the states. García Valseca began his publishing career by publishing comic books. His first newspaper was a sports publication from Mexico City, and his business expanded by an average of one provincial newspaper annually from 1941 to 1964.

In 1973 newspapers in the chain were published in fifteen Mexican states and carried well over one-fourth of the total circulation of all daily general-interest newspapers. Most of them carried the title *El Sol,* followed by the name of the city where they were published. In 1973 over twenty newspapers were so titled. In 1972 it was reported that the government took over controlling interest in the García Valseca chain through calling in a large outstanding debt owed to the chief investment agency of the federal government, the National Development Bank. The debt became equity in a finance agency in which the government controls the majority of the stock, and through the takeover the finance agency became the majority stockholder in the chain. García Valseca resigned for health reasons, although his name continued to appear as president and director general. It was reported, however, that administrative and financial personnel representing the finance agency were gaining a foothold through the controlling stock.

The second largest chain controls at least seven daily newspapers and is owned by the O'Farrill family. The leading newspaper in the chain is *Novedades,* published in Mexico City and having a circulation of 122,000 in 1973. *Novedades* grew in three decades from a sensational tabloid to a high-quality newspaper and ranks just behind *Excélsior* in importance. Also included in the O'Farrill chain are the *News,* an English-language daily, and *Diario de la Tarde,* both published in the capital and considered among the major general-interest dailies. In the 1960s four more dailies became part of the chain and were all called *Novedades. Novedades de Campeche* began in 1973. In addition to its more than half a dozen dailies, the O'Farrill organization owns twenty magazines and an influential radio chain and has holdings in the television industry.

El Día, an independent daily established in the capital in 1962, is known for its high percentage of hard news, which often includes verbatim excerpts from important foreign speeches and government communiqués. Although it is regarded as one of the fifteen major dailies in the capital, its circulation remains small—65,000 in 1973—and it is limited mainly to members of liberal professions, university students, and those who consider themselves intellectuals.

Mexican newspapers have frequently been criticized by those who would have the press become more controversial and less dependent upon the government for subsidies and as a news source. Padding the newspapers with "soft" news, as opposed to "hard" news—that based on events of crucial relevance—has been one of the most frequent criticisms.

Another criticism of the newspapers has been the lack of responsibility or accountability. This is reflected in the suspicion and cynicism of many readers, who consider information in newspapers largely unreliable. More specifically they criticize the poor quality of news reporting, the poor training received by journalists and subsequent lack of professionalism, and the highly political character of the press and loss of objectivity in reporting.

In addition, there are many things that undermine the independence of the press and tie it to other interests. The fact that news space may be bought in most newspapers in the form of *gacetillas* (paid publicity stories) is very important. Since these are not labeled as advertising when they appear, they are indistinguishable from news stories. In 1972, when a Mexican editor criticized the practice of selling *gacetillas,* he declared that the second headline at the top of the front page of

Excélsior could sell for 8,000 pesos (12.5 pesos equal US$1).

Because many editors and columnists are employed only part time and because the earnings of even experienced journalists are low, many newspapermen take on second jobs. Frequently such positions are with the firms that prepare and disseminate publicity releases. Also common among newsmen as a means of earning added income is the collection of *igualas*, monthly gratuities from the organizations on their beats, a practice accepted among both business and governmental concerns. This payoff from a news source often comes to the beat reporter or to the page editor for his cooperation and, in fact, one duty of a government press officer may be to distribute *igualas*. In the newspaper business this is called "to work the hook" *(trabajar el gancho)* because government publicity offices hang current releases on a wall in the reception room.

Working the hook provides many journalists with enough income and fringe benefits to live very well. Depending upon the financial resources of the organization, *igualas* usually averaged about 1,000 pesos (the equivalent of US$80) per beat per month in the early 1970s. In addition to regular salaries and monthly gratuities, some journalists received clandestine bonuses above the usual *iguala*, salaries as officers in a newspaperman's union, gifts, or other fringe benefits. Access to the Journalists Club in Mexico City was one of these benefits. A new building constructed in the early 1960s, it housed government-approved reporters' and editors' unions as well as a library, a ballroom, a restaurant, and conference rooms.

Newspaper circulation is largely limited to the urban population. During the mid-1960s it was estimated that there was an average of five newspapers for every three families in the Federal District, whereas in Campeche, Hidalgo, Oaxaca, and Zacatecas, for example, 90 percent of the families had no available newspaper. This means that about half the people are dependent on radio rather than newspapers for basic national and international information.

MAGAZINES

There is no published list of Mexican periodicals, and the exact number is unknown. The main card catalog of the National Archives (Hemeroteca Nacional) contains entries for thousands of small news sheets that have appeared and then lapsed into oblivion. Moreover, before every election a spate of magazines appears around nominating time, ostensibly to promote certain Institutional Revolutionary Party (Partido Revolucionario Institucional—PRI) candidates for office. In the late 1960s it was estimated that there were well over 1,800 periodicals published, of which only 100 circulated nationwide. Of the 1,800, close to 500 were weeklies; 250, fortnightly; and well over 800, monthlies; the balance were quarterlies and journals published at irregular intervals.

There were about 450 periodicals in 1900. Almost half of these were general information; about 30 percent were political, and another 12 to 13 percent were literary. Twelve percent were devoted to scientific and technical subjects. The revolution brought about expansion of the periodical press and also changed its character appreciably. Most magazines had been established since the revolution. By the early years of World War II about the same proportion were devoted to general information, a much smaller percentage were political or literary, and the proportion devoted to scientific and technical subjects were more than twice as high. In the 1970s the majority of magazines were of general appeal, although substantial numbers specialized in religious, technical, scientific, cultural, literary, political, juvenile, sports, and labor articles.

As in the case of the newspapers, the Federal District has been the undisputed magazine publishing center of the nation; Guadalajara and Veracruz ranked next. Circulation figures were highly unreliable, however, perhaps because many magazines inflated the figures supplied to the government in order to receive as high a quota of paper as possible from PIPSA. This surplus could then be sold to publications that had not received an allotment. It is believed that advertisers and advertising agencies commonly discount unverified circulation claims by anywhere from 35 to 50 percent, and the skepticism spreads even to those few publications who do offer verification.

Spanish-language editions of foreign magazines are prominent on Mexican newsstands. In fact, the highest circulation of any magazine— 415,000 a month for 1973—was claimed by *Selecciones del Reader's Digest*. Before its demise in the 1960s, *Life en Español* had been third highest; its sales were approximately 186,000 in 1967. When *Life en Español* ceased publication, it was supplanted by a conservative news magazine published in New York City, *Visión*. Another popular digest has been *Temas*, also published in New York.

Two leading news magazines have been *Tiempo* and *Siempre*. *Tiempo* —distributed in the United States as the *Hispano Americano*—is modeled on *Time* magazine and has tended to be progovernment and anticlerical. *Siempre* is a left-wing magazine that claimed a weekly circulation of 120,000 in 1969. The *Revista de Revistas*, owned by *Excélsior*, changed from a staid literary weekly to an attractive magazine covering current events in the late 1960s. Another weekly published by *Excélsior* was *Jueves de Excélsior*.

Mexico publishes as many specific interest or specialized magazines as any Latin American country, if not more. *Teleguía*, for example, is a television news weekly that claimed a circulation of 335,000 in 1973. *Revista Industrial* is the leading trade journal, but there are at least twelve others. The National Foreign Trade Bank (Banco Nacional de Comercio Exterior) publishes a monthly, in both English and Spanish, entitled *Comercio Exterior* that gives informative reports on economic conditions. *Review of the Economic Situation in Mexico* is a government publication with a similar format. *Trimestre Económico*, published by the Economic Culture Fund (Fondo de Cultura Económica), is one of the best economic publications in all of Latin America. Another monthly economic bulletin is *CEMLA*, published by the Latin American Center of Monetary Studies (Centro de Estudios Monetarios Latinoamericanos), a publishing house for a number of journals and books.

Another large group of specialized journals are those published by various university facilities and social science research centers. *Anuario Indigenista*, published by the Inter-American Indigenist Institute (Instituto Indigenista Interamericano) in Mexico City, is one of the best known Spanish-language anthropological journals in the Western Hemisphere. *Revista Mexicana de la Sociología* is another high-quality research journal devoted to sociological topics. For those with a specific interest in law and order there are at least six scholarly journals on the topic. Government agencies, in addition to the academic community, put out numerous weekly and monthly journals.

There are a large number of popular women's journals, aimed at the urban middle class. A number of these magazines are non-Mexican. *Buen Hogar*, a Spanish-language edition of the magazine *Good Housekeeping* published in the United States, enjoys a large market among Mexican women. The biweekly *Vanidades*, with editorial offices in New York, is circulated throughout Mexico and claimed a Mexican circulation of 129,000 in 1973. Women's magazines based in Mexico include *Kena, Feminidades, Nueva Vida*, and *Bienestar*. Most such magazines attempt to act as confidant and guide to their readers, using the familiar rather than the formal form of address and providing self-help manuals on cooking, marriage, and childbearing.

BOOK PUBLISHING

As of mid-1968 there were about 120 publishers in the country. Very few firms were engaged solely in publishing, however, and in most cases their other activities—book wholesaling and retailing—were financially more important than publishing. The Economic Culture Fund was one of the few firms engaged solely in publishing. Originally devoted to books on economics, in the late 1960s the fund carried a more balanced list in the social sciences and humanities. D. E. Herrero and Editorial Patria, both old, established publishing and sales firms, covered a variety of fields, and César Cicerón, another substantial firm, carried a list that concentrated mainly on low-priced popular books.

The Economic Culture Fund was still partially subsidized in the mid-1970s as were all firms in the book industry, because they paid no taxes other than social security taxes for their employees and excess profits taxes. Since the revolution adequate copyright laws have been enacted, but a fair portion of the book business is in pirated books, mostly from abroad, where royalties do not have to be paid. Foreign firms operating in Mexico are generally in wholesaling; the others have been almost entirely taken into Mexican control.

Textbook publication is financially the most important part of the industry's output. Textbooks for primary and secondary schools are almost entirely by Mexican authors, but for advanced curricula, especially in scientific and technical fields, including law, foreign texts are quite common. In addition to textbooks, the Ministry of Public Education has engaged in other publication efforts, often in philosophy and religion. In the early 1960s the government began a free textbook program, and during the last decade gave many contracts to private publishers. The publishers had the sole responsibility for production; distribution was handled by the government. The government also regulated the contents and, where applicable, the prices of textbooks.

Mexico is one of four countries in Latin America that can be said to have important book industries, and Argentina and Mexico are the chief book exporters in the region. Spain still supplies a large part of the imports into the region and into Mexico. The present-day book industry in Mexico stems largely from the disruption of the civil war in Spain and from World War II, when traditional sources of supply could not meet Mexican demands; Mexican publishers and sellers moved in to substitute domestic products for foreign ones and grew rapidly. Mexico does not levy duties on incoming books, nor does it impose a quota system, although there are import charges on books with elaborate bindings.

In 1974 a controversy arose over whether to restrict the importation of books. Involved in the debate were Mexico's publishing companies, the national chambers of the editorial industry and graphic arts, the secretary of public education, and the secretary of industry and commerce. Proposed legislation would limit the number of books imported in order to correct an unfavorable balance between domestically published and imported books. Those in favor of the proposed legislation stated that Mexican publishers were in competition with those abroad who could publish books more cheaply and who were aided by government subsidies. Moreover, Mexican books were denied entry into certain Latin American countries because of strict censorship. One commentator on the subject noted that, whereas the United States was free to export an unlimited number of books printed in Spanish to Mexico, Mexico was limited to exporting duty free only 1,500 copies of any book printed in English. Although the gap between imports and exports had continued to grow—from US$12.5 million in 1971 to US$28 million in 1974—many still favored unlimited importing. They considered the measure a blow to the free circulation of information and ideas between nations and a step toward cultural isolation.

RADIO AND TELEVISION

The broadcasting media continued to play an important role in the communications network in the early 1970s. The low literacy rate and isolation in the rural areas made radio a particularly vital element (see

The Government and the Media, this ch.). In 1974 there were 654 radio stations and 162 television stations. About one-fourth of the total number of stations were used to carry literacy programs. Except for these and a few government programs, however, both television and radio have been largely privately owned, commercially operated entertainment media.

Radiobroadcasting began in 1923, and television followed twenty-seven years later. In both cases initial development was impeded by low per capita income, mountainous terrain, poor transportation, and problems related to development of the industry. Early listening and watching were in public or semipublic places because receivers were scarce and expensive. This may still be the case in rural areas or in squatter settlements on the edges of cities, where one family may purchase a television set and charge the neighbors for viewing. Moreover, it is not uncommon to find people grouped in the streets of a provincial town, watching—but not hearing—the latest program through a showcase window.

Radiobroadcasting continued to show vitality and growth in the early 1970s. In 1961 there were 414 broadcasting stations, and this number had jumped to 592 a decade later. They were nearly all privately owned and operated under government license. An estimated 12 million to 13 million sets were in use, although these figures do not include the considerable number of pocket-sized transistor radios in use. One source estimated the number of radio receivers at 261 per 1,000 inhabitants, a fairly high average for Latin America. This figure apparently refers only to standard-size sets, so that the actual number is probably greater. With the exception of the southwestern corner of Mexico, radio transmitters provide near-saturation of potential audiences in both the city and the country.

Radiobroadcasting is financed on a commercial basis, with little or no apparent subsidization from the government. Programming for most radio stations features soap operas and radio request programs with sporting events in third place. In the capital this order of preference may be reversed during the bull-fighting season, when the majority of listeners prefer the fight broadcasts above other Sunday afternoon programs. One market-research firm reported that, during a selected period of time, eight of the top-ten radio programs were soap operas; the remaining two were comedy skits. Advertising—radio's sole means of support—is also a prominent feature of the broadcasting day. Article 67 of the 1960 Federal Law of Radio and Television prescribes a "prudent balance" between the time allocated for programming and commercials. This vague wording, however, allowed advertisers to absorb as much as twenty minutes per hour.

Although the vast majority of radio stations were privately owned commercial stations, government provision allowed for the establishment of certain noncommercial "cultural stations." There were at least a dozen such amplitude modulation (AM) stations, largely run by state governments or universities. Among these were stations in Jalisco, Chihuahua, Jalapa, San Luís Potosí, Guanajuato, Sonora, and Mexico City. There were also several shortwave and frequency modulation (FM) cultural stations. Radio Gobernación, under the Ministry of Government, was the only station operated by the federal government in 1974. It carried speeches of importance, such as state-of-the-union messages and comments by foreign dignitaries, as well as agricultural and educational programs.

Television has grown faster than any other medium. Moreover, its accelerated growth since the mid-1960s has clearly made it the most important communication medium throughout the urban areas. The number of stations has grown from one in 1950, owned by Romulo O'Farrill, to close to 162 in 1974, including two educational stations and four cable television stations. As of 1973 there were 5 million television sets and a potential audience of 25 million. There were eight stations in Mexico City alone.

Television in Mexico was largely an operation of one network (Telesistema Mexicana). In 1974 ninety-seven stations were affiliated with this network. It began as a merger of O'Farrill's station and two others in the early 1950s. By 1965 Telesistema Mexicana had two microwave networks, covering 80 percent of the country's population, and owned or controlled forty of the fifty television stations. In the late 1960s Telesistema Mexicana still owned all three of Mexico City's commercial stations, although in 1968 two new private commercial television stations came into being and, since, then, several other networks have been formed by business groups in Monterrey and Mexico City.

In the early 1970s one of the television stations devoted exclusively to cultural programming was Channel 11 in Mexico City, operated by the National Polytechnical Institute. Twenty-seven other stations were affiliated with this government-owned station. The programming was similar to educational television elsewhere and featured French and English lessons, documentary films on travel and scientific subjects, lectures on Mexican literature and music, Mexican film classics, and classical music. During the late 1960s its power was amplified, expanding its radius of receivers, and it began transmitting in color.

For the most part, however, television is used for entertainment purposes, transmitting United States as well as Mexican productions. At Televicentro, the headquarters of Telesistema Mexicana, about 174 hours of live programs and the same number of filmed programs are produced per week. Included in this are about fifty half-hour soap operas, as well as situation comedies, dramas, and mysteries. In addition to the domestic market, Mexican television producers have been developing markets for packaged programs in the Dominican Republic, Puerto Rico, Central America, Venezuela, Perú, Colombia, Ecuador, Argentina, and

Chile. The largest foreign market continues to be the United States. This market is supplied through the Spanish International Broadcasting Company, operating Channel 41 in San Antonio, Texas, and Channel 34 in Los Angeles, California, on ultrahigh frequency (UHF). About seventy programs a week go to each station.

Much of the cable television programming was picked up from the United States. This has been one of the few instances in the world where a live signal was transmitted directly to a largely foreign audience. In 1973 it was estimated that 60 percent of the cable television viewers were Mexicans, contrary to the belief that the majority were other North Americans living in Mexico. In the case of one cable television company, in 1973 Cablevisión viewers in Mexico City paid the equivalent of US$10.40 per month on a twelve-hour-a-day basis. Although the numbers of subscribers were few, they were usually the better educated and more affluent Mexicans. Among the more popular programs were Johnny Carson's "Tonight Show," "All in the Family," "The Mary Tyler Moore Show," sports events, and motion pictures—especially biblical films of the Cecil B. De Mille era.

In an uncharacteristic action aimed at restricting programming, Mexican authorities banned thirty-seven imported series in mid-1974. These included such programs as "Ironside," "The Fugitive," "The FBI," and "The Avengers" and were banned on the grounds that they were so violent as to be considered harmful influences on the country's youth. The programs were being aired on a commercial network operating several stations. Mexican officials blamed these programs in part for the accelerating wave of leftist activity.

The Mexican government has undertaken a program to increase and improve television broadcasting through a system of microwave lines that would carry television and other forms of telecommunications to all towns of more than 2,500 people. The system would consist of 203 repeater stations and fifty-five terminal stations. One of the major components of the system was Mexico's first, and the world's largest, satellite communications ground station, built in Tulancingo, Hidalgo, in the late 1960s. This system would give Mexicans direct telephone, telex, and television communication with Europe, and with other Latin American countries as well. Money for this program has been borrowed from various countries, including the Federal Republic of Germany (West Germany), Italy, the Netherlands, France, Switzerland, Canada, the United States, and Japan. A Japanese company built the ground station. The final completion of the inter-American communications network was scheduled for 1975.

In spring of 1974 the Ministry of Communications and Transport announced that the Mexican government had signed a contract to use Channel 5 in Mexico City to exchange programs via the inter-Atlantic satellite. The television channel was to transmit government-produced programs to several other countries in Latin America in order to strengthen commercial, cultural, and news exchange within the Western Hemisphere.

FILMS

In the early 1970s there were an estimated 2,700 theaters in Mexico, having a total estimated seating capacity of 1.75 million. Mexican filmmaking reached its peak in the 1940s and early 1950s when the industry achieved an unprecedented level of financial and artistic success. Mexican films were acclaimed at international film festivals. They dominated the Latin American market—largely because World War II eliminated the United States as a competitor. Moreover, the United States government supplied the Mexican film industry with financial aid, technical equipment, and raw film stock. The boom in Mexican films attracted talent from throughout the Western hemisphere, including Argentina, Chile, Colombia, Cuba, Spain, and Venezuela. Equally important was the impressive supply of talent available. Delores del Río, Pedro Armendáriz, María Félix, Cantínflas (Mario Moreno), and Jorge Negrete were all performers in that era.

As a result of this prosperity, six film studios operated in Mexico City in 1946—CLASA, Tepeyac, Azteca, México-Films, Cuauhtémoc, and Churubusco. Only one of these, Churubusco, survived the crisis in the Mexican film industry from 1950 to 1959 and still existed in 1974. This was probably because of the financial and technical aid received by this company from both Mexican and foreign sources. The National Cinematographic Bank, a government agency, had been formed to give aid to the film companies, but by 1957 so many companies were in financial trouble that the bank declared it could not possibly help all of them. During this time, Churubusco combined with the stockholders of Azteca, and this began the merger that led to the closing of the latter company.

Despite some successes, the Mexican film industry has not achieved the creativity and brilliance that marked its earlier years. During the 1960s it suffered from the loss of some of its major directors and actors. Moreover, such a huge backlog of films was built up that when a new director of the bank was appointed in 1970, he outlined a plan for reorganizing and restructuring the Mexican cinema. Among his five proposals were: more coproduction with other countries to help finance the cost of making quality films; more efficient coordination of the three avenues of film distribution and publicity; the opening of a center for training young filmmakers; using the facilities at Churubusco; building up of the government-owned television station's production center at Churubusco in order to provide educational and cultural programming; and expansion of facilities to house a film library, vaults for preserving motion pictures, a theater for the public showing of these films, and a library of books and periodicals devoted to films. As of 1974 several of these proposals had been completed or were being carried out.

Despite the decline in the quality of Mexican films and the growing popularity of television, film attendance has increased. Prices of tickets are closely controlled by the government and depend upon the category of the film. Prices may range as high as the equivalent of US$2, but in the rural areas it is possible to see a film for as little as a few cents. A Sunday family outing often consists of going to see films. Moreover, since films are not dubbed but kept in the original language with subtitles, many students use them for extracurricular language practice.

INTERPERSONAL COMMUNICATION

An American observer of interpersonal communications in Mexico in the early 1970s, Evelyn P. Stevens, noted that a soft-spoken style, marked by a high degree of evasiveness and indirectness, is characteristic of the people. Adults of both sexes are expected to speak softly, frequently giving the appearance of sharing secrets. Loudness is considered abrasive and offensive, and one who is addressed in such tones is expected to retaliate aggressively.

In addition to placing a positive value on being soft-spoken, Mexicans employ circumlocution in a further effort to cushion the listener. Directness in questioning or answering and bold flat statements are interpreted as being rude and vulgar and carrying threatening overtones. Writing about his countrymen one Mexican asserted that "on our lips the Spanish language becomes an instrument of roundabout indirect allusion, of definition by approximation." Such circumlocution is accompanied by redundancy and flowery embellishments, even in the most routine business conversations. Frequently, the result is a tendency to use many words to say very little. This has been hilariously exploited by the popular Mexican comedian, Cantínflas. Throughout Mexico and much of the rest of Latin America, redundancy laced with vagueness is called a *cantinflismo*.

ACTIVITIES OF FOREIGN GOVERNMENTS

Many foreign countries maintained cultural and information centers where their national languages were taught. Among these were Great Britain, France, West Germany, Israel, Japan, the Soviet Union, and the United States. There were other nations that had cultural and educational exchanges with Mexico that were operated by cultural attachés; others, such as Canada, maintained separate libraries and information centers. The Soviet Union had an active cultural exchange program. In 1972, for example, such shows as the Moscow Circus and the Leningrad Music Hall Troupe performed in various cities in Mexico. An exchange of students was planned for November 1974; five young Mexicans planned to visit the Soviet Union, and three Soviet youths were scheduled to visit Mexico.

The governments of Mexico and Poland promulgated a cultural agreement in 1972; under its terms "Polish Weeks" were held in various cities throughout Mexico. An exhibit of Polish graphic arts was also circulated. There was increasing cultural involvement with the People's Republic of China (PRC), and in 1972 the PRC sent a table tennis team and a volleyball team for exhibition games.

The United States Information Service (USIS) maintained an extensive program in Mexico, which included one of its three book publishing programs in Latin America. There were sixteen USIS binational centers engaged, for the most part, in English teaching programs. Most also had libraries of American books and other materials obtained through USIS. USIS had access to all the means of mass communication in Mexico. It distributed material on a regular basis to newspapers, radio, and television and published a locally produced monthly magazine to be sent to Mexican educators. In 1972 USIS maintained contact with seventy-eight radio and 105 television stations, placing Voice of America news and commentaries, documentary films, and newsclips at their disposal.

CHAPTER 12

FOREIGN RELATIONS

Mexico's attitude toward the outside world has traditionally been defensive, reserved, and cautious. In terms of security, it has a northern neighbor it can do little about and southern neighbors it need do little about. During the first fifty years of independence Mexico suffered a sequence of foreign onslaughts, the greatest losses and humiliations having been suffered in the Mexican-American War (1846–48) and under the French-imposed empire of Maximilian (1861–67).

Relations with the United States have always been the cornerstone of Mexican foreign policy. Porfirio Díaz, whose long dictatorship (1867–1911) witnessed a massive increase in United States investment and influence in the country, is said to have lamented, "Poor Mexico. So far from God and so close to the United States." Nationalism in general, and resentment toward the United States in particular, were both cause and effect of the Mexican Revolution of 1910. Opposition to the favored position of United States interests in the country was among the grievances that sparked the rebellion. And the success of the revolution reinforced the sense of national cultural distinctiveness and engendered popular support for a foreign policy that stressed national prerogatives and independence.

Domestic instability during the first two decades after the revolution made national self-assertion difficult and left the country vulnerable to external pressures. It was unable to prevent such United States incursions as the Pershing expedition and the occupation of Veracruz, and claims settlements continued to favor United States citizens over Mexicans (see ch. 3). In the 1930s, however, two factors contributed to a change in United States-Mexican relations and to the emergence of a more effective Mexican foreign policy: the deterioration of the peace in Europe, which in turn inspired United States adoption of the Good Neighbor Policy; and the consolidation of the Mexican revolution, expressed in the institutionalization of the revolutionary party and the concentration of power in the central government. These factors enabled the Mexican government to carry out, for example, the nationalization of the United States-owned oil fields in 1938.

For a brief period after World War II Mexico assumed an "internationalist" posture. At the San Francisco conference in 1945, preceding the establishment of the United Nations (UN), Mexico advocated expanded powers for the General Assembly, elimination of the Security

Council veto, protection of human rights, explication of the rights and duties of states, and elimination of domestic jurisdiction as a limitation on the security functions of the UN.

Aside from that period, however, Mexico has continuously stressed the principles of nonintervention and of the inviolability of the sovereignty of nation-states. Even during the Díaz regime these principles were expressed by Mexican delegates to The Hague peace conferences and the Pan-American conferences, along with nonrecognition of territorial conquest; pacific settlement of disputes; equality of rights between foreigners and nationals; the unlawfulness of the forceful collection of debts; and the nonresponsibility of the state for damages from civil strife.

Resistance against foreign military influence has been a particularly persistent tenet of Mexican policy. In the early years of the revolution President Venustiano Carranza refused to admit foreign military bases and opposed collective intervention in any form in domestic affairs. After World War II the civilian leadership was able to circumscribe the military as an autonomous political force, and participation in the United States Mutual Security Act program was rejected. Mexico is the only Latin American country that has refused to participate in the military assistance program established by that act.

In the post-World War II period Mexican foreign policy has exhibited a relatively high degree of continuity and independence. It has consistently opposed, for example, United States attempts to fashion the Organization of American States (OAS) into an anticommunist alliance.

Nevertheless, Mexican opposition to United States policies has generally been couched in legalistic rather than moral or ideological terms. The latitude of the country's independent posture continues to be circumscribed by the important role of the United States in its economy. The United States accounts for almost two-thirds of Mexico's foreign trade and more than two-thirds of its foreign investment.

While Mexico's military budget since World War II has been low, so has that of the foreign ministry. The country has not taken full advantage of its potential for an activist role in global organizations. It has refused a seat on the UN Security Council since 1946 and, in order to protect its own infant industries through high tariffs, it has refused to join the General Agreement on Tariffs and Trade (GATT). Aside from participation in the Latin American Free Trade Association (LAFTA) and initiatives leading to the Treaty of Tlatelolco (1967) that barred nuclear arms from Latin American signatory states, it has assumed neither a leading nor a mediating role in inter-American affairs. The extensive travels in Latin America and elsewhere of President Adolfo López Mateos in the early 1960s and of President Luís Echeverría in the early 1970s have been exceptions. Despite expressions of solidarity with all third world countries, bilateral relations with African and Asian states have been limited.

As a consequence of its own experiences in the nineteenth and early twentieth centuries, Mexico has firmly adhered to the Drago Doctrine, which prohibits the use of armed force for the collection of a public debt. Mexico's own contributions to inter-American international law include the Carranza Doctrine, which provides that citizens and foreigners are entitled to equal treatment in such matters as the payment of claims; the revival of an old Spanish law asserting the government's right to nationalize the "subsoil"; and the Estrada Doctrine, which calls for automatic recognition of existing governments, although it has not been observed in the cases of Spain and Chile.

In his annual address to the National Congress in September 1974, President Echeverría reiterated the foundations of the country's foreign policy.

The regime's foreign policy is inspired by the best traditions of our doctrine and international practice. Its objective is to defend Mexico's legitimate interests within the context of the universal struggle for peace, liberty, social justice, and common progress. We affirm that we do not hold ideological prejudices and that we always act in a spirit of the most open and clear communication. We contribute with our behavior and with the reiteration of our pacifist theses to a strengthening of political pluralism, which is an unavoidable result of the principle of national sovereignty. Proud of the coexistence the Mexican people have created with particular effort and heroism, we defend the right of all nations to shape their destinies freely and we therefore reject all forms of foreign meddling in their affairs.

RELATIONS WITH OTHER LATIN AMERICAN COUNTRIES

The Central American countries separated from Mexico shortly after independence, and in the ensuing years Mexico occasionally loomed as the "Colossus of the North" for its southern neighbors. A boundary dispute with Guatemala over the district of Chiapas was resolved in Mexico's favor. The cession of the disputed area to Mexico in 1882 was confirmed by treaty in 1899. The disposition of Belize, formerly British Honduras, remains an unresolved issue between Mexico and Guatemala. Should Great Britain relinquish her claim to the colony, Mexico would oppose its annexation by Guatemala in favor of self-determination for the population of Belize.

The disruption of international trade patterns during World War II resulted in a significant increase in Mexico's trade with the Central American countries. The volume of trade dropped precipitously after the war, however, and did not grow much again until the 1960s. The increased trade since the 1960s has been attributed to Mexican interest in the diversification of its markets and fears of losing the Central American market as a consequence of the accelerated economic integration of the region. The balance of trade has been highly favorable to Mexico, and the increased Mexican presence in the area has led a number of periodicals in Central America to warn of Mexican "imperialism."

As a consequence of its proximity to the United States, its isolation during the formative years of the revolution, and its distance from the

South American states and the relative instability of their governments, Mexican bilateral relations with the South American states have traditionally been limited. Except during World War II trade with all of Latin America has never accounted for more than 12 percent of Mexico's exports nor more than 5 percent of its imports. Mexico's principal involvement in the political affairs of the region has been as a refuge for political exiles.

In the early 1960s President López Mateos began to deviate from this tradition of self-imposed diplomatic isolation. He met with many Latin American heads of state and traveled to Peru, Argentina, and Chile. A trip to Bolivia had also been scheduled, but the pilot was afraid to land in La Paz. His successor, President Gustavo Díaz Ordaz, limited his state visits to Central America, but President Echeverría has traveled extensively throughout Latin America.

In June 1974 President Echeverría toured Ecuador, Peru, Argentina, Brazil, and Venezuela, in part to urge the acceleration of regional economic integration and the lifting of the economic blockade against Cuba. At the United Nations Law of the Seas Conference in Caracas, he advocated recognition of a twelve-mile territorial sea and of a two-hundred-mile patrimonial sea over which the state exerts economic jurisdiction. And he expressed his government's support for free access to the sea for South America's landlocked countries, Bolivia and Paraguay.

In Argentina Echeverría signed a manifesto creating a committee to draft an instrument to ensure the right to free analysis and research in the Western Hemisphere. In Brazil he agreed to create permanent committees for a joint Mexico-Brazil commission to evaluate opportunities for trade. He encouraged the Venezuelan government in its attempts to regain control over basic resources and offered the technological cooperation of Mexican Petroleum Petróleos Mexicanos—PEMEX) and the Mexican Oil Institute.

Relations with Chile became an important issue in domestic politics in the early 1970s. The Echeverría government had expressed great sympathy with the government of socialist President Salvador Allende. The overthrow of that government by a military junta in September 1973 and the death of Allende aroused public outrage in Mexico. Since that time Echeverría has been an outspoken critic of the violation of human rights in Chile and of alleged United States complicity in the undermining of the Allende government. Mexico has welcomed refugees from Chile and has urged the junta to release those members of Allende's cabinet who remain in prison. Finally, in November 1974 Mexico severed diplomatic relations with Chile. In Peru Echeverría advocated the establishment of an exclusive Latin American economic organization to foster Latin American cooperation on price setting for raw materials and commodity exports and science and technology.

Mexico's relations with Cuba have passed through four stages since the Cuban revolution. The initial attitude of the Mexican government toward the government of Fidel Castro was one of great sympathy and recognition of the goals common to the Mexican and Cuban revolutions. The second stage, which began with the strengthening of Cuban-Soviet ties in late 1961, was characterized by Mexico's withdrawal of outspoken support for Castro and the maintenance of formal ties only, with minimal contact. The phase that began in 1968 saw a sequence of unpleasant incidents between the two countries, causing a significant deterioration of relations. Since 1971, however, relations have improved markedly.

RELATIONS WITH THE UNITED STATES

Historically, four phases of diplomatic intercourse can be discerned in Mexican-United States relations. From 1822 until 1917 most diplomatic interchange concerned territorial boundary disputes, which resulted in three United States military interventions and Mexico's loss of nearly half of its territory. The second phase of diplomatic activity arose from the Mexican Constitution of 1917, which contained many socioeconomic provisions impinging upon private United States investments in Mexico. During this period diplomatic relations between the United States and Mexico were subjected to great stress (see ch. 3).

During and immediately after World War II, a third phase of unprecedented military and technical cooperation between the two nations occurred. In the fourth phase (since 1952), Mexico has attempted to follow a nonaligned position vis-à-vis United States involvement in the cold war. Mexico maintains cordial relations with the United States but follows a relatively independent hemispheric and international course consistent with its ideological formulation of foreign policy.

During World War II Mexico participated in and supported all hemispheric collective defense agencies. In 1942 Mexico severed all diplomatic relations with the Axis powers and declared war. Reciprocal military and political agreements were signed by the two nations. In the Americas, Mexico received the second largest lend-lease installments from the United States, US$38 million. Economic cooperation was evidenced by the creation of a joint commission in 1943 to make recommendations to meet any economic problem arising in either nation's production level. The Water Treaty of 1944 provided for joint flood-control and water conservation projects and the allocation of water from the Rio Grande and the Colorado River. In the immediate postwar years, the United States and Mexico continued to further economic and technical cooperation.

Mexico's refusal to enter into a bilateral military assistance agreement with the United States in 1952 marked the fourth phase of relations between the two nations. In the context of the cold war, Mexico has felt obliged to steer a difficult course of asserting independence from the United States, as popular sentiment has demanded, without placing intolerable strain on their basically cordial relations.

The push and pull of domestic nationalism and the realities of power in the international system have led to such political strategies as the position of the Mexican foreign minister at the Organization of American States (OAS) conference in Punta del Este, Uruguay, in 1962. He introduced the thesis, later seized upon by the majority as justification for the expulsion of Cuba from the OAS, that a Marxist-Leninist regime was incompatible with participation in that organization; but he voted against the expulsion of Cuba on procedural grounds. There have been obvious limits to the amount of independence Mexico could effectively exercise, but the country has generally succeeded in appearing to concede less than in fact it was necessary to concede.

In economic relations, Mexico has attempted since the 1930s to assert control over foreign investment. The country has placed complex limitations on imports and has required 51 percent Mexican ownership of any corporation based in the country. It has also attempted to diversify the sources of foreign capital entering the country. Nevertheless, foreign investment has remained overwhelmingly of United States origin— about 74 percent in the early 1970s—and of the country's 400 largest corporations, more than half were in reality owned or heavily influenced by non-Mexican interests. Furthermore, the country has remained highly dependent on United States tourists for the provision of its foreign currency reserves.

Mexico has continued from time to time to advance the program of mexicanization of United States-owned concerns operating in the country, but it has paid well for the foreign shares. In 1974 the state purchased 11 percent of International Telephone and Telegraph's shares in its subsidiary, Indetel, increasing Mexican ownership to 51 percent.

A border dispute, caused by the shifting course of the Rio Grande, that had dragged on for years was finally settled in 1963 in Mexico's favor. Another dispute, however, had remained unresolved and, together with other boundary uncertainties, was not settled until 1970. The excessively high saline content of the Colorado River as it crossed into Mexico, resulting from irrigation projects on the United States side of the border, had been viewed by Mexico as a violation of the Water Treaty of 1944 and international law.

Another persistent irritant in bilateral relations has been the alleged mistreatment of Mexican migratory laborers in the United States. The *bracero* (field-worker) program, whereby the number of Mexican laborers to be seasonally employed in the United States and the conditions of their employment were set forth in bilateral agreements, was terminated by the United States Congress in 1965 under pressure from domestic labor unions. Since that time the illegal status of the Mexican workers who have continued to cross the border in great numbers has subjected them to greater exploitation. The Mexican government has sought the reinstatement of some arrangement whereby the dignity of the Mexican workers might be respected by United States employers and customs officials. The United States government would like the Mexican government to cooperate in curtailing the entry of illegal Mexican immigrants.

Since the meeting of presidents Franklin Roosevelt and Manuel Avila Camacho during World War II, an institutionalized arrangement has been established whereby the new president of either country is invited to pay a state visit to the other. In keeping with this custom, President Echeverría met with President Richard Nixon in Washington in 1972 and with President Gerald Ford on both sides of the border in 1974. As a consequence of the meeting with President Nixon, the two governments concluded an agreement in 1973 for the resolution of the Colorado River issue. There was no indication in 1974 of progress toward the solution of the problem of migrant laborers.

RELATIONS WITH OTHER COUNTRIES

Mexico maintains diplomatic relations with most of the countries of the world, irrespective of the nature of their governments. During the first four years of the Echeverría administration relations were established with several additional countries, including the People's Republic of China (PRC), Barbados, Tanzania, Guyana, Romania, the German Democratic Republic (East Germany), New Zealand, the Commonwealth of the Bahamas, Cyprus, Malaysia, Hungary, Bulgaria, Algeria, and Albania.

One of the few exceptions to the country's adherence to the Estrada Doctrine, of recognizing governments on a de facto rather than a de jure basis, has been the case of Spain. During the Spanish civil war, Mexico welcomed a large number of Spanish republican refugees, who have since become Mexican citizens. Since that time Mexico has recognized the Spanish republican government-in-exile, located in Mexico City, and has refused to establish formal contact with the Francisco Franco government in Madrid. On the possibility of establishing diplomatic relations with Spain, President Echeverría commented in 1974: "There is much affinity between Mexico and Spain. We are very proud of our Spanish roots, but it will probably be the next Mexican and Spanish administrations which will determine this."

As a consequence of the persistent friction between the Roman Catholic Church and the state throughout much of Mexico's history, the country does not maintain relations with the Vatican. President Echeverría, however, paid a visit to Pope Paul VI in 1974.

Commercial and cultural affairs dominate Mexico's bilateral relations with countries beyond the Western Hemisphere. The exportation of Mexican culture, such as folkloric troupes and art exhibits, and the interest displayed by foreign scholars in Mexican archaeology and ethnology have been sources of national pride. There has also been a fairly large market in the country's upper and middle classes for the cultural products of other nations. The French language and literature

265

have been particularly influential among intellectuals.

Mexico has viewed the Western European countries—Italy, the Federal Republic of Germany (West Germany), France, and Great Britain in particular—as alternate sources of foreign investment in its drive to lessen its dependence on United States capital. The country has also sought to diversify its trading relationships and, in fact, the United States proportion of its total foreign trade dropped from about 86 percent in 1950 to about 60 percent in the early 1970s (see ch. 15).

In the Orient, Japan has been a major source of investment capital as well as the country's main trading partner. Trade with India and Indonesia has also been significant. Among the Middle Eastern countries Mexico's strongest ties have been with Lebanon, probably as a result of its large population of Lebanese immigrants. Trade with most of the third world states has been minimal as production for export has been competitive rather than complementary.

Mexico has tended, however, to identify with the third world countries on most issues of international trade. It participated in the fourth conference of nonaligned states in Algiers in 1973. In 1974 it assured members of the Organization of Petroleum Exporting Countries that it would market its recently discovered oil at the prices set by that organization. In July 1974 President Echeverría called for a common front of all third world countries to obtain better raw material prices.

Alleging Soviet interference in its internal affairs, Mexico severed relations with the Soviet Union in 1930. Leon Trotsky was later given political asylum in Mexico and resided there for three years before he was assassinated in 1940. Relations were renewed in 1942. Since that time relations have generally been cordial but distant, involving little friction but also little contact, and trade with Eastern Europe has been inconsequential. In 1972, however, Mexico concluded banking agreements with Poland, Romania, and Yugoslavia in an effort to boost trade with those countries; Mexico also signed a commercial treaty with the PRC in 1973.

President Echeverría's travels in 1972 and 1973, undertaken to promote Mexico's political and economic interests as well as to defend the position of the third world against pressure from the great powers, included state visits to Japan, Great Britain, Belgium, France, the Soviet Union, and the PRC. The highlight of the tour was said to have been agreement by France and the PRC to sign the Second Protocol of the Treaty of Tlatelolco, though the French agreement was with "reservations." One of Echeverría's missions in Western Europe was the establishment of closer ties between LAFTA and the European Economic Community (EEC). In the Soviet Union he affirmed that cordial relations would be maintained "without fear of any kind and certain that the Soviet Union would not export its revolution to Mexico, nor Mexico export its revolution to the Soviet Union."

In February 1974 President Echeverría traveled to West Germany, Italy, Austria, and Yugoslavia, where financial, commercial, scientific, technological, and cultural agreements were signed. In Vienna he signed a cooperation agreement with the International Atomic Energy Organization to use nuclear power to produce electricity. Great Britain was making an effort to expand commercial ties with Mexico in the 1970s. It was announced in 1974 that Queen Elizabeth would visit Mexico in 1975 to reciprocate President Echeverría's visit to Great Britain.

INTERNATIONAL ORGANIZATIONS AND COMMITMENTS

The country views its participation in international and regional organizations as a reassertion of commitment to the principles of international cooperation and peace. Foreign policy in relation to these bodies indicates a nonaligned and isolationist view of what the proper functions of international organizations should be. Within these organs, Mexico asserts a strictly legalistic and juridical approach to the problems of international peace. Self-development by sovereign nations is the best guarantee of the effective operation of international conciliatory agencies. As an example, the country proudly points to Benito Juárez, the first Mexican statesman to enunciate the principles of nonintervention and self-determination as the cornerstones of Mexican foreign policy. Mexican participation in international bodies does not extend beyond these doctrines.

The Inter-American System

Mexico has been a member, though not necessarily a very active one, of most of the global or Western Hemisphere organizations constituted since The Hague Conference of 1899. In the Western Hemisphere Mexico is a party to the Inter-American Treaty of Reciprocal Assistance (commonly known as the Rio Pact) and a member of the OAS, the Inter-American Development Bank, and LAFTA.

The country has rarely taken a leading role as a spokesman for the interests of Latin America as a whole, but it has followed a more persistently independent course than most of the Latin American states, especially in opposition to United States security policies in the hemisphere. Mexican objections to the use of the OAS as an anticommunist alliance became apparent in the early 1950s. The Caracas Conference of 1954, spearheaded by the United States, adopted a resolution stating that the domination and control of any American state by international communism was to be deemed a threat to all American states. This anticommunist resolution met with an abstention from Mexico, which claimed that this declaration compromised the principle of nonintervention.

At the Seventh Meeting of Consultation of Foreign Ministers at San José, Costa Rica, in 1960, the United States stressed the danger presented by Cuba to hemispheric security. Mexican Foreign Minister Manuel Tello stated that the Cuban experience demanded patience on the part of the American states and that their task would be to make Cuba feel that its destiny was in the Americas. The Mexican government took exception to the Declaration of San José by claiming that collective action would endanger the principle of nonintervention when an alleged case was not clearly an extracontinental threat to peace and security.

After the abortive invasion of Cuba in April 1961, the United States requested a meeting of consultation of the OAS to consider the threat by the Soviet Union and Cuba to hemispheric security. Mexico opposed the calling of such a meeting. Despite this opposition, the eighth meeting was held in Punta del Este, Uruguay, and by the necessary two-thirds majority vote Cuba was suspended as an OAS member. Mexico opposed this move claiming that it was juridically impossible under the existing OAS Charter to exclude a member state from the organization. Mexico insisted that such procedure could occur only after amending the charter. This meeting concluded with a resolution suspending trade with Cuba, on which Mexico abstained from voting.

At the Ninth Meeting of Foreign Ministers in July 1964, a mandatory declaration for member states to suspend diplomatic and economic relations with Cuba was issued. Mexico vigorously denounced this as intervention and refused to adhere to the OAS ruling. In 1967 the country refused to vote in favor of expanding economic sanctions imposed upon Cuba, while it supported, at this same conference, a resolution that called for the immediate reporting to the UN of any aggressive action on the part of Cuba.

By the time of the Quito Conference in 1974, six Latin American countries besides Mexico were maintaining diplomatic and commercial relations with Cuba despite the OAS ban, and a majority of the member states favored the lifting of the ban. Mexico voted with the majority, but the vote fell short of the two-thirds majority required to nullify the 1964 resolution.

Mexico has long been an advocate of the latinization of the OAS. Several items in the Protocol of Amendment to the Charter, signed in Buenos Aires on February 27, 1967, designed to strengthen cooperation in social and economic affairs and to dilute the political role of the Permanent Council, had been proposed by the Mexican delegation. The country's foreign policy regards the OAS as an embodiment of the juridical principles of nonintervention and self-determination. As such, the participation of the United States in this body is viewed by some Mexican foreign policymakers as inimical to these doctrines. In this view, United States involvement in the cold war impinges upon the development of a truly integrated Latin America. Mexico has vigorously opposed the creation of a permanent OAS military organ.

The Dominican Republic crisis of 1965 further illustrates Mexican opposition to inter-American collective intervention in the internal affairs of American states. At that time, Mexico affirmed that the sole justification of its military forces has been to defend and protect its own institutions and processes. To expand this to provide personnel for an

268

inter-American military force would be a violation of the Bogotá Charter, which expressly prohibits the use of force to settle disputes, asserts the doctrine of nonintervention, and guarantees the juridical equality of all states. These provisions constitute the essence of Mexican foreign policy as well.

The country was instrumental in formulating the Treaty of Tlatelolco for the proscription of nuclear arms in Latin America. Mexico became a signatory on February 14, 1967. According to then-Subsecretary of Foreign Affairs Alfonso García Robles, Mexican support of this treaty has the twin objectives of excluding nuclear arms from Latin America and taking the first step toward the general and complete disarmament of the world. Mexico also supports the economic integration of Latin America and a political confederation in which only Latin American nations can participate. Mexico has become one of the leading proponents of Latin American integration based upon a purely Latin American directorate.

President Díaz Ordaz enthusiastically supported the summit meeting of Latin American chiefs of state at Punta del Este in April 1967, and he stated that at this level of decisionmaking in concerted action, Latin America would arrive at economic integration in the near future. Likewise, President Echeverría has stressed that "Latin America must achieve greater unity, above all economically," and he has proposed the formation of Latin American multinational companies organized in the manner of cooperatives, engaged in purchasing as well as marketing.

President Echeverría's frustrations with the OAS have been frequently and forcefully articulated. In his address to the National Congress in September 1974 he said, "The OAS is more inoperative every day. It cannot achieve strength of any kind unless it carries out a basic reform of its structure and methods and confronts the reality of political pluralism. It must not insist on remaining a theatrical backdrop for undisguisable hegemonic maneuvers." At the various meetings of the organization since Echeverría assumed the presidency in 1970, Mexico has urged consideration of Panamanian sovereignty over the canal that divides its territory, the drafting of a code to regulate the activities of transnational corporations, the transfer of technology at reasonable cost, and the lifting of the sanctions against Cuba.

Global Organizations

Mexico was not a charter member of the League of Nations but was a member at the time of the demise of that agency. One reason for the delay in joining was Mexican opposition to Article 21 of the league covenant, which termed the Monroe Doctrine a "regional arrangement" and provided for its internationalization. Mexico expressed reservations against this article on the basis that it was a unilateral declaration and it violated the juridical principles of nonintervention.

The UN serves as an outlet for Mexican foreign policy statements and is viewed as an embodiment of the principles of international law and cooperation. The country has not contributed financial assistance or personnel, however, to the UN collective security operations.

Mexico has been one of the most active UN members in the area of defining the principles of nonintervention. In an address before the General Assembly, Subsecretary for Foreign Affairs García Robles stated that the principle of nonintervention is an incontrovertible and inviolable doctrine guaranteed by the Charter of the United Nations. As a member state, Mexico was at the forefront in pressing the adoption of the declaration concerning the "Inadmissibility of Intervention into the Internal Affairs of States and the Protection of Their Independence and Sovereignty." This was passed by the General Assembly on December 21, 1965, by a unanimous vote. Mexico's consistently reiterated position before the UN is that the organization does not have to concern itself with Mexican affairs because Mexico's own development permits it to avoid all international problems. Mexico has taken no position in the UN that would compromise its commitment to nonintervention and self-determination. Its foreign policy holds that there can be no international peace if these principles are not observed by all nations.

While eschewing a seat on the UN Security Council and assuming a low profile on most issues relating directly to the cold war, Mexico has taken an active role in promoting disarmament, denouncing colonialism, and focusing attention on the problems of underdevelopment. It has participated enthusiastically, for example, in the affairs of the United Nations Conference on Trade and Development (UNCTAD).

Addressing the third UNCTAD conference in Santiago in April 1972, President Echeverría urged the adoption of a "charter of economic duties and rights of states." The charter was meant to include the demands of the Chilean government for the renunciation of economic pressure as a political tool and the prohibition of the interference of multinational corporations in the internal affairs of host countries. Urging support for this charter has been a major theme of Echeverría's extensive exercise of personal diplomacy since that time. Another theme emphasized by the Mexican delegation in the UN General Assembly in 1974 was the urgency of progress toward nuclear disarmament.

Mexico's consistently good standing with the international lending institutions has been highly beneficial to its economic development programs. Mexico has sought to obtain most of its credit from these institutions rather than through private banks or bilateral aid programs and has become one of the largest borrowers from the International Bank for Reconstruction and Development (IBRD, commonly known as the World Bank).

FOREIGN POLICY DECISIONMAKING

Primary responsibility for the formulation of foreign policy lies with the president of the republic. His decisions are supplemented and

270

implemented by the Secretariat of Foreign Affairs, headed by a secretary and two subsecretaries appointed by the president. Foreign office personnel are drawn primarily from the professional sector of the Institutional Revolutionary Party (Partido Revolucionario Institutional —PRI). Attorneys and engineers constitute the largest groups of professionals on the upper levels of the foreign ministry, although some ambassadors have risen through the ranks of the foreign service. Lower positions are usually filled by professional civil servants in the small foreign service. Appointment to the foreign service, in some cases through competitive examination, carries much prestige; and the prestige of the ministry is in turn enhanced by the appointment of noted intellectuals to the ambassadorial ranks. Such appointments, however, carry a certain risk of embarrassment to the government. The renowned poet and essayist Octavio Paz, for example, appointed ambassador to India by the government of Díaz Ordaz, received considerable international publicity when he resigned in protest after the Tlatelolco Massacre in 1968 (see ch. 10).

There is no formally constituted intelligence agency existing within the foreign affairs secretariat. The military is primarily responsible for such services through its own intelligence apparatus. A number of foreign economic matters are dealt with by other departments and entities. The secretariat of finance, for example, issues import and export permits, and the National Development Bank (Nacional Financiera) deals with controversies concerning foreign investments.

Despite the general continuity in support for certain broad principles of national and international law, both style and content of foreign policy have varied somewhat from one administration to the next. The administrations of Adolfo Ruiz Cortines (1952–58) and Díaz Ordaz (1964–70) were characterized by a low profile and little innovation in foreign affairs, but those of López Mateos (1958–64) and Echeverría have witnessed a greater degree of national self-assertion.

To the extent that public opinion focuses on foreign policy, there has generally been a broad constituency for a nationalistic stance and opposition to United States influence. The only powerful groups that seek to influence foreign policy on a regular basis, however, are those having a direct interest in foreign trade and investment. University students and intellectuals are frequent advocates of foreign policy positions, but without the support of other groups they can bring little pressure to bear on decisionmaking.

SECTION III. ECONOMIC

CHAPTER 13

CHARACTER AND STRUCTURE
OF THE ECONOMY

Mexico, at the end of 1974, was completing twenty-five years of impressive economic growth, but the government was confronted with problems of inflation and uneven distribution of wealth. During the period 1950 through the 1960s the gross domestic product (GDP) had grown at rates averaging between 6 and 7 percent annually, and the per capita income had increased fivefold. The growth rates in 1970, 1972, and 1973 exceeded the average growth rates for all of Latin America, the United States, and Western Europe.

Still classified by the United Nations (UN) as a developing country in 1974, Mexico's economy was led by industry and trade, characteristics of developed nations. Agriculture had contributed an ever-decreasing share to the GDP since 1950 although it employed the largest percentage of the labor force. Industrial production includes most consumer goods and many intermediate and capital goods. Agriculture, including livestock, is well diversified with no strong reliance on one or two products, although corn is the most widely grown crop (see ch. 14).

Although Mexico is a relatively wealthy country, it has not been able to eliminate poverty or to improve income distribution, especially between rural and urban inhabitants (see National Accounts, this ch.). The other major worry in the 1970s was inflation. Until the 1970s Mexico experienced little or no inflationary pressure. The cost-of-living index during the 1950s and 1960s rose by no more than 5 percent annually, and thus the inflationary pressure of the 1970s was a new phenomenon for most of the population. Although the pressure was not as severe as in some other countries, it was sufficiently high to cause concern to the government and to stimulate discontent in the labor force. Inflationary pressures first became evident in 1970, and by 1973 the national retail price index had risen by more than 20 percent over 1972; by late 1974 it appeared that the index would increase another 11 percent for the year. The prices of some foods had doubled, and more and more commodities, including nonconsumer goods, were coming under strict price controls as the government became determined to combat the inflationary spiral.

Some of the factors that contributed to Mexico's rapid economic

273

development were a long period of political stability; diversified natural resources, including minerals, petroleum, and agricultural raw materials; a sophisticated financial system; a professional and competent corps of government officials with considerable decisionmaking authority; and geographic proximity to the United States, which provided a ready market for Mexican exports and permitted a heavy flow of tourism to Mexico that brought in much-needed foreign exchange. Exports are diversified and include sugar, cotton, shrimp, chemicals, fruit, coffee, and machinery (see ch. 15).

The government is deeply involved in the economy. It operates numerous state corporations, provides basic services and infrastructure, regulates credit and the flow of funds to the economy, sets minimum wages, and maintains price supports for certain agricultural products coupled with price controls on many consumer and industrial products.

Despite the important role of the government in certain areas, such as petroleum, however, state-owned firms account for only about 10 percent of total industrial production. The economy is not centrally controlled, and economic plans are merely guidelines. The dynamic private sector dominates the economy, and within it highly visible foreign investment that gravitated to the most dynamic industries has resulted in restrictions being placed on the degree of ownership of Mexican companies by foreign firms.

The labor movement is relatively highly organized, and a close relationship exists between government and most labor leaders (see ch. 10). The Constitution and several labor laws protect all workers and encourage them to organize for greater benefits than the minimum standards outlined by law. An estimated 2 million workers—one-seventh of the labor force—belonged to industrial and commercial unions in 1974. Profit sharing has been mandatory since 1962, and a new far-reaching profit-sharing formula was prepared in late 1974, which called for 8 percent of a company's pretax profits to be divided among all its workers. Although labor laws cover most aspects of worker-management relations, collective bargaining is the basic mechanism for improving wages and working conditions. Wage bargaining tends to be on a company level but sometimes is on an industry basis. In 1974 organized labor successfully attempted nationwide bargaining and won an across-the-board wage increase of 22 percent under the threat of a general strike.

Business organizations articulate and promote the views and interests of private enterprise. Mexican law requires most private firms and merchants to belong to a management association, and this requirement enhances the strength of such organizations. Among the more influential management organizations are the National Confederation of Chambers of Commerce (Confederación Nacional de Cámaras de Comercio—CONCANACO), the Confederation of Industrial Chambers (Confederación de Cámaras Industriales—CONCAMIN), and the National Chamber of Transformation Industries (Cámara Nacional de la Industria

274

de Transformación—CANACINTRA). In addition to representing the general interest of their members in their relations with the government, they perform numerous services, such as arbitration between members in disputes, educational seminars on economic problems of the nation, and improvement of labor-management relations. Of smaller numerical strength but exercising considerable influence are the Mexican Bankers Association, the Mexican Association of Insurance Institutions, and the Mexican Employers Confederation. There are also numerous smaller associations organized on an industrywide basis. An estimated 400,000 firms belong to business organizations.

Many Mexican companies are family owned and operated, even those that have grown into corporations. The most striking example is found in Monterrey, where over 60 percent of the industrial firms are family owned. In contrast to the experience in other Latin American countries where family-operated companies tend to be less progressive, a high percentage of the family members in the management hierarchy of Mexican firms are well trained in technical and business administration. Such companies rank among the most influential and dynamic in Mexico. One study further indicated that firms founded by European immigrants to Mexico have become leaders in their industries.

NATIONAL ACCOUNTS

Beginning in 1969 national accounts statistics were set up in accordance with guidelines used by the UN and have been expressed in terms of GDP. Until 1969 accounts were maintained in terms of the gross national product (GNP). During the decade of the 1960s the GNP growth rate averaged 7.1 percent annually; the industrial, trade, and construction sectors grew at faster rates and the other sectors of the economy at slower rates. In 1970 the GDP growth rate was 7.7 percent, but the rate fell in 1971 to 3.7 percent as a direct result of governmental anti-inflationary policies to reduce pressures on prices and the balance of payments. In 1972 there was a rapid recovery to 7.5 percent, and preliminary data for 1973 indicated a rate of 7.3 percent and an absolute GDP of about 550 billion pesos (12.5 pesos equal US$1). In late 1974 indications were that the GDP growth rate for that year might not exceed 6 percent.

The composition of the GDP has undergone a vast change since 1950. The largest share, nearly one-third, is contributed by trade, including tourism (see table 8). The growth of this sector is attributable to the promotion of the purchase of consumer goods, particularly durables, by easy financing and credit. Manufacturing has become the second most important sector, spurred by a governmental policy encouraging industrialization (see ch. 14). The growth of trade and manufacturing has occurred mainly at the expense of the agricultural sector. Although it provides employment for the largest percentage of the population, agriculture has been the slowest growing sector, averaging under 4 percent annually and in some years growing at less than 2 percent. Whereas agriculture, including forestry and fishing, contributed 25 percent of the GDP in 1950, by 1973 its share was under 11 percent. The contribution of the other sectors has remained more or less constant.

The average per capita income has increased steadily, notwithstanding population growth, and was estimated at about the equivalent of US$744 in 1972. Despite the relatively high per capita figure, income in Mexico is very unevenly distributed, and the redistribution of income in order to improve the living standards of more persons is one of the dominant concerns of the government. Income diversity is most significant on a regional basis. The highest per capita levels are found in the Federal District, Baja California, and urban areas of other states along the United States border. The lowest per capita income is found in the largely rural states of Chiapas, Oaxaca, Tlaxcala, Hidalgo, Guanajuato, San Luís Potosí, and Zacatecas, located in the center and south of the country. Numerous studies and income comparisons have borne out the thesis that income levels in Mexico may be among the most widely varying in the world, and the gap between the highest and lowest income is constantly widening.

In 1969, when the average annual per capita income was the equivalent of about US$645, almost 18 percent of the population had a per capita income below US$75. In 1970 an estimated 42 percent of the economically active population received incomes under US$40 per month, and 2 percent had incomes over US$400 per month. In 1972 the minister of finance, in a statement calling for more equal distribution of wealth, contended that 10 percent of the population received 50 percent of the total income in the country while at the other extreme 50 percent of the population received only 10 percent of the income. Another study in 1972 revealed that annual rural per capita income was one-fourth the national average of the equivalent of US$744 and that the per capita income of the upper 30 percent of the population was equivalent to US$1,400, which was on a par with per capita incomes of many industrialized nations.

GOVERNMENT ROLE IN THE ECONOMY

The Mexican government follows a policy of maintaining a mixed economy and playing an active role. The government is an investor, a provider of substantial credit, and an entrepreneur. At the same time private interests are promoted, encouraged, and protected but often curtailed. The direct participation of the government is accomplished mainly by means of government corporations and autonomous agencies. It has the primary or dominant role in certain sectors: petroleum, railroads, electricity, communications, irrigation, steel manufacturing, aviation, and petrochemicals. It plays an extensive role in finance by means of more than thirty public credit institutions and operates the largest agricultural marketing and retailing organization. When private

Table 8. Mexico, Gross Domestic Product by Sector, 1969–73
(in percent)

Sector	1969	1970	1971	1972	1973[1]
Trade, including tourism	32.0	32.2	32.0	31.3	32.3
Manufacturing	22.5	22.8	23.7	24.0	23.1
Agriculture, forestry, and fishing	11.9	11.6	12.1	11.4	10.1
Rental of dwelling	6.3	6.2	5.9	7.0	....[2]
Government	5.6	5.5	6.1	6.1	6.1
Mining and petroleum	5.2	5.1	4.4	4.3	4.4
Transportation, utility, and communications	4.8	4.9	5.0	4.7	5.3
Construction	4.7	4.7	4.7	5.0	5.0
Finance	1.7	1.7	1.6	2.3	....[2]
Other	5.3	5.3	4.5	3.9	13.7
TOTAL	100.0	100.0	100.0	100.0	100.0

[1] Preliminary figures.
[2] Included in Other.

firms need financial assistance or when certain legal requirements so stipulate, the government may become a partner in the company. About 550,000 people were employed in all the state-owned enterprises in 1974, and the total number of firms in which the government has some participation was variously estimated at between 240 and 350, although one government spokesmen suggested that there might be over 900 in 1974.

Indirectly the government has acted to influence the level and direction of private investment by such means as concessions for the exploitation of minerals, exclusion of imports competing with domestic products, and the granting of fiscal and tax incentives and benefits. When the import demand for any product reaches a certain level, the government attempts to stimulate its domestic production by bringing it to the attention of manufacturers and promising protection from competition once production commences. Under the budget law and a practice dating back to 1897, the government may grant fiscal subsidies to an entire industry or to a few specific firms in the industry. The fiscal subsidy consists of the forgiveness of taxes due, but in return the recipients must agree in writing to increase production, employment, and investment. Generally these subsidy agreements are not made public, and the beneficiaries are unknown.

Although the federal government has acted with increasing effectiveness to determine the rate and direction of economic growth, it has done so without formal national development plans. Systematic planning has been limited to regional and sectoral development. Between 1930 and 1952 planning documents consisted mainly of general-purpose statements having little effect on actual policy. Under the government of President Adolfo Ruiz Cortines (1952–58) an attempt was made to coordinate the investment programs of the federal government with those of the decentralized agencies, and under President Adolfo Lopéz Mateos (1958–64) the responsibility for overall planning was given to the Ministry of the Presidency. Details of plans, however, are never published, and their drafts are not formally adopted although their recommendations are usually followed. The newly created Mexican Development Institute announced in mid-1974 that the country's medium-range goals would include an average annual GDP growth rate of between 7.5 and 8 percent, a reduction of the population growth rate from 3.5 percent to 2.5 percent, the creation of at least 700,000 new jobs annually to cope with rising unemployment and underemployment, and increasing exports by 15 percent annually (see ch. 2).

Regional development programs have been more successful. The more important are the river basin commissions, such as the Papaloapán Basin Commission, a semiautonomous entity created in 1947 originally as a flood control agency for the Papaloapán River basin, which straddles the Gulf Coast and South Pacific regions. Gradually it evolved into a regional development authority with programs for irrigation, drainage, sanitation, electricity, communications, agriculture, and industry. Another successful river basin commission was the Tepalcatepec Commission, originally created in 1947 to serve parts of the states of Michoacán and Jalisco but later, in 1960, expanded into the much larger River Balsas Commission. Other such regional commissions include the Fuerte River Commission, the Grijalva River Commission, the Lerma-Chapala-Santiago Commission, and the Tehuantepec Isthmus Commission (see fig. 1; ch. 2).

PUBLIC FINANCE

The public sector consists of the federal government, the autonomous government entities, the state enterprises, and local governments including states, the Federal District, and municipalities. Only some of the government enterprises and autonomous agencies have been brought under central budgetary control; as of 1974 they included the sixteen largest, such as Mexican Petroleum, the Federal Electricity Commission, the National Railways of Mexico, and the various social welfare institutes. Except for fiscal year (FY) 1975 their combined share of the annual central budget usually exceeded the amount established for the operations of the federal government. Except for credit, educational, and cultural institutions, the budgets of the agencies and enterprises not under central budgetary control are reviewed and approved by the Ministry of National Properties, which also has the right to restructure the organization of those agencies. Budgets of state financial organizations are approved by the Ministry of Finance and Public Credit, and the Ministry of Education and Culture oversees the educational and cultural institutions. The fiscal year generally is the calendar year although some government agencies use a fiscal year of July 1 to June 30.

Since 1970 budget estimates have been moving rapidly upward,

although some of the increase was caused merely by changes in accounting procedures. Whereas in 1970 the central budget was 72.2 billion
pesos, proposed expenditures increased to nearly 80 billion pesos for
1971, rose to over 122 billion pesos in 1972, soared to almost 174 billion
pesos in 1973, and was established at 231 billion pesos for 1974. The 1975
budget was established at 299 billion pesos. There is always a wide
discrepancy, however, between budgetary estimates and actual outlays
because most congressionally approved budgetary forecasts characteristically underestimate both revenues and expenditures and are subsequently revised upward at the discretion of the executive. For example,
in 1970 actual revenues and expenditures were over 109 billion pesos
rather than the 72.2 billion pesos approved in the budget. In spite of the
wide deviation between estimates and actual expenditures, the fiscal
policy of the government has been conservative, and there are frequently
small surpluses in the current account. The capital account, however,
usually has a deficit, which is made up by domestic and foreign
borrowing.

According to the Constitution the budgetary laws and administrative
regulations rest with the legislature, and responsibility for the preparation and execution of the budget lies with the executive. The budget law,
the Organic Law of the Federal Expenditures Budget, provides for the
annual enactment of a law of revenues and a law of expenditures before
any money can be collected or spent. Control of the Law of Expenditures
is constitutionally in the hands of the Chamber of Deputies, and jurisdiction over revenues is shared with the Senate. In practice, however,
initiative in fiscal matters is taken by the executive. Both the revenue
and the expenditure bills are prepared by the Ministry of Finance and
Public Credit for introduction to the legislature, and very little change is
made in the budgetary recommendations by congress.

The estimate of expenditures is presented with various analytical
breakdowns: by ministry, by function, and by consolidated capital
expenditures. The Ministry of Education and Culture received the
largest share of the federal government's budget—almost 34 percent in
1972. The Ministry of Hydraulic Resources received the next largest
share in 1972—almost 14 percent, mainly for irrigation and flood control.
Public works received over 10 percent, mainly for highway construction.
Although some military expenses are not included in the defense budget,
defense was allotted over 7 percent, one of the lowest percentages of
any Latin American country's budget, and agriculture and livestock
obtained about 4 percent, mainly for research on improved techniques in
crop and livestock production. (see ch. 17). The balance was divided
among all other ministries. Functionally the combined budgets of the
federal government and the decentralized agencies indicated that the
largest share, about 30 percent, went for industrial development, 19
percent was earmarked to amortize the public debt, 12 percent was for
welfare and social security, and 8 percent went to development of natural

resources. Agriculture and energy development received the major shares of capital expenditures, 18 percent and 12 percent, respectively, in the 1974 budget.

As much as 40 percent of the federal government's current budget is transferred to other agencies and to the states by the federal ministries as subsidies to help make up their operating deficits. The National Railways of Mexico is the governmental entity with the largest operating deficit, and a long-range goal is to make it self-supporting (see ch. 15). A few other agencies—mainly entities performing public service functions —receive substantial subsidies, but most of the autonomous organizations are self-financing.

Before 1972 the budget did not include sources of revenue other than taxes and fees for services. From 1972 onward the budget included all sources of income, including loans. The largest single source of revenue for the federal government is the income tax, which brings in about 30 percent of total federal government income. Loans, both foreign and domestic, bring in about 20 percent of total receipts, miscellaneous production and excise taxes 13 percent, import duties 12 percent, a gross receipts tax over 8 percent, and all other taxes, plus fees for services and sale of goods, the balance. The combined income of those autonomous agencies under budgetary control comes mainly from their operations, as much as 73 percent of the total; transfers from the federal government accounted for about 22 percent, and miscellaneous sources for the small balance.

Tax laws are comprehensive and amended frequently; they are generally moderate. The average tax burden during the 1969–71 period was just over 7 percent of GNP, the second lowest percentage of forty-eight nations studied by the International Monetary Fund. By 1974 the tax burden was about 13 percent of GNP, still a relatively low level for a rapidly developing country. A survey taken by the Ministry of Finance and Public Credit in the early 1970s indicated that 78 percent of the taxpayers were unfamiliar with the workings of the tax bureau, and 86 percent claimed that they could not understand the tax laws. As a result of the survey, the texts of the tax laws were rewritten for clarity, and nationwide publicity campaigns were undertaken to explain the workings of tax administration. Informative audits are made of taxpayers' books to point out irregularities that could cause legal difficulties if the audit were investigative in nature.

In 1973 regional tax offices were established to improve tax collections, resolve problems at local levels, and coordinate liaison among federal, state, and municipal tax authorities. Until 1973 all tax matters had to be resolved in Mexico City by personal visits of taxpayers. Professional tax accountants have been hired since 1973 to serve as inspectors, a national tax register has been compiled, computers are used to gather information, and pardons for past tax evasion are granted if the taxpayer files a revised and corrected tax return. The names of prominent persons who are tax delinquents are publicized in the media in order to embarrass them into paying. As a result of these various measures tax revenue increased by one-fourth in 1973 without any new taxes being levied. New tax legislation introduced in late 1974, however, would sharply increase levies beginning in 1975.

Fewer than two dozen taxes were in effect in the early 1970s, and the income tax was the most important. Mexico has had an income tax for many years but the one in effect in 1974 dated from 1965 with later amendments. In FY 1972 over 190,000 individuals and 200,000 business entities filed income tax declarations. Businesses are subject to a single income tax depending upon annual taxable income, but individuals are taxed on the basis of two different tax schedules; one applies to income derived from personal services, and the other is for income from capital investment. Numerous allowable deductions and exemptions apply to both individuals and businesses, and the highest tax rate was 42 percent on taxable income over 500,000 pesos. In 1973 over 60,000 taxpayers reported incomes exceeding that figure.

Customs taxes, both import and export, are complex. Import duties are a combination of a specific duty based upon weight or quantity plus an ad valorem rate assessed on either the invoice value or an official valuation made by customs authorities. Export duties, which are levied on only a few items and tend to be ad valorem, are occasionally lifted in order to stimulate exports of the product but are then reimposed when exports increase. A gross receipts tax, which dates from 1947, is levied on all gross receipts derived from sales, rentals of goods and property except land and buildings, and the rendering of services. The minimum tax rate in effect in 1974 was 4 percent, but the rate ranges up to 10 percent for some luxury goods, such as automobiles, jewelry, and furs. A certain portion of the gross receipts tax collected by the federal government is returned to states and municipalities in exchange for their agreement not to levy local taxes on commerce and industry.

States and municipalities have the right to impose only certain kinds of taxes, such as those on property, agricultural products, livestock, public markets, and public amusements. The Constitution prohibits them from imposing taxes that restrict interstate trade, and they are not permitted to incur debt that is not self-liquidating, thus limiting their borrowing power. On various occasions national tax conventions are held by federal, state, and local tax officials to coordinate the overall tax system so that there is little overlapping or duplication. In 1974 representatives of the states and municipalities met to develop a projected law to make municipal revenues uniform nationwide.

The public debt has been growing rapidly; at the end of 1973 the foreign debt was estimated at the equivalent of over US$7 billion, more than twice the external debt at the end of 1970, and was projected to rise to over US$11 billion by the end of 1974. The extent of the domestic debt was unknown. The debt has been growing mainly to provide capital for infrastructure, although some new debt has been earmarked to refinance older debts falling due. Mexico has been able to service its debt for many years; there has been no default since 1917, and its credit rating is very high, enabling it to obtain sufficient financial resources, including the placing of Mexican bonds in international markets.

The major portion of the foreign debt—nearly 70 percent of the total—has been incurred by the various decentralized agencies. The federal government accounts for the balance of the foreign debt, but it also guarantees the debt of the other agencies. Private foreign banks held the largest share of the external debt at the beginning of 1973, over 41 percent, but since 1971 the government has been following a policy of attempting to obtain capital initially from international lending institutions and secondarily through bond issues; so the percent of the credits supplied by private foreign banks should be decreasing. Since 1971 more of the foreign debt has been contracted on a long- or medium-term basis and at lower interest rates. Before that time short-term loans of less than five years predominated, and interest rates generally were 9 percent or higher.

BALANCE OF PAYMENTS, FOREIGN ASSISTANCE, AND INVESTMENT

Since 1940 imports have far exceeded exports, resulting in unfavorable balances of trade but not in amounts sufficient to cause overall balance-of-payments difficulties. During the 1962-73 period there was a net surplus in the balance of payments every year except 1965. The overall surplus was the equivalent of US$200 million in 1971, US$265 million in 1972, and US$122 million in 1973 despite a record deficit of US$1,331 billion in the current account. Although the gap between imports and exports is a continual threat to the balance of payments, the trade deficit is almost always covered by receipts from tourism and incoming capital, and international reserves continue to rise. In mid-1974 total international reserves were over US$1.5 billion, a historic high.

Mexico is one of the few countries where a very high percentage of foreign exchange earnings comes from tourism (see ch. 15.). Large-scale public investment programs have contributed to the growth of tourism; for example, Mexico has the most extensive highway network in Latin America to take advantage of the fact that most of the foreign travel is by automobile from the United States. Incoming capital, the other key element offsetting the deficit in the current account, consists of foreign investment, long-term credits and loans from abroad, and remittances from Mexican nationals living and working in the United States. Personal remittances were sharply curtailed as a source of foreign exchange when the formal farm labor program between Mexico and the United States was discontinued in 1964 but have since grown again as the number of Mexican citizens legally admitted to the United States has increased (see ch. 2.).

All of the foreign assistance that Mexico receives is the form of loans and credits. The largest single source has been the International Bank for Reconstruction and Development (IBRD, commonly known as the World Bank). Through mid-1974 the World Bank had provided over US$1.7 billion for about thirty major projects. The first World Bank loan to Mexico was made in 1949, and since then the bank has been so closely associated with Mexico's economic development that Mexico became the second leading recipient of bank funds by 1973. The major World Bank loans have been for power projects, agriculture, railroads, and highway construction. One of the World Bank's associated agencies, the International Finance Corporation, had provided about US$55 million to companies dealing in textiles, steel, cement, and tourism.

The Inter-American Development Bank (IDB) has provided the second largest share of credits. Through mid-1974 almost US$960 million had been provided, more than half of which was for the agricultural sector, principally irrigation and land improvement. Other loans from the IDB were for potable water systems, education, technical research, and small and medium-sized industries. The United States was the next leading source of funds, supplying about US$800 million through 1973; the bulk of the assistance from the United States, over US$620 million, was in more than 100 Export-Import Bank loans. Several loans totaling US$109 million were provided under the Foreign Assistance Act, part of the funds being channeled to Mexico through the Social Progress Trust Fund administered by the IDB.

Extensive loans have been received from other foreign governments and from private foreign banks. In 1974, for example, the Bank of America provided the equivalent of US$100 million to Mexican Petroleum for expansion purposes, and the Federal Electricity Commission and the National Bank of Public Works and Services (Banco Nacional de Obras y Servicos Publicos) each received a like sum from a consortium of international banks.

Foreign investment in Mexico is another source of incoming capital. Whereas formerly the Mexican government considered private foreign investment exploitative, particularly in the sense of an overly rapid exhaustion of nonrenewable natural resources, it now considers foreign investment complementary to domestic investment provided it follows certain prescribed rules. At the time of the 1910 Revolution foreign investment totaled about US$1.5 billion, 70 percent of which was in railroads and mining. During the 1920s and 1930s the level of foreign investment declined steadily as a result of expropriation of petroleum properties and foreign-owned farming land, the nationalization of the railroads, and the loss of interest by foreign companies in investing in Mexico. By the beginning of World War II less than US$450 million remained of former foreign investment in the country. During and after the war, particularly as foreign investors got over the fear of expropriation, foreign capital began to return in large quantities and was estimated to have reached the level of between US$3.2 billion and US3.5 billion by 1973.

Although the United States had provided less than 40 percent of total foreign investment in Mexico at the start of the revolution, by 1973 it had provided nearly 80 percent; an estimated 1,000 United States companies were operating in Mexico in 1973. The Federal Republic of Germany (West Germany) was in second place with about US$600 million invested in Mexico, the United Kingdom had about US$150 million, and France had about US$80 million; the balance was made up of smaller investments from other countries. In 1974 there were indications that Japanese firms were planning to make substantial investments. The overwhelming percentage of foreign investment in 1973 was in manufacturing, an estimated 90 percent of the total. About 6 percent was in mining, and the balance was invested in all other activities.

A nonretroactive new foreign investment law, the Law to Promote Mexican Investment and to Regulate Foreign Investment, became effective in 1973, and the National Commission on Foreign Investment was created to interpret and implement it. The new law codified all previous legislation concerning investment and added some new features. Generally foreign investment is welcome when it complements local capital, when it develops new areas of economic activity, when it contributes to exports, or when it reinvests profits in the country. There are no restrictions on expatriation of profits or convertibility of foreign exchange. Foreign investment is not permitted in sectors controlled by the state, such as petroleum, railroads, or telecommunications, or in financial institutions, radio, television, or forestry. Land within a strip that is thirty miles wide along seacoasts and sixty miles wide along international borders may not be purchased by individual foreigners or foreign-owned companies. The only legal method of acquiring land in those areas, which amount to 43 percent of the national territory, is through a trust set up by a Mexican financial institution with the express permission of the Ministry of Foreign Relations.

Generally foreign companies may not control more than 49 percent of the equity of any corporation, but exceptions may be made by the National Commission on Foreign Investment. Initial indications were that the commission was applying the new law fairly and flexibly. In some industries the equity share is set lower than 49 percent for foreign participants: 40 percent in secondary petrochemical operations and motor vehicle parts manufacturers and 34 percent in minerals companies. When the government takes over the majority share of a company, it usually purchases controlling shares at a fair price.

At about the time that the new foreign investment law was passed, a corresponding law was approved that controls payments for foreign technology. All companies must register technology contracts with the National Registry of Technology Transfer before approval is given. The rules are flexible and apparently designed to obtain the best deal possible. During the first year of operation the single most prevalent reason for refusal of permission to negotiate a technology contract was the excessive cost of royalty payments.

Some Mexican firms have started to open affiliates in other countries, and at least eighty of them were operating abroad in 1974. The largest number, about sixty, had established themselves in Central American countries to take advantage of the Central American Common Market.

Banking, Credit, and Currency

The monetary and financial system of Mexico has grown rapidly and achieved a level of sophistication unrivaled in developing countries. The use of money and the practice of saving and borrowing had reached most of the population, and miscellaneous credit institutions, both public and private, have grown to serve the needs of the nation. By setting overall banking and credit policy the government determines the allocation of financial resources and the direction in which it wishes the economy to move. The financial structure of Mexico changed substantially during the twentieth century, and by 1974 it was composed of a central bank, public development banks, public credit institutions, private commercial banks private investment banks, savings and loan associations, mortgage banks, insurance companies, and a securities market. Jointly, these financial institutions employ over 120,000 people.

The Bank of Mexico (Banco de México), the country's central bank, whose shares are owned by the federal government and other banks, was created in 1925 but functioned like a commercial bank until it divested itself of commercial activities during the 1933–38 period. The primary functions of the Bank of Mexico are to regulate the money supply, regulate the foreign exchange market, serve as a reserve bank and discount house for private deposit banks and other designated financial institutions, establish and administer reserve requirements, serve as the fiscal agent of the federal government, and establish policies governing the activities of the National Banking Commission, which supervises all banking institutions and determines their compliance with central bank regulation. The Bank of Mexico, which has ten branches, is not truly independent, its actions being subject to the approval of the Ministry of Finance and Public Credit, but it does exert a powerful role in developing priority areas of the economy by means of its monetary and credit policies. Although it provides very little direct credit, the bank does administer several special-purpose funds, which are channeled to the private sector through intermediary borrowing institutions. These funds are used both as a guarantee against default on the part of borrowers in these specific activities and to discount paper acquired by private institutions in extending credit to these borrowers.

Of the more than two dozen government financial institutions apart from the central bank, the largest and most important is the National Development Company (Nacional Financiera—NAFIN; literally, National Financier). Originally created in 1934 to help restore liquidity to the banking system, its first objectives were to subsidize and sell real estate taken by banking institutions as collateral for loans. A 1940 reconstruction of NAFIN redefined its objectives: to promote investment companies, to act as an investment company itself, to oversee the issuance of public securities and direct the operations of stock exchanges, to be the legal depository of government securities, to act as the fiduciary of the federal government and its dependencies, and to act as the agent and adviser of states and municipalities in the issuance, recall, and conversion of their public securities. The reorientation toward industrial promotion had a tremendous effect on NAFIN's growth, and by 1974 it was the major supplier of funds for industry and the major issuer of securities.

All public agencies must obtain NAFIN's approval before borrowing abroad. NAFIN itself will borrow abroad and relend to the decentralized agencies for such infrastructure investments as irrigation, highways, seaports, and telecommunications and will also lend to public and private enterprises for expansion purposes. At the specific request of the government and where private money seems loath to enter, NAFIN will purchase stock of a company and take an equity position in its operations. When this occurs, NAFIN places an employee in the associated company to restrict the firm to less risky ventures than might otherwise be undertaken. Like the Bank of Mexico, NAFIN acts as trustee for several special-purpose funds that have been created by the government to assist in the development of certain industrial areas. These funds are used to supplement the resources of private credit institutions and to reduce lenders' risks by guarantee arrangements to cover defaults.

In mid-1974 there were three government development banks catering exclusively to the agricultural sector. The oldest, the National Agricultural and Livestock Credit Bank (Banco Nacional de Crédito Agrícola y Ganadero), founded in 1926, specialized in working-capital loans to small-scale farmers, particularly in conjunction with supervised technical assistance. The National Ejidal Credit Bank (Banco Nacional de Crédito Ejidal), established in 1935, was created to aid farmers working communal lands by providing unsecured short-term crop loans (see ch. 14). The National Farm Bank (Banco Nacional Agropecuario) was founded in 1965 to specialize in credit to groups or associations of farmers rather than to individuals. In mid-1974 the government announced that it was studying the possibility of merging the three agricultural banks into one institution.

The National Bank of Public Works and Services was created in 1966 by a merger of two predecessor institutions. It is the second largest government bank in assets, exceeded only by NAFIN. The bank finances most public works projects, federal and residential construction, transportation, and development of municipalities. Numerous other government credit institutions provide financing to such diverse sectors or

286

activities as foreign trade, cooperatives, small retailers in Mexico City, consumer loans to military personnel, the motion picture and sugar industries, and credit unions. The National Pawnshop, which serves as a small credit institution, dates back to the colonial period.

Only eight of the numerous prerevolutionary private banks survived the revolutionary period, but there has been a proliferation of private financial institutions since then, especially since 1940. By 1974 there were over 200 private credit institutions with over 2,500 branches and agencies in the country, permitting most borrowers and lenders to have access to the national money and capital market. Part of the reason for the large number of financial institutions is the limitation placed by banking laws on combining certain functions. Except for the functions of savings and trust operations, no single institution can combine any two of the commercial, investment, capitalization, or mortgage functions usually carried out by private banks. This limitation has caused the organization of banking groups in which each institution in the group offers a different service although all are linked by common ownership.

Among the major private institutions the largest banking group is the Commerce Bank of Mexico (Banco Comercio de México), which was composed of thirty-five different affiliated banks with more than 500 branches in 1974. The group also operated subsidiary mortgage banks, insurance companies, and a financial and trust institution. It also was the first Latin American bank to hold an equity position in a London international merchant bank. The National Bank of Mexico (Banco Nacional de México), the second largest institution, maintained 400 branches in Mexico and a correspondent relationship with 1,500 international banks. It also heads a consortium of two Mexican and five foreign institutions that owns Intermex, an institution headquartered in London that serves as a conduit for obtaining funds to relend in Mexico.

In terms of resources, the private development banks are of greater importance to the industrial sector than are the commercial banks. The private investment banks obtain most of their funds from selling their own bonds, notes, and certificates of deposit to the public and are permitted to make loans for longer periods than are commercial banks. Most of the development banks, which are called *financieras*, are organized by commercial banks in association with major industrial enterprises. Mortgage banks finance and guarantee residential and public construction and grant mortgage loans to private individuals. Capitalization banks handle a small portion of private credit operations; their main function is to permit potential small businessmen to accumulate sufficient capital to get started. Savings and loan banks were designed to enable low-income families to finance home ownership but, because of unsatisfactory results, a 1971 amendment to the banking law provides for their gradual disappearance through merger with other institutions.

Although sixty foreign banks operated in Mexico in 1974, only one, the First National City Bank, was permitted to receive deposits from the public. All the others must bring in their own operating capital and may not borrow within Mexico.

More than six dozen insurance companies, both private and public, operate in the country. Their portfolios fall under the provisions of the reserve requirements imposed by the Bank of Mexico, and their activities are inspected by the National Insurance Commission. A requirement that a certain portion of their portfolios be in low yielding government securities enables the government to obtain funds at moderate cost. Mexico is one of the top users of insurance, particularly life insurance, in Latin America, and insurance companies have grown rapidly.

A stock exchange of some sort, either formal or informal, has existed in Mexico City since 1894. Legislation passed in 1932 empowered the Ministry of Finance and Public Credit to establish formal securities exchanges, and subsequently it created one in Mexico City in 1933, another in Monterrey in 1950, and a third in Guadalajara in 1960. Since 1940 NAFIN has been specifically charged with developing the exchanges, although the National Securities Commission, founded in 1946, actually regulates the marketing of securities. Despite the existence of the exchanges, more securities are traded over the counter than through the exchanges; average volume of trading on the three exchanges during a six-month period in 1971 and 1972, for example, was under 65,000 shares per day. Ten times that amount was traded over the counter. The main reason for the large over-the-counter trading is that almost all banks conduct their transactions directly with buyers and sellers, bypassing the securities exchanges.

Fixed income securities rather than stocks predominate in both formal and over-the-counter trading; 90 percent of total transactions are in government bonds, mortgage bonds, financial bonds, and other instruments with a fixed rate of interest. Over 400 firms list their stocks on the exchanges, but the shares of only a few dozen are actively traded. Many of the family-owned companies do not use the exchanges as a means of obtaining financing because they fear a dilution of their interests. Instead they sell a few shares from time to time to establish a reference point for the value of their holdings in order to use them as personal collateral in obtaining bank loans. New legislation containing fiscal benefits was being prepared in late 1974 to encourage more firms to use the stock market to raise needed capital and to stimulate investment in stocks by individual investors.

The supply of credit to the economy is controlled by the government. During inflationary periods the Bank of Mexico increases the percentage of total resources that financial institutions must deposit with it as reserves and also enters into special arrangements with such institutions for voluntary additional deposits to be invested in government securities. Credit is directed toward specific sectors through the setting of ratios of loan portfolios by end purposes and the establishment of priorities. In 1974, for example, priority was to be given to loans for agriculture and livestock, new industrial plants, export expansion, tourism, and the building of shopping centers in border cities to attract United States clientele. Also, in the early 1970s commercial banks in the Federal District were limited to lending no more than 25 percent of new resources to commerce, whereas banks located elsewhere in the country had no such limitation.

The government is the largest source of credit to agriculture; in 1974 it set aside 14 billion pesos for loans within that sector. Some farmers obtain credit within the industry, sugar mills lend funds to sugarcane growers, and equipment and supply outlets provide credit to their clients. NAFIN is the only source of long-term industrial credit, although the private development banks usually extend their short- and medium-term loans when they fall due, especially for well-established firms with a close relationship to the financial institution. Interest rates on loans vary greatly. Commercial banks cannot charge more than 12 percent but usually require a portion of the loan to be kept in the borrower's account as a compensating balance. The development banks have no upper limitation, but their interest rates during the early 1970s generally ranged between 13 and 15 percent.

An increasing number of consumers are resorting to the use of credit cards to boost their purchasing power. An estimated 650,000 general bank credit cards were in circulation in 1973 along with an unknown number issued by travel and entertainment clubs and large department stores. One study indicated that 28 percent of credit card sales would not have been made if the customer had had to pay cash for the merchandise. The state of México permits the use of credit cards to pay traffic fines.

The unit of currency is the peso, divided into 100 centavos; the official symbol for the peso is $, which causes frequent confusion with United States dollars. Accordingly, many merchants, stores, media, and government publications utilize slightly different symbols, M$N or $MN, to denote pesos, the MN denoting national money (moneda nacional). Pesos come in paper banknotes of 1, 5, 10, 20, 50, 100, 500, and 1,000 denominations and in one-peso coins. Some older five-peso coins are still in circulation as well as gold coins in denominations of 2, 2½, 5, 10, 20, and 50 pesos. Gold coins are worth much more than face value. Fractional centavo currency comes in coins of 1, 5, 10, and 20 centavos.

The peso is one of the world's more stable currencies, and the International Monetary Fund uses it to help support other currencies. It is the strongest currency in Latin America, and the government considers the prestige of the peso an asset to be preserved. Accordingly a fundamental part of monetary policy is the free convertibility and absolute maintenance of the peso-dollar exchange rate. Since April 19, 1954, the exchange rate of the peso has been 12.50 pesos equal US$1, and both currencies circulate freely in towns and cities on both sides of the Mexican-United States border. Pesos are known to be accepted by merchants as far north as Phoenix, Arizona. Although the peso-dollar exchange rate has remained constant, on three separate occasions through 1973 the gold par value of the peso was lowered and thereby theoretically devalued.

CHAPTER 14

AGRICULTURE AND INDUSTRY

In the mid-1970s the largest percentage of the labor force was engaged in agriculture, which accounted for more than half of all export earnings, but industry contributed more to the gross domestic product (GDP) (see ch. 13). Agricultural production and the marketing of produce is made complex by the country's geography and the differing forms of farm organization and land tenure. Although agricultural productivity had increased markedly since the end of World War II, it had barely kept pace with population growth. Using the average production of the 1961–65 period as a base of 100, the per capita index of food production in 1973 was only 104. When nonfood agricultural products were included, the per capita index of production had actually fallen to 97 over the same period. Heavy public investments had been made in agriculture, particularly irrigation and flood control projects, and additional land was constantly being brought into production.

After more than fifty years of agrarian reform there were more than 2.8 million farming units, but half of all agricultural production was accounted for by only 4 percent of the number of farms, generally those that escaped the reform process, which have become the most efficient. About 1 percent of the farms produced all of the agricultural exports, and another 15 percent produced most of the food for the urban areas; the vast majority were either subsistence farms or produced only for nearby markets. According to a study released in 1974 by the Center for Agrarian Research (Centro de Investigaciones Agrarias), half of all farm units generated only between 50 and 80 pesos per month of income (12.5 pesos equal US$1).

Although there were many infant industries before World War II, the process of industrialization acquired momentum with the outbreak of hostilities because of the scarcity of imported goods. Many older plants operated at full capacity, and new producers entered the market. After the war there was a widespread belief in the need to industrialize the nation at any cost, and the policy of the government has been to channel a high proportion of the nation's capital resources, both public and private, into industry.

The result has been impressive; domestic production meets almost all consumer needs and produces many capital and intermediate goods. Considerable attention has been devoted to the creation of industry in support of agriculture: fertilizers, pesticides, and the transformation of

291

raw materials into processed foods or into finished or semifinished nonfood products. Industry has also promoted the growth of a middle class, although it is doubtful that it can continue to accommodate as high a proportion of unemployed or underemployed agricultural workers as it did in the past (see ch. 2).

Manufacturing and construction led industrial growth, and only mining has not experienced substantial growth although it is an important contributor to export earnings. Mining, however, appears to have received a stimulus in the early 1970s as a result of higher world prices for most minerals. Many new exploitation projects were being announced in 1973 and 1974.

The need for energy is met by the government, which controls the petroleum and natural gas industries and the production of electricity. A crash exploration program for new petroleum fields was undertaken in 1973 when consumption was far outpacing production and imports were required. Most of the electricity is generated by costly thermal plants, but some of the largest, most recent projects are hydroelectric complexes taking advantage of the relatively untapped rivers.

LAND TENURE

Land use statistics vary among sources, but all of them indicate a fairly high percentage of idle cultivable land, an anomaly for a country with a rapidly increasing population. Of about 494 million acres of surface area, only about 40.7 million acres were under crop cultivation in 1973, between 195 million and 212 million acres were pastures, and as many as 108.7 million acres were in forests; the balance was idle or unusable land. The total potentially arable land for crop cultivation has been estimated to be as high as 91 million acres, but this includes land covered by dense jungles and arid land requiring much irrigation. More reasonable figures for cultivable land range between 74 million and 86.5 million acres. Much of the usable uncultivated land is in the southern part of the state of Veracruz, along the coast of the state of Guerrero, and in the states of Tabasco, Chiapas, Campeche, and Quintana Roo. Of the various zones of the country, the North has the lowest proportion of idle land as it contains the highest proportion of irrigated lands; nonetheless, large areas have remained unused because of their distance from the sources of water (see ch. 2).

A further complication is that the ratio of harvested area to planted croplands is low. Because of such factors as plots lying fallow, plant disease and pests, flooding, drought, frost, lack of equipment or farm help at harvesttime, or off-farm employment by the farmowner, as much as 44 to 50 percent of the planted croplands may not be harvested in any given year.

The major part of the pastureland is located on steep slopes. Only about 42 million acres of pastureland are on plains or low hills, the most suitable kind of land for cattle raising. Uncertainty exists as to the exact extent of forests. Population pressure and expansion of livestock raising have encroached on forests in some areas, and some land that is called forested is actually arid land on which plants and bush or brush yield some forest products.

Article 27 of the Constitution of 1917, the Agrarian Code of 1934, and the Agrarian Code of 1942 had served as the legal basis for agrarian reform, and by the end of 1970 about 204.5 million acres of cropland, pastures, and undeveloped government-owned land had been redistributed to villages and private individuals; the figures for redistributed land included some that had been redistributed more than once. Under these laws there was a proliferation of small farms, with little increase in total productivity. On May 1, 1971, the new Federal Law of Agrarian Reform became effective, which went beyond mere redistribution provisions; the thrust of the new law was to encourage the use of modern production.

In 1910, when the revolution began, 97 percent of the land was owned by 830 people or corporations, 2 percent was held by 500,000 small- and medium-scale farmers, and the balance was owned by municipalities. An estimated 3.5 million peasants were landless. By 1970, after more than fifty years of agrarian reform, nearly 2.9 million people owned land or had usufructuary rights to it. At the same time, however, because of population increase in the same period, the number of landless peasants had climbed to 4.5 million, a circumstance that caused even the government to conclude that a considerable portion of the rural population might never receive land of its own.

Landholdings may be privately, communally, or publicly owned. Farms may be worked by the owner, by sharecroppers, by landless wage-earning peasants, by *colonos* (colonists settled on public land), or by members of *ejidos* (see Glossary).

A farmer working *ejido* land is termed an *ejidatario*. The *ejidos* have historical antecedents in the communal organization of landholdings that characterized many Indian groups before the Spanish conquest and the revolution restored such a method of landholding to prominence. The *ejido* rather than the individual peasant was made the legal proprietor of the land to prevent loss of the land by the new recipients, who might be encouraged to sell or mortgage their rights. The 1971 law gave *ejidos* juridical status with the right to enter into contracts like other commercial enterprises or to engage in small-scale industry, mining, forestry, handicrafts, and tourism in addition to agriculture. The functions and responsibilities of *ejido* officials are spelled out in the law, and their term of office is limited to three years with one reelection.

Ejido land may be farmed on a cooperative basis, or the land may be distributed among the residents with usufructuary rights. In 1970 there were about 18,000 *ejidos*, of which about 14,000 were worked on the basis of usufruct and 4,000 were operated collectively. The *ejidos* owned about 40 percent of the land in the country. Most of the collective *ejidos* are located in the southern portion of the country. Even on the *ejidos* operating under the usufruct principle, woodlands and pastures must be used collectively.

An *ejidatario* who receives the usufruct of a parcel of land may dispose of the produce of his cropland as he wishes and may continue to work the holding until he either loses the usufruct or assigns his right to one designated successor, who in turn must agree to accept the obligation to support the dependents of the original user. The designated successor can be anyone but usually is the eldest son. The usufruct is lost if the *ejidatario* does not work the allotted land for two consecutive years, if he acquired the land by succession and fails to support the original user's dependents, if he has an interest in land elsewhere, or if he uses the land for growing narcotic plants or other illegal purposes. The maximum amount of land an *ejidatario* can work is twenty-five acres if it is irrigated and fifty acres if it is dry land. In 1972 there were an estimated 1.86 million parcels of *ejido* land being worked individually, with an average size of about sixteen acres.

Until the practice was legalized in 1971, many *ejidatarios* illegally augmented the size of their allotments by renting plots from other *ejidatarios*. Illegal renting was done on a wide scale, and in recognition of its reality the law was amended. In some areas the land is rented to farmers outside the *ejido* who plant commercial crops on the plot and then hire the *ejidatario* to cultivate and harvest them.

In 1972 there were about 960,000 so-called private farmers, a term used in Mexico to mean an independent farmer who works privately owned land. The maximum amount of land that can be held as private property depends on the use to which the land is put, higher limits being established for the production of certain specified crops. Generally, the limitation is 100 hectares (247 acres) of irrigated land or the equivalent thereof in dry land. Enough pastureland may be owned to support 500 head of cattle or the equivalent in smaller animals. Private landowners receive a certificate of inaffectability that usually, but not always, renders the holding free from expropriation.

In the early 1970s about 40,000 private farms were over 250 acres, and about 500 were over 125,000 acres. These latter farms usually contained land not suitable for expropriation and redistribution. Many of the medium-sized private farms are worked under unified management to obtain maximum production and the most efficient use of pooled machinery. Owners of private property can transfer title by sale or inheritance. Some landowners acquire more land than the law allows and hold it in the names of members of their family.

There is an undetermined number of sharecroppers working part of the private lands. Once made, sharecropping arrangements between the tenant and the landowner tend to remain stable for years and even decades. A personal relationship usually develops between the two, and a degree of economic security binds them. The tenant is available to work the owner's land when help is required, and the owner lends the tenant

294

money or food until harvesttime. There are also an unknown number of *colonos*, individuals who are resettled on federally owned land under government sponsorship. When the *colonos* discharge their repayment obligation, they receive title to their plots and thus become small private landholders. In 1974 the major government-sponsored resettlement programs were in Campeche, where the *colonos* received a small house in addition to the plot of land. Additionally, it was estimated that in the early 1970s there were as many as 4 million day laborers, of whom perhaps as many as 700,000 operated small plots of land of their own. A survey indicated that most of the day laborers were young—two-thirds were between the ages of twelve and thirty-four years, and most were children of *ejidatarios*.

TECHNIQUES, RESEARCH, AND TRAINING

Although most farmers no longer practice shifting (rotating) cultivation because of the growing use of fertilizers and irrigation, this form of agriculture is still found in the states of Colima, Chiapas, Guerrero, Oaxaca, Campeche, Tabasco, and Veracruz and in the Yucatán Peninsula. In Veracruz shifting cultivation is carried out on steep hillsides where poor soils prevent continuous farming. Most Veracruz farmers also have other plots on flatter ground and view their hillside plots as supplemental. After a few years the hillside plot loses its fertility, and it is left fallow for several years while a new plot is cleared. In Campeche shifting cultivation, including slash-and-burn agriculture, is the dominant form of land use, and much valuable forestland is lost annually.

In some areas of the country, soil conservation is practiced efficiently. In the southwestern part of the state of Tlaxcala, where soils are poorly drained, the maintenance of drainage systems has developed into a routine voluntary community project. The annual consumption of fertilizer has been constantly increasing, and fertilizer was being applied to about 40 percent of the cropland in the early 1970s; 1 million tons were consumed in 1974. Fertilizer needs are met almost entirely by domestic companies, one government-owned firm dominating the industry. Fertilizer is maintained in warehouses in various rural areas by government banks, which are then able to provide it almost immediately to farmers seeking bank credit to purchase it.

Plowing is done with animal or mechanical power. Most farmers plant seeds directly in their fields by hand, but some vegetable farmers start their crops in seedbeds and then transplant the seedlings. More than one crop may be planted in the field, as is usually the case with corn, squash, and beans. Commercial fertilizer is applied by those farmers who can afford it, and those who cannot usually use animal manure mixed with bits of straw and kitchen refuse.

The use of agricultural machinery and equipment has also been increasing constantly. There were more than 95,000 tractors in use in the country in 1971, but demand was exceeding production capacity in 1974. There are four large companies and dozens of smaller firms making agricultural equipment.

Irrigation plays a prominent role; about 80 percent of all water use in the country is for agriculture, and about three-fourths of all government investment in agriculture traditionally has been for irrigation projects. Statistics on irrigation vary, but about 10.5 million acres were estimated to be in government irrigation districts in 1973, 2.47 million acres were under some form of private irrigation, and 1.38 million acres of additional land were under development in that year. In 1974 two major irrigation projects totaling 585,000 acres, were announced for the Pánuco Basin and the state of Sinaloa.

About 55 percent of the total irrigation has been in the northwestern portion of the country. The thrust of future new projects, however, will be in the central and southern parts of the country. The new Federal Water Law of 1972 brought together various forms of water legislation under one heading and a centralized water management. Rights and priorities are defined, and the Ministry of Hydraulic Resources is authorized to operate all projects that use public funds. The new law limited the right to irrigation at government expense to fifty acres per private farm. If more land than that is being irrigated on a farm by a government irrigation system, then the excess land could be expropriated. Although much farmland is under irrigation not all of the irrigated land is planted. In some cases, irrigation is insufficient because of water loss by evaporation, filtration of soil into the irrigation canals, and leakage. Other soils have become too saline, particularly in the Mexicali area of the Baja California Peninsula and lack sufficient drainage or require costly nutrients in addition to water.

To accommodate the need for irrigation in areas where major projects are not feasible, such as isolated villages, the National Plan for Small Irrigation Works was initiated in 1967. These small works consist of drilling wells and irrigating areas under 2,500 hectares (6,175 acres). By the end of the program's first stage in 1970, over 321,000 acres had been placed under irrigation in various parts of the country, and the second stage, scheduled for completion by 1976, envisaged irrigating an additional 432,000 acres.

Crop research in the early 1970's was well organized, particularly for crops benefiting from irrigation. The two main national research institutions were the National Institute of Agricultural Research and the National Institute for Livestock Research. Several specialized research organizations were the Institute of Technological Research, the Institute of Sugar Production, and the Mexican Coffee Institute. The International Maize and Wheat Improvement Center, partly financed by international contributions, was world renowned; its work during the 1940s and 1950s did much to improve yields of these two basic crops.

The National Agricultural School at Chapingo, well recognized throughout the Western Hemisphere, and other institutions offered university-level courses in agriculture and veterinary medicine. An agricultural extension service had operated for many years, but it had undergone numerous reorganizations, and its staff was too small to provide much of an impact. Priority was given to helping small-scale private farmers and *ejidos*. Many banks and farm input suppliers had hired technicians to assist their farm clients who did not receive government assistance.

CROPS

A large variety of crops is grown, for both consumption and export (see table 9). Mexico is self-sufficient in many products, although in some years imports of usually surplus crops are required when the harvest is low because of adverse climatic conditions. Corn, the staple food, for example, is produced in quantities usually sufficient to meet domestic demand and leave some for export, but in 1972 and 1973 corn imports were needed. The largest share of acreage, usually as much as half the total cropland, is devoted to corn cultivation; in 1973 over 17.3 million acres were planted in corn. About half the corn acreage is in Central Mexico, which is the focus of subsistence agriculture (see ch. 2). As irrigated land in the North is opened, corn production is moving there and achieving remarkable yields. The yield on irrigated cornland is more than double the yield on unirrigated land. Still, more than 80 percent of the corn crop depended upon natural rainfall in the early 1970s.

Cotton has been one of the most important crops both as a source of foreign exchange and for its role in the economy. Cotton farmers were pioneers in moving into commercial agriculture and introducing modern farming methods. Mexico usually accounts for about 3 percent of world cotton production and 5 percent of total world cotton exports. The acreage planted in cotton has been declining, but the yield per acre has been increasing, partially offsetting the decline in cultivated areas. As much as 2.5 million acres had been planted in cotton during the 1950s, but total acreage was down to 1 million acres by 1974 as many cotton farmers shifted to other crops because of higher prices. Cotton is the most heavily irrigated crop; more than 90 percent is grown under irrigation, and the leading cotton-growing areas are in Sonora, Sinaloa, Baja California, and what is known as the La Laguna area, bordering the states of Durango and Coahuila. Cotton also is raised in Chiapas, where the yields are very high but constant attention must be given to prevention of insect damage.

Sugarcane is another major crop. The rate of per capita domestic consumption of sugar is one of the highest in the world, but exports are also maintained at fairly high levels. Sugarcane is grown in about fifteen states, but the major concentrations are in coastal areas, mainly in Veracruz, which accounts for about 45 percent of the total production. In the early 1970s there were about 90,000 cane growers in the country,

85,000 of whom were *ejidatarios* whose small plots accounted for about half of the estimated 1 million acres planted in sugarcane. There were sixty-six sugar mills in the country in 1972, employing about 45,000 workers. During the height of the cane harvest as many as 2 million people may be employed.

Difficulties have, however, been experienced by the industry. The government controlled about twenty-one of the sugar refineries in 1972, mainly as a result of loan defaults by the previous millowners. For many years the government had imposed low sugar prices for the benefit of consumers, but this prevented many of the older mills from installing modern machinery and equipment. Cane growers are paid by the percentage of the sugar yield extracted from the cane by the mills, with a guaranteed minimum percentage; however, few refineries have been able to achieve the established minimum percentage, and many of them are also in debt to the growers.

In the early 1970s the cane growers who belong to regional organizations joined forces to pressure the government into restructuring and modernizing the sugar industry. A fund of 3.8 billion pesos was established by the government to build new mills and renovate older ones, but industry sources contend that many of the refineries are too inefficient to be worth modernizing. In addition to the large quantities of white sugar produced, between 115,000 and 118,000 tons of locally consumed brown sugar and about 1 million tons of molasses are estimated to be produced annually.

Wheat production is concentrated in irrigated areas of the North, the northeast, and the Bajío (see ch. 2). Although wheat is grown on only about 5 percent of the cultivated land, yields are very high because of irrigation, the use of improved seeds, genetic research, and fertilizer and pesticide applications. The yield per acre went up nearly fivefold between 1943 and 1973, and Mexican wheat seed is exported to numerous countries. Despite the government's desire for the country to become self-sufficient in wheat, burgeoning consumption by the growing middle class, coupled with the shift to oilseed production by some wheat farmers in the early 1970s, caused the need to import wheat. It was estimated that as much as 1 million tons would have to be imported in the 1975 crop year. A special incentive fund for wheat producers created in late 1972 was expected to help increase the production of wheat and reduce the need for imports.

The principal seed grain is sorghum, about half of which is produced under irrigation. Production in the 1972 and 1973 crop years was badly hurt by storms in the Tamualipas growing area (see ch. 2). Beans are another essential part of the people's diet and, although much of the production comes from small plots, the use of improved seed, insecticides, and fertilizers has helped to increase yields. Numerous oilseeds are grown, but the emerging preference is for soybeans, which can be double-cropped with wheat. Soybeans are also grown on former

298

Item	1969	1970	1971	1972	1973
Bananas	986	1,136	1,219	1,280	865
Barley	285	238	305	294	300
Beans	899	1,000	1,000	800	900
Cacao	24	29	29	31	30
Chick-peas	167	157	170	180	180[1]
Coconuts	n.a.	932	1,080	1,300	n.a.
Coffee	173	184	192	198	210
Corn	8,596	11,176	9,850	8,926	9,500 ✓
Cotton	552	391	322	403	412
Grapes	128	144	219	225	n.a.
Henequen (sisal)	147	158	122	136	140
Lemons	n.a.	199	207	210	n.a.
Mangoes	205	209	216	520	n.a.
Melons and cantaloupes	176	190	207	210	n.a.
Oats	41	63	34	28	55
Onions	146	144	194	200	n.a.
Oranges	882	940	927	1,650	1,660
Peanuts	72	77	70	63	75
Peppers, chili	256	265	248	250	n.a.
Potatoes	377	600	650	680	460[1]
Potatoes, sweet	132	155	158	161	n.a.
Rice	417	399	410	430	450
Safflower seed	168	197	390	300	320
Sesame seed	165	182	185	160	120
Sorghum	1,605	2,738	2,200	1,700	1,900
Soybeans	283	240	250	360	510
Sugar	2,393	2,400	2,402	2,476	2,600
Tobacco	74	69	65	82	65
Tomatoes	675	783	855	950	987[1]
Watermelons	227	190	200	200	n.a.
Wheat	2,058	2,262	1,861	1,780	2,000

n.a.—not available.
[1] Food and Agriculture Organization estimate.

cottonlands in Sonora and in new farming areas in Oaxaca, Campeche, and Veracruz.

Coffee continues to be another major crop—raised by 300,000 families —although it is grown only in the Gulf Coast and South Pacific regions, mainly in Chiapas, Veracruz, and Oaxaca. About one-third of total coffee production comes from the Chiapas Highlands. Mexican coffee usually commands a slightly higher price in world markets, and more than half the annual production is exported. Tobacco is a specialty crop of 13,000 farmers, 11,000 of whom are located in the state of Nayarit. Certain varieties are raised exclusively for export, and other varieties are sold only on the domestic market. In November 1972 the government nationalized the leaf tobacco processing and exporting companies and formed a single firm called Mexican Tobacco (Tabacos Mexicanos), owned 52 percent by the government and 24 percent each by the former companies and the tobacco farmers. The new firm has sole authority to market all crude tobacco.

Henequen, the source of sisal fiber, is the major crop of Yucatán. Henequen products, such as twine, rope, rugs, and wall and floor coverings, have been exported since 1802. Mescal plants, technically known as *agave azul tequilena*, grow in parts of the states of Jalisco, Nayarit, and Michoacán on land that cannot support other crops, and the leaves of the plant are used to produce the popular drink tequila (see Manufacturing and Construction, this ch.). Mexico is a leading producer of cacao, from which cocoa and chocolate are derived. Fruits and vegetables taken together account for about 20 percent of the total value of crop production but occupy only about 7 percent of the cultivated area. Large quantities of more than thirty fruits and vegetables are exported to the United States; the more important are tomatoes, cucumbers, eggplant, stringbeans, asparagus, strawberries, onions, and green peppers. The state of Sinaloa is the main producing area for export-oriented fruits and vegetables although the area around the city of Irapuato in the state of Guanajuato produces most of the strawberries.

LIVESTOCK

Mexico ranks among the major beef producing and exporting nations. Export controls are imposed to safeguard sufficient domestic supplies. In 1973, for example, nearly 1.4 billion pounds of beef were produced, but only 80 million pounds were exported, a considerable drop from previous years. In addition to beef, large numbers of live cattle are exported to the United States: 824,000 head in 1973. There were an estimated 26 million head of cattle in the country in 1973, and they were concentrated in two general areas: the semiarid northern states (located near the United States), from which most of the live cattle are exported, and the tropical grasslands of the coastal states in the south, where most of the beef for the domestic market originates. In the coastal areas of the south, mainly along the Gulf Coast, many of the pastures are improved with guinea grass and other species and can support as much as ten times the number of cattle as the same acreage in the north. Until 1973 beef cattle ranchers could not legally plant crops on their land as this would be grounds for expropriation under the agrarian reform law. On September 21, 1973, a new regulation was issued that permitted livestock producers to use part of their land for certain crops—mainly grain and forage crops.

Diseases cause a high annual loss of cattle, but the government operates several programs to combat hoof-and-mouth disease, brucellosis, screwworm, and ticks. Some of these programs are carried out in conjunction with the United States.] Closely related to livestock production are the tanning and leather industries. About 3 million hides are tanned annually, but in some years rawhides have to be imported when domestic supplies decrease. The tanning industry is located almost entirely in the three cities of Mexico City, Guadalajara, and León.

About 10 million cattle produce milk. No more than 2.5 million of these are dairy cattle; the rest are crossbreeds whose milk yields are low but sufficient to provide the rancher with a small daily income. The full-time dairy ranches usually have pastures of irrigated alfalfa and import high-producing animals to upgrade their herds. Despite continual increases in the number of dairy cows and in milk production, the demand far exceeds the supply, and substantial imports of powdered milk and other milk products are required.

There were more than 13 million pigs and hogs in 1973, and their numbers are growing steadily. Many farmers raise hogs as a sideline, but there are numerous commercial hog farms concentrated in the Bajío and more recently in the northwest irrigation districts, where grains are fed to the hogs. More than 8 million goats can be found in the North and Central Plateau. Goat meat is popular among rural people, and goat milk is used fresh and made into cheese. The numbers of sheep in the country have been declining and were down to 5.5 million in 1972. Sheep are raised in high, cool elevations, but there are declining numbers of full-time shepherds, and the availability of good pastureland has decreased. As a result of the decrease in sheep, wool imports have started to increase. Equines—horses, mules, asses, and donkeys—numbered about 10 million in 1972. The load capacity of the ubiquitous burro can be as much as 500 pounds.

One of the fastest growing segments of the livestock industry has been poultry farming. Commercial poultry farms have as many as 50,000 layers and use the most modern production technology. The growth was so fast that there was an oversupply of poultry and eggs in both 1971 and 1972, and the government had to restrict production because cold-storage facilities were overburdened with unsold poultry meat. From about 231 million chickens in 1971 flocks were down to an estimated 214 million at the end of 1972, and a further decrease was anticipated for 1973 until supply and demand were more evenly balanced. Poultry farmers also raise about 5 million turkeys annually.

Mexico is the world's largest exporter of honey although it is only the third largest producer. There are a few large firms specializing in apiculture, and many farmers produce honey as a sideline. In some areas, such as Yucatán, which produces 30 percent of the honey, apiarists have formed marketing cooperatives. Elsewhere middlemen travel around the countryside collecting small amounts of honey for resale to the large exporters. During the flowering cycle of such crops as avocados, alfalfa, lima beans, onions, cabbage, squash, nuts, melons, and strawberries insect pollination is required, and many farmers rent beehives on a temporary basis from apiarists. A survey revealed that, when beehives are placed directly in the fields and orchards, yields improve dramatically.

FISHING AND FORESTRY

Mexico's fisheries, like those of many other Latin American countries, have remained underdeveloped, despite the fact that Mexico possesses a long coastline and rich offshore resources. The recorded catch in 1973 was 330,000 tons, but the marine resources are sufficient to support a much larger industry. Although fishing accounts for less than 1 percent of the GDP, it is an important foreign exchange earner because of exports of shrimp and lobster, the most valuable part of the catch. Mexico's waters contain a fish population of varied species rather than large schools of single finfish. The more important fish taken from the Pacific are lobsters, shrimps, croakers, albacore, skipjacks, and anchovies, and the Gulf of Mexico and the Caribbean waters provide shrimp, jewfish, croaker, snapper, mackerel, snook, and mullet.

The government has taken an interest in improving the fishing industry. It owns a holding company called the Mexican Fishing Products Company that markets about 15 percent of total fish and shellfish production. The company sells its own catch plus that of fishing cooperatives; licenses for certain species—shrimp, lobster, abalone, clam, croaker, grouper, and sea turtle—are reserved for fishing cooperatives. Private individuals may not catch these species. In 1970 there were more than 200 cooperatives with about 25,000 members. *Ejidatarios* living along the shores of lagoons, estuaries, and inshore waters may also form fishing cooperatives. On the other hand, five species—marlin, sailfish, shad, dolphin, and roosterfish—are reserved for individual fishermen.

The government opened thirty technical schools in 1972 to train workers, technicians, and sea research personnel. More financing is to be made available to the fishing industry, and a program to construct 500 modern refrigerated fishing vessels was under way in 1973 and 1974. The fishing fleet in 1972 was composed of 1,500 vessels, 800 of which were older than fifteen years and almost obsolete. The new vessels will be sold to cooperatives under favorable terms and will replace the oldest vessels. The country claims 200 miles of waters as patrimonial, which permits free passage of foreign vessels but reserves minerals and marine resources to Mexico (see ch. 2). Foreign vessels may be licensed to fish in patrimonial waters if 50 percent of the crew are Mexican citizens.

The government also maintains fish breeding stations for fingerlings, which are stocked in reservoirs and lakes. Trout and carp are the most popular freshwater fish stocked. One interesting aspect of stocking began in 1972 when millions of tadpoles were released into irrigation canals and small ponds in rural areas all over the country. When full grown, the frogs will serve as a source of protein for rural families. Bullfrogs have been found to contain more protein than chicken or fish and to have a lower fat content.

Forest exploitation has tended to be destructive; there has been widespread cutting and burning since the colonial era. The exact area of forests is unknown as various surveys have resulted in differing figures, but according to preliminary results of a long-term national forestry inventory, there were about 100 million acres in the early 1970s. Only about 9 percent of the forests were on state or federal land; 18 percent were located on land owned by *ejidos*, and the large balance was privately or municipally owned.

By value, about 70 percent of forest products are sawn wood and lumber, 25 percent are pulp and paper products, and the balance is firewood, charcoal, and miscellaneous. Among the miscellaneous products, many of which are exported, are oil of turpentine, turpentine, pitch, chicle, seeds, istle fiber (used in basketry), leaves, and rhizomes (rootstocks). About two-thirds of the forests are in hardwoods, and one-third is composed of softwoods. The most abundant and valuable trees are pine and oak.

Since 1926 several forestry laws have been passed aimed at the rational exploitation of the forest resources, and the long-range National Forestry Plan was issued in 1965. The Forestry Fund, operated by the Bank of Mexico, receives logging and concession fees and finances conservation expenses and the exploitation of forest resources by the government. Special permits are needed to engage in forestry operations, and there are no more than 35,000 people in the industry. No timber at all may be cut in the states of Morelos, Puebla, and Hidalgo, which have suffered from unlicensed exploitation. Most of the licensed exploitation is in the state of Durango, where there are large pine forests.

MINING AND PETROLEUM

Although mineral production accounts for a small share of the GDP—about 2 percent in the early 1970s—mineral exports usually account for between 10 and 15 percent of total annual exports. Mexico long has been a producer of minerals (nearly all of the twenty-nine states have commercial reserves of minerals) and numerous new projects under way in the early 1970s should increase the importance of mining to the country by the end of the decade. The upsurge of international demand for minerals in 1973 and 1974 coupled with higher prices caused the industry to push forward with the development of previously deferred projects costing billions of pesos.

During the early 1950s about 95 percent of the Mexican mining industry was foreign owned. The government then began fostering a gradual "Mexicanization of mining," as the official policy was termed.

By 1970 Mexican-owned companies were accounting for 90 percent of total mineral production, and it was believed that 98 percent of the industry was in Mexican hands in 1974. Foreign companies can be minority stockholders, and many have joined with Mexican companies or the Mexican government to form new companies to conform with Mexican law. The government has also decreed that certain minerals may not be exported but may only be used to meet domestic needs. These include iron, coal, and tin.

A large range of minerals, both metallic and nonmetallic, are produced (see table 10). The most valuable mineral is zinc, which is the leading mineral export. Zinc production is fairly steady, exhibiting no sharp annual increases or decreases. The second most valuable mineral export is fluorspar. Mexico is the world's leading producer of this mineral, which is a translucent multicolored mineral used as an industrial flux or made into hydrofluoric acid.

The second most valuable mineral produced for domestic use during the early 1970s was copper but, when some of the new exploitation projects are developed, copper should become the leading mineral. There are large copper deposits in the state of Sonora; two of them contain 1.6 billion tons and 700 million tons, respectively. Preliminary exploitation began in 1974, and full production is scheduled for 1977. Iron ore was the third most valuable mineral; most of the exploitation was in the North, where coking coals are also found, but larger deposits exist in Colima and Michoacán on the Pacific coast, and the government was taking the initiative in joint ventures for their development. Most coal comes from the state of Coahuila.

Silver deposits are found throughout the country, but the main producing areas are in Chihuahua, Hidalgo, Zacatecas, and Durango. Once the world's leading silver producer, Mexico ranked only fourth by 1973 as the main deposits started to decline. Rising world prices, however, promised to stimulate production from lower grade deposits, although prices received by producers are set by the Bank of Mexico, sometimes on a monthly basis and sometimes on a daily basis. Durango and Chihuahua are the major gold-producing states, but gold is recovered mainly as a by-product of other minerals, as most gold deposits have been nearly exhausted.

Dome sulfur deposits discovered on the Isthmus of Tehuantepec during the 1920s are of importance and have made Mexico one of the world's major producers and exporters, although an increasing proportion of the output is being employed by the country's rapidly expanding fertilizer industry. Of more recent development has been the establishment of the largest operation in the world for the evaporation of marine salts, on the west coast of the peninsula of Baja California. Almost all of that production is exported to chemical companies on the Pacific coast of the United States. Hundreds of small entrepreneurs operating

Table 10. *Mexico, Production of Selected Minerals, 1969–72*
(in thousands of metric tons unless otherwise indicated)

Item	1969	1970	1971	1972
Aluminum, refined	32	34	40	39
Antimony	3	4	3	3
Arsenic	6	7	9	4
Barite	176	319	280	261
Calcite	4	5	8	4
Celestite (strontium minerals)	18	25	35	24
Coal	2,458	2,959	3,552	3,264
Copper	66	61	63	78
Diatomite	11	23	22	9
Feldspar	83	86	99	98
Fluorspar (fluorite)	988	978	1,181	1,040
Gold[1]	5,617	6,166	4,694	4,543
Graphite	43	56	51	55
Gypsum	1,219	1,219	1,298	1,497
Iron ore	2,097	2,612	2,353	2,672
Lead	171	177	157	162
Manganese	60	99	96	103
Natural gas[2]	609,056	665,026	633,416	660,000
Petroleum, crude[3]	149,661	156,530	155,912	161,000
Salt	3,890	4,153	4,360	4,558
Silica (quartz and glass sand)	282	356	393	404
Silver[4]	42.9	42.8	40.1	37.5
Sulfur	1,717	1,381	1,178	944
Zinc	253	266	265	272

[1] Kilograms.
[2] Million cubic feet.
[3] Thousand barrels.
[4] Million ounces.

on both coasts of the mainland produce sufficient salt to meet domestic needs.

Under the Constitution as amended, the exploration, production, refining, and distribution of petroleum and natural gas and the manufacture and sale of basic petrochemicals are a government monopoly. These activities are conducted by Mexican Petroleum (Petróleos Mexicanos—PEMEX), a state company with more than 70,000 employees; PEMEX is one of the largest taxpayers in the country and exerts a major force on the economy. At one time PEMEX contracted with private firms for services such as well drilling, reimbursement being made in the form of a percentage of the crude oil discovered. The last of these service contracts were terminated by the end of 1969, however, and PEMEX has since been conducting all of its own exploration and exploitation.

Consumption of petroleum has been increasing faster than production, and Mexico, once a net exporter, was importing large quantities of crude and refined products by 1974. The basic reason for the slow production increase has been the financial status of PEMEX. Consumer prices were frozen for fifteen years before 1974, but wages were not, and PEMEX's profits had declined to the point where only the most urgent investments were being made and long-term developments were being postponed. By the end of 1973 tested reserves were down to 5.4 billion barrels, only enough for about seventeen years of exploitation at then current consumption rates. With an increase in consumer prices in 1974 and an infusion of foreign loans, PEMEX was embarking on major exploration projects including offshore drilling and once again appeared on the way to self-sufficiency. The most promising new fields appeared to be in an area straddling the borders of Chiapas and Tabasco. The major production areas had previously been in the northeast between the cities of Reynosa and Matamoros and along the Gulf Coast around the cities of Tampico, Tuxpan, Poza Rica, and Veracruz.

PEMEX had a rapidly expanded transportation network for the transportation of its products from the 4,500 producing oil and gas wells in 1974. Thousands of miles of crude oil pipelines and twenty-one tankers each accounted for about half of the transportation of crude oil to the refineries, and other pipelines, tankers, trucks, and railcars owned by PEMEX handled the transportation of the finished products. The refining capacity of the several refineries was about 592,000 barrels per day in 1974, not enough to handle demand. A new 150,000-barrel-per-day refinery, however, was scheduled to begin operations in 1975 at the city of Tula. Further plans for refinery expansion should bring capacity up to 1.1 million barrels per day by 1977.

Natural gas reserves in 1970 were believed to be sufficient for about two decades, but production was declining in the gas fields near Reynosa, and there was growing concern in 1974. Natural gas is piped from Reynosa fields to the northern industrial zone around Monterrey, and Mexico City and Central Mexico are supplied with gas from Tabasco and northern Veracruz. The country is virtually self-sufficient in the production of industrial gases, such as nitrogen, oxygen, hydrogen, argon, acetylene, and carbon dioxide. These gases are produced by private firms in a competitive and dynamic industry.

MANUFACTURING AND CONSTRUCTION

Mexican industry produces a wide range of items, about 80 percent of all manufactured products sold in the country (see table 11). Most of the growth has resulted from high protective import barriers. The 1970 census indicated that there were over 119,000 manufacturing establishments employing five or more workers, but the majority were small shops where the employers generally lack the knowledge and financial resources needed for the improvement of techniques. Productivity was low in a great many of the firms.

Over 57 percent of all manufacturing enterprises were concentrated in apparel and food-processing industries—54,000 food processors and

	1969	1970	1971	1972	1973
Item (in thousands of metric tons):					
Caustic soda	154	171	171	169	185
Cement	6,674	7,126	7,390	8,600	9,800
Paper	818	897	908	n.a.	1,070
Phosphoric acid	262	225	342	402	419
Pig iron	1,695	1,645	1,683	1,890	n.a.
Soaps	378	411	407	456	n.a.
Steel ingot	3,420	3,881	3,821	4,400	4,700
Sulfuric acid	1,070	1,233	1,442	1,518	1,737
Item (in thousands):					
Radios	941	1,015	921	n.a.	n.a.
Refrigerators	181	241	244	281	307
Television sets	413	431	391	443*	497*
Tires	3,372	3,555	3,986	4,610	n.a.
Vehicles	165	189	208	228	283
Washing machines	113	197	191	217	177*

n.a.—not available.
*Sales figures only.

14,000 apparel and shoe manufacturers. There were also 9,000 metal products firms and over 8,000 nonmetallic mineral products companies. Some of the small firms, however, have shown much dynamism, and in almost every industry cases can be cited where small shops have expanded to become major producers.

The location of industry has been a matter of increasing concern to planners. There has been a heavy concentration of plants in and around the capital, Monterrey, and Guadalajara tending to aggravate runaway urbanization and its attendant social problems. In many cases plants are uneconomically located with respect to resources because skilled labor is more readily available in these industrial cities or owner-managers prefer urban life with all its amenities for their families. The government has been constructing industrial parks in 110 cities in an effort to attract industry to other areas, and in 1972 it started to offer fiscal benefits to companies locating in designated zones, the benefits varying by zone. Since the Federal District remains the hub of economic activity, it appears that the states in the vicinity of the capital will benefit most from the attempts to diversify industrial location. In fact, there was a small industrial boom in the early 1970s in the states of Querétaro, Puebla, México, and Morelos, and the state of Hidalgo was making a strong bid to attract its share of new industry.

One highly successful industrial diversification program involving foreign firms has been the Border Industry Program. Started in the 1960s, this program permits foreign companies setting up assembly operations in towns and cities along the United States-Mexican border to import free of duty all component parts if the assembled product is then reexported. A key feature of this program is that the company must have a counterpart plant outside Mexico to which it sends the assembled product. Some plants located in free zones in Baja California, however, may sell part of their production locally. By mid-1974 over 530 firms, almost all from the United States and employing over 65,000 people, were involved in such assembly operations. Some of the companies were contracting out their overcapacity workload to Mexican companies supplying several thousand additional workers. About 40 percent of the plants were assembling parts for the electronics industry, and another 30 percent were apparel factories. A 1972 decree permitted the establishment of such assembly plants away from the border, and the original name, Border Industry Program, has been informally changed to the In-bond Industry Program.

In value of production, the food, beverages, and tobacco sector is the most important industrial activity, contributing almost 30 percent of the total value in 1970. This is followed by machinery and metals with 13 percent, chemicals with 12 percent, and textiles and clothing with 8 percent each. Although many of the food-processing plants in the 280,000-employee industry are engaged in the preparation of simple products such as tortilla dough, there is a growing market for brand name products prepared and packaged for convenience, and the few large producers are expanding their share of the market. There are about 2,200 beverage firms, only 210 of them making soft drinks; most beverage companies are distillers and brewers. The wine and brandy industry is concentrated in the state of Aguascalientes, where good quality grapes are grown. An important contributor to the economy of the state of Jalisco are more than two dozen distillers of tequila, one of the native drinks of Mexico originating in that state. Brewing, one of the older established industries, has been distinguished for its efficient operation and the excellence of its product.

The steel industry is one of the oldest in Latin America; the first plant was established in 1903. The industry experienced a strong upward trend in production between 1960 and 1973 except for 1971 and was operating at near capacity of 5 million tons by 1974. Various new projects were scheduled for completion by 1980 to bring capacity up to 10 million tons. This 45,000-employee industry contained about ten important steel companies and numerous smaller firms producing steel products from ingots bought from the larger companies. The largest, Blast Furnaces of Mexico (Altos Hornos de México), primarily state owned, accounts for about 40 percent of total steel production. A new government-owned steel company was under construction in 1974 at the Las Truchas iron ore deposits in Michoacán, about 460 miles from Mexico City. Scheduled for completion in 1976 or 1977, its initial capacity will be 1.5 million tons, and it will be the largest single industrial investment ever undertaken by a Mexican government. The first phase of the project alone was estimated to cost over 6.1 billion pesos. The project also requires the construction of a 160-mile railroad and a new seaport at the mouth of the Balsas River.

In the automotive field there has been notable expansion, despite government regulations making the finished product more costly than if imported. The regulations, however, have stimulated a multitude of small plants—more than 350—producing parts and subassemblies and have undoubtedly helped the general level of technical capability of Mexican industry. Each automotive firm's output is regulated by government-set quotas, which may be increased when the company can demonstrate that it can compensate through exports for the foreign exchange that would be required to import any parts needed for the expanded production. There are seven companies making vehicles, but the leading producer is Volkswagen, reflecting in part the popularity of smaller cars.

Government policy has played a prominent role in the development of the chemical industry, one of the most dynamic industrial sectors. Petro-chemical production is divided between the government and private capital; PEMEX extending its monopoly to the first stages of production but leaving subsequent processing steps to private enterprise. In 1960 the Mexican petrochemical industry was nonexistent. By 1974 its list of products was long and was steadily being increased. PEMEX operated some sixty petrochemical plants, and there were more than 200 private companies in the early 1970s. In some chemical products such as syn-thetic fibers, private industry has assumed the leading role. About 750 companies employing 38,000 people composed the pharmaceutical seg-ment of the chemical industry, but fifty-six companies controlled three-fourths of production. The government exerted an influence on the industry by purchasing more than one-fourth of total annual production under its various social and welfare programs.

As is commonly the case in developing countries, textiles were the earliest area of industrialization. Owing to this and to inadequate re-investment and modernization during a long period of years, by 1945 much of the equipment was antiquated and inefficient. The problem was complicated by the opposition of strongly organized unions to the intro-duction of new techniques and the difficulties experienced in retraining workers to operate new equipment. In an effort to encourage moderni-zation of the textile industry, the government permitted the importation of duty-free textile machinery during the 1960s, and by the end of the decade about three-fourths of the 1,850 textile companies were automated. Despite the change to modern equipment, however, the industry, which employed some 160,000 workers, was still hampered by high labor costs. Some companies, such as embroidery firms, farmed out piecework to housewives who worked in their homes rather than at the factory. Although textile firms were located all over the country, the manufactured clothing industry is concentrated in Mexico City, Guadalajara, and Irapuato.

Shoemaking was a handicraft industry dating from colonial times but in the early 1970s footwear was made by 800 large shoe factories using highly mechanized equipment and about 3,000 small and medium-sized artisan workshops using, for the most part, hand labor. There were an estimated 160,000 people employed in the footwear industry.

The paper and pulp industry was another of the major industries, with over sixty-three companies employing 19,000 workers. Despite high growth trends the industry could not meet demand, and costly imports were required. In 1966 domestic firms could supply 80 percent of pulp and paper demand, but by the mid-1970s they were able to meet only two-thirds of demand. There were insufficient supplies of raw materials for the production of paper; plants were located away from the source of raw materials, thereby raising transportation costs; and productivity per employee was low because too many kinds of low-volume paper were manufactured, over 400 varieties in 1970. In addition to conventional pulpwood, much cheap paper was made from nonwood cellulose materials, such as bagasse, wheat and barley straw, and cotton waste. Bagasse, the residue from the sugar refineries, is considered a basic material to satisfy the country's future requirements for newsprint.

The Mexican glass industry received its first major impulse from the scarcities of World War II, and since then sizable investments have increased capacity to the point where some kinds are exported. Mexican glass products are sold throughout Central America, and some Mexican flat glass has entered the United States market.

A state-owned company, the National Railroad Car Factory, is capable of supplying most railroad cars and equipment except for some locomotives and specialized gear. Its capacity exceeds its requirements, and some freight cars are exported. The country's shipyards mainly construct fishing vessels and were operating at full capacity during the 1972–74 period.

The production of such consumer durables as domestic appliances, radios, and television sets has been stimulated by a policy of protectionism, and most appliances are made entirely from domestically manufactured parts. The forty-four firms making consumer durables can meet almost the entire domestic demand.

In 1973 total installed capacity of the twenty-nine existing cement plants was more than 10 million tons, and most companies had been operating at between 80 and 90 percent of capacity since 1960. Several new cement plants were under construction, and expansion was contemplated for older ones so that capacity could be raised to 12 million tons by 1975.

The construction industry was robust, employing as many as 730,000 people in the early 1970s and contributing almost 5 percent to the GNP. Current construction displayed a broad spectrum of materials and techniques. Although much construction was still carried out using crude materials and labor-intensive methods, Mexican manufacturers were able to provide a diversity of excellent building materials, and the country had numerous splendid examples of advanced architecture and engineering. Much of the construction activity was dependent upon government contracts; between 65 and 70 percent of all construction investment since 1950 was for federal programs. Many firms were established by a group of engineers for the purpose of obtaining a contract and were disbanded afterwards. Government contracts were awarded only to firms that were members of the National Chamber of the Construction Industry. In 1973 more than 4,650 companies were registered with the chamber, and these were believed to be about 80 percent of the existing construction companies. Some firms specialize only in a particular kind of construction, and others bid on any project. Most construction firms maintained a small number of permanent employees and either hired or subcontracted needed labor for a specific job.

ELECTRIC ENERGY

Electric energy capacity has been growing at annual rates of between 10 and 15 percent since 1960; demand has kept pace with growth and in some years has exceeded it. During 1973, for example, there was not enough electricity produced for all of the needs of the Mexico City metropolitan area, and some residential sections suffered frequent power cutoffs. New projects scheduled for completion during 1974 should alleviate the difficulties and raise total electric generating capacity to 9.2 million kilowatts by the end of that year.

An autonomous government agency, the Federal Electricity Commission, created in 1937, provided most of the electricity in the country and was in charge of planning, promoting, and administering the government's power policy. In the early 1970s the commission was supplying about 85 percent of total electric power; the balance was generated by the plants belonging to industrial firms and the few remaining privately owned electric companies selling power to the public.

In all there were nearly 2,300 power plants, large and small, in operation; 2,000 of these, with about 1.2 million kilowatts of capacity, belonged to industrial firms and generated electricity mainly for their own use. A few of the larger company-operated plants, particularly those of mining firms, supplied electricity to the surrounding areas. Eventually all of the private electric companies were to be absorbed by the Federal Electricity Commission.

Most of the power plants in 1973 were fueled by oil or gas. The balance were hydroelectric, coal-fueled, or geothermal plants. Some of the natural gas-fueled plants were being converted to oil during 1973 and 1974 in order to assure a sufficient reserve of natural gas for industrial use. Much of the industry in Monterrey, for example, uses natural gas as the prime source of its energy. Only about one-third of Mexico's hydroelectric potential was being utilized during the 1970s, and further use of this resource was planned. About seventy-five miles south of Mexicali in Baja California was a 75,000-kilowatt geothermal plant using super-heated steam coming from depths of 4,000 feet. This plant, located at a site called Cerro Prieto, was supplying the state of Baja California with 25 percent of its electricity needs in 1974, and expansion of the plant could provide all future needs of the state until 1984, according to estimates. There were about 120 geothermal sites in central and northwest Mexico, and the success of the Cerro Prieto plant encouraged government experts to explore the possibility of tapping them. By January 1974 over 4,000 tons of proven reserves of commercially exploitable uranium had been verified, and the National Nuclear Energy Institute had plans for the future development of nuclear fuels. The first nuclear powered-plant, with a capacity of 670,000 kilowatts, was under construction at Laguna Verde, Veracruz, and was scheduled for completion by 1977.

Electricity produced is either fifty cycles, 125 volts or sixty cycles, 110 volts. Under a long-range program to end in 1977 all power is being converted to sixty cycles, and until then all electrical equipment must be capable of being operated on either fifty or sixty cycles. Industry consumes the largest share of electricity—almost 54 percent. Residential use accounts for 17 percent, and the balance is for all other uses. At the beginning of 1971 about 59 percent of the houses in the country had access to electricity. The percentage ranged from as high as 95 percent of the houses in the Federal District to as low as 28 percent in Oaxaca. In that year the government announced a six-year program to bring electricity to as many as 9,000 small towns and villages.

CHAPTER 15

TRADE AND TRANSPORTATION

Mexico's foreign trade expanded steadily after 1940 and more rapidly after 1960. The country has been able to diversify its export base, no single commodity accounting for more than 10 percent of total exports. Imports, composed mainly of raw materials and intermediate and capital industrial goods, have far exceeded exports and, although causing an annual negative trade balance, have not caused balance-of-payments difficulties (see ch. 13). Earnings generated by the Mexican tourist industry have helped to offset the negative trade balances, and the government considers the growth of tourism one of the priority areas in the economy.

The dominant trading partner has been the United States, but the founding of the Latin American Free Trade Association (LAFTA) in 1961 gave an impetus to shift some trade to Latin America. Also, more attention is being given to expanding trade with Japan and Europe in order to counterbalance commercial dependency on the United States. Mexico has been a party to relatively few trade agreements; it is not a member of the General Agreement on Tariffs and Trade (GATT) although it became an official observer in 1973, and the few trade agreements it has signed, apart from LAFTA, have had little effect on trade patterns.

The domestic trading and service community is fairly widespread, and there has never been the social stigma attached to trading activities that exists in some other Latin American countries. The courtesy that is customary in Mexican social relations is extended to business dealings. Business relations are generally free of ethnic implications, and the prevailing business values and methods of operations are similar to those in most industrialized economies.

Mexico's land transportation systems, both rail and road, are comprehensive, and the secondary and tertiary road network continues to expand, incorporating hitherto isolated communities into the national fabric. Because of the importance of tourism from the United States, much attention has been placed upon improving north-south highways, and all federal roads are patrolled by aid and rescue squads. Aviation is well developed, although relatively little air freight is carried; most air service is passenger traffic. Maritime transportation is the weakest link in the transportation network but is still generally satisfactory. Since most trade had been overland with the United States, less attention had been paid to developing the seaports and a national merchant marine. Increased emphasis, however, was being placed on maritime transport in the 1970s.

The merchandising of consumer goods is becoming mass oriented with respect to price, sales techniques, and terms of credit. Few families are completely outside the market economy despite the large numbers of poor farmers. With a rising standard of living since World War II, foodstuffs and other subsistence items are tending to occupy a place of declining relative importance in the composition of retail trade.

FOREIGN TRADE

Mexico is one of the major trading nations of the world; the value of its foreign trade is constantly increasing. Preliminary figures indicate that exports reached over US$2.4 billion in 1973 while imports soared to US$4.1 billion. Mexico has consistently experienced a balance-of-trade deficit that has usually been covered by income from invisibles, such as tourism and private foreign investment. The 1973 deficit, however, was of record proportions and caused concern to Mexican officials as a portent of the future. Numerous government-sponsored export promotion measures exist, and increased emphasis was being given to them in 1974.

The National Foreign Trade Bank (Banco Nacional de Comercio Exterior) finances, promotes, and aids in export marketing. The bank operates a subsidiary marketing company that provides information about conditions of foreign markets and transport problems and makes special studies on products and specific markets. The special Fund for the Promotion of Manufactured Exports set up in 1962 by the Bank of Mexico permits manufacturers to sell on credit to overseas customers and provides certain kinds of export credit insurance. By 1973 this fund was financing about one-fourth of all exports of manufactures. The Mexican Foreign Trade Institute coordinates the activities of all public and private organizations participating in foreign trade. Commercial counselors are stationed at some Mexican embassies and consulates to help Mexican exporters seek clients and to obtain the reduction of restrictions against Mexican exports. A study revealed that Mexican exports have increased rapidly in every country where commercial counselors have been sent. Additionally, numerous government-sponsored trade missions composed of officials and businessmen are sent to countries where the market appears favorable, as was the case in 1974 when missions went to nearly every Latin American and Arab country to sell Mexican products and technology. The government will also help Mexican firms to attend foreign trade fairs and expositions, and financial incentives are given to companies forming export consortia and also to firms providing export services to smaller manufacturers. In late 1974 the government agreed to subsidize the cost of stockpiling products in overseas warehouses.

Export licenses are required for certain items to ensure that domestic needs are met first, as occurred with oilseeds in 1973; to control export prices, such as those for coffee; to conform to an international agreement, such as that concerned with textiles; or to enable export duties to be levied, as is the case with some minerals. Generally, despite the restrictions, the policy of encouraging and diversifying exports has been successful. Mexico has been able to reduce the risk of payment crises stemming from the fall in the world price of one or two commodities by widening the base of exports (see table 12). No single export commodity constitutes as much as 10 percent of total exports.

Together all agricultural products account for about half of total exports, and all manufactured goods account for 30 to 40 percent. Minerals account for the balance. Since 1967 the growth in exports has been mainly in manufactured goods, and a large share of that increase has been from the success of the In-bond Industry Program whereby foreign firms may import component parts for assembly and reexport (see ch. 14).

Mexico has become the leading Latin American exporter of shrimp, machinery, and zinc. It is an important exporter of meat, but faster

Table 12. Mexico, Exports of Selected Products, 1970–73
(in millions of U.S. dollars)

Product[1]	1970	1971	1972	1973[2]
Miscellaneous small manufactures	175	233	359	790
Miscellaneous agricultural products	66	102	241	...[3]
Sugar	90	91	102	115
Chemicals	78	80	100	...[3]
Spare parts for machinery	43	69	88	175
Cotton	124	120	77	111
Miscellaneous processed foods	57	57	75	...[3]
Coffee	86	81	74	135
Shrimp	63	69	74	82
Textiles	39	50	73	...[3]
Miscellaneous minerals[4]	70	53	72	...[3]
Miscellaneous livestock and fishing	15	15	69	...[3]
Fresh meat	42	42	59	57
Zinc	57	48	56	...[3]
Iron and steel	29	47	47	19
Fluorspar	24	29	41	38
Fresh fruit	26	30	33	35
Tomatoes	108	90	32	40
Other	181	168	153	860
TOTAL	1,375[5]	1,474	1,825	2,457

[1] Listed in descending order of value in 1972.
[2] Preliminary figures.
[3] Included in Other.
[4] Excluding precious metals.
[5] Items do not add to total because of rounding.

growth is hindered by quarterly meat export quotas imposed to ensure domestic supplies. Textile exports, which would otherwise increase more rapidly, conform to the principles contained in a multilateral agreement called the Long-Term Arrangements Regarding International Trade in Cotton Textiles to which Mexico is a signatory. Although Mexican coffee usually commands a higher price than most other coffees, Mexico joined in 1974 with the Central American countries of El Salvador, Costa Rica, Guatemala, and Honduras in establishing a common coffee export marketing company in order to support export prices and avoid separate competing sales.

Mexico is heavily dependent upon the importation of capital goods and raw materials to sustain its industrial development (see ch. 14; table 13). At one time such imports accounted for about half of the total, and by the early 1970s they made up more than 80 percent. Although Mexico was once a fairly sizable exporter of grains, by 1973 it was importing such cereals as wheat, corn, sorghum, barley, and oats. These imports were occasioned by increased consumption coupled with several bad crop years. Concerned over the growing magnitude of imports but unable to curtail them because they were needed, in 1974 the government sponsored a four-month-long exhibit of approximately 7,500 products that were being imported in large quantities in order to bring them to the attention of Mexican manufacturers in the hope that some or most of the items could be manufactured domestically.

About 65 percent of all items in the tariff code are subject to a prior import license requirement, and orders may not be placed until the

Table 13. Mexico, Imports of Principal Products, 1970–73
(in millions of U.S. dollars)

Product[1]	1970	1971	1972	1973
Nonelectric machinery	} 822	760	{ 667	828
Electrical machinery			{ 321	415
Motor vehicles and spare parts	196	208	258	319
Chemicals	104	134	257	312
Cereals	58	18	83	224
Petroleum and gas	56	94	126	217
Iron and steel	30	23	84	173
Scientific equipment	14	23	87	113
Plastics	...[2]	...[2]	71	87
Railroad cars and parts	18	8	45	71
Clothing	10	14	47	63
Paper and pulp	63	56	42	44
Asbestos, phosphates, and clays	9	10	31	44
Others	1,081	1,059	616	1,175
TOTAL	2,461	2,407	2,735	4,085

[1] Listed in descending order of magnitude in 1973.

[2] Included with chemicals.

license is granted. Licenses are usually not granted for imports that compete with domestic products in price, quality, or delivery time, for which a similar domestic product can be substituted, or that are deemed not convenient for the economy. For many items licenses have never been granted, and most importers know this and do not submit applications. Licenses are approved or denied by consulting committees, each of which is responsible for a section of the customs tariff. The consulting committees are composed of representatives of the industries involved and of government officials. Licenses are customarily decided upon within thirty days and, if approved, are valid for six months. If the import is to come from a country that is a member of LAFTA and is a product that has been accorded a tariff concession, then no import license is required. In mid-1974 the government was studying the possibility of eliminating the consulting committees because of numerous alleged cases of conflict of interest on the part of the industries' representatives.

For many years the government has attempted to control illegal imports across the United States-Mexican border but has been generally unsuccessful because of the length of the border and the limited number of customs officials. Some success was achieved in the early 1970s by reducing customs duties on whiskeys, liquors, and wines, thereby making it unprofitable to smuggle such items into the country. In 1973 the government initiated a policy of giving customs officials a share of the value of seized contraband in the hope that this would stimulate initiative and stifle a tendency toward corruption.

The United States has almost always been Mexico's most important trading partner. Mexico was the United States' fifth best customer and sixth leading supplier during the early 1970s. The United States purchases between 65 and 70 percent of annual Mexican exports and supplies about the same percentage of imports. Main exports to the United States include sugar, coffee, shrimp (one-third of all United States shrimp imports), minerals, meat and livestock, and fresh fruit and vegetables. Imports from the United States are chiefly industrial and electrical machinery, motor vehicles, chemicals and, since 1970, cereals.

Since 1972 Mexico has been attempting to strengthen its commercial ties with other Latin American countries and with Japan in an effort to reduce its dependence on the United States as a trading partner. In 1973 the rest of Latin America as a whole and Japan were each taking about 7 percent of Mexico's exports, and each was supplying Mexico with about 5 percent of its total imports. Most of the balance of the trade was with Canada, the Federal Republic of Germany (West Germany), Italy, and France. In 1973 a commercial agreement was signed with the People's Republic of China (PRC) granting reciprocal rights to seaport facilities in each other's territory and most-favored-nation status for tariff purposes. In 1974 some eighty Mexican firms exhibited their products at an industrial show in Peking.

LATIN AMERICAN FREE TRADE ASSOCIATION

Mexico was a founding member of the Latin American Free Trade Association (LAFTA), which came into being on June 1, 1961, on the basis of a multilateral agreement known as the Montevideo Treaty. Argentina, Brazil, Chile, Paraguay, Peru, and Uruguay were the other original members, and Ecuador and Colombia joined in late 1961, Venezuela in September 1966, and Bolivia in January 1967. As originally conceived LAFTA was to have the objective of expanding members' markets by the elimination of barriers to trade—particularly tariffs. Since Mexico had built its industrial sector on the basis of tariff protection, many businessmen were initially opposed to the country's becoming a member. It joined LAFTA mainly upon the constant urging of forward thinking economists and technicians in the government who were able to convince both President Adolfo López Mateos and the business community that the organization would be beneficial to Mexico.

As of 1973 a total of over 11,150 general tariff concessions had been negotiated among LAFTA members, which were applicable to all members, and 7,400 nonextensive concessions, which were not applicable to all, had been granted on a bilateral basis between certain members. Only about one-third of all tariff concessions had ever been used by 1974 because many of them were for products not yet manufactured by the recipient countries. Still, intrazonal trade had increased from a level of US$360 million in 1961 to over US$2 billion in 1973. Mexico experienced a trade surplus within LAFTA every year except 1973 and, along with Argentina and Brazil, dominated the market.

An unusual but successful trade liberalization mechanism under LAFTA is the use of what are termed complementation agreements. Representatives of specific industrial sectors, such as pharmaceuticals, machine tools, or chemicals, negotiate on behalf of their countries agreements for free trade on particular products of that industry. The agreements usually include the assignment of production rights whereby the signatories specify which country will manufacture a specific product. This ensures a wider market without the threat of undue competition. Twenty such complementation agreements applicable to nearly 2,800 items had been negotiated by mid-1974. Mexico was a member of fourteen of the agreements covering about 750 items.

Dissatisfaction with the rate of progress and the benefits accruing to them as members of LAFTA had led Bolivia, Chile, Ecuador, Colombia, and Peru in mid-1969 to sign the Andean Subregional Economic Integration Agreement, commonly called the Cartagena Agreement, to form an association within LAFTA leading to the Andean Common Market. Venezuela, which had participated in the original negotiations, joined in December 1973, Mexico indicated interest in developing special ties with the Andean Common Market, and the Andean-Mexican Commission was established in late 1972.

Because of concern that full free trade among all LAFTA members could not be achieved by the original deadline of 1972, an amendment to the basic LAFTA treaty pushed back the free-trade target date to 1980, and a series of special meetings was taking place in 1974 to study new ways to revitalize LAFTA. The Mexican permanent representative to LAFTA stated in 1974 that his country not only favored a revision of the Montevideo Treaty to take into account subregional groupings and to freeze all tariff duties at current levels but also to institute an automatic tariff-cutting mechanism not subject to annual negotiation, which would vary according to each member's stage of development. Mexico also favored the elimination of all nontariff restrictions and the negotiation of special marketing agreements for agricultural products.

DOMESTIC TRADE

Commerce, both wholesale and retail, has been the dynamic sector of domestic trade, contributing an ever-increasing share to the gross domestic product (GDP) while services have tended to level off. The last commercial census, taken in the mid-1960s, indicated that there were more than 352,000 commercial establishments in the country ranging from large department stores to small family shops selling a few basic commodities. The number of establishments offering personal services, such as restaurants, motion picture theaters, barbershops, and laundries, was about 142,000. Very few families remain completely out of the market economy, and even the portion of the rural population that engages in subsistence agriculture receive some cash payments. Nonmonetary arrangements such as barter are the exception.

Business activities are governed by the Civil Code, the Commercial Code, or the Law of Commercial Companies. The most common form of business organization is the sole proprietorship. An individual engaged in business must be registered in a commercial register and must be a member of an appropriate chamber of commerce or industry. He must also maintain certain prescribed books of accounts. Partnerships may be of three types: general, limited, and stock-issuing. In a general partnership all partners have unlimited liability to third parties, and each partner is active in the company. This form is generally used where the business is small. In a limited partnership only the active members have unlimited liability, and the nonactive partners are liable only up to the amount they contributed to the company. A stock-issuing partnership is similar to a limited partnership in that the capital is represented by shares of stock owned by active and nonactive partners. The active partners are fully liable for the company's debts, and the nonactive partners are liable only for the payment of the value of their shares.

An intermediate form of business organization between partnerships and corporations is the limited liability corporation. The liability of all members, active or nonactive, is limited to their contributions. The shares are generally not negotiable but may be transferred under certain circumstances, and the company may not have more than twenty-five shareholders. There are detailed regulations for corporations. At least five stockholders are required for a corporation to be formed. Any foreigner who is a founding stockholder of a corporation requires a prior permit from the Ministry of Foreign Relations and must agree not to invoke the protection of his government insofar as his interests in the corporation are concerned.

Numerous producer, consumer, and public service cooperatives are covered by special legislation. Cooperatives may be formed by at least ten members and operate with a variable capital under a simple name for the benefit of their members, who have limited liability. A new from of business organization, the development holding company *(sociedad de fomento)*, was created in 1973. Such a company may own any number of other firms and consolidate their profits and losses for tax purposes. The government hopes that such companies will attract better skills and have easier access to financing than would any of the component firms. This type of company is considered ideal for a foreign company seeking a Mexican partner.

The channels of trade are numerous and present a wide spectrum of commercial practices ranging from traditional to the most advanced. The best organized marketing system for agricultural products is located in the state of Sinaloa and is often cited as a model to be copied elsewhere in the country. There, all of the private farmers belong to the statewide Confederation of Farmer Associations, which carries out marketing studies, furnishes marketing information, supplies seeds to its members, provides fertilizers and pesticides, and then markets its members' produce, except for rice and chick-peas, which are marketed through national associations of producers of those crops.

The largest department stores in the country have integrated the distribution of consumer goods by becoming involved in varying degrees in the manufacture and wholesaling of articles they retail. Numerous appliance discount houses have developed ties with manufacturers to produce merchandise under house brands.

Supermarkets have expanded rapidly in all the large cities and suburbs and have branched out into distributing nonfood items. Some supermarket chains act as wholesalers to such institutions as hospitals and hotels. The public markets continue to play a significant role and in most cities have been rehoused in sanitary structures. Mexico City alone has 240 public markets. The markets have held their own against the inroads of the supermarkets because they usually have fresh fruits and vegetables daily and cater to lower income groups by selling miscellaneous low-cost nonfood merchandise. Some markets are reserved for retail sales by small producers, and middlemen are not permitted to operate in them. Many Mexican housewives prefer the warm atmosphere of the public market to the impersonal relations of a supermarket. One major public market in Mexico City was experimenting successfully in 1974 with sales on Sundays in wholesale lots to retail customers. There are also several nonfood markets in Mexico City and other cities that specialize in such categories of merchandise as handicrafts, household goods, or flea market items.

In order to help the small wage earner cope with rising food prices, a government entity, the National Company of Popular Subsistences (Compañia Nacional de Subsistencias Populares—CONASUPO), operates a chain of stores selling basic commodities at reasonable prices to members of labor unions, governmental workers, the military, and the general public. CONASUPO also provides *ejidos* (see Glossary) with standardized buildings stocked with basic food items and trains *ejido* personnel to operate the stores (see ch. 14). An extension of the CONASUPO program is a system called markets on wheels, initiated in Mexico City in 1972, in which mobile vans make weekly stops at designated street corners in selected residential neighborhoods and sell basic necessities at discount prices. More than 1,500 companies operate retail stores for the benefit of their employees. Many labor-management contracts provide for the establishment of such company outlets, and a new government entity was created in 1974 to provide financial backing for them.

Peculiar to the Monterrey marketing area are *despensas*, home delivery distribution systems for nonperishable foods. The system developed during the revolution as a means of ensuring an adequate food supply for factory workers; about 250,000 people were participating during the early 1970s, and the system accounted for about 10 percent of total food sales in the area. Under the system families submit monthly orders through their employers to the *despensa* outlet, usually a private wholesaler, who delivers the orders to their homes within two weeks. The employers deduct money from the employees' salaries and forward it along with the order blanks directly to the *despensa*.

At the bottom of the distribution system are the petty merchants in whom the country abounds. These are the people, generally women, who either operate out of very tiny shops, market stalls, or push carts or are ambulatory and sell a small quantity of a limited number of items. The ambulatory vendors generally provoke the anger of established merchants, and periodically merchant organizations call upon local authorities to exclude peddlers from city streets, usually to no avail.

Storage facilities are generally adequate in the country except at some seaports where cargo is in open storage. The Mexican border city of Nuevo Laredo and the United States city of Laredo completed plans in 1974 for a joint warehousing and distribution complex. The National Warehouse Company, created by the government in 1936, manages nearly 760 warehouses scattered in 280 cities and towns throughout the country with a total capacity of about 4 million tons. Private storage facilities can accommodate about 3 million tons. CONASUPO has a project whereby it helps *ejidos* build warehouses in a standard design and then rents space in the facilities to enable the *ejidos* to pay off the cost of the buildings. In mid-1974 the government decided to place the National

Warehouse Company under the administrative control of CONASUPO.

Most weights and measures are in the metric system, although English measures are known and sometimes cited. One local land measure used in Yucatán is the *mecate*, equivalent to one-tenth of an acre.

TOURISM

Mexico is one of the world's most richly endowed tourist destinations, and the foreign exchange generated by tourism is of vital importance to the balance of payments. In some years, as in 1971, tourism earned more income than exports. Cognizant of this fact, the government has been granting a high priority to the promotion of tourism, and numerous fiscal incentives exist to enlarge and improve tourist facilities.

The number of people visiting Mexico increases constantly; in 1971 some 2.3 million tourists arrived, in 1972 this figure rose to 2.9 million, and in 1973 an estimated 3.4 million people visited the country. More than 80 percent of the total came from the United States. In addition to the tourists, who are defined as persons visiting the country for more than three days, there are vast numbers of what are termed border crossers, or persons who spend a short time in the cities and towns just below the United States border. These persons shop, eat, and go sightseeing without the need of a tourist card and thus do not enter the statistics; however, it was known that over 30 million such border crossers visited the city of Tijuana alone in 1973.

The income from tourism and border crossing has an economic impact in all the border cities and in Mexico City, Acapulco, Taxco, Guadalajara, Monterrey, and Cuernavaca. The gross income from tourism, including border business, was estimated at nearly US$1.9 billion in 1973. This was partially offset by the spending of Mexican tourists abroad, but net earnings from tourism were believed to be about US$1 billion. Direct employment generated by the tourist industry in 1972 was about 320,000 workers, not counting those engaged in making handicrafts to be sold to tourists as souvenirs. In the beginning of 1973 there were 163,000 hotel rooms in the country, about one-third of which met the standards of sophisticated international travelers. The rest catered to middle and lower income tourists and to the vast number of Mexican families who travel on vacation. In some areas domestic tourism accounts for a large share of the industry; 65 percent of the tourism in the state of Jalisco, where the city of Guadalajara is located, is said to be generated by domestic vacationers.

Related to tourist receipts, but not counted as part of them, are the expenditures of the thousands of foreigners who have retired to Mexico on pensions and social security. The country has been very successful in attracting these persons, most of whom are United States citizens. A special immigrant status is accorded them—that of retired income holder, which permits them to reside in the country and to make investments in Mexican securities but not to engage in lucrative employment.

Several government agencies are involved in stimulating the tourist industry, and in 1974 the Interministerial Executive Commission on Tourism was created to coordinate the activities of all the agencies. The National Fund for Tourism was also established in that year, taking over the functions of a previous promotional entity, to develop the infrastructure of major tourist complexes, including land development, water, power, roads, and airports, and to supervise the privately built hotels through strict zoning regulations. The Mexican Tourist Council maintains offices in several United States cities and helps arrange group tours in addition to giving out individual tourist cards. A large number of international organizations hold their conventions in Mexico; over 400 international conventions were held in 1971. The United States joined with Mexico in 1974 in an experimental project to encourage European tourists to visit both countries during the same tour. Mexico and the Organization of American States jointly operate the Inter-American Tourism Training Center in Mexico City to train tourist personnel from the other Latin American countries.

TRANSPORTATION

In spite of extensive mountainous terrain Mexico has one of the most comprehensive transportation networks of any country in Latin America (see fig. 3). Although suffering some deficiencies, the railroad and highway systems link all economically important areas to the capital and to the major seaports and connect with the United States at twelve border cities. Air transport serves most population centers with either scheduled or nonscheduled service. Less attention has been paid to shipping because so much of the foreign trade is overland (with the United States).

Roads and highways have undergone rapid expansion and in 1972 served about 40 percent of the national territory. A government survey indicated that road transportation is used almost exclusively for both passengers and freight up to distances of about 160 miles; for trips over that distance rail and air transportation start to predominate. The highway system is an intricate network of federal, state, and local roads almost all of which are suitable for year-round use except for some rural dirt roads. Total highway mileage in 1972 was nearly 78,000, over 25,000 miles of which were paved, most of the balance being of all-weather surfaces. About 21,000 miles of highways including toll roads were under federal jurisdiction, an equal amount was designated as state highways, and the balance were local roads.

Federal highways are those that are entirely built and maintained by the federal government. All actual highway construction is done by contractors, but all maintenance work is done by government personnel. The highway contracting business has become a highly competitive field, and there are over 700 private engineering firms specializing in road construction. Not only are federal roads built to meet domestic needs, but many are designed to encourage the flow of United States tourists. Three major federal highway projects were the 1,154-mile Baja California Dorsal Highway, also known as the Transpeninsula Highway, going from Tijuana on the United States border to Cabo San Lucas at the southern tip of the peninsula; the 1,700-mile Trans-Mexico Highway paralleling the United States border from Tijuana to Matamoros on the Gulf of Mexico; and the 1,800-mile Pacific Coast Highway from Tijuana to Tapachula on the Guatemala border. The Baja California Dorsal Highway opened in 1973, and an estimated 2 million vehicles traversed it during the first year of operation, a figure that Mexican authorities had not expected to be reached until 1979, and taxing existing facilities for motorists but augering economic growth for the southern portion of the peninsula.

State highways are built and maintained by state highway boards, but 50 percent of their cost is borne by the federal government, which must approve all state highway construction plans. The greatest increase in road mileage has been in local roads, which are opening up hitherto isolated communities and lowering the cost of transporting agricultural products from farm to market. There are three categories of local roads, differentiated by the method of financing. So-called tripartite roads are local roads that are planned and built by the federal government, construction costs being split three ways among the federal and state governments and either municipalities or those private persons who benefit from the road. Once constructed, tripartite roads are transferred to the state highway boards for full maintenance costs. Rural roads are the designation given to local roads linking small villages to the nearest main road. Rural roads are planned, built, and financed entirely by the federal government, but their maintenance is the responsibility of the town. Finally, there is the category of hand-labor roads, which are low-standard rural roads built entirely by hand laborers from nearby communities, who are paid by the federal government in a combination of cash, food, and medicines. Over 300,000 local laborers were utilized in this program during 1973, and its popularity caused the government to believe that 500,000 people could be accommodated in 1974.

In 1972 about 2.15 million vehicles were registered in Mexico; their number had been increasing at a rate of about 9 percent annually. More than 554,000 were trucks, and over 34,500 were buses. Most of the trucks are owned by small independent haulers who are given permits by either federal or state authorities to operate between certain cities and towns and only along fixed routes. Government regulations also set freight rates, but there is much rate cutting among truckers, and many of them are said to operate with expired permits or with no permission at all.

The Mexican railroad system is in general an integrated net of six different lines, most of whose trackage is standard gauge. Five of the railroads are owned by the government, and the sixth, the Western

Railroad of Mexico (Ferrocarril Occidental de México), is a private short line operating in the state of Sinaloa and offering only freight services. The two largest railroads, the National Railways of Mexico (Ferrocarriles Nacionales de México) and the Pacific Railroad (Ferrocarril de Pacífico) are autonomous government agencies under a common management. The other three government lines, the Chihuahua-to-Pacific Railroad (Ferrocarril de Chihuahua al Pacífico), the Sonora-Baja California Railroad (Ferrocarril Sonora-Baja California), and the United Railroads of the Southeast (Ferrocarriles Unidos del Sureste), are directly part of the Ministry of Communications and Transport.

The total length of the railroad system in 1973 was about 14,700 miles. Most of the more than 1,050 locomotives were diesel, but nearly 20 percent required replacement because of obsolescence. More than 26,500 freight cars of all kinds and around 2,000 passenger cars were also in service. The National Railways of Mexico operated about 70 percent of the total trackage and carried about 80 percent of total freight and passenger traffic. The railroad connects with the United States at such cities as Ciudad Juárez, Laredo, Piedras Negras, Reynosa, and Matamoros and with Central America via Guatemala. Passengers can switch and continue traveling in either direction with a minimum of difficulty. The Chihuahua-to-Pacific Railroad was the most difficult line to construct, taking fifty-eight years to cross the rugged Sierra Madre Occidental mountains; it also connects with the United States at Ojinaga, across from Presidio, Texas.

The government railroads suffer continual deficits; in 1973 the overall deficit was 1.9 billion pesos (12.5 pesos equal US$1). Freight rates generally are fair and generate profits, but passenger fares were deliberately kept low as a social measure for a fifteen-year period ending in 1974. More than 40 million passengers are transported annually. The deficits incurred by passenger service more than wiped out revenues generated by freight operations. The wage bill was also very high; the government railroads employed over 83,000 people in 1974 in addition to paying pensions to 24,000 retired workers. After reevaluating its railroad policy, the government decreed higher passenger and freight rates commencing in August 1974 in hopes of making the railroads self-supporting. An equipment modernization program was also started to improve efficiency of operations.

Most of the railroad freight traffic consists of minerals—25 percent of the total—nonperishable products, forestry products, and heavy industrial materials. Perishable products and valuable industrial merchandise have been taken over by other means of transportation. In 1974, the government began to study the possibility of constructing an electrified rapid rail service across the Isthmus of Tehuantepec connecting the Pacific port of Salina Cruz with the gulf port of Coatzacoalcos as an alternative route between Europe and Asia for valuable cargo then transiting the Panama Canal. In addition to the new railroad line, both seaports would have to be enlarged to accommodate large ships for containerized cargoes.

Aviation came early to Mexico. Several Mexican pilots are recognized as being among the early aviation pioneers, flying long before World War I. Among the foremost was Juan Pablo Aldasoro, who built the first airplane in Mexico in 1909. Air postal service was inaugurated in 1917, and scheduled commercial airlines date from the 1920s. Topography that delayed road construction was the most important factor in the growth of domestic aviation. The government has been constantly constructing and improving airfields in order to help unite the distinct regions of the country, and by 1974 there were few population centers of any consequence that were not served on either a scheduled or a nonscheduled basis. There were 29,000 miles of air routes in the country in that year.

There were over 1,200 airfields and airstrips in 1974; 200 were government owned, and the remainder were privately operated. Twenty-nine of the airports could accommodate long- and medium-range jet aircraft, thirty-one could handle short-range aircraft, and the large balance have facilities only for light, single-engine aircraft. Nine of the airports accounted for 75 percent of total passenger traffic in the early 1970s: Acapulco, Guadalajara, La Paz, Mazatlán, Mérida, Mexico City, Monterrey, Puerto Vallarta, and Tijuana. Under the terms of the long-range National Airport Plan, developed in the mid-1960s, seventy-five airports are to be improved and modernized. The Mexico City International Airport, obsolete after twenty years of use, was to be used only for domestic traffic, and a new international airport was under construction forty miles north of the city.

In the early 1970s there were seventy-seven domestic airlines, but two of them dominated the industry. The largest was Air Mexico (Aeroméxico), formerly named Aeronaves de México. It was owned 100 percent by the federal government and provided both domestic and international service. The other was Mexican Aviation (Mexicana de Aviación), which had 10-percent government ownership. It operates mainly domestically but also flies to a few cities in the United States. Near bankruptcy in 1967, it later became profitable under conservative management by doubling its routes without a concomitant increase in its payroll. The rest of the airlines are either small feeder airlines operating only regionally or nonscheduled airlines, including air taxis. The commercial airlines operated a total of about 240 aircraft of all types, and an additional 2,200 civil aircraft were owned by corporations and private persons. Government agencies owned about 240 aircraft for official use. Twenty-seven foreign airlines provide international service to and from Mexico.

Port facilities have grown less rapidly, but the government was placing greater emphasis on shipping in the 1970s, and major improvements were planned or already under way. The country has more than fifty ports;

thirty-six of them are deepwater ports, but none has a good natural harbor. The dredging of some harbors is inadequate, cargo-handling facilities at some ports are underequipped, the financial management of the ports is not coordinated, and administrative responsibility is disseminated among twelve government and private agencies; nevertheless, port conditions are considered generally satisfactory. In an attempt to tighten up port administration the government began in 1972 to place port operations under the jurisdiction of the General Directorate of Port Operations, a dependency of the Ministry of the Navy. Five of the seaports are free ports and will remain under the jurisdiction of the Ministry of Finance and Public Credit. A yearlong study of the twelve largest seaports was finished in 1972 to determine their dredging requirements for the next twenty years.

Five of the ports handle 80 percent of total tonnage: Tampico, Veracruz, Guayamas, Mazatlán, and Manzanillo. Tampico primarily handles petroleum and petroleum products because a major oil refinery is located nearby. It is also important as an outlet for mineral exports. Veracruz is the major general cargo port, most of its imports being destined for Mexico City. Guaymas is the most important port on the Pacific, but its large capacity is not fully utilized because the extra trip around the peninsula of Baja California makes it less attractive for some shippers than other Pacific ports. Other seaports are Coatzacoalcos on the Gulf Coast and Acapulco on the Pacific.

Mexican merchant marine vessels totaled over 650,000 gross registered tons in 1973. The major portion, 350,000 tons, consisted of twenty oil tankers belonging to Mexican Petroleum (Petróleos Mexicanos—PEMEX), which mainly served Mexican seaports and seldom made overseas trips. The Mexican Maritime Transportation Company (Transportación Marítima Mexicana—TMM), partially owned by the government, had thirty-three oceangoing vessels. TMM had two subsidiaries, the Mexican Pacific Line (Linea Mexicana de Pacífico), which operated eight vessels out of Pacific ports, and Anáhuac Maritime Transports (Transportes Marítimas Anáhuac), which maintained irregular coastal services between Mexican and United States ports. Mexico hopes that growth of its merchant marine will be stimulated by the LAFTA Water Transportation Agreement, effective May 28, 1974, which reserves all freight going between members to vessels belonging to any of them.

Coastal shipping has gained some importance, carrying almost as much cargo as does ocean shipping and more passengers. In 1971, for example, coastal ships handled over 10.6 million tons of freight, and 13 million tons were carried as international freight. Coastal vessels work up and down the gulf and Pacific ports, and ferries operate between the peninsula of Baja California and the mainland and between the Yucatán Peninsula and the offshore islands. Tampico, Salina Cruz, Coatzacoalcos, and Tuxpan are the major coastal shipping ports. Most inland rivers are shallow;

there are only an estimated 2,000 miles of navigable inland waterways. A state-owned company was created in 1970 to provide service on the Grijalva, San Pedro, Tonalá, and Usumacinta rivers, all in the south of the country.

The growth of the cities has caused serious urban congestion—particularly in and around the Federal District. The automobile is the main cause of congestion. One government study of downtown Mexico City revealed that, although 56 percent of the vehicles going in and out of the center were cars, they carried only 13 percent of total passengers whereas buses, constituting only 11 percent of the vehicles, carried 52 percent of the passengers. A surprising 14 percent of the people walked to work, and taxis, trucks, and streetcars, including a subway, carried the balance.

The bus situation in Mexico City is chaotic. All buses are privately owned and are given permits to operate on specific routes, each route having its own internal administration. The route administrator collects all fares from the drivers, deducts salaries of the drivers and other costs, and then turns the balance over to the owners. There are no time schedules and no transfer system. Drivers race one another in order to pick up as many fares as possible, and a new fare must be paid each time a passenger changes buses at connecting routes. Sometimes drivers take alternate streets that are not on their assigned routes. Buses on each route are either first- or second-class and have different fares for each category. The licenses to operate along a route are usually passed on within a family by inheritance and are seldom sold to outsiders.

Trolleys still operate in Mexico City, Veracruz, and some other cities. Most trolleys are ancient vehicles purchased from defunct trolley companies in other countries. They are slow and frequently break down, but they provide an inexpensive means of urban transportation for the very poor. In Mexico City they are operated by a municipal company. Taxis are numerous and generally inexpensive; some are permitted to charge a higher rate and to operate from stands near major hotels provided that the driver speaks at least one foreign language. One unusual kind of taxi is the *pesero; peseros* ply between fixed points and are permitted to pick up and discharge passengers anywhere along the route for a one-peso fare. A twenty-six-mile-long subway system, called the Metro, was in operation in Mexico City in 1974, serving forty-eight stations and transporting about 1.5 million people daily. A similar subway system was under construction in Guadalajara in late 1974.

TELECOMMUNICATIONS

Mexico is considered to have the best telecommunication system in Latin America. Most of the systems are government operated. There were about 1.89 million telephones in the country in 1973, and about 97 percent of the service was provided by Mexican Telephones (Teléfonos de México—TELMEX). Although TELMEX is government operated, it has about 150,000 private shareholders, who hold a minority share of the company. TELMEX has been carrying out a long-range extension program designed to increase the number of telephones in service to about 4 million by 1980. About fifty cities have direct dialing systems, and about 1,700 other towns and cities have manual operations. Some of the larger cities are connected directly to the United States and Canadian telephone systems. Microwave telephone connections exist between the large cities and many of the smaller Mexican towns and to all Central American capitals.

The telegraphic, radiotelegraphic, and telephonic networks are integrated. Land telegraph lines cover more than 92,000 miles, and many of the lines have been relocated along highways in order to reduce maintenance costs and long interruptions of service. Mexico enjoys worldwide satellite communication by means of a ground station located at Tulancingo in the state of Hidalgo. The ground station was the first one built in a Latin American country and is one of the largest in the world.

The postal system is comprehensive and provides all classes of service between some 5,100 post offices in the country. Delays started to occur in the late 1960s, however, and many businesses resorted to messengers to deliver important mail. In 1973 the government started to mechanize postal operations in order to speed up service and prevent further deterioration.

SECTION IV. NATIONAL SECURITY

CHAPTER 16

PUBLIC ORDER AND INTERNAL SECURITY

Most Mexicans are inclined to place law and order above civil rights; being imprisoned is, however, not always viewed with a social stigma or contempt because many of Mexico's heroes and revered leaders were confined at one time or another. But there is a fear, especially among older citizens, of a return to the violence that followed the 1910 Revolution (see ch. 3).

The country has a strong family orientation focused on the authority of the father and extends the image of the father figure to the president and other high government officials. People are expected to obey rules and those in positions of authority, although in turn individual rights are not supposed to be abused by those authorities (see ch. 5).

The largest part of the workload of the federal courts consists of *amparo* actions, legal devices that are designed to protect individuals and ensure procedural fairness whenever administrative or legislative actions or laws threaten constitutionally guaranteed rights. Pending the outcome of an *amparo* procedure, an adverse administrative or judicial decision is noneffective. The right to file *amparo* suits is exercised quite liberally by Mexicans at all levels of society.

The legal power of the federal government tends to be substantially greater than that of the states. The Constitution requires the states to enforce federal laws, and the states are also required to follow the federal penal codes in establishing their own codes. Nevertheless, literal transfer has not been effected or required, and differences persist. For example, although capital punishment is prohibited in the federal code, not all states have abolished the death penalty.

Prisons are generally overcrowded, and prisoners have little to occupy their time, particularly in cities experiencing a large influx of rural migrants. In 1974 an estimated 54,000 people were in all kinds of prisons and jails, either serving sentences or awaiting the conclusion of their trials on felony charges. A substantial number of people were also serving time for misdemeanors, many because they could not afford to pay fines instead. The maximum sentence that can be imposed for minor infractions is fifteen days.

At any given time there are apt to be several hundred aliens imprisoned. These are mainly young middle-class youths, generally from the

United States but including Canadians and Europeans, who have run afoul of the strict Mexican laws on drugs and narcotics. In mid-1974 more than 500 United States citizens were among aliens being held.

Popular sentiment among Mexicans fosters fear of their own system of justice but, according to Mexican penologists, legal proceedings are generally fair and impartial. Of all persons brought to trial during the forty-year period ending in 1969, about 49 percent were convicted and sentenced to prison terms. The percentage of convictions ranged from a high of nearly 71 percent of persons charged with homicide to lows of 42 percent for rape and 34 percent for abuse of confidence, a charge covering such crimes as embezzlement, misuse of trust funds, or using private information for personal gain. Police actions have been more open to criticism than have decisions of the courts, but the police image was being improved through better training and use of more scientific laboratory equipment.

Threats to the internal security of the nation during the late 1960s and early 1970s stemmed mainly from massive antigovernment student demonstrations and isolated guerrilla and terrorist activities by both leftist and rightist groups unhappy with governmental economic and political policies. Condemned for their activities by most segments of the media and society as being contrary to the goals of the revolution, the terrorist bands were being methodically sought out and their members either killed or captured by combined police and military action (see ch. 17).

LEGAL SYSTEM

There are separate criminal codes and codes of criminal procedure for the Federal District and the individual states. The laws for the Federal District are also applicable to territories but, when the remaining territories of Baja California Sur and Quintana Roo became states in late 1974, it was assumed that they would adopt their own codes and procedures. Because portions of the codes for the Federal District and the territories are applicable nationwide in some circumstances, they are sometimes referred to as federal codes although, strictly speaking, they are not.

The federal criminal code in effect in 1974 dated from 1931 with later amendments. It went far to modernize previous law, eliminating such remnants from earlier codes as special privileges for certain social groups. Juvenile delinquency was singled out for special attention, and new provisions were made for controlling traffic in narcotics and dealing with corruption, pandering, and espionage. Crimes are broadly categorized: those against persons, those against property, those against the state, those against public morals, and those against public health.

Capital punishment was prohibited by the 1931 federal penal code and, although the Constitution permits the death penalty for parricide, abduction, and highway robbery, it does not require that the penalty be imposed. Kidnapping, depending upon the form, calls for no less than five years and no more than thirty years in prison plus a fine. Various forms of assault are specified, each with a different sentence, and homicide is treated in accordance with presumed motive. Severe penalties are imposed upon those who are charged with violation of constitutional guaranties of persons. They range from fines to lengthy imprisonment. Individual rights cannot ordinarily be suspended but may under special circumstances be set aside temporarily. Those circumstances are contained in Article 29 of the Constitution and are detailed in the Law of Social Dissolution enacted in 1941, whereby the executive can suspend individual rights. Such rights were first suspended from June 2, 1942, until the end of World War II in 1945; since the war the law has been used only in cases of violent riots or strikes.

As one of the most advanced of the developing countries, Mexico has experienced a growing need to deal with more sophisticated crimes, such as fraud or embezzlement, and amendments to the penal code have reflected this need. Mexico grants political and diplomatic asylum. Aliens may not be deported without judicial determination, although the president may issue a deportation order if deemed necessary for public safety. Mexican nationals may not be extradited by foreign countries unless they have been naturalized citizens for less than two years or unless there is a specific treaty between Mexico and the requesting nation. Persons must be extradited from one Mexican state to another if the penalty for the alleged crime is at least one month in prison.

The most distinctive feature of the Mexican legal system is the writ of *amparo*, which has no exact English equivalent although it is similar to a writ of habeas corpus and other legal doctrines, such as injunctions (see ch. 9). It has broad scope, protecting individual rights and effecting restitution. The *amparo* is considered Mexico's contribution to jurisprudence. It has been adopted in part by several other Latin American countries, and some of its provisions have been included in Article 8 of the United Nations Universal Declaration of Human Rights.

The *amparo* doctrine was introduced more than a century ago. It stems from the Yucatán Constitution of 1841 and was incorporated on a national basis in the 1847 Reform Act (Acta de Reformas). Made more explicit in the 1857 Constitution, it was additionally detailed in the 1917 Constitution and in the laws of *amparo* published since then. An *amparo* may be sought by any citizen for the redress of an infringement of his civil rights, or it may be brought by a governmental authority claiming infringement upon its jurisdiction by another authority. The *amparo* may be brought by an individual against the act of any official, tribunal, police officer, legislature, or bureaucrat. *Amparo* proceedings are usually in writing but on occasion may be presented orally. A writ of *amparo* is issued only by a federal judge unless no federal judge can be located and an emergency exists; in that case state judges are empowered to issue the writ.

Writs of *amparo* take one of three forms—direct, indirect, and constitutional. A direct *amparo* is brought against a judgment of any court or administrative tribunal and seeks a reversal of the decision based upon a denial of due process or misapplication of the law to the facts in the particular case. Indirect *amparos* are used either against actions, or to force actions by nonjudicial authorities, such as police or government employees. Such *amparos* closely resemble a writ of habeas corpus, a writ of mandamus, or an injunction. The most interesting form of *amparo* is the constitutional *amparo*, also called *amparo* against the laws. It permits individuals to enjoin the enforcement of a law against them on the grounds of a defect in the law. It does not attack the basic constitutionality of the law itself, however; if the decision is in favor of the plaintiff, it is applicable only to the person or persons who are parties to the suit. No class action suits are permissible, and each person aggrieved by a law must file a separate *amparo* for redress, as the defective law remains valid until corrected by the legislature. Judicial precedents, however, may be established by the Supreme Court of Justice by deciding the same way in similar cases a number of times. When established, judicial precedents become binding upon all courts and administrative tribunals, and the precedent in effect nullifies the law under attack.

A flood of *amparo* suits in the early 1970s was causing a backlog in all courts. Many cases of little or no legal merit were being introduced by litigants who knew that the case would be dragged on before being resolved against them. In 1974 the president of the Supreme Court of Justice stated that such an abuse of the right of *amparo* was preferable to imposing limitations on the introduction of *amparo* suits. He contended that the solution to the growing backlog was to establish additional courts and judgeships.

Another distinctive feature of the Mexican legal system dating back to the nineteenth century is the Public Ministry. This institution exists at the federal, state, and municipal levels. At the federal level the Public Ministry is headed by the attorney general. The Public Ministry performs both investigative and accusative functions. Agents of the Public Ministry are called *fiscales* because one of their principal functions in the early days of the country was the enforcement of fiscal levies by attorneys of the crown. Later they were charged with suppressing crime and initiating procedures in criminal cases. Investigative agents of the Public Ministry are usually assigned to police stations to determine the facts in a given case, but they may be assigned to such places as hospital emergency rooms to investigate cases of persons suffering trauma as the result of an assault. Investigative agents turn their findings over to a central office where a determination is made whether to bring an accusation before a competent authority. The representatives of the Public Ministry then become public prosecutors acting as the accusing party in criminal cases.

336

The public prosecutor's duties are spelled out in procedural codes: he is the watchman over prompt and just administration of justice; he must represent the public but at the same time act to preserve the accused person's rights; and if the rights of the accused are violated, he must see that reparations are made. Public prosecutors are independent of the courts and may not be censured or instructed by the judiciary. Since the Public Ministry represents the public, the office may not be sued by defendants found innocent who believe themselves to have been unjustly accused. Other functions of the Public Ministry are to serve as legal adviser to the executive branch and to command the Judicial Police.

LAW ENFORCEMENT AGENCIES

Police forces exist on the federal, state, and municipal levels and, owing to lack of integration, their activities are frequently duplicated. The main federal police force is called the General Directorate of Police and Traffic (Dirección General de Policía y Transito), which is part of the Ministry of Government. The Directorate is divided into several divisions: preventive police, riot police, auxiliary police, traffic police, and the division of investigation, which was formerly called the Secret Service. The total personnel of the General Directorate of Police and Traffic in 1974 was about 22,000, including 500 policewomen.

Also on the federal level are the Judicial Police, who are under the command of the Public Ministry and are empowered to give orders to other police, such as the traffic police, to assist them in an emergency. The Federal Highway Police, numbering about 1,400, patrol along federally designated highways; their main function is to investigate automobile accidents. Other government ministries and agencies maintain small police forces; these include the Ministry of Public Health, the National Railways of Mexico, the Ministry of Hydraulic Resources, and Mexican Petroleum.

Each of the states and the Federal District has its own police force. In addition to enforcing state laws in their jurisdictions, the police forces also assist in enforcing federal laws. Large cities have special units, such as the park police or foreign language police. At the level of the small municipality, police work is less intricate, and the pace is generally slow except on weekends when rural dwellers come to town for church, marketing, celebration, and drinking that may lead to fighting and violence. Municipal police forces in state capitals are under the command of state governors.

There are numerous small private police forces. Many banks, department stores, hotels, and other similar institutions pay the salaries of uniformed or plainclothes guards and investigators, assigned to them by the commercial police branch of the police force. The Bank of Mexico, for example, maintains a private police force of over 120 armed men. The police assigned to department stores sometimes arrest debtors and keep them locked up in the store jail until their families pay the debt.

Legislative action has not been able to change this practice.

In large urban areas such as Mexico City there are several police precincts each having jurisdiction over a specified part of the city. The precinct is called a police delegation, and a typical delegation has between 170 and 200 preventive police assigned to it. The delegation is under the command of a *comandante*, usually an officer with the rank of first captain (all police ranks correspond to military ranks). Lesser officers, usually lieutenants, are in charge of each eight-hour shift and are assisted by first sergeants, second sergeants, and corporals. Most of the men operate out of the command headquarters, which is called a *comandancia*, but part of the company is stationed at fixed points throughout the police delegation, usually at small two-man kiosks accessible to the public. Assisting the preventive police are auxiliary police who patrol the streets on the night shift; auxiliary police operate only during the night shift. Agents of the Public Ministry assigned to the delegation have their offices at the *comandancia*, and many of the *comandancias* also have a first aid post on the premises with a doctor or medical technician in attendance. Most of the *comandancias* have two kinds of cells; large communal cells, usually without bunks, hold numerous persons sentenced for misdemeanors (separate communal cells exist for men and women), and small cells with bunks are used to confine persons under arrest for felonies during the preliminary investigation.

Police units in all jurisdictions tend to be short of funds and equipment and to be undermanned. Securing a sufficient number of police has been a long-standing problem, as the shortage of training resources also has been. The General Directorate of Police and Traffic operates a police academy where intensive courses of from four to six months are given to selected new recruits and advanced training is provided for some officers and men. The Federal Highway Police unit runs a small training school for its personnel. The Technical Institute of the Public Ministry was authorized by the Ministry of Public Education in 1974 to give graduate-level courses in criminology that would be recognized as valid throughout the country.

A few states have academies for state police; the best are those in the states of Nuevo León, Jalisco, and México. Courses at state academies usually last for four months. News media have criticized the overall lack of police training and the methods of selecting police officers. In cities and other localities where no formal training courses are provided, the media point out that policemen are appointed upon the recommendation of local politicians. Many persons without any background in crime prevention obtain police jobs.

Numerous cases of police incompetence, immorality, and corruption were brought to the attention of the public during 1974 by the government as part of its effort to halt such abuses. In August 1974 the General Directorate of Police and Traffic announced that its Board of Honor had just completed investigation of nearly 800 cases in which police had been charged with criminal acts and that all but fifty-five of those charged had been convicted. The announcement was in response to an editorial in a leading newspaper reporting that the frequency of cited cases of police immorality and brutality was becoming alarming and that sixty-eight innocent people had been killed by police over the past twenty months.

COURTS AND PROCEDURES

The judiciary consists of federal, state, and municipal courts and several special tribunals. Federal courts have jurisdiction in both civil and criminal cases arising from enforcement of federal laws; in all admiralty cases; in cases where the federal government is a party; in suits between states; in suits between a state and the federal government; in suits between a state and private citizens residing in another state; in all constitutional cases; in all cases involving diplomatic or consular personnel; in cases involving state laws that infringe upon the authority of the federal government; and in all cases where federal laws infringe upon states' rights.

The federal judiciary consists of the Supreme Court of Justice, circuit courts, district courts, and courts of the Federal District. The Supreme Court of Justice—the highest court—is composed of twenty-one justices called ministers and five auxiliary judges, all appointed by the president of the republic with the consent of the Senate. Supreme court members serve until they resign or retire, at age seventy or earlier because of illness. One of the members serves as president of the court. Justices may meet in plenary session, though ordinarily the work flow takes place through four chambers dealing respectively with criminal, civil, administrative, and labor matters. Five justices are assigned to each chamber. A fifth chamber, called the auxiliary chamber and composed of the five auxiliary judges, takes the overload from any chamber and hears any kind of case.

Most supreme court justices have been successful lawyers for at least five years and have served previously as judges of lower federal courts. There have been very few political appointments to the supreme court, and it enjoys a good reputation in the country. All lower federal court judges are appointed by the supreme court, which makes for a relatively independent judiciary. In addition to having both original and appellate jurisdiction in legal matters, Article 97 of the Constitution grants the court the right to initiate an investigation into the conduct of any federal judge, any electoral violations, or any acts that might be a violation of individual guaranties. This power, however, has been used sparingly.

Circuit courts are the next level of federal courts; there were ten such courts in 1974 with a total of fifty-seven judges. Circuit court judges are appointed by the supreme court for a term of six years; most of them have previously served as district judges. In *amparo* actions and in original jurisdiction cases not reserved to the supreme court, circuit judges sit as a full court, and the court is called a collegiate circuit court. In all other cases the judges sit individually, hearing appeals from lower courts, and the court is referred to as a unitary circuit court. In *amparo* cases the circuit court is the final court of appeal unless the case is that of a constitutional *amparo;* unless Article 22, which prohibits extreme or unusual punishment, is alleged; or unless the conflict is between the federal and a state government.

District courts are the courts of first instance in most matters relating to federal law. There were fifty-six district courts in 1974, each composed of one judge, although supernumerary judges may be appointed by the supreme court if the case load so warrants. Eight of the district courts were located in the Federal District; three specialized in criminal law cases, three handled administrative and labor law cases, and two dealt only with civil cases. The president of the supreme court announced in late 1974 that ten additional district courts would be created in the country, one of which would be another criminal court for the Federal District. Most district court judges have been supreme court clerks before their appointment.

The highest courts in the Federal District and any territory are known as superior courts. Their members are appointed by the president of the republic with the consent of the Chamber of Deputies. They in turn appoint judges to the courts of first instance and other lower courts within their jurisdiction. Although the Constitution provides that the only special tribunals will be those of the armed forces, a number of exceptions have been made. These special tribunals are part not of the judiciary but rather of the executive branch. Decisions of the tribunals, however, may be appealed through the federal judiciary system. Among the special tribunals are juvenile tribunals, tax courts, electoral commissions, and various labor boards. Federal juvenile tribunals in the Federal District functioned under the jurisdiction of the Ministry of Government, and a 1965 constitutional amendment called for all states to establish similar institutions under state governments. In late 1974 a new law was passed calling for the creation of guardianship councils to replace federal juvenile tribunals. These tribunals deal with minors under eighteen years of age. Children under the age of twelve who are brought before these tribunals may be sent to foster homes or ordered to be kept under close watch by their families. If over twelve years of age, the minor may be sent to a correctional institute or school. The juvenile tribunals consist of three judges, who are usually educators, doctors (particularly psychologists), and lawyers.

The Constitution allows the states to organize their own judiciaries, and they generally follow the pattern set in the Federal District. Members of state superior courts, sometimes popularly referred to as state supreme courts, are usually appointed by the governors with the consent of the state legislatures. They in turn appoint members of lower state courts. State courts generally have both original and appellate jurisdiction over state laws, although in cases between private parties the plaintiff may, if he chooses, use state courts rather than federal courts in matters involving the application of federal laws. Municipalities, depending on size, may have both judges of first instance and justices of the peace. The justices of the peace, also called police judges, are assigned to police *comandancias* and generally work around the clock in shifts, fining, jailing, or releasing persons accused of misdemeanors. If jailed they may be punished with not more than fifteen days of incarceration.

Related to the judiciary are the public notaries. In Mexico they are civil law professionals whose records and documents are prima facie evidence of the legal acts and proceedings contained therein. Public notaries are appointed on the basis of competitive examinations and they serve until death or resignation. Theirs is a full-time occupation. The number of public notaries in the country is fixed by law and varies with the population. They may perform marriages, officiate at other civil proceedings, and draft wills, deeds, property transfers, and articles of incorporation. They may also be asked to act in cases requiring arbitration.

All public notaries and federal and state judges must be lawyers. Since 1929 lawyers have been known as *licenciados en derecho;* before that time they were called *abogados.* A degree and a license plus registration in the Central Registry of Professionals are required in order to practice law. A preparatory school degree is required for entrance to law school (see ch. 6). Courses last five years; the first two years consist of political science and economics courses, and the last three years cover legal subjects. A student must then write a thesis to obtain his degree. After the degree is granted, a six-month clerkship is required before the license is issued. Mexican lawyers do not have to belong to a bar association, although the prestigious Mexican Bar Association, founded in 1760, is the oldest in the Western Hemisphere.

Except where an offender has been apprehended in flagrante delicto, when anyone can make an arrest, and in cases where the need is vital and no judicial authority is available, arrest and detention must be preceded by the issuance of a warrant by a competent judicial authority. For a warrant to be issued, there must be reasonable cause to presume the guilt of the accused, and the crime must be one for which imprisonment would be the penalty. The accused is entitled to legal counsel from the moment of arrest, and detention cannot exceed three days without a formal order of commitment with the specification of the charges. The accused must be set free on demand while awaiting trial if he can pay bail, which is set according to his status and the gravity of the offense. Bail may not be permitted if the offense carries a prison term of more than five years as a penalty.

Detention awaiting trial must be as short as possible, and in no case may the pretrial detention period exceed the maximum prison term applicable to the crime. The place of detention while awaiting trial must be separate from the place for serving sentences, but in practice this requirement is often not met. The offender must be represented by legal counsel during the trial. If he does not already have an attorney, he may choose one from a list presented by the court; if he fails to choose one of these, the court will appoint a public defender.

Trials are usually open, unless their subject matter is regarded as injurious to public morals, order, or security. Jury trials are not usual in Mexico, but they may be held if the crime is against the safety of the nation or if the penalty involved exceeds one year in prison. If the court orders a jury trial, the jurors called must serve if they are literate and are residents of the place where the offense was committed. Before, during, and after the trial the accused has legal recourse to the *amparo*, through which he can secure relief from false arrest, improper procedure, false witness, extreme or unusual punishment, or any other violation of his rights, including those relating to procedural fairness.

PENAL SYSTEM

The Constitution and succeeding laws require that the federal and state governments organize penal systems on the basis of labor, training, and education as a means of effecting the social readjustment of the prisoner. The institutions have been slowly moving toward that goal. If a penal facility in any of the states is inadequate or if there are none, the state may make an agreement with the federal government for a prisoner to serve his sentence in a federal establishment. Most of the states had signed such agreements by 1974. The responsibility for overseeing and regulating the serving of sentences resides with the penal administration rather than with the courts. Although most state prisons are headed by civilian employees, the wardens of the federal prisons in 1974 were military officers, who were introducing military discipline.

The most important federal prison is the Penitentiary for the Sentenced, located in the Federal District. Built in 1958 to house 1,000 prisoners, it has rather elaborate facilities—schools, medical clinics, a library, an auditorium, athletic fields, and shops where trades are taught. Before 1958 most federal prisoners were kept in the Lecumberri Penitentiary, also located in the Federal District. An old building, constructed in 1910, it had a distasteful reputation. When the new penitentiary was constructed, Lecumberri was renamed the Preventive Jail of the City and has been used since then to house only persons detained and awaiting trial. It is overcrowded; the original capacity was 800 prisoners, but over 3,700 were incarcerated in late 1974, and the number has seldom dropped below 3,000. The Federal District also contained four centers of reclusion, each with a capacity for 250 people; the Women's Jail, housing 600 women who are either awaiting trial or serving sentences; three smaller jails serving three of the delegations of the Federal District; and thirteen jails located in the various *coman-dancias*.

The practice of transporting criminals to a federal penal colony has been in existence since 1860, when vagrants and pickpockets were sent to Yucatán to work on farms. In 1974 there were only two such colonies in use, and they were defended on the grounds that they represent colonies of regeneration rather than places of punishment. Only the most dangerous criminals or those serving the longest sentences are sent to penal colonies. The most famous colony is located on the María Islands about seventy miles offshore in the Pacific Ocean. During the 1960s the penal colony averaged about 1,000 prisoners and an equal number of government employees and families of both. Married prisoners are permitted to have their families with them and are provided with thatched houses. Unmarried prisoners live in dormitories, but all can move freely on the main island except that they must attend roll call twice daily. Prisoners work to develop the island's resources and labor in lime quarries, salt fields, lumber mills, on sisal plantations, and in miscellaneous workshops or engage in other agricultural pursuits such as cattle raising. During the decade of the 1960s only three crimes were committed at the penal colony, and no one attempted to escape.

All states have state penitentiaries. Some are old and overcrowded; some are modern and fairly large. Among the best state prisons are those in Sonora, Durango, Michoacán, Jalisco, and México. The penitentiary in the state of México was built in 1967 and has a capacity of 800 people. It has a large staff including psychologists, psychiatrists, and doctors. Every prisoner either works, in shops or on the prison farm, or goes to school. Municipal jails, numbering about 2,350 in the early 1970s, hold persons under sentence, on trial, or under investigation for federal, state, or local crimes. Some municipal jails are fairly large; the one at Tampico, for example, houses 400 people and has separate sections for women and younger defendants. Most municipal jails, however, are of primitive construction and have little or no correctional activities; some of them lack toilet and water facilities. In some villages the prisoners work on such public projects as street cleaning and gardening. Escape attempts are rare from the village and small town jails, and in some cases the prisoners' families are permitted to move in with them.

Life in Mexican prisons and jails generally is less disciplined than in other countries. In many state prisons, especially in rural areas where most of the prisoners tend to be peasants rather than professionals or hardened criminals, informality is common and the prisoners themselves help the warden and guards maintain order. Little friction exists between prisoners and guards, and the guards frequently perform small services for the prisoners in exchange for tips. Prisoners with skills are permitted to make items and sell them; others provide such services as barbering or shoe repairing. Prisoners who can afford it are permitted to furnish their quarters with items brought from the outside, and they sometimes hire other inmates to work as personal servants. Some prisons permit commercial workshops to operate on the premises; space is leased by private firms who engage prisoners to work in their shops.

Prisoners are usually on their own during the day to work, loaf, or engage in sports as most penal institutions do not have full-time organized activities. Sports-minded inmates usually form intramural leagues for baseball and soccer with daily games. Idle inmates frequently fight among themselves; fighting is the most prevalent reason for being sent to solitary confinement. Families and relatives are usually permitted to make visits twice a week. On Sundays, one of the days set aside for visits, prisons take on a festive air as entire families laden with food, clothing, and other gifts spend the day with the prisoners, freely roaming around the grounds. In women's prisons and in women's sections of state prisons, mothers are permitted to have small children with them at all times. Mexican penologists believe that the family visits and the children's residing with their mothers contribute to strong family ties and are in keeping with the role of the family in Mexican society (see ch. 5).

Male inmates of Mexican penal institutions have the right to conjugal visits. Wives are usually permitted to spend up to two hours every two weeks alone with their husbands in their cells, compartments, or in special rooms. Some prisons permit wives to spend the entire night with their husbands, and in others girl friends or prostitutes are allowed to visit single inmates. No conjugal visits, however, are permitted women inmates. Only brothers or fathers may be alone with women prisoners.

During the mid-1960s the penitentiary in the state of México experimented with a program whereby prisoners who were nearing the end of their sentences—usually three months away—were taken on unguarded field trips to places of historic and cultural interest. Some of the more exemplary prisoners were permitted to spend weekends with their families. As of mid-1974 not one convict who participated in those programs had escaped, and the experiment had been adopted by nineteen other prisons.

INCIDENCE OF CRIME

Complete data are not available on all infractions of the law, although crime stories receive almost excessive press coverage daily. Data on minor infractions usually are not compiled, and numbers of unreported crimes must be presumed to exist as well as crimes that do not go through formal judicial procedures, such as those dealt with by private police. A study by a Mexican sociologist of all available crime statistics for a forty-year period through the late 1960s indicated that three kinds of crimes accounted for over 71 percent of the total reported. The leading crime was injury—assault and battery—against persons, almost 32 percent of the total. Robbery accounted for over one-fourth, and homicides for almost 15 percent. Sex-related crimes accounted for nearly 6 percent; property damage, for nearly 3 percent; fraud, for over 2 percent; abuse of confidence (embezzlement), for under 2 percent; and all other crimes for the balance.

Among the miscellaneous crimes was rustling; as late as 1974 cases of cattle rustling were still being reported throughout the countryside. One band apprehended in the state of Morelos confessed to having stolen over 2,000 head before being caught. Kidnappings were increasingly reported during the late 1960s and early 1970s; some of the kidnappings were believed to be the work of dissident political groups, but many others were carried out by common criminals, who took advantage of the citizens' fears of terrorists.

Drug abuse and narcotics traffic were other kinds of crimes increasingly reported in the early 1970s and were of growing concern to the government. In 1974 a leading newspaper claimed that the use of drugs by Mexicans had increased 300 percent in a five-year period, and another source stated that the number of users had increased 350 percent between 1966 and 1971 and that the amount of drugs being consumed had increased by 500 percent. The most popular narcotics were marijuana, opium, cocaine, peyote, and mushrooms that produce hallucinatory effects. A 1973 confidential survey of about 700 students at various secondary schools indicated that 15 percent had admitted taking drugs and 3 percent admitted to being constant users. Not only was the government concerned with the increasing use of drugs by Mexicans, but it was disturbed by the effect that narcotics smuggling into the United States would have upon relations with its northern neighbor. The government was stepping up both its internal efforts and its cooperation with United States authorities to stem the flow of narcotics. Mexican police and army elements annually destroy thousands of acres of marijuana and opium poppies, but farmers still manage to grow them in isolated mountainous areas or even scattered throughout their cornfields. Shoot-outs between police and narcotics pushers are frequently reported in the press. From 1971 through 1974 the police had arrested over 10,000 people accused of trafficking in illegal narcotics.

Crimes committed by juveniles generally occur in urban areas; there is almost no juvenile crime reported in rural areas or small towns. There are many youth gangs in Mexico City and other urban areas. Almost every secondary school has a problem with student gangs. A survey of over 2,000 students in various preparatory schools in the Federal District in 1973 revealed that nearly one-third had been robbed by other students and 7 percent admitted that they had joined school gangs for self-protection. A favorite tactic of young gangs is to follow a person seen leaving a bank and rob him. Professional thieves specialize in house burglary, which is usually committed by a small band skilled in opening or breaking locks. The second most prevalent kind of crime committed by the professional thief is picking pockets, either alone or with the help of an associate who distracts the victim. Pickpockets find it easy to operate in crowded buses and churches and at the numerous fiestas and public ceremonies where crowds gather.

In rural areas the most prevalent crimes are injuries or homicides caused by passionate outbursts, usually the result of inebriation. Violent crimes by peasants are related to land disputes, water rights, family feuds, disputes between rival villages, and insults to women. The weapon is usually a machete, knife, or dagger. Few rural crimes occur during the daytime, when men are working their fields; most take place during the period between 6:00 P.M. and 6:00 A.M. and on weekends and holidays.

Automobile accidents are classified as crimes according to the penal code, and drivers are usually held by the police. Although 24,000 serious automobile accidents were reported in 1970 on federally designated highways alone, the accident rate in Mexico is not high. In 1969, the last year for which comparative statistics were available, for example, the automotive accident rate in Mexico was forty-nine per 1,000 vehicles, the second lowest rate in the Western Hemisphere. The death rate from motor vehicle accidents is also extremely low, only two people per 1,000 vehicles.

Two areas of the country where large numbers of crime were being reported in the 1970s were the state of Guerrero and the city of Netzahualcóyotl, which is part of the metropolitan area of the Federal District. The rising incidence of crime in Guerrero, especially in the famous resort city of Acapulco, stimulated a two-hour general work stoppage in mid-September 1974 that was followed by a demonstration by several thousand irate citizens clamoring for stronger police action. Reacting to the demands of the citizenry, police and soldiers conducted street shakedowns of suspicious persons and car searches to confiscate weapons. In Netzahualcóyotl, the majority of whose inhabitants were poor, armed gangs roamed the streets at will. One report indicated that Netzahualcóyotl had only one policeman per 7,600 inhabitants, and most crimes went unpunished.

Of every 100 people charged with a crime during the forty-year period ending in 1969, ninety-two were men, and eight were women. Assault, robbery, and homicide were the leading crimes committed by men; women committed a variety of crimes, none predominating. Prostitution per se is not illegal in Mexico, but soliciting clients is a crime. Prostitutes must be registered and periodically examined. If found diseased, they are sent to hospitals for treatment. Many prostitutes, however, do not register and practice their profession illegally.

INTERNAL SECURITY

Organized violence shows a more local or regional than national pattern. No group had been able to elicit more than a local response to its urgings, partly owing to the lack of national issues; partly to the distrust of outside leadership, particularly on the part of Indian communities; partly to the reluctance of local leaders to subordinate their authority to a unified command; and partly to the absence of any person with sufficient charisma to weld the various factions into a national movement. None of the guerrilla groups had very specific goals; all issued such general statements as "better distribution of wealth," "unfinished Revolution of 1910," "challenge to a new middle class that is subverting the revolution's goals," or "bureaucrats who are traitors to the revolution."

Organized threats to internal security have stemmed mainly from two sources, student demonstrations and guerrilla activities. In 1974 a ban on student protests dating from 1971 was still in effect and being enforced, perhaps indicating the government's continuing concern over a latent source of discontent that at one time was serious enough to force the government to call upon the military to assist the police in maintaining order. Although the government did not publicly state its concern, guerrilla and terrorist activities were sufficient to cause the government to increase the internal mobility of the military in 1974 (see ch. 17). Spontaneous riots by hundreds of persons protesting the rising cost of living occurred in Oaxaca in October 1974, leaving two dead and 200 arrested. Several smaller, economically generated, spontaneous protests also occurred in cities around the country during 1974, in connection with labor's demand for a general wage increase (see ch. 13). Such more or less unorganized disorders had seldom occurred before.

Student demonstrations, once strong enough to threaten the holding of the 1968 Olympic Games in Mexico City, have not been serious enough since June 1971 to cause concern to the government (see ch. 10). There have been frequent short outbursts of violence at many universities, but the issues were local, and the protests were not directed against the government. Before 1968 almost all student demonstrations had been small, nonpolitical, generally peaceful, and designed to correct local grievances. The police seldom had to be called upon, and the issues failed to arouse students at other universities.

In mid-1968 a minor clash between rival preparatory school students in Mexico City was mishandled by authorities, who called in the riot police. University leaders at the National Polytechnical Institute received permission a few days later to protest the overreaction by the police in handling the secondary students. Their meeting coincided with a celebration of the anniversary of the Cuban revolution by the more politically minded students from the National Autonomous University of Mexico. The two groups intermingled; the protesters soon got out of hand, and they were dispersed by the riot police. During the next few days students from all universities and secondary schools went into the streets; on July 29, 1968, the army was called out to quell disturbances, and numerous members of the Mexican Communist Party were arrested as a precautionary measure. The student demonstrations did not stop despite the presence of the troops in the city. Throughout August 1968 as many as 400,000 people of different ideologies participated in continual antigovernment protests. By September the army had arrested several thousand students; and on October 2, 1968, soldiers, unable to control the situation, finally fired upon the demonstrators, killing dozens. That action effectively ended the 1968 student protest.

In June 1971 an estimated 10,000 students in Mexico City demonstrated, protesting numerous grievances but chiefly the continued imprisonment of students arrested during the 1968 demonstrations. The protests were broken up by the police and by large numbers of young men—calling themselves "the falcons"—who suddenly arrived on the scene armed with poles and clubs. The falcons were alleged by the media to be either thugs in the employ of the police or extreme rightists. Shots were fired, causing several deaths, and the government subsequently placed a ban upon any further student protests. A call by student leaders for an antigovernment demonstration in mid-1974 elicited almost no response, and political analysts were writing off the students as a further threat to internal security in the foreseeable future.

In contradistinction to the quiescence of the student movement, the activities of urban terrorists and rural guerrillas had not subsided by 1974, but they were not believed to pose any serious threat to the government (see ch. 10). The terrorists and guerrillas belonged to a number of small groups that acted independently. Two groups were fairly large and appeared to be better organized than the others. The various groups were not under any centralized command and did not coordinate their activities. Some of the groups had names; others appeared to be formed by disgruntled youths on an ad hoc basis to commit a few terrorist acts. Some crimes that the media played up as being perpetrated by terrorists are believed to have been committed by nonpolitical criminals. Some criminals have used the names of actual guerrilla groups to cover their activities. In mid-1974 about 300 people were in jails as a result of engaging in terrorist activities, but all had been charged as common criminals by the government.

Generally the various subversive groups have engaged in two kinds of crimes, kidnappings and bank robberies. In urban areas such as Monterrey and Guadalajara, many prominent businessmen are heavily guarded as a result of assaults and kidnappings that began in 1971. A curfew was in force for several months during 1974 in Guadalajara; an unanticipated result of the curfew was the decrease in common crimes. Wealthy persons or their relatives and some foreign diplomats have been kidnapped either to embarrass the government or to extract ransom. In what may have been the most audacious kidnapping, the father-in-law of President Luis Echeverría was kidnapped in Guadalajara in late August 1974 and held for more than a week before being released unharmed. In Guerrero the leading gubernatorial candidate was kidnapped by rural guerrillas in mid-1974 and held for a lengthy period of time until freed by army troops after a gun battle with the rebels in September. The United States consul general and the honorary British consul in Guadalajara were kidnapped during 1973 and freed after ransoms were paid. Some kidnapped victims were not freed but were found dead by authorities.

Beginning in 1974, however, the guerrillas appeared to be taking a different approach; rather than engaging in kidnappings and bank robberies, they were ambushing police and setting off explosives in urban areas. During 1974 an estimated thirty policemen were killed in ambushes in various cities. In June 1974 several fires were started in government buildings in Oaxaca after telephone warnings by terrorists; bombs exploded in governmental buildings in Guadalajara in July 1974, and bombs were hurled at a newspaper building in Puebla in August 1974. On November 18, 1974, thirteen bombs exploded, almost simultaneously, at government buildings, political party headquarters, banks, and stores in Mexico City, Guadalajara, and Oaxaca.

Two groups appeared to be the strongest and to have attracted the most national attention. The 23 of September Communist League, named after the date of the first clash with army troops in Chihuahua and reportedly formed in Guadalajara from remnants of other groups, was operating in various urban areas and was believed to be closest to a national movement. In September 1974 more than thirty of that group's members were captured in Quintana Roo while picking up a load of armaments they had cached there, and two months earlier five of its leading members had been captured in Mexico City after a shoot-out with the police. In December 1974, however, the group claimed responsibility for robbing two banks in Mexico City and killing five policemen during the incidents.

The other group that commanded attention operated in rural areas of the state of Guerrero. Active since 1967, in 1974 the group called itself the Poor People's Party and was estimated to number between 250 and 500 people. Numerous terrorist acts had been credited to it, including sporadic clashes with the army that caused deaths on both sides but, since Guerrero has a long history of banditry, it was often difficult to differentiate between activities of outlaws and those of revolutionaries.

Among other groups involved in terrorist incidents was the Revolutionary Action Movement, which was led by a small group of students who were trained abroad and returned to Mexico to foment insurrection; most of its leaders were captured in 1971. The National Liberation Movement, active in Monterrey, committed numerous bank robberies until its headquarters was discovered by police in 1972. The Revolutionary Student Front was believed responsible for several bank robberies in the state of Jalisco, and the Revolutionary Front of Socialist Action was blamed for bank robberies in Aguascalientes. Several of the members of the latter group when captured claimed to be loosely associated with the guerrillas in Guerrero. Another group active in Guerrero was the Revolutionary Armed Forces; it has a separate women's command that admitted to being responsible for the kidnapping and murder of a wealthy woman in Acapulco in 1974.

Several small groups active in the states of Tabasco, Chiapas, and Chihuahua have never taken formal names, and captured members have denied any relationship to other terrorist groups. Other groups have surfaced intermittently as authors of several attacks, but their actions have not been dramatic. Some of these groups are: the Independent Popular Front; the National Revolutionary Civic Association; the People's Revolutionary Armed Vanguard; the Emiliano Zapata Peasant Brigade, allegedly linked to the 23 of September Communist League; the Leninist Spartacus League; the Workers Brigade of Armed Struggle; and the Armed Communist League. The Mexican Communist Party has had no apparent links to any terrorist organizations, and its membership in 1973 was estimated at fewer than 5,000 people, a result of a long history of internal leadership disputes.

In addition to the leftist guerrilla bands, at least two rightist terrorist groups were also active in the early 1970s. The Center of Armed Revolutionary Action had assaulted several government telegraph offices, and a group calling itself Sangre, which means blood, was reported to have killed numerous leftists in the state of Guerrero in 1974 in reaction to the activities of guerrillas operating in that state. Of some concern to Mexican authorities was the existence in the jungle areas near the Guatemalan border of an unknown number of Guatemalan guerrillas in hiding. Occasional firefights had taken place between the Guatemalan guerrillas and the Mexican police and army during the early 1970s, and the guerrillas had attacked a small civilian airstrip in 1972, destroying several aircraft and taking some equipment.

CHAPTER 17

THE ARMED FORCES

In the mid-1970s the armed forces played a deceptively inconspicuous part in the national scene. The army, larger than the air force and navy combined, was much smaller in relation to the national population than the armies of most other Latin American countries, and the budgets were far lower per capita than those of nearly all other countries in the region. Both manpower and budgets absorbed far smaller proportions of the national total than during the 1920s and 1930s when the army had been a key factor in politics and the presidents had been generals. The last of the generals to occupy the presidency had relinquished office in 1946, and since that time the number of senior military officers occupying cabinet posts, seats in the legislature, and state governorships steadily declined.

The role of the army in the mid-1970s, like the more limited supporting roles of the other armed services, was unusual in the sense that Mexico's geographical location and historical events had reduced the danger of armed invasion to a minimum. Military forces were used primarily to maintain internal order and in such civic action functions as roadbuilding and preventive medicine campaigns that made the presence of the central government favorably known in remote parts of the country. In the performance of these functions the army maintained a close relationship with the political party that had held the reins of government for nearly half a century.

The decline in overt political activity by the military since the late 1930s had been accompanied by a progressive increase in professionalism and an improvement in the conditions of service. Military schools were expanded, and pay raises and improvements in fringe benefits were frequent. The absence of a potential threat of invasion made it possible to devote a minimum of the limited budgets to tanks and guns and a maximum to the training and well-being of personnel. In the late 1960s and early 1970s officers were recruited largely from the middle and lower middle classes, but a considerable number were of working-class origin, and the enlisted personnel recruited were often illiterate peasants with little hope of finding good civilian jobs. Service life offered a fair degree of comfort, security, and the promise of upward social mobility.

The improvement in conditions of service has had the effect of identifying the interests of the military with those of the party in power. The sense of common interest has further been enhanced by the fact that the army was generally thought of as a national entity devoted to pursuit and preservation of the ideals and goals of a revolution that had been successfully institutionalized by the dominant party.

Although the basic relationship between the military and the central government in the mid-1970s was less one of identity of interests than one of interests kept carefully in balance, the armed forces were generally contented, and a majority of their leaders were dedicated to preservation of the political status quo. There had been a considerable increase in guerrilla insurgency and other forms of civil unrest during the late 1960s and 1970s, and a resurgence in military security activity was believed by some observers to have taken place. In the mid-1970s, however, there was no clear evidence that the military was seeking significant political influence.

ORGANIZATION

The Ministry of War and Marine, which had exercised control over the armed forces since the early independence period, was replaced in 1937 by the Ministry of Defense. Two years later, naval activities were placed under the independent Ministry of Marine. In addition to the navy the new ministry was made responsible for the merchant marine and other maritime functions, such as maritime works, dredging, lighthouses, and fisheries. The military air arm did not achieve significant status until World War II when, after undergoing several changes in organization and denomination, it became the Mexican air force in 1944. Although it does not possess separate ministerial status, it holds a quasi-autonomous position within the Ministry of Defense. Traditionally, the positions of minister of defense and minister of marine are occupied by generals and admirals. These officials under civilian presidents have not played the important policymaking roles that they sometimes were able to assume during the 1920s and 1930s.

The most recent published estimates available during the mid-1970s indicated that the army constituted about three-fourths of the armed forces strength of between 70,000 and 80,000 officers and men. During the 1960s the total increased at a rate estimated at slightly under 2 percent annually, as compared with a population growth rate of 3.5 percent.

In addition to being the oldest and largest of the armed services, the army has been the most visible and has played the most significant role in the country's development. The missions of the navy and the air force have been limited ones supporting that of the army. Their personnel systems, training programs, conditions of service, and roles in society have not differed materially from those of the senior service. In general, the navy and air force have supported political actions initiated by the army.

Army

The strength of the army declined from some 100,000 in 1920 to 50,000 in 1930 and remained at that level until about 1950. Small increases were reported during the 1950s and 1960s, and most recent estimates available in 1974 placed the number of officers and men on active duty at 54,000. Several of the estimates, however, fixed the number at 60,000 or 65,000. Estimates of the ratio of enlisted men to officers varied from six to one to twelve to one, and a considerable number or both officers and men were reported engaged in administrative desk activities.

In the late 1960s and early 1970s the major equipment was made up of medium tanks, armored cars, and howitzers. For the most part, firepower consisted of the arms carried by troops.

There were two infantry brigades, one of which was an elite presidential guard with a strength of about 4,000 men, one infantry group, about fifty independent infantry battalions, twenty mounted cavalry battalions, and one mechanized cavalry regiment. There were also artillery, antiaircraft, engineer, and other support units. Troops were garrisoned in the Federal District and in thirty-five military zones in a troop dispersal pattern established in 1924. There was a military zone for each of the twenty-nine states, the two then-existing territories, and one for the Federal District, except that there were two zones each for the states of Oaxaca, Guerrero, and Veracruz. The zone headquarters was usually, but not invariably, in the state capital.

Air Force

The strength of the air force was estimated in 1974 at 6,000 officers and men, as compared with about 5,000 during the mid-1960s. The register included an airborne brigade with a strength of about 1,800. Like the army, the air force is widely dispersed throughout the country.

During the early 1970s nearly half of the more than 200 aircraft were listed as combat planes, but many of these were not rated as combat ready. These consisted primarily of jet fighter-bombers, several years old. In addition to the combat-ready craft, a considerable number of training planes were capable of use for ground support or for reconnaissance missions. The bulk of the air fleet consisted of training planes, transports, and helicopters. Among the newest of the aircraft were helicopters and some small Avaran transport planes acquired from Israel in 1973.

Navy

Jane's Fighting Ships, 1972–73 credited the navy with a personnel complement of 11,600, including 2,300 officers. The service maintains a small air arm and seven companies of naval infantry, or marines. Estimates of naval strength during the 1950s and 1960s vary considerably, but the rate of growth of naval manpower during that time appears to have been greater than that of the other services.

The major naval schools and installations are located in Veracruz, the country's principal port, and there are four naval districts on each coast. The Atlantic district headquarters are located in Tampico, Tamaulipas; Veracruz, Veracruz; Ciudad del Carmen, Campeche; and Isla de Mujueres, Quintana Roo. Those on the Pacific are in Puerto Cortés, Baja California; Guaymas, Sonora; Manzanillo, Colima; and Icacos, Guerrero.

The largest naval vessels are two 2,100-ton destroyers, mounted with five-inch guns. They are capable of a flank speed of thirty-four knots and have a cruising range of 6,000 miles at fifteen knots. The fleet also includes two frigates, two gunboats, one small troop transport, and numerous fleet and escort minesweepers and coastal and river patrol boats. The twenty-five to thirty planes assigned to the fleet air arm include reconnaissance planes and helicopters. A training ship and a repair ship were commissioned, and twenty-one modern torpedo boats were on order from the United Kingdom in 1974.

The Mexican navy is unlikely to be required to perform minesweeping functions, but the minesweepers are suitable for coastal patrol duties. All vessels were acquired from the United States with the exception of the transport, which was built in Spain, and two patrol boats, which were built in Mexican shipyards.

Paramilitary Components

Every eighteen-year-old Mexican male is obligated to undergo one year of military training. In the early 1970s there were estimated to be about 250,000 young men engaged in this kind of service, as provided in the National Military Service Act of 1942. They are referred to as conscripts (*conscriptos*), but the terminology is misleading. These trainees are not conscripted into the army; their connection with the regular armed forces is limited to a few hours of training each Sunday morning under a junior army officer.

During this period the men march about a parade ground, a stadium or open field, or even on the street of the town or city. Rifles and uniforms are seldom issued. Conscripts completing the period of training remain in an active reserve until the age of thirty-eight, but this reserve component is a manpower pool rather than a trained cadre.

Little military competence is achieved; the program, however, costs the government almost nothing although the program has an importance that bears little relationship to national defense. It is above all a means of instilling a sense of being a part of discharging an obligation to the nation, which is a part of the revolutionary mystique.

Obligatory military service also has a highly practical use. The conscript completing his year of service is given a certificate of service called a *cartilla* (little card) that is afterward revised periodically by army officials to whom he must report each change of residence. It must be presented when applying for a passport or in connection with a variety of matters involving government action. It is a permanent identity card and a means by which the government assembles and keeps current a great deal of information concerning its adult male population. Because it is awarded for performance of a patriotic obligation, it is carried with pride.

The second paramilitary force is a rural militia organized loosely into rural guards or defense groups. In the early 1970s these groups had a total of about 80,000 mounted and 40,000 infantry members. They originated during the period of agrarian reform that followed the revolution, a time during which landowners resisted the division of hacienda lands and formed forces known as "white guards" to harass and panic the peasantry. Defense groups formed spontaneously and requested and received arms from the government as institutionalized equivalents of the posses of the southwestern United States. In the 1926 conflict between the state and the Roman Catholic Church, the defense groups sided with the state and served as guides and couriers for the army, a service that they performed admirably because of their intimate familiarity with the local terrain. In 1929 they were officially incorporated into the army under the name of Rural Defense Corps.

Until 1955 only *ejidatarios* (farmers working community land) were permitted to enroll in the defense groups. Later, some colonists and small farmers were admitted, but the units have been raised within the *ejidos* (see Glossary), whose local governments have remained basically responsible for the conduct of the unit.

Under terms of an extensive 1955 reorganization, rural guard units cannot be transferred from territory under their jurisdiction, and only on direct orders from the military zone commander may they take part in emergency action outside that territory. Members do not wear uniforms and are issued hand-me-down carbines of a make and caliber different from those in use by most regular units.

Guardsmen receive no pay but are eligible for medical care in the event of wounds or injuries suffered in the line of duty. Enlistment is for periods of three years and is open to men between the ages of eighteen and fifty. The basic unit, an eleven-man *peletón* (platoon), may be formed by any local organizer on petition to the minister of defense. The authority of these units originates with the Ministry of Defense, however, and they receive their orders through commissioned officers of the local military zone.

Guard units sometimes engage in operations against cattle thieves and drug dealers, but their most effective role in the maintenance of public order consists of service as guides and informers. When a civil disturbance occurs in a remote area, it first comes to the attention of the local guard unit, but line forces usually are called in to quiet it.

Prestige is attached to membership in the rural guards who represent the central government in the local community and who are of considerable value to it at little cost. Considerable trust is placed in this armed peasantry, and the risk to the central authority is minimal; the communal landholders of the *ejidos* have a limited title to their farms that itself depends on the stable power of the government in Mexico City. Guardsmen are so little known outside the *ejidos* that their existence is often ignored in summary statements concerning the Mexican armed forces, but they play a political as well as a tactical role of probably greater significance than that of the conscripts engaged in their year of compulsory paramilitary training.

BUDGETS AND EXPENDITURES

Armed forces budgets during most of the era that has followed World War II have been among the lowest in Latin America and have progressively declined, both in relation to the total Mexican population and in relation to the expenditures of the other countries of Latin America, a region of relatively low military expenditure. This had not always been the case, for in 1917 the military budget had amounted to 72 percent of the total allocated by the central government, and the proportion had remained above 60 percent until after 1921. Thereafter, it declined to 32 percent in 1930, to 21 percent in 1940, to 10 percent in 1950, and to 7 percent in 1956. It remained at approximately that level throughout the 1960s, and in 1972 it was reported at 7.4 percent of the total as compared, for example, with 33.6 percent for education. During 1974 the Latin American countries as a whole were estimated to be budgeting about 16 percent of their central government funds for defense purposes.

The precise budget data reported are often incorrectly interpreted, for many or most observers believe budgets and expenditures for defense to be the same as those for the armed forces. Since the establishment of the Ministry of Marine in 1939, however, naval budgets and expenditures have been reported separately under the allocations and expenditures of that ministry. During the 1960s and early 1970s the navy was assigned half or more of the budgets of the new ministry, which ranged from 2 to 4 percent of the national total.

In addition, the relationship between the amount of funds budgeted and the amount expended has been an unusual one. The overall totals of central government expenditures during the 1960s and early 1970s have exceeded budget allocations by as much as 50 percent (see ch. 13). During the years 1961 through 1971, however, defense expenditures averaged 5.6 percent of the total rather than the approximately 7 percent budgeted. The consistent annual shortfall suggests a particularly careful scrutiny on the part of civilian administrations over the manner in which the appropriated money is spent.

Although military budgets and expenditures have remained constant as proportions of national totals, these national totals have risen and actual amounts budgeted and expended by the military have risen correspondingly. According to a survey of Latin American defense expenditures based on constant 1970 prices, the level for Mexico rose irregularly from a base of 100 in 1961 to 178 in 1971. The rate of increase was eighth among the nineteen Latin American countries counted.

MISSION AND OPERATIONS

The Constitution of 1917 and organic statutes of the armed forces assign to the military responsibility for defending the sovereign independence of the country, maintaining the rule of its constitution and laws, and preserving internal order. This formal definition of responsibility is very similar to that of other countries of Latin America, but in Mexico the most significant of the responsibilities that make up the mission of the armed forces has proved to be the preservation of internal order.

Mexican as well as foreign observers have noted that the great size and power of the neighbor to the north makes effective preparation for resistance to armed invasion impossible and that the small size and limited power of the neighbor to the south makes preparation for defense unnecessary. There are no offshore territories in need of protection, and there is general awareness that armed invasion of Mexico by sea or air would be resisted by the United States. The regular disposition of Mexican army and air force units includes no particular concentration along land or sea frontiers.

There remains the theoretical possibility of invasion in the form of infiltration but, in practice, Mexican arms are employed for suppressing rural and urban guerrilla activity, riots and other forms of civil unrest, and in general for the preservation of public order. The army plays the leading part; the navy and air force assist by patrolling the coastlines and airspaces. The navy is concerned primarily with patrol functions that in other countries are performed by coast guards, and the air force mission supplements that of the army, of which it is a part. Air force transport planes give needed mobility to army units, and parachute units can quickly provide help in the preservation of order in remote rural localities.

All three services are frequently called upon to perform ceremonial functions, and as much as one-fourth of the combined strength of the army and air force is sometimes assembled for parades in Mexico City. Military units participate in activities of the Inter-American Geodetic Survey, and the navy's small fleet includes one oceanographic vessel. The army is responsible for the registration of firearms and is used extensively to control the illicit drug traffic; the administration of President Luís Echeverría placed some customs posts under the control of middle-grade army officers along the United States border.

In its preeminent role of preserving internal order, the army performs functions assigned primarily to the civilian police in other countries, and army personnel have been quoted as saying that the nature of their activities sometimes made them feel more like policemen than soldiers.

There is an interweaving of the activities of the two forces. The two frequently engage in joint operations, and in the Federal District there is a significant interlocking of organizations. Army officers serve regularly as chiefs of the judicial police, security police, district police, riot police, motorized police brigade, traffic police, and the federal penitentiary forces.

In rural parts of the country the dominance of the army in public order becomes a matter of practical expediency whenever the number of individuals involved in the disturbance places the incident beyond control of the small local police unit or when a search of wide areas is required, as in cases of cattle rustling (see ch. 13). In addition, it is the zone army commander rather than civilian authority who commands the paramilitary rural defense guards whose services are sometimes called upon (see Organization, this ch.). Moreover, the chain of command and communication linking the central government, the zone army commander, and the local army units is a more direct and effective one than that linking the central authority, the state governor, and the local police.

In urban localities the army has been called in to suppress civil disturbances of several kinds. The best known of these incidents, known as the "Tlatelolco Massacre," occurred on the eve of the 1968 Olympic Games, which were held in Mexico City, and involved students from the National Autonomous University of Mexico in a series of related incidents. An estimated 10,000 troops occupied the university campus at one point, and a riot at Tlatelolco resulted in numerous fatalities. Other student disturbances involving the use of troops occurred in the Federal District in 1957, in Morelia in 1966, in Hermosillo in 1967, and in Tlaxcala in 1973 (see ch. 16).

The army is also employed to supervise elections, to maintain order during electoral disorders, to prevent the collapse of local administrations, and to settle disputes between rival political factions. Troops were called in to settle a 1958–59 strike of railroad workers and to maintain order during the 1972 elections of petroleum workers in the Veracruz fields. In 1972 the army engaged in operations against Guatemalan guerrillas operating from or retreating into Mexican territory (see ch. 16).

In the countryside much of the army's activity has been directed against subversive and guerrilla activities, frequently involving kidnappings. The countermeasures have been quick and effective. In 1965 an attack on a garrison resulted in the death of the commanding officer and several soldiers and civilians. Within twenty-four hours troops and aircraft were on the scene. The attackers were efficiently hunted down, and their unit was destroyed.

During the late 1960s and early 1970s much of the rural disorder occurred in Guerrero, a state with a largely rural and widely dispersed population and a tortuous terrain that had been marked by unrest since colonial days. Between 300 and 500 guerrillas were estimated to be active in the state, most of them under the leadership of Lucio Cabañas, a former schoolteacher, who was killed in a shoot-out with troops late in 1974. On several occasions in this campaign the army demonstrated its capability for mobility by promptly assembling a substantial proportion of its total effective strength in the guerrilla zone. In 1974 its engagement in a firefight brought about the release of a senator after he had been held captive by Guerrero guerrillas for more than 100 days (see ch. 16).

Although Mexicans tend to assume a somewhat benevolent attitude toward internal guerrilla activities in other countries, the government has taken prompt action against such activities at home. The frequent use of the army rather than the police in many of these operations is attributed to the closer association of the army with the central government as well as to its greater tactical capacity. The ability of the army to act promptly and effectively against civil disorder, while maintaining a generally favorable public image, is largely attributable to its civic action program, which accomplishes numerous useful and welcome works in the countryside.

As early as 1921 some nineteen military labor battalions were organized for use in road construction, irrigation projects, and repairs of railroad systems and telegraph lines. Other civic action programs were initiated in later years, and the first organic law of the army and navy made civic action an official part of the army's mission; it prescribed the use of army personnel in works of a public character that bore some relationship to military needs. Civic action and related activities have been most numerous and most effective in isolated rural areas. During the 1960s and early 1970s they were of particular importance in the countryside of the states of Chihuahua, Guerrero, and Yucatán.

The army and occasionally the other services have been used in projects as diverse as the construction of schools and hospitals, reforestation, antimalarial services, distribution of food and water supplies, and disaster relief throughout the country, particularly in the rural villages of communal landholders. A large part of the funds of the Ministry of Defense are expended directly or indirectly on civic action projects. The Ministry of Defense is not hesitant to call attention to this important phase of the army's mission. An attractive forty-seven-page pamphlet with photographs in color describing its civic action accomplishments was in wide circulation in 1974.

POLITICAL ROLE

The military journal *Revista del Ejercito* has publicized the slogan Militar, Si; Militarista, No ("Military, Yes; Militarist, No") as descriptive of the present-day Mexican army. The slogan is valid to the extent that the army has developed a fairly high degree of professionalism during a period in which its overt political activity and influence have progressively declined. The overt political role had become so inconspicuous during the late 1960s and early 1970s that casual observers commenting on the army's political role simply described it as nonpolitical. Others, looking more thoroughly into the relationship between the military and the civilian political administration, were not always in full agreement on their findings, but there was a consensus that the army continued to be of important political significance in its performance of what has been termed its residual political role.

During the 1920s and 1930s the presidents of Mexico had been revolutionary generals, and ranking military officers filled a large proportion of party positions. The last of the general presidents left office in 1946, and that date is sometimes pointed to as marking the end of military domination of politics (see Social Composition, Recruitment, and Training, this ch.).

In reality the decline in military domination was a gradual process over a considerable period of time; 1946 was a significant date only in a symbolic sense. By that time the overt political clout of the military was already heavily eroded. President Lázaro Cárdenas (1934–40) had been a general of the revolution, but his program of social reform did not meet with the approval of some of his old military comrades. President Manuel Avila Camacho (1940–46) had been a general but not a general of the revolution. A major during that period, he had been made brigadier at a later date. The difference was an important one to the revolutionary elite who opposed his election.

Cárdenas did much to professionalize the army. He retired many senior officers and reduced the number of troop units, however, and during his term of office the number of military men holding important appointive and elective political offices declined substantially. The downward trend in political activity by the military continued under Camacho, who used the World War II emergency as a means for compelling the army to devote itself exclusively to its military functions. Military budgets were pared sharply, and in 1945 more than 500 revolutionary generals were retired.

After the Revolution of 1910 the first political movements were led by revolutionary generals. A new generation of civilian politicians emerged, however, and some civilians were among the leaders of a government party formed in 1929 as a fusion of local political machines dominated for the most part by military figures. This group, which became the Institutional Revolutionary Party (Partido Revolucionario Institucional—PRI) in 1946, was still in power in the mid-1970s (see ch. 10). In 1938 President Cárdenas officially made the army one of the four sectors constituting the government party, a move protested by some of his advisers as giving it too important a political role; Cárdenas is said to have replied that, on the contrary, he was reducing its status to one in four.

Soon after taking office, President Camacho terminated the army's formal position within the party, and thereafter it was never again an institutional part of the political mechanism, although it has since that time been represented in the "popular" sector. Army influence, however, did not end immediately. In 1946, when the first of the civilian presidents assumed office, a general was named to head the government party, which at that time was reconstituted as the PRI. Generals continued to head the party during most of the years up to 1970. The trend that commenced in the late 1920s was one in which an originally dominant military was led gradually to transfer its power to a government political party that was increasingly under civilian domination.

In this process, politically ambitious officers were co-opted individually by directing their ambitions into the party where they could achieve political goals through acceptability to it rather than as leaders of a military power bloc. During the 1950s and 1960s, however, the number of military men holding political office progressively declined. In 1948 some fifteen officers were governors of states, for example, but by 1969 only two state governors were military men. Moreover, *Who's Who in Mexican Government*, published in 1969, which listed the biographies of 245 important political figures, included only eighteen military men. In the late 1960s and early 1970s, however, officers continued to influence political decisions by acting in staff and advisory capacities, and it has been common policy of high-ranking government officials and party leaders to recruit officers as their personal aides.

In converting the military from a possible adversary to a client and partner, the government has created an atmosphere favorable to the performance by the military of what is sometimes called its residual political role. This role involves primarily the preservation of internal order, but it is one in which at some point the function shifts from simple police action against disturbances to one of action against political manifestations hostile to the government.

In performance of this residual role the thirty-five army zone commands are of particular significance, for it is these units that must suppress rural guerrilla and subversive activity and perform other police actions necessary to the preservation of order in the countryside (see Mission and Operations, this ch.). Moreover, the zone commanders serve as important sources of interest articulation and political intelligence; they are well-equipped to inform the central government concerning local political opinion, and the peasant leader discontented with the treatment given him by the local government can appeal to the central government through the zone commander.

The general commanding the zone is named directly by the president on the recommendation of the minister of defense. Within the zone, the general is the direct representative of the president through the minister and, when necessary, a counterpoise to the state governor. He is useful as an adviser to the local civilian administration, for his troop units and the paramilitary rural guards under his command in the farm villages are often better sources of information than the civilian police. In the event of a grave political crisis, he may take over the governor's office until a replacement is named.

A zone commander usually is transferred after a maximum of three or four years in his post. The rotation of officer assignments is standard procedure in most of the world's military organizations, but the periodic transfers of generals commanding Mexico's military zones may be at least in part a precautionary move to avoid the development of too close a sense of identification with the locality or too substantial a local political following.

The function of suppressing political actions that are hostile to the central government is supplemented by the useful and welcome civic action projects performed by the usually cheerful and cooperative zone troops. Civic action assignments are performed in all parts of the country and by all armed services. They are most numerous and most effective, however, in the remote countryside where they have the dual effects of contributing to social and economic progress and of reminding rural people of the power and the usefulness of the government in Mexico City (see Mission and Operations, this ch.).

In the large cities the army is less concerned with civic action and political intelligence matters and more concerned with matters directly related to the preservation of order. In general, its residual political role is one of providing a force of proven loyalty and of sufficient strength to provide effective support to the government when necessary. The ability of the government to rely on army officers for the performance of such functions as the heading of important police units, the replacement of state governors, and the supervision of elections is of first importance.

Despite the erosion of the army's overt political role, one academic observer in 1972 expressed the opinion that it remained of greater political significance than any of the opposition parties. Another observer pointed out that the peaceful erosion of the overt political role was made possible by the long domination of the political scene by a single party; under a two-party or multiparty rule it would have been unlikely.

During the 1960s and the early 1970s the balance of positions and interests that existed between the civilian government and the PRI on the one hand and the army and related services on the other hand was not so stable that both sides did not feel in need of reassurance. Government and party officials repeatedly lauded the military for its high degree of professionalism, for its respect for civil authority, and for its civic action accomplishments. Service spokesmen regularly announced their continued loyalty to and support of the Constitution and the government. At the same time, the two sides exchanged ritual assurances of continued devotion to the goals of the revolution.

In the early 1970s some observers believed that a pronounced increase in internal disorder since the late 1960s had been accompanied by a resurgence in political activity by the military. Other observers contended that the military remained unswervingly loyal to the government and that it was more in the public eye simply because the rise in unrest gave it more work to do.

During the early 1970s the formerly dominant political role of the army had become an inconspicuous one, and it had become common practice for some observers to describe it as nonpolitical. Others chose to describe the part played as a residual one based on the army's ability to maintain internal order and the government's confidence in the army's continuing support of its policies and programs. The existing political system relied heavily on the army's performance of its residual political role, and any effort to reduce or expand this role would be conducive to political instability.

SOCIAL COMPOSITION, RECRUITMENT, AND TRAINING

The Mexican armies of the nineteenth century were frequently havens for thugs and bandits, and the army of the revolutionary period was a people's force constituted from guerilla bands. The revolutionary generals became a political elite, and some later amassed considerable fortunes, but many of the officers as well as the men of the revolution came from peasant or working-class backgrounds.

With the growth of the army professionalism during the postrevolutionary years the social position of the officer tended to rise, and in the mid-1970s he was generally recognized as having middle-class status. His origin, however, was often somewhat lower. Among the 1955 graduates of the military academy who in 1974 were at the important midcareer point in their army service, the sons of military men were the most numerous. Sons of shopkeepers and white-collar workers ranked next; and the sons of manual workers, in fourth place, outnumbered the sons of all professionals combined. There was also a scattering of officers whose parents had been peasants.

Most of those entering the military academy had come from urban homes, particularly from Mexico City, where the military academy was located, where the annual academy entrance examinations were held, and where the well-dressed and well-trained army contingents were most frequently seen. Most of the remainder came from Central Mexico and the South Pacific. A moderate number came from the North, but only a few had lived in the North Pacific and the Gulf Coast regions.

The motivation of the midcareer officers in seeking an army career had seldom involved the romantic ideals of military service. Rather, it had been the prospect of a free education, upward social mobility, and considerable security (see Conditions of Service, this ch.). Soaring university enrollments since the 1950s have reflected the desire of children of the more prosperous families for a university education leading to a civilian career in one of the professions. The officers who had entered the academy because of an intrinsic desire for a service career were for the most part sons of army personnel, and the considerable number of these second-generation army men indicated the emergence of and increasingly self-perpetuating officer corps.

The individual enlisting for a three-year period of army service has been traditionally a peasant or a city dweller unable to find work because of insufficient schooling. In the late 1960s and early 1970s industrial employers were increasingly demanding a minimum of a completed primary education.

In the villages it has been common practice to encourage or compel delinquent youths to enter the army, and the often illiterate and undisciplined recruits seem to be unpromising material. The improving conditions of service, however, have made it possible to fill the ranks with generally contented and satisfactory volunteers without resorting to conscription. Reenlistments are frequent, and many who attain a noncommissioned officer grade remain in the army until retirement. Most of the recruits are of mestizo blood, but a considerable minority are Indians, and barracks life and in-service schooling have combined to mix cultures and bring the recruits into the mainstream of national life. Upon discharge, soldiers of rural origin seldom return to their native villages.

The oldest and largest of the service schools for the training of officers is the military academy, formally called the Heroic Military College (Heróico Colegio Militar). Established in 1822, the academy had occupied various sites in the Federal District and in 1974 was located in the Potopla section. Construction of a new campus in the San Pedro Martír section had commenced, however, and was scheduled for completion in 1976. It was to have accommodations for over 2,000 cadets—considerably more than the 1974 enrollment.

The naval academy, formally known as the Heroic Naval Military School (Heróica Escuela Naval Militar), is in Veracruz, where the bulk of the country's naval facilities are located. It includes a program for the schooling of marine corps officers and a small school of naval aviation. The air academy, the School of Military Aviation (Escuela de Aviación Militar), is located at Zapopan in the state of Jalisco.

During the late 1960s and early 1970s the graduating classes numbered 300 to 350 at the military academy, sixty to seventy at the air academy, and fifty to sixty at the naval academy. Recruitment of candidates for the schools represents no problem; in 1965 applicants to the military and naval academies outnumbered admissions by proportions of six to one and fifteen to one, respectively.

The military academy was largely neglected during the nineteenth century and was allocated sufficient funds for effective operation only after the Revolution of 1910 at a time when army professionalization was on the rise and numerical strength was being reduced. By the early 1970s an estimated 90 percent of all officers on active duty in the armed forces were graduates of service academies.

Applicants for admission to the military academy must be Mexican by birth, single, between the ages of sixteen and twenty-one, and at least five feet three inches in height. A substantial matriculation fee (500 pesos in 1970) is charged. Applicants must present documentary evidence of proficiency in language and mathematics and must have completed the three-year secondary or secondary-technical level or equivalent basic course of study at the middle school level (see ch. 6). They must also complete physical, psychological, and aptitude tests held in the Federal District. Candidates are selected on the basis of their documentary evidence and test scores.

The course of study is four years in duration and corresponds to the curriculum in the upper cycle of middle school and the first year or two at the university level. The curriculum includes military, liberal arts, and general studies, as well as physical education. During the first year a common program is studied; during the remaining years the cadet engages in specialized study for entry to the infantry, cavalry, artillery, combat engineers, or administration. Upon graduation, he is commissioned as a second lieutenant in the appropriate arm or service.

Officers continue professional training throughout their careers. In particular, schools for cavalry, infantry, and artillery are grouped together in the Center for Application and Perfection of the Armed Forces Officers (Centro de Aplicación y Perfeccionamiento para Oficiales de las Armas). Courses are of one year's duration. The air and naval academies provide postgraduate training for commissioned personnel.

Numerous other small facilities provide specialized in-service officer training. A graduate school for engineers was established the same year as the military academy. Other schools, a majority established in the 1930s, include units for officers who did not attend the military academy and a school of military communications. The army provides its own training for medical personnel and operates highly regarded schools for doctors and nurses. In addition, Mexican officers are frequently sent abroad for specialized or advanced study, a majority to the United States and a few to other Latin American countries and Europe. During the mid-1960s about sixty officers were posted abroad annually for further professional schooling.

At the apex of the graduate school program for the army and air force is the Higher War College (Escuela Superior de Guerra). This institution offers courses in the basic areas of advanced arms and services, command and general staff, and higher war studies. Higher War College attendance is important to the progress of the officer's career, and a large and increasing proportion of those attaining general officer rank have completed the command and general staff course of study.

In the mid-1970s a three-year curriculum was designed to prepare combat officers for command staff duties and officers of the supporting services for technical staff duties. In a separate course, air officers were trained for corresponding assignments. A one-year course in higher war studies was open to selected civilians as well as to officers of the rank of lieutenant colonel and above and the equivalent in all services and offered nonmilitary as well as military courses in a program of study of matters related to national security.

In 1974 the armed services did not maintain basic training camps for enlisted recruits, but a wide variety of in-service programs was available to enlisted personnel as well as to officers. The 1936 organic legislation for the army and navy made primary schooling obligatory for enlisted men and noncommissioned officers who had not completed this cycle of education. Because so large a proportion of the recruits were illiterate, however, the principal thrust of the program was directed toward literacy training. In 1962 some 31,000 soldiers and dependents became literate, and in 1965 the army's literacy effort was redefined as part of the national program. Army literacy centers were to give instruction not only to service personnel and their dependents but also to illiterate civilians, particularly in rural localities.

Once assigned to a unit the enlisted man commences to receive on-the-job instruction, and there are opportunities to attend technical schools operated by the services and their branches. Particular emphasis is placed on the training of noncommissioned officers who are periodically able to attend courses at different levels to further their career development. In addition, schools at the various posts provide training in which enlisted personnel can acquire skills in agriculture and industry that will facilitate employment in civilian life. A small number of first sergeants who have completed the noncommissioned officers' school are offered a special course of training at the military academy that leads to a second lieutenant's commission.

The progressive expansion and intensification of educational programs and the increase of professionalism in the armed services during the middle decades of the twentieth century have resulted in the appearance of a large number of professional journals, a majority published monthly or every two months. *Armas: Revista Militar* is a magazine of general interest to service personnel. *Revista del Ejercito, Revista General de la Armada de México,* and *Revista del Heróico Colegio Militar* are the professional journals of the army, the navy, and the military academy, respectively. Among the other publications are journals concerned with military justice, the cavalry, the army communications service, and matters of interest to retired officers.

CONDITIONS OF SERVICE

Rank Structure and Promotions

The rank structure in army commissioned officer grades in Mexico corresponds to that in the United States, except that the rank of captain is divided into two levels and lieutenant general is the highest rank designated (see table 14). The army system applies also to the air force, and in the navy equivalent ranks range to vice admiral.

The army register does not include the rank of warrant officer; the senior enlisted man is the first sergeant. Following him in order are second sergeant, corporal, private first class, and private. The first and

Table 14. Mexico, Army Commissioned Officer Grades

Mexican Grade	United States Equivalent Rank .
General de división	Lieutenant General
General de brigada	Major General
General brigadier	Brigadier General
Coronel	Colonel
Teniente coronel	Lieutenant Colonel
Mayor	Major
Capitán primero (first captain) .... ⎫ Capitán segundo (second captain) .... ⎭	Captain
Teniente	First Lieutenant
Subteniente	Second Lieutenant

Source: Adapted from Lyle N. McAlister, Anthony P. Maingot, and Robert A. Potash, *The Military in Latin American Sociopolitical Evolution: Four Case Studies,* Washington, 1970, p. 225.

second naval ranks are warrant officer and chief petty officer. Following them in order are petty officer first and second class, corporal (an army rank also used in the navy), and seaman.

The graduate of the military academy customarily serves two years as a second lieutenant and three years as a first lieutenant. Service during this five-year period is obligatory. Time served in grade for subsequent promotions varies, and quality of performance becomes a factor. Officers promoted through the grade of lieutenant colonel must pass a medical examination and a computer-graded academic examination. Finally, physical fitness must be demonstrated by an 8.7-mile (fourteen-kilometer) march by infantrymen or a course on horseback for cavalrymen. In 1974 some 3,000 officers in the grades of second lieutenant through lieutenant colonel were examined for promotion.

Promotions to the ranks of colonel and above require Senate confirmation and are limited by the number of vacancies available. Voluntary retirement is possible after twenty years of service, and compulsory retirement for age in grade varies from forty-eight years of age for first lieutenants to sixty-five years of age for lieutenant generals. Dismissals and demotions in rank must be under process of military law.

Liberal retention and promotion policies are followed, and there are relatively large numbers of armed forces officers in the upper echelons of service registers, particularly at the general and flag officer levels. In 1974 there were an estimated 300 army officers with the rank of brigadier general or higher.

This pattern is traceable to the revolutionary period when officers were made or promoted informally, frequently on the field of battle, in a process known popularly as *por dedo* (by finger, or by pointing at). Civilian governments since 1946 have sought to bring about officer contentment and support by a policy of relatively easy promotion coupled with one of forced retirement of senior officers in order to make promotions possible.

There are pragmatic as well as political reasons for the maintenance of officer corps with a high proportion of senior officers. The logistical dispersion of the armed forces into a great many small units throughout the country in the many military zones and naval districts creates a corresponding need for commanding officers with appropriate rank. In addition, the ceremonial and representational functions are important elements in the armed forces mission, and possession of senior rank facilitates the performance of these functions. In the mid-1970s a lieutenant general and a vice admiral served as military and air attaché and as naval attaché in Washington, and a flag officer served as attaché in London.

Pay and Benefits

Pay is regulated by law and is subject to periodic adjustment. Base compensation is the same at equivalent ranks in all branches of the service and is supplemented by various forms of compensation and fringe benefits. In the mid-1960s, for example, the monthly base pay for commissioned officers ranged from the equivalent of US$134 for a second lieutenant to US$450 for a lieutenant general. For officers holding certain positions, supplemental pay ranged from US$8 for a company commander to US$792 for the minister of defense. Representation allowances ranged from US$16 for a zone chief of staff to US$176 for the minister of defense. In addition, differential pay is awarded both officers and men for service abroad and in certain parts of the country; and personnel engaged in flying, paratroop, or demolition-unit activities receive risk pay.

Pay raises were frequent during the 1950s and 1960s, and the general level of military compensation rose at a rate much faster than that of the cost of living, which in Mexico ascended only moderately until the early 1970s, years that were marked by a sharply increased inflationary trend. President Adolfo López Mateos after entering office in 1958 increased military salaries by 10 percent during each of the six years of his administration. Substantial additional increases marked the term of President Gustavo Díaz Ordaz (1946–70), and a spate of left-wing terrorism was believed to have been the immediate cause of a further general increase declared by President Luís Echeverría in late 1973.

The rates of officer pay are generally similar to those in other Latin American countries. The salary of company grade personnel is comparable to that of white-collar workers or skilled laborers, but the salaries of field grade and general officers permit them to live in progressively greater degrees of comfort. The practice of moonlighting is common among younger officers, however, and the illegal practice of holding a second job in the public sector is occasionally reported. In the mid-1960s one young officer estimated the number of his colleagues

368

holding other employment at one-fourth of the officer corps, and other estimates ran higher. Dissatisfaction with pay is given as a primary reason for the fairly high rate of resignations among commissioned personnel who have completed five years of obligatory service, but the multiple pay increases of the 1960s and early 1970s have presumably reduced the rate of resignation because of dissatisfaction over pay.

The base pay of enlisted personnel is modest, and soldiers also frequently moonlight. Some supplementary pay is also available to them, however, and the income of the recruit is usually higher than that of the farmworker or the unskilled urban laborer whose wages are extremely low (see ch. 2). Moreover, the soldier or sailor has relatively little need for money; most of the goods and services he would need to purchase in civilian life are provided by the government.

Fringe benefits are estimated at 40 percent of base pay for officers and are much higher for enlisted personnel who receive free food, shelter, and uniforms. Army messes, usually maintained at the battalion level, are staffed by competent personnel trained at the Cooks' and Bakers' School. The ample and nutritious menu follows the prevailing dietary pattern of the country.

A housing program for officers was initiated in 1952, and during the term of President López Mateos (1958–64) more than 1,500 units were constructed at a cost of over 100 million pesos (12.5 pesos equal US$1). Military personnel may participate in a cooperative housing fund to which the government also makes contributions; the accumulated deposits can be withdrawn on retirement or disbursed to survivors if death occurs while the participant remains on active duty.

Beginning in the early 1960s an extended construction program was aimed at replacing the frequently primitive and inadequate quarters on military posts throughout the country. The new buildings have not invariably been of first quality, but they have been of modern construction and design and often have included officer, troop, and family housing. By 1970 new housing units had been built at most of the major installations.

Since 1960 an accelerated program has resulted in the construction of numerous post exchanges and commissary stores where lower prices are available for food, toilet articles, and other necessary goods. The most extensive of the improvements to military facilities were installed at the army post in Monterrey during the mid-1930s. A hospital, theater, library, and gymnasium and schools and gardens were constructed for personnel and their families. An officers' club included party rooms and a swimming pool; and a cooperative store complex included a restaurant, grocery store, market, bakery, pharmacy, and clothing and dry goods store. All housing units had electric wiring, purified water supply, gas heating, and baths. The Monterrey installation served as the prototype for several other military communities subsequently constructed.

Fringe benefits for enlisted men include a variety of small schools at which they can receive in-service training in skills that may later prove useful in civilian life. Schools called *hijos del ejercito* (children of the army) that were established in the late 1930s provide education for military dependents, and several small military boarding institutions prepare the sons of officers for entrance to the military academy. These considerable fringe benefits are of importance to the morale of the Mexican soldier who is enabled to keep his family close to him.

The National Bank of the Army and Navy, established in 1946, provides low-cost credit and life insurance policies on favorable terms to military personnel. Army hospitals, among the best in Mexico, provide free service for dependents as well as for personnel, and pharmaceutical products are available free or at low cost. Career personnel may retire on 75 percent of pay after twenty years and at full pay after thirty years of service.

Military Justice

Discipline is not severe in the armed forces, and maintaining order is not a major problem. The serviceman has a background in which deference to authority is traditional, and obedience to superiors is accepted without question as an aspect of military life. The soldier must accept a degree of regulation of conduct that somewhat circumscribes his freedom, however, and violations of military law and regulations meet with treatment somewhat more stringent than those governed by civil codes.

Military courts and tribunals are convened as needed; there is no permanent military court system. Army and navy judge advocate's corps have cognizance over all military legal matters. Courts operate under provisions of the Code of Military Justice, a compilation that closely resembles the Unified Code of Military Justice of the United States.

The Constitution of 1917 recognizes military jurisdiction over cases involving matters of military discipline, 1855 legislation having assigned to civilian courts jurisdiction over common crimes and civil cases involving military personnel. The Constitution also stipulates that a civilian implicated in a military crime or violation must be tried by a civil authority.

The Code of Military Justice does not define crimes against military discipline; however, these are commonly recognized to be absence without leave, desertion, insubordination, abuse of authority, self-infliction of wounds to avoid service, violation of military honor, rebellion, and treason. The Supreme Court of Justice resolves disputes over the competence of military courts, and military personnel who feel that their rights have been violated may seek an injunction *(amparo)*. In addition, it has jurisdiction over disputes between military courts and courts of the federal or state systems.

In the colonial period a system of *fuero militar* (military privileges) that had been developed in Spain was extended to the New World.

During the early years of independence this *fuero militar* made military personnel virtually immune to civil authority and was an important incentive to army enlistment. This special status was largely eliminated by the Constitution of 1857, and in the modern Mexican armed forces the separateness of military legal jurisdiction has become a disability to the extent that service personnel are excepted from many civilian constitutional guarantees and a relatively swifter and more rigorous system of justice is imposed on them. Punishments by military courts are not unduly harsh, however, and the broad discretionary authority of commanding officers in matters of discipline limits the calling of courts-martial to cases involving serious offenses. Neither the rules nor their enforcement are so rigorous as to have an adverse effect on the generally satisfactory state of army morale. Moreover, senior officers to some extent enjoy an ad hoc immunity from trial in civilian courts, and when military punishment is meted out it often takes the form of a simple reprimand.

Morale

During the course of half a century the Mexican military has increasingly placed emphasis on the man rather than the gun. The decline in military budgets has been accompanied by an allocation of increasing proportions of those budgets to the professionalization and welfare of personnel rather than the acquisition of armaments that would bear little relevance to the armed forces' real mission.

In the early 1920s President Alvaro Obregón initiated a program to improve housing, mess, and recreational facilities and to expand and improve educational and training facilities for what was still essentially the revolutionary army. The process was continued by succeeding military presidents and, after 1946, by civilian chief executives. At first the program was designed to facilitate the improvement of order and discipline in the army and to ensure its loyalty to a still insecure central government. Later, the focus of intent shifted to include maintaining loyalty to the dominant political party, but the consequence was a continued improvement in troop morale (see Political Role, this ch.).

The modest circumstances of the homes from which the enlisted men and many of the officers have been recruited make them particularly receptive to the advantages offered by service life. This receptiveness is demonstrated by the ability of the services to recruit sufficient enlisted personnel on a volunteer basis, and by the broad margin by which applicants for enrollment in the academies for officer training outnumber the academy vacancies (see Social Composition, Recruitment, and Training, this ch.).

Patriotism and esprit de corps among officers are instilled throughout their service careers by training, ceremonies, hortatory addresses, service publications, and constant association with brother officers. "Heroic" was included in the name of the Heroic Military College as a reminder of the Niños Heroes (Heroic Children)—the military academy cadets who died in the defense of Chapultepec during the war with the United States. The sense of patriotism and pride in membership in their service by enlisted personnel are cultivated no less diligently.

The mystique of the revolution has an ambivalent effect on morale. On the one hand, the revolutionary concept of national purpose and unity inhibits the growth of a sense of military elitism or a sense of the military as a separate entity. On the other hand, the concept encourages pride in membership in the army as a part of society as a whole. This sense of linkage has been an important asset to civilian political leaders in their efforts to fashion the armed forces into a competent and loyal instrument of the government (see Political Role, this ch.).

Although the level of morale in the Mexican armed forces is probably much higher than in most Latin American countries, some factors militate against high morale. Some inescapable frustration, among officers in particular, results from the nature of the Mexican military mission. Most of their training and much of their day-to-day activity involve the acquisition and practice of skills that are unlikely ever to be employed in the defense of their country against invasion. A corollary frustration results from the limited inventory of armament.

The generally favorable attitude of the civilian population toward the army has contributed to high troop morale. The army's police role in maintaining public order has seriously affected this favorable attitude only in the case of radical student groups who dislike it as an instrument of a disliked central government. In the mid-1970s, however, the activist students were a minority in the student population (see ch. 6). The army's relationship with other sectors of the urban population was a comfortable one, and in the countryside its civic action program made it regarded as a friend (see Mission and Operations, this ch.).

UNIFORMS, INSIGNIA, AND AWARDS

On service uniforms, officers display rank insignia on shoulder straps in the army and on the sleeve cuff in the navy. The air force wears the uniform and insignia of the army. Noncommissioned officers' insignia are worn on the upper or lower sleeve.

Officers' insignia of rank in the army and air force are indicated by bars, stars, or embellished stars. A second lieutenant wears one gold bar; a first lieutenant, two; a second captain, 2½; and a first captain, three. Field grade starts with one gold star for a major, two for a lieutenant colonel, and three, set in a triangle, for a colonel. General officers wear silver stars with the addition of a semicircular laurel wreath enclosing the eagle of the national arms. A brigadier general has one star; a major general, two; and a lieutenant general, three.

Naval officers' insignia of rank are worn as gold stripes above the sleeve cuff (or on shoulder boards), the uppermost stripe incorporating a braid loop some two inches in outer diameter. The number and pattern of stripes correspond to United States equivalents. Warrant officers wear one gold stripe without the loop, and members of the marine corps are distinguished by red piping on insignia of rank.

Noncommissioned officers' insignia of rank consist primarily of horizontal stripes worn on the sleeve. The army displays the stripes in the color of a man's branch of service worn above the elbow. Red signifies infantry; blue, cavalry; and purple, artillery. A private first class has one short stripe worn vertically; and a corporal, one full stripe worn horizontally. Sergeant second class has two stripes; and a sergeant first class, three. The navy uses the rank of corporal, designated by a white chevron on the upper sleeve. Petty officers wear white stripes at the cuff—one for petty officer second class and two for first class. A chief petty officer has three stripes.

The army has a blue dress uniform and a service uniform of field green similar to that of the United States, but a shade darker. Suntan khaki is used for hot weather. The navy, including the marine corps, uses standard dark blue or white. There are a variety of dress, service, and field uniforms for all services. Army jackets are standard single-breasted models, worn with straight trousers except in the field. Cavalry officers may wear breeches and boots. Navy officers use the blue double-breasted coat similar to that of the United States Navy, but more fitted and with two rows of five buttons each. White uniforms are worn in hot weather. There is also a khaki work uniform that is worn with shoulder boards. Uniforms for enlisted men closely resemble United States service wear.

Headgear ranges from the conventional peaked service cap to field overseas caps or steel helmets. Helmets resemble the French design of derby crown and narrow, sloping brim. Senior officer service caps have visor decorations that become more elaborate with higher rank.

The army uses branch insignia, mostly appropriate heraldic devices in brass worn on the lapel, and the navy has a variety of cloth specialist badges that supplement rank insignia. The ornaments of both services in many cases closely resemble United States equivalents. There are also a number of badges to indicate special duties or accomplishments, and these are worn mostly over the right breast pocket. There is a distinctive emblem for graduates of the military academy, and others indicate presidential service, general staff corps, aides, and the like.

The eagle emblem of the national coat-of-arms is used extensively for decoration and is incorporated as a central theme for buttons, cap ornaments, wings, and other items of apparel. Officers purchase their own uniforms; enlisted men receive a standard issue, which in addition to uniforms includes equipment and personal items. Uniforms and accessories are comfortable and of generally good quality; they adequately meet the needs of the individual, and the serviceman, for the most part presents a neat and professional appearance.

Mexico makes extensive use of awards and decorations, and the military forces are particularly conscious of the numerous national symbols of official recognition for both military and civil distinction. There are several strictly military decorations and numerous awards for individual accomplishment of a professional, academic, or technical nature. Military personnel are eligible for any national decoration, many of which may also be presented to foreign nationals.

The country's highest award is the Mexican Order of the Aztec Eagle. Created in 1933, it is presented in six grades, the highest of which, the Grand Collar, is given only to heads of state. Of the military decorations, the most important, in order of precedence, are the Mexican Legion of Honor, the Cross of Military Merit, the Heroic Valor Medal, and the War Cross.

The Cross of Military Merit for army use was created in 1902 and is in three classes. The crosses are gold for officers and bronze for enlisted men. The Heroic Valor Medal or Cross was established in 1926 and also is in three classes. The Decoration for Naval Merit was established in two classes in 1926. The Decoration for Merit in Air Service has three classes, gold, silver, and bronze, and was created in 1929. In addition, the Decoration for Technical Military Merit was created in 1926, a first class for Mexicans and a second class for foreigners who have assisted in developing the armed forces. Also in 1926 the Cross for Fidelity was established in four classes, and in 1911 the Cross for Pensioners was created.

There are various other awards to recognize long and meritorious service or special accomplishment in such fields as engineering, sports, or teaching in military schools. Commemorative campaign medals have been issued to participants in the significant battles, campaigns, and wars in the country's history. They were struck and issued to participants in the resistance to the United States invasion of 1914, for example, for convoy and patrol duty during World War II, and for service in the Far East with the Mexican expeditionary air force in the Pacific in 1945.

FOREIGN INFLUENCES

As a consequence of the highly independent Mexican foreign policy, which stresses national identity, self-determination, and avoidance of intervention, foreign influences on the armed forces are studiously avoided. The size and power of the neighbor on its northern border, however, make some United States influence unavoidable. The foreign news section of *Revista del Ejercito*, the army's principal professional journal, contains frequent reports on United States military developments. In addition, some Mexican officers receive training in the United States, and some arms are purchased there.

Mexico remained neutral in World War I, and several United States divisions were assigned to border duty as a precaution against possible hostile activity in that quarter. Mexico entered World War II in 1942, however, and was the only Latin American country other than Brazil to send men into combat. In 1945 volunteer Air Force Fighter Squadron 201 received training in the United States and was deployed to Pracos Air Force Base in the Philippines. The contingent engaged in the strafing of Japanese installations in the Philippines and Formosa, and eight Mexican lives were lost.

Some military sentiment was expressed in favor of at least token representation in the United Nations forces in Korea in the early 1950s, and in 1962 a considerable number of officers urged Mexican participation in the Organization of American States (OAS) naval blockade and air surveillance of Cuba. Civilian authority, which had previously ruled against a military request for more extensive participation in World War II, did not permit involvement in Korea and Cuba.

During World War II the Plan of Integral Defense linked the operations of the Fourth United States Army and the Mexican Pacific Command. The Joint United States-Mexico Defense Commission, established in 1942, administered the military phase of lend-lease operations through which Mexico received—and later determined to retain and purchase—tanks, aircraft, radar equipment, and other modern matériel valued at about US$18 million. The commission continues in existence as a significant point of contact.

Mexico is a party to the 1947 Inter-American Treaty of Reciprocal Assistance (Rio Pact). It led the opposition to proposals for creation of a standing military component within the OAS that were presented at the OAS Bogotá Conference in 1948, however, and has since resisted other proposals aimed at creation of any inter-American military or police force.

In 1951, when the United States proposed military defense assistance pacts to most of the countries of Latin America, only Mexico declined. The military establishment had urged acceptance, which would probably have meant acquisition of much modern matériel, but once again the officers were overruled by civilian authority.

BIBLIOGRAPHY

Section I. Social

Adams, Richard N., et al. *Social Change in Latin America Today.* New York: Random House, 1960.

Adolph, José B. "The South American Macho: Myths and Mystique," *Impact of Science on Society* [Paris], XXI, No. 1, January-March 1971, 83–92.

Aguirre Beltrán, Gonzala. "La Integración de la población negra en la sociedad mexicana," *Economía y Ciencias Sociales* [Caracas], X, No. 2, April-June 1968, 5-21.

Álba, Victor. *The Mexicans: The Making of a Nation.* New York: Praeger, 1967.

Alexander, Robert. *Today's Latin America.* (2d ed.) New York: Anchor Books, Doubleday, 1968.

Anderson, Arthur J. O. *Rules of the Aztec Language.* Salt Lake City: University of Utah Press, 1973.

Aramoni, Aniceto. *Psicoanálisis de la dinámica de un pueblo.* Mexico City: Universidad Nacional Autónoma de México, 1961.

Archer, Ules. *Mexico and the United States.* New York: Hawthorne Books, 1973.

Arzápalo, Ramón. "The Social Role of the Indigenous Languages of Mexico and Guatemala," *Canadian Journal of Linguistics* [Toronto], XIV, No. 2, Spring 1969, 133-141.

Atlas of Mexico. Austin: Bureau of Business Research, University of Texas, 1970.

Ávila, Manuel. *Tradition and Growth: A Study of Four Mexican Villages.* Chicago: University of Chicago Press, 1969.

Baerresen, Donald W. *The Border Industrialization Program of Mexico.* Lexington, Massachusetts: D. C. Heath, 1971.

Bailey, Helen M., and Nasatir, Abraham P. *Latin America: The Development of Its Civilization.* Englewood Cliffs: Prentice-Hall, 1960.

Balán, Jorge; Browning, Harley L.; and Jelin, Elizabeth. *Men in a Developing Society: Geographic Social Mobility in Monterrey, Mexico.* (Latin American Monographs, No. 30.) Austin: University of Texas Press, 1973.

Banco Nacional de Comercio Exterior. *Mexico, 1970: Facts, Figures, and Trends.* (5th ed.) Mexico City: 1970.

Bannon, John F., and Dunne, Peter M. *Latin America: An Historical Survey.* Milwaukee: Bruce Publishing, 1963.

Barkin, David. "El desarrollo económico y la distribución del ingreso: estudio de caso," *Anuario Indigenista* [Mexico City], XXIX, December 1969, 125-138.

Beals, Ralph. "Social Stratification in Latin America." Pages 342–360 in Dwight Heath and Richard N. Adams (eds.), *Contemporary Cultures and Societies of Latin America.* New York: Random House, 1965.

Béjar Navarro, Raúl. "Prejuicio y discriminación racial en México," *Revista Mexicana de Sociología* [Mexico City], XXXI, No. 2, April-June 1969, 417-433.

Bell, Betty (ed.) *Indian Mexico: Past and Present.* Los Angeles: Latin American Center, University of California, 1967.

Bellar, Jacob. *Jews in Latin America.* New York: Jonathan David Publishers, 1969.

Belshaw, Michael. "Aspects of Community Development in Rural Mexico," *Inter-American Economic Affairs*, XV, No. 4, Spring 1962, 71-94.

————. *A Village Economy: Land and People of Huecorio.* New York: Columbia University Press, 1967.

Beltran del Río, Abel. "Mexico: An Economy at the Crossroads," *Wharton Quarterly*, VI, No. 1, Fall 1971, 20-24.

Benítez, Fernando. *The Century after Cortés.* Chicago: University of Chicago Press, 1965.

Benítez Zenteno, Raúl. "Sobrepopulación, subdesarrollo y política de población en México." Mexico City: Universidad Nacional Autónoma de México, June 15, 1973 (mimeo.).

Bennett, Robert. "Economics: Mexico." Pages 168–173 in Donald E. J. Stewart (ed.), *Handbook of Latin American Studies;* XXXV: Social Sciences. Gainesville: University of Florida Press, 1973.

Benson, Nettie Lee (ed.). *Mexico and the Spanish Cortés, 1810–1822: Eight Essays.* Austin: University of Texas Press, 1966.

Benton, William. *The Voice of Latin America.* New York: Harper and Row, 1965.

Berle, Adolf A. *Latin America: Diplomacy and Reality.* New York: Harper and Row, for the Council on Foreign Relations, 1962.

Bermúdez, María. *La vida familiar del mexicano.* Mexico City: Antigua Lebevia Robredo, 1955.

Bernstein, Harry. *Modern and Contemporary Latin America.* New York: Lippincott, 1952.

Blakemore, Harold. *Latin America.* (Modern World Series.) London: Oxford University Press, 1966.

Blum, Albert A., and Thompson, Mark. "Unions and White-Collar Workers in Mexico," *Industrial and Labor Relations Review*, XXVI, October 1972, 646–659.

Bobb, Bernard E. *The Viceregency of Antonio María Bucareli in New Spain, 1771–1779.* Austin: University of Texas Press, 1962.

Booth, George C. *Mexico's School-Made Society.* New York: Greenwood Press, 1969.

Borah, Woodrow, and Cook, Sherburne F. *The Aboriginal Population of Central Mexico on the Eve of the Spanish Conquest.* Berkeley: University of California Press, 1963.

————. "Marriage and Legitimacy in Mexican Culture," *California Law Review,* LIV, No. 2, May 1966, 946-1008.

Born, Esther. *The New Architecture in Mexico.* New York: William Morrow, 1937.

Bowman, Mary J. (ed.) *Readings in the Economics of Education.* Paris: United Nations Educational, Scientific and Cultural Organization, 1968.

Braden, Charles S. *Religious Aspects of the Conquest of Mexico.* Durham: Duke University Press, 1930.

Brandenburg, Frank. *The Making of Modern Mexico.* Englewood Cliffs: Prentice-Hall, 1964.

Breese, Gerald. *Urbanization in Newly Developing Countries.* Englewood Cliffs: Prentice-Hall, 1966.

Browning, Harley L., and Feindt, Waltraut. *Selectivity of Migrants to a Metropolis in a Developing Country: A Mexican Case Study.* (Offprint Series, No. 97.) Austin: Institute of Latin American Studies, University of Texas, 1970.

Burland, C. A. *The Gods of Mexico.* New York: G. P. Putnam's Sons, 1967.

Bushnell, G.H.S. *Ancient Arts of the Americas.* London: Thames and Hudson, 1965.

Bushwood, J. S. *The Romantic Novel in Mexico.* Columbia: University of Missouri Press, 1954.

"Business Holidays in 1973 Are Listed for 135 Nations." *Commerce Today,* III, No. 6, December 25, 1972, 45-50.

Butland, Gilbert J. *Latin America: A Regional Geography.* (3d ed.) New York: John Wiley and Sons, 1972.

Butterworth, Douglas S. "From Royalty to Poverty: The Decline of a Rural Mexican Community," *Human Organization,* XXIX, No. 1, Spring 1970, 5-11.

————. "A Study of the Urbanization Process Among Mixtec Migrants from Tilantongo in Mexico City." Pages 98–113 in William Mangin (ed.), *Peasants in Cities: Readings in the Anthropology of Urbanization.* Boston: Houghton Mifflin, 1970.

Calderón de la Barca, Fanny. *Life in Mexico.* London: Chapman and Hall, 1843.

Callcott, Wilfrid H. *Church and State in Mexico, 1822-1852.* New York: Octagon Books, 1965.

————. *Liberalism in Mexico, 1857-1929.* Hamden, Connecticut:

Archon, 1965.

Calvert, Peter. *Mexico*. (Nations of the Modern World.) New York: Praeger, 1973.

Cárdenas, Leonard, Jr. *The Municipality in Northern Mexico*. (Southwestern Studies, No. 1.) El Paso: Texas Western Press, 1963.

Cardoso, Fernando Enrique, and Reyna, José Luís. *Industrialización, estructura ocupacional, y estratificación social en America Latina*. Santiago: Instituto Latinoamericano de Planificación Económica y Social, 1966.

Carlos, Manuel L. *Politics and Development in Rural Mexico: A Study of Socioeconomic Modernization*. New York: Praeger, 1974.

Carlos, Manuel L., and Brokensha, David. "Agencies, Goals, and Clients: A Cross-Cultural Analysis," *Studies in Comparative International Development*, VII, No. 2, Summer 1972, 130-155.

Carrasco, Pedro. "Tarascan Folk Religion: Christian or Pagan?" Pages 3–15 in Walter Goldschmidt and Harry Hoijer (eds.), *The Social Anthropology of Latin America: Essays in Honor of Ralph Leon Beals*. Los Angeles: University of California, 1970.

Caso, Alfonso. *La comunidad indígena*. Mexico City: Secretaría de Educación Pública, 1971.

Caso, Antonio. "Land Tenure Among the Ancient Mexicans." *American Anthropologist*, LXV, No. 4, August 1963, 863-878.

Castillo, Isidro. *México y su revolución educativa*. Mexico City: Academia Mexicana de la Educación, 1965.

Cepeda Villareal, Rodolfo. "Certain Aspects of Mexican Labor Laws, Especially as They Affect Foreign-Owned Business," *California Western Law Review*, VI, Spring 1970, 234-246.

Cerna, Manuel M., and Ramírez, Rafael. *Adalid de la educación rural*. Mexico City: Cuadernos de la Lectura Popular, 1967.

Cervantes de Salazar, Francisco. *Life in the Imperial and Loyal City of Mexico in New Spain*. Austin: University of Texas Press, 1953.

Chase, Gilbert. *Contemporary Art in Latin America*. New York: Free Press, 1970.

Cheetam, Nicholas. *Mexico: A Short History*. New York: Crowell, 1971.

Chevalier, François. *Land and Society in Colonial Mexico: The Great Hacienda*. Berkeley: University of California Press, 1963.

Chevalier, Michel. *Mexico: Ancient and Modern*. (Trans., Thomas Alpers.) London: J. Maxwell, 1864.

Clark, Sydney. *All the Best in Mexico*. New York: Dodd, Mead, 1970.

Cline, Howard F. *Mexico: Revolution to Evolution,* New York: Oxford University Press, 1963.

———.*The United States and Mexico*. (Rev. ed.) Cambridge: Harvard University Press, 1963.

Coe, Michael D. *The Maya*. New York: Praeger, 1966.

———. *Mexico*. New York: Praeger, 1962.

———. "A Model of Ancient Community Structure in the Maya

Lowlands," *Southwestern Journal of Anthropology*, XXI, No. 2, Summer 1965, 97-114.

Colby, Benjamin N. *Ethnic Relations in the Chiapas Highlands of Mexico*. Santa Fe: New Mexico Press, 1966.

Cole, J. P. *Latin America: An Economic and Social Geography*. London: Butterworth, 1970.

Cole, William E., and Sanders, Richard D. *Growth and Change in Mexican Agriculture*. Knoxville: Center for Business and Economic Research, University of Tennessee, 1970.

Colegio de México. Centro de Estudios Económicos y Demográficos. *Dinámica de la Población de México, 1970*. Mexico City: 1970.

Collier, Jane Fishburne. *Law and Social Change in Zinacantan*. Stanford: Stanford University Press, 1973.

Collis, Maurice. *Cortés and Montezuma*. London: Faber, 1954.

Considine, John J. (ed.) *The Church in the New Latin America*. Notre Dame: Fides, 1964.

———. *New Horizons in Latin America*. New York: Dodd, Mead, 1958.

———. *Social Reform in the New Latin America*. Notre Dame: Fides, 1965.

Cortés, Hernán. *Conquest: Dispatches of Cortés from the New World*. (Ed., Harry M. Rosen.) New York: Grosset and Dunlap, 1962.

Corwin, Arthur F. *Contemporary Mexican Attitudes Toward Population, Poverty, and Public Opinion*. Gainesville: University of Florida Press, 1963.

Costiloe, Michael P. *Church Wealth in Mexico: A Study of the "Juzgado de Capellanias" in the Archbishopric of Mexico, 1800-1856*. Cambridge: University Printing House, 1967.

Covarrubias, Miguel. *Mexico South*. New York: Knopf, 1954.

Covill, H. W., and Grubb, K. *World Christian Handbook, 1962*. London: World Dominion Press, 1962.

Crawford, William Rex. *A Century of Latin American Thought*. (Rev. ed.) Cambridge: Harvard University Press, 1961.

Creel, George. *The People Next Door: An Interpretive History of Mexico and the Mexicans*. New York: John Day, 1926.

Crow, John A. *Mexico Today*. (Rev. ed.) New York: Harper and Row, 1972.

Crumrine, Lynne Scoggins. *Ceremonial Exchange as a Mechanism in Tribal Integration Among the Mayos of Northwest Mexico*. Tucson: University of Arizona Press, 1969.

Cumberland, Charles C. *Mexico: The Struggle for Modernity*. New York: Oxford University Press, 1968.

Cummings, Ronald G. *Water Resource Management in Northern Mexico*. Baltimore: Johns Hopkins University Press, 1972.

Davidson, David M. "Negro Slave Control and Resistance in Colonial Mexico, 1519-1650," *Hispanic American Historical Review*, XLV, No. 3, August 1966, 235-253.

Davis, Harold. *Latin American Thought*. Baton Rouge: Colonial Press, 1972.

Davis, Kingsley. "Population." Pages 116-131 in L. B. Young (ed.), *Population in Perspective*. New York: Oxford University Press, 1968.

———. *World Urbanization, 1950-1970*, I: Basic Data for Cities, Countries, and Regions. (Population Monograph Series. No. 4.) Berkeley: Institute of International Studies, University of California, 1969.

Davis, Russell G. *Scientific, Engineering, and Technical Education in Mexico*. New York: Education and World Affairs, 1967.

De la Haba, Luís. "Mexico: The City that Founded A Nation," *National Geographic*, CXLIII, No. 5, May 1973, 638-670.

Demographic Yearbook, 1972. New York: United Nations, Department of Economic and Social Affairs, Statistical Office, 1973.

Derossi, Flavia. *The Mexican Entrepreneur*. (Development Center Studies.) Paris: Organization for Economic Cooperation and Development, 1971.

Díaz, May N. *Tonolá*. Berkeley: University of California Press, 1966.

Díaz del Castillo, Bernal. *Historia verdadera de la conquista de la Nueva España*. Mexico City: Ediciones Mexicans, 1950.

Diccionario encylopédico abreviado. Madrid: Espasa-Calpe, 1957.

Dooley, Francis Patrick. "Cristeros, Calles, and Mexican Catholicism." Unpublished doctoral dissertation. College Park: University of Maryland, 1972.

Dovring, Folke. "Land Reform and Productivity in Mexico," *Land Economics*, XLVI, No. 3, August 1970, 264-274.

Dow, James. "Keeping Indians in Their Place: A System of Peasant Exploitation in Central Mexico." (Unpublished paper obtained from U.S. Department of State, Office of External Research, Foreign Affairs Research Documentation Center, No. FAR 16716-P.) Washington: November-December 1972.

Duncan, W. Raymond. "Education and Political Development: The Latin American Case." Pages 125-149 in Thomas J. La Belle (ed.), *Education and Development: Latin America and the Caribbean*. (Latin American Studies Series, No. 18.) Los Angeles: Latin American Center, University of California, 1972.

Dunne, Peter M. *Juan Antonio Balthasar: Padre Visitador to the Sonora Frontier, 1744-1745, Tucson: Arizona Pioneers' Historical Society, 1957.*

Dusenberry, William H. *The Mexican Mesta: The Administration of Ranching in Colonial Mexico*. Urbana: University of Illinois Press, 1963.

"Economic Roundup: General Economic Conditions in Mexico," *Comercio Exterior de México*, [Mexico City], XVII, No. 2, February 1971, 22-27.

Edmonson, Munro S., et al. *Synoptic Studies of Mexican Culture.* New Orleans: Middle American Research Institute, Tulane University, 1957.

Elder, Glen. "Family Structure and Educational Attainment: A Cross-National Analysis," *American Sociological Review*, XXX, No. 1, February 1965, 81-96.

Elliott, Sean M. *Financing Latin American Housing.* (Special Studies in International Economics and Development.) New York: Praeger, 1968.

Elu de Leñero, María del Carmen. *Hacia dónde va la mujer mexicana? Proyecciones a partir de los datos de una encuesta nacional.* Mexico City: Instituto Mexicano de Estudios Sociales, 1969.

Erasmus, Charles J. *Man Takes Control.* Minneapolis: University of Minnesota Press, 1961.

————. "Monument Building: Some Field Experiments," *Southwestern Journal of Anthropology*, XXI, No. 4, Winter 1965, 277-301.

————. "Thoughts on Upward Collapse: An Essay on Explanation in Anthropology," *Southwestern Journal of Anthropology*, XXIV, No. 2, Summer 1968, 170-193.

Esquenazi-Mayo, Roberto. "Prose Fiction: Mexico." Pages 363-369 in Henry E. Adams (ed.), *Handbook of Latin American Studies*, XXXII: Humanities. Gainesville: University of Florida Press, 1960.

Estados Unidos Mexicanos. Dirección General de Estadístico. *Anuario Estadístico de los Estados Unidos Mexicanos, 1968-1969.* Mexico City: Talleres Gráficos de la Nación, 1971.

————. *IX Censo General de Población, 28 de Enero de 1970, Resumen Abreviado.* Mexico City: Talleres Gráficos de la Nación, 1972.

Esteva Fabregat, Claudio. "Familia y matrimonio en México: el patrón cultural," *Revista de Indias* [Madrid], CXV-CXVI and CXVII-CXVIII, 1969, 173-278.

Ewing, Russell C. (ed.) *Six Faces of Mexico.* Tucson: University of Arizona Press, 1966.

Fagg, John E. *Latin America: A General History.* New York: Macmillan, 1963.

Family Planning in Five Continents. London: International Planned Parenthood Federation, 1969.

Fehrenbach, T. R. *Fire and Blood: A History of Mexico.* New York: Macmillan, 1973.

Fernández, Justino. *Mexican Art.* London: Spring Books, 1965.

Foland, Francis. "Mexico: A Country of Craftsmen." (Unpublished paper obtained from U.S. Department of State, Office of External Research, Foreign Affairs Research Documentation Center, No. FAR 14598). Washington: August 1971.

Ford, Norman D. *Fabulous Mexico.* (9th ed., rev.) Greenlawn, New York: Harlan Publications, 1973.

Foster, George. *Tzintzuntzan: Mexican Peasants in a Changing World.*

Boston: Little, Brown, 1967.

Foster, Mary Le Cron. *The Tarascan Language*. Berkeley: University of California Press, 1969.

Fox, David J., and Robinson, D. J. *Cities in a Changing Latin America: Two Studies of Urban Growth in the Development of Mexico and Venezuela*. Mexico City: Latin American Publications Fund, July 1969.

Foy, Felician A. (ed.) *1968 National Catholic Almanac*. Paterson, New Jersey: St. Anthony's Guild, 1968.

Friedrich, Paul. *Agrarian Revolt in a Mexican Village*. (Anthropology of Modern Societies Series.) Englewood Cliffs: Printice-Hall, 1970.

Fromm, Erich, and Maccoby, Michael. *Social Character in a Mexican Village*. Englewood Cliffs: Prentice-Hall, 1970.

García Granados, Rafael. "Mexican Father Mosaics," *Mexican Art and Life*, No. 5, January 1939, 2–8.

Gates, Gary R., and Gates, Marilyn. "Uncertainty and Development Risk in Pequeña Irrigación Decisions for Peasants in Campeche, Mexico," *Economic Geography*, XLVIII, No. 2, April 1972, 135-152.

Germidis, Dimetrios A. *The Construction Industry of Mexico*. (Technical Papers.) Paris: Development Center, Organization for Economic Cooperation and Development, 1972.

Gibson, Charles, *The Aztecs Under Spanish Rule: A History of the Valley of Mexico, 1519-1810*. Stanford: Stanford University Press, 1964.

Gicovate, Bernard. "Spanish American Poetry." Pages 247-260 in Roberto Esquenazi-Mayo and Michael C. Meyer (eds.), *Latin American Scholarship Since World War II*. Lincoln: University of Nebraska Press, 1971.

Gillin, James. "Ethos Components in Modern Latin American Culture," *American Anthropologist*, LVII, No. 3, June 1955, 488-500.

Goldberg, David. "Background, Dimensions of Women's Roles and Fertility: Some Data from Turkey and Mexico." (Unpublished paper obtained from U.S. Department of State, Office of External Research, Foreign Affairs Research Documentation Center, No. FAR 17306-P.) Washington: April 1973.

Goldschmidt, Walter, and Hoijer, Harry (eds.). *The Social Anthropology of Latin America: Essays in Honor of Ralph Leon Beals*. Los Angeles: University of California, 1970.

de Gemezgil, María Wisa Rodríguez Sala. "Imagen del científico entre los adolescentes Mexicanos," *Revista Mexicana de la Sociología* [Mexico City], XXXI, No. 1, January-February 1971, 147-167.

Gonzáles Salazar, Gloria. *Problema de la mano de obra de México: Subempleo, requisitos educatívos y flexibilidad ocupacionál*. Mexico City: Instituto de Investigaciones Económicas, 1971.

González Casanova, Pablo. *Democracy in Mexico*. (Trans., Danielle Salti.) New York: Oxford University Press, 1970.

————. "The Evolution of the Mexican Class System." Chapter 6 in Joseph Kahl (ed.), *Comparative Perspectives on Stratification: Mexico, Great Britain, Japan.* New York: Little, Brown, 1968.

————. "Mexico: Dynamics of an Agrarian Revolution." Pages 467–485 in James Petras and Maurice Zeitlin (eds.), *Latin America: Reform or Revolution?* Greenwich, Connecticut: Fawcett Publications, 1968.

González-Cosío, Arturo. *México: cinquenta años de revolución,* II. Mexico City: Fondo de Cultura Económica, 1961.

González Ramirez, Manuel R. *La Iglesia mexicana en cifras. Mexico City: Centro de Investigación* y Acción Social, 1969.

Gracia de Mejia, Martha Olga. *Mujer: Participación y planificación familiar.* (Trabajo presentado en el Seminario Regional para los Paises del Hemisferio Occidental de la Mujer y Planificación Familiar, Naciones Unidos, Santo Domingo, Repúblico Dominicana Mayo 1973, Selecciónes de Población.) Bogotá: Population Reference Bureau, Oficina Regional para América Latina, n.d.

Greenberg, Martin Harry. *Bureaucracy and Development: a Mexican Case Study.* (Studies in International Development and Economics.) Lexington, Massachusetts: D.C. Heath, Lexington Books, 1970.

Griffen, William B. *Cultural Change and Shifting Populations in Central Northern Mexico.* (Anthropological Papers of the University of Arizona, No. 13.) Tucson: University of Arizona Press, 1969.

————. Notes on Seri Indian Culture, Sonora, Mexico. Gainesville: University of Florida Press, 1959.

Guerrero, Raúl. *Historia general del arte mexicano.* Mexico City: Editorial Hermes, 1962.

Guerrero Galván, Jesús. "A Mexican Painter Views Modern Mexican Paintings." Pages 1–9 in *Inter-America* (Short Series II). Albuquerque: University of New Mexico Press, 1942 (pamplet).

Haddox, John H. *Antonio Caso: Philospher of Mexico.* Austin: Univeraity of Texas Press, 1971.

Hale, Charles A., and Meyer, Michael C. "Mexico: The National Period." Pages 115–119 in Roberto Esquenazi-Mayo and Michael Meyer (eds.), *Latin American Scholarship Since World War II.* Lincoln: University of Nebraska Press, 1971.

Hall, Barbara J. *Mexico in Pictures.* (Visual Geography Series.) New York: Sterling Publishing, 1973.

Hamill, Hugh M., Jr. *The Hidalgo Revolt: Prelude to Mexican Independence.* Gainesville: University of Florida Press, 1966.

Handbook of Middle American Indians. I: Natural Environment and Early Cultures. (Gen. ed., Robert Wauchope; vol. ed., Robert C. West.) Austin: University of Texas Press, 1964.

Handbook of Middle American Indians. VI: Social Anthropology. (Gen. ed., Robert Wauchope; vol. ed., Manning Nash.) Austin: University of Texas Press, 1967.

Handbook of Middle American Indians, VII-VIII: Ethnology. (Gen.

ed., Robert Wauchope; vol. ed., Evon Z. Vogt). Austin: University of Texas Press, 1969.

Hanke, Louis. *Mexico and the Caribbean.* Princeton: Van Nostrand, 1959.

Haring, C. H. *The Spanish Empire in America.* New York: Harcourt, Brace and World, 1963.

Harner, Evelyn L. *Changing Patterns of Education in Latin America.* (Research Memorandum RM60TMP-54.) Santa Barbara: Technical Military Planning Operation, General Electric Company, 1960.

———. "The Mexican Example," *Education, LXXXII, No. 1, September 1961, 53-55.*

Hasbrouk, Louise Seymour. *Mexico: From Cortés to Carranza.* New York: D. Appleton, 1918.

Hayner, Norman S. *New Patterns in Old Mexico.* New Haven, Connecticut: College and University Press, 1966.

Heath, Dwight B. (ed.) *Contemporary Cultures and Societies of Latin America.* New York: Random House, 1965.

Heath, Dwight B., and Adams, Richard N. *Contemporary Cultures and Societies of Latin America.* New York: Random House, 1965.

Heath, Shirley Brice. *Telling Tongues: Language Policy in Mexico, Colony to Nation.* New York: Center for Education in Latin America, Columbia University, Teachers College Press, 1972.

Hernández, Pedro E., and Jenkins, Quentin. "Sociology: Mexico, Central America, and the Caribbean." Pages 439-450 in Donald E. J. Stewart (ed.), *Handbook of Latin American Studies, XXXV: Social Sciences.* Gainesville: University of Florida Press, 1973.

Herring, Hubert. *A History of Latin America from the Beginnings to the Present.* (3d ed.) New York: Knopf, 1968.

Hill, A. David. *The Changing Landscape of a Mexican Municipio: Villa Las Rosas, Chiapas.* (Department of Geography Research Paper, No. 91.) Chicago: University of Chicago Press, 1964.

Hobart, Lois. *Mexican Mural.* New York: Harcout, Brace and World, 1963.

Hofstadter, Dan (ed.). *Mexico, 1946-73.* New York: Facts on File, 1974.

Horowitz, Irving Louis. *Masses in Latin America.* New York: Oxford University Press, 1970.

Houtart, François, and Pin, Emile. *The Church and the Latin American Revolution.* (Trans., Gilbert Barth.) New York: Sheed and Ward, 1965.

Howard, George P. *Religious Liberty in Latin America?* Philadelphia: Westminster Press, 1944.

Howells, W. W., et al. *The Maya and Their Neighbors.* New York: Appleton-Century-Crofts, 1962.

Hughes, Lloyd H. *The Mexican Cultural Mission Program.* Paris: United Nations Educational, Scientific and Cultural Organization, 1950.

Hunt, Lacy H., III. "Industrial Development on the Mexican Border," *Business Review*, February 1970, 3-12.

Ichaso, Marilyn. "Theater in Mexico," *Americas*, XXIV, No. 9, September 1972, 8-15.

Ingham, John M. "Ethnology: Middle America." Pages 69-78 in Donald E. J. Stewart (ed.), *Handbook of Latin American Studies*, XXXV: Social Sciences. Gainesville: University of Florida Press, 1973.

Institute of International Education. *Undergraduate Study Abroad.* New York: 1966.

Inter-American Development Bank. *Economic and Social Progress in Latin America: Annual Report, 1972.* Washington: IDB, n.d.

———. *Economic and Social Progress in Latin America: Annual Report, 1973.* Washington: IDB, n.d.

———. *Socio-Economic Progress in Latin America: Annual Report, 1971.* Washington: IDB, 1972.

———. *Socio-Economic Progress in Latin America: Social Progress Trust Fund Tenth Annual Report, 1970.* Washington: IDB, 1971.

———. *Statistical Data on the Latin American and Caribbean Countries, 1972.* Washington: IDB, n.d.

International Labour Organisation. International Labour Office. *Indigenous Peoples.* Geneva: ILO, 1953.

———. *Labor Force Projections. 1965-85: Latin America.* Geneva: ILO, 1971.

"An International Project for the Financing of Education." (Paper presented at Latin American workshop sponsored by the Center for Education and Development Studies of Harvard University, January 29 to February 1, 1973, in Cartegena, Colombia.) Washington: Inter-American Development Bank, n.d. (mimeo.).

International Yearbook of Education, 1968. Geneva: International Bureau of Education, 1969.

Isbister, John. "Urban Employment and Wages in a Developing Economy: The Case of Mexico," *Economic Development and Cultural Change*, XX, No. 1, October 1971, 24-46.

Iturriaga, José E. *La Estructura social y cultura de México.* Mexico City: Fondo de Cultura Económica, 1951.

Ivie, Stanley D. "A Comparison in Educational Philosophy: José Vasconcelos and John Dewey," *Comparative Education Review*, X, No. 3, October 1966, 404-417.

James, Earle K. "Church and State in Mexico," *Annals of the American Academy of Political and Social Science*, CCVIII, March 1940, 112-120.

James, Preston. *Latin America.* (4th ed.) New York: Odyssey Press, 1969.

Jara, Francisco G. "La Estratificación rural en México," *Revista Mexicana de Sociología* [Mexico City], XXXII, No. 3, May-June 1970, 691-707.

Jeffries, Charles. *Illiteracy: A World Problem.* New York: Praeger, 1967.

Jennings, Jesse D., and Norbeck, Edward (eds.). *Prehistoric Man in the New World.* Chicago: University of Chicago Press, 1964.

Jiménez, Rueda. *Herejías y supersticiones en la Nueva España.* Mexico City: Imprenta Universitaria, 1946.

Johnson, Allan Griswold. "Modernization and Social Change: Attitudes Towards Women's Roles in Mexico City." Unpublished doctoral dissertation. Ann Arbor: University of Michigan, 1972.

Johnson, William W. "The Enduring Indians," *Holiday,* XXXII, No. 4, October 1962, 92-103.

––––––. *Heroic Mexico.* New York: Doubleday, 1968.

Johnson, William W., and the Editors of *Life. Mexico.* (World Library.) New York: Time, 1966.

Kahl, Joseph A. *Comparative Perspectives on Stratification: Mexico, Great Britain, Japan.* Boston: Little, Brown, 1968.

––––––. *The Measure of Modernism: A Study of Values in Brazil and Mexico.* Austin: University of Texas Press, 1968.

Kasdon, L. M., and Kasdon, N. S. "Television: Vehicle for Literacy Training in Mexico," *Adult Leadership,* XVI, No. 3, September 1967, 91–92.

Kelly, Francis C. *Blood Drenched Altars.* Milwaukee: Bruce Publishing, 1935.

Kelly, Isabel. *Educational Anthropology: An Introduction.* New York: Wiley, 1965.

––––––. *Folk Practices in North Mexico: Birth Customs, Folk Medicine.* Austin: University of Texas Press, 1965.

Kenedy, Thomas B. (ed.) *Official Catholic Dictionary.* New York: Kenedy and Sons, 1968.

Kiev, Ario. *Curanderísmo: Mexican-American Folk Psychiatry.* New York: Free Press, 1972.

King, Joseph P. *The World and Its Peoples: Mexico.* New York: Greystone Press, 1964.

King, Richard G. *Provincial Universities of Mexico: An Analysis of Growth and Development.* New York: Praeger, 1972.

Knudson, Jerry W. "Anti-Semitism in Latin America (1): Barometer of Social Change," *Patterns of Prejudice* [London], VI, No. 5, September-October 1972, 1-11.

Koth, Marcia, et al. *Housing in Latin America.* (MIT Report, No. 1.) Cambridge: MIT Press, 1965.

Krieger, Ronald A. *Mexico: An Economic Survey.* New York: First National City Bank, 1971.

La Belle, Thomas J. (ed.) *Education and Development: Latin America and the Caribbean.* (Latin American Studies Series, No. 18.) Los Angeles: Latin American Center, University of California, 1972.

Lajoie, Lucen F. (ed.) *Who's Notable in Mexico City.* Mexico City;

Who's Who in Mexico, 1972.

Latapi, Pablo. *Educación nacional y opinión pública.* Mexico City: Centro de Estudios Educativos, 1966.

Latapi, Pedro. "Secundario Obligatorio? Un Precepto Inútil," *Excélsior* [Mexico City], IV, No. 20,926, July 14, 1974, A 6-9.

Lavine, Harold. *Central America.* New York: Time, 1964.

Leal, Luis. "Prose Fiction: Mexico." Pages 446-458 in Donald E. J. Stewart (ed.), *Handbook of Latin American Studies,* XXXV: Humanities. Gainesville: University of Florida Press, 1972.

————. "Spanish American Novel and Short Story." Pages 227–246 in Roberto Esquenazi-Mayo and Michael C. Meyer (eds.), *Latin American Scholarship Since World War II.* Lincoln: University of Nebraska Press, 1971.

Leal de Araujo, Lucila, "Extension of Social Security to Rural Workers," *International Labour Review* [Geneva], CVIII, No. 4, October 1973, 295-312.

Leonard, Olen E., and Loomis, Charles (eds.). *Latin American Social Organizations and Institutions.* East Lansing: Michigan State College Press, 1953.

León-Portilla, Miguel. *The Broken Spears: The Aztec Account of the Conquest of Mexico.* Boston: Beacon Press, 1962.

Leslie, Charles. *Now We Are Civilized.* Detroit: Wayne State University Press, 1960.

Lesser, Harriet Sara. "The History of the Jewish Community in Mexico, 1912-1970." Unpublished doctoral dissertation. New York: New York University, 1972.

Lewis, Oscar, *The Children of Sánchez.* New York: Random House, 1961.

————. *Five Families.* New York: Basic Books, 1959.

————. *Life in a Mexican Village: Tepoztlán Restudied.* Urbana: University of Illinois Press, 1963.

————. "Manuel in the Thieves' Market," *Harper's Magazine,* CCXXII, No. 1333, June 1961, 66-76.

————. "Urbanization Without Breakdown: A Case Study," *Scientific Monthly,* LXXV, No. 7, July 1952, 31–41.

Lindquist, Sven. *The Shadow: Latin American Faces the Seventies.* (Trans., Keith Bradfield.) (Pelican Latin American Library.) Harmondsworth, Middlesex, England: Penguin Books, 1972.

Lipset, Seymour Martin. "Values, Education, and Entrepreneurship." Pages 76–124 in Thomas J. La Belle (ed.), *Education and Development: Latin America and the Caribbean.* (Latin American Studies Series, No. 18.) Los Angeles: Latin American Center, University of California, 1972.

Littwin, Lawrence. *Latin America: Catholicism and Class Conflict.* Encino, California: Dickinson Publishing, 1974.

López Cámara, Francisco. *El Desafío de la clase media.* Mexico City:

Editorial Joaquín Mortiz, 1971.

Lowry, Dennis T. "Radio, TV, and Literacy in Mexico," *Journal of Broadcasting*, XIV, No. 2, Spring 1970, 239–244.

McCann, Eugene C. "Anglo-American and Mexican Management Philosophies," *MSU Business Topics*, XVIII, No. 3, Summer 1970, 28-37.

Maccoby, Michael. *Social Change and Social Character in Mexico and the United States*, I. (CIDOC, Cuaderno 55.) Cuernavaca, Mexico: Centro Inter-Cultural de Documentación, 1970.

Maccoby, Michael, and Foster, George M. "Methods of Studying Mexican Peasant Personality: Rorschach, TAT, and Dreams." *Anthropological Quarterly*, XLIII, No. 4, October 1970, 225-242.

McDougall, Charlotte, "Mexico City," *Canadian Geographical Review* [Ottowa], LXXXV, No. 4, October 1972, 142-149.

McHenry, John Patrick. *A Short History of Mexico*. New York: Doubleday, 1962.

McQuown, Norman A. "The Indigenous Languages of Latin America," *American Anthropologist*, LVII, No. 3, June 1955, 501-570.

Maddox, James. "Education in Tepoztlan." Pages 257–264 in J. W. Hanson and Cole S. Brembeck (eds.), *Education and the Development of Nations*. New York: Holt, Rinehart and Winston, 1966.

Maddox, James G. *Mexican Land Reform*. (American Universities Field Staff Reports, Mexican and Caribbean Area Studies, IV, No. 5.) New York: AUFS, July 1957.

Madsen, William. *The Virgin's Children*. Austin: University of Texas Press, 1960.

Madsen, William, and Madsen, Claudia. *A Guide to Mexican Witchcraft*. (2d ed.) (Minutiae Mexicana Series.) Mexico City: Editorial Minutiae Mexicana, 1972.

Mallet, Alfredo. "Diversification or Standardization: Two Trends in Latin American Social Security," *International Labour Review* [Geneva], CI, No. 5, January 1970, 49-83.

Marett, Robert. *Mexico*. New York: Walker, 1971.

Martínez Domínguez, Guillermo. "Integración y desarrollo de la industria eléctrica de México: La Obra 1965–70," *Trimestre Económico* [Mexico City], XXXVIII, No. 150, April-June 1971, 433-448.

Martínez Ríos, Jorge. *El Perfil de México en 1980*, III. Mexico City: Siglo XXI Editores, 1972.

May, Jacques M., and McClellan, Donna L. *The Ecology of Malnutrition in Mexico and Central America*. New York: Hafner Publishing, 1972.

Mecham, J. Lloyd. *Church and State in Latin America*. Chapel Hill: University of North Carolina Press, 1966.

Mendez Napoles, Oscar. *Planeación de la educación en México*. Mexico City: Universidad Nacional Autónoma de México, 1970.

Mendieta y Núñez, Lucio. "La Cuestión racial en América," *Humanitas* [Monterrey], XIII, 1972, 485-507.

"The Mexican M.D.'s," *Newsweek*, LXXXIV, No. 2, July 8, 1974, 49.

Mexico. Banco Nacional de Obras y Serviciós Públicos. *Programa Buena Vivienda: Mejoramiento de Vivienda*. Mexico City: 1970.

Mexico. Dirección General de Estadística. *Anuario Estadístico de los Estados Unidos Mexicanos, 1968–1969*. Mexico City: Talleres Gráficos de la Nación, 1971.

"Mexico: Las iniciativas sobre población van tomando forma," *Población* [Bogotá], IV, No. 5, 1973, 1-4.

"Mexico Works on Its Economy," *Investors Reader*, LX, No. 3, February 7, 1973, 23–27.

Meyer, Michael C. *Huerta: A Political Portrait*. Lincoln: University of Nebraska Press, 1972.

Miles, Beryl. *Spirit of Mexico*. London: John Murray, 1961.

Miller, Clyde. "Film Makers of Churubusco," *Américas*, XXVI, No. 4, April 1974, 15-20.

Miller, Frank C. *Old Villages and a New Town: Industrialization in Mexico*. Menlo Park, California: Cummings Publishing, 1973.

Milne, Jean. *Fiesta Time in Latin America*. Los Angeles: Ward Ritchie Press, 1965.

Mitchell, James E. *The Emergence of a Mexican Church: The Associate Reformed Presbyterian Church of Mexico*. South Pasadena, California: William Carey Library, 1970.

Morales Coello, Eduardo. "Mexico: Notas sobre política de recursos humanos en el desarrollo económico y social," *La Educación*, XIII, No. 51 and 52, July-December 1968, 55-61.

Moreira, J. Roberto. "Education and Development in Latin America." Pages 7–44 in Thomas J. La Belle (ed.). *Education and Development: Latin America and the Caribbean*. (Latin American Studies Series, No. 18.) Los Angeles: Latin American Center, University of California, 1972.

Morgan Guaranty Trust. *Banking and Public Holidays Throughout the World, 1973*. New York: 1972.

Mueller, Marnie W. "Changing Patterns of Agricultural Output and Productivity in the Private and Land Reform Sectors in Mexico, 1940–1960," *Economic Development and Cultural Change*, XVIII, No. 2, January 1970, 252-266.

Muñoz, Humberto; de Oliveira, Orlandina; and Stern, Claudio. *Categorías de migrantes y nativos y algunos de sus caracteristicas socioeconomicas: Comparación entre las ciudades de Monterrey y México*. Mexico City: Universidad Nacional Autónoma de México, 1971.

Munro, Dana G. *The Latin American Republics: A History*. New York: Appleton-Century-Crofts, 1960.

Murray, Paul V. *The Catholic Church in Mexico*. Mexico City: Aldina, 1965

Myers, Charles Nash. *Education and National Development in Mexico*. Princeton: Industrial Relations Section, Princeton University, 1965.

Nash, Joe. *A Guide to Mexico: Then and Now.* New York: International Publications Service, 1966.

Navarrete, Ifigenía M. de. "Income Distribution in Mexico." Pages 133–172 in Enrique Pérez López, et al, *Mexico's Recent Economic Growth: The Mexican View.* (Trans., Marjorie Urquidi.) (Latin American Monographs, No. 10.) Austin Institute of Latin American Studies, University of Texas, 1967.

Needler, Martin C. "Political Aspects of Urbanization in Mexico." Pages 287–299 in Arthur J. Field (ed.), *City and Country in the Third World.* New York: Schenkman Publisher, 1970.

———. *Politics and Society in Mexico.* Albuquerque: University of New Mexico Press, 1971.

Nelson, Cynthia, *The Waiting Village: Social Change in Rural Mexico.* Boston: Little, Brown, 1971.

Nevins, A. J. (ed.) *Maryknoll Catholic Dictionary.* New York: Dimension Books, 1965.

The New Catholic Encyclopedia, IX. New York: McGraw-Hill, 1967.

Nicholson, Irene. *Mexican and Central American Mythology.* London: Paul Hamlyn, 1967.

———. *The X in Mexico.* London: Faber and Faber, 1965.

Nida, Eugene A. "The Relationship of Social Structure to the Problems of Evangelists in Latin America," *Practical Anthropology,* V, No. 3, May–June 1958, 101–123.

Nomland, John Barrington. "Contemporary Mexican Theatre, 1900-1950." Unpublished Ph.D. dissertation. Los Angeles: Hispanic Languages and Literature, University of California, 1957.

Norman, James. *Terry's Guide to Mexico.* New York: Doubleday, 1972.

Ocampo, Londoño Alfonso. "La universidad abierta de la UNAM (México)," *La Educación,* XVIII, No. 65, January-April 1973, 7–14.

Odell, Peter R., and Preston, Dwight. *Economies and Societies in Latin America: A Geographical Interpretation.* New York: John Wiley and Sons, 1973.

Oficina Internacional del Trabajo. *Las empresas de América Latina ante el problema vivienda obrera.* Geneva: 1972.

Olivera, Sedano. *Aspectos del conflicto religioso de 1926 a 1929: sus antecedentes y consecuencias,* Mexico City: Instituto Nacional de Antropología y Historia, 1966.

Olizar, Marynka, *Guía a los mercados de México.* (5th ed.) Mexico City: n. pub., 1968.

Organización de los Estados Americanos. *Boletín estadístico.* (No. 99.) Washington: September 1973.

Organización de los Estados Americanos. Instituto Interamericano de Estadística. *América en Cifras 1970, Situación Cultural: Educación y Otros Aspectos Culturales.* Washington: 1971.

———. *América en Cifras 1972, Situación Cultural: Educación y Otros Aspectos Culturales.* Washington: 1973.

————. *América en Cifras 1972, Situación Demográfica: Estado y Movimiento de la Población.* Washington: 1972.

————. *América en Cifras 1972, Situación Física: Territorio y Clima.* Washington: 1972.

————. *América en Cifras 1972, Situación Social: Hogar, Habitación, Mejoramiento Urbano, Previsión Social, Asistencia Médica y de Salud, y Trabajo.* Washington: 1973.

Organización Panamericana de la Salud. *Salud y población.* (Publicación Científica, No. 232.) Washington: 1971.

Organization for Economic Cooperation and Development. *Statistics of the Occupational and Educational Structure of the Labour Force in 53 Countries.* Paris: 1969.

Organization of American States. *Youth in Latin America: Realities and Expectations.* Washington: 1974.

Paddock, John. *Ancient Oaxaca: Discoveries in Mexican Archeology and History.* Stanford: Stanford University Press, 1966.

Padilla Aragón, Enrique. *México: Desarrollo con pobreza.* Mexico City: Siglo Viente, 1969.

Pan American Health Organization. *Annual Report of the Director.* (Official Document No. 116.) Washington: 1972.

————. *Facts on Health Progress, 1971.* (Scientific Publication, No. 227.) Washington: 1971.

————. *Health Conditions in the Americas, 1965-1968.* (Scientific Publication, No. 207.) Washington: 1970.

————. *Reported Cases of Notifiable Diseases in the Americas, 1969.* (Scientific Publication, No. 247.) Washington: 1972.

Parkes, Henry Bamford. *A History of Mexico.* Cambridge: Houghton Mifflin, 1938.

Parry, J. H. *The Spanish Seaborne Empire.* New York: Knopf, 1966.

Paz, Octavio. *The Labyrinth of Solitude.* New York: Grove Press, 1961.

Pennington, Campbell. *The Tarahumara of Mexico.* Salt Lake City: University of Utah Press, 1963.

Pike, Fredrick B. (ed.) *The Conflict Between Church and State in Latin America.* New York: Knopf, 1964.

Pitt-Rivers, Julian. "Mestizo or ladino?" *Race* [London], X, No. 4, April 1969, 463-477.

"Population Year in Review, 1972." *Population Bulletin,* XXVIII, No. 6, December 1972, 1-10.

Powell, Philip W. *Soldiers, Indians, and Silver.* Berkeley: University of California Press, 1952.

Pozas, Ricardo, and Pozas, Isabel H. de. *Los Indios en las clases de México.* Havana: Casa de las Americas, 1971.

Puffer, Ruth Rice, and Serrano, Carlos V. *Patterns of Mortality in Early Childhood.* Washington: Pan American Health Organization, 1973.

Quirk, Robert E. *The Mexican Revolution, 1914–1915: The Convention*

of Aguascalientes. Bloomington: University of Indiana Press, 1960.
————. *Mexico.* (Modern Nations in Historical Perspective.) Englewood Cliffs: Prentice-Hall, 1971.

Ramos, Joseph R. *Labor and Development in Latin America.* New York: Columbia University Press, 1970.

Ramos, Samuel. *Profile of Man and Culture in Mexico.* (Trans., Peter G. Earle.) Austin: University of Texas Press, 1962.

Rand McNally. *The International Atlas.* New York: 1969.

Ranis, Peter. *Five Latin American Nations: A Comparative Political Study.* New York: Macmillan, 1971.

Reck, Gregory George. "Goodbye, Ixoxolotl: Acculturation of a Mestizo-Indian Village in Mexico." Unpublished doctoral dissertation. Washington: Catholic University, 1972.

Redfield, Robert. *The Folk Culture of Yucatán.* Chicago: University of Chicago Press, 1941.

Reed, Irving B., et al. *The Latin American Scene of the Seventies: A Basic Fact Book.* (Monographs in International Affairs.) Coral Gables: Center for Advanced International Studies, University of Miami, 1972.

Reed, Nelson. *The Caste War of Yucatán.* Stanford: Stanford University Press, 1964.

Rengert, Arlene C. *Who Moves to Cities? A Multivariate Examination of Migrants from Rural Mexico.* (U.S. Department of State, Office of External Research, Foreign Affairs Research Paper, No. FAR 17310–P.) Washington: April 1973.

Represas, José. "Agro-Industry: Key to Rural Development," *Mexican-American Review* [Mexico City], XL, June 1972, 19-23.

Restrepo Fernandez Iván. "El caso de los jornaleros agrícolas en México," *Aportes* [Paris], XXIII, January 1972, 53-61.

Reyes, Nevarez Salvador. "El Machismo en México," *Mundo Nuevo* [Paris], XLVI, April 1970, 14-19.

Rhodes, Robert I. "Mexico: A Model for Capitalist Development in Latin America," *Science and Society,* XXXIV, No. 1, Spring 1970, 61-77.

Richard, Robert. *The Spiritual Conquest of Mexico.* Berkeley: University of California Press, 1966.

Rippy, J. Fred. *Latin America: A Modern History.* Ann Arbor: University of Michigan Press, 1958.

Riviére, P.G. "The Honor of Sánchez," *Man* [London], II, No. 4, December 1967, 569-583.

Roberts, Robert E. "Modernization and Infant Mortality in Mexico," *Economic Development and Cultural Change,* XXI, No. 4, Pt. 1, July 1973, 655-669.

Roberts, Robert E., and McBee, George W. "Modernization and Economic Development in Mexico: A Factor Analysis Approach," *Economic Development and Cultural Change,* XVI, No. 4, July 1968, 603-612.

Robertson, William Spence. *History of the Latin American Nations.*

(Rev. ed.) New York: D. Appleton, 1930.

Robinson, Harry. *Latin America: A Geographic Survey*. New York: Praeger, 1967.

Rodman, Selden. *The Mexico Traveler: A Concise History and Guide*. New York: Meredith Press, 1969.

Roemer, Milton J. "Development of Medical Services Under Social Security in Latin America," *International Labour Review* [Geneva], CVIII, No. 1, July 1973, 1-23.

Rolle, Andrew F. *The Lost Cause: The Confederate Exodus to Mexico*. Norman: University of Oklahoma Press, 1965.

Romanell, Patrick. *Making of the Mexican Mind*. Lincoln: University of Nebraska Press, 1952.

Romano, Agustín. "La Política indigenista de México y la antropología aplicada," *America Indígena* [Mexico City], XXIX, No. 4, October 1969, 1065-1076.

Romanucci-Ross, Lola. *Conflict, Violence, and Morality in a Mexican Village*. Palo Alto, California: National Press, 1973.

Ross, Edward A. *The Social Revolution in Mexico*. New York: Century, 1923.

Ross, John B. *The Economic System of Mexico*. Stanford: California Institute of International Studies, 1971.

Ross, Patricia Bent. *Mexico*. Sacramento: California State Department of Education, 1964.

Ross, Stanley R. (ed.) *Is the Mexican Revolution Dead?* New York: Knopf, 1966.

Roys, Ralph L. *The Indian Background of Colonial Yucatán*. (Publication No. 58.) Washington: Carnegie Institute, 1943.

Ruddle, Kenneth, and Odermann, Donald (eds.). *Statistical Abstract of Latin America, 1971*. Los Angeles: Latin American Center, University of California, December 1972.

Ruíz, Ramón Eduardo. *Mexico: The Challenge of Poverty and Illiteracy*, San Marino: Huntington Library, 1963.

Russell, Richard J., and Kniffen, Fred B. *Culture Worlds*. New York: Macmillan, 1951.

Russett, Bruce. *World Handbook of Social and Political Indicators*. New Haven: Yale University Press, 1964.

Rycroft, W. Stanley. *Religion and Faith in Latin America*. Philadelphia: Westminister Press, 1958.

Rycroft, W. Stanley, and Clemmer, Myrtle M. *A Factual Study of Latin America*. New York: Office for Research, Commission of Ecumenical Mission and Relations, United Presbyterian Church in the U.S.A., 1958.

Sabloff, Jeremy A., and Willey, Gordon R. "The Collapse of Maya Civilization in the Southern Highlands: A Consideration of History and Process," *Southwestern Journal of Anthropology*, XXIII, No. 4, Winter 1967, 311-336.

Sanders, William T. "The Central Mexican Symbiotic Region: A Study in Prehistoric Settlement Patterns." Pages 115–127 in Gordon R. Willey (ed.), *Prehistoric Settlement Patterns in the New World*, New York: Wenner-Gren Foundation for Anthropological Research, 1956.

Sarfatti, Magali. *Spanish Bureaucratic-Patrimonialism in America*. (Politics of Modernization Series, No. 1.) Berkeley: Institute of International Studies, University of California, 1966.

Schmiedehaus, W. "A Beleaguered People: The Mennonites of Mexico," *Landscape*, IV, No. 1, Summer 1954, 13-21.

Scott, Robert E. *Mexican Government in Transition*. Urbana: University of Illinois Press, 1964.

Séjourne, Laurette. *Thought and Religion in Ancient Mexico*. New York: Grove Press, 1960.

Sekulic, Stojam. "Siete afirmaciones erroneas sobre iberoamerica," *Communidades* [Madrid], IV, January-April 1969, 42-55.

Selby, Henry A. *Zapotec Deviance: The Convergence of Folk and Modern Sociology*. Austin: University of Texas Press, 1973.

Senior, Clarence. *Land Reform and Democracy*. Gainesville: University of Florida Press, 1958.

Severo, Richard. "The Flight of the Wetbacks," *New York Times*, CXXIII, No. 42414, March 10, 1974, 6, 17, 77-84.

Shafer, Robert J. *Mexican Business Organizations: History and Analysis*. Syracuse: Syracuse University Press, 1973.

Simon, Kate. *Mexico: Places and Pleasures*. (Rev. ed.) New York: World Publishing, 1971.

Simpson, Lesley B. *Many Mexicos*. (4th ed., rev.) Berkeley: University of California Press, 1967.

Solís, Leopoldo. *La realidad económica mexicana*. Mexico City: Siglo XX, 1970.

Solis Garza, Hernán. *Los Mexicanos del norte*. Mexico City: Editorial Nuestro Tiempo, 1971.

Sosa Vásquez, Esperanza, et al. "Nursing Resources in Mexico," *International Nursing Review* [Geneva], XX, No. 1, January–February 1973, 2–24.

South American Handbook, 1974. (Golden Jubilee Ed.) (Ed., John Brooks.) Bath, England: Trade and Travel Publications, 1974.

Stakman, E.C., et al. *Campaigns Against Hunger*. Cambridge: Harvard University Press, 1967.

A Statement of the Laws of Mexico in Matters Affecting Business. (4th ed., rev.) Washington: General Secretariat, Organization of American States, 1970.

Statistical Yearbook, 1973. New York: United Nations, Department of Economic and Social Affairs, 1974.

Stavenhagen, Rodolfo. *Agrarian Problems and Peasant Movements in Latin America*. Garden City: Doubleday, Anchor Books, 1970.

————.Classes, Colonialism, and Acculturation." Pages 235-288 in

Irving Louis Horowitz (ed.), *Masses in Latin America*. New York: Oxford University Press, 1970.

Stein, Stanley J., and Stein, Barbara H. *The Colonial Heritage of Latin America: Essays on Economic Dependence in Perspective*. New York: Oxford University Press, 1970.

Steiner, Henry Malcolm. "The Mexican Border Industrialization Program," *Texas Business Review*, XLV, No. 7, July 1971, 145-149.

Stokes, William S. "Social Classes in Latin America." Pages 51-70 in Peter G. Snow (ed.), *Government and Politics in Latin America: A Reader*. New York: Holt, Rinehart and Winston, 1967.

Stoltman, Joseph P., and Ball, John M. "Migration and the Local Economic Factor in Rural Mexico," *Human Organization*, XXX, No. 1, Spring 1971, 47-56.

Stoppelman, Joseph. *People of Mexico*. London: Phoenix House, 1964.

"The Stork vs. the Steel Mill," *Forbes*, CXII, August 15, 1973, 33-35.

Stout, Joseph Allen. *The Liberators: Filibustering Expenditions into Mexico, 1848–1862, and the Last Thrust of Manifest Destiny*. Los Angeles: Western Lore Press, 1973.

Stycos, J. Mayone. *Human Fertility in Latin America*. Ithaca: Cornell University Press, 1968.

Tamayo, Jorge L. *Atlas geográfico general de México*. Mexico City: Instituto Mexicano de Investigaciones Económicas, 1962.

Tannenbaum, Frank. *Mexico: The Struggle for Peace and Bread*. New York: Knopf, 1964.

———. *Ten Keys to Latin America*. New York: Knopf, 1963.

Tax, Sol (ed.). *Heritage of Conquest*. Glencoe: Free Press, 1952.

Teja-Zabre, Alfonso. *Breve historia de México*. Mexico City: La Impresora, 1935.

Thomas, Alfred B. *Latin America: A History*. New York: Macmillan, 1956.

Thomas, Norman. "La Posición lingüística y geográfica de los indios zoques," *Instituto de Ciencias y Artes de Chiapas* [Mexico City], XIX, No. 1, January–June 1970, 15-39.

Thompson, J. Eric S. *The Civilization of the Mayas*. (Popular Series, Anthropology, No. 25.) Chicago: Chicago Natural History Museum, 1958.

Thompson, Richard A. "Stochastic and Structure: Cultural Change and Social Mobility in A Yucatec Town," *Southwestern Journal of Anthropology*, XXVI, No. 4, Winter 1970, 354-374.

———. "Structural Statistics and Structural Mechanics: The Analysis of Compadrazgo," *Southwestern Journal of Anthropology*, XXVII, No. 4, Winter 1971, 381-403.

Timmons, Wilbert H. *Morelos of Mexico*. El Paso: Texas Western College Press, 1963.

" 'To Harness What Nature Gives Us,' An Interview with Luis Echeverría, President of Mexico," *Impact of Science on Society*

[Paris], XXII, Nos. 1 and 2, January-June 1972, 43-52.

Tomme, Clark. *The Mexican Venture*. New York: Oxford University Press, 1953.

Toor, Frances. *Mexican Folkways*. New York: Crown Publishers, 1947.

Treviño, Elizabeth Borton. *Mexico*. New York: Farrar, Straus, and Giroux, 1970.

Tucker, William P. "Las Elites Mexicanas," *Aportes* [Paris], XIII, No. 11, July 1969, 103–106.

Tuohy, William S., and Ames, Barry. *Mexican University Students in Politics: Rebels Without Allies*. (Monograph Series in World Politics, No. 3.) Denver: University of Denver, 1970.

Turner, Frederick C. *Catholicism and Political Development in Latin America*. Chapel Hill: University of North Carolina Press, 1971.

―――. "The Compatibility of the Church and State in Mexico." *Journal of Interamerican Studies*, IX, No. 4, October 1967, 591-602.

―――. *The Dynamics of Mexican Nationalism*. Chapel Hill: University of North Carolina Press, 1968.

Ulmer, Melville J. "Who's Making It in Mexico?", *New Republic*, CLXV, No. 13, September 25, 1971, 21-23.

Unikel, Luis. "The Process of Urbanization in Mexico: Distribution and Growth of Urban Population." Pages 247–302 in Francine F. Rabinovitz and Felicity M. Trueblood (eds.), *Latin American Urban Research*, I. Beverly Hills: Sage Publications, 1971.

Unión Panamericana. *Los Libros de Texto de las Escuelas Primarias de América*. Washington: 1964.

Unión Panamericana. Instituto Interamericano de Estadística. *América en Cifras 1967, Situación Cultural: Educación y Otros Aspectos Culturales*. Washington: 1969.

―――. *América en Cifras 1967, Situación Demográfica: Estado y Movimiento de la Población*. Washington: 1968.

United Nations. *Population and Vital Statistics Report: Data Available as of 1 April 1974*. (Statistical Papers, Series A, XXVI, No. 2.) New York: UN, 1974.

―――. *Social Change and Social Development Policy in Latin America*. New York: UN, 1970.

United Nations. Economic Commission for Latin America. *Education, Human Resources, and Development in Latin America*. New York: UN, 1968.

United Nations Educational, Scientific and Cultural Organization. *World Survey of Education*, II: Primary Education. Geneva: UNESCO, 1958.

―――. *World Survey of Education*, III: Secondary Education. New York: International Documents Service, 1961.

―――. *World Survey of Education*, IV: Higher Education. New York: UNESCO Publications Center, 1966.

————. *World Survey of Education*, V: Educational Policy, Legislation, and Administration, Paris: UNESCO, 1971.

U. S. Agency for International Development. *Population Program Assistance*. Washington: AID, October 1970.

U. S. Agency for International Development. Bureau for Latin America, Office of Development Programs. *Summary Economic and Social Indicators: 18 Latin American Countries*. Washington: AID, 1972.

U. S. Department of Commerce. Bureau of International Commerce. *Establishing a Business in Mexico*. (Overseas Business Reports, OBR 72-027.)

U. S. Department of State. *Background Notes: Mexico* (No. 7865.) Washington: GPO, March 1971.

U. S. Embassy in Mexico City. *Mexican Government Plans Significant Expansion in Housing Program* (Department of State Airgram, A-210.) Mexico City: April 18, 1972.

————. *Preparatory Meetings for Fourth Inter-American Housing Congress*, (Department of State Airgram, A-227.) Mexico City: May 8, 1973.

Universidad Autónoma de Puebla. "A la Opinión Pública: El Nuevo Rol de la Universidad," *Excélsior* [Mexico City], V, No. 20925, July 1974, A–13.

Uribe Villegas, Oscar. "Indígenas monoligües en la población de México en 1960," *Aportes* [Paris], XIV, October 1969, 69-79.

Vallier, Ivan. "Religious Elites: Differentiations and Developments in Roman Catholicism." Chapter 6 in Seymour M. Lipset and Also Solari (eds.), *Elites in Latin America*. New York: Oxford University Press, 1967.

Vargas Galindo, Sergio, and Goldberg, David. "The Economic Experience of Migrants to Mexico City." (Paper obtained from U. S. Department of State, Office of External Research, Foreign Affairs Research Paper, No. FAR 18773-P.) Washington: 1973 (mimeo.).

Vasconcelos, José. *Breve historia de México*. Mexico City: Ediciones Rotas, 1938.

Veliz, Caludio (ed.). *Latin America and the Caribbean: A Handbook*. New York: Praeger, 1968.

Vogt, Evon Z. *The Zinacantecos of Mexico: A Modern Maya Way of Life*. New York: Holt, Rinehart and Winston, 1970

Von Winning, Hasso, and Adams, Richard E. V. "Archaeology: Middle America." Pages 26–46 in Donald E. J. Stewart (ed.), *Handbook of Latin American Studies*, XXXV: Social Sciences. Gainesville: University of Florida Press, 1973.

Wallace, Thompson. *The People of Mexico*. New York: Harper and Row, 1921.

Webb, Kempton E. *Geography of Latin America: A Regional Analysis*. (Foundations of World Regional Geography.) Englewood Cliffs:

Prentice-Hall, 1972.

West, Robert C., and Augelli, John P. *Middle America: Its Lands and Peoples*. Englewood Cliffs: Prentice-Hall, 1966.

Whetten, Nathan. *Rural Mexico*. Chicago: University of Chicago Press, 1948.

Whiteford, Andrew H. *Two Cities of Latin America: A Comparative Description of Classes*. New York: Doubleday Anchor Books, 1964.

Wilgus, A. Curtis, and D'Eca, Raul. *Latin American History*. (College Outline Series.) New York: Barnes and Noble, 1967.

Wilke, Raymond. *San Miguel: A Mexican Collective Ejido*. Stanford: Stanford University Press, 1971.

Wilkie, James W. *The Mexican Revolution: Federal Expenditures and Social Change Since 1910*. (2d ed., rev.) Berkeley: University of California Press, 1970.

Willey, Gordon R. "Mesoamerica." Pages 84-105 in Robert J. Brainard and Gordon R. Willey (eds.), *Courses Toward Urban Life*. Chicago: Aldine, 1962.

Williams, Mary W.; Ruhl, J.; and Miller, Russell E. *The People and Politics of Latin America*. Boston: Ginn, 1958.

Winnie, William W., Jr. "Estimate of Inter-State Migration in Mexico, 1950–1960: Data and Methods," *Anthropologica* [Caracas], No. 14, June 1965, 38–60. (Reprinted and translated by Latin American Center, University of California at Los Angeles.)

Wolf, Eric R. "Aspects of Group Relations in a Complex Society: Mexico." Pages 85–101 in Dwight Heath and Richard N. Adams (eds.), *Contemporary Cultures and Societies of Latin America*. New York: Random House, 1965.

————. *Sons of the Shaking Earth*. Chicago: University of Chicago Press, 1959.

Wood, James. "Church and State in Latin America," *Journal of Church and State*, VIII, No. 2, Spring 1966, 45-52.

Worcester, Donald E., and Schaeffer, Wendell G. *The Growth and Culture of Latin America*. New York: Oxford University Press, 1956.

The World and Its Peoples: Mexico. New York: Greystone Press, 1964.

World of Learning, 1973–74, II. London: Europa Publications, 1973.

Worldmark Encyclopedia of the Nations: America (Ed., Moshe Y. Sachs.) New York: Worldmark Press, Harper and Row, 1967.

Year Book of Labour Statistics, 1970. Geneva: International Labour Office, 1970.

Year Book of Labour Statistics, 1973. Geneva: International Labour Office, 1973.

Zorita, Alonso de. *Life and Labor in Ancient Mexico*. New Brunswick: Rutgers University Press, 1963.

(Various issues of the following periodicals were also used in the preparation of this section: *Américas* [Washington], January 1970-February 1974; *Bolsa Review* [London], January 1972-June 1974;

Christian Science Monitor [Boston], January 1972-June 1974; *Financial Times* [London], January 1973-April 1974; *Latin America: A Weekly Political and Economic Report* [London], January 1971-April 1974; *New York Times*, January 1971-July 1974; *Noticias* [New York], January 1973-April 1974; *Población* [Bogotá, Colombia], 1970-74; *Times of Americas* [Washington], March 1968-June 1974; *Translations on Latin America* [Washington], January 1970-June 1974; and *Washington Post*, January 1971-July 1974.)

Section II. Political

Agor, Weston H., and Suárez, Andres. "The Emerging Latin American Political Subsystem," *Changing Latin America*, XXX, No. 4, 1972 153-166.

Alcaraz, Rodolfo. "Sesenta años de periodismo mexicano," *Historia y Sociedad* [Mexico City], IV, 1966, 107–125.

Archer, Jules. *Mexico and the United States*. New York: Hawthorne Books, 1973.

Aztiz, Carlos A. "Mexico's Foreign Policy: Disguised Dependence," *Current History*, LX, No. 393, May 1974, 220-224.

Aztiz, Carlos A., and McCarthy, Mary F. (eds.) *Latin American International Politics: Ambitions, Capabilities, and the National Interest of Mexico, Brazil, and Argentina*. Notre Dame: University of Notre Dame Press, 1969.

Bailey, Norman A. *Latin America in World Politics*. New York: Walker, 1967.

Baker, Richard D. *Judicial Review in Mexico: A Study of the Amparo Suit*. (Latin American Monographs, No. 22.) Austin: University of Texas Press, 1971.

Ball, Margaret M. *The OAS in Transition*. Durham: Duke University Press, 1969.

Bizzarro, Salvatore, "Mexico Under Echeverría," *Current History*, LXVI, No. 393, May 1974, 212-216, 224.

Blair, Calvin P. "Mexico in the World Economy," *Current History*, LXVI, No. 393, May 1974, 217-219, 224.

Brandenburg, Frank. *The Making of Modern Mexico*. Englewood Cliffs: Prentice-Hall, 1964.

Broadcasting Stations of the World. (25th ed.) Washington: Foreign Broadcast Information Service, 1972.

Burgoa, Ignacio. *El juicio de amparo*. (3rd ed.) Mexico City: Editorial Porrua, 1950.

Burnett, Ben G., and Johnson, Kenneth F. (eds.) *Political Forces in Latin America: Dimensions of the Quest for Stability*. Belmont, California: Wadsworth Publishing, 1968.

Callahan, James M. *American Foreign Policy in Mexican Relations*. New York: Macmillan, 1932.

Calvert, Peter. *Mexico*. (Nations of the Modern World.) New York: Praeger, 1973.

Camp, Roderich Al. "The Cabinet and the Técnico in Mexico and the United States," *Journal of Comparative Administration*, III,

August, 1971, 188-214.

Cancino, Francisco Cuevas. "The Foreign Policy of Mexico," Pages 643–671 in Joseph E. Black and Kenneth W. Thompson (eds.), *Foreign Policies in a World of Change.* New York: Harper and Row, 1963.

de Carlos, Ann Wyckoff. *Mexico's National Liberation Movement: The MLD.* Stanford: Institute of Hispanic American and Luso-Brazilian Studies, Stanford University Press, 1963.

Carlos, Manuel L. *Politics and Development in Rural Mexico: A Study of Socioeconomic Modernization.* New York: Praeger, 1974.

Carlos, Manuel L., and Brokensha, David. "Agencies, Goals, and Clients: A Cross-Cultural Analysis," *Studies in Comparative International Development,* VII, No. 2, Summer 1972, 130-155.

Castaneda, Jorge. *Mexico and the United Nations.* New York: Manhattan Publishing, 1958.

Castro Leal, Antonio. "El Pueblo de México espera: Estudio sobre la radio y la televisión." *Cuadernos Americanos* [Mexico City], CL, January-February 1967, 90.

Chilcote, Ronald. "The Press in Latin America, Spain, and Portugal: A Summary of Recent Developments," *Hispanic American Report* (Special Issue), 1963.

Clagett, Helen L., and Valderrama, David M. *A Revised Guide to the Law and Legal Literature of Mexico.* (Latin American Series, No. 38.) Washington: Library of Congress, 1973.

Cline, Howard F. *Mexico: Revolution to Evolution, 1940 to 1960.* New York: Oxford University Press, 1963.

———. *The United States and Mexico.* (Rev. ed.) Cambridge: Harvard University Press, 1963.

Cole, Richard Ray. "The Mass Media in Mexico: Ownership and Control." Unpublished Ph.D. dissertation. Minneapolis: University of Minnesota, 1972.

———. *The Mexican Press System: Selected Aspects of Growth, Control, Ownership.* Chapel Hill: University of North Carolina, 1973.

Connell-Smith, Gordon. *The Inter-American System.* London: Oxford University Press, 1966.

Considine, John J. (ed.) *The Church in the New Latin America.* Notre Dame: Fides, 1964.

Couturier, Edith B. "Realism, Nationalism, and Legalism in Mexican Foreign Policy." Chapter 6 in Harold E. Davis and Larman C. Wilson (eds.), "Latin American Foreign Policies: An Analysis." Washington: American University, 1971 (unpublished manuscript).

Corwin, Arthur F. *Contemporary Mexican Attitudes toward Population, Poverty, and Public Opinion.* Gainesville: University of Florida Press, 1963.

Crow, John A. *Mexico Today.* (Rev. ed.) New York: Harper and Row, 1972.

Cumberland, Charles C. "Mexico Since Cárdenas." Pages 285–346 in

Richard N. Adams, et al, *Social Change in Latin America Today: Its Implications for United States Policy.* New York: Harper, for Council on Foreign Relations, 1960.

———. *Mexico: The Struggle for Modernity.* New York: Oxford University Press, 1968.

Díaz Rangel, Eleazar. *Pueblos Sub-informados.* Caracas: Imprenta Universitaria de Caracas, 1967.

Dizard, Wilson P. *Television: A World View.* Syracuse: Syracuse University Press, 1966.

Editor and Publisher International Year Book. New York: Editor and Publisher, 1973.

Emery, Walter B. "Broadcasting in Mexico," *Journal of Broadcasting,* VIII, No. 3, Summer 1964, 251-261.

———. "A Comparative Study of Broadcasting Law and Regulations in Mexico and the United States," *Journal of Broadcasting,* VIII, No. 2, Spring 1964, 185-202.

———. *National and International Systems of Broadcasting: Their History, Operation, and Control.* East Lansing: Michigan State University, 1969.

Erlandson, Erling Halvard. "The Press in Mexico, with Special Considerations of Economic Factors." Unpublished Ph.D. thesis. Chicago: Northwestern University, 1963.

Fabela, Isidro. *Buena y mala vecindad.* Mexico City: n. pub., 1963.

Fagen, Richard R., and Tuohy, William S. *Politics and Privilege in a Mexican City.* Stanford: Stanford University Press, 1972.

Feldman, Mark B. "U.S. Relations with Canada and Mexico." (Paper presented at the Annual Meeting of the American Society of International Law.) Washington: April 1974.

Foro Internacional [Mexico City], XIV, No. 4, April-June 1974.

García Rivera, Emilio. *El cine mexicano.* Mexico City: Ediciones Era, 1963.

Garza, David T. "Factionalism in the Mexican Left: The Frustration of the MLN," *Western Political Quarterly,* XVII No. 3, September 1964, 751–760.

Gil, Federico. *Latin American-U.S. Relations.* New York: Harcourt, Brace Jovanovich, 1971.

Goldhamer, Herbert. *The Foreign Powers in Latin America.* Princeton: Princeton University Press, 1972.

González Casanova, Pablo. *Democracy in Mexico.* (Trans., Danielle Salti.) New York: Oxford University Press, 1970.

González Pedrero, Enrique (ed.). *Los Medios de communicación de masas en México.* (Serie Estudios 10.) Mexico City: Facultad de Ciencias Políticas y Sociales, Universidad Nacional Autónoma de México, 1969.

Gordon, Wendell C. *The Expropriation of Foreign-Owned Property in Mexico.* Washington: American Council on Public Affairs, 1941.

Graham, David L. "Mexico Looks at Castro," *Nation*, CXCII, No. 13, April 1961, 284-285.

Green, David. *The Continent of Latin America: A History of the Myths and Realities of the Good Neighbor Policy.* Chicago: Triangle Books, 1971.

Greenberg, Martin Harry. *Bureaucracy and Development: A Mexican Case Study.* (Studies in International Development and Economics.) Lexington, Massachusetts: D. C. Heath, Lexington Books, 1970.

Hackett, Charles W. *The Mexican Revolution and the United States, 1910-1926.* Boston: World Peace Foundation, 1926.

Handbook of Middle American Indians, VI: Social Anthropology. (Gen. ed., Robert Wauchope; vol. ed., Manning Nash.) Austin: University of Texas Press, 1967.

Hansen, Roger D. *The Politics of Mexican Development.* Baltimore: Johns Hopkins University Press, 1971.

Herman, Donald L. *The Comintern in Mexico.* Washington: Public Affairs Press, 1974.

Hill, Duane W., and Johnson, Kenneth F. "A Cross-Cultural Approach to Political Alienation," *Rocky Mountain Social Science Journal,* II, No. 1, May 1965, 137-171.

Hofstadter, Dan (ed.). *Mexico, 1946-73.* New York: Facts on File, 1974.

Johnson, John J. (ed.) *Continuity and Change in Latin America.* Stanford: Stanford University Press, 1964.

Johnson, Kenneth F. "Ideological Correlates of Right Wing Political Alienation in Mexico," *American Political Science Review,* LIX, No. 3, September 1965, 656–664.

————. *Mexican Democracy: A Critical View.* Boston: Allyn and Bacon, 1971.

Karst, Kenneth L. *Latin American Legal Institutions: Problems for Comparative Study.* Los Angeles: Latin American Center, University of California, 1966.

Lewis, Oscar. *The Children of Sánchez.* New York: Random House, 1961.

————. *Five Families.* New York: Basic Books, 1959.

————. *Pedro Martínez.* New York: Random House, 1964.

Liebman, Arthur. "Student Activism in Mexico," *Annals of the American Academy of Political and Social Science.* CCCXCV, May 1971, 159-170.

Lowry, Dennis T. "Broadcasting's Expanding Social Role in Mexico," *Journalism Quarterly,* XLVI, No. 2, Summer 1969, 332-336.

————. "Radio, TV, and Literacy in Mexico," *Journal of Broadcasting,* XIV, No. 2, Spring 1970, 239-244.

MacLachlan, Colin M. "Modernization of Female Status in Mexico: The Image of Women's Magazines," *Revista Interamericana* [Puerto Rico], IV, No. 2, Summer 1974, 246-257.

Madrazo, Carlos A. *Seis temas de México.* Mexico City: Comisión

Editorial del Frente Nacional Progresista, 1968.

Maldonado, Braulio. *Comentarios políticos*. Baja California: B. Costa-Amie Editor, 1960.

Marett, Robert. *Mexico*. New York: Walker, 1971.

Mecham, J. Lloyd. *Church and State in Latin America*. Chapel Hill: University of North Carolina Press, 1966.

————. "Latin American Constitutions: Nominal and Real," *Journal of Politics*, XXI, No. 2, May 1959, 258-275.

————. *A Survey of United States-Latin American Relations*. New York: Houghton Mifflin, 1965.

Medal, Consuelo. "El Periodista como orientador social." Unpublished Ph.D. dissertation. Mexico City: Escuela Nacional de Ciencias Políticas y Sociales, Universidad Nacional Autónoma de México, 1965.

Merrill, John C. *"Gringo": The American as Seen by Mexican Journalists*. (Latin American Monographs, No. 23.) Gainesville: University of Florida Press, 1963.

————. *A Handbook of the Foreign Press*, Baton Rouge: Louisiana State University Press, 1959.

México de Hoy [Mexico City], XVII, No. 182, December 1965.

Navarro, Juan Sánchez. "Discurso del Presidente de la Confederación de Camaras Industriales en México." Acapulco: March 1960 (mimeo.).

Navarro, Mendoza. "Mexico," *International Social Science Journal*, XIX, No. 2, 1967, 114-123.

Needleman, Carolyn, and Needleman, Martin. "Who Rules Mexico? A Critique of Some Current Views on the Mexican Political Process," *Journal of Politics*, XXXI, No. 4, November 1969, 1011-1034.

Needler, Martin C. "Mexico's Growing Pains," *Current History*, LXVI, No. 393, May 1974, 193-194, 231.

————. *Politics and Society in Mexico*. Albuquerque: University of New Mexico Press, 1971.

Needler, Martin C. (ed.) *Political Systems of Latin America*. Princeton: Van Nostrand, 1970.

Nixon, Raymond B., and Tae-youl, Hahn. "Concentration of Press Ownership: A Comparison of 32 Countries," *Journalism Quarterly*, XLVIII, Spring 1971, 15-16.

Norris, Renfro Cole. "A History of La Hora Nacional: Government Broadcasting Via Privately Owned Radio Stations in Mexico." Unpublished Ph.D. dissertation. Ann Arbor: University of Michigan, 1963.

Opie, Redvers. "Mexico's President Plans for Progress," *Banking*, LXIII, No. 9, March 1971, 42-43.

Organization of American States. General Secretariat. Charter of the *Organization of American States as Amended by the Protocol of Buenos Aires in 1967*. (OAS Official Records, Series, A, 2d rev.) Washington: 1968.

Padgett, L. Vincent. *The Mexican Political System*. Boston: Houghton

Mifflin, 1966.

―――. "Mexico's One-Party System: A Re-Evaluation," *American Political Science Review*, LI, No. 4, December 1957, 995-1008.

Pan American Union. *Books and Libraries in the Americas*. Washington: Organization of American States, 1963.

―――. *Books in the Americas*. Washington: Organization of American States, 1960.

―――. *Constitution of the United States of Mexico, As Amended to 1964*. Washington: Organization of American States, 1964.

―――. *Eighth Meeting of Consultation of the Ministers of Foreign Affairs, Punta del Este, Uruguay, January 23-31, 1962*. Washington: PAU, 1962.

―――. *Round Table on International Cooperation for Library and Information Services in Latin America*. Washington: Organization of American States, 1966.

―――. *Seventh Meeting of the Consultation of Ministers of Foreign Affairs, San Jose, Costa Rica, August 22-29, 1960*. Washington: PAU, 1960.

―――. *The Tenth Inter-American Conference, Caracas, Venezuela, March 1-28, 1954: Report of the Pan American Union on the Conference*. Washington: PAU, 1964.

Peñalosa, Fernando. *The Mexican Book Industry*. New York: Scarecrow Press, 1957.

Perissinotto, Giorgio. "Educational Reform and Government Intervention in Mexico," *Current History*, LXVI, No. 393, May 1974, 208-211, 226.

Poitras, Guy, and Denton, Charles. "Bureaucratic Performance: Case Studies from Mexico and Costa Rica," *Journal of Comparative Administration*, III, August 1971, 169-187.

The Political and Socio-Economic Role of the Military in Latin America, Appendix III: Guatemala, Haiti, Mexico, Coral Gables: Center for Advanced International Studies, University of Miami, 1972.

Porter, Alejandro. "Return of the Wetback," *Transaction*, XI, No. 3, March-April 1974, 40-46.

"President Ford Meets with President Echeverría of Mexico," *Department of State Bulletin* [Washington], LXXI, No. 1847, November 18, 1974, 661-667.

"Public Administration," *Comercio Exterior de México* [Mexico City], XVII, No. 2, February 1971, 29-31.

Publishers' International Yearbook. (Ed., Alexander P. Wales.) (5th ed.) London: Alexander P. Wales, 1968.

Publishers World. *Libraries and Their Holdings*. New York: 1965.

Publishers' World: 1965 Yearbook. New York: R.R. Bowker, 1965.

Ranis, Peter. *Five Latin American Nations: A Comparative Political Study*. New York: Macmillan, 1971.

Rippy, J. Fred. *The United States and Mexico.* New York: Knopf, 1926.

Rives, G.L. *The United States and Mexico, 1821–1848.* 2 vols. New York: Charles Scribner's Sons, 1913.

Roberts, C. Paul, and Kohda, Takado (eds.). *Statistical Abstract of Latin America.* (10th ed.) Los Angeles: Latin American Center, University of California, 1967.

Rosenbaum, H. John, and Cooper, Glenn M. *Arms and Security in Latin America: Recent Developments.* (International Affairs Series, No. 101.) Washington: Woodrow Wilson International Center for Scholars, December 1971.

Rotha, Paul. *The Film Till Now: A Survey of World Cinema.* London: Spring Books, 1967.

Scott, Robert E. *Mexican Government in Transition.* Urbana: University of Illinois Press, 1964.

Simoní, Guillermo Enriquez. *La Libertad de prensa en México una mentira rosa.* Mexico City: B. Costa-Amie Editor, 1967.

Smith, Bruce L., and Smith, Chitra N. *International Communication and Political Opinion: A Guide to the Literature.* Princeton: Princeton University Press, 1956.

Snow, Peter G. (ed.) *Government and Politics in Latin America.* New York: Holt, Rinehart and Winston, 1967.

Sommerlad, F. Lloyd. *The Press in Developing Countries.* Sydney: Sydney University Press, 1966.

Stevens, Evelyn P. "Mexican Machismo: Politics and Value Orientations." *Western Political Quarterly,* XVIII, No. 4, December 1965, 848–857.

————. *Protest and Response in Mexico.* Cambridge: MIT Press, 1974.

Taylor, Philip B. "The Mexican Elections of 1958: Affirmation of Authoritarianism?" *Western Political Quarterly,* XIII, No. 3, September 1960, 722-744.

Teeters, Nigley K. *Penology from Panama to Cape Horn.* Philadelphia: University of Pennsylvania Press, 1946.

Tucker, William P. *The Mexican Government Today.* Minneapolis: University of Minnesota Press, 1958.

Turner, Frederick C. *Catholicism and Political Development in Latin America.* Chapel Hill: University of North Carolina Press, 1971.

————. *The Dynamics of Mexican Nationalism.* Chapel Hill: University of North Carolina Press, 1968.

United Nations Educational, Scientific and Cultural Organization. *Professional Associations in the Mass Media: Handbook of Press, Film, Radio, and Television Organizations.* Paris: UNESCO, 1959.

U. S. Congress. 90th, 1st Session. Senate. Committee on Foreign Relations. *Survey of Alliance for Progress, 9 October 1967.* Washington: GPO, 1967.

U. S. Department of State. *Background Notes: Mexico.* (No. 7865.) Washington: GPO, March 1971.

————. *Bulletin*, XVII, No. 432, October 12, 1947.

————. *Bulletin*, XLIX, No. 1265, September 23, 1963.

U. S. Department of State. Office of the Geographer. *International Boundary Study: British Honduras-Guatemala Boundary*. (Series No. 8.) Washington: GPO, July 21, 1961 (mimeo.).

U. S. Department of State. Office of the Legal Advisor. *Treaties in Force on January 1, 1967*. (Publication No. 8188.) Washington: GPO, 1967.

U. S. United States Information Agency. Office of Research and Assessment. *Sales Figures for Mexican Book Publishing Program*. (U. S. Department of State, Office of External Research, Foreign Affairs Research Paper, No. FAR 18296-G.) Washington: May 1973.

————. *VOA Listening Habits and Program Preferences Reported by Transistor Contest Entrants in Five Latin American Countries*. (U. S. Department of State, Office of External Research, Foreign Affairs Research Paper, No. FAR 18295-G.) Washington: September 1972.

Utton, Albert E. (ed.) *Pollution and International Boundaries: US-Mexico Environmental Problems*. Albuquerque: University of New Mexico, 1973.

Veliz, Claudio (ed.). *Latin America and the Caribbean: A Handbook*. New York: Praeger, 1968.

Vernon, Raymond. *The Dilemma of Mexico's Development*. Cambridge: Harvard University Press, 1963.

Viya, Miko. *La Televisión y yo: Crónica de la televisión mexicana*. Mexico City: B. Costa-Amie Editor, 1970.

Wells, Alan. *Picture Tube Imperialism? The Impact of Television on Latin America*. Maryknoll, New York: Orbis Books, 1972.

Willis, Colin. "Entrenched Press Corruption Challenges Mexican Editor," *Editor and Publisher*, July 3, 1972, 14.

Wolf, Eric R. "The Indian in Mexican Society," *Alpha Kappa Deltan*, XXX, No. 1, Winter 1960, 3-6.

World of Learning, 1973-74. (24th ed.) London: Europa Publications, 1973.

World Radio TV Handbook, 1974. (28th ed.) (Ed., J. M. Frost.) Hvidovre, Denmark: World Radio TV Handbook, 1974.

Yates, Paul Lamartine. *El desarrollo regional de México*. Mexico City: Banco de México, 1962.

Zea, Leopoldo. *El hombre y la cultura en nuestros días*. Mexico City: Universidad Nacional Autónoma de México, 1959.

Zimmerman, Irene. *A Guide to Current Latin American Periodicals: Humanities and Social Sciences*. Gainesville: Kallman Publishing, 1961.

(Various issues of the following periodicals were also used in the preparation of this section: *Christian Science Monitor* [Boston], September-December 1974; *Excélsior* [Mexico City], July-December

1974; *Foreign Broadcast Information Service, Daily Report: Latin America* [Washington], September-December 1974; *Latin America* [London], July-October 1974; *Mexican Newsletter* [Washington], July-August 1974; *New York Times* [New York], May 1973-December 1974; *Time Magazine* [New York], June 1971; *Times of the Americas* [Miami], August-October 1974; *Quarterly Economic Review* [London], 1974; and *Washington Post*, August-December 1974.)

Section III. Economic

Abercrombie, K. C. "Agricultural Mechanisation and Employment in Latin America," *International Labour Review* [Geneva], CVI, No. 1, July 1972, 11-46.

Adams, Dale W. "Agricultural Credit in America: A Critical Review of External Funding Policy," *American Journal of Agricultural Economics*, LIII, No. 2, May 1971, 163-172.

Ahluwalia, Montek S. "Income Inequality: Some Dimensions of the Problem," *Finance and Development*, XI, No. 3, September 1974, 2-8.

Álba, Victor. *Historia del movimiento obrero en América Latina.* Mexico City: Libreros Mexicanos Unidos, 1964.

Alcalá Quintero, Francisco. "México y su relación con el mercado común centroamericano," *Foro Internacional* [Guanajuato, Mexico], XV, No. 2, October 1973, 175-203.

————. "A Promising Perspective: Japan-Mexico Trade Relations," *Pacific Community* [Tokyo], II, No. 4, July 1971, 732-741.

————. "The Tasks of the National Foreign Trade Bank," *Comercio Exterior de México* [Mexico City], XVIII, No. 1, January 1971, 8, 21.

Alcazar, Marco Antonio. *Los Agrupaciones Patronales en México.* Mexico City: El Colegio de México, 1970.

Alisky, M. "CONASUPO: A Mexican Agency Which Makes Low-Income Workers Feel Their Government Cares," *Inter-American Economic Affairs*, XVII, Winter 1974, 47-59.

Araiza, Luis. *Historia del movimiento obrero mexicano.* Mexico City: n. pub., 1964.

Asociación Latinoamericana de Libre Comercio. *Estudio sobre la maquinaria agricola en los paises de la ALALC.* Buenos Aires: Secretaria de ALALC, 1970.

Aubey, Robert T. "Regional Credit and the Mexican Financial System," *Growth and Change*, II, No. 4, October 1971, 25-33.

Baer, Werner. "The Role of Government Enterprises in Latin America's Industrialization." (Paper prepared for Conference on Fiscal Policy for Industrialization in Latin America, February 17-20, 1971.) Gainesville: University of Florida Press, 1971 (mimeo.).

Baerresen, Donald W. *The Border Industrialization Program of Mexico.* Lexington, Massachusetts: D.C. Heath, 1971.

Baerresen, Donald W., et al. *Latin American Trade Patterns.* Washington: Brookings Institution, 1965.

Balance of Payments Yearbook, 1966-72, XXIII. Washington: International Monetary Fund, 1972.

Ball, D.A. "Permanent Tourism: A New Export Diversification for Less Developed Countries," *International Development Review*, XIII,No. 4, 1971, 20-23.

Ballance, R.H. "Mexican Agricultural Policies and Subsistence Farming,"*American Journal of Economics and Sociology*, No. 3, July 1972, 295-306.

Banco de Londres y México. *100 años de banca en México: primer centenario de la banca de depósito en México, 1861–1964.* Mexico City: Cía. Impresora y Litográfica Juventud, 1964.

Banco de México. *Informe Anual, 1972.* Mexico City: 1973.

Banco Nacional de Comercio. *Cuestiones Económicas Nacionales, 1955–1970.* Mexico City: 1971.

Banco Nacional de Comercio Exterior. *Mexico: The New Government's Economic Policy.* Mexico City: 1971.

———. "Transnational Corporations and Multinational Companies," *Comercio Exterior de México* [Mexico City], XVII, No. 2, December 1971, 5-9, 15.

Barkin, David. "Agricultural Development in Mexico: A Case Study of Income Concentration," *Social Research*, XXXVII, No. 2, Summer 1970, 306-320.

Barkin, David, and King, Timothy. *Regional Economic Development: The River Basin Approach in Mexico.* London: Cambridge University Press, 1970.

Basch, Antonín, and Kybal, Milic. *Capital Markets in Latin America.* New York: Praeger, 1970.

Belshaw, Michael. *A Village Economy: Land and People of Huecorio.* New York: Columbia University Press, 1967.

Beltran del Río, Abel. "Mexico: An Economy at the Crossroads," *Wharton Quarterly*, VI, No. 1, Fall 1971, 20-24.

Bennett, Robert L. *The Financial Sector and Economic Development: The Mexican Case.* Baltimore: Johns Hopkins Press, 1965.

Benviniste, Guy. *Bureaucracy and National Planning: A Sociological Case Study in Mexico.* New York: Praeger, 1970.

Beteta, Mario Ramón. *El sistema bancario mexicano y el banco central.* Mexico City: Centro de Estudios Monetarios Latinoamericanos, 1964.

Bett, Virgil M. *Central Banking in Mexico: Monetary Policies and Financial Crises, 1864–1940.* Ann Arbor: University of Michigan Press, 1957.

Biggs, Huntley H. "The Dualistic Approach to Mexican Agricultural Development: Irrigation Development and the Puebla Project." (Paper presented at the Economic Development Section, Rocky Mountain Social Science Association Meeting, April 28, 1972, in Salt Lake City.) Fort Collins: Department of Economics, Colorado State University, 1972 (mimeo.).

Billingsley, Ray V.; Armero-Tapia, Luis de; and Moore, Donald. *An Economic Analysis of Supervised Credit for Rubber Producers in the*

El Palmar Region of Mexico. (International Programs Information Report) College Station: Department of Agricultural Economics and Sociology, Texas A. and M. University, n.d.

Bird, Richard M., and De Wulf, Luc Henry. "Taxation and Income Distribution in Latin America: A Critical Review of Empirical Studies," *Staff Papers*. XX, No. 3, November 1973, 639-682.

Brandenburg, Frank. *The Making of Modern Mexico*. Englewood Cliffs: Prentice-Hall, 1964.

Brothers, Dwight S. "Mexican Policy Toward Foreign Investment." (Paper presented at the Dubrovnik Conference of the Development Advisory Service of Howard University, June 20-26, 1970.) Washington: 1970, (mimeo.).

Brothers, Dwight S., and Solís M., Leopoldo. *Mexican Financial Development*. Austin: University of Texas Press, 1966.

"Business Boomlet on Mexico's Border," *Business Week*, No. 2211, June 22, 1972, 38.

Butler, Robert W., Jr. "Trade Conflict: The Mexican Canadian Yarn War of 1969-70," *Inter-American Economic Affairs*, XXV, No. 1, Summer 1971, 21-30.

Cable, Vincent. "Mexico: The role of Foreign Investment," *Bank of London and South America Review* [London], VIII, No. 92, August 1974, 457-466.

Calderon Martínez, Antonio. "La promoción de las exportaciones en México," *Comercio Exterior* [Mexico City], XX, No. 1, January 1970, 37-45.

Cale, Edward O. *Latin American Free Trade Association: Progress, Problems, Prospects*. Washington: GPO, 1969.

de Calvo, Doreen, E.C. "Tourism in Latin America," *Bank of London and South America Review* [London], III, No. 28, April 1969, 200-212.

Camarena, P. "The Runaways: Multinational Companies on the Mexican Border," *Free Labor World* [Brussels], CCXLV, November 1970, 16-19.

Caso Bercht, Jorge. *El Mercado de Acciones en Mexico*. Mexico City: Centro de Estudios Monetarios Latinoamericanos, 1971.

Cepeda Villareal, Rodolfo. "Certain Aspects of Mexican Labor Laws, Especially as They Affect Foreign-Owned Businesses," *California Western Law Review*, VI, Spring 1970, 234-246.

"Changes in Coffee Marketing," *Review of the Economic Siutation of Mexico* [Mexico City], L, No. 580, March 1974, 111-115.

Chelliah, Raja J. "Trends in Taxation in Developing Countries," *International Monetary Fund Staff Papers*, XVIII, No. 2, July 1971, 254-331.

Christman, John H. "Bank Charge Cards: Growing Share of Higher Stakes," *Mexican-American Review* [Mexico City], XXXVII, No. 6, June 1970, 8-13.

———. "Sugar Industry Goes Bittersweet," *Mexican-American Review*

[Mexico City], XXXVII, No. 11, November 1969, 10-14.

Cole, J.P. *Latin America: An Economic and Social Geography*. London: Butterworth, 1970.

Cole, William E., and Sanders, Richard D. "Income Distribution, Profits, and Savings in the Recent Economic Experience of Mexico." *Inter-American Economic Affairs*, XXIV, No. 2, Autumn 1970, 49-63.

Comisión Federal de Electricidad. *Plantas generadoras y localidades con servicio*. Mexico City: CFE, 1972.

Comité Interamericano de Desarrollo Agrícola. *Estructura Agraria y Desarrollo Agrícola en México*, I-II. (Trabajos de investigación sobre tenencia de la tierra y Reforma Agraria, No. 18.) Mexico City: 1970.

Cummings, Ronald G. *Water Resource Management in Northern Mexico*. Baltimore: Johns Hopkins Press, 1972.

De la Haba, Luis. "Mexico: The City that Founded a Nation," *National Geographic*, CXLIII, No. 5, May 1973, 638-670.

Derossi, Flavia. *The Mexican Entrepreneur*. (Development Center Studies) Paris: Organization for Economic Cooperation and Development, 1971.

Díaz, Heliodoro, and Felstehausen, Herman. *Communication and Institutional Change in Mexican Agricultural Development*. (LTC No. 98.) Madison: Land Tenure Center, University of Wisconsin, January 1974.

Dorner, Peter (ed.). *Land Reform in Latin America: Issues and Cases*. Madison: Land Economics, University of Wisconsin, 1971.

Dovring, Folke. "Land Reform and Productivity in Mexico," *Land Economics*, XLVI, No. 3, August 1970, 264-274.

Dozier, Craig L. "Agricultural Development in Mexico's Tabasco Lowlands: Planning and Potentials," *Journal of Developing Areas*, V, No. 2, October 1970, 61-72.

Durán T., Marco Antonio. "Acotaciones para una definición de la Reforma Agraria en México," *Aportes* [Paris], No. 22, October 1971, 6-22.

———. "Apuntes acerca de la política Agrícola Méxicana," *Trimestre Económico* [Mexico City], XXXVII, No. 147, July-September 1970, 525-536.

The Economist Intelligence Unit. *Quarterly Economic Review: Mexico, Annual Supplement 1974*. London: 1974.

Ellis, Philip B. *Changes in Agriculture and Settlement in Coastal Chiapas, Southern Mexico*. (Occasional Papers, No. 2.) Glasgow: Institute of Latin-American Studies, University of Glasgow, 1971.

"Energy in Latin America," *Economic Bulletin for Latin America*, XV, No. 2, 1970, 3-93.

Ericson, Anna-Stina. "An Analysis of Mexico's Border Industrialization Program," *Monthly Labor Review*, XCIII, No. 5, May 1970, 35-40.

Erikson, John R. "Wage Change and Employment Growth in Latin

American Industry." (Research Memorandum, No. 36.) Williamstown, Massachusetts: Center for Development Economics, Williams College, June 1970 (mimeo.).

Escobedo, Gilberto. "The Response of the Mexican Economy to Policy Actions," *Federal Reserve Bank of Saint Louis Monthly Review*, LV, No. 6, June 1973, 15-23.

Evans, John S. "Mexican Border Development and Its Impact Upon the United States," *South Eastern Latin Americanist*, XVI, No. 1, June 1972, 4-10.

"Factories on the Border," *Monthly Review Federal Reserve Bank of San Francisco*, December 1971, 212-216.

"Fast Moving Mexico Hits a Roadblock," *U.S. News and World Report*, LXXIII, No. 14, October 1972, 34-36.

Flores, Edmundo. *Tratado de economía agrícola.* Mexico City: Fonda de Cultura Económica, 1964.

Food and Agriculture Organization. *Annual Fertilizer Review, 1971.* Rome: FAO, 1972.

————. *Government Marketing Policies in Latin America.* Rome: FAO, 1967.

————. *The State of Food and Agriculture, 1970.* Rome: FAO, 1970.

Frederick, Kenneth D. "Production Controls Under the International Coffee Agreements," *Journal of Inter-American Studies*, XII, No. 2, April 1970, 255-270.

Freithaler, William O. *Mexico's Foreign Trade and Economic Development. New York: Praeger, 1968.*

Furtado, Celso. *Economic Development of Latin America.* (Cambridge Latin American Studies Series.) Cambridge: Cambridge University Press, 1970.

Gamble, Stephen Holland. *The Despensa System of Food Distribution: A Case Study of Monterrey, Mexico.* New York: Praeger, 1970.

García Maldonado, Edmundo. *El Mercado Nacional de Valores: el mecanismo de inversión en México.* Mexico City: Editorial Libros de México, 1964.

Gates, Gary R., and Gates, Marilyn. "Uncertainty and Development Risk in Pequeña Irrigación Decisions for Peasants in Campeche, Mexico," *Economic Geography*, XLVIII, No. 2, April 1972, 135-152.

Germidis, Dimetrios A. *The Construction Industry in Mexico.* (Technical Papers.) Paris: Development Center, Organization for Economic Cooperation and Development, 1972.

Glade, William P., Jr., and Anderson, Charles W. *The Political Economy of Mexico.* Madison: University of Wisconsin Press, 1963.

Goldsmith, Raymond W. *The Financial Development of Mexico.* Paris: Development Center, Organization for Economic Cooperation and Development, 1966.

González y González, Javier. "Projection of Foreign Investment in Mexico," *Mexican-American Review* [Mexico City], XXXIX, No. 9,

September 1971, 47-60.

Gordon, Michael W. "The Contemporary Mexican Approach to Growth with Foreign Investment: Controlled but Participatory Independence," *California Western Law Review*, X, No. 1, Fall 1971, 1-46.

Goreux, Louis M., and Manne, Alan S. (eds.) *Multi-Level Planning: Case Studies in Mexico.* Amsterdam: North-Holland Publishing, 1973.

Greenberg, Martin Harry. *Bureaucracy and Development: A Mexican Case Study.* (Studies in International Development and Economics.) Lexington, Massachusetts: D.C. Heath, Lexington Books, 1970.

Griffin, Keith B. (ed.) *Financing Development in Latin America.* London: Macmillan, 1971.

Griffiths, Brian. *Mexican Monetary Policy and Economic Development.* New York: Praeger, 1972.

Grunwald, Joseph, and Musgrove, Philip. *Natural Resources in Latin American Development.* Baltimore: Johns Hopkins University Press, 1970.

Haney, Emil B., Jr. *The Nature of Shifting Cultivation in Latin America.* (LTC No. 45) Madison: Land Tenure Center, University of Wisconsin, May 1968.

Hansen, Roger D. *Mexican Economic Development: The Roots of Rapid Growth.* (Studies in Development Progress, No. 2.) Washington: National Planning Association, 1971.

——. *The Politics of Mexican Development.* Baltimore: Johns Hopkins University Press, 1971.

"How to Plan an Ammonia Fertilizer Producing Operation," *World Petroleum* XLI, No. 1, January 1970, 5-52.

Hunt, Lacy H., III. "Industrial Development on the Mexican Border," *Business Review*, February 1970, 3-12.

Ingenieria Hidráulica en México [Mexico City], XXII, No. 3, 1968.

Inter-American Center of Tax Administrators. *Papers and Report of the Seventh General Assembly, Guatemala City, May 1973.* Panama City: Executive Secretariat, CIAT, 1973.

——. *Tax Incentives in the American Countries.* (Doc. V-A/1.) Rio de Janeiro: Executive Secretariat, CIAT, 1971.

Inter-American Development Bank. *The Process of Industrialization in Latin America.* Washington: IDB, n.d.

——. *Statistical Data on the Latin American and Caribbean Countries, 1972.* Washington: IDB, n.d.

Inter-American Development Bank. Latin American Free Trade Association. *La industrial naval en la ALALC.* Buenos Aires: Instituto para la Integración de América Latina, 1971.

International Bank for Reconstruction and Development. *The Economic Development of Mexico.* Baltimore: Johns Hopkins University Press, 1953.

International Labour Organisation. "The Settlement of Labour Disputes in Mexico," *AIFLD Review*, III, No. 3, 1971, 32-58.

418

International Monetary Fund. *Twenty-Fifth Annual Report on Exchange Restrictions, 1974.* Washington: IMF, 1974.

International Monetary Fund and International Bank for Reconstruction and Development. *Direction of Trade Annual, 1969-1973.* Washington: IMF-IBRD, 1974.

"Irrigation Projects: The Basin of Agricultural Progress," *Review of the Economic Situation of Mexico* [Mexico City], XLVIII, No. 559, June 1972, 184-191.

Isbister, John. "Urban Employment and Wages in a Developing Economy: The Case of Mexico," *Economic Development and Cultural Change,* XX, No. 1, October 1971, 24-46.

James, Dilmus. "Used Automated Plants in Less Developed Countries: A Case Study of a Mexican Firm," *Inter-American Economic Affairs,* XXVII, No. 1, Summer 1973, 31-46.

Johnston, Roger D. "Should the Mexican Government Promote the Country's Stock Exchange?", *Inter-American Economic Affairs,* XXVI, No. 3, Winter 1972, 45-60.

Jud, G. Donald. "Tourism and Economic Growth in Mexico Since 1950," *Inter-American Economic Affairs,* XXVIII, No. 1, Spring 1974, 19-44.

Katz, Bernard S. "Mexican Fiscal and Subsidy Incentives for Industrial Development," *American Journal of Economics and Sociology,* XXXI, No. 4, October 1972, 353-359.

Keesing, Donald B. "External Finance and the Requirements of Full Modernization in Mexico." (Research Memorandum, No. 54.) Williamstown, Massachusetts: Center for Development Economics, Williams College, April 1974 (mimeo.).

————. "Structural Change Early in Development: Mexico's Changing Industrial and Occupational Structure from 1895-1950," *Journal of Economic History,* XXVIII, No. 4, December 1969, 716-738.

Kemmerer, Edwin Walter. *Inflation and Revolution: Mexico's Experience of 1912-1917.* Princeton: Princeton University Press, 1940.

King, Timothy. *Mexico: Industrialization and Trade Policies Since 1940, Industry and Trade in Some Developing Countries.* London: Oxford University Press, for the Development Center of Organization for Economic Cooperation and Development, 1970.

Kling, Merle. *A Mexican Interest Group in Action.* Englewood Cliffs: Prentice-Hall, 1964.

Koehler, John E. *Economic Policymaking with Little Information and Few Instruments: The Process of Macro Control In Mexico.* (Rand Paper, No. P-4769.) N. pl.: Rand Corporation, January 1972.

Krieger, Ronald A. *Mexico: An Economic Survey.* New York: First National City Bank, 1971.

Lavell, A. M. "Regional Industrialization in Mexico: Some Policy Considerations," *Regional Studies* [London], VI, September 1972, 343-362.

Lentnek, Barry. "Economic Transition from Traditional to Commercial Agriculture: The Case of El Llano, Mexico," *Annals of the Association of American Geographers*, LIX, March 1969, 65-84.

"Limitations on Foreign Capital in Certain Basic Industries," *Comercio Exterior de México* [Mexico City], XVI, No. 8, August 1970, 2-3.

McCann, Eugene C. "Anglo-American and Mexican Management Philosophies," *MSU Business Topics*, XVIII, No. 3, Summer 1970, 28-37.

McDougall, Charlotte. "Mexico City," *Canadian Geographical Review* [Ottawa], LXXXV. No. 4, October 1972, 142-149.

Manning, Richard C., and Ela, Ofelia M. *An Economic Evaluation of Irrigation Rehabilitation Projects in Mexico.* (Report No. E.C.-180.) Washington: International Bank for Reconstruction and Development and International Development Association, September 1971.

Martínez Domínguez, Guillermo. "Integración y desarrollo de la industria eléctrica de México: La Obra 1965–70," *Trimestre Económico* [Mexico City], XXXVIII, No. 150, April-June 1971, 433-454.

May, Herbert K., and Fernández Arena, José Antonio. *Impact of Foreign Investment in Mexico.* Washington: National Chamber Foundation, n.d.

Meek, Wilber T. *The Exchange Media of Colonial Mexico.* New York: King's Crown Press, for Columbia University, 1948.

Mexican Income and Commercial Receipts Tax Law. Chicago: Commerce Clearing House, 1972.

"Mexicana Reinstates Dallas Service as Part of Expansion," *Aviation Week and Space Technology*, XCVII, No. 2, November 13, 1972.

Mexico. Banco Nacional Agropecuario. *Organización, politica, y financionamiento, 1965–1970.* Mexico City: 1970.

Mexico. Banco Nacional de Obras y Servícios Públicos. *Informe Anual, 1971.* Mexico City: 1972.

Mexico. Comisión Nacional de Valores. *Los bancos y el Mercado de Valores en 1971–1972.* Mexico City: 1973.

———. *Memoria Anual, 1972.* Mexico City: 1973.

Mexico. Secretaría de Agricultura y Ganadería Secretaría de Hacienda y Crédito Público, and Banco de México. *Projections of Supply of and Demand for Agricultural Products in Mexico to 1965, 1970, and 1975.* (Trans., Israel Program for Scientific Translations.) Jerusalem: Israel Program for Scientific Translations for Economic Research Service, U.S. Department of Agriculture, 1966.

Mexico. Secretaría de Comunicaciones y Transportes. *Memoria de Labores, 1970.* Mexico City: 1970.

Mexico. Secretaría de Comunicaciones y Transportes. Dirección General de Ferrocarriles en Operación. *Estadística Ferroviaria Nacional, 1971.* Mexico City: 1973.

Mexico. Secretaría de Hacienda y Credito Público. *Presupuesto General de Egresos de la Federación, 1972.* Mexico City: 1972.

Mexico. Secretaría de Industria y Comercio. Dirección General de

Estadística. *Estadística Industrial Anual, 1970.* Mexico City: 1972.

Mexico. Secretaría de Obras Públicas. *Informe de Labores 1 Septiembre de 1971 al 31 Agosto de 1972.* Mexico City: Talleres Gráficos de la Nación, 1972.

Mexico. Secretaría de Recursos Hidráulicos. *Informe de Labores, 1972-1973.* Mexico City: Talleres Gráficos de la Nación, 1973.

Mexico in Pictures. (Visual Geography Series.) New York: Sterling Publishing, 1973.

Mexico, 1970: Facts, Figures, and Trends. Mexico City: Banco Nacional de Comercio Exterior, 1970.

"Mexico Works on Its Economy," *Investors Reader,* LX, No. 3, February 7, 1973, 23-27.

Milenky, Edward S. *The Politics of Regional Organization in Latin America: The Latin American Free Trade Association.* New York: Praeger, 1973.

Minerals Yearbook, 1971, III: Area Reports, International. Washington: GPO, for U.S. Department of the Interior, Bureau of Mines, 1973.

Moore, Ernest D. *Evolución de las instituciones financieras en México.* Mexico City: Centro de Estudios Monetarios Latinoamericanos, 1963.

Motoring in Mexico. (19th ed.) Washington: General Secretariat, Organization of American States, 1972.

Mueller, Marnie W. "Changing Patterns of Agricultural Output and Productivity in the Private and Land Reform Sectors in Mexico, 1940–1960," *Economic Development and Cultural Change,* XVIII, No. 2, January 1970, 252-266.

Nassef, El Sayed Mohamed Abdel Mabood. *Monetary Policy in Developing Countries: The Mexican Case.* Rotterdam: University of Rotterdam, 1972.

Navarrete, Ifigenía M. de. *Política fiscal de México.* Mexico City: Universidad Nacional Autónoma de México, 1964.

Olizar, Marynka. *Guía de los mercados de México.* (5th ed.) Mexico City: n. pub., 1968.

Opie, Redvers. "The Mexican Economy: Performance and Prospects," *Banking,* LXII, No. 11, May 1970, 53-54.

———. "Mexico's President Plans for Progress,"*Banking,* LCIII, No. 9, March 1971, 42-43.

———. "The New Mexican Labor Law." *Banking,* LXIII, No. 5, November 1970, 54, 92.

Organización de los Estados Americanos. Instituto Interamericano de Estadística. *América en Cifras 1974, Situación Económica,* II: Industria. Washington: Secretaría General, Organización de los Estados Americanos, 1974.

Organization of American States. Department of Legal Affairs. General Legal Division. *Mining and Petroleum Legislation in Latin America.* (2d ed.) Washington: Pan American Union, 1969.

Organization of American States. General Secretariat. *Copper.* (Commodity Series.) Washington: Pan American Union, 1971.

Pan American Union. *Constitution of the United Mexican States, 1917 (As Amended).* Washington: PAU, 1964.

——. *A Statement of the Laws of Mexico in Matters Affecting Business.* Washington: PAU, 1964.

Pan American Union. General Secretariat, Organization of American States. Inter-American Committee for Agricultural Development. *Inventory of Information Basic to the Planning of Agricultural Development in Latin America: Mexico.* Washington: PAU, 1964.

"Paper Industry," *Review of the Economic Structure in Mexico* [Mexico City], XLVII, No. 549, August 1971, 303-309.

Pérez López, Enrique, et al. *Mexico's Recent Economic Growth: The Mexican View.* (Trans., Marjorie Urquidi.) (Latin American Monographs. No. 10.) Austin: Institute of Latin American Studies, University of Texas, 1967.

"Perspectives of Inflation: Deceleration in the Offing," *Review of the Economic Situation of Mexico* [Mexico City], L, No. 580, March 1974, 105-110.

Pick's Currency Yearbook, 1973 (Ed., Franz Pick.) New York: Pick Publishing, 1973.

Production Yearbook, 1972, XXVI. Rome: Food and Agriculture Organization, 1973.

Puente Leyva, Jesús. "Planeación y desarrollo en México," *Mundo Nuevo* [Buenos Aires], LVI, February 1971, 10-14.

Puga, William B. (ed.) *Electrical World: A Directory of Electrical Utilities in Latin America, Bermuda, and the Caribbean Islands, 1969-70.* New York: McGraw-Hill, 1969.

Pulgar, M. "Mexico's Economic Success Story," *Banker* [London], CXX, September 1970, 982-987.

Ramos Garza, Oscar. "Doing Business in Mexico." Pages 137-158 in *Private Investors Abroad: Problems and Solutions in International Business in 1972.* Dallas: Southwestern Legal Foundations, International and Comparative Law Center, 1972.

Restrepo Fernandez, Iván. "El caso de los jornaleros agrícolas en México," *Aportes* [Paris], XXIII, January 1972, 53-61.

Reyes Heroles, Jesús. "México y su petroleo," *Cuadernos Americanos* [Mexico City], XXIX, No. 3, May-June 1970, 7-28.

Reynolds, Clark W. "Changing Trade Partners and Trade Policy in Mexico: Some Lessons for Developing Countries," *Food Research Institute Studies,* IX, No. 1, 1970, 3-41.

——. *The Mexican Economy: Twentieth-Century Structure and Growth.* New Haven: Yale University Press, 1970.

Rhodes, Robert I. "Mexico: A Model for Capitalist Development in Latin America," *Science and Society,* XXXIV, No. 1, Spring 1970, 61-77.

Riviera R., José. "Profit Sharing under Legislation." (Management

Bulletin, No. 57.) New York: American Management Association, 1964.

Ronfeldt, D. *Atencingo: The Politics of Agrarian Struggle in a Mexican Ejido.* Stanford: Stanford University Press, 1973.

Ross, John B. *The Economic System of Mexico.* Stanford: California Institute of International Studies, 1971.

Ross, Stanford G., and Christensen, John B. *Tax Incentives for Industry in Mexico.* Boston: George H. Ellis, for Harvard Law School, International Program in Taxation, 1959.

Rourke, B. E. "Short-Range Forecasting of Coffee Production." *Food Research Institute Studies in Agricultural Economics,* IX, No. 3, 1970, 197-214.

Ruiz Equihua, Arturo. *El encaje legal: instrumento fundamental de la política monetaria mexicana contemporanea.* Mexico City: Editoria Cultura, 1963.

Santillán López, Roberto, and Rosas Figueroa, Aniceto. *Teoría general de las finanzas públicas y el caso de México.* Mexico City: Universidad Nacional Autónoma de México, 1962.

Scheffler, Winifred. "Folding Money: Made in Mexico," *Mexican-American Review* [Mexico City], XXXVII, No. 3, March 1970, 8-13.

Schmitter, Philippe C., and Haas, Ernst B. *Mexico and Latin American Economic Integration.* (Research Series, No. 5.) Berkeley: Institute of International Studies, University of California, 1964.

Schotta, Charles, Jr. "The Money Supply, Exports, and Income in an Open Economy: Mexico, 1939-1963," *Economic Development and Cultural Change,* XXXII, No. 4, October 1963, 652-673.

Scott, Robert E. "Budget Making in Mexico," *Inter-American Economic Affairs,* IX, No. 2, Autumn 1955, 3-21.

Shafer, Robert J. *Mexican Business Organizations: History and Analysis.* Syracuse: Syracuse University Press, 1973.

————. *Mexico: Mutual Adjustment Process.* Syracuse: Syracuse University Press, 1966.

Sheahan, John. *Trade and Employment: Industrial Exports Compared to Import Substitution in Mexico.* (Research Memorandum, No. 43.) Williamstown, Massachusetts: Center for Development Economics, Williams College, December 1971.

Solís, Leopoldo. "Mexican Economic Policy in the Postwar Period: The Views of Mexican Economists," *American Economic Review,* LXI, No. 3, Pt. 2, June 1971, 2-67.

Solís, Manjarrez, Leopoldo. *La Económica Mexicana.* Mexico City: Fondo de Cultura Económica, 1973.

"Spread of U. S. Plants to Mexico Brings a Boom—and Complaints," *U. S. News and World Report,* LXXII, No. 13, March 27, 1972, 57-59.

A Statement of the Laws of Mexico in Matters Affecting Business. (4th ed., rev.) Washington: General Secretariat, Organization of American States, 1970.

Stavenhagen, Rodolfo. "A Land Reform Should Answer the Questions It Raises." *Ceres* [Rome], II, No. 6, November-December 1969, 43-47.

"The Steel Industry: Promising Future," *Review of the Economic Situation in Mexico* [Mexico City], XLVII, No. 553, December 1971, 430-437.

Steiner, Henry Malcolm. "The Mexican Border Industrialization Program," *Texas Business Review*, XLV, No. 7, July 1971, 145-149.

Stewart, Donald E. J. (ed.) *Handbook of Latin American Studies*, XXXV. Gainesville: University of Florida Press, 1973.

Tamayo, Jorge L. "Necesidad de una política forestal realista en México," *Investigación Económica*, XXX, No. 117, January-March 1970, 107-130.

Tancer, Robert S. "Tourist Promotion in Mexico," *Law and the Social Order 1972*, No. 4, 1972, 559-579.

Tannenbaum, Frank. *Mexico: The Struggle for Peace and Bread.* New York: Knopf, 1964.

Thompson, Kenneth W. "The Green Revolution: Leadership and Partnership in Agriculture," *Review of Politics*, XXXIV, No. 2, Spring 1972, 174-189.

Ulmer, Melville J. "Who's Making It in Mexico?", *New Republic*, CLXV, No. 13, September 25, 1971, 21-23.

United Nations Conference on Trade and Development. *Insurance Legislation and Supervision in Developing Countries.* New York: UN, 1972.

United Nations. Economic Commission for Latin America. *Economic Survey of Latin America 1970.* New York: UN, 1972.

United Nations. Industrial Development Organization. *Small-Scale Industry in Latin America.* New York: UN, 1969.

U.S. Agency for International Development. *Land Reform in: Brazil, Northeast; Cuba; Guatemala; Mexico.* (AID Spring Review of Land Reform, 2d ed., VII.) Washington: AID, June 1970.

U.S. Agency For International Development. Bureau for Program and Management Services. Office of Financial Management. *Latin America: Economic Growth Trends.* Washington: AID, July 1973.

U.S. Agency For International Development. Bureau for Program and Policy Coordination. Office of Statistics and Reports: *AID Economic Data Book: Latin America.* Washington: AID, July 1971.

U. S. Department of Agriculture. Economic Research Service. *The Agricultural Situation in the Western Hemisphere: Review of 1972 and Outlook for 1973.* (ERS-Foreign 351.) Washington: USDA, April 1973.

―――. *The Latin American Farmer.* (ERS-Foreign 257.) Washington: GPO, 1969.

U.S. Department of Commerce. Bureau of International Commerce. *Establishing a Business in Mexico,* by Paul S. Flores. (Overseas Business Reports, OBR 72-027.) Washington: GPO, July 1972.

————. *Foreign Trade Regulations of Mexico*, by Walter Haidar. (Overseas Business Reports, OBR 72-072.) Washington: GPO, December 1972.

U.S. Department of Commerce. Domestic and International Business Administration, *Mexican Paper Industry Recovering from 1970/71 Slump*. (Pulp, Paper, and Board Quarterly Industry Report.) Washington: GPO, January 1973.

————. *World Trade Outlook for Latin America*. (Overseas Business Reports, OBR 74-20.) Washington: GPO, June 1974.

U.S. Department of Commerce. International Marketing Information Service. *Electronic Data Processing Equipment: Mexico*. (World Markets for U.S. Exports, IMIS 70-212.) Washington: USDC, June 1970.

————. *Food Processing, Packaging Equipment: Mexico*. (World Markets for U. S. Exports, IMIS 70-207.) Washington: USDC, May 1970.

U.S. Department of Labor. Bureau of Labor Statistics. *Labor Law and Practice in Mexico*. (BLS Report, No. 240.) Washington: GPO, 1963.

U.S. Department of the Treasury. *Foreign Credits by the United States Government: Status of Active Foreign Credits of the United States Government and of International Organizations as of December 31, 1972*. Washington: GPO, 1973.

U.S. Embassy in Mexico City. *Mexican Import Licensing System*. (Department of State Airgram, A-305.) Mexico City: May 24, 1972.

————. *Mexican In-Bond Industry Program*. (Department of State Airgram, A-478.) Mexico City: September 17, 1973.

U.S. Federal Power Commission. *World Power Data: Capacity of Electric Generating Plants and Production of Electric Energy, 1969*. Washington: GPO, 1972.

"U.S. Mexican Trade Sets New Records," *Foreign Agricultural Trade of the United States*, August 1974, 79-89.

U.S. National Council on Marine Resources and Engineering Development. *Marine Science Activities of the Nations of Latin America*. Washington: GPO, 1968.

Urrutia Millan, Rafael. *Algunos aspectos fiscales y comerciales de México*. Mexico City: Sela, 1966.

Vega Manzo, Javier. "El seguro de crédito de exportación en México," *Técnicas Financieras* [Durango, Mexico], IX, No. 6, July-August 1970, 635-643.

Venezian, Eduardo L., and Gamble, William. *The Agricultural Development of Mexico: Its Structure and Growth Since 1950*. New York: Praeger, 1969.

Vernon, Raymond. *The Dilemma of Mexico's Development*. Cambridge: Harvard University Press, 1963.

Vernon, Raymond (ed.). *Public Policy and Private Enterprise in Mexico*. Cambridge: Harvard University Press, 1964.

Vilaplana, Victor A. "The Forbidden Zones in Mexico," *California Western Law Review*, X, No. 1, Fall 1973, 47-81.

Viscaya Canales, Isidro. "Internal and External Factors in the Development of Monterrey as an Industrial Center," *South Eastern Latin Americanist*, XVI, No. 1, June 1972, 1-4.

Walton, John. "Political Development. A Regional Assessment of Contemporary Theories," *Studies in Comparative International Development*, VII, No. 1, Spring 1972, 39-63.

Watanabe, Susumu. "Constraints on Labour-Intensive Export Industries in Mexico," *International Labour Review* [Geneva], CIX, No. 1, January 1974, 13-46.

Watters, R. F. *Shifting Cultivation in Latin America*. (Food and Agriculture Organization Forestry Development Paper, No. 17.) Rome: FAO, 1971.

Weckstein, R. S. "Evaluating Mexican Land Reform," *Economic Development and Cultural Change*, XVIII, No. 3, April 1970, 391-409.

Weitz, Raanan (ed.). *Rural Development in a Changing World*. Cambridge: MIT Press, 1971.

Werrett, Rosemary. "Mexico: Drawing in the Reins on Foreign Investment," *Columbia Journal of World Business*, IX, No. 1, Spring 1974, 88-97.

West, Robert C., and Augelli, John F. *Middle America; Its Lands and Peoples*. Englewood Cliffs: Prentice-Hall, 1966.

Wilken, Gene C. "Drained-field agriculture: An Intensive Farming System in Tlaxcala, Mexico," *Geographical Review*, LIX, No. 2, Spring 1969, 215-241.

Wilkie, James W. *The Mexican Revolution: Federal Expenditure and Social Change Since 1910*. (2d ed., rev.) Berkeley: University of California Press, 1970.

Wilkleman, Don, and Hansen, David. "Idle Land: An Anomaly in Mexican Resource Use," *Land Economics*, XLVII, No. 3, August 1971, 289-296.

Williams, Simon, and Miller, James A. *Credit Systems for Small-Scale Farmers: Case Histories from Mexico*. (Studies in Latin America Business, No. 14.) Austin: University of Texas, 1973.

Winberry, John J. "Ferrocarril de Chihuahua al Pacifico: Mexico's Newest Railroad," *Social Science Quarterly*, LIV, No. 4, March 1974, 804-873.

Wionczek, Miguel S. "Foreign Banking in Mexico," *Banker* [London], CXX, September 1970, 985-1001.

———. "Foreign-Oriented Enclave in a Rapidly Industrializing Economy: Sulphur Mining in Mexico." Pages 264-311 in Raymond F. Mikesell (ed.), *Foreign Investment in the Petroleum and Mineral Industries*. Baltimore: Johns Hopkins University Press, for the Resources for the Future, 1971.

———. "La inversion extranjera privada en México: Problemas y Perspectivos," *Comercio Exterior* [Mexico City], XX, No. 10, October 1970, 816-824.

———. "The Rise and the Decline of Latin American Economic Integration," *Journal of Common Market Studies* [Oxford], IX, No. 1, September 1970, 49–66.

Wionczek, Miguel S. (ed.) *Economic Cooperation in Latin America, Africa, and Asia: A Handbook of Documents.* Cambridge: MIT Press, 1969.

———. *Latin American Economic Integration.* (Praeger Series on International Economics and Development.) New York: Praeger, 1966.

Witte, Ann Dryden. "Employment in the Manufacturing Sector of Developing Economies: A Study of Mexico, Peru, and Venezuela." Unpublished doctoral dissertation. Raleigh: North Carolina State University, 1971.

World Bank. *World Bank Annual Report, 1974.* Washington: International Bank for Reconstruction and Development, 1974.

———. *The World Bank Group in the Americas.* Washington: May 1974.

Wright, Harry K. *Foreign Enterprise in Mexico: Laws and Policies.* Chapel Hill: University of North Carolina Press, 1971.

Wygard, Edward J. "The Industrialization of Mexico." Pages 586–596 in Claudio Veliz (ed.), *Latin America and the Caribbean: A Handbook.* New York: Praeger, 1968.

Yates, Paul Lamartine. *Regional Development in Mexico and the Decentralization of Industry.* Mexico City: Banco de México, 1960.

Zanotti, John P. "Mexico's Forbidden Zones: The Presidential Decree of April 29, 1971," *Law and the Social Order 1973,* No. 3, 1973, 455-479.

(Various issues of the following periodicals were also used in the preparation of this section: *Bank of London and South America* [London], July 1973-July 1974; *Boletín de la Integración* [Buenos Aires], August 1972-May 1974, *Bolsa Review* [London], April 1972-September 1974; *Brazil Herald* [Rio de Janeiro], April-September 1974; *Business Latin America* [New York], December 1972-July 1974; *Christian Science Monitor* [Boston], February 1971-September 1974; *Comercio Exterior* [Mexico City], January 1970-August 1973; *Commerce Today* [Washington], July 1973-April 1974; *Excélsior* [Mexico City], July-September 1974; *Financial Times* [London], March 1973-September 1974; *Foreign Agriculture* [Washington], May-August 1974; *Latin American Free Trade Association Newsletter* [Montevideo], December 1973-June 1974; *Latin American Integration* [Buenos Aires], January-June 1974; *Mexican American Review* [Mexico City], February 1971-June 1974; *Monthly Bulletin of Agricultural Economics and Statistics* [Rome], February-July 1974; *New York Times,* May 1972-September 1974; *Pan American Coffee Bureau Bulletin* [New York], January-July 1974; *Review of the Economic Situation in Mexico*

[Mexico City], June 1972-June 1974; *Times of the Americas* [Washington], May-August 1974; *Translation on Latin America* [Washington], October 1970-September 1974; *Wall Street Journal* [New York], July 1972-April 1974; *Washington Post*, August 1971-September 1974; and *Washington Star News*, February-September 1974.)

Section IV. National Security

Alisky, Marvin (ed.) *Who's Who in Mexican Government*. Tempe: Center for Latin American Studies, Arizona State University, 1969.

The Americana 1968 Yearbook. New York: Americana, 1969.

Baker, Richard D. *Judicial Review in Mexico: A Study of the Amparo Suit*. (Latin American Monographs. No. 22.) Austin: University of Texas Press, 1971.

Baldwin, Fletcher N., Jr. "A Constitutional Comparison: Mexico, the United States, and Uganda," *California Western Law Review* [San Diego], X, No. 1, Fall 1973, 82-104.

Barber, Willard F., and Ronning, C. Neale. *Internal Security and Military Power*. Columbus: Ohio State University Press, 1966.

Barck, Oscar T., Jr., and Blake, Manfred. *Since 1900: A History of the United States in Our Times*. New York, Macmillan, 1947.

Barkenbus, Jack N. "The Trans-Peninsular Highway: A New Era for Baja California," *Journal of Interamerican Studies*, XVI, No. 3, August 1974, 259-273.

Bettiol, G. "Aspectos Políticos de Derecho Penal Comparado," *Criminalia* [Mexico City], XXXI, No. 1, January 1965, 33-38.

Brandenburg, Frank. *The Making of Modern Mexico*. Englewood Cliffs: Prentice-Hall, 1964.

Brinsmade, Lyon L. "Mexican Law: An Outline and Bibliography of English Source Materials Relating to Certain Aspects," *International Lawyer*, IV, No. 4, October 1972, 829-857.

Brown, Thomas A. *Statistical Indications of the Effect of Military Programs on Latin America*. (Document No. P-4144.) Santa Monica: Rand Corporation, July 1969.

Buckley, William F., Jr. "Down Mexico Way," *National Review*, August 25, 1970, 910.

Buentello y Villa, Edmundo. "Prisiones," *Criminalia* [Mexico City], XXXV, No. 4, April 30, 1969, 302-314.

Busey, James L. *Latin America: Political Institutions and Processes*. New York: Random House, 1964.

Butte, Woodfin L. "Strict Liability in Mexico," *American Journal of Comparative Law*, XVIII, 1970, 805-830.

Campos Huttick, Ricardo. "Los accidentes de tránsito: problema de salud pública," *Salud Pública de México* [Mexico City], XV, No. 1, January-February 1973, 9-41.

Carranca y Rivas, Raul. "La readaptación social de los sentenciados," *Pensamiento Político* [Mexico City], VII, May 1971, 25-44.

Carter, Constance Ann Crowder. "Law and Society in Colonial Mexico: Audiencia Judges in Mexico Society from the Tello de Sandoval Visita General, 1543–1547." Unpublished Ph.D. dissertation. New York: Columbia University, 1971.

Clagett, Helen L. *Administration of Justice in Latin America.* New York: Oceana Publications, 1952.

————. *A Guide to the Mexican States.* Washington: Library of Congress, 1947.

Clagett, Helen L., and Valderrama, David M. *A Revised Guide to the Law and Legal Literature of Mexico.* (Latin American Series, No. 38.) Washington: Library of Congress, 1973.

Cramer, James. *Uniforms of the World's Police.* London: Cassells, 1968.

Dupuy, Trevor Nevitt. *Almanac of World Military Power.* Dunn Loring, Virginia: T. N. Dupuy Associates, 1970.

"The Fearsome Falcons," *Time,* XCVII, June 21, 1971, 33.

Fix Zamudio, H. "Juicio de amparo Mexicano y la enseñanza del derecho procesal," *Revisto Iberoamericano de Derecho Procesal* [Madrid], 1971, 361.

"Fourth State of the Nation Report," *Mexican Newsletter* [Mexico City], No. 24, September 1, 1974.

Gallegos, Anibal. *Mis amigos: delincuentes.* Mexico City: B. Costa-Amie Editor, 1966.

García Ramírez, Sergio. *El artículo 18 constitucional.* Mexico City: Universidad Nacional Autónoma de México, 1967.

Gillingham, Harrold E. *Mexican Decorations of Honour.* New York: American Numismatic Society, 1940.

Glick, Edward B. *Peaceful Conflict.* Harrisburg: Stackpole Books, 1967.

González Casanova, Pablo. *La democracia en México.* Mexico City: Ediciones ERA, 1965.

Gott, Richard. *Rural Guerrillas in Latin America.* (Rev. ed.) London: Penguin Books, 1973.

Hansen, Roger D. *The Politics of Mexican Development.* Baltimore: Johns Hopkins University Press, 1971.

Hayman, Elizabeth. "Military Power and Political Change in Latin America," *Survival* [London], XV, No. 2, March-April 1973, 65–73.

Hayner, Norman S. *New Patterns in Old Mexico.* New Haven, Connecticut: College and University Press, 1966.

Herman, Donald L. *The Comintern in Mexico.* Washington: Public Affairs Press, 1974.

de la Hidalgo, Luis. "Justicia Popular: Tribunal de lo contencioso administrativo en el Distrito Federal," *Pensamiento Politico* [Mexico City], VII, August 1971, 467-92.

James, Preston. *Latin America.* (4th ed.) New York: Odyssey Press, 1969.

Jane's Fighting Ships, 1972-73. (Ed. Raymond V. B. Blackman.)

London: McGraw-Hill, 1972.

Johnson, John J. *The Military and Society in Latin America*. Stanford: Stanford University Press, 1964.

Johnson, John J. (ed.) *Continuity and Change in Latin America*. Stanford: Stanford University Press, 1964.

————. *The Role of the Military in Underdeveloped Countries*. Princeton: Princeton University Press, 1962.

Johnson, Kenneth F. *Mexican Democracy: A Critical View*. Boston: Allyn and Bacon, 1971.

Kalijarvi, Thorsten V. *Central America: Land of Lords and Lizards*. Princeton: Van Nostrand, 1962.

Karst, Kenneth L. *Latin American Legal Institutions: Problems for Comparative Study*. Los Angeles: Latin American Center, University of California, 1966.

Kozolcyyk, Boris. *Law and the Credit Structure in Latin America*. (Rand Memorandum, Rm–4918–RC.) Santa Monica: Rand Corporation, 1966.

Ladman, Jerry R. "A Model of Credit Applied to the Allocation of Resources in a Case Study of a Sample of Mexican Farms," *Economic Development and Cultural Change*, XXII, No. 2, January 1974, 279-301.

Law and Judicial Systems of Nations. Washington: World Peace Through Law Center, 1968.

Liebman, Arthur. "Student Activism in Mexico," *Annals of the American Academy of Political and Social Science*, CCCXCV, May 1971, 159-170.

Lieuwen, Edwin. *The "Fuero Militar" in New Spain, 1764–1800*. Gainesville: University of Florida Press, 1957.

————. *Generals vs. Presidents*. New York: Praeger, 1964.

————. *Mexican Militarism: The Political Rise and Fall of the Revolutionary Army, 1910–1940*. Albuquerque: University of New Mexico Press, 1968.

Lozoya, Alberto Jorge. "The Mexican Army Today," *International Journal of Politics*, I, Nos. 2 and 3, Summer-Fall 1971, 272-285.

McAlister, Lyle N.; Maingot, Anthony P.; and Potash, Robert A. *The Military in Latin American Sociopolitical Evolution: Four Case Studies*. Washington: Institutes for Research, Center for Research in Social Systems, 1970.

Marett, Robert. *Mexico*. New York: Walker, 1971.

Margiotta, Franklin D. "Changing Patterns of Political Influence: The Mexican Military in Politics." (Unpublished paper presented at the Annual Meeting of the American Political Science Association.) New Orleans: September 1973.

Martindale-Hubbell Law Directory. *Digest of the Laws of Foreign Countries: Mexico*. Chicago: R. R. Donnally and Sons, 1973.

Mexico. Secretaría de Comunicaciones y Transportes. *Memoria de*

Labores, 1970. Mexico City: 1970.

Mexico in Pictures. (Visual Geography Series.) New York: Sterling Publishing, 1973.

Mexico, 1970: Facts, Figures, and Trends. Mexico City: Banco Nacional de Comercio Exterior, 1970.

The Military Balance, 1973-74. London: International Institute for Strategic Studies, 1973.

Millan Morales, Roman. *La Criminalidad en la decimatercera delegación del Ministerio Público.* Mexico City: Universidad Nacional Autónoma de México, 1963.

de Mora, Juan Miguel. *Las Guerrillas en México y Genaro Vásquez Rojas.* Mexico City: Editora Latino Americano, 1971.

Needler, Martin C. *Politics and Society in Mexico.* Albuquerque: University of New Mexico Press, 1971.

Needler, Martin C. (ed.) *Political Systems of Latin America.* Princeton: Van Nostrand, 1964.

"1970 Mexican Law Symposium," *California Western Law Review,* VI, 1970

Norman, James. *Mexico.* (American Republics Series, No. 14.) Washington: Organization of American States, 1965.

―――. "The Sociable Jails," *Holiday,* XXXII, No. 10, October 1962, 62-67.

Pierson, William W., and Gil, Federico G. *Governments of Latin America.* New York: McGraw-Hill, 1957.

Piña y Palacios, Javier. "La Colonia Penal de los Islas Marías," *Criminalia* [Mexico City], XXXVI, No. 5, May 31, 1970, 199-308.

―――. "La Colonia Penal de los Islas Marías," *Criminalia* [Mexico City], XXXVI, No. 6, June 30, 1970, 311-428.

The Political and Socio-Economic Role of the Military in Latin America, Appendix III: Guatemala, Haiti, Mexico. Coral Cables: Center for Advanced International Studies, University of Miami, 1972.

Poppino, Rollie E. *International Communism in Latin America.* Glencoe: Free Press, 1964.

Price, John A. *Tijuana: Urbanization in a Border Culture.* Notre Dame: University of Notre Dame Press, 1973.

"The Price of Freedom," *Time,* CI, May 21, 1973, 57.

Quiroz Cuarón, Alfonso. *La criminalidad en la república mexicana.* Mexico City: Universidad Nacional Autónoma de México, 1958.

Quiroz Cuarón, Alfonso, and Quiroz Cuarón, Raul. *El Costo Social del Delito en México.* Mexico City: Libreria y Ediciones Botas, 1970.

"Una Reforma Integral de los Tribunales para menores del Distrito Federal," *Criminalia* [Mexico City], XXXIX, Nos. 7 and 8, July-August 1973, 221-228.

"Reformas y adiciones al Decreto que crea Dirección de Pensiones Militares," *Salud Pública de México* [Mexico City], XV, No. 1,

January-February, 1973.

Riding, Alan. "Rumors About the Army," *Financial Times* [London], February 13, 1974, 9.

Roberts, C. Paul, and Kohda, Takado (eds.). *Statistical Abstract of Latin America*. (10th ed.) Los Angeles: Latin American Center, University of California, 1967.

Rodríguez Manzanera, Luis. "El crimen como maxima expresión de patología social," *Salud Público de México* [Mexico City], XV, No. 1, January-February 1973, 59-66.

———. "Indices de Drogadición a Nivel de Bachillerato en México, D.F," *Criminalia* [Mexico City], XXXIX, Nos. 3 and 4, March-April 1973, 51-75.

———. *El polígrafo*. Mexico City: Gráfica Panamericana, 1965.

Ronfeldt, David F. *The Mexican Army and Political Order Since 1940*. (Document P-5089.) Santa Monica: Rand Corporation, September 1973.

"Rough Arm of the Law," *Economist*, July 10, 1965, 37-38.

Salazar, Rosendo. *Del militarismo al civilismo en nuestro Revolución: esbozo de una lucha que duró trienta y cinco años por la consecuen-cación de gobiernos no militares*. Mexico City: Libro Mexicano, 1968.

Schwarz, Carl E. "Exceptions to the Exhaustion of Administrative Remedies Under the Mexican Writ of Amparo: Some Possible Applications to Judicial Review in the United States," *California Western Law Review*, VII, No. 3, Spring 1971, 331-354.

Sellers, Robert C. *The Reference Handbook of the Armed Forces of the World*. Garden City: Robert C. Sellers and Associates, 1968.

Snaden, James N. "Mexico's Fourth Largest City: A Research Note," *Latin American Studies Association Newsletter*, IV, No. 1, March 1973, 33-34.

Stauffer, Elam K., and Blase, Melvin G. "Institutional Disequilibria in the Development Process," *Economic Development and Cultural Change*, XXII, No. 2, January 1974, 265-278.

Stevens, Evelyn P. *Protest and Response in Mexico*. Cambridge: MIT Press, 1974.

"The Stork vs. the Steel Mill," *Forbes*, CXII, August 15, 1973, 33-35.

Tina Ramírez, Felipe. *Leyes fundamentales de México, 1808-1957*. Mexico City: Editorial Porrua, 1957.

"Troubles on the Via Pacifico," *Time*, XCVII, April 19, 1971, 23-24.

Turner, Frederick C. *The Dynamics of Mexican Nationalism*. Chapel Hill: University of North Carolina Press, 1968.

United Nations. *Freedom from Arbitrary Arrest and Exile*. New York: UN, 1959.

———. *International Review of Criminal Policy*. New York: UN, 1961

———. *Latin American Seminar on the Prevention of Crime and the Treatment of Offenders*. New York: UN, 1954.

United Nations Educational, Scientific and Cultural Organization.

433

World Survey of Education, V: Educational Policy, Legislation, and Administration. Paris: UNESCO, 1971.

U. S. Agency for International Development. *Summary Economic and Social Indicators: 18 Latin American Countries*. Washington: AID, 1972.

U. S. Arms Control and Disarmament Agency. *World Military Expenditures, 1971*. Washington: GPO, July 1972.

U. S. Department of Commerce. Domestic and International Business Administration. *Marketing in Mexico*, by Paul S. Flores. (Overseas Business Reports, OBR 74-58.) Washington: GPO, November 1974.

U.S. Department of State. *Diplomatic List*. (Publication No. 7894.) Washington: GPO, May 1974.

U.S. Department of State. Bureau of Intelligence and Research. *Latin American Military Expenditures, 1967-71*, Pt. II. Washington: GPO, October 1973.

U.S. Department of State. Office of the Legal Adviser. *Treaties in Force on January 1, 1967*. (Department of State Publication, No. 8188.) Washington: GPO, 1967.

Veliz, Claudio (ed.). *Latin America and the Caribbean: A Handbook*. New York: Praeger, 1968.

de Vries, Henry P., and Rodríquez-Novas, José. *The Law of the Americas*. Dobbs Ferry: Oceana Publications, 1965.

Weiskoff, Richard. "Income Distribution and Economic Growth in Puerto Rico, Argentina, and Mexico," *Review of Income and Wealth*, XVI, No. 4, December 1970, 303-332.

Wilkie, James W. *The Mexican Revolution: Federal Expenditure and Social Change Since 1910*. Berkeley: University of California Press, 1970.

Williams, Mary Wilhelmine. *The People and Politics of Latin America*. New York: Ginn, 1945.

The Worldmark Encyclopedia of the Nations: America. (Ed., Moshe Y. Sachs.) New York: Worldmark Press, Harper and Row, 1967.

Yearbook on International Communist Affairs, 1974. (Ed., Richard F. Staar.) Stanford: Hoover Institution Press, 1974.

(Various issues of the following periodicals were also used in the preparation of this section: *Excélsior* [Mexico City], June–October 1974; *Washington Post*, August–October 1974; and *Washington Star News*, February-October 1974.)

GLOSSARY

amparo—A category of legal actions that guard individual civil rights. Literally, *amparo* signifies protection, assistance, or a human refuge.

Bajío—Literally, flatland; a series of interconnecting basins in Central Mexico.

Central Mexico—Geographic region; a highland area consisting of ten states and the Federal District. It is the economic heartland of the country and contains nearly one-half of the population.

china poblada—Literally, Chinese girl from Puebla. The national women's costume, it displays the red, green, and white national colors. The costume is named for a mythical Chinese princess said to have been brought in captivity to the city of Puebla, where she achieved great popularity.

compadrazgo—Relationship contracted by a godfather with the parents of a child for whom he stands sponsor.

compadre—A ritualized relationship between a father and his child's godfather.

curandero—Native healer.

ejidatrio—A communal landholder.

ejido—System of communal land tenure.

fiscal year (FY)—Generally, same as calendar year, but some government agencies and state enterprises use twelve months other than calendar year as a fiscal year.

Fracture Belt—Area of Central Mexico in which the country's highest mountains, many of them volcanic, are located. The area is subject to severe earthquakes.

Gulf Coast—Geographic region; consists of the states of Veracruz, Tabasco, Campeche, Yucatán, and Quintana Roo.

jacal—A primitive hut often made of mud and brush or corn stalks and in some cases cheap materials.

México—The Spanish name for Mexico, Mexico City, and the state of México. It is also the Spanish name of one of the valleys in the central part of the country.

municipio—Literally, municipality; political subdivision below the state level that corresponds roughly to a county in the United States.

North—Geographic region; consists of the states of Chihuahua, Coahuila, Durango, Neuvo León, San Luís Potosí, Tamaulipas, and Zacatecas.

North Pacific—Geographic region; consists of the states of Sonora, Sinaloa, Nayarit, Baja California, and Baja California Sur.

Northern Plateau—The generally arid and barren high plateau lying between the Sierra Madre Oriental and the Sierra Madre Occidental to the north of Central Mexico.

padrino—Godfather.

peso—Unit of currency. Official symbol is $; unofficial symbol in M$N. Rate of exchange has been stable; 12.5 pesos equaled US$1 from 1954 to late 1974.

PRI—Partido Revolucionario Institucional (Institutional Revolutionary Party). The dominant political party since 1929, it was originally designated the National Revolutionary Party (Partido Revolucionario Nacional—PRN). Its name was changed in 1937 to the Mexican Revolutionary Party (Partido Revolucionario Mexicano—PRM) and in 1946, to the PRI.

South Pacific—Geographic region; consists of the states of Colima, Guerrero, Oaxaca, and Chiapas.

Tlatelolco Massacre—The name given to a 1968 uprising of university students that was suppressed by federal troops and in which numerous lives were lost.

World Bank Group—Consists of the International Bank for Reconstruction and Development (IBRD) and its two financial affiliates, the International Finance Corporation (IFC), which became operational in 1956, and the International Development Association (IDA), which became operational in 1960. IFC works specifically with the private sector in developing countries, and IDA operates in the same sectors and with the same policies as the IBRD but provides credits only to the poorer developing countries and on easier terms than conventional IBRD loans.

Zócalo—The central plaza in Mexico City around which many colonial buildings are located; also used for central plazas in many other cities and towns.

INDEX

Acapulco: 36, 329, 346

acculturation of Indians: 101, 106–108, 112, 217; "passing", 86, 107

adobe: 169, 171

adult education: 155, 246

advertising: broadcasting, 253; controls on, 245; in print, 243, 248, 250

Aeroméxico: 243, 328

agreements and treaties: ix, 67, 329, 375; border areas, 261; nuclear arms, 260; trade, 313, 318; water rights, 263

agriculture (see also crops; exports; labor force; landownership; migratory workers in the United States: viii, 80, 291–303; budget, 279; credit, 289; gross domestic product, 275, 276, 277; income, 183, 273, 291; Indians and, 90–91, 101; schools, 148, 151; worker organizations, 80

Aguascalientes (state): 9, 27, 308; city, 325

Agustín, José: 194, 195

air force: 351, 352, 353, 357, 375; insignia, 372; schools, 264, 265

airlines and airfields: 328

alcoholic beverages: 23, 166, 300

Aldama, Juan: 61, 62

Aldasoro, Juan Pablo: 328

Alemán, Miguel: 43, 82

alien residents (see also foreign-born persons): landownership, 73, 213, 284; rights, 38, 72, 261, 320, 333, 335

Allende, Ignacio: 61, 62

Allende Institute: 152

Alliance for Progress: 151

Alvarado, Pedro de: 52

Alvarez, Juan: 67

amparo, writ of: 214–215, 333, 335–336, 339, 340, 342, 370

Anahuac, Republic of: 63

Anahuac University: 152

Andean Common Market: 318

anthropology: 198, 203, 206, 251

ants: 25

archeology: 191, 198, 199, 265

architecture: 33, 199; churches, 130–131, 200; modern, 205–207

area: vii, 27

Argentina: 262

armed forces: ix, 5, 120, 271, 342, 351–375; defense budget, 279

army: awards, 374; insignia and uniform, 372, 373; politics and, 80, 82, 83, 232, 234, 351–352, 353, 359–363; under the porfiriato, 71

Arreola, Juan José: 194

art: 199–208; folk type, 203, 207–208; murals, 201, 202

associations and organizations: artists guilds, 202; business management, 274; Civil Association (A.C.), 181; commerce and industry, 181, 228, 249, 274; construction industry, 311, 319; farmers, 320; regional clubs, 120

Austria: 266–267

Authentic Party of the Mexican Revolution (PARM): 235

automotive vehicles: 33, 309, 324, 330; accidents, 346; imports, 316, 317

Autonomous University of Guadalajara: 135, 150, 151, 153, 175, 176

aviation (see also air force): 313, 328

Avila, Roberto: 186

Avila Camacho, Manuel: 81, 82, 234, 265, 360

awards and decorations, military: 373–374

Ayala, Daniel: 209

Aztecoidan language: 103

Aztecs: 51, 53, 100, 188; architecture, 199, 200; artifacts and skills, 21, 208; religion, 23, 195

Azuela, Mariano: 193

Baja California (state): 9, 12, 14, 15, 24, 55, 177, 324; agriculture, 296, 297; area and population, 27, 102; industry, 308; minerals, 21, 312; people, 94, 95; ports, 36, 354

Baja California Sur (state): 9, 21, 27, 214

Bajío: 17–18, 298

Ballet Folklórico: 185, 192, 210

Balsas River: 17, 19, 309

Bank of America: 283

Bank of Mexico: 285, 288, 304, 314, 337

banks and banking (see also credit): 285–288,

los halcones: 238, 348

handicrafts: 21, 41, 207; Indian, 91, 101, 183

health *(see also* diet and nutrition): 173–179

Hebrew language: 128

henequen industry: 35, 208, 299, 300

herbs. *See* pharmacopoeia plants

Hernández, Luisa Josefina: 196

Herrán, Saturnio: 201

Hidalgo (state): 9, 303, 304; area and population, 27, 29; Cornish immigrants, 94; Indians, 89, 100

Hidalgo y Costilla, Miguel: 61, 62, 63, 125

higher education *(see also* National Autonomous University of Mexico; National Polytechnical Institute; state universities): 1, 135, 148–155; employment and, 45; publishing, 150, 251; teachers, 160–161; university subjects, 198; War College, 365

Hokan language: 102

holidays *(see also* fiestas): 181–182

homeopathic medicine: 174

honey: 301

hospitals: 173, 175, 176, 370

housing: 2, 89, 168–173; military, 369; urban, 119, 163

Huastec Indians: 96, 97

Huave Indians: 98

Huerta, Victoriano: 74, 75, 76

Huichol language: 102

hurricanes: 19

igualas: 249

iguanas: 24

illiteracy. *See* literacy

immigrants. *See* migration

imports: ix, 271, 314, 316; balance of payments, 282, 313; books, 252; controls, 264, 277, 281; licenses, 317

IMSS. *See* Mexican Social Security Institute

In-bond Industry Program: 307–308, 315

income: per capita, 112, 116, 183, 273, 276; uneven distribution, 273, 276

independence from Spain: 62–64

India: 266, 271

Indians *(see also* acculturation of Indians; and names of specific ethnic groups and languages): 23, 55, 61, 87, 88–94, 102, 167, 172, 225, 364; cultural and artistic contributions, 191, 193, 198, 199, 203; education, 107, 137, 217; interethnic relationships, 103–106; population, 85, 88, 96, 97–98, 106; religion, 100, 124, 125, 128, 130–131

Indonesia: 266

industry *(see also* mining industry; petro-

leum and natural gas): viii, 40, 303–312; government regulation, 79; interest groups, 228; locations, 31–32, 34; profit-sharing, 274; subsidies, 280

inflation: 3, 273, 368

INFONAVIT (worker housing): 172

inheritance *(see also ejidos):* 122

Inquisition: 58, 61, 63, 65

insects: 25

insurance: 275, 288, 314

Institutional Revolutionary Party (PRI) *(see also* National Executive Committee): 4, 50, 82, 114, 116, 211, 217, 220, 226, 229, 249, 271, 360, 361; armed forces and, 232, 351, 362; control of the government, 219, 221, 225, 234, 235; elections, 222, 223; image, 227–228

Inter-American Development Bank: 267, 283

interest rates: 289

International Monetary Fund: 289

international organizations and memberships *(see also* Organization of American States; United Nations): viii, 267–269

International Telephone and Telegraph: 264

iron and steel industry: 308, 315; ore production, 304, 305, 308

irrigation: 17, 20, 30, 35, 279, 292, 296, 297

Israel: 353

ISSSTE (government employees social security): 180

Italy: 266, 317; immigrants, 94

Iturbide, Agustín de: 63, 64

Ixtacihuatl (mountain): 13

jade: 21

jai alai: 187

Jalisco (state): 9, 27, 103, 322, 338, 343; folk art, 208; minerals, 21, 22

Japan: 255, 257, 266, 284; trade, 317

Jesuit missionaries: 54, 55, 58, 59, 102, 127

jewelry: 21, 208

Jews: 95, 127

Juárez, Benito: 49, 67, 68, 182, 267; presidency, 69, 70, 213, 228

jury trials: 342

justice. *See* court system

juvenile delinquency: 334, 340, 345

Kekchi Indians: 96

kidnapping: 335, 345, 348, 349, 358

kindergarten: 141–142

labor force *(see also* employment): viii, 3, 40–45, 183; agriculture, 28, 80, 115, 180, 298; migratory workers, 11, 264, 265, 282;

Park, 158, 188, 206; crime, 346, 347, 348, 349; housing, 169, 170; justice system, 214, 334, 340, 342; markets, 320; mass media, 4, 242, 243, 246, 248; Netzahual-cóyotl, 30, 31; population, 27, 31, 32, 95; power needs, 311, 312; publishing, 250, 251; religious groups, 127, 128; schools and universities, 148, 151, 206, 207; television, 254; traffic and transportation, 330; Xochomilco Park, 23; Zócalo, 33

Mezquital Valley: 100

Michoacán (state): 9, 21, 27, 343: Indians, 95, 100, 208

middle class: 109, 113, 114, 182, 183, 292, 363

middle-level schools: 135, 138, 139, 145–148, 150, 151, 157, 159, 246, 345

migration: 72, 178; from outside, 12, 37–38, 94, 266; to urban areas, 30, 111, 119, 137, 170, 173

migratory workers in the United States: 38, 264, 265, 282; wetbacks, 11, 47

Miguel Alemán Reservoir: 19

military aid and foreign influences: 260, 263, 374–375

milk: 164, 165, 301

minerals: 8, 20–22, 208, 304, 305–306; exports, 303, 315, 317

mining industry: 43, 72, 277, 292, 303–306; laws for, 59–60

ministries (see also Public Ministry): 216

Ministry of Agrarian Reform: 217

Ministry of Agriculture: 151

Ministry of Communications and Transport: 245, 255, 327

Ministry of Defense: 352, 355, 359

Ministry of Education and Culture: 278, 279

Ministry of Finance and Public Credit: 216, 278, 279, 285, 288, 329

Ministry of Foreign Relations: 284, 320

Ministry of Government: 216, 222, 245, 254; courts, 340; police, 337

Ministry of Health and Welfare: 174, 176, 178, 245

Ministry of Hydraulic Resources: 279, 337

Ministry of Industry, Commerce, and Fisheries: 207, 216

Ministry of Marine: 352, 356

Ministry of National Properties: 218, 278

Ministry of Public Education (SEP): 107, 134, 135, 338; budget, 217; mass media and, 245; textbooks, 252

Ministry of Public Health: 337

Ministry of the Navy: 329

Ministry of the Presidency: 278

Ministry of Tourism: 217

Mixe Indians: 93, 98, 99

Mixtec Indians: 98, 99

MLN. See National Liberation Movement

Moncayo, Pablo: 209

Monsiváis, Carlos: 195

Monterrey: 31, 34, 72, 325; army post, 369; despensas, 321; health, 176; industry, 172, 275, 288, 307, 311; mass communication, 247, 254; people, 113, 119; schools, 148, 151, 157, 161

Montes de Oca, Antonio: 195

Montezuma II: 51, 52

mordidas: 43

Morelia: 151, 325

Morelos (state): 9, 27, 94, 303, 345; Dam, 16

Morelos, José María: 61, 63, 125

Morones, Luis: 78, 80, 229

Morrow, Dwight: 79

mortality: 37, 176, 177; infant, viii, 2, 36

mulattoes: 56, 94

Murillo, Gerardo: 201, 207

museums: 198, 203, 206

music: 184, 208–209

NAFIN. See National Development Company

Nahua Indians: 50, 98

Nahuatl-speakers: 51, 96, 99, 100; religion, 94

name: country, 8; people surnames, 89

Napoleon II: 69, 70

narcotics. See drug abuse and narcotics

Narváez, Panfilo: 52

National Action Party (PAN): 226, 235, 236

National Autonomous University of Mexico: 135, 140, 150, 152, 153, 158, 161, 175, 198, 205; sports, 186, 188; student activism, 232, 234, 238, 347; University City, 206, 207

National Bank of Mexico: 287

National Bank of Public Works and Services (BNOSP): 173, 286

National Confederation of Campesinos (CNC): 80, 225, 230, 231, 234

National Confederation of Workers (CNT): 229

national congress: 214, 235

National Development Bank: 243, 247, 271

National Development Company (NAFIN): 285–286, 288, 289

National Ejidal Credit Bank: 217, 230, 286

National Executive Committee (CEN): 225, 234, 235

National Indian Institute: 107

National Liberation Movement (MLN): 236, 237

443

446

PUBLISHED AREA HANDBOOKS

550–65	Afghanistan	550–39	Indonesia
550–98	Albania	550–68	Iran
550–44	Algeria	550–31	Iraq
550–59	Angola	550–25	Israel
550–73	Argentina	550–69	Ivory Coast
550–169	Australia	550–30	Japan
550–170	Belgium	550–34	Jordan
550–66	Bolivia	550–56	Kenya
550–20	Brazil	550–50	Khmer Republic (Cambodia)
550–168	Bulgaria	550–81	Korea, North
550–61	Burma	550–41	Korea, Republic of
550–83	Burundi	550–58	Laos
550–166	Cameroon	550–24	Lebanon
550–96	Ceylon	550–38	Liberia
550–159	Chad	550–85	Libya
550–77	Chile	550–163	Malagasy Republic
550–60	China, People's Republic of	550–172	Malawi
550–63	China, Republic of	550–45	Malaysia
550–26	Colombia	550–161	Mauritania
550–67	Congo, Democratic Republic of (Zaire)	550–79	Mexico
		550–76	Mongolia
550–91	Congo, People's Republic of	550–49	Morocco
550–90	Costa Rica	550–64	Mozambique
550–152	Cuba	550–35	Nepal, Bhutan and Sikkim
550–22	Cyprus	550–88	Nicaragua
550–158	Czechoslovakia	550–157	Nigeria
550–54	Dominican Republic	550–94	Oceania
550–155	East Germany	550–48	Pakistan
550–52	Ecuador	550–46	Panama
550–150	El Salvador	550–156	Paraguay
550–28	Ethiopia	550–92	Peripheral States of the Arabian Peninsula
550–167	Finland	550–42	Peru
550–29	Germany	550–72	Philippines
550–153	Ghana	550–162	Poland
550–87	Greece	550–160	Romania
550–78	Guatemala	550–84	Rwanda
550–82	Guyana	550–51	Saudi Arabia
550–164	Haiti	550–70	Senegal
550–151	Honduras	550–86	Somalia
550–165	Hungary	550–93	South Africa, Republic of
550–21	India	550–171	Southern Rhodesia
550–154	Indian Ocean Territories		

450